7 Prob.
1,3,6
8 Ex 4
Pr 1,2

Chpt. 6
Ex 6
Prob 10

Managerial Accounting

3d EDITION

CARL L. MOORE, MA, CPA

College of Business and Economics

Lehigh University

ROBERT K. JAEDICKE, PhD

Graduate School of Business

Stanford University

Published by

A92 **SOUTH-WESTERN PUBLISHING CO.**

Cincinnati   Chicago   Dallas   New Rochelle, N.Y.   Burlingame, Calif.   Brighton, England

ISBN: 0-538-01920-4

Library of Congress Catalog Card Number: 79-153115

2 3 4 5 6 7 8 9 H 0 9 8 7 6 5 4 3 2

Printed in the United States of America

Preface

The objective in this edition of *Managerial Accounting,* as in the earlier editions, is to explain how accounting data can be interpreted and used by management in planning and controlling business activities. The major purpose of this book is to show how accounting can help to solve the problems that confront those who are directly responsible for the management of the enterprise. At the same time, attention is given to the use of accounting data by investors and potential investors whenever appropriate.

Some changes have been made in the basic structure by regrouping certain topics to aid the student in his overall understanding of the subject matter. The book consists of three parts. Part I discusses the financial statements and the interpretation of financial data, and Parts II and III explain how accounting data are used in planning and controlling business activities.

In this edition both job order and process cost accounting are covered in one chapter, Chapter 11. Materials and labor cost control are discussed in Chapter 12, and manufacturing overhead control is discussed in Chapter 13. Standard cost is incorporated in both Chapters 12 and 13.

Many of the chapters have been revised extensively. Chapter 1, for example, combines the material on financial statements that was previously covered in two chapters. The chapter on asset and equity structure (Chapter 3 in the earlier editions) has been eliminated, but much of the subject material has been retained and included in Chapters 2, 3, and 5. Problems in accountability are given more attention in this edition (Chapters 2 and 3) with the latest Accounting Principles Board Opinions being included whenever appropriate.

Quantitative methods and organizational behavior are given much more attention in this edition. Chapter 9 has been completely rewritten to include responsibility accounting and to show how responsibility accounting can operate to exert a subtle control over managerial behavior. Statistical techniques that can be used to estimate and control costs are discussed in Chapter 10. The quantitative methods that were discussed in the last chapter of the earlier editions are now moved forward to Chapter 16 and are incorporated in the treatment of costs and managerial decisions. The chapters on budgets have been moved to the end of the book to show how the predicted results of all planning and decision-making activities are brought together in a master budget plan.

This book is intended for a one-semester or a one-quarter course for students who expect to use accounting data in their future occupations. We believe that accounting majors will benefit from this material as much as those students who are studying other fields in business and economics but who are not going to be professional accountants. After all, the professional accountant must be as familiar with the use of data as he is with its collection and presentation. It is important for him to know the *why* as well as the *how*. The student should use this book after having had a one-semester or two-quarter course in the introductory principles of accounting. Students who need a review of introductory accounting are referred to the appendixes that deal concisely with the accounting cycle. Also students who are not familiar with the present value concept should study Appendix D before Chapters 2, 5, or 19 are covered.

The chapters may be assigned in sequence, or they may be assigned in a different order, depending upon the background of the class and the objective of the course. If the students have a good background in accounting fundamentals and have covered financial statement analysis in another course, they may start with Chapter 7. Chapters 2, 3, and 4 which deal with important special topics are not essential to an understanding of the later chapters. Students who have been exposed to job order and process cost accounting will not have to spend much time on Chapter 11. When Chapter 15 has been completed, the remaining chapters may be assigned according to the preferences of the instructor. If desired, certain chapters may be combined and treated as one unit. Chapters 5 and 6 may be assigned as a unit on statement analysis, Chapters 12 and 13 may be assigned for control over product costs, and Chapters 20 and 21 may be assigned for budgets.

Questions, exercises, and problems are given at the end of the chapters. Present value tables are given at the back of the book for use in working some of the problems in Chapters 3 and 19. The questions may be used as a basis for classroom discussion, or they may be used by the students as study guides. Essential points are included in the questions in the order in which they are presented in the chapters. The exercises are simple problem situations to help the student apply the concepts discussed in the chapters. The problems are more rigorous than the exercises and are usually listed in order of difficulty or according to the amount of time required for a solution. Many of the exercises and problems are new.

The authors acknowledge with gratitude the many helpful comments received from teachers and students who have used the second edition. Particular recognition is given for the help received from Professors Robert C. Becker, Auburn University; Donald D. Bourque, Syracuse University; Francis M. Brady, Lehigh University; William J. Bruns, Jr., University of Washington; Neal M. Feldman, University of Massachusetts; V. D. Gardner, Utah State University; John Gehman, Moravian College; Max G. Hensel, University of Wisconsin at Green Bay; James B. Hobbs, Lehigh University; Clarence H. Jackman, California State Polytechnic College; Alfred P. Koch, Lehigh University; Frederick Lang, De Paul University; Eldon L. Schafer, Syracuse University; Lawrence Schkade, University of Texas at Arlington; Edwin J. Schmidlein, Southern Illinois University; James E. Stewart, Wright State University; Robert L. Stone, Lehigh University; and Robert L. Virgil, Washington University.

CARL L. MOORE
ROBERT K. JAEDICKE

Contents

PART III—LONG-RANGE PLANNING

Introduction

Managerial accounting, sometimes referred to as management accounting, is a division of accounting that deals specifically with how accounting data and other financial data can be used in the management of business or non-business entities. Managerial accounting primarily serves the needs of internal management, and, as a result, it is relatively free from many of the restrictions that are imposed when presenting accounting information to outsiders. It is not bound by rules and regulations issued by any organization or governing body. There are certain types of data and applications that are most useful to management, but the specific application in a given situation depends to a large extent upon the needs and preferences of the individual manager who is to receive the information.

Managerial accounting is also free to extend beyond the boundaries of accounting and may draw upon economics, finance, statistics, operations research, or other disciplines as necessary in providing accounting and financial information that can be used by management in planning and directing the affairs of an enterprise. In short, managerial accounting has a strong pragmatic orientation and is not forced to operate within boundaries established by generally accepted principles and procedures that govern financial accounting.

THE OBJECTIVE OF MANAGEMENT

If managerial accounting is expected to serve management, it will be necessary to consider the goals of management. What does management seek to achieve? It may appear that management is striving only to increase business volume or to maximize profits, but this may not be so.

Many enterprises do not even attempt to produce profits. A governmental agency may be primarily concerned with giving a needed service to the public. Individuals may also form an association for the purpose of promoting some common ideal. The success of the enterprise is measured by the realization of an established common goal rather than in economic terms. However, the economic realities cannot be ignored. In any type of enterprise the management will have to use its resources in such a way that the desired goals will be attained in an efficient manner.

A governmental unit, for example, may make use of the profit concept in measuring whether or not resources have been used effectively and efficiently in achieving its objectives. Plans may be made with profit goals included and with activity conducted accordingly. Performance may then be rated by comparing the results with the resources and effort dedicated to the achievement of the objectives. This is an extension of the rate-of-return measurement commonly employed by business management.

A commercial enterprise, of course, is normally interested in profits, and the management is judged according to its ability to earn profits from the resources entrusted to its care. Owners and potential investors look at the rate of return earned upon the investment and the relative risk involved, and in making an evaluation they compare current results with the results of past years as well as those reported by similar business organizations. In this textbook, the problems of management will be examined for the most part from the viewpoint of a manager of a profit-making entity.

The managers who are elected or appointed by the owners as trustees in the skillful management of invested resources cannot carry out this assignment without the cooperation of others. Modern management recognizes that business enterprise is also responsible to many persons who belong to diverse groups. For example, the general public expects to receive dependable products at a fair cost, and the employees depend upon the business for a means of livelihood. In addition, the business is expected to be a good neighbor in the communities in which it operates. Various groups must be given recognition along with the owners and the creditors who have invested tangible resources in the enterprise. It is now generally understood that the interests of each group are best served by the harmonious reconciliation of all interests. Hence, the objective of maximizing the rate of profit must be accomplished within socially and legally accepted bounds.

THE WORK OF MANAGEMENT

The management accomplishes its objectives by working through people. The efforts of many individuals are combined in an organization. The top-level management, as it is called, assumes responsibility for overall planning and policy formation. Decisions that affect the business as a whole are made in a corporate form of organization by the president, the vice-presidents, and other officers. The work of the organization is divided so that each officer has authority to act in a given area of activity. For example, one vice-president may be in charge of production, while another is in charge of sales.

Managers at the top level are unable to make all of the decisions. They are assisted by lower levels of management who make specific decisions in prescribed areas. A vice-president in charge of production may delegate the authority for plant operation to superintendents, each of whom assumes responsibility for the operation of a given plant. The plant superintendent may also delegate a part of his authority to section superintendents, who in turn depend upon departmental foremen who are responsible for operations at the departmental level. Company policy is thus established and carried out through a hierarchy of managerial personnel extending from the president to the department foremen. This division of work throughout the organization applies not only to production but to other functional areas as well.

In carrying out its work, the management must make choices or decisions. Some decisions, such as those involving the location of a plant, the expansion of facilities, the addition of a product line, and the capital structure, are made at the higher management levels. Within prescribed areas, less far-reaching decisions are made by executives who are charged with the responsibility for a certain segment of the enterprise. For example, the manager of the stores of raw materials in a plant may be given authority to decide when certain material stocks are becoming depleted and when new orders should be placed.

PLANNING AND CONTROL DECISIONS

The decisions of the management may be classified as planning and control decisions. An enterprise must have its course charted and must be given direction in the light of future expectations. The planning decisions may be incorporated in a budget of future expected sales, cost of sales, operating expenses, and profit; or plans may involve a selection of a new product line to be sold or an investment in new equipment. Plans standing by themselves, of course, are not enough. There must be a follow-through. Steps must be taken to put the plans into operation and to see that they are being carried out as intended. Actual operations will have to be directed and controlled if the plans are to be realized. Sometimes as operations progress it will be necessary to revise the plans and to direct activities along a different course from that originally contemplated. The decisions that pertain to the direction of actual business activity may be looked upon as decisions of control.

Both planning and control decisions are made at all levels of management. Top-level management, for example, may investigate new investment opportunities and may plan for the future by accepting or rejecting certain proposals. When a course of action has been decided upon, the results will be measured and compared with the original plan. Operations will be directed so that unfavorable tendencies will be eliminated or at least minimized. Whenever necessary, the initial plan will be altered to fit a change in circumstances.

A foreman may likewise make planning and control decisions within his own jurisdiction. It may be up to him to plan the work within his department and to assign men to different tasks so that the production quota will be met, and he too will guide operations in accordance with established plans.

A firm does not have complete freedom of choice in making decisions. Limitations are imposed by conditions in the market place and by other outside influences. Any given company may find it necessary to adjust itself to the demand for its products, the relative scarcity of productive factors, their cost, and other conditions that prevail. Basic managerial decisions of business enterprise have often been classified under three general headings as decisions with respect to:

(1) The methods of production.
(2) The quantities to be produced and the prices to be charged.
(3) The combination of products to be produced.

Under methods of production, management considers whether it should manufacture the products that it will sell or buy them in completed form for resale. Some of the component parts entering into the final products may be purchased from other companies or they may be manufactured by the company itself. There is also the question as to how the productive factors should be combined. Should machinery and equipment be used in place of labor, for example, and if so, in what proportion? What type of machinery and equipment is required, how can it be used to best advantage, and when should equipment be replaced? These are only a few examples of the many decisions falling under this category.

Management must also consider the size of the operation. What quantities are to be produced? In order to handle a given volume of business, the firm must have adequate resources. These resources must be in balance so that there will be sufficient cash for the payment of creditors, inventory of products to deliver to customers, facilities to support the planned production, etc. Furthermore, before making *any* plans, management must have some understanding of how resources flow in and out of the business and how they are converted into different forms. Prices and costs are examined in relationship to the volume of business conducted, and decisions are made that will tend to maximize the rate of return on the resources invested.

If there is more than one product to be considered, management has to select the combination that appears to be the most profitable. Each line of product has a certain selling price, and there are costs identifiable with each line. When products are sold in combination, it may be better to concentrate attention on the line that yields the greatest profit. Further analysis may show, however, that profits can be improved by selling products in a combination that does not necessarily maximize the sale of the most profitable line.

These decisional classifications are given for the sake of convenience. In practice, one type of decision cannot be isolated from another. There are combinational aspects, it will be noted, in the decision of how to produce; and the quantity to be produced will depend upon the methods of production, the combinations selected, and the prices. The classification given does not pertain to manufacturing alone but could be just as well applied to an enterprise that sells services rather than products to its customers. Nor will the decisions in every case involve capital investment. For example, machinery and equipment may have to be acquired and will enter into the decisional process. On the other hand, no investment of this sort may be needed.

CLASSIFICATION OF DECISIONS BY FUNCTION AND TIME ELEMENT

Managerial decisions may sometimes be classified under given functions such as sales, production, finance, etc. A decision may be spoken of as a sales decision or as a production decision. A decision to concentrate sales effort in a given area would be primarily a sales decision, whereas a decision to use a certain method in manufacturing would be primarily a production decision. The breakdown of decisions according to function and activity is possible in many cases.

However, there is some risk in the classification of decisions by function. Not all decisions can be classified. In some instances, decisions that appear to fall within a functional area will have a widespread effect upon the entire operation. It would seem, for example, that the decision to manufacture a part instead of buying it would be a production decision. Yet, the effect may extend beyond the production area. By producing parts, the company may be competing with its former suppliers. This in turn may have an effect upon sales, particularly if excess parts produced are sold on the market. It is also possible that the costs of administering the business will increase if parts are manufactured. Before going ahead with its plans, management should make certain that it has considered the total effect of these plans upon the enterprise as a unit.

It is also possible to classify decisions according to time element. Certain decisions have an effect for only a relatively short period of time, while others are so long-range as to have an impact extending many years into the future. A budget for the coming year would be a short-range plan. Likewise, an estimate of expected cash collections during the next three months would be a plan of short duration. On the other hand, a plan to construct a new plant or to lease properties would probably commit the enterprise to a course of action extending several years into the future. Decisions having an influence over a relatively long period of time are spoken of as long-range decisions.

THE NEED FOR INFORMATION

The management depends upon information in making decisions. A large part of this information is provided within the framework of the managerial organization itself. There are channels of communication extending from the top level of management to the lower levels and conversely from the lower levels to the top. Policies and instructions are transmitted to subordinates, who in return report to their superiors, showing how well they have discharged the tasks assigned to them. Without these channels of communication, effective business management would be impossible.

The management also depends upon information that is furnished by specialists. Accountants, attorneys, economists, marketing specialists, and others provide information and advise the management with respect to various phases of the business. The attorneys, for example, point out how certain transactions should be handled to conform with governmental laws and regulations and interpret various stipulations laid down by governing units. The economists provide information with respect to general economic conditions, and the marketing specialists point out effective ways to promote and distribute products.

THE CONTRIBUTION OF THE ACCOUNTANT

The accountant is expected to furnish financial information. It will also be his responsibility to maintain the financial records of the business and to prepare the financial statements that show how the business has progressed over a period of time and what its financial position is at any given time. In addition, the accountant will combine financial data in various ways in the preparation of reports that serve as a guide to management.

The accountant is not only a service arm to the management but is a part of the management. The controller of a company, for example, is responsible for the management of the accounting function, selecting ways to process accounting data and methods of presentation. In the accounting area itself, the principles of management are applied. What combination and quantity of reports should be prepared, how should they be prepared, and what is the best method of collecting data? By the nature of his work, the accountant is drawn into the management of the business and often plays an important part in shaping the decisions made for his company.

PLANNING

Budgeting and planning in general have already been pointed out as highly significant management functions. The accountant helps to bring together the budget estimates and coordinates them into a comprehensive plan for the future. Sales estimates expressed in physical units are translated into dollars. Production requirements are planned, costs are determined, and all phases of the business operation are interlocked to form a master guide. By following this plan, the management will be able to predict the results of business operation and the financial position at some later date.

Accounting data can also be adapted to fit special situations. A question may arise as to whether or not a particular part should be manufactured or purchased. Assume that the part can be purchased from an outside supplier at a cost of $14. Perhaps the part can be manufactured for less than the purchase price. A special study may reveal that if the part were manufactured, costs would be incurred as follows:

	Unit Cost
Cost of materials needed to make the part	$ 6.50
Labor cost of parts manufacture	4.20
Increase in other manufacturing costs and costs of administration	2.10
Additional cost incurred if part is manufactured	$12.80

No additional facilities are required to make the part. Apparently, the part should be made because the addition to cost is $1.20 less than the cost to purchase. But this is only part of the problem. There may be other factors, such as the ability of the company to make parts of the quality desired, its capacity to make the required quantity, and the effect on the market situation. Perhaps there are other alternatives. The company may find that facilities can be put to even better use in some other undertaking.

A store manager may consider the advantages and the disadvantages of remaining open after normal working hours. Additional sales volume may be anticipated, but there are also additional costs attached to keeping the store open. Sales that would not be made otherwise may be estimated at $8,000 for the extra hours. The cost of the products sold would be about $5,500. Therefore, the store operation could contribute $2,500 to other costs and to profits during those hours. But the costs to keep the store open must be considered. Total wages will be higher, and there will be higher heat and light costs.

Estimated increase in wages $1,100
Estimated increase in heat and light costs 150
Total estimated cost increase $1,250

From the accounting data given, there is a net advantage of $1,250 in remaining open after hours. To obtain this advantage there are risks. Bad weather may cause the sales to fall below the estimate or may push the cost of heating beoynd the estimate made. If competing stores in the area are open, the manager may be virtually forced to remain open. Nevertheless, the profit and loss effect will be recognized and can be evaluated as one of the major factors in arriving at a decision.

CONTROL

During the course of operation, measurements can be made and related to the budget to see if operations are being carried out as intended. The manager of a department, for example, will prepare a budget of the costs for which he is responsible. The actual costs will then be compared with the budgeted costs, and the information derived can be applied in better control over costs and in better future budgeting. To illustrate, a simple budget is given for a department managed by Henry Wills, with actual results of operation.

Department A
Manager—Henry Wills
Operations Report
For the Month of March, 1972

			Actual	
	Budget	Actual	Over	Under
Materials used	$21,400	$21,200		$200
Labor	13,100	15,600	$2,500	
Indirect materials and supplies .	2,850	2,800		50
Travel and entertainment	650	750	100	
Heat and light	150	200	50	
Repairs and maintenance	300	250		50
Miscellaneous	50	100	50	
Total	$38,500	$40,900	$2,700	$300

Assuming that the budget fits the level of operations with which it is compared, attention is immediately called to labor cost. What has caused the large variance? Perhaps labor rates are higher than shown in the budget, more labor time has been used, or possibly a combination of rate and time differences has caused the problem. In any event, the management is aware of the problem and can investigate further to see what can be done to correct it. In many instances a monthly report will not be sufficient. Sometimes a report of weekly or even daily costs may be required so that the costs can be brought under control more quickly.

THE BASIS FOR ACCOUNTABILITY

The accountant obtains information about the financial affairs of a business from its accounting system. The accounting system consists of the sum total of the methods and the procedures employed in the accumulation and the organization of financial data for a business enterprise. It is designed by the accountant to fit the peculiar needs of the business unit to which it applies. Within the system, there are certain checks and controls that tend to protect business properties from intentional or unintentional loss and that aid in the detection of errors in the processing of the data itself.

The accountant is concerned with financial transactions as they pertain to a given business unit or entity, not with the aggregate transactions of an industry, a segment of the economy, or the economy as a whole. The business unit is also looked upon as an entity separate and apart from the persons or the organizations that have an interest in it. Accounting is performed for the entity as such.

Business transactions of a financial nature are analyzed by the accountant and are recorded, classified, and combined with similar transactions. The process of recording, classifying, and combining is spoken of as the *accounting process* or as the *accounting cycle*. The accounting process is explained in Appendixes A, B, and C. From an orderly summation of business events, financial statements and reports are prepared for use by various individuals and organizations who are interested in the financial affairs of the enterprise. Often financial data are projected into the future or are adapted so that they can be more useful in the decision-making process.

THE USE OF ACCOUNTING DATA

The focus in the introduction has been on the idea that management needs data in making decisions. The remainder of this textbook is devoted to showing how accounting data can be used as an aid in decision making and control. A decision maker may be a business manager or he may be a potential investor or lender. Accounting data are useful to both the insider and the outsider; hence, the use of data by both types of users will be considered. For the most part, however, the problems of business management will receive attention. Problems that arise in the collection and the processing of data are not of primary concern. The important problem is the *use* of data, and this use will be emphasized.

Questions

1. What is managerial accounting?

2. Why is managerial accounting relatively free from restrictions?

3. Explain in general how governmental units can make use of the profit concept.

4. What objectives in addition to profit are important to management?

5. How are the objectives of management discharged?

6. How does a planning decision differ from a control decision?

7. Give examples of planning decisions that would be made (a) at top management levels and (b) at lower levels of management.

8. Basic managerial decisions have often been classified under three general headings. Identify and discuss each of the three decisional classifications.

9. Can managerial decisions also be classified according to functional area and length of time? Explain how these classifications may overlap.

10. Where does management get the information it needs?

11. How does the accountant make a contribution to business management?

12. Is the accountant a manager in his own right? How?

PART ONE   FINANCIAL RELATIONSHIPS

Chapter 1

FINANCIAL STATEMENTS

Financial statements and financial relationships will be discussed in this chapter and in the next few chapters. Much of the material in these chapters is fundamental to both financial accounting and managerial accounting because financial accounting is (1) the foundation for managerial accounting, and (2) a contribution in itself to better business management.

Top management is responsible for the financial statements that are published and distributed to stockholders and to the public at large. These statements are a basis for the evaluation of the firm and its management. Financial analysts and other persons interested in making investment decisions examine these statements and the relationships between and within the statements. Management is quite aware of this evaluation process and tries to maintain a proper balance in the financial structure and operations of the firm.

The financial statements often contain summarized information. Summarized data, such as an inventory of merchandise or the depreciation of equipment shown in one amount, can help management to obtain an overall view of the enterprise. However, much more information is needed in planning and controlling the various segments of the entity. In the case of inventory, for example, it is important to know the quantities of different types of inventory, costs, estimated selling prices, and the effect of adding or dropping certain lines. Managerial accounting extends beyond financial accounting to use data selectively with the central objective being to serve the needs of management.

THE BASIC FINANCIAL STATEMENTS

Financial statements and reports are prepared from the accounting records according to the peculiarities and needs of the business to which they pertain. Two of the most widely recognized statements, the balance sheet and the income statement, which are prepared for almost every business entity, will be discussed in this chapter. Most persons having an interest in the financial affairs of a business will expect to receive the basic information contained in these two statements.

In addition, a statement of retained earnings may be prepared for a corporation to show the changes in retained earnings during the year, and an illustrative statement is given later in the chapter. Also, a statement of changes in financial position should be presented. This statement will be discussed in Chapter 7.

The balance sheet. The *balance sheet* is a listing of the resources of a business together with the equities or interests of creditors and owners in those resources. The resources of a business are the properties and the property rights possessed and are called the *assets* of the business. An individual or a group of individuals having a claim against the assets is said to have an equity in the business. The interest of the owners in the assets is called the *owners' equity*. Creditors' interests in the assets are called *liabilities*. The combined interests of the owners and creditors are referred to simply as *equities*. The balance sheet is a statement of the financial position of an enterprise at a given date, and it reflects the result of all recorded accounting transactions since the enterprise was formed. In a sense, the balance sheet is a cumulative record. Assets, when acquired, are listed on the balance sheet and are held as such in one form or another until they are either used or transferred out of the business. The equities of both creditors and owners are also continually changing as a result of various transactions, and the status of the equities as well as the assets at any given time is revealed on the balance sheet. The balance sheet for a particular date tells what the assets and the equities are at that time, but it does not tell what caused them to change nor does it tell when the change took place. However, by examining a series of balance sheets, it is possible to detect changes in asset and equity structure. Relationships between the various items can be determined, and trends may be discovered. Information revealed by the statements can then be applied in planning for the future.

The income statement. The *income statement,* sometimes called a statement of income, a statement of income and expense, a profit and loss statement, or an operating statement, is dynamic. It shows the results of operations for a company during a certain interval of time. The inflow of assets resulting from selling products and services to customers is measured in revenue accounts. The outflow of assets identified with the products and services provided to customers is measured in expense accounts. The net increase or decrease in net assets resulting from this activity, that is, the difference between revenue and expense, is designated as net income or net loss. A net increase in net assets, net income, is added to the owners' equity on the balance sheet at the end of the measured time interval. On the other hand, a net decrease in net assets, net loss, is deducted from the owners' equity. Neither the balance sheet nor the income statement stands alone. The statements interlock or articulate. Data appearing on the income statement are tied in with data reported on the balance sheet.

The interlocking effect. The relationship of the balance sheet and income statement is derived from the balance sheet equation. An expanded form of this equation is given below to show how the balance sheet and the income statement are related.

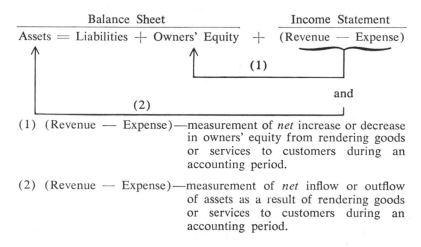

(1) (Revenue — Expense)—measurement of *net* increase or decrease in owners' equity from rendering goods or services to customers during an accounting period.

(2) (Revenue — Expense)—measurement of *net* inflow or outflow of assets as a result of rendering goods or services to customers during an accounting period.

The equation as presented above is somewhat oversimplified but is essentially true. Revenue and expense accounts measure aggregate increases or decreases in assets, but no specific assets are identified. More precisely it may be stated that *net* assets (assets — liabilities) are increased or decreased when revenues and expenses are recognized. Sometimes assets are received with a corresponding liability being recorded until goods or services are delivered. When the goods or services are delivered, the liability is reduced and revenue is recorded. For example, a deposit in the form of cash may be received from customers with a liability being recorded for the obligation to deliver goods or services in the future. Eventually, when the goods or services are delivered, the liability is removed and revenue is recognized.

Often the relationship between the assets and the revenues and expenses is direct. For example, assets such as cash or accounts receivable are usually increased at the time sales revenue is recorded. At the same time, cost of goods sold is recorded as an expense and the inventory (asset) is reduced. The ability to see how a transaction affects both statements is not only essential to an understanding of accounting but is most helpful in managing a business.

SOME BASIC CONCEPTS

In the preparation of financial statements certain accounting concepts are observed, some of which are discussed in the following paragraphs.

The going concern. In accounting, the assumption is made that a business will continue to operate in the future and that it will not cease doing business, sell its assets, and make final payments to creditors and owners. Therefore, it is said that accounting is carried out on a *going concern basis*. The plant assets, for example, are not normally adjusted to liquidation values. Presumably the plant assets will not be sold but will be used in future business operations. On the balance sheet given for Hamilton Products, Inc., on page 22, the building and equipment, for example, are shown at a net amount of $240,900. This does not mean that they can be sold for that amount. The valuation of $240,900 is the undepreciated cost to be carried forward to future years. As the building and equipment are used in conducting operations, a cost of using them will be recognized in the determination of net income or net loss.

There are, of course, circumstances in which the going concern assumption would not apply. If a business is to be discontinued, a different type of statement could be prepared and assets could be revalued at amounts that would possibly be realized upon their sale. However, this would be a special case, and the business would not be a going concern but would be a "quit concern."

Cost. Cost is conventionally used as the basis for accountability. Assets when acquired under normal circumstances are recorded at the price arrived at by negotiation between two independent parties dealing at arm's length. Simply stated, the *cost* of an asset to the purchaser is the price that he must pay now or later to obtain it. The fair value of the asset is not relevant in recording the transaction. A purchaser may acquire an asset at a cost that is greater or less than the fair value determined in the market place. If so, he accounts for the asset at his cost, value notwithstanding.

Accounting for costs is an extremely complex process. In conducting business operations, assets lose their original identity, that is, they are converted into some other form. For example, materials used in a chemical process often cannot be identified as such in some end product produced.

Costs are traced through operations, wherever possible, as the assets are transferred or converted in the course of operations.

One of the principal objectives in accounting for costs is the measurement of profits and losses. The costs attached to the products or services sold are matched against the consideration received from the customers in the determination of profits or losses. This is not always easy to do. For example, several product lines may be produced together, with one particular cost common to all lines. The assignment of the cost to any one line is difficult at best, with further complexities being introduced when attempts are made to apportion the cost attached to any one line between the cost of the goods or services sold and the cost remaining on hand as inventory.

The realization concept. The profits and losses of a business are measured as the difference between the consideration received from customers and the costs attached to the products or services given in exchange. In conventional accounting, profits are not recognized unless they are realized. For the most part, realization depends upon an agreement with a customer to pay a stipulated amount for the product.

The point at which the revenue is realized will vary depending upon circumstances. The amount of the consideration received from the customer is frequently looked upon as being realized when title to the items sold is vested in the customer. At that point there is an enforceable claim against the customer. It is not necessary that the consideration be in the form of cash; the promise of the customer to make eventual payment is sufficient. In some cases, profit realization and cash realization go together. For example, a barber will realize the amount to be received from the customer as he gives the customer service, and he will realize the consideration in cash immediately after the service has been given. For all practical purposes, it can be said that the barber would be entitled to measure profits as cash is realized. On the other hand, when merchandise is delivered to customers on installment sales, there may be considerable doubt as to whether or not the promise of the customer to make eventual payment will be fulfilled. Profits on installment sales may be looked upon as realized when cash is collected.

In some cases, profits are realized before delivery is made to the customer and before cash is collected. For example, a shipbuilder may build a vessel on government contract. As the work progresses, profits may be realized by matching costs for the percentage of work completed against a corresponding percentage of the amount of the consideration to be received. This method of accounting for profits, spoken of as the *percentage-of-completion* method, is sometimes used by contractors who build highways, buildings, bridges, and other structures and properties that are completed over a relatively long period of time.

Periodicity. The income statement has already been revealed as a statement pertaining to a given period of time only. Ideally, no measurement of net income or net loss should be made while a business is still actively conducting operations. A more accurate measurement of the net income or the net loss could be made after a company had ceased doing business and had sold all of its assets and had paid off all of its liabilities. The net income or loss would then be the difference between the amount ultimately realized by the owners and their initial investment. As a practical matter, however, measurements must be made while the business is in progress and the results must be reported periodically.

Ordinarily revenues and expenses are measured over a period of one year. This year does not necessarily correspond with the calendar year but instead may correspond with the natural cycle of business activity. Logically, a fiscal year should end with the close of a cycle of business activity, that is, when inventories and accounts receivable are at a minimum but before new inventory is acquired for another cycle of sales and subsequent collections. For example, a department store may choose a year extending from March 1 of one year to February 28 (or 29) of the next calendar year. The Christmas sales and the January sales for the same season will then fall within the same year, and the inventories and the accounts receivable will generally be low just before merchandise is purchased for spring and summer sales. The year chosen for financial measurements is called the *fiscal year* or *fiscal period*.

Although a year is generally the longest period of time used in making measurements, it is possible to take measurements over shorter time intervals, such as a quarter of a year or a month. During the year, an income statement may be prepared for both a given month and for the year to date, or for a quarter of a year and the year to date. Sometimes the data for a corresponding period in the previous year will be presented along with the current data, thus making comparison possible.

Matching. A reasonably accurate measurement of the net income or the net loss for a fiscal period depends upon the matching of expenses against related revenues. The matching of revenues and expenses is difficult. With a going concern there is always the possibility that a revenue or an expense should have been recognized in a previous fiscal period or that it should have been deferred until some future period. If expenses have not been properly offset against revenues, the resulting net income or net loss for the fiscal period will be reported incorrectly.

The revenues and the expenses pertaining to a fiscal period may have to be estimated. A company might sell a product under an agreement to guarantee against defects and furnish future maintenance and repair services. Not only must the estimated liability to the customer be recognized, but the expense of giving this service should be estimated and offset against the revenue resulting from the initial sales transaction. The cost of giving this service to the customer is related to the sales transaction; therefore, the estimated expense and liability should be recorded during the period in which the sale was made.

A company may also enter into a program of research and development, expecting to receive future benefits. The costs that are expected to benefit future fiscal periods should be deferred and matched against the revenues of the later fiscal periods. But what portion of the costs should be deferred and matched against the revenues of any given year? There are many similar situations in which matching must be done on an estimated basis. Estimates will have to be made on a judgment basis using information available.

Consistency. Not only are the results of an accounting system dependent in many cases upon estimates, but also they will be influenced by the choice of an accounting method and the consistency with which it is applied. For example, inventories may be accounted for on a first-in, first-out basis, a last-in, first-out basis, or by some other means.

The *first-in, first-out* method of costing inventories or, in abbreviated form, the *fifo* method occurs when the older costs are traced through to the cost of goods sold while more recent costs are identified with the inventories at the end of the period. On the other hand, the more recent costs may be traced through to the cost of goods sold, with the older costs being held as inventories at the end of the period. This method of costing is called the *last-in, first-out* method or, in abbreviated form, the *lifo* method. Inventory costs may also be averaged, with the cost of goods sold and the inventories at the end of the period on an average cost basis according to the particular averaging technique employed. The distinction between the costs to be matched against revenues as cost of goods sold and the costs to be held as inventories is highly important in the income determination process. One method of accounting for the flow of costs cannot be labeled as the correct method to the exclusion of all others. Yet, the choice of a particular method and the way in which it is carried out over the years will have an influence on the profits reported as well as on the inventory cost for the balance sheet.

Assume, for example, that a company keeping its inventory records on a fifo basis computed its cost of goods sold for a year as shown below:

Inventory, January 1 (50,000 units @ $2)	$ 100,000
Purchases:	
January to June (150,000 units @ $3)	450,000
July to December (200,000 units @ $4)	800,000
Cost of goods available	$1,350,000
Less: Inventory, December 31 (40,000 @ $4)	160,000
Cost of goods sold	$1,190,000

If the company had decided for some valid reason to change its method of accounting for inventories and had shifted to the lifo method of costing inventories at the beginning of the year, it would compute a different cost of goods sold and a different inventory cost at the end of the year. The results might have appeared as follows:

Inventory, January 1 (50,000 units @ $2)	$ 100,000
Purchases:	
January to June (150,000 units @ $3)	450,000
July to December (200,000 units @ $4)	800,000
Cost of goods available	$1,350,000
Less: Inventory, December 31 (40,000 units @ $2)	80,000
Costs of goods sold	$1,270,000

The cost of goods sold is higher by $80,000 than it would have been without the change. Unless this is pointed out, the reader of the financial statements in making a comparison with the previous years might reach an inaccurate conclusion as to why the cost of goods sold had increased.

An accounting method or procedure once chosen should be followed consistently from year to year. Consistency in accounting is not advocated just for the sake of consistency, but instead is advocated because of the confusion that would result if profits or losses were to be calculated on a different basis each year. Desirable changes should be made, of course; but when changes are made, the effect of such changes upon the financial statements should be fully disclosed.

The accrual principle. Revenues and expenses are accounted for on the accrual basis. *Revenue* is defined as the consideration (measured in monetary terms) received for rendering goods and services. Revenue is usually recognized when the following conditions are satisfied:

(1) The amount of revenue must be capable of objective measurement.

(2) The earning process must be reasonably complete or complete enough so that the cost of completion can be determined.

(3) The revenue must be realized.

Revenue is not necessarily recognized at the time cash is collected. For example, goods and services are often sold on credit terms. At some later date collections will be made from the customers, but collections of cash are not a realization of revenue. Instead, the collections are a realization in cash of the asset, accounts receivable, which was increased at the time revenue was recorded, that is, at the date when goods or sevices were delivered and billed.

Occasionally, customers will pay in advance for goods and services that will be delivered later. The advance payments have not been earned and cannot be recorded as revenue. The company in accepting these advance payments is obligated to the customers until it makes delivery. As deliveries are made, the liability is reduced and revenue is earned. If the accounting records have not been kept up-to-date during the fiscal period, adjusting entries will be made at the end of the period so that the portion of the advance earned will be shown as revenue with the portion still owed to the customers being shown as a liability.

When merchandise is sold on the installment plan, there may be some question as to whether or not revenue should be recognized when deliveries are made to the customers. The collections may not be made according to plan, and the merchandise may have to be repossessed. Under the circumstances, there may be a justification for the recognition of revenue as collections are made. At that time there is no question about the realization of the revenue.

Reductions in revenue should be offset against the corresponding revenue recorded. Cash discounts and allowances granted to customers should be estimated and deducted from the related revenue. The loss is related to the revenue and not to the period of time in which the discount or the allowance is finally granted.

Similarly, expenses are carefully matched against related revenues and are not necessarily recognized when cash payments are made for goods and services. An expense occurs when the asset leaves the business as a result of revenue-producing activity and not when cash payments are made to creditors. The cost of the asset becomes expense in the fiscal period that benefits from the use of the asset. For example, supplies may be purchased on credit terms. At the time of purchase the supplies are recorded as an asset, and a liability to the creditor is recorded. When payment is made for the supplies, the liability to the creditor is reduced. But the payment is not related to the use of the supplies. As the supplies are used in earning revenue, the cost of the portion used should be recorded as expense with the supplies asset account being reduced by a corresponding amount. Often expenses will have to be estimated. Goods and services may be delivered with an agreement that defects will be corrected or that future services will be given without charge. The costs to correct the defects and to furnish the additional services should be estimated and deducted as expenses in the same period in which the related revenue is recorded.

The problem of matching expenses against revenues in the income determination process is a challenging problem. The identification of revenue with a given interval of time is not an exact process, nor is it a simple matter to identify expenses with the resulting revenues. Judgments and estimates will have to be made in many cases, using the best information that is available to management.

Conservatism. Usually the accountant takes a conservative position. Revenue is generally not recognized by recording value increases that may take place on unsold products or merchandise, even if it can be demonstrated that the items in question can be sold at the current market prices in excess of their cost. The principles of valuing assets at cost and recognizing revenue only when the sale is made go hand in hand. If market increments were recorded, assets would be reflected at market value and not at cost.

On the other hand, losses may be recorded when market prices decline below costs. This inconsistency in the application of accounting principles has been justified on the basis of conservatism. As a rule the accountant is skeptical of claims that assets are worth more than cost but will be more inclined to accept evidence that assets may be realized at even less than cost. Conservatism can be carried too far, however. It has merit in that the readers of the balance sheet are not led to expect that marketable securities, for example, can be realized at cost when in reality the current market prices are below cost. But excessive undervaluation can make the business appear to be in poor financial condition when such is not the case. Investment may be discouraged if a business appears to be less valuable than it is. The accountant must recognize that persons can be injured by understatements as well as by overstatement.

Valuation. The reader of the balance sheet should be acquainted with the principles of valuation that are commonly applied in arriving at the dollar amounts shown for the various assets and equities. Sometimes the basis of valuation will be indicated in the body of the statement or in accompanying footnotes. In many cases, however, the basis of valuation will not be given, it being assumed that the reader is familiar with conventional practices. Recently, the conventional practices of valuation have been criticized. Questions have been raised as to whether or not assets should be valued at cost on the balance sheet when there is evidence that the assets are worth considerably more or less than cost.[1] Or is the profit for a fiscal period properly measured when historical costs are matched against revenues as expenses in the period of sale? The valuation problem cannot be separated from the problem of income determination. In the last few years, a great deal of attention has been focused on the problem of presenting financial information in a way that will best serve the interests of both the investors and the management. Some conventional practices have been challenged.

BALANCE SHEET CLASSIFICATIONS

A condensed balance sheet for Hamilton Products, Inc., at September 30, 1972, is illustrated on the following page.

Both the assets and the equities are usually listed separately and are not reduced by offsetting one against the other. This holds true even though specific assets may be pledged to secure the payment of a debt such as notes payable or bonds payable, for example. Ordinarily the debt-holder will receive payment in cash and will lay claim to the assets pledged only if the debtor defaults. The equity holders are said to have an *undivided interest* in the total assets. Thus the equities are looked upon as a measurement of the extent of the rights of any individual or entity in the total assets, but not to any particular asset. In the statement given for Hamilton Products, Inc., the holders of the long-term notes payable do not have a $60,000 interest in cash, accounts receivable, inventories, or any other specific asset. They do, however, have a $60,000 claim against the assets in total.

On the balance sheet the assets and the equities are listed under classifications according to their general characteristics. Similar assets or similar equities are listed together, so that it is a relatively simple matter to make a comparison of one classification with another or to make comparisons within a classification. Some of the most commonly used classifications are listed below:

Assets	*Equities*
Current assets	Current liabilities
Investments	Long-term liabilities
Plant assets	Deferred revenues
Intangible assets	Other liabilities
Other assets	Owners' equity

Current assets. The *current assets* include cash and other assets that in the normal course of events are converted into cash within the operating

---

[1] See Robert T. Sprouse and Maurice Moonitz, *A Tentative Set of Broad Accounting Principles for Business Enterprises*, Accounting Research Study No. 3 (New York: American Institute of Certified Public Accountants, 1962).

Hamilton Products, Inc.
Balance Sheet
September 30, 1972

Assets

Currents assets:

Cash		$ 36,230	
Marketable securities at cost (market value, $42,650)		41,320	
Notes receivable		5,000	
Accounts receivable	$ 71,570		
Less: Allowance for discounts, returns, allowances, and doubtful accounts	3,620	67,950	
Inventories		96,210	
Prepaid insurance		1,670	$248,380
Investment in stock of Bayberry, Inc.			50,000

Plant assets:

Land		$ 17,800	
Building and equipment	$288,200		
Less: Accumulated depreciation	47,300	240,900	258,700

Intangible assets:

Organization expense		$ 6,200	
Goodwill		27,500	33,700

Other assets:

Advances to company officers ..			11,400
Total assets			$602,180

Equities

Current liabilities:

Bank loans		$ 15,000	
Accounts payable		38,790	
Accrued payroll and other expenses		26,220	
Estimated income taxes payable .		33,800	$113,810
Long-term notes, due November 30, 1981			60,000
Deferred rental revenues			3,800

Owners' equity:

Capital stock, $10 par value, 5,000 shares issued and outstanding		$ 50,000	
Premium on stock		31,200	
Retained earnings		343,370	424,570
Total equities			$602,180

cycle. A manufacturing enterprise, for example, will use cash to acquire inventories of materials that are converted into finished products and sold to customers. Cash is collected from the customers, and the circle from cash back to cash is called an *operating cycle*. In a merchandising business, one part of the cycle is eliminated. Materials are not purchased for conversion into finished products. Instead, the finished products are purchased and are sold directly to the customers.

Several operating cycles may be completed in a year, or it may take more than a year to complete one operating cycle. The time required to complete an operating cycle depends upon the nature of the business.

It is conceivable that virtually all of the assets of a business can be converted into cash within the time required to complete an operating cycle. But a current asset is an asset that is converted into cash within an operating cycle *in the normal course of events*. Assets such as buildings, machinery, and equipment that are used in conducting the business will not be converted into cash in the normal course of operations. They are held because they provide useful services for the business and are excluded from the current asset classification.

On the other hand, a manufacturer or a dealer who holds assets such as buildings, machinery, and equipment for resale to customers in the regular course of his business will include these items in the inventory under the classification of current assets. The manufacturer or dealer does not hold these assets for his own use but holds them as an inventory of product in the expectation that the assets will be converted into cash in the normal course of operations. An automobile dealer, for example, will have company cars that are not to be sold but are to be used in operating the business. These cars are not included in the inventory. But the cars that are held for resale to customers are an inventory of product that should be listed under the current assets.

In many cases, the operating cycle will not extend beyond a year. However, there are exceptions. An inventory of liquor in the distilling industry must be aged, for example, and may be shown as a current asset even though it will not be converted into cash within the next year. It qualifies as a current asset inasmuch as it is converted into cash in the normal course of events within the operating cycle of the business.

Investments. *Investments* are funds in cash or security form held for a designated purpose or for an indefinite period of time. This classification would include investment in the stocks or the bonds of another company, real estate or mortgages held for income-producing purposes, and investments held for a pension or other special fund.

Plant assets. The assets such as land, buildings, machinery, and equipment that are to be used in business operations over a relatively long period of time are often classified as *fixed assets* or more specifically as plant assets or as plant and equipment. It is not expected that these assets will be sold and converted into cash as are inventories. Plant assets produce income indirectly through their use in operations.

On the balance sheet for Hamilton Products, Inc., the land is shown separately at $17,800; the buildings and the equipment are shown at both the gross amounts and at the net amounts after deducting accumulated depreciation. Land does not have a limited useful life and is not reduced by depreciation. However, the cost of buildings, equipment, and other plant assets having a limited useful life are matched against revenues during the fiscal periods in which they are used.

Adjustments are usually not made in conventional accounting practice to restate plant assets at current replacement costs or at net realizable values. Plant assets, unlike the inventories, are not to be sold in the normal course of operations. Instead, they will be used in performing the work of the business enterprise. The investment in plant assets should be recovered gradually as the assets are used in producing profits, but it is not expected that the investment will be recovered by direct sale as is the case with inventory.

In accounting for profits, the replacement cost of a plant asset and its net realizable value are not generally considered; yet in special decision-making situations these valuations can be applied. When equipment is to be replaced, for example, the management will consider the current replacement cost and the amount that should be realized upon the sale or trade-in of the present equipment. During the course of operations, recognition may also be given to the possibility that new equipment may cost more in the future. Profits that would otherwise be distributed to the owners as dividends may be retained to the extent of the anticipated increase in replacement costs. By following this policy, the company hopes to be able to retain the *purchasing power* of its initial investment.

Intangible assets. Other fixed assets that lack physical substance are often referred to as *intangible assets*. The intangible assets consist of valuable rights, privileges, or advantages. Although the intangibles lack physical substance, they have value. Sometimes the rights, privileges, and advantages of a business are worth more than all of the other assets combined.

Typical items included as intangible assets are patents, franchises, organization expense, and goodwill. *Patents* give the business an exclusive privilege of using a certain process in manufacturing. *Franchises* permit a company to handle a given product or to operate within a given territory or along a certain route. To become incorporated, a company must incur certain costs, such as the initial incorporation fee to the state and the cost of legal services in connection with the formation of the corporation. These costs are the costs of the privilege of having a corporation and are designated as *organization expense*. A company is said to possess *goodwill* if it can earn a higher-than-normal rate of return upon invested resources. The higher rate of return may be caused by various factors such as managerial skill, popular acceptance of the products, or some other favorable circumstance. In setting a selling price for a prosperous business, it is recognized that the business as such may be worth more than the fair market value of the properties listed on the balance sheet as reduced by the liabilities. In other words, a value is placed on the anticipated earnings above an established normal level.

Goodwill is usually recorded only when it is purchased. Frequently goodwill is recorded when a profitable business is acquired or when there is a change in the form of ownership. In the balance sheet given for Hamilton Products, Inc., goodwill is shown at $27,500. Perhaps the business was at one time a sole proprietorship and developed goodwill valued at $27,500. When the business was incorporated, stockholders purchased ownership interests and in doing so recognized and paid for goodwill. Or Hamilton Products, Inc., may have purchased some other business, paying in excess of the values of the listed properties transferred less the liabilities assumed. This additional payment was made for anticipated future earnings above a normal level, or in short was a payment for goodwill.

If the intangible asset has a limited life, its cost should be written off on the income statements over the fiscal periods during which it yields benefits. For example, a franchise may enable a company to operate over a given route for only a stipulated period of time. The cost of the franchise should then be written off during the estimated fiscal periods that will benefit.

Other assets. There are other assets that cannot be classified as current assets, investments, plant assets, or intangible assets. These assets are listed as other assets. Frequently the other assets consist of advances made to company officers, cost of buildings in the process of construction, and miscellaneous funds held for special purposes.

Current liabilities. On the equity side of the balance sheet, as on the asset side, a distinction is made between current and long-term items. The *current liabilities* are obligations that are to be discharged within the normal operating cycle of the business and in most circumstances are liabilities that are to be paid within the next year by using the assets now classified as current. The amounts owed under current liabilities often arise as a result of acquiring current assets, such as inventory, or acquiring services that will be used in current operations. The amounts owed to trade creditors arising out of the purchase of materials or merchandise are shown as accounts payable. If the company is obligated under promissory notes that support bank loans or other amounts owed, the liability is shown as notes payable. Other current liabilities may include the estimated amount payable for income taxes and the various amounts owed for wages and salaries of employees, utility bills, payroll taxes, local property taxes, and other services.

Long-term liabilities. Debts not falling due until more than a year from the balance sheet date are generally classified as *long-term liabilities*. Notes, bonds, and mortgages are often listed under this heading. If a portion of the long-term debt is to become due within the next year and is to be paid, it should be removed from the long-term debt classification and shown under current liabilities with a caption such as "current installment of long-term debt payable." This reclassification will not be necessary, however, if the debt is to be refunded. Hamilton Products, Inc., has a long-term debt of $60,000 evidenced by notes that will not become due until November 30, 1981. No portion of this debt is to be paid during the next fiscal year; therefore, the entire amount is shown separately and is excluded from the current liability classification.

Other liabilities. Liabilities, like assets, cannot always be classified as being either current or long-term. In some cases the creditors will not expect to receive payment either in the near or the distant future.

Deferred revenues. Customers may make advance payments for merchandise or services. The obligation to the customers will, as a general rule, be settled by delivery of the products or services and not by cash payment. Advance collections received from customers are usually classified as *deferred revenues*, pending delivery of the products or services. On the balance sheet given for Hamilton Products, Inc., rent has been collected in advance from the tenants who have leased space in the building. When Hamilton Products, Inc., gives rental service to the tenants, the obligation will be removed from the balance sheet. The rentals will then be realized and shown on the income statement.

Owners' equity. The *owners' equity* in a corporation is subdivided:

(1) One portion represents the amount invested by the owners directly, plus any portion of retained earnings converted into paid-in capital.
(2) The other portion represents the retention of net earnings in the business.

This rigid distinction is necessary because of the nature of a corporation. Ordinarily the owners of a corporation, that is, the stockholders, are not personally liable for the debts contracted by the company. A stockholder may lose his investment, but creditors usually cannot look to his personal assets for satisfaction of their claims. Under normal circumstances, the owners may withdraw as cash dividends an amount measured by the corporate earnings. This rule gives the creditors some assurance that a certain portion of the assets equivalent to the owners' investment cannot be arbitrarily withdrawn. Of course, this portion could be depleted because of operating losses.

The investment by the owners or the paid-in capital may also be divided into two portions. One portion of the investment is the legal minimum that must be invested according to the corporate charter as approved by the state. Each share of stock may be assigned a par value such as $1, $5, or $10 per share. For each share issued, the stipulated value is to be received by the corporation. This minimum investment is generally labeled as *capital stock*. Any amount invested in the corporation that is in excess of par value is shown separately and is labeled as *premium on stock* or as *paid-in capital in excess of par value*.

Sometimes shares are not assigned a par value. The state may require that the entire amount received from the sale of no-par stock be held as the legal minimum investment, in which case the total amount received would be credited to capital stock. In some states, however, no-par shares are virtually equivalent to par-value shares for accounting purposes in that they are assigned a stated value per share. Any amount received in excess of the stated value can be classified as *paid-in capital in excess of stated value*.

Ordinarily, the premium on stock or the paid-in capital in excess of stated value is not reduced as a result of dividend distributions. Many states, however, allow dividends to be charged against this portion of the owners' investment, but some states require that the source of such dividends be revealed to the stockholders.

If stock is issued at less than its par value or its stated value, it is issued at a discount. Some states will not permit the issuance of stock at a discount, while other states will hold the stockholders liable to creditors to the extent of the stock discount if the corporation cannot meet the claims of its creditors.

The accumulated net earnings of a corporation are shown under a separate heading such as *retained earnings* or *reinvested earnings*. As a general rule, this portion of the owners' equity may be voluntarily reduced by the distribution of dividends to the stockholders and, of course, involuntarily by losses. Net losses in excess of retained earnings are shown as a deduction in the owners' equity section and are labeled as a *deficit*.

The owners' equity in an unincorporated business is shown more simply. The interest of each owner is given in total, with usually no distinction being made between the portion invested and the accumulated net earnings. The creditors are not concerned about the amount invested because, if necessary, they can attach the personal assets of the owners. The owners' equity in a partnership may appear as follows:

Owners' equity:
William Dobbs, Capital $128,000
Clifford Wells, Capital 87,000
Total owners' equity $215,000

INCOME STATEMENT CLASSIFICATIONS

The income statement, like the balance sheet, is a classified statement. An income statement for Hamilton Products, Inc., for the fiscal year ended September 30, 1973, is illustrated on the following page.

Operating revenues. The revenues resulting from the predominant activities of the business are listed first and are called the *operating revenues.* The gross operating revenues are often reduced by customer returns and allowances and cash discounts in arriving at net operating revenues. Hamilton Products, Inc., earns gross operating revenue by making sales to customers, and this revenue has been reduced by returns and allowances, and cash discounts, in arriving at the net sales shown on the statement at $935,260.

Cost of goods sold. If a company is engaged in selling material goods, the cost of the goods sold is computed and is deducted from the net sales to obtain the gross margin. The cost of goods sold can be computed quite easily in two steps as follows:

(1) Inventory of finished goods available at the beginning of the fiscal period $+$ Cost of goods manufactured or purchased during the fiscal period $=$ Cost of goods available for sale during the fiscal period

(2) Cost of goods available for sale during the fiscal period $-$ Inventory of finished goods available at the end of the fiscal period $=$ Cost of goods sold

Gross margin. The gross margin of $363,130 is equal to the net sales of $935,260 reduced by the cost of goods sold of $572,130. *Gross margin*

Hamilton Products, Inc.
Income Statement
For the Year Ended September 30, 1973

Net sales		$935,260
Cost of goods sold		572,130
Gross margin		$363,130
Selling expenses:		
Sales salaries	$68,350	
Advertising	34,280	
Travel and entertainment	9,370	
Freight and delivery	4,620	
Depreciation	7,760	$124,380
General and administrative expenses:		
Officers' salaries	$42,500	
Office salaries	32,580	
Taxes	8,740	
Insurance	1,880	
Utilities	8,130	
Uncollectible accounts expense	9,400	
Depreciation	6,450	109,680
Total operating expenses		$234,060
Net operating income		$129,070
Other revenue and expense:		
Interest and dividends earned	$ 6,200	
Rent revenue	19,400	
	$25,600	
Less: Interest expense	5,200	20,400
Net income before income taxes		$149,470
Estimated income taxes		74,720
Net income after income taxes		$ 74,750
Gain on sale of investment in Bayberry, Inc., net of tax on the gain of $9,400		8,340
Net income to retained earnings		$ 83,090

measures the difference between the net revenue realized from the sale of goods and their cost. No final profit has been earned at this point, of course, because there are operating expenses and other revenues and expenses that must be considered. However, the gross margin is significant. The relationship between the gross margin and net sales may be expressed as a percentage. A comparison of gross margin percentages between years may reveal that selling prices are increasing or decreasing relative to the cost of goods sold. Or it may reveal a change in the mix of products sold. Under certain conditions, gross margin percentages can also be used to estimate the amount of inventory that should be available.

If an inventory has been destroyed or stolen, an insurance claim can be established by using the typical gross margin percentage to estimate the amount of the inventory loss. The cost of the goods sold up to the time of the loss is estimated to be equal to the complement of the gross margin percentage multiplied by net sales. The estimated cost of goods sold is then subtracted from the cost of the goods that were available for sale to arrive at an estimated cost of the inventory at the time of the loss. The cost of the goods available for sale is equal to the cost of the inventory at the beginning of the fiscal period and the cost of purchases or goods manufactured to the point of the loss.

Operating expenses. The expenses of operating the business are then classified according to functional purpose and are deducted from the gross margin to arrive at the net operating income. Expenses of promoting, selling, and distributing products are classified as *selling expenses* and include such items as advertising, sales commissions, delivery expense, sales supplies used, travel and entertainment, and sales office rent. The general expenses of business administration are classified as *general and administrative expenses* and include such items as officers' salaries, office salaries, office supplies used, taxes, insurance and uncollectible accounts expense.

Other revenue and expense. Various incidental or miscellaneous revenues and expenses not related to the main operating purpose of the business are combined with the net operating income in the computation of net income before income taxes. In this example, interest, dividends, and rents were earned, and interest expense was incurred.

Income taxes. Corporate federal income taxes are as much an expense for an incorporated business as any other operating expense. Yet they are usually shown separately near the bottom of the statement because (1) they are based upon the taxable net income or loss for the period, and (2) they are usually a significant amount.

Extraordinary gains and losses. Certain gains or losses such as the gain or loss on the sale of investments and a loss by fire are usually nonrecurring items and are shown net of income taxes in arriving at the net income to be transferred to retained earnings. These unusual gains and losses, if not shown separately, would tend to distort the results from normal activity.

BALANCE SHEET, END OF FISCAL YEAR

A balance sheet for Hamilton Products, Inc., is given at the end of the fiscal year, September 30, 1973.

Hamilton Products, Inc.
Balance Sheet
September 30, 1973

Assets

Current assets:

Cash		$ 39,650	
Marketable securities at cost (market value, $44,240)		43,510	
Notes receivable		3,000	
Accounts receivable	$ 76,950		
Less: Allowance for discounts, returns, allowances, and doubtful accounts	5,210	71,740	
Inventories		94,760	
Prepaid insurance		1,840	$254,500
Investment in bonds of Kohl Bros., Inc.			65,000
Plant assets:			
Land		$ 17,800	
Building and equipment	$327,800		
Less: Accumulated depreciation	73,510	254,290	272,090
Intangible assets:			
Organization expense		$ 6,200	
Goodwill		27,500	33,700
Other assets:			
Advances to company officers			12,700
Total assets			$637,990

Equities

Current liabilities:

Bank loans		$ 4,500	
Accounts payable		39,440	
Accrued payroll and other expenses		26,170	
Estimated income taxes payable		48,750	$118,860
Long-term notes, due November 30, 1981			60,000
Deferred rental revenues			3,600
Owners' equity:			
Capital stock, $10 par value, 5,000 shares issued and outstanding		$ 50,000	
Premium on stock		31,200	
Retained earnings		374,330	455,530
Total equities			$637,990

A STATEMENT OF CHANGES IN RETAINED EARNINGS

The *statement of changes in retained earnings* connects the owners' equity in retained earnings as shown on the balance sheet with the results as shown on the income statement. Other additions or deductions are also shown in the computation of retained earnings at the end of the fiscal period.

A statement of changes in retained earnings is given below for Hamilton Products, Inc.

Hamilton Products, Inc.
Statement of Changes in Retained Earnings
For the Year Ended September 30, 1973

Balance of retained earnings at September 30, 1972	$343,370
Add: Net income for the year	83,090
	$426,460
Less: Dividends	52,130
Balance of retained earnings at September 30, 1973	$374,330

The dividends are a distribution of earnings to the stockholders and are not an expense of doing business. Hence, they are deducted on the statement of changes in retained earnings.

Questions

1. Who is primarily responsible for the financial statements that are published and distributed to stockholders?

2. How is the income statement related to the balance sheet?

3. What do revenue and expense accounts measure?

4. What is meant by matching? Give illustrations to show why matching is difficult.

5. A piece of equipment used in the shop can be sold and converted into cash within the normal operating cycle of the business. Why isn't the equipment classified under current assets?

6. American Company pledged its accounts receivable as security for a bank loan in the amount of $18,000. The accounts receivable are all deemed collectible and are reported on the balance sheet as follows:

Accounts receivable, net of loan payable to the bank in the
amount of $18,000 .... $7,800

Criticize this presentation and tell how you would report the accounts receivable and the loan.

7. Roland Williams, Inc., paid an attorney $2,500 to incorporate a business formerly conducted by Roland Williams as a proprietorship. How should this cost be reported?

8. Cayuga Enterprises, Inc., purchased all of the assets of Mansfield Tool Company and assumed all of its liabilities. At the date of purchase, the tangible assets of Mansfield Tool Company were valued at $168,000. The liabilities amounted to $46,000. The stockholders of the purchased company received $153,000 in payment. How should the excess of the purchase price over the fair market value of the net assets be reported? What factors should have been taken into account in arriving at the purchase price?

9. Why is the owners' equity section of a corporate balance sheet divided into two distinct portions? Why isn't this distinction made for a proprietorship or a partnership?

10. Value is added to products as they are being manufactured. Why doesn't the accountant record these value increments while the products are going through the manufacturing process?

11. Why does the accountant tend to take a conservative position? Can conservatism be carried too far? Explain.

12. Are the dividends to stockholders classified as an operating or a non-operating expense? Explain.

13. Why do some accountants believe that gross margin and net income on operations should not be designated on an income statement? Is there any advantage in showing the gross margin, net operating income and detailed expenses?

14. How does a statement of retained earnings connect an income statement with a balance sheet?

Exercises

1. Thomas Eberly owns and operates The Gift Haus. On June 30, 1972, cash in the amount of $2,420 is on deposit in a bank account established for the business. Customers owe $7,060, and the total amount is estimated to be collectible. The inventory of merchandise can probably be sold for $11,200. The cost of the inventory, however, was $9,350, and this is approximately the amount that would have to be paid to replace it. Equipment cost $14,330. Accumulated depreciation on the equipment amounted to $4,960. The equipment has a fair market value of $16,500. The Gift Haus owes the bank $2,500 on a loan and owes trade creditors $3,740 for merchandise purchased.

Required: Prepare a balance sheet at June 30, 1972, for The Gift Haus.

2. The accounting records of Georgia Reproductions, Inc., show the following balances as of February 29, 1972:

Cash	$24,300
Prepaid insurance	840
Accounts payable	5,480
Inventory	11,410
Land	12,000
Building	84,000
Accumulated depreciation—Building	12,100

Long-term bank note, including installment of $5,000 due on
    August 31, 1972 25,000
Interest payable 650
Goodwill 15,000
Equipment 38,600
Accumulated depreciation—Equipment 8,250
Wages payable 3,240
Retained earnings 61,800
Organization expense 1,000
Accounts receivable 9,370
Capital stock 80,000

Required: Prepare a classified balance sheet as of February 29, 1972.

3. The president of Green Pond Supplies, Inc., has prepared a balance sheet as of October 31, 1972, to support a request for additional bank credit.

Green Pond Supplies, Inc.
Balance Sheet
October 31, 1972

Assets

Cash .... $ 5,280
Accounts receivable 12,350
Inventory 14,810
Equipment and fixtures 32,000
Goodwill 5,000

Total assets $69,440

Equities

Accounts payable .... $ 3,660
Accrued expenses payable 1,830
Bank notes payable, due November 30, 1972 15,000
Capital stock 20,000
Retained earnings 28,950

Total equities $69,440

An examination of the records reveals that $2,200 of the accounts receivable are likely to be uncollectible. The inventory is shown on the balance sheet at fair market value. The cost of the inventory, however, amounts to $11,300. The equipment and fixtures are shown at the estimated amount that would be received if the equipment and fixtures were sold. The cost of the equipment and fixtures was $24,500, and at October 31, 1972, the accumulated depreciation was $7,300. The president of the company, recognizing that the company has an established business reputation, recorded goodwill at $5,000 with a corresponding credit to retained earnings.

Required: Prepare a revised balance sheet for Green Pond Supplies, Inc., at October 31, 1972.

4. Financial data pertaining to the operations of Ashley Products, Inc., for the year, 1972, are given at the top of the next page.

(1) Wages and salaries of $19,300 were earned during the year by the employees. Payments of wages and salaries during the year amounted to $20,100.

(2) During 1971, rent of $1,500 was paid for the four months of January to April, 1972, and shown on the balance sheet at December 31, 1971, as prepaid rent. During 1972, rent payments of $4,500 were made for May, 1972, to February, 1973, inclusive.

(3) Other operating costs of $18,500 were incurred for 1972. Payments of $17,000 were made during the year for operating costs incurred in both 1971 and 1972.

(4) Sales to customers in 1972:

$$\begin{array}{ll}
\text{Cash sales} \dots\dots\dots\dots\dots\dots & \$\ 22,000 \\
\text{Credit sales} \dots\dots\dots\dots\dots\dots & 135,000
\end{array}$$

(5) Collections in the amount of $79,000 were made on customer accounts.

(6) Merchandise costing $87,000 was delivered to customers for sales made during the year. Purchases of merchandise during the year amounted to $91,000, and payments made to creditors for merchandise purchased amounted to $90,000. Inventory on hand on January 1, 1972 amounted to $7,000.

Required: Prepare an income statement for Ashley Products, Inc., on an accrual basis for the year, 1972.

5. Malcolm McPherson has received a charter for McPherson, Inc. He and his associates invested $140,000 in cash for capital stock. Store space was rented on May 1, 1972, and a payment of $6,000 was made for rent covering the two years from May 1, 1972, to April 30, 1974. Equipment costing $68,000 was purchased. A down payment of $25,000 was made on the equipment, and the balance was financed by a noninterest note due on May 1, 1978. Cash of $85,000 was paid for an inventory of merchandise, and operating expenses of $26,000 were paid during the fiscal year ended April 30, 1973. Eighty percent of the cost of the inventory was sold to customers during the fiscal year for $115,000. Collections of $91,000 have been made from the customers during the year. Cash of $58,000 has been disbursed near the end of the fiscal year to replenish part of the stock of merchandise sold. Additional merchandise costing $17,000 has also been acquired but not paid for by the end of the fiscal year. Depreciation on the equipment has been estimated for the first fiscal year at $7,500. Income taxes are estimated at 50 percent of net income before taxes.

Required: From the information given, prepare an income statement for the first fiscal year and a balance sheet at the end of the fiscal year.

6. A balance sheet for Gregg-Hall, Inc., is given at the top of the next page.

Transactions for the fiscal year ended June 30, 1973, are summarized below:

(1) New equipment costing $5,000 was acquired on July 1, 1972, and was financed by long-term notes payable with interest of 8 percent per year.

(2) Purchases of merchandise during the fiscal year amounted to $74,000. Payments of $81,000 were made on accounts payable.

(3) All of the inventory on hand at the beginning of the fiscal year plus 75 percent of the dollar cost of merchandise purchased during the year was sold to customers on credit terms for $120,000.

Gregg-Hall, Inc.
Balance Sheet
June 30, 1972

Assets		Equities	
Cash	$15,400	Accounts payable	$ 8,200
Inventory	18,000	Capital stock	25,000
Equipment, net of accumu-		Retained earnings	16,500
lated depreciation of			
$8,700	16,300		
Total assets	$49,700	Total equities	$49,700

(4) Collections from customers amounted to $112,000.
(5) Bills received for various costs of operation such as wages, insurance, property and income taxes, and rent amounted to $38,000. All of these bills with the exception of a bill in the amount of $1,000 for insurance for the fiscal year ended June 30, 1974, pertain to the fiscal year ended June 30, 1973. Payments of $27,000 were made on operating costs, and included in the payments is the payment for the insurance mentioned above.
(6) Depreciation expense has been estimated at $2,000.
(7) Dividends were paid to the stockholders in the amount of $6,000.

Required: Prepare in summary form an income statement for the year ended June 30, 1973, and a balance sheet at June 30, 1973.

7. On July 1, 1971, Brighton Shoes, Inc., was incorporated upon the investment of $130,000 in cash and $90,000 in equipment. The entire amount invested was credited to capital stock. Depreciation of $8,000 is to be deducted each fiscal year on the equipment.

During the first fiscal year, the corporation purchased merchandise for resale at a cost of $112,000. Payments to merchandise creditors amounted to $96,000.

Sales on account to customers amounted to $133,000, of which $95,000 was collected in cash. It is estimated that about $3,000 of the amount owed by customers will be uncollectible. The cost of the merchandise delivered to customers was $77,000.

Operating expenses of $23,400 were paid. Included in this amount are payments for rent, taxes, and insurance in the amount of $1,900 that apply to the second fiscal year. Expenses accrued in the first fiscal year but unpaid at June 30, 1972, amounted to $2,600.

Income taxes are estimated at 40 percent of net income before taxes. One-half of the earnings after income taxes were paid out as dividends.

Required: Prepare in summary form an income statement, a statement of retained earnings, and a balance sheet for the first annual report.

8. A balance sheet for Ferngold Builders, Inc., at September 30, 1971, is given at the top of the next page.

Transactions for the fiscal year ended September 30, 1972, are summarized below:

(1) Customers were billed $252,000 for services rendered during the year.
(2) Collections of $263,000 were made on accounts receivable.

Ferngold Builders, Inc.
Balance Sheet
September 30, 1971

Assets

Cash	$ 73,200
Accounts receivable	64,100
Inventory	58,500
Equipment, net of accumulated depreciation	68,000
Total assets	$263,800

Equities

Accounts payable	$ 37,200
Accrued expenses payable	8,300
Capital stock	120,000
Retained earnings	98,300
Total equities	$263,800

(3) Advance deposits of $17,000 were received from customers for work to be performed after September 30, 1972.

(4) Materials and supplies were purchased on account at a cost of $143,000. The inventory at September 30, 1972, amounted to $53,800.

(5) Payments for materials and supplies amounted to $168,000.

(6) Operating expenses of $47,200 were incurred for the fiscal year ended September 30, 1972. The accrued expenses payable at September 30, 1972, amounted to $9,400.

(7) Depreciation was recorded in the amount of $5,500.

(8) Dividends of $12,000 were declared and paid during the fiscal year.

(9) Income taxes were estimated at 50 percent of net income before taxes and were unpaid at the end of the fiscal year.

Required: Prepare an income statement and a statement of retained earnings for the fiscal year ended September 30, 1972. Prepare a balance sheet for September 30, 1972.

Problems

1–1. The income statement for Blair Allison, presented below, has been prepared on a cash basis. Cash receipts from customers have been reported as revenue, and cash disbursements for merchandise purchased and for the costs of operation have been reported as expense. Adjustments have been made for the inventory on hand at both the beginning and at the end of the year.

The customers were billed $142,300 for merchandise delivered to them during the fiscal year. Included in net sales on the income statement is $1,700 earned and collected during the year as interest on temporary investments held. Also included in net sales is $8,200 collected in advance from customers who will receive deliveries during the next fiscal year.

Merchandise purchased during the year had a gross cost of $87,000. Purchase returns were $1,200 and discounts taken on purchases amounted to $1,600.

There was no liability to employees for salaries and wages at April 30, 1971, but at the end of the current fiscal year the employees had earned $2,300 that had not been paid to them.

The liability for property taxes has increased by $900 during the year ended April 30, 1972. Rent is at the rate of $400 a month, and payments of rent have been made up to and including July 31, 1972. The insurance premium of $4,200 gives coverage from May 1, 1971, to April 30, 1974.

Allison borrowed $30,000 from Farmers' Bank on an 8 percent note on March 31, 1972. Interest for 90 days was deducted in advance. Allison recorded the note at the amount of cash received.

Payments of $10,000 plus interest were made on equipment during the year. Both the payment on the equipment and the interest for the fiscal year of $1,500 were included in miscellaneous expense. It has been estimated that depreciation on the equipment for the fiscal year should amount to $4,000.

Blair Allison
Income Statement
For the Year Ended April 30, 1972

Net sales		$152,200
Cost of goods sold:		
Inventory, May 1, 1971	$ 21,300	
Purchases	84,200	
Cost of goods available for sale	$105,500	
Less: Inventory, April 30, 1972	23,100	82,400
Gross margin		$ 69,800
Operating expenses:		
Salaries and wages	$ 18,400	
Property taxes	2,300	
Advertising	5,400	
Travel and entertainment	1,100	
Rent	6,000	
Insurance	4,200	
Utilities	1,600	
Office expense	2,100	
Miscellaneous expense	11,700	52,800
Net income		$ 17,000

Required: Prepare an income statement for Blair Allison on an accrual basis for the year ended April 30, 1972. Blair Allison operates as a sole proprietor.

1–2. David Bernstein has operated a merchandising business as a sole proprietor and on July 1, 1971 formed a corporation to be designated as Shoreline Shop, Inc. The assets contributed by Bernstein are listed below at their appraised values on July 1:

Land	$ 14,000
Building	83,000
Fixtures	53,000
Prepaid insurance, expires at December 31, 1971	600
Inventory	11,700
Cash	6,400
	$168,700

The corporation assumed the mortgage of $22,000 on the building. Goodwill was valued at $50,000.

Other stockholders have invested $74,000 in cash in return for shares of stock.

Transactions for the fiscal period ended June 30, 1972, are summarized as follows:

(1) Merchandise costing $112,000 was purchased. The merchandise delivered to customers cost $94,400. Payments of $94,000 were made to merchandise creditors.

(2) Sales of $238,000 were made to customers on credit terms, and $196,000 was collected from the customers. Uncollectible accounts have been estimated at $3,500.

(3) Cash payments in addition to those made to suppliers of merchandise were:

Wages and salaries	$37,300
Payroll taxes	2,100
Advertising	15,500
Insurance, expires at June 30, 1972	600
Property taxes	1,300
Fixtures	2,000
Interest	1,500
Supplies	3,200
Utilities	2,300
Repairs	1,700
Dividends	25,000
	$92,500

Wages of $800 were accrued at June 30, 1972, and supplies of $1,400 were on hand at June 30, 1972. New fixtures costing $20,000 were acquired on April 30, 1972, with $18,000 of the cost financed by a note due on March 31, 1975. Depreciation on the building is recorded at $4,000, and depreciation is recorded on the fixtures at $6,000. Interest of $800 was accrued at June 30, 1972.

Required: From the information given, prepare financial statements for Shoreline Shop, Inc., for the fiscal period ended June 30, 1972.

1–3. The unadjusted ledger account balances for Heron Container Company at December 31, 1972, are given at the top of the next page.

Additional information:

(1) On the sales made to customers in 1972, it is estimated that $2,600 will not be collectible. No provision has been made for these uncollectible accounts. It is also estimated that customers will return merchandise and receive credit of $720 in addition to the returns already recorded.

(2) Additional interest of $170 has accrued on marketable securities.

(3) The supplies were counted at the end of the year and assigned a cost of $3,840. The supplies inventory should be shown at this amount, and the remaining amount shown in the ledger account should be shown as supplies used.

(4) Facilities have been rented throughout the year at a rental rate of $500 a month. Rent has been paid to September 30, 1972.

	Debits	Credits
Cash	$ 24,260	
Marketable securities	15,000	
Accounts receivable	38,700	
Allowance for doubtful accounts		$ 1,250
Inventory, 12/31/72	42,630	
Supplies	12,670	
Prepaid insurance	2,600	
Machinery and equipment	72,500	
Accumulated depreciation		16,300
Accounts payable		18,920
Wages payable		3,250
Payroll tax payable		1,940
Capital stock		65,000
Retained earnings		29,700
Sales		295,400
Sales returns	1,630	
Cost of goods sold	152,100	
Wages and salaries	42,600	
Payroll taxes	2,880	
Advertising	13,720	
Rent	4,500	
Insurance	2,000	
Repairs and maintenance	3,250	
Utilities	1,670	
Interest and dividends received		950
	$432,710	$432,710

(5) The machinery and equipment less residual salvage value of $7,500 are to be depreciated on a straight line basis at a rate of 8 percent per year.

(6) Income taxes are to be estimated at 40 percent of net income before taxes. (Round to nearest $10.)

Required: Prepare an income statement for 1972, and a balance sheet for December 31, 1972.

1-4. A balance sheet for Island Frames, Inc., as of May 31, 1972, is given below and at the top of the next page.

Island Frames, Inc.
Balance Sheet
May 31, 1972

Assets

Cash		$ 27,400
Marketable securities		17,000
Accounts receivable	$38,200	
Less: Allowance for doubtful accounts ..	3,400	34,800
Inventory		37,650
Prepaid insurance		150
Equipment	$83,000	
Less: Accumulated depreciation	17,500	65,500
Total assets		$182,500

Equities

Accounts payable	$ 18,300
Accrued wages payable	800
Payroll tax liability	350
Estimated income tax payable	6,200
Total liabilities	$ 25,650
Capital stock	120,000
Retained earnings	36,850
Total equities	$182,500

Transactions for the fiscal year ended May 31, 1973, are summarized below:

(1) Sales to customers, $214,600.

(2) Accounts receivable in the amount of $2,000 were written off during the year as uncollectible.

(3) Collections from customers during the year amount to $216,300.

(4) Credits were granted to customers for merchandise not meeting exact specifications. The credits were in the amount of $1,700.

(5) Dividends of $500 were received on the marketable securities.

(6) Merchandise costing $158,200 was purchased on account.

(7) Payments of $159,600 were made on accounts payable.

(8) Inventory at the end of the fiscal year had a cost of $31,800.

(9) Insurance accrues at the rate of $50 a month. Payments to the insurance company during the year amounted to $300.

(10) Equipment costing $8,000 with accumulated depreciation of $2,500 was sold during the year for $7,500.

(11) Wages expense, $11,300.

(12) Payroll tax expense, $550.

(13) Payments for wages, $11,500.

(14) Payments for payroll taxes, $700.

(15) It has been estimated that customers owing $2,600 on sales made during the fiscal year will not be able to pay their accounts.

(16) Depreciation expense, $3,500.

(17) Other operating expenses for the fiscal year in the amount of $8,700 were paid.

(18) Payments on income taxes, $7,000.

(19) Income taxes for the fiscal year have been estimated at $9,300.

(20) Dividends amounting to $8,000 were paid to the stockholders.

Required: Prepare an income statement for the fiscal year ended May 31, 1973, and a balance sheet at May 31, 1973.

1–5. A balance sheet for Trumbauer Products, Inc., as of May 31, 1972, and an income statement for the fiscal year ended May 31, 1973, are given on the next page.

An examination of the records reveals the following:

(1) Collections from customers during the fiscal year were recorded as sales. Billings to the customers for the fiscal year amounted to $164,200. All customers' accounts are estimated to be collectible.

(2) Cash payments for merchandise during the fiscal year were reported as cost of sales. Purchases made during the fiscal year cost $92,500, and the inventory at the end of May, 1973, was assigned a cost of $29,600.

Trumbauer Products, Inc.
Balance Sheet
May 31, 1972

Assets

Cash	$ 21,200
Accounts receivable	34,600
Inventory	32,100
Furniture and fixtures	43,000
Patents	16,000
Total assets	$146,900

Equities

Accounts payable	$ 11,800
Expenses payable	3,200
Income taxes payable	9,200
Capital stock	90,000
Retained earnings	32,700
Total equities	$146,900

Trumbauer Products, Inc.
Income Statement
For the Year Ended May 31, 1973

Sales		$161,300
Cost of goods sold		96,800
Gross margin		$ 64,500
Operating expenses:		
Wages and payroll taxes	$14,500	
Advertising	8,000	
Rent	5,600	
Insurance	1,200	
Dividends	6,000	
Income taxes	13,000	
Other expenses	2,200	50,500
Net income		$ 14,000

(3) Included as a part of advertising expense is the cost of advertising materials in the amount of $1,500 that will not be used until June and July, 1973.

(4) Furniture and fixtures were all acquired on May 31, 1972, and are to be depreciated at a rate of 10 percent per year after making an allowance for a residual salvage value of $8,000. Patents are to be amortized in equal amounts over four years beginning on June 1, 1972.

(5) Other expenses accrued as of May 31, 1973, but not recorded, amounted to $500. The liability for expenses payable on May 31, 1972, was paid during the fiscal year with a charge being made to the liability account.

(6) Dividends were declared and distributed to stockholders in the amount of $6,000.

(7) The income taxes shown on the income statement were properly computed. Payments on income taxes during the fiscal year totaled $17,500.

Required: Prepare a corrected income statement, a statement of retained earnings, and a balance sheet at May 31, 1973, from the data given.

Chapter 2

PROBLEM AREAS
IN ACCOUNTABILITY—I

Generally accepted principles of accounting serve as guidelines in accounting practice. These principles of accounting are not principles in the sense that they are natural laws, as in the case of the physical sciences. Accounting is an art, not a science, and both skill and judgment are required in adapting principles to the individual situation. Accounting data are presented on financial statements in various ways depending on the employment of the principles.

Through years of experience, research, and study, generally accepted accounting principles have been developed. In some cases, alternative treatment of these principles are appropriate; one alternative may be as acceptable as another. In other cases, there are areas of considerable disagreement with strong arguments to support each alternative. Often the selection of an accounting alternative will have a material effect on the financial statements.

In relatively recent years, the American Institute of Certified Public Accountants (AICPA) has published research studies in accounting in an attempt to resolve the more difficult issues. In addition, an Accounting Principles Board (APB) has been formed to study controversial areas and issue opinions. Although these opinions do not have the force of law, they do provide strong support for a practitioner who follows the recommendations.

The accountant is obviously concerned with variations in accounting treatment, but management must also be knowledgable in this area. Financial data can be collected and arranged in various ways. It has been said that figures don't lie but liars can figure. Differences in reporting, however, are honest differences that arise because of alternatives that are selected in presenting financial data. Furthermore, as will be discussed at length in later chapters, data must be used selectively and combined in various ways to serve the different needs of internal management. Information that may be useful in controlling operations, for example, may not be suitable in a decision-making situation.

COST OR MARKET

One area of major interest is asset valuation. The basis selected for reporting assets on the balance sheet affects not only the balance sheet but also the income statement. Customarily, most assets are accounted for on a cost basis. The asset, when acquired, is recorded at cost; as it is used in the revenue producing process, an appropriate portion of the cost is matched against revenue as expense.

If there is a decline in market value while the asset is held, the initial cost in some cases may not be the best basis for accountability. In the case of marketable securities and inventories, for example, losses resulting from reduced market values are usually recognized when the market values decline. On the other hand, a gain in market value is usually not recognized while the asset is held. As pointed out in the last chapter, this inconsistency in accounting is justified on the grounds of conservatism.

Marketable securities. Often cash in excess of current needs is temporarily invested in marketable securities. The investment is made so that a return can be earned on cash that would otherwise be idle; it is assumed that the securities can readily be converted to cash should the need arise. While the securities are held, market values may fluctuate. Temporary changes in market values need not be recognized in the accounts; but if a market decline is considered to be permanent, the securities should be reduced from cost to the lower market value.

So that the reader of the financial statements may make his own judgment, marketable securities are often shown on the balance sheet in one of two ways:

(1) On the cost basis, with the market value in parentheses, e.g.,
   U.S. Government and other securities at cost
   (at market quotations December 31, 1972,
   $1,342,000) $1,682,000

(2) At the lower of cost or market, with the higher valuation in parentheses, e.g.,
   U. S. Government and other securities at the
   lower of cost or market (at cost, $1,682,000) $1,342,000

Investments in securities are often material in amount, particularly in the case of pension trusts and investment companies. In these circumstances it is customary to list the individual securities on a separate schedule, showing both the costs and the current market values.

It has been suggested that securities should be stated at current market values on the balance sheet regardless of whether the current market value is above or below cost. Thus, as market values change, gains and losses would be reported on securities which are held as well as those sold. These gains or losses may be designated as *holding gains or losses*.

To illustrate, it is assumed that a company has been reporting holding gains or losses consistently over the years and that the net income for the current year, excluding holding gains or losses, amounted to $3,400,000. Marketable securities were shown on the balance sheet at the beginning of the year as follows:

Marketable securities at market value (original cost, $300,000) $372,000

The same securities were held throughout the year, and the market value at the end of the year was $662,000 or $290,000 higher than it was at the beginning of the year. The holding gain of $290,000 may be reported on the income statement as follows:

Net income before holding gains and losses	$3,400,000
Add: Gain from holding securities that have appreciated in value during the year	290,000
Net income	$3,690,000

The balance sheet at the end of the year would show the marketable securities at current market values as follows:

Marketable securities at market value (original cost, $300,000) $662,000

It should be recognized that market values can move in either direction; if there were a decline in market values, a holding loss would be shown on the income statement and the lower market values would be shown for the securities on the balance sheet.

The selection of a valuation method can be quite important in measuring income and in setting forth the financial position of the company. Regardless of the method selected for financial reporting purposes, management should have complete information and understand how a difference in valuation can affect the results.

Inventory valuation. Inventories, like marketable securities, are conventionally valued at the lower of cost or market. Some question has also been raised as to whether or not inventories should be shown at current market values with holding gains being recognized on the inventories held.

In practice holding losses are typically recognized when market values decline below cost, but holding gains are usually not recognized. This inconsistency is justified on the grounds that the reader of the statements should not be led to anticipate gains that may not be ultimately realized through an arms-length transaction with a buyer.

Materials, for example, that are used in operations or merchandise purchased for resale may be written down to the current cost of replacement if such cost is lower than the cost of acquisition. Products which are partially or completely processed would have a market value equivalent to the current cost of materials, labor, and overhead necessary to reproduce the product to its present stage of completion. If the current costs of reproduction are lower than the actual costs incurred, the product may be reduced to the lower market value with a loss being recognized during the fiscal period of the market decline.

Within broad limits, market values may be derived in various ways. The American Institute of Certified Public Accountants has defined an upper and lower limit for market value.[1]

> "As used in the phrase *lower of cost or market*, the term *market* means current replacement cost (by purchase or by reproduction, as the case may be) except that:
>
> (1) Market should not exceed the net realizable value (i.e., estimated selling price in the ordinary course of business less reasonably predictable costs of completion and disposal); and
>
> (2) Market should not be less than net realizable value reduced by an allowance for an approximately normal profit margin."

Assume, for example, that a product sells for $20 a unit and that it costs $1 to deliver each unit to a customer. One partially completed unit is held in inventory at the end of the year, and the cost of labor and overhead required to complete the product has been estimated at $3. The net realizable value is computed below:

Selling price		$20
Less:		
Cost of disposal	$1	
Cost of completion	3	4
Net realizable value		$16

Market value should be no higher than the net realizable value, in this case, $16.

---

[1] *Accounting Research and Terminology Bulletins* (Final ed.; New York: American Institute of Certified Public Accountants, 1961), p. 31.

Assume further that a normal profit margin of $5 can be expected from the sale of each unit. The lower limit of net realizable value reduced by an allowance for an approximately normal profit margin is computed below:

Net realizable value $16
Less: Normal profit margin 5
Net realizable value less normal profit margin $11

The market value to be compared with cost in setting a valuation at the lower of cost or market cannot be higher than $16 or lower than $11. These are the boundaries for market value. For example, if reproduction cost were $15 and if this amount were lower than cost, the inventory would be valued at a market value of $15 per unit. This amount lies within the limits. However, a reproduction cost of $17 that is lower than cost would be too high. The market value would be set at the upper limit of $16. Also a reproduction cost of $10 would be too low, and the inventory would be valued at $11 if $11 were lower than cost.

With inventories reported at the lower of cost or market, the balance sheet may show a conservative valuation; but there is a possibility that profits may be shifted from one year to another.

Assume, for example, that Company A purchased 100,000 units of merchandise in 1972 at a unit cost of $3 and that 80,000 units were sold during that year for $5 a unit. In 1973, another 100,000 units were purchased at the same cost, and 80,000 units were again sold at the same price. On a cost basis, profits on the sales for the two years would be computed as follows:

Company A
Statement of Gross Margin
For the Years 1972 and 1973

	1973	1972
Sales	$400,000	$400,000
Cost of goods sold:		
Inventory, January 1	$ 60,000	—0—
Purchases	300,000	$300,000
Cost of goods available	$360,000	$300,000
Less: Inventory, December 31	120,000	60,000
Cost of goods sold	$240,000	$240,000
Gross margin	$160,000	$160,000

The gross margin for each of the two years was the same, as would be expected with no change in the selling price, the cost, or the volume sold.

Suppose, however, that the suppliers of Company A reduced the price of the item to $2 before December 31, 1972, but no purchases were made at this price. The inventory at December 31, 1972, at the lower market value, would be shown at $40,000, not $60,000. This would also be the value shown for the inventory at the beginning of 1973. At the beginning of 1973, the suppliers returned to the former price of $3. Statements of gross margin, as given below, show that a greater gross margin was made in 1973, yet there was no difference between the operations of the two years. Thus, conservative valuations on the balance sheet may not always produce conservative results on the income statements.

Company A
Statement of Gross Margin
For the Years 1972 and 1973

	1973	1972
Sales	$400,000	$400,000
Cost of goods sold:		
Inventory, January 1	$ 40,000	—0—
Purchases	300,000	300,000
Cost of goods available	$340,000	$300,000
* Less: Inventory, December 31	120,000	40,000
Cost of goods sold	$220,000	$260,000
Gross margin	$180,000	$140,000

* Includes only merchandise purchased during the year.

INVENTORY COSTING

The problem of assigning costs to inventories can also be troublesome. Materials and merchandise for resale are purchased in various quantities at different prices throughout the year. The question then arises as to what costs can be matched against revenue in the calculation of net income and what costs should be attached to the inventory remaining at the end of the year. Some logical method of accounting for the costs should be decided upon and followed consistently.

A decision may be made to charge the older costs of materials to the cost of products manufactured and to charge the older costs of products manufactured to the cost of goods sold. The more recent costs would then remain as inventory cost. This costing method is labeled appropriately as the first-in, first-out method (fifo).

Assume, for example, that a company had an inventory of merchandise at the beginning of the year consisting of 800 units of a given item with a unit cost of 60 cents. A record of the purchases made throughout the year is given below:

January	1,000 units @	$ .70
March	500 units @	.80
June	1,500 units @	.90
September	2,500 units @	1.00
November	2,000 units @	1.05

A count of the stock on hand at the end of the year revealed that there were 2,900 units available.

According to the first-in, first-out inventory method, the costs of the beginning inventory and the purchases made earliest in the year would be shown as the cost of the goods sold. The more recent costs would be identified with the ending inventory, as shown in the table below:

	Number of Units	Unit Cost	Total Cost
Cost of goods sold:			
Inventory at January 1	800	$ .60	$ 480
Purchases:			
January	1,000	.70	700
March	500	.80	400
June	1,500	.90	1,350
September	1,600	1.00	1,600
Cost of goods sold			$4,530
Number of units sold	5,400		
Inventory at December 31:			
Purchases:			
September	900	1.00	$ 900
November	2,000	1.05	2,100
Cost of inventory			$3,000
Number of units in inventory	2,900		

The inventory cost has been determined by starting with the most recent purchase and working back through the year until all of the units in the inventory have been costed. At the end of the year there were 2,900 units on hand, but only 2,000 units were purchased in November. Therefore, only 2,000 of the inventory units can be assigned the November cost. The remaining 900 units will bear the cost incurred in September.

The cost of materials or merchandise may be accounted for in exactly the opposite way. The earlier costs may be held in inventory while the more recent costs are considered to be the cost of materials used in manufacturing or the cost of finished products sold. This method of inventory costing is called the last-in, first-out method (lifo). Using the same example, the costs would be accounted for as shown in the table on the next page.

	Number of Units	Unit Cost	Total Cost
Inventory at December 31:			
Inventory at January 1	800	$ .60	$ 480
Purchases:			
January	1,000	.70	700
March	500	.80	400
June	600	.90	540
Cost of inventory			$2,120
Number of units in inventory	2,900		
Cost of goods sold:			
Purchases:			
June	900	.90	$ 810
September	2,500	1.00	2,500
November	2,000	1.05	2,100
Cost of goods sold			$5,410
Number of units sold	5,400		

In this case, the inventory costs were determined by adding the costs of the earliest purchases in succession to the beginning inventory cost, until 2,900 units were accounted for. Note that during a period of rising prices the last-in, first-out method tends to produce a higher cost of goods sold than the first-in, first-out method. This would be expected, considering that the higher recent costs are being charged off as the cost of goods sold. However, if the inventory is being depleted, earlier costs that are lower in price will be charged off as the cost of goods sold. In this case, the cost of goods sold will not consist of higher recent costs.

Inventories may also be accounted for by computing average costs. An average cost may be determined in various ways. For example, there may be several purchases during a month at different unit costs. An average cost for the month may be computed and used in costing inventories by the fifo or lifo principle. Sometimes a running average is kept with a new average cost being computed each time units are purchased.

DEPRECIATION

Plant assets such as buildings, machinery, and equipment are often used in business operations for many years before being deemed worn out, obsolete, or inadequate. The entire cost of a plant asset cannot be properly charged to any one year as expense. Instead, the cost should be spread over the years in which the plant asset is in service, that is, the cost should be charged as expense to the periods that benefit from the use of the asset. The cost charged to operations during a fiscal period is referred to as *depreciation*. Frequently, depreciation charges are substantial; and the selection of a depreciation method and the estimates that are made will have a material effect on the net income or net loss to be reported.

A plant asset is in effect a collection of potential services that will be released over the months and years that lie ahead. A building, for example, will provide a working area for individuals and space for various materials and tools used in business operations. Service may be received from the building at a relatively uniform rate over the years of its life; and the cost of the building less the estimated salvage recovery at the end of its useful life may be assigned equally to each year that the building is in use. When the cost is assigned equally to each year, the depreciation method is referred to as the *straight-line method*.

Straight-line depreciation can be defended as being logical if it is assumed that the asset in question will release as much service in one year as in another. Sometimes, however, the services are released in an irregular pattern. A truck, for example, may be driven 30,000 miles in one year and only 15,000 miles in another year. The cost of the truck less its estimated residual salvage value may be assigned to operations in proportion to the units of service rendered. If it is estimated that the truck will have a useful life of 100,000 miles, then 30 percent of the cost subject to depreciation may be charged to the year in which it was driven 30,000 miles. Only 15 percent of this cost may be assigned to the year in which the truck was driven 15,000 miles. When depreciation is based on physical units of service, the depreciation method is referred to as the *production-unit method*.

Sometimes it is believed that greater amounts of depreciation should be charged to the early years in the life of the asset with smaller amounts being charged to later years. This concept is often defended on the grounds that the resale value of a plant asset tends to decline rapidly at first and then level off in later years. But depreciation, as the term is used in accounting, is not an attempt to scale plant assets down to their approximate market value. It is, instead, a means of matching the costs of services obtained from a plant asset against the resulting revenues. A fast write-off is also defended as a means of equalizing the costs of plant asset operation over the life of the asset. In the early years, depreciation will be high, but repair and mainte nance costs will be low. In later years, depreciation will be low, but repairs and maintenance may increase. It is assumed that the combined annual costs of repairs, maintenance, and depreciation will be about the same each year over the life of the asset. This may or may not be true in practice.

Two accelerated (fast write-off) methods of depreciation, the sum-of-the-years-digits method and the double-rate method, are often used.

The *sum-of-the-years-digits method* (SYD method) is illustrated by assuming that a unit of equipment costing $60,000 has a useful life of ten years with an estimated residual salvage value of $5,000 at the end of that time. Using the straight-line method of depreciation, 1/10 of $55,000 or $5,500 would be deducted each year as depreciation. If the SYD method is used, the digits for each of the ten years, that is $1 + 2 + 3 + 4 + \ldots\ldots + 10$, are added to produce a denominator of 55 for an allocating fraction. Then, the numerator for that fraction will be 10 in the first year, 9 in the second year, 8 in the third year, etc. Depreciation for each year would be computed as shown below:

Year	Cost Subject to Depreciation		Allocating Fraction		Depreciation
1	$55,000	×	10/55	=	$10,000
2	55,000	×	9/55	=	9,000
3	55,000	×	8/55	=	8,000
4	55,000	×	7/55	=	7,000
5	55,000	×	6/55	=	6,000
6	55,000	×	5/55	=	5,000
7	55,000	×	4/55	=	4,000
8	55,000	×	3/55	=	3,000
9	55,000	×	2/55	=	2,000
10	55,000	×	1/55	=	1,000

The *double-rate method* makes use of a rate that is twice the straight-line rate, hence the term "double rate." The double rate is applied to the remaining undepreciated cost each year. No allowance is made for residual salvage in making the calculation. The total cost will never be written off, inasmuch as the rate is calculated on a balance remaining after deducting depreciation for previous years. The total cost, however, should not be reduced to an amount lower than the estimated residual salvage value of the asset.

If the equipment in the previous example were depreciated by the double-rate method, the rate would be 20 percent, that is, twice the 10 percent rate used in writing off the cost over ten years by the straight-line method. The depreciation for the first year would be $12,000 (20 percent of $60,000). In the second year the 20 percent rate would be applied to the undepreciated cost of $48,000 ($60,000 minus $12,000) in arriving at a depreciation charge of $9,600. Depreciation for each year would be computed as shown on the next page.

DEPRECIATION AND INCOME TAXES

Depreciation is a very important factor in the computation of income taxes. For several years the taxpayer has been permitted to deduct accelerated depreciation for tax purposes. In addition, the government has

Year	Cost	Accumulated Depreciation (Beginning of the Year)	Undepreciated Cost (Beginning of the Year)	Depreciation*
1	$60,000	—	$60,000	$12,000
2	60,000	$12,000	48,000	9,600
3	60,000	21,600	38,400	7,680
4	60,000	29,280	30,720	6,144
5	60,000	35,424	24,576	4,915
6	60,000	40,339	19,661	3,932
7	60,000	44,271	15,729	3,146
8	60,000	47,417	12,583	2,528
9	60,000	49,945	10,055	2,528
10	60,000	52,473	7,527	2,527

* Rounded off to even dollars. The double-rate method will not reduce the asset to zero, nor will it reduce the asset to its estimated residual salvage value which in this case is $5,000. In order to maximize the amount of the cost written off as depreciation in the earliest years of the asset's life, the time will come when a change from the accelerated method to the straight-line method will have to be made. In this example for instance, the remaining undepreciated cost of $12,583 at the end of the seventh year was reduced by the estimated residual salvage value of $5,000; and the difference of $7,583 was written off by the straight-line method over the remaining three years. Had the double-rate method been continued in use, the amount of depreciation for the eighth year would have been only $2,517 (20% × $12,583).

encouraged a more rigorous study of the depreciation problem by the publication of estimated lives of various types of properties and has issued guidelines to enable the taxpayer to compare his operations with typical conditions in his industry group.

There is a very definite advantage in the use of accelerated depreciation for tax purposes, an advantage that cannot be overlooked. Large depreciation deductions in the early years reduce the income taxes for those years. In the last example, depreciation for the first year by the double-rate method was $12,000 as compared to $5,500 by the straight-line method. If the tax rate is 50 percent, the company can save income taxes of $3,250 in that year by using the double-rate method, that is, it can save 50 percent of the $6,500 difference in depreciation. Sometimes the argument is made that a company can only deduct its cost in the long run and that if large amounts of depreciation are claimed in early years there will be very small amounts that can be claimed in later years. The conclusion is made that there is no advantage in a fast depreciation method. This argument overlooks the very important fact that a dollar saved today is much more important than a dollar saved in the future. The dollar saved today can be put to work immediately to earn a return, whereas the future dollar cannot be invested until the saving is realized. Accelerated depreciation creates a tax shield that enables the company to retain more resources in the early years than it can by the straight-line method, resources that can be reinvested for more profits.

If there is reason to believe that income tax rates will be higher in the future, it may be better to take smaller depreciation deductions in the present so that larger deductions will be available in later years. The decision will depend upon returns that can be earned from available resources as compared with the anticipated future tax savings.

LEASE OR PURCHASE

Various plant assets such as buildings, machinery, and equipment needed for business operation are usually financed by borrowing, whether the purchase is outright or whether the item is rented under a long-term lease agreement. Leasing may be looked upon as a form of financing. It is a means by which assets needed by the business can be acquired. It is not necessary for the company to own the assets if it can have the use of them. The costs to lease, however, may be more than the costs to own. The lessor is well aware of the risks of ownership and may set his rental fee accordingly. Business management should compare the costs of renting with the costs of ownership. If the costs of renting are higher and if management elects to rent, it is paying a premium to avoid the risks that are inherent in the ownership of property.

When property is purchased, the cost of the property is recorded in the accounting records. If debt has been incurred to finance property acquisition, the amount of the debt will be recorded as a liability. Both the property and the outstanding debt will appear on the balance sheet.

Under ordinary circumstances, a rented property is not recorded as an asset, and no liability is recorded for future rental payments. The rentals are charged to operations in the fiscal periods to which they apply.

In some cases, however, a long-term lease agreement may be similar to a purchase contract. The lease may extend over the useful life of the property and may not be canceled except in very unusual circumstances. Perhaps the property is peculiarly constructed to suit the needs of the lessee, and the lessee is expected to pay taxes, insurance, and other costs that are normally incurred by a property owner. Under these circumstances, the present value of the future rental payments should be capitalized, that is, shown as the cost of the property on the balance sheet. The present value of the future rental payments should also be recorded as a liability. Property taxes, insurance, and the various costs to operate the property should not be capitalized, of course, but should be charged to operations.

(See Appendix D for a discussion of the present value concept.) The cost of the property should be written off to depreciation over its useful life, and the liability should be reduced as rental payments are made.[2]

The present worth or value of all of the future payments on a lease is equivalent to long-term debt incurred to finance the purchase of property. If debt is incurred in connection with the acquisition of property, the owner will list the asset on his balance sheet at cost and will also record the long-term debt as a liability. Company A, for example, purchased equipment at a cost of $400,000 and financed the purchase by long-term notes payable that mature in five years. The equipment and notes would appear on the balance sheet as follows:

Company A
Partial Balance Sheet
Date of Acquisition of Equipment

Assets

Equipment $400,000

Equities

Notes payable, due in 5 years $400,000

If Company A had the use of this equipment under a long-term lease agreement, it would obtain the same benefits from the use of the property and would be obligated to make the lease payments just as it would be obligated to pay a debt incurred to purchase the property. Logically, the leased property should be recorded as an asset, and a liability for future lease payments should be recognized.

The general practice in the past has been to call attention to lease agreements in footnotes to the financial statements rather than to recognize the leased properties as assets on the balance sheet and the future lease payments as long-term debt on the balance sheet. Although there is no solid support for capitalization, lease capitalization has been receiving much attention in recent years.

Lease capitalization. The general procedures that are employed in capitalizing lease payments are illustrated by assuming that Hassler Products,

---

[2] See *Reporting of Leases in Financial Statements of Lessee,* Accounting Principles Board Opinion No. 5 (New York: American Institute of Certified Public Accountants, 1964).

Inc., is planning to lease equipment that has an estimated life of ten years. This equipment has been constructed to meet specifications stipulated by Hassler Products, Inc. A payment of $300,000 is to be made at the end of each of the next ten years. The lessor has made provision for interest at eight percent in setting the rental payments. Hence, the ten annual payments are discounted to a present value at a discount rate of eight percent.

Present value of lease:

Present value of 10 annual payments of $300,000 ($300,000 × 6.710 present value of $1 received or paid annually for 10 years at 8%. See Table II on page 701.) $2,013,000

A summary balance sheet for Hassler Products, Inc., at the beginning of the lease may appear as follows:

Hassler Products, Inc.
Balance Sheet
Date—Beginning of Lease

Assets

Current assets	$ 4,312,600
Plant assets:	
Land	183,400
Building	3,865,200
Equipment (10-year lease with annual payments of $300,000. The annual payments are discounted at 8%)	2,013,000
Total assets	$10,374,200

Equities

Current liabilities	$ 2,732,100
Liability on lease agreement:	
Lease rentals payable (10-year lease with annual payments of $300,000. The annual payments are discounted at 8%)	2,013,000
Owners' equity	5,629,100
Total equities	$10,374,200

The cost of the leased property will be written off to depreciation over its useful life, following the same procedures that are employed for property that is owned. Depreciation may be deducted by the straight-line method or by any other acceptable depreciation method that has been adopted by the company.

Using the data from the illustration, and assuming the straight-line method of calculating depreciation is used, depreciation expense each year would be

$201,300. The entry to record depreciation for each of the ten years is presented below.

```
Depreciation Expense ...................... 201,300
     Accumulated Depreciation ...............         201,300
To record depreciation for the first year.
```

The liability will be reduced as rental payments are made. Interest at the rate of 8 percent will be computed on the liability at the beginning of the year, and the balance of the $300,000 payment will be applied to reduce the principal of the debt. For example, interest for the first year is $161,040 (8 percent of $2,013,000). The entry to record the rental payment for the first year is given below.

```
Lease Rentals Payable ...................... 138,960
Interest Expense .......................... 161,040
     Cash ...................................         300,000
To record payment of rental for the first year.
```

After the payment has been made at the end of the first year, the debt will be reduced to $1,874,040 ($2,013,000 minus $138,960). The debt of $1,874,040 is the present value of the remaining nine annual payments of $300,000 with a slight difference due to rounding the present value factor in the table ($300,000 × 6.247 present value of $1 received or paid annually for nine years at 8 percent discount rate). In subsequent years interest computations will be made on the debt outstanding at the time, and the debt will be reduced by the balance of the rental payments.

The total amount of the charges to revenue—interest and depreciation—during the life of the leased assets will equal the total amount paid in rent. The following table supports this statement.

Charges to Revenue

Year	Depreciation	Interest	Total	Payment
1	$ 201,300	$161,040	$ 362,340	$ 300,000
2	201,300	149,923	351,223	300,000
3	201,300	137,917	339,217	300,000
4	201,300	124,950	326,250	300,000
5	201,300	110,946	312,246	300,000
6	201,300	95,822	297,122	300,000
7	201,300	79,488	280,788	300,000
8	201,300	61,847	263,147	300,000
9	201,300	42,795	244,095	300,000
10	201,300	22,272 *	223,572	300,000
	$2,013,000	$987,000	$3,000,000	$3,000,000

* Based on the data given, the interest cost for the tenth year would be $22,218, difference due to rounding.

At the end of the life of the property the liability will be completely eliminated, and the property will have been written off to operations through depreciation charges.

In making a decision as to whether the equipment should be leased or purchased, management may compute the present value of the lease payments after making adjustments for income taxes. This value can then be compared with the cost to purchase the property.

Assume, for example, that Hassler Products, Inc., can either lease the equipment with annual payments of $300,000 at the end of each year for ten years or can purchase the equipment for $1,980,000.[3] If the property is purchased, depreciation will be deducted for income tax purposes by the SYD method. (The sum of the digits from 1 to 10 is 55 and will be used as the denominator of the allocating fraction. In the first year, 10/55 of $1,980,000 or $360,000 will be deducted as depreciation, 9/55 of $1,980,000 or $324,000 will be deducted in the second year, and so forth.) It is assumed (1) that the equipment will have no residual salvage value at the end of ten years, and (2) that the full amount of the annual lease payment is allowable as a deduction for income tax purposes. The difference between the depreciation deduction and the lease payment is the tax deduction advantage or disadvantage of the lease. The income tax, estimated in this example at 50 percent of net income before income taxes, is computed on this difference. It is then added to or deducted from the total lease payment in the computation of the lease payment as adjusted for the income tax advantage or disadvantage. The adjusted lease payments are discounted to a present value using as a discount rate the interest rate after income taxes on borrowed money. Assume that Hassler Products, Inc., can ordinarily borrow at an 8 percent interest rate. The interest rate after 50 percent income taxes is 4 percent. The after-tax interest rate of 4 percent is used to discount the lease payments as adjusted for the income tax on the advantage or disadvantage of a lease payment deduction or a depreciation deduction. The sum of the present values of the lease payments is compared with the cost to own the property. If the present value of the adjusted lease payments is less than the cost to purchase the property, the company should lease; if it is greater, the company should purchase the property.

The computation of the present value of the lease payments for Hassler Products, Inc., as adjusted for the income tax effect, is shown on the following page.

---

[3] If the purchase is financed, the present value of the debt payments should be compared with the present value of the net lease payments. The present value of lease payments will not necessarily be equal to the cost of purchasing the property because of different financing agreements and various options within either a purchase or lease agreement.

(1) Year	(2) Lease Payment	(3) Depreciation (If Purchased)	(4) Tax Advantage (Disadvantage) of Lease (2) — (3)
1	$300,000	$360,000	($ 60,000)
2	300,000	324,000	(24,000)
3	300,000	288,000	12,000
4	300,000	252,000	48,000
5	300,000	216,000	84,000
6	300,000	180,000	120,000
7	300,000	144,000	156,000
8	300,000	108,000	192,000
9	300,000	72,000	228,000
10	300,000	36,000	264,000

(5) Tax on Advantage (Disadvantage) 50% × (4)	(6) Lease Payments Net of Income Tax Effect (2) — (5)	(7) Present Value Rate	(8) Present Value of Net Lease Payments, 4% Discount Rate (6) × (7)
($ 30,000)	$330,000	0.962	$317,460
(12,000)	312,000	0.925	288,600
6,000	294,000	0.889	261,366
24,000	276,000	0.855	235,980
42,000	258,000	0.822	212,076
60,000	240,000	0.790	189,600
78,000	222,000	0.760	168,720
96,000	204,000	0.731	149,124
114,000	186,000	0.703	130,758
132,000	168,000	0.676	113,568

Present value of lease payments
(net of income tax effect) ... $2,067,252

Cost to purchase property $1,980,000

A comparison of the present value of the net lease payments of $2,067,252 with the purchase cost of $1,980,000 indicates that Hassler Products, Inc., should purchase the equipment. Sometimes, however, a lease may be preferred because it involves less risk than property ownership; or there may be services given with a lease that are not available if the property is purchased.

In recent years, leasing has received favorable attention notwithstanding the fact that it may be relatively expensive. Leasing provides advantages such as: (1) reduced business risk, (2) reduced income taxes, and (3) increased borrowing capacity.

Reduction of business risk. A lease may be preferred because it involves less risk than property ownership. A company that engages in a certain line of activity accepts the hazards connected with that type of business and has confidence in its ability to cope with them. But this same company may be unwilling to assume the risks of property ownership. The responsibility for handling real estate, machinery, or equipment investments will be left to some other enterprise if possible.

The property owner is to an extent a speculator. He hopes that he can purchase the property at favorable prices and that with proper handling it can be traded or sold at a later date for no less than the unrecovered cost. Property may become obsolete. Equipment, in particular, may become outmoded before it wears out. When new models come out, the owner may not be able to replace without loss. The renter may avoid these risks. Under many lease agreements, the renter will receive up-to-date models of equipment when they become available.

Income tax advantage. If property is owned, there may be a loss of purchasing power when the price level effect is taken into account. It is sometimes argued that the full amount of a rent payment can be deducted in the computation of income taxes; whereas, when property is owned, only the original cost of the property can be deducted over the years as depreciation. If the price level rises and if the tax rate is high, the company may not recover the original purchasing power invested. In recent years, however, income tax provisions with respect to depreciation have been liberalized, permitting larger proportionate depreciation deductions during the early years of property use. This fast recovery of a substantial portion of the cost tends to compensate for losses that might occur because of price level changes and tends to compensate for the tax advantage claimed for a lease.

Increased borrowing capacity. Business management may believe that the company will have a greater borrowing capacity if it leases. When property is owned, it must be shown on the balance sheet with the other assets. Also the debt incurred to finance the property will be listed with the liabilities. The nonliquid assets may appear to be large in relation to the liquid assets, and the debt may appear to be large. As a result, prospective credit grantors may be reluctant to furnish additional credit. However, as stated earlier, leased property should also be shown on the balance sheet.

Management is in error when it fails to see that the lease has the same effect as other forms of debt financing. Prospective creditors generally recognize that the lease imposes a fixed charge for interest and debt amortization. The company may find that it will not be able to increase its borrowing capacity by leasing property. Credit grantors will tend to look at a lease agreement as a form of debt financing.

Questions

1. Why are marketable securities often valued at the lower of cost or market but not at market values that are in excess of cost?

2. Are inventories customarily valued at current market values with gains or losses being recognized while the inventories are held?

3. What is meant by saying that the inventory is valued at the current cost of reproduction?

4. What is net realizable value?

5. Define the upper and lower limits of market value for inventories as established by the American Institute of Certified Public Accountants.

6. If inventories are valued at the lower of cost or market, is there a possibility that profits may be shifted from one year to another? Explain.

7. Explain briefly the principle of the first-in, first-out inventory method and the principle of the last-in, first-out inventory method.

8. When is it appropriate to charge depreciation to operations by the straight-line method?

9. Explain how double-rate depreciation is computed.

10. What is the advantage in deducting depreciation for income tax purposes by an accelerated method?

11. Explain how leased property can be capitalized and shown on the balance sheet.

12. Explain how leased property under certain conditions can be virtually equivalent to property that is purchased.

13. How can an economic decision be made as to whether property should be leased or purchased?

14. When a company leases property is it in a better position to borrow money than if the property had been purchased and financed? Explain.

15. Why might a company prefer to lease property when it might be less expensive to purchase?

Exercises

1. Weller Holmes, Inc., is in the process of building up a fund for the future expansion of business operations. According to the plans of management, approximately $150,000 will be needed by 1972 to begin construction. Cost and market prices at the end of 1971 are given for the securities held by the fund at the end of 1971.

No. of Shares	Security	Cost Per Share	Market Price, 12/31/71
1,000	Andover Mills, Inc.	42	51
1,500	Creighton Metals	26	37
500	Dunn Fixtures	33	46
300	Lisle Chemical	63	71

The securities are to be converted to cash in June, 1972. At that time market prices were as follows:

Andover Mills, Inc. 38
Creighton Metals 14
Dunn Fixtures 21
Lisle Chemical 58

Required: (1) Show how the expansion fund investments would be shown on the balance sheet at December 31, 1971, if valued at current market values.

(2) If the investments had been valued at the lower of cost or market on December 31, 1971, how would they appear on the balance sheet at that date?

(3) Assume that the investments were realized in June, 1972, at the current market prices. How much cash was realized?

2. There is some difference of opinion among the executives of Hawthorne Styles, Inc., as to how the current assets should be valued on the balance sheet. One member of the management group believes that both the marketable securities and inventories should be shown at cost with current market values given parenthetically. The controller favors showing these assets at the lower of cost or market with the higher valuations being shown parenthetically. The treasurer, on the other hand, believes that these assets should be shown at current market prices, whether the market prices are above or below cost. Data with respect to the current assets follow:

Cash $130,000
Marketable securities:
    Cost 542,000
    Market 915,000
Accounts receivable 264,000
Inventory of 15,000 items,
    each costing $50 ....
Current market price,
    $47 each ....
Cost to sell and deliver
    each unit, $2 ....

Required: Prepare the current asset section of a balance sheet under each of the three conditions stated.

3. Data with respect to the purchase and sale of merchandise during 1972 are given for Hammond Dial Company.

Cost of inventory on hand at January 1, 1972
    (10,000 units) $180,000

Purchases:
    March—5,000 units @ $23 115,000
    June —8,000 units @ $25 200,000
    Sept. —7,000 units @ $26 182,000

Sales were made as follows:

Jan. and Feb. .... 8,000 units
Apr. and May .... 4,000 units
July and Aug. .... 4,000 units
Oct. and Dec. .... 9,000 units

All sales were made at a price of $26 a unit, and this is the current price at the end of the year. It costs $1 to deliver each unit to the customer.

Required: (1) Compute the cost of goods sold for the year and the inventory value at the end of the year using the lifo inventory method.

(2) Compute the cost of goods sold for the year and the inventory value at the end of the year using the fifo inventory method with inventory valued at the lower of cost or market.

4. Worthing Enterprises, Inc., constructed a new plant at a cost of $15,000,000 and placed the plant in service at the beginning of 1972. The plant was estimated to have a useful life of 20 years with an estimated salvage value of $3,000,000 at the end of the 20 years. The company expects earnings, before deducting depreciation on the plant or income taxes, of $4,800,000 each year. Income taxes are estimated at 40 percent of net income before taxes.

Required: (1) Compute depreciation for each of the next 3 years by both the straight-line method and the double-rate method.

(2) What tax advantage can be expected in each of the next 3 years by using double-rate depreciation on the tax return instead of straight-line depreciation?

5. Filtration equipment is being installed by Marcello Chemicals, Inc., at a cost of $940,000. The equipment is expected to have a useful life of 5 years with a residual salvage value of $100,000 at the end of the five years. Mr. Marcello wants to see the pattern of depreciation deductions for each of the five years by (1) the straight-line method, (2) the SYD method, and (3) the double-rate method. If the double-rate method is used, the remainder of the cost to be written off to reduce the equipment to the residual salvage value will be written off in the fifth year.

Required: (1) Prepare the schedules of depreciation requested by Mr. Marcello.

(2) Which of the three depreciation methods offers the most advantage from an income tax point of view? Why?

6. Benjamin Levitz plans to lease certain equipment to be used in productive operations. Under the lease agreement, he is expected to pay $85,000 when the equipment is installed and to pay $75,000 at the beginning of each of the next 10 years. This means that he must pay a total of $160,000 when the equipment is installed. Included in the lease payments is a provision for interest at the rate of 8 percent a year.

Required: (1) Show the capitalized value of the leased equipment on the balance sheet after the equipment has been installed with the initial payments made as required. Show the liability under the lease agreement.

(2) After payment has been made at the beginning of the second year, show the liability under the lease agreement. How would the leased equipment appear

at that time assuming that straight-line depreciation has been deducted with no allowance for residual salvage value?

Problems

2–1. The marketable securities of Allied Chemical Corp. were reported on the balance sheets at December 31, 1961 and 1962 as follows:

	December 31	
	1962	*1961*
Marketable securities at cost (quoted market value at end of 1962—$77,742,644 and 1961—$89,725,434)	$16,877,609	$16,934,095

No marketable securities were purchased during 1962, but securities costing $56,486 were sold for $80,000.

The net income before taxes in 1962 was reported at $61,704,964 with no adjustment made for unrealized market value changes. The net income before taxes for 1961 was $57,978,128.

Required: (1) Show how marketable securities would have appeared on the balance sheets at December 31, 1961 and 1962, if reported at current market values.

(2) Show the net income before taxes for 1962 as adjusted for unrealized market appreciation. (Assume for problem purposes that all market value changes have been recognized on the income statements for past years.)

2–2. McGraw Feed Company, Inc., carries substantial inventories in soybeans, wheat, and other grains and hedges commodities to the extent practicable to minimize risk due to market fluctuations.

The inventories are reported at the lower of cost or market as shown below:

	June 30	
	1972	*1971*
Inventories	$50,950,276	$43,930,985

Current replacement cost of these inventories in excess of the inventory basis used in the financial statements was $1,497,000 at June 30, 1972, and $2,423,000 at June 30, 1971.

Net income before taxes for the fiscal year ended June 30, 1972, was reported at $8,217,319.

Required: If net income had been consistently reported at current replacement cost over the years, how much net income before taxes would have been reported for the fiscal year ended June 30, 1972?

2–3. Finch Products, Inc., manufactures a component used in air purification equipment. This component is manufactured in two operations. Detail with respect to the inventories on hand at October 31, 1972, is given on the next page. The cost of manufacturing each unit in Operation #2 amounted to $7.00. The cost of the materials used is included in the unit cost of Operation #1.

On October 31, 1972, it was estimated that the materials could be replaced at a cost of $6.00 per unit. To reproduce the work in process (including the cost

64

	Number of Units in Inventory	Unit Cost
Materials	8,000	$ 9.00
Work in process, complete as to all work in Operation #1	5,800	15.00
Finished goods	6,300	22.00

of materials) would cost $11.00 per unit. The cost of further processing in Operation #2 would amount to $5.00 a unit. The component can be sold for $35.00 a unit on October 31, 1972 with costs to sell and ship estimated at $2.00 per unit.

Required: (1) Compute the cost of the inventories at October 31, 1972.

(2) Determine the net realizable value of the inventories at October 31, 1972.

(3) Determine the cost to replace or reproduce the inventories at October 31, 1972.

2–4. Boyd Fasteners, Inc., constructed a new plant at Greensboro. The building cost $7,100,000 and was estimated to have a useful life of 20 years with a residual salvage value of $800,000 at the end of 20 years. Equipment costing $6,000,000 with an estimated useful life of 10 years and a residual salvage value of $500,000 was installed early in January, 1972. Operations were started shortly after the equipment was installed.

Early in January, 1973, additional equipment costing $1,500,000 was installed. This equipment was estimated to have a useful life of 10 years with a residual salvage value of $400,000.

During 1973, the plant reported a net income on manufacturing operations of $5,000,000 before deducting depreciation or income taxes. Income taxes are 40 percent of net income before taxes.

The plant superintendent plans to report net income on the financial statement by deducting depreciation by the straight-line method. The SYD method will be used in computing income taxes. Taxes as computed on the tax returns will be deducted on the income statement as income tax expense for the year.

Required: (1) Determine the net income after income taxes for 1973 using the method outlined above. Show both the depreciation and income tax expense as separate items in your computation.

(2) What would the tax expense have been for the year if the tax had been computed on the net income reported after deducting straight-line depreciation?

2–5. A balance sheet for Roswell Block Company at June 30, 1972, shows assets on an original cost basis as shown below:

Cash	$ 1,946,000
Marketable securities (at cost, market value, $5,135,000)	2,380,000
Accounts receivable	2,467,000
Inventories	1,872,000
Land	115,000
Plant and equipment, net of accumulated depreciation .	1,624,000
Total assets	$10,404,000

Net income for the fiscal year ended June 30, 1972, was reported at $1,875,000.

Management believes that valuations shown on the balance sheet are completely out of date. As a result, a rate of return computed on the total assets has little significance considering that the net income for the most part has been measured in current dollars while the assets are stated on an original cost basis. Marketable securities, for example, have current market values well in excess of cost. Inventories if replaced at current prices would amount to $2,346,000. The plant and equipment has been used for many years. The estimated current value of the plant and equipment after allowing for accumulated depreciation is $8,648,000. Land has been currently appraised at $220,000.

A large part of the asset appreciation can be attributed to past years, but $1,242,000 of the total appreciation took place during the fiscal year ended June 30, 1972.

Required: (1) Restate the assets at current market values and restate the net income to include holding gains during the year.

(2) What was the percentage of net income as given to the total assets stated on a cost basis?

(3) Compute the percentage of net income (including holding gains for the year) to total assets stated at current market values.

2–6. Montgomery Ward reported total assets of $881,949,674 at February 3, 1965. Current liabilities and deferred credits amounted to $235,699,648. There were no long-term liabilities, and the capital stock and retained earnings amounted to $646,250,026.

The company has lease obligations on property used in operations, but the leases were not capitalized on the balance sheet. Notes accompanying the financial statements state that minimum annual rentals of $25,332,000 must be paid at the end of each fiscal year for the next 25 years.

Required: (1) Capitalize the long-term leases on February 3, 1965, at 8 percent.

(2) Restate the total assets, liabilities, and owners' equity at February 3, 1965, with the long-term leases capitalized.

(3) What effect will the capitalization of leases have on the net income before taxes for the fiscal year ended in January 1966, if the full amount of the rental can no longer be deducted as expense? Assume that depreciation will be deducted by the straight-line method with no allowance for residual salvage value.

2–7. Machinery to be used in operations can be purchased at a cost of $4,500,000. This equipment is expected to have a useful life of 5 years with an estimated residual salvage value of $300,000 at the end of 5 years.

The manufacturer of this equipment agrees to furnish this equipment to customers under a leasing plan with an initial payment of $1,500,000 required and additional payments of $1,500,000 a year due at the end of each year over a period of 4 years.

Yates Supply Company is considering the purchase of this machinery. Before making a decision the management wants to know whether or not the leasing arrangement should be accepted. If purchased, depreciation will be deducted by the SYD method. Yates Supply Company can borrow at an interest rate of 8 percent after taxes. Income taxes are at the rate of 40 percent of net income before taxes. Under the lease arrangement, Yates Supply Company would deduct the full amount of the lease payments for tax purposes.

Required: Should Yates Supply Company purchase the machinery or lease it? Show computations.

2–8. Bates Machine Company, Inc., plans to acquire equipment and fixtures that can be purchased from Myers and Coburn, Inc., at a cost of $6,500,000. It is estimated that the equipment will have a useful life of 10 years with a residual salvage value of $1,000,000 at the end of 10 years.

Bates Machine Company, Inc., can purchase the equipment and fixtures with resources that are available, or it can lease the property through an agreement with a finance company. If the property is leased, a payment of $1,000,000 must be made at the beginning of each of the next 10 years. Interest at the rate of 8 percent is included in the payments after taxes.

For income tax purposes, depreciation will be deducted by the SYD method if the property is purchased. If the property is leased, the full amount of the lease payment will be deducted. Income taxes are at the rate of 40 percent of net income before taxes.

Required: From an economic point of view, should the company purchase the equipment and fixtures or lease them?

2–9. The board of directors of McCabe Mills, Inc., is in a position where equipment that is essential to the manufacturing operation must be replaced at an estimated cost of $5,000,000. The company does not have funds available for replacement, and additional capital stock cannot be issued without the risk to the present stockholders of giving up control.

The purchase can be financed at 8 percent interest with interest payments due at the end of each year. A down payment of $500,000 must be made when the equipment is purchased, and the $4,500,000 principal of the loan becomes due at the end of 10 years.

Another equipment manufacturer agrees to lease comparable equipment to McCabe Mills upon payment of $400,000 when the lease is signed and annual payments of $800,000 due at the end of each of the next 10 years. For income tax purposes, the lease is to be treated as a purchase with deductions allowed for depreciation and interest.

One member of the board of directors favors leasing, pointing out that the company can avoid long-term financing; and if the need should arise in the future, it will be easier to borrow with no long-term debt on the balance sheet.

The equipment is estimated to have a useful life of 10 years with no residual salvage value at the end of 10 years. Income taxes are at the rate of 40 percent of net income before taxes.

Required: (1) Compute the present value of the total payments to be made under each plan including the tax effect of depreciation deducted by the straight-line method and interest as a tax deduction under each plan.

(2) Comment upon the reason why one of the board members prefers the leasing plan.

2–10. Zale and Morrison, Inc., plan an expansion program. Equipment costing $33,000,000 will be acquired as a part of the expansion program. The equipment may be depreciated over a period of 10 years with no allowance being made for residual salvage value. For income tax purposes, the depreciation will be deducted by the SYD method. Plans are being made to finance the equipment with equipment notes that become due at the end of 5 years. Interest at the rate of 8 percent must be paid at the end of each year on the notes. Notes of

$25,000,000 will be issued, and $8,000,000 will be paid when the equipment is acquired.

Under an alternative financing plan, the equipment may be leased with an initial payment of $3,000,000 to be made when the lease is signed. At the end of each of the next 5 years, Zale and Morrison must pay $7,000,000 in rentals. Title to the property is transferred to Zale and Morrison at the end of 5 years upon the payment of an additional $500,000. The lease is to be capitalized on the balance sheet using a rate of 8 percent for capitalization. Depreciation on the total cost as capitalized is to be deducted over 10 years by the SYD method.

Required: Compare the financing plans on a present value basis. Include the total effect of income taxes estimated at 40 percent of net income before taxes. Under the leasing plan, assume that the company will exercise the option to buy the property at the end of 5 years. Interest under the lease is included in the annual payments of $7,000,000 and is to be deducted in the computation of income taxes.

Chapter 3

PROBLEM AREAS
IN ACCOUNTABILITY—II

There are several other problem areas in accountability in addition to assets, as discussed in the preceding chapter. Some of these areas are identified below and discussed in this chapter.

(1) Revenue recognition.

(2) Expense recognition.

(3) Extraordinary gains and losses.

(4) The dilution of earnings.

(5) Business combinations.

REVENUE RECOGNITION

The earning process extends over the entire period of time that goods and services are produced for and delivered to customers. There are at least three points in time when revenue could be recognized.

(1) When goods or services are produced.

(2) When goods or services are delivered to customers.

(3) When cash is collected from the customers.

Ideally, perhaps, revenue should be recognized as goods or services are produced. The total revenue is not earned when the customer receives the goods or service. Instead, it is earned gradually over the entire production and delivery cycle.

As a practical matter, however, this approach poses certain difficulties. It may be that revenue cannot be measured precisely or objectively until some outsider recognizes the value increments by agreeing to pay a stated price for the goods or services. A reliable measurement of the worth of goods or services may not be available until a sale takes place.

In some cases the accountant will make an exception to the general rule that revenue should be recognized at the point of transaction with a customer. If there is little reason to question that the goods or services will be accepted by customers at a fixed price, revenue may be recognized during the course of the productive operation. For example, in mining precious metals such as gold, revenue may be recognized as the gold is mined. There is a definite market for gold at an established price. In situations like this, the inventories should be valued at sales value with reductions made for cost of delivery and costs to complete the productive operation.

Ordinarily, the accountant recognizes revenue on a legalistic basis at the point when the title to goods is transferred or when services are rendered in exchange for the customer's promise to pay a stated price. At this point there is an enforceable agreement, and the revenue can be measured objectively according to the terms of the transaction.

At the other extreme it may be argued that revenue should not be recognized until cash is collected from the customer. Until that time, there is some uncertainty with respect to the ultimate collectibility of the accounts receivable from customers. But if cash collections are reported as revenues, the revenue to be reported each year will depend upon the pattern of cash collections and will not necessarily be related to the earning process. In accounting, revenue is generally recognized before it is realized in the form of cash, but there are exceptions. Small businesses where cash is received at approximately the same time that goods are delivered or services rendered may report revenue on a cash basis; also, if business is conducted on an installment sales basis, revenue may be recognized as collections are received from the customers. With installment selling, there may be considerable doubt about the collectibility of the accounts.

An example to illustrate the recognition of revenues and expenses under installment selling is given. Assume that appliances costing $40,000 were sold to customers during 1972 on installment sales contracts. The cost of the appliances to the dealer were $28,000 (70 percent of the selling price). In a normal sales situation, the total revenue and expense would be recorded at the point of sale, and a gross margin of $12,000 would be recognized. In installment selling, however, the profits are recognized as cash is collected. Assume further that $15,000 has been collected from the customers in 1972 and that $20,000 has been collected in 1973. Revenues and expenses would be reported as shown below:

	Cash Collections	Revenue	Cost of Goods Sold	Gross Margin
1972	$15,000	$15,000	$10,500	$4,500
1973	20,000	20,000	14,000	6,000

The cost of goods sold for each year is equal to 70 percent of the revenue recognized. Other expenses that are related to the sales and collections should also be matched against revenue in the determination of net income.

EXPENSES AND RELATED LIABILITIES

In the income measurement process, assets consumed in the earning process are matched against revenues as expenses. Sometimes, an expense is recorded directly along with a related liability. In certain situations, accountants are not in agreement as to whether or not an expense and liability should be recognized at all; in other situations the area of disagreement may be limited to the *amount* to be shown for the expense and liability.

Deferred income taxes expected to become due for payment in future years are an example of controversy over the amount to be shown for the expense and liability. The difficulty arises from differences between expenses shown on income tax returns and on financial statements as a result of such policies as using different depreciation methods for income tax and annual reporting.

Assume that accelerated depreciation is deducted on the income tax returns but that straight-line depreciation is deducted on the financial statements. For tax purposes the depreciation deductions will be larger in the earlier years of the life of a plant asset than in the later years. As a result, income taxes will be lower in the earlier years than they would be otherwise. In later years when the depreciation deductions are smaller under accelerated depreciation than they would be with straight-line depreciation, the company may have to pay more income taxes than it would with straight-line depreciation. In the meantime, however, the company has conserved resources that would otherwise be paid out in income taxes; and these resources can be invested to earn more profits.

It is difficult at best to estimate the flow of benefits from a plant asset. The problem is often resolved by assuming that the benefits flow in at a uniform rate and that depreciation should be deducted in the accounting records accordingly. Perhaps the benefits to be derived from a plant asset should be defined more broadly to include not only the benefits from the physical use of the property but also the tax benefits from depreciation. The income tax differences could then be included as a part of the depreciation on the financial statements. However, this is not accepted in conventional practice.

An example is given on page 72 to show how the use of different depreciation methods for tax and annual reporting will give rise to deferred income taxes. Equipment costing $30,000 with an estimated useful life of 5 years with no residual salvage value was acquired. Depreciation is to be deducted by the sum-of-the-years-digits method on the tax return and by the straight-line method in the accounting records. Differences in depreciation and income taxes are given below for the 5 years on the assumption that income taxes are equal to 40 percent of net income before income taxes.

| | Depreciation | | Differences | |
Years	Tax Return	Income Statement	Depreciation	Income Taxes
1	$10,000	$6,000	$4,000	$1,600
2	8,000	6,000	2,000	800
3	6,000	6,000	—0—	—0—
4	4,000	6,000	(2,000)	(800)
5	2,000	6,000	(4,000)	(1,600)

A summary of the information from the tax return and the income statement for the first year follows. The net income before depreciation and income taxes on both the tax return and the income statement is assumed to be $50,000.

	Tax Return	Income Statement
Net income before depreciation and income taxes	$50,000	$50,000
Depreciation	10,000	6,000
Net income before income taxes	$40,000	$44,000
Income taxes (40%)	16,000	17,600
Net income after income taxes	$24,000	$26,400

Note that the tax on the income statement is $1,600 more than it is on the tax return and that the total tax is equal to 40 percent of the reported net income before income taxes. If only the currently due tax of $16,000, as reported on the tax return, were reported as tax expense for the year, the readers of the financial statements could be misled into believing that the tax was a lower percentage of net income before tax. Although the current amount to be paid on income taxes is only $16,000, the company may have to pay the additional $1,600 in income taxes in a later year when there is no further advantage from accelerated depreciation.

A journal entry is given below to record the income taxes for the first year.

Income Tax Expense	17,600	
Current Income Taxes Payable		16,000
Deferred Income Taxes		1,600
Estimate of income taxes chargeable against income of the first year.		

At the end of the first year deferred taxes would be shown in the balance sheet as a noncurrent liability of $1,600, assuming no other entries to the account and no previous balance. If there were no change in tax rates over the remaining four years, the account balance at the end of the second year would be $2,400 (the combined tax difference for the two years). At the end of the third year the balance would remain unchanged; at the end of the fourth year it would be reduced to $1,600; and at the end of the fifth year there would be no balance.

A summary of the information from the tax return and the income statement for the fifth year follows. The net income before depreciation and income taxes on both the tax return and the income statement is assumed to be $50,000.

	Tax Return	Income Statement
Net income before depreciation and income taxes	$50,000	$50,000
Depreciation	2,000	6,000
Net income before income taxes	$48,000	$44,000
Income taxes (40%)	19,200	17,600
Net income after income taxes	$28,800	$26,400

A journal entry is given below to record the income taxes for the fifth year.

Income Tax Expense	17,600	
Deferred Income Taxes	1,600	
Current Income Taxes Payable		19,200
Estimate of income taxes chargeable against income of the fifth year.		

There is some disagreement in the accounting profession as to whether or not deferred income taxes should be recognized. The Accounting Principles Board of the American Institute of Certified Public Accountants recommends that a provision be made for deferred income taxes. However, some members of the profession question this and believe that only the income taxes that are computed on the returns should be recorded as income tax expense for the year, and that no provision should be made for deferred income taxes. At the present time, the problem of how to handle deferred income taxes has not been completely resolved. In any event, management should understand how the problem arises and should consider what it means in terms of the future and in terms of the attitudes of customers, stockholders, and other interested persons.

EXTRAORDINARY GAINS AND LOSSES

It is expected that a company will derive net income year after year in its normal operations. The net income from normal recurring activity should be clearly designated so that it can be distinguished from the unusual or nonrecurring type of gains and losses known as *extraordinary items*. An extraordinary item, such as the gain or loss from the sale of a plant asset less the income tax effect, should be shown separately on the income statement.

It is important to remember two things with regard to extraordinary items. First, extraordinary items that are adjustments relating to earlier fiscal periods may be shown as an adjustment to the opening balance of retained earnings, rather than as an item on the income statement. An error, for example, may have been made in reporting net income in some earlier year. Perhaps an estimate was made of the cost to settle a damage claim, and the exact amount was not determined until a later year. The amount of the correction pertains to the earlier year.

Secondly, the reader of the financial statements may be misled if the distinction between net income from normal operations and from extraordinary items is not made clear or if information is only partially given.

For example, a company with 100,000 shares of stock outstanding may report that it has earned $3.20 a share in 1972 and $4.00 a share in 1973. Apparently the company has increased its earnings per share by 25 percent, and the public may expect earnings of at least $4.00 a share in future years. While it may be true, in one respect, that earnings per share have increased from $3.20 to $4.00, there is more to be revealed.

Assume that net income has been reported for the two years as follows:

	1973	1972
Net income after income taxes, before extraordinary items	$240,000	$320,000
Gain on sale of land, less income tax on the gain	160,000	—0—
Net income	$400,000	$320,000
Net income per share of stock (100,000 shares outstanding)	$4.00	$3.20

With more information available, it is evident that the increase in earnings per share resulted from the sale of land. The net income per share on normal activity was only $2.40, and the gain from the sale of land amounted to $1.60 per share. The fact that on a normal operating basis the company did not earn as much per share in 1973 as it did in 1972 should be clearly revealed to the stockholders.

DILUTION OF EARNINGS

The earnings per share of stock are often quoted in evaluating the performance of a company. Management, who is aware of this yardstick used to measure earning power, will generally make every effort to keep the earnings per share from decreasing. The potential investor must understand how earnings per share were computed, as illustrated in the example given for extraordinary items. Both management and the investor should be aware of the potential dilution of earnings that can result from financing transactions.

During a period of relatively high interest costs, a company may obtain a lower interest rate by issuing *convertible debt*. The debt is issued with a provision that it can be converted to capital stock under stated conditions. The investor is generally willing to accept a smaller interest return in exchange for the conversion privilege. He avoids the risk of an investment in common stock and obtains a reasonably good return on his investment. If the stock sells above the conversion price, he can exercise his conversion option and obtain the advantages of stock ownership.

The conversion option creates a problem in the measurement of earnings per share. While the debt is outstanding, there is no effect on the earnings per share. Yet, a shadow is cast over the earnings per share by the possibility that they will be reduced when the conversion option is exercised. Management must consider this factor in selecting a financing arrangement, and the investor must recognize this possibility when investing in the company.

The dilution effect is illustrated by assuming that a company with 1,000,000 shares of common stock outstanding throughout the year has reported a net income of $4,500,000 for the year. The actual earnings per share amount to $4.50 ($4,500,000 ÷ 1,000,000 shares). However, convertible debt is outstanding that gives the holder an option of converting the debt to common stock, and, if all of the debt is converted, the number of outstanding shares will be increased to 1,100,000. Also, if the debt is converted, interest charges will cease. Assume in this case that the interest after income taxes on the convertible debt amounted to $150,000 a year.

The net income after income taxes is adjusted as shown below:

Actual net income	$4,500,000
Add: Effect of interest reduction after income taxes	150,000
Adjusted net income (assuming the conversion of all debt to common stock)	$4,650,000

The earnings per share are shown not only on the basis of the number of shares of stock outstanding but also on the basis of full conversion of the debt to common stock.

Earnings per share of outstanding stock, assuming no conversion of debt ($4,500,000 ÷ 1,000,000 shares) $4.50

Earnings per share, assuming full conversion of debt to common stock ($4,650,000 ÷ 1,100,000 shares) $4.23

With full disclosure, both management and the investor are in a better position to make decisions.

BUSINESS COMBINATIONS

Another important problem of accountability arises when two or more companies combine. For example, if one company is acquired by another, the question arises as to how the net assets of the acquired company should be valued. Two methods have emerged for accounting for the net assets acquired: (1) the purchase method, and (2) the pooling of interests method.

When the net assets of a particular company are acquired for a cash purchase, there is no particular problem of valuation. That is, if cash is paid for the outstanding stock of the acquired company, the cash purchase price becomes the basis for the valuation of the net assets acquired. This is called a *purchase* treatment. However, a problem can arise when the outstanding shares of the acquired company are obtained by the buyer issuing shares (or other securities) in exchange for the stock of the acquired company. When this happens, the question arises as to whether the net assets acquired should be valued at their historical book value—in which case the accounting method is referred to as a *pooling of interests*, or whether the value of the net assets acquired should be based on the market value of the shares issued—in which case the accounting method is referred to as a purchase.

It is quite possible that the market value of the shares issued in exchange for the shares of the acquired company may be different from the book value of the net assets acquired. In many cases the market value of the shares will exceed the book value of the net assets acquired. If this is the case, and if a purchase method is used, the individual assets are recorded by the acquiring company at their appraised (current) value and any positive difference between the market value of the shares issued and the appraised value of the net assets would be recorded as goodwill by the acquiring company.

On the other hand, if a pooling of interests method is used, the net assets are recorded at their book value and any goodwill that might exist is not recorded since neither appraisal values nor the market value of the shares issued is used in the pooling of interests treatment. An example is given on the next page illustrating the basic difference between the two different methods of accountability.

Assume that Company P acquired the net assets of Company S by an exchange of stock which has a market value of $100,000 and a par value of $10,000. The former shareholders of Company S will then receive Company P stock in exchange for Company S stock. Summarized balance sheets for the two companies just prior to acquisition are given below:

Balance Sheets
Date of Purchase

	Company P	Company S
Assets		
Current assets	$600,000	$50,000
Plant assets	300,000	30,000
Total assets	$900,000	$80,000
Equities		
Current liabilities	$100,000	$20,000
Capital stock, paid-in capital, and retained earnings	800,000	60,000
Total equities	$900,000	$80,000

The basis of the acquisition of Company S was determined as follows:

Current assets	$ 50,000
Plant assets—appraised value	50,000
Goodwill	20,000
Total asset value	$120,000
Less: Liabilities to be assumed by purchaser	20,000
Price	$100,000

A balance sheet is given below for the new company assuming that the acquisition is accounted for as a purchase.

	Company P	Acquisition of Company S	Company P (After Acquisition)
Assets			
Current assets	$600,000	$ 50,000	$ 650,000
Goodwill		20,000	20,000
Plant assets	300,000	50,000	350,000
Total assets	$900,000	$120,000	$1,020,000
Equities			
Current liabilities	$100,000	$ 20,000	$ 120,000
Capital stock, paid-in capital, and retained earnings	800,000	100,000	900,000
Total equities	$900,000	$120,000	$1,020,000

The acquisition of Company S, using the purchase treatment, would have been recorded by Company P as follows:

Current Assets	50,000	
Plant Assets (appraisal values used)	50,000	
Goodwill	20,000	
Current Liabilities (assumed)		20,000
Capital Stock		10,000
Paid-In Capital		90,000

Acquisition of assets of Company S and assumption of liabilities. Capital stock issued in exchange.

As can be seen, the above treatment reflects not only the appraised value of the plant assets but also the goodwill of $20,000 that is calculated as follows:

Acquisition price based on market value of stock		$100,000
Net tangible assets acquired:		
Current assets	$ 50,000	
Plant assets	50,000	
	$100,000	
Liabilities assumed	(20,000)	80,000
Goodwill (intangible asset)		$ 20,000

When a pooling of interests method is used the net assets are recorded at their book value rather than at a value based on the market value of the stock of Company P. The Accounting Principles Board of the American Institute of Certified Public Accountants has stated that the necessary requirements for a combination to be viewed as a pooling of interests are that the acquiring company should preferably issue only common stock with voting rights for substantially all of the voting common stock of another company, the shareholders should have the same proportionate interests as before, and there should be no break in the continuity of ownership.

Using the same example as before, the balance sheet for Company P immediately after the date of pooling would be presented as shown at the top of the next page.

In the example, the asset base for the pooling of interests is $40,000 lower than in the case of the purchase. This is because in the pooling the net assets are recorded at their book value whereas in the case of the purchase treatment the market value of the common stock is the basis for establishing the value of the net assets. Where the purchase treatment is used, the tangible assets are recorded at their appraised values. In the example, this added $20,000 to the plant asset accounts. The difference between the appraised value of the net tangible assets received and the

	Company P	Acquisition of Company S	Company P (After Acquisition)
Assets			
Current assets	$600,000	$50,000	$650,000
Plant assets	300,000	30,000	330,000
Total assets	$900,000	$80,000	$980,000
Equities			
Current liabilities	$100,000	$20,000	$120,000
Capital stock, paid in capital, and retained earnings	800,000	60,000	860,000
Total equities	$900,000	$80,000	$980,000

market value of the common shares issued (in this example, $20,000) is recorded as goodwill.

THE ATTITUDE OF MANAGEMENT

Management tends to favor the pooling of interests treatment. With a pooling of interests, the assets are combined at their book values with no adjustments being made for changes in fair market values of the assets or for the recognition of goodwill. Assuming that the net assets are undervalued, the asset and net asset base for the combined operation will tend to be lower for a pooling of interests treatment than for a purchase treatment. Assuming the same net income in either case, the rate of return on assets or net assets will tend to be higher with a lower asset base under the pooling of interests treatment. Inasmuch as management is sometimes evaluated on a rate-of-return basis, it is evident that the management will typically prefer a lower asset base.

In a purchase transaction if the net assets are undervalued, goodwill will usually be recognized and recorded on the balance sheet as an asset. Past practice has been to show goodwill on the balance sheet year after year with no provision for amortization. The Accounting Principles Board recognizes that goodwill may not retain its value as an asset indefinitely and has stated that goodwill should be amortized over its useful life and in no case should the amortization period be in excess of 40 years.

CONSOLIDATED STATEMENTS

In many business combinations, the companies acquired retain their identities, but in the annual report, the results of the combined operations are shown by using *consolidated financial statements*. That is, under appropriate circumstances consolidated financial statements are prepared for the group of companies as one economic unit. A company holding a controlling interest in another company is called a *parent company*. The company whose stock is held is called a *subsidiary company*. On a consolidated balance sheet the assets and equities of the parent and the subsidiary companies are combined. *However, the owners' equity of the subsidiary companies applicable to the parent's share of stock ownership is eliminated against the investment.*

The balance of the owners' equity in the subsidiary company after eliminating the parent's share is shown on the consolidated balance sheet as the *minority interest*. There is a minority interest only when the parent company holds less than 100 percent of the stock of the subsidiary company. The minority interest is the interest of the stockholders other than the parent company in the subsidiary company.

If there is a difference between the book value of the net assets acquired and the amount of the investment by the parent company, this difference will be shown as goodwill resulting from the acquisition if a purchase method is used in accounting for the combination. This is illustrated below.

Condensed balance sheets for Company P and Company S on July 1, 1972, the date that Company P acquired 90 percent of the stock of Company S at a cost of $245,000, are shown below:

Balance Sheets
July 1, 1972

	Company P	Company S
Assets		
Investment in Company S	$245,000	—
Other assets	500,000	$300,000
Total assets	$745,000	$300,000
Equities		
Liabilities	$145,000	$ 50,000
Owners' equity:		
Capital stock	200,000	150,000
Retained earnings	400,000	100,000
Total equities	$745,000	$300,000

A consolidated balance sheet at the date Company P acquired a 90 percent interest in Company S is given on the next page.

Note that the other assets and the liabilities of the two companies are combined. It is assumed that there are no intercompany borrowing or lending transactions. If there were, the amount would be eliminated from the receivables of the lending company and from the payables of the borrowing company.

Company P and Subsidiary S
Consolidated Balance Sheet
July 1, 1972

Assets

Goodwill	$ 20,000
Other assets	800,000
Total assets	$820,000

Equities

Liabilities	$195,000
Minority stockholders' interest in Company S	25,000
Owners' equity:	
Capital stock	200,000
Retained earnings	400,000
Total equities	$820,000

The excess of the investment cost over 90 percent of the owners' equity of Company S is shown as goodwill.

Investment in Company S	$245,000
Less: 90% of the owner's equity of Company S (90% of $250,000)	225,000
Goodwill	$ 20,000

The minority stockholders' share in Company S is shown separately.

Total owners' equity—Company S	$250,000
Less: 90% interest purchased by Company P (90% of $250,000)	225,000
Minority interest	$ 25,000

The owners' equity in Company P is carried forward as the owners' equity for the consolidation. This same elimination will be made in future years so long as Company P holds a 90 percent interest.

The income statements will also be consolidated in subsequent years. Intercompany sales and purchases will be eliminated, and intercompany profits included in the inventory of any company in the combination will be eliminated. For example, assume that Company P sold merchandise to Company S during the next fiscal year for $300,000. All of this merchandise *was sold* by Company S during the fiscal year to outsiders. Company S, however, owed $80,000 to Company P at June 30, 1973.

Income statements for the two companies for the fiscal year ending June 30, 1973, as well as a consolidated income statement for Company P and Company S are shown on the next page.

On the consolidated income statement, the total sales for both companies of $1,950,000 are reduced by the sales between the companies of $300,000.

Income Statement
For the Year Ended June 30, 1973

	Company P	Company S
Net sales	$1,350,000	$600,000
Cost of goods sold	800,000	400,000
Gross margin	$ 550,000	$200,000
Operating expenses	380,000	130,000
Net income	$ 170,000	$ 70,000

Company P and Subsidiary S
Consolidated Income Statement
For the Year Ended June 30, 1973

Net sales	$1,650,000
Cost of goods sold	900,000
Gross margin	$ 750,000
Operating expenses	510,000
	$ 240,000
Less: Minority stockholders' share of net income	7,000
Consolidated net income	$ 233,000

Cost of goods sold for the two companies is also combined and reduced by $300,000.

The minority stockholders' interest of 10 percent in the profits of Company S is deducted in computing the consolidated net income. The consolidated net income is added to the parent company's retained earnings to arrive at consolidated retained earnings, and the minority share of net income is added to the minority interest on the consolidated balance sheet.

Balance sheets for the two companies at June 30, 1973, as well as a consolidated balance sheet at the same date are shown on the next page. Goodwill in the amount of $5,000 has been amortized. The $5,000 is included in the operating expenses of Company P with a resulting decrease in Retained Earnings and a corresponding decrease in the investment account. An entry also has been made by Company P to record its share of profits of Company S.

Investment in Company S	63,000	
Retained Earnings		63,000
To record 90% of profits of Company S (90% of $70,000)		

	Company P	Company S
Assets		
Investment in Company S	$ 303,000	—
Other assets	700,000	$425,000
Total assets	$1,003,000	$425,000
Equities		
Liabilities	$ 170,000	$105,000
Owners' equity:		
Capital stock	200,000	150,000
Retained earnings	633,000	170,000
Total equities	$1,003,000	$425,000

Company P and Subsidiary S
Consolidated Balance Sheet
June 30, 1973

Assets	
Goodwill	$ 15,000
Other assets	1,045,000
Total assets	$1,060,000
Equities	
Liabilities	$ 195,000
Minority stockholders' interest in Company S	32,000
Owners' equity:	
Capital stock	200,000
Retained earnings	633,000
Total equities	$1,060,000

The assets of the two companies are combined with the accounts receivable of $80,000 from Company S as shown by the records of Company P being eliminated against the accounts payable of $80,000 to Company P as shown by the records of Company S. This elimination is reflected in the consolidated balance sheet by other assets being combined and reduced by $80,000 and liabilities being combined and reduced by $80,000. The investment in Company S is eliminated to the extent of 90 percent of the owner's equity of Company S at the *acquisition date*. Goodwill is shown at $15,000 as reduced by amortization. The minority interest of $25,000 at the beginning of the year is increased by the minority stockholders' share of the net income of Company S (10 percent of $70,000) and is shown on the consolidated balance sheet at $32,000. The capital stock of the parent company is shown as capital stock on the consolidated balance sheet. The consolidated retained earnings are the retained earnings of the parent company increased by the parent company's share of the subsidiary company's net income ($570,000 + 90 percent of $70,000 = $633,000).

The consolidation procedure with respect to goodwill, consolidated retained earnings, and the minority interest is illustrated below.

	Company P		Company S		
	Investment in Company S	*Retained Earnings*	*Capital Stock*	*Retained Earnings*	*Minority Interest, Company S*
(After closing) balances at June 30, 1973 ...	$240,000	$570,000	$150,000	$170,000	
Division of Company S's net income between parent and minority interest		63,000		(70,000)	$ 7,000
Elimination of 90% of owners' equity of Company S *at acquisition date* against investment account ...	(225,000)		(135,000)	(90,000)	
Minority interest in Company S at date of acquisition			(15,000)	(10,000)	25,000
Goodwill	$ 15,000				
Consolidated retained earnings		$633,000	—0—	—0—	
Minority interest					$32,000

On a consolidated balance sheet, the minority stockholders' interest is sometimes shown as a liability. More frequently, as shown in the preceding illustration, it is shown as a separate item between the liabilities and the owners' equity in the parent company. There has been a recent trend to look at the consolidated statements from the viewpoint of *all* stockholders rather than from the viewpoint of the parent company stockholders alone. Thus, the minority interest is considered to be a part of the owners' equity. Owners' equity is then divided into two portions: controlling stockholders' interest and minority shareholders' interest.

Questions

1. Name at least three points in time when revenue may be recognized.

2. Why does the accountant generally recognize revenue on a legalistic basis when the title to goods is transferred or when services are rendered in exchange for the customer's promise to pay a stated price?

3. Under what circumstances would deferred income taxes be recognized and recorded on the balance sheet?

4. Assuming that a company must pay the same amount in income taxes over the years, what advantage is there in using an accelerated depreciation method for income tax purposes?

5. What are extraordinary gains and losses?

6. Why should extraordinary gains and losses be handled separately when computing the earnings per share of stock?

7. How can a company obtain an advantage by the issuance of convertible securities? Are there any disadvantages?

8. Why might there be a potential dilution of earnings as a result of issuing convertible securities?

9. Explain how earnings per share should be reported when convertible securities are outstanding.

10. In a business combination formed by purchase, why must there be a new basis of accountability?

11. Why is there no new basis of accountability in a pooling of interests?

12. When may a business combination be treated as a pooling of interests?

13. Why would management prefer to have a business combination treated as a pooling of interests?

14. Why must transactions between companies in a business combination be eliminated in the preparation of consolidated financial statements?

15. What is the minority interest?

16. How is the minority stockholders' share of net income computed?

17. Can goodwill arising from a consolidation be amortized?

Exercises

1. Pine Grove Farms raises and processes a certain food product that is sold for a fixed price of 42 cents a pound under a price support program. There was no inventory on hand at January 1,1971, and during 1971 Pine Grove completely processed 2,186,000 pounds of which 1,658,000 pounds were sold at the set price. In 1972, 2,631,000 pounds were completely processed with 485,000 pounds remaining on hand at the end of the year. At the beginning of 1972, the growers' association had to accept a lower fixed price per pound of 36 cents. Total costs of operation in 1971 amounted to $633,940 with $153,120 of this cost being identified with the inventory on hand at the end of the year. Total costs of operation in 1972 amounted to $789,300 with $145,500 of this cost being identified with the inventory on hand at the end of the year.

Required: (1) Prepare summary income statements for each of the two years with income determined at point of sale and inventories valued at cost.

(2) Prepare summary income statements for each of the two years with income recognized as the food product is produced and with inventories valued at current market prices.

2. Hi-Value Stores began operations in 1971, selling merchandise on the installment plan. During the first year sales were recorded at $5,840,000, and during 1972 sales were recorded at $6,175,000. Cost of goods sold and operating expenses for the two years follow.

1971—$3,504,000
1972— 3,705,000

In 1971, cash collections from customers amounted to $3,240,000. Collections on sales during 1972 are given below.

On 1971 sales—$1,720,000
On 1972 sales— 3,875,000

Required: Prepare summary income statements with revenue and expense recognized at point of sale. Also prepare summary income statements with revenue and expense recognized as collections are made from the customers.

3. Bushkill Stores, Inc., reports revenues and expenses as sales are made to customers. For income tax purposes, however, the installment method is used. Revenues and expenses are recognized as collections are made from customers. Bushkill Stores, Inc., began business operations in 1970.

Business data for 1970, 1971, and 1972 are given below.

	1970	*1971*	*1972*
Sales (annual basis)	$6,580,000	$7,225,000	$7,836,000
Cost of goods sold and expenses (accrual basis)	3,948,000	5,057,500	5,485,200
Net income before income taxes	$2,632,000	$2,167,500	$2,350,800

Cash collections:

	1970	*1971*	*1972*
On 1970 sales	$4,170,000	$1,080,000	$ 770,000
On 1971 sales	—	3,647,000	2,825,000
On 1972 sales	—	—	3,752,000

Income taxes are at the rate of 40 percent of net income before taxes.

Required: (1) Prepare journal entries to record income taxes for each of the three years with deferred income taxes being recognized.
(2) Determine the balance of deferred income taxes at the end of each of the three years.

4. In 1971, Dixon Equipment Company reported a net income after taxes on regular operating activity of $12,642,000. During the year a gain of $8,250,000 after taxes was made on the sale of an investment in Bruder Films, Inc. Dixon Equipment Company had 15,000,000 shares of common stock outstanding in 1971. In 1971, a damage suit against the company was dismissed. In 1968, the income statement showed a deduction for estimated damages in the amount of $1,500,000. Correction has been made at the bottom of the income statement in 1971. The annual report for 1971 shows earnings per share at $1.49.

Required: Comment on the earnings per share reported and recompute earnings per share.

5. On July 1, 1971, Fishman Realty Company borrowed $5,000,000 with interest at 7 percent a year. Under terms of the debt agreement, the debt can be converted to common stock. If the conversion privilege is exercised, 100,000 additional shares of stock will be issued. During the fiscal year ended June 30, 1972, the company earned $25,600,000 after income taxes at 40 percent of net income before taxes on 8,000,000 shares of common stock outstanding during the year.

Required: Show how the earnings per share should be reported for the fiscal year ended June 30, 1972.

6. A merger agreement has been worked out by the directors of Castile Industries, Inc., and Watkins Manufacturing Company. The stockholders of Watkins Manufacturing Company are to receive common stock of Castile Industries, Inc., in exchange for their stock. Balance sheets of the two companies are given below in summarized form just prior to the merger on October 31, 1972.

Balance Sheets
October 31, 1972

	Castile Industries Inc.	Watkins Manufacturing Company
Assets		
Cash	$ 642,000	$ 121,000
Accounts receivable	783,000	376,000
Inventory	1,346,000	526,000
Land	482,000	73,000
Buildings and equipment, net of depreciation	1,843,000	387,000
Total assets	$5,096,000	$1,483,000
Equities		
Liabilities:		
Accounts payable	$ 587,000	$ 257,000
Notes payable	750,000	—
Total liabilities	$1,337,000	$ 257,000
Owners' equity:		
Capital stock	450,000	120,000
Retained earnings	3,309,000	1,106,000
Total equities	$5,096,000	$1,483,000

Required: (1) From the information furnished, prepare a balance sheet for the merged companies at October 31, 1972.

(2) Does it appear that Castile Industries, Inc., purchased Watkins Manufacturing Company? Give your reason.

7. On July 1, 1972, Hogan Tool Company purchased 90 percent of the outstanding capital stock of Blue Mountain Company at a cost of $6,000,000. Cash payment was made for the stock. Any excess of the purchase price over the net book value of the stock acquired is to be treated as goodwill. Balance sheets for each of the companies in summary form at July 1, 1972, are given at the top of the next page.

Required: Prepare a consolidated balance sheet in summary form at date of acquisition showing goodwill and the minority interest as separate items.

Balance Sheets
July 1, 1972
(In Thousands of Dollars)

	Hogan Tool Company	Blue Mountain Company
Assets		
Cash	$10,925	$ 802
Assets other than cash	47,983	5,829
Total assets	$58,908	$6,631
Equities		
Liabilities	$12,143	$1,231
Capital stock	18,500	2,000
Retained earnings	28,265	3,400
Total equities	$58,908	$6,631

Problems

3–1. Over the years Decker Appliances Company has sold their merchandise on the installment plan with payments from customers being spread over several months. Experience has shown that customers frequently do not follow through with their payment plans and that merchandise must be repossessed. In the past, revenue was recorded at point of sale with allowance being made for losses on contract defaults.

Management is considering a change of policy which would include reporting revenue as collections are made on the installment sales. Costs will be matched against revenue by using an estimated percentage of cost to the total sales price of the merchandise.

All adjustments have been made for prior years. Data for 1971, the year the installment method of reporting income was started, are given along with data for 1972 and 1973.

	Billed Price of Merchandise Delivered Under Installment Contracts	Cost of Goods Delivered and Estimated Costs of Operation
1971	$6,840,000	$4,104,000
1972	7,600,000	4,940,000
1973	8,170,000	5,719,000

Collections for 1971, 1972, and 1973 are reported below:

1971	$4,100,000
1972:	
On 1971 sales	1,460,000
On 1972 sales	3,540,000
1973:	
On 1971 sales	315,000
On 1972 sales	2,670,000
On 1973 sales	4,050,000

Required: Show how net income would be reported by the installment method for each of the three years.

3–2. For several years Strachey Parts Company has been a supplier of an essential component used by a large manufacturer of industrial equipment. The selling price per unit has remained at $45 over the years. Production costs are also stable. The parts manufacturer is reasonably sure of a market for this component even though sales fluctuate from year to year.

In 1971, Strachey Parts Company produced 1,000,000 units with costs as follows:

Materials	$27,250,000
Labor and overhead	11,480,000

The materials, labor, and overhead costs are product costs. For example, in 1971 each unit of product cost $38.73 [(27,250,000 + 11,480,000) ÷ 1,000,000]. Shipping and administrative costs amounted to $800,000 and were not assigned as product costs. In 1971, the company delivered 600,000 units of product to the customer. There were no units on hand at the beginning of the year.

In 1972, the company manufactured 750,000 components and delivered 1,000,000 components to the customer. Costs of production for 1972 are given below.

Materials	$20,437,500
Labor and overhead	8,610,000

Costs of shipping and administration for the year amounted to $920,000.

Required: (1) Prepare an income statement for each year, recording income as deliveries are made to the customer. (Ignore income taxes.)

(2) Prepare an income statement for each year, recognizing income as the component is produced with inventories adjusted to current sales value. (Ignore income taxes.)

3–3. On January 1, 1971, Wunder Products, Inc., was formed. Machinery and equipment to be used in production was acquired at a cost of $4,800,000. This equipment is estimated to have a useful life of 5 years with a residual salvage value of $600,000 at the end of 5 years.

Management plans to deduct straight-line depreciation for financial reporting purposes and accelerated depreciation on the income tax returns. The tax differences will be reported on the balance sheet each year as deferred income taxes.

Before selecting a depreciation method for tax purposes, the management would like to see a projection of the income tax effect for 5 years, comparing the SYD method with the double-rate method. If double-rate depreciation is deducted, a switch to straight-line depreciation will be made after 3 years of double-rate depreciation have been deducted.

The income tax rate is estimated at 40 percent of net income before income taxes.

Required: (1) Prepare a schedule showing the income differences each year and the balance in deferred taxes at the end of each year with SYD depreciation deducted on the tax returns.

(2) Prepare a similar schedule with depreciation deduction on the tax returns by the double-rate method.

(3) Which accelerated method is more advantageous for tax purposes?

3–4. During the past 5 years Burlington Appliances, Inc., has been reporting net income for income tax purposes on the installment plan with income being recognized as collections are received on the installment contracts. On published financial reports, however, revenues and expenses are recognized as sales are made to customers.

The cost of merchandise and other costs of installment selling are equal to 65 percent of the contract sales price. Income taxes are at the rate of 40 percent of net income before taxes.

Data pertaining to the installment sales for the past 5 years are given below.

Years	Net Income Before Income Taxes (Published Income Statement)	Cash Collections
1	$3,500,000	$ 4,740,000
2	4,200,000	6,830,000
3	5,250,000	12,620,000
4	6,300,000	18,400,000
5	6,650,000	21,300,000

Required: (1) Give journal entries to record income taxes and deferred taxes for each of the five years.

(2) Determine the balance of deferred taxes for the balance sheet at the end of the fifth year.

3–5. Data abstracted from the income statements and the statements of changes in retained earnings for 1971 and 1972 are given for Kell Products Company.

	1972	1971
Income statements:		
Net income after income taxes before extraordinary gains and losses	$16,099,051	$13,989,049
Add gain on sale of securities less income taxes	—	2,694,445
Net income for the year	$16,099,051	$16,683,494

The statement of change in retained earnings for 1972 in addition to showing net income for the year and dividends shows the write-off of an investment in Barton Corporation of $7,493,039 net of tax benefit.

Earnings per share were reported as follows:

	1972	1971
Earnings per share from operations	$5.10	$4.51
Earnings per share from extraordinary items	—	.87
Total earnings per share	$5.10	$5.38
Number of shares of common stock outstanding	3,156,676	3,101,784

Required: What would the earnings per share have been in 1972 if the write-off of the investment in Barton Corporation had been properly shown as an extraordinary item on the income statement?

3–6. The treasurer of Summit Transportation Company is making plans to finance an equipment replacement program. With debt financing, he finds that the company can borrow $20,000,000 with an interest rate of 8½ percent a year. However, if the debt agreement includes a provision for the conversion of the debt to common stock under stipulated conditions, the interest can be reduced to 7 percent a year.

At the present time, there are 8,000,000 shares of common stock outstanding. If the debt is issued granting a privilege of conversion to common stock, 1,000,000 additional shares would be issued if all conversion rights were exercised.

The company expects a net income of $32,000,000 before deducting interest and income taxes next year. Income taxes are estimated at 40 percent of net income before income taxes.

In planning for the financial needs of the company, the treasurer must maintain balance in the equity structure by financing in various ways. Sometimes it will be better to issue additional capital stock, and sometimes it will be better to borrow funds under various options.

In this particular situation, the treasurer would like to know what the earnings per share would be with the conversion privilege included in the debt agreement and without the conversion privilege included.

Required: Based on the estimated net income for the next year, compute the earnings per share if the 8½ percent debt is issued and if the 7 percent debt is issued.

3–7. Northwest Machine Company acquired all of the assets of Montana Mills, Inc., in exchange for 180,000 shares of Northwest Machine Company common stock with a par value of $1 per share. Northwest Machine Company is to assume all of the liabilities and obligations of Montana Mills, Inc.

At the date of acquisition, Northwest Machine Company had a market value of $63 per share. The market value of the shares involved in the exchange then amounted to $11,340,000.

The owners' equity section of the balance sheet for each company, immediately after acquisition is given below:

	Northwest Machine Company	Montana Mills, Inc.
Common stock, no par value ...	$ 4,112,000	$ 400,000
Additional paid-in capital	39,836,000	2,190,000
Retained earnings	90,703,000	4,257,000
Total stockholders' equity	$134,651,000	$6,847,000

It is agreed that the combination shall be treated as a pooling of interests and that the stated capital of the combination will remain unchanged.

Required: (1) Show how the owners' equity section of Northwest Machine's consolidated balance sheet would appear immediately following the transaction when the acquisition is accounted for as a pooling of interests.

(2) Assume that the combination was accounted for as a purchase. How would the owners' equity section of Northwest Machine appear on a consolidated balance sheet immediately following acquisition?

3–8. On August 31, 1971, Huntington Mills, Inc., purchased 90 percent of the capital stock of Paden Products, Inc., at a cost of $3,336,000. Income statements for the two companies are given at the top of the next page for the fiscal year ended August 31, 1972.

Income Statements
For the Year Ended August 31, 1972
(In Thousands of Dollars)

	Huntington Mills, Inc.	Paden Products, Inc.
Net sales	$26,340	$14,170
Cost of goods sold	$11,480	$ 6,430
Operating expenses	6,150	4,290
Total expenses	$17,630	$10,720
Net income	$ 8,710	$ 3,450

During the fiscal year, Paden Products sold merchandise costing $2,130,000 to Huntington Mills for $3,480,000. All of this merchandise was subsequently resold to outsiders by Huntington Mills.

Condensed balance sheets at August 31, 1972 are given below:

Balance Sheets
August 31, 1972
(In Thousands of Dollars)

	Huntington Mills, Inc.	Paden Products, Inc.
Assets		
Cash	$ 3,294	$ 780
Accounts receivable, Huntington Mills, Inc. .	—	860
Accounts receivable, other	5,282	2,419
Inventories	4,174	2,165
Investment in Paden Products, Inc.	3,315	—
Plant and equipment, net of accumulated depreciation	5,775	3,041
Total assets	$21,840	$9,265
Equities		
Accounts payable—Paden Products, Inc.	$ 860	
Accounts payable—other	3,780	$2,365
Capital stock	4,200	750
Retained earnings	13,000	6,150
Total equities	$21,840	$9,265

Net income of $3,450,000 for the fiscal year has been closed to retained earnings of Paden Products. No other entries have been made to the stockholder equity accounts of Paden Products during the fiscal year.

Required: Prepare a consolidated income statement for the fiscal year and a consolidated balance sheet at August 31, 1972. (Goodwill resulting from the consolidation in the amount of $21,000 has been amortized by Huntington Mills by a charge on the income statement and a credit to the investment account.) No entry has been made, however, by Huntington Mills, Inc., to record its share of net income from Paden Products, Inc.

3–9. On November 1, 1972, Haupert Liner Company purchased 80 percent of the common stock of Barrett Manufacturing Company. To finance the purchase, Haupert Liner Company issued additional common stock and used proceeds from the sale amounting to $1,540,000 to purchase the Barrett stock. The excess of the acquisition cost of Barrett stock over the net book value is to be shown as goodwill on the consolidated balance sheet.

Balance sheets for the two companies in summary form are given at November 1, 1972. Haupert Liner Company has received the proceeds from the issuance of its stock but has not yet paid for the stock of Barrett Manufacturing Company.

Balance Sheets
November 1, 1972

	Haupert Liner Company	Barrett Manufacturing Company
Assets		
Cash	$3,160,000	$ 148,000
Other assets	5,232,000	1,697,000
Total assets	$8,392,000	$1,845,000
Equities		
Liabilities	$ 584,000	$ 215,000
Capital stock and paid-in capital in excess of stated value of stock	3,600,000	350,000
Retained earnings	4,208,000	1,280,000
Total equities	$8,392,000	$1,845,000

Required: (1) Prepare a balance sheet for Haupert Liner Company on November 1, 1972, after cash payment has been made for the capital stock of Barrett Manufacturing Company.

(2) Prepare a consolidated balance sheet for the two companies at date of acquisition.

3–10. Lakeland Sales Corporation purchased 90 percent of the outstanding stock of Reeves Machine Company at a time when the total owners' equity in Reeves Machine Company amounted to $5,800,000. Included in this amount was retained earnings of $3,460,000. Lakeland Sales Corporation paid $6,820,000 for the investment and since that date has amortized a portion of the goodwill, deducting the amount amortized against the investment account.

In 1972, Reeves Machine Company sold merchandise to Lakeland Sales Corporation for $3,580,000. The cost of this merchandise to Reeves Machine Company was $2,132,000. Lakeland Sales Corporation sold all of this merchandise to outsiders during the year and had no merchandise from Reeves Machine Company on hand at the beginning of the year.

Included in the accounts receivable of Reeves Machine Company is $165,000 owed by Lakeland Sales Corporation. The same amount is included in the accounts payable of Lakeland Sales Corporation as the amount owed to Reeves Machine Company.

Income statements in summary form for 1972 are given on the next page.

Income Statements
For the Year, 1972

	Lakeland Sales Corporation	Reeves Machine Company
Net sales	$15,463,400	$8,246,100
Cost of sales	$ 7,825,600	$5,115,800
Operating and other expenses	3,683,100	1,772,400
Total expenses	$11,508,700	$6,888,200
Net income	$ 3,954,700	$1,357,900

Balance sheets in summary form at December 31, 1972 follow:

Balance Sheets
December 31, 1972

	Lakeland Sales Corporation	Reeves Machine Company
Assets		
Cash	$ 1,652,600	$ 315,400
Accounts receivable	1,368,400	323,400
Inventories	1,126,700	538,200
Investment in Reeves Machine Company	6,500,000	
Plant assets, net of accumulated depreciation	7,975,500	7,959,000
Total assets	$18,623,200	$9,136,000
Equities		
Accounts payable	$ 512,900	$ 217,300
Other liabilities	682,300	486,700
Capital stock and premium on stock	3,500,000	2,340,000
Retained earnings	13,928,000	6,092,000
Total equities	$18,623,200	$9,136,000

Required: Prepare consolidated financial statements for Lakeland Sales Corporation and its subsidiary. Lakeland Sales Corporation has not recorded its share of the net increase in retained earnings of Reeves Machine Company.

Chapter 4

PRICE LEVEL CHANGES

The dollar that is used as a standard of measurement in accounting possesses a given amount of purchasing power at any particular time, but this purchasing power does not remain constant with changes in time. In contrast, the physical units of measurement, such as the foot, the gallon, and the ton, remain constant as standards of measurement with changes in time. This peculiarity of the dollar makes it difficult to evaluate financial data. Over a period of time, financial measurements are made in terms of a dollar that varies in value. When data are carried forward from the past and combined with current data, the combined result is a measurement in dollars of mixed value.

Three general approaches are often recommended for dealing with the problem of changes in the purchasing power of the dollar.

(1) Abandon historical costs and use replacement costs.
(2) Match current costs against revenue.
(3) Adjust historical financial data by applying published index numbers.

In this chapter, all three approaches are discussed, but primary attention will be focused on the adjustment of historical financial data by applying published index numbers.

GENERAL AND SPECIFIC PRICES

A price level may be explained as:

(1) The price level for a specific type of asset. The price of specific assets may change independently of the movement of prices of other goods and services because of market characteristics peculiar to the assets in question.
(2) The price level for a mixture of goods and services throughout the economy, or general price level. Since the prices of *all* goods and

services do not fluctuate simultaneously, technically there is no such thing as a general price level. However, the term is a convenient way to refer to the weighted average prices of selected goods and services in the economy.

It is extremely difficult, if possible at all, to measure the effect of price level changes on each individual or business entity. Each person or entity purchases different goods or services in various quantities at various times and will be affected in different ways. About the best that can be done is to measure the impact of price level changes by means of an average of prices for goods or services that are most commonly used.

Approximate measurements of general price level changes may be made by using published indices. Two widely recognized index series are the Consumer Price Index published by the Bureau of Labor Statistics, Department of Labor, and the Gross National Product Implicit Price Deflator used by the Department of Commerce to measure changes in the Gross National Product. The gross national product implicit price deflator is more comprehensive and for that reason may be a better indicator of general price movement.

When prices go up in general, there is *inflation*. Conversely, when prices go down, there is *deflation*. However, all goods and services are not affected in the same way. The prices of some goods and services may be relatively stable over the years while the prices of others will fluctuate greatly.

Most individuals are well aware of the problem of changing price levels in their own personal lives. During a period of inflation, earnings from the past that are held in the form of cash lose their purchasing power. The holder of cash does not retain the purchasing power that he earned. For example, a worker earning a wage of $200 a month at a time when this amount was considered to be a living wage would be able to command at that time all the goods and the services that he would need for a month. But if he saved the $200 in cash and spent it at a later date when $200 a week was considered to be a living wage, he would find that he could buy only the goods and the services that he would need for a week. He then suffered a loss because of the decrease in the purchasing power of his dollars.

A borrower, on the other hand, may gain by inflation. A loan taken at a lower price level will provide the borrower with resources that have relatively higher purchasing power than the resources that will later be used to repay the loan at a higher price level. This gain in purchasing power goes to the borrower. Conversely, the lender loses purchasing power by lending relatively valuable dollars in comparison to those that he receives in repayment. The effect will be the opposite in a period of deflation.

ABANDONMENT OF HISTORICAL COSTS

One method that has been suggested for dealing with the problem of price changes in financial reporting involves a departure from historical costs. Assets such as inventories, investments in stock, and plant assets are ordinarily held for a relatively long period of time. The costs that were incurred to obtain these assets in the past—the historical costs—may be out of date when compared with current costs. On a balance sheet the costs from some past period may be combined with current costs, and the total of the mixed costs will have little if any real significance. The problem may not be too serious in the case of inventories if the investment in inventories is turned over rapidly. But an investment in stock and in plant assets will often be held over a period of many years during which time there may be substantial variations in cost. When this is the case, the assets should be restated at current *replacement costs*, which, as the term implies, are the costs to replace the assets currently in use.

Inasmuch as goods and services are acquired and used at different times, it is difficult to measure income and to report financial results in a meaningful way. What is profit? Has a profit of $20,000 been realized from the sale of goods at $30,000 if the goods were acquired for $10,000 at an earlier date? To continue business as before, the merchant may have to pay $18,000 to replace the goods sold.

Profit Measurement

	Historical Cost (Current Revenue Minus Original Costs)	Replacement Cost (Current Revenue Minus Replacement Costs)
Sales revenue	$30,000	$30,000
Cost of goods sold and operating expenses ..	10,000	18,000
Profit	$20,000	$12,000

Conventionally, profit is measured as the difference between sales revenue and the original costs of the services and products sold. However, this conception of profit makes no provision for a continuation of business operations on the same scale as before. Perhaps profits should be looked upon as a difference between revenue and original cost with provision being made for reentry into the market for another selling cycle. In short, the profit would be the difference between sales revenue and the cost to replace the goods and services sold.

In the example, it is assumed that the merchant plans to continue business on the same scale as before. He must then replace the inventory that he sold, and the cost of replacement is $18,000. Hence, on a true *going concern basis* the profit is only $12,000. The balance sheet is also distorted when current costs and old costs are mingled, with the result that the rate of return computed on total assets as well as other financial statement relationships are distorted.

If replacement costs are used to measure the effect of price changes, appraisals must be made periodically to determine the replacement costs. The difference between the replacement cost and the original cost may be analyzed, if desired, to determine how much of the difference can be attributed to the trend in general prices and how much of the difference can be attributed to the particular nature of the market for the specific asset in question. A variety of factors in the market will influence price. A certain portion of the price change may be attributed to improvement and technological innovations but, in some cases, exact replacement may not even be possible.

The replacement cost method offers the advantages of being tailored to the peculiarities of a particular company and to the specific assets on an individual basis. However, replacement costs may be criticized for being too subjective.

MATCHING CURRENT COSTS AGAINST REVENUES

This approach to the price level problem does not deal with the problem directly. Instead, it is an attempt to get around the problem.

Sometimes the effect of price level changes is minimized during a period of rising prices by matching the most recent costs against revenues. The argument for this procedure is that net income is more accurately determined if both the revenues and the costs are on the same dollar basis. Furthermore, there can be no objection that the historical cost principle has been violated. Actual incurred costs are accounted for.

Adjusted lifo method. The matching of the most current costs against revenue is implicit in the lifo inventory method. When this method is used, the costs of the most recent purchases are matched against revenues as cost of goods sold, and the older costs remain on the balance sheet as inventory. Under the lifo method, assuming that the beginning inventory is not depleted, the current costs are charged against revenue on the income statement; but the balance sheet inventory costs are out-of-date. Ideally, both the income statement and the balance sheet should show current costs. Thus, some adjustment will have to be made to restate the older costs at current dollar amounts.

In the example given below, the fifo inventory method is compared with the lifo method. It is assumed in each case that 500 units of merchandise were first purchased at a cost of $1.50 per unit. Another 500 units were acquired later at a cost of $2 per unit. During the year, 500 units were sold at a unit price of $3.

Fifo Inventory Method

Income Statement (Partial)		Balance Sheet (Partial)	
Sales (500 units @ $3)	$1,500	Inventory	
Cost of goods sold		(500 units @ $2)	$1,000
(500 units @ $1.50)	750		
Gross margin	$ 750		

Lifo Inventory Method

Income Statement (Partial)		Balance Sheet (Partial)	
Sales (500 units @ $3)	$1,500	Inventory	
Cost of goods sold		(500 units @ $1.50)	750
(500 units @ $2)	1,000		
Gross margin	$ 500		

The fifo method matches older costs against current revenues and thus may be less desirable from the income statement point of view when prices are rising. On the other hand, the current costs are shown as inventory on the balance sheet. Under the lifo method, the opposite situation prevails. The balance sheet showing older costs is inadequate, but on the income statement current costs are matched against revenues.

In some circumstances, the lifo inventory method may not result in matching current costs against revenue. If the quantity sold, for example, is in excess of the current quantity purchased, older costs will be mixed with current costs in the cost of goods sold.

The advantages of both the fifo method and the lifo method can be obtained by using current costs for *both* statements. This treatment, as illustrated below, is a departure from conventional practice.

Income Statement (Partial)		Balance Sheet (Partial)	
Sales (500 units @ $3)	$1,500	Assets	
Cost of goods sold		Inventory	
(500 units @ $2)	1,000	(500 units @ $2)	$1,000
Gross margin	$ 500		
Gain from holding inventory	250		
Gross margin (operations)		Equities	
and holding gain	$ 750	Retained earnings	$ 750

The retained earnings from operations would be accumulated in the conventional way, and the inventory would be valued at fifo which gives a figure closest to current cost. However, lifo is used on the income statement, giving a breakdown between *operating* income and *holding* gains. The operating income results from sales made to customers, and the holding gain is the difference between the current value of the inventory and the original cost.

Accelerated depreciation. Accelerated depreciation methods are usually favored because of the income tax advantage, but they may also be favored as a means of matching current costs against revenues. If a large part of the cost of a plant asset can be written off as depreciation during a few years, it is hoped that the bulk of the cost can be matched against revenue before the price level has changed to any appreciable extent. Whether this will work out in practice or not depends upon the movement of the price level.

The income tax advantage from accelerated depreciation methods arises because depreciation deductions in the early years of a plant asset are larger than they are under the straight-line method. During these years, the net income and the income taxes for each year are lower than they would be under the straight-line method of depreciation. With a lower income, the company is able to use more resources for a longer period because the tax payment is delayed. Furthermore, if the net income is used as a guide in dividend policy, the dividends are likely to be lower. The advantage may be only temporary. In the long run, of course, the company can only recover the cost of its investment. In later years, the depreciation deductions are smaller and the net income and the income taxes each year will be larger under accelerated depreciation. But, in the meantime, the company has additional resources available that can be reinvested to earn a return. Perhaps losses because of change in the price level can be avoided or at least held to a minimum.

The advantage of accelerated depreciation is illustrated by assuming that Company A and Company B each earned $250,000 before deducting depreciation and income taxes. Company A used accelerated depreciation and deducted $100,000 in depreciation on equipment that it had purchased at the beginning of the year. Company B purchased equipment having the same cost at the same time but took depreciation on a straight-line basis.

Company A had paid $25,000 less in income taxes than Company B as a result of deducting $50,000 more in depreciation. The depreciation deduction operated as a tax shield. Company A, with a smaller income tax, will thus have $25,000 more cash with which to work.

Assume further that each company distributed all of its net income to the shareholders as dividends. Company A reported a net income of only

$75,000 and paid that amount in dividends, while Company B reported a net income of $100,000 and paid that amount in dividends. Company A had a smaller income tax by $25,000 and paid $25,000 less in dividends than Company B. As a result, Company A retained $50,000 more in resources. It may be that Company A will eventually pay more income taxes in certain years than Company B. However, in the meantime Company A has more resources to use.

	Company A (Accelerated Depreciation)	Company B (Straight-Line Depreciation)
Net income before depreciation and income taxes	$250,000	$250,000
Less: Depreciation	100,000	50,000
Net income before income taxes	$150,000	$200,000
Income taxes (50% rate)	75,000	100,000
Net income after income taxes	$ 75,000	$100,000
Add: Depreciation	100,000	50,000
Net inflow of current resources from operations	$175,000	$150,000

It should not be presumed from the foregoing discussion that accelerated depreciation is to be preferred to straight-line depreciation for financial reporting purposes. If plant assets yield services over the years at a uniform rate, then each year should bear an equal amount of the cost. On the other hand, if the services are received irregularly, a case could be made for charging off the cost of the plant assets accordingly. Accelerated depreciation methods in common use are not flexible and in many cases cannot be looked upon as a means of matching expenses against revenues according to the flow of benefits received from the use of the assets. Nevertheless, accelerated depreciation can yield short-term benefits in tax accounting and can be used as an aid in managerial planning.

PRICE LEVEL—INDEX ADJUSTMENTS

The price level problem may be approached by converting the dollars having mixed purchasing power to dollars having current purchasing power. This method, unlike the replacement cost method, does not introduce a new basis of accountability. Historical costs are still accounted for in the conventional way but the historical costs are brought up to date by means of an index adjustment. All dollars will then be restated on a common basis, that is, they will be uniform dollars of purchasing power. Published price indexes can be used in converting dollars to a common denominator of value. The conversion operation itself is simple. The difficulty lies in the selection of an index series that will accomplish the desired result without adding further distortions.

The price level adjustments restate financial data in terms of the current dollar of purchasing power.[1] Past dollar amounts are brought up-to-date by the application of an index number multiplier. For example, inventory costing $6,000 when the price index was 120 would be restated in current dollars at an index of 150 as shown below.

$$\$6,000 \times 150/120 = \$7,500 \text{ cost of inventory in dollars of the 150 price index}$$

The current index number is the numerator of the multiplier fraction, and the index number at the time of the transaction is the denominator.

The adjustment procedure makes it possible to:

(1) Compute the gains and losses caused by changes in the purchasing power of the dollar and

(2) To compare financial statements that have been restated in uniform current dollars of purchasing power.

THE CHARACTER OF ASSETS AND EQUITIES

Not all assets and equities respond to changes in the price level in the same way. Some assets tend to adjust themselves automatically to changes in the price level. Tangible goods will usually go up or down in price in rough correspondence to the general price pattern. But cash and claims to cash remain at fixed dollar amounts without regard to shifts in the price level.

Monetary items. Cash and claims to cash as well as liabilities stated in a fixed number of dollars are referred to as monetary items. The monetary items at any given time are always stated in current dollars of purchasing power without adjustment.

The individual who has $100 today possesses $100 of purchasing power measured in today's dollars. This is not changed by the fact that he may have received the $100 when prices were lower and when he could have purchased $110 worth of goods or services as measured by the current dollar. Comparative balance sheets expressed in *current* dollars of purchasing power will show $110 in cash on the balance sheet at the point of time at which the cash was received. Remember that the original $100 was then worth $110 in terms of *today's* dollar. On the current balance sheet the $100 is shown as $100. It has a purchasing power of $100 at the present time. The individual lost $10 in purchasing power by holding cash.

---

[1] See *Reporting the Financial Effects of Price-Level Changes,* Accounting Research Study No. 6 (New York: American Institute of Certified Public Accountants, 1963).

Accounts receivable from customers and investments in bonds are similar to cash. The monetary amount is fixed. Liabilities such as accounts payable, wages payable, taxes payable, mortgage payable, and bonds payable are also expressed in fixed dollar amounts as a general rule. If an individual incurs a debt of $5,000 when the price index is 100 and repays it when the index is 110, he has a purchasing power gain of $500. At the time of repayment, the debt amounted to $5,000 in current dollars of purchasing power. But the original debt of $5,000 had a purchasing power of $5,500 when it was incurred as measured in the dollars used to repay the debt, that is, the current dollars of purchasing power.

Nonmonetary items. Assets and equities that cannot be stated in fixed monetary amounts are referred to as nonmonetary items.

Tangible items such as buildings, machinery, and inventories of materials or products awaiting resale tend to sell at higher or lower dollar amounts at different times. For example, a residence costing $8,000 in 1940 may sell for $16,000 at the present time, although it has been used and is no longer modern. The $8,000 in 1940 is not equivalent to $8,000 today, nor is it necessarily equivalent to $16,000 either. Probably there are other reasons explaining the increase in price. The neighborhood may be attractive, the house may have been well kept, or some additions may have been made that justify the higher price. However, in price level adjustment procedure the $8,000 cost would be converted to a current basis by application of the current index number in relation to the index number in 1940 to arrive at an amount that may be more or less than $16,000. The technological changes in the house or other factors do not enter into the adjustment.

Investments in stocks or bonds may have the characteristics of fixed monetary claims or they may be similar to tangible properties. Bonds usually are a claim to a fixed quantity of dollars and would, therefore, be similar to cash. An investment in common stock, however, is not a stated claim to any given quantity of dollars but is an ownership claim to the assets of a business and would be somewhat similar to an investment in tangible property.

The owners' equity, with the exception of preferred stock that may be callable in a fixed number of dollars, is a nonmonetary item. The common stock and the retained earnings are not fixed in dollar amounts but will vary as a result of many factors, including price level changes.

FINANCIAL STATEMENTS AND INDEX CONVERSIONS

To illustrate the price level conversion procedure, it is assumed that Pellinger, Inc., began business at the beginning of 19A and that it has conducted operations during 19A and 19B. Price index data follow:

Price index at the beginning of 19A 100
Average price index during 19A and at the end of 19A 120
Average price index during 19B and at the end of 19B 150

In order to simplify the example, some artificial assumptions have been made. Under normal conditions, the price index would probably not increase from 100 to 150 in two years. Furthermore, there would probably be changes from month to month which would make it unlikely that the average price index for a year would be the same as at the end of that year. However, the adjustment procedure can be illustrated without going into the detailed month by month computations.

At the beginning of 19A, the stockholders of Pellinger, Inc., invested $60,000. Plant equipment costing $130,000 was purchased, a down payment of $30,000 was made, and the $100,000 balance was financed by bonds payable. An inventory of merchandise was purchased at a cost of $24,000.

Unadjusted financial statements are given in summary form for 19A and 19B. The assets and equities are classified as monetary or nonmonetary items on the balance sheets rather than in the conventional current and noncurrent categories to emphasize the important distinctions in price level accounting. Of course, the balance sheets can be presented in the conventional manner and probably would be for financial reporting purposes.

Pellinger, Inc.
Summary Income Statements
For the Years 19A and 19B

	19A	19B
Sales	$900,000	$1,200,000
Cost of goods sold	$450,000	$ 600,000
Other expenses, excluding depreciation	350,000	450,000
Depreciation	10,000	10,000
Total expenses	$810,000	$1,060,000
Net income	$ 90,000	$ 140,000

The gains and losses resulting from changes in the purchasing power of the dollar are to be computed for the two years, and the financial statements are to be restated in terms of the dollar at the end of 19B. A gain or loss in purchasing power arises from holding monetary assets and equities while the general purchasing power of the dollar increases or decreases.

Pellinger, Inc., for example, began operations in 19A with $60,000 and ended the year with $90,000 in *net current* monetary assets. Transactions affecting the net current monetary assets during the year are converted, as shown on page 106, to uniform dollars of purchasing power at the end of 19A. The uniform dollars of purchasing power of the net current monetary assets

Pellinger, Inc.
Summary Balance Sheets
December 31, 19A and 19B

	19A	19B
Assets		
Monetary assets:		
Cash and accounts receivable	$180,000	$210,000
Nonmonetary assets:		
Inventory (fifo method)	40,000	50,000
Plant assets, net of accumulated depreciation	120,000	110,000
Total assets	$340,000	$370,000

	19A	19B
Equities		
Monetary equities:		
Accounts payable and other current claims payable	$ 90,000	$ 80,000
Bonds payable	100,000	100,000
Nonmonetary equities:		
Capital stock	60,000	60,000
Retained earnings	90,000	130,000
Total equities	$340,000	$370,000

at the end of 19A are compared with the unadjusted amount. If the unadjusted amount is less than the adjusted amount, there has been a loss in purchasing power. Conversely, if the unadjusted amount is greater than the adjusted amount, there has been a gain in purchasing power. In this case, the difference between the adjusted amount of $91,200 and the unadjusted amount of $90,000 expressed in mixed dollars of purchasing power is the loss in purchasing power on net current monetary assets for 19A *stated in dollars of purchasing power at the end of 19A*. This loss of purchasing power occurred in 19A and has been stated in 19A dollars. All measurements, however, are to be made in terms of the most recent dollar, that is, the dollar at the end of 19B. Hence, the loss of purchasing power in 19A measured in 19A dollars must be restated in terms of purchasing power at the end of 19B, and this computation is shown below the transactional analysis.

The income statement for 19A shows sales in purchasing power dollars of 19A. Other expenses were also incurred at this price level. Inventory costing $24,000 was acquired at the beginning of 19A and was converted to the dollars that were current at the end of 19A. The summary balance sheets show an inventory of $40,000 at the end of 19A. Inventory has thus increased by $16,000 ($40,000 — $24,000) during the year indicating that purchases exceed cost of goods sold by $16,000 and amount to $466,000 ($450,000 + $16,000). The purchases of $466,000 were made at prices that prevailed during 19A and at the end of 19A. No conversion is required. The company paid $30,000 for plant assets at the beginning of the year, and this amount is converted to end-of-year dollars.

Purchasing Power Loss—19A
Net Current Monetary Assets

	Unadjusted Data, 19A	Multiplier	Adjusted Data 19A Dollars (End of Year)
Net current monetary assets, beginning of 19A	$ 60,000	120/100	$ 72,000
Add:			
Sales	900,000	120/120	900,000
	$960,000		$972,000
Less:			
Purchases:			
Beginning of 19A	$ 24,000	120/100	$ 28,800
During 19A	466,000	120/120	466,000
Other expenses	350,000	120/120	350,000
Plant asset acquisition	30,000	120/100	36,000
	$870,000		$880,800
Net current monetary assets, end of 19A:			
Adjusted			$ 91,200
Unadjusted	$ 90,000		90,000
Purchasing power loss on net current monetary assets, 19A dollars (end of year)			$ 1,200

Restatement of the Purchasing Power
Loss in 19B Dollars (End of Year):

$1,200 \times \dfrac{150}{120} = $1,500$ purchasing power loss measured in 19B dollars (end of year).

A similar computation of the purchasing power gains or losses on net current monetary assets for 19B is given below and at the top of the next page.

Purchasing Power Loss—19B
Net Current Monetary Assets

	Unadjusted Data, 19B	Multiplier	Adjusted Data 19B Dollars (End of Year)
Net current monetary assets, beginning of 19B	$ 90,000	150/120	$ 112,500
Add:			
Sales	1,200,000	150/150	1,200,000
	$1,290,000		$1,312,500

	Unadjusted Data, 19B	Multiplier	Adjusted Data 19B Dollars (End of Year)
Less:			
Purchases	$ 610,000	150/150	$ 610,000
Other expenses	450,000	150/150	450,000
Dividends	100,000	150/150	100,000
	$1,160,000		$1,160,000
Net current monetary assets, end of 19B:			
Adjusted			$ 152,500
Unadjusted	$ 130,000		130,000
Purchasing power loss on net current monetary assets, 19B dollars (end of year)			$ 22,500

Offsetting the losses in purchasing power from current monetary transactions are the gains in purchasing power from the bonds payable obligation. The computation follows:

	Unadjusted Bonds Payable, 19A Dollars (Beginning of Year)	Multiplier	Adjusted Bonds Payable, 19A Dollars (End of Year)
19A:			
Bonds payable	$100,000	120/100	$120,000
Less: Unadjusted bonds payable			100,000
Gain in purchasing power, 19A (19A dollars)			$ 20,000
Gain in purchasing power expressed in 19B dollars (end of year):			

$20,000 \times 150/120 = $25,000 gain in purchasing power, 19B dollars (end of year)

19B:			
Bonds payable	$100,000	150/100	$150,000
Less: Unadjusted bonds payable			100,000
Accumulated gain in purchasing power by the end of 19B			$ 50,000
Less: Purchasing power gain in 19A (19B dollars) ..			25,000
Purchasing power gain in 19B			$ 25,000

The purchasing power gains and losses for the two years as measured in 19B dollars are summarized on the next page.

		19A	19B
Purchasing power loss, net current monetary assets		($ 1,500)	($22,500)
Purchasing power gain, bonds payable		25,000	25,000
Net purchasing power gain		$23,500	$ 2,500

These net gains are shown separately on the adjusted income statement for each year and are accumulated in a separate section of retained earnings on the adjusted balance sheets.

The income statement for 19A is restated in current purchasing power dollars, that is, in the dollars at the end of 19B. The computations are shown below:

	Unadjusted	Multiplier	Adjusted
Sales	$900,000	150/120	$1,125,000
Cost of goods sold:			
Purchases at the beginning of the year	$ 24,000	150/100	$ 36,000
Purchase made in 19A (less inventory at the end of the year)	426,000	150/120	532,500
Cost of goods sold	$450,000		$ 568,500
Other expenses, excluding depreciation	350,000	150/120	437,500
Depreciation	10,000	150/100	15,000
Total expenses	$810,000		$1,021,000
Net income from operations	$ 90,000		$ 104,000
Net gain in purchasing power			23,500
Net income and purchasing power gain			$ 127,500

The income statement for 19B requires adjustments for cost of goods sold and depreciation. All other revenues and expenses are on a current dollar basis. The cost of goods sold of 19B is adjusted as follows:

	Unadjusted	Multiplier	Adjusted
Cost of goods sold of 19B:			
Inventory at the beginning of the year	$ 40,000	150/120	$ 50,000
Purchases in 19B (sold in 19B)	560,000	150/150	560,000
Cost of goods sold	$600,000		$610,000

The depreciation of $10,000 pertains to the plant assets acquired at a price index of 100 and is $15,000 when stated in dollars at the price index of 150.

The income statements for the two years as restated in 19B dollars (end of year) are given on the following page.

Pellinger, Inc.
Summary Income Statements
(Uniform Dollars of Purchasing Power
as of December 31, 19B)
For the Years 19A and 19B

	19A	19B
Sales	$1,125,000	$1,200,000
Cost of goods sold	$ 568,500	$ 610,000
Other expenses, excluding depreciation ..	437,500	450,000
Depreciation	15,000	15,000
Total expenses	$1,021,000	$1,075,000
Net income from operations	$ 104,000	$ 125,000
Net gain in purchasing power	23,500	2,500
Net income and purchasing power gain (loss)	$ 127,500	$ 127,500

The unadjusted income statements give the impression that the company had a higher net income in 19B. When the income statements are restated in uniform dollars of purchasing power, however, the increase in net income from operations is revealed to be smaller.

The balance sheets are restated in current dollars (dollars at the end of 19B) as shown on the following page.

Note that all items on the 19A balance sheet are on an old dollar basis and must be restated. It was stated earlier that monetary assets and equities are automatically stated in dollars of current purchasing power. This is true *for any given time*. The monetary assets and equities on the 19A balance sheet are in 19A dollars. But these dollars must be adjusted if the statements are to be expressed in 19B dollars. The nonmonetary items are stated in the dollars of purchasing power that were current when they were initially recorded. The index at that time is the denominator of the multiplier to be used in restating the dollar amounts.

The adjusted balance sheets, as well as the income statements, reveal that the company did not do quite as well as the unadjusted statements indicate. Some of the differences do not represent real increases or decreases but, instead, are differences that are partially attributable to a change in the level of prices. For example, cash and receivables increased from $180,000 at the end of 19A to $210,000 at the end of 19B. In terms of purchasing power, however, the $180,000 in cash and receivables at the end of 19A was equivalent to $225,000 measured in 19B dollars. Although there was an increase in cash and receivables from $180,00 to $210,000 as measured in absolute dollars, there was a loss of purchasing power during 19B. A comparison of other amounts on financial statements will

Pellinger, Inc.
Summary Balance Sheets
(Uniform Dollars of Purchasing Power as of December 31, 19B)
December 31

	19A			19B		
Assets	*Unadjusted*	*Multiplier*	*Adjusted*	*Unadjusted*	*Multiplier*	*Adjusted*
Monetary assets:						
Cash and accounts receivable	$180,000	150/120	$225,000	$210,000	150/150	$210,000
Nonmonetary assets:						
Inventory (fifo method)	40,000	150/120	50,000	50,000	150/150	50,000
Plant assets, net of accumulated depreciation	120,000	150/100	180,000	110,000	150/100	165,000
Total assets	$340,000		$455,000	$370,000		$425,000
Equities						
Monetary equities:						
Accounts payable and other current claims payable	$ 90,000	150/120	$112,500	$ 80,000	150/150	$ 80,000
Bonds payable	100,000	150/120	125,000	100,000	150/150	100,000
Nonmonetary equities:						
Capital stock	60,000	150/100	90,000	60,000	150/100	90,000
Retained earnings:						
*Operations	90,000		104,000	130,000		129,000
Accumulated purchasing power gains on net monetary items .			23,500			26,000
Total equities	$340,000		$455,000	$370,000		$425,000

* Adjusted amounts taken from adjusted income statements for the two years. The adjusted retained earnings from operations at December 31, 19B are computed below:

Balance, January 1, 19B	$104,000
Adjusted net income, 19B	125,000
	$229,000
Less: Dividends, 19B	100,000
Balance, December 31, 19B	$129,000

also be more meaningful if the statements are converted to uniform dollars of purchasing power.

THE PRICE LEVEL AND INVESTMENT POLICY

During a period of rising prices, a company will suffer losses in purchasing power by holding cash and cash claims instead of assets that tend to follow price level movements. If net income is used as a guide to the amount of dividends, then depreciation charged against operations will not result in the retention of assets having a purchasing power equivalent to the original amount invested. Over the years the dollars invested may be recovered, but these dollars will not have the purchasing power of the dollars invested. Amounts equal to depreciation as adjusted for changes in prices may be reinvested in plant assets or other assets that tend to follow the price level. In this way, the purchasing power of the original investment will not be lost, provided, of course, that the price level continues to rise and that the subsequent investment follows the price level.

As a matter of policy, a company may attempt to maintain the original purchasing power invested in plant assets by reinvesting an amount equivalent to the price-level-adjusted depreciation each year. There is, of course, no assurance that the company will not suffer price level losses by following this policy. In general, the prices of plant assets tend to move with the price level. If further price level increases are anticipated, an amount equal to the depreciation as adjusted to current dollars may be reinvested in plant assets, which tend to follow the price level.

In making plans, management will have to take some position with respect to the movements in the general level of prices. If it is believed that prices will become higher in the future, inventories will be built up through current purchases and more will be invested in plant assets. During a period of anticipated price increases, there will be less reluctance to incur debt. Conversely, if it seems that the price level will go down, cash and cash claims will be held and the purchases of inventories and plant assets will be kept at a minimum.

DIVIDEND POLICY

The net income reported for the year is only one element, although an important one, in the formation of dividend policy. A company may have sufficient net income to permit a legal declaration of dividends, but the assets may not be in a form suitable for distribution to the stockholders. Or the board of directors may wish to hold assets so that the company can expand without issuing additional stock or debt.

Aside from the factors just mentioned, there is some doubt as to whether or not the reported net income can be accepted as net income available to the stockholders. During a period of rising prices, older costs may have been matched against revenues, with the result that net income is higher than it would be otherwise. On the income statement illustrated below, no adjustments were made for increased costs of replacements or for increases in the price level.

Net sales	$9,500,000
Cost of goods sold	5,700,000
Gross margin	$3,800,000
Operating expenses including depreciation of $200,000	2,000,000
Net income before income taxes	$1,800,000
Income taxes	900,000
Net income after income taxes	$ 900,000

The board of directors declared a dividend of $500,000, intending to retain a portion of the earnings for the year. To continue operations, however, the company will have to replenish its inventory at costs that are 10 percent higher. Also, depreciation restated on a current dollar basis should be recorded at $300,000 in total. The income statement adjusted to a current dollar basis appears below:

Net sales	$9,500,000
Cost of goods sold	6,270,000
Gross margin	$3,230,000
Operating expenses including depreciation of $300,000	2,100,000
Net income before income taxes	$1,130,000
Income taxes	900,000
Net income after income taxes	$ 230,000

According to the adjusted statement, the board of directors not only distributed current earnings but also unintentionally distributed earnings from past years. Note also that the income taxes are higher in relation to the net income before taxes.

During a period of falling prices, the net income will be lower when older and higher costs are matched against revenues. To illustrate, an income statement prepared in the conventional manner is presented below:

Net sales	$7,000,000
Cost of goods sold	4,800,000
Gross margin	$2,200,000
Operating expenses including depreciation of $200,000	1,400,000
Net income before income taxes	$ 800,000
Income taxes	400,000
Net income after income taxes	$ 400,000

The merchandise sold can be replaced at 90 percent of the cost shown above, and depreciation should be adjusted downward by 20 percent. A revised statement reflecting the lower current costs appears below:

Net sales	$7,000,000
Cost of goods sold	4,320,000
Gross margin	$2,680,000
Operating expenses including depreciation of $160,000	1,360,000
Net income before income taxes	$1,320,000
Income taxes	400,000
Net income after income taxes	$ 920,000

The changes in the price level tend to distort the results. With an increasing price level, the company may appear to be more prosperous than it really is. Conversely, during a general decline in prices, the situation may appear to be worse than it is. In the formation of its dividend policy, the directors should consider the effect of changes in the price level and should not rely entirely upon profits reported in the conventional manner.

Questions

1. Explain what is meant by a change in the general level of prices.

2. Name two index series that are used to measure changes in the general price level.

3. During a period when prices are increasing, does an individual or business benefit by holding cash? Explain.

4. How does a borrower benefit during a period of increasing prices?

5. What are replacement costs? Is the replacement cost the same as the price level adjusted cost? Explain.

6. Are current costs matched against revenues when the fifo inventory method is used? Explain.

7. As a general rule, are older costs or more recent costs shown on the balance sheet when the lifo inventory method is used?

8. Explain how current costs can be shown on both the income statement and on the balance sheet under the lifo inventory method.

9. How can accelerated depreciation methods reduce the impact of price level changes?

10. Distinguish between monetary items and nonmonetary items.

11. Dollar amounts from the past are brought up-to-date by the application of an index number multiplier. What index number is used as the numerator of the multiplier fraction? the denominator of the multiplier?

12. Company X incurred a debt of $90,000 when the price index was at 150. One year later, the debt was still outstanding, and the price index was at 200. Compute the gain or loss in purchasing power during the year.

13. Company Y held cash and accounts receivable amounting to $60,000 at the beginning of the year when the price index was at 100. During the year, revenue of $100,000 was realized at a price index of 120. Expenses of operation amounting to $70,000 were paid at a price index of 140. At the end of the year, the price index was 150. Compute the gain or loss in purchasing power for the year from the information furnished.

14. At the end of the year, Company Z had cash of $40,000 and inventory of $50,000. Both the cash and the inventory were obtained when the price index was at 100. The price index at the end of the year was 140. Show how the cash and the inventory would appear on a balance sheet stated in current dollars of purchasing power at the end of the year.

Exercises

1. Charles Daubert, Inc., reported a net income after income taxes of $127,000 in 1972. Cost of goods sold included costs incurred in past years and amounted to $280,000. Analysis reveals that at the present time it would cost $370,000 to replace these goods. Depreciation on the original cost of plant assets amounted to $30,000. Based on replacement cost, the depreciation should have been shown at $50,000.

Required: How much of the net income for 1972 could be distributed to the stockholders as dividends with provision made for the retention of resources necessary for continuance of the business on the same scale as before?

2. During the past year, Hansen Brothers, Inc., has increased its inventory in anticipation of increased sales in the next year. Perpetual inventory records are not maintained. In the past year, 230,000 units of product were sold at a unit price of $16. Inventory and purchase data follow:

	Number of Units	Unit Cost	Total Cost
Inventory balance at the beginning of the year	35,000	$ 9.00	$315,000
Purchases:			
January	50,000	9.50	475,000
March	70,000	10.00	700,000
June	70,000	11.00	770,000
October	30,000	12.00	360,000
December	20,000	12.50	250,000

Required: (1) Compute the gross margin using the fifo method of accounting for inventory costs. Determine the cost of the inventory at the end of the year.

(2) Compute the gross margin using the lifo method of accounting for inventory costs. Determine the cost of the inventory at the end of the year.

(3) Show how the inventory would appear on the balance sheet if the lifo inventory were adjusted to a current cost basis at the end of the year. What effect would this adjustment have on the equity side of the balance sheet?

3. George Biddle had $240,000 in savings when he retired. At that time the price index was 120. The savings have been held in bonds and in savings and loan accounts with an average interest yield of 8 percent a year. Mr. Biddle believed that he could live modestly and comfortably from the return on his

(margin note, handwritten): change is value of the measuring unit — change is real value

savings. Ten years after his retirement, he has $240,000 in bonds and savings and loan accounts, and the price index stands at 180.

Required: (1) Compute the value of Mr. Biddle's capital ten years after retirement in dollars of purchasing power *at the time he retired.*
(2) Determine his annual income ten years after retirement in dollars of purchasing power *at the time he retired.*

4. Wilson Serfass purchased a tract of land at a cost of $90,000 when the price index was at 75. He anticipated that the city of Hilliard would expand in this direction and that the land could be sold to developers at a considerable profit. Because of industrial developments and housing projects in neighboring towns, Hilliard has not grown as much as anticipated in the past 10 years. The property now is worth $100,000 and the price index is now at 120.

Required: Adjust the cost of the land to a current price basis by index numbers. Does this amount agree with the current value of the land?

5. Pearson and Wagner, Inc., constructed a building when the price index was at 100. The company borrowed $7,200,000 to finance construction costs. Management anticipated that the price level would increase so that the debt could be paid in cheaper dollars. At the present time, the price index is at 60.

Required: (1) When the debt was incurred, it was shown on the balance sheet at $7,200,000. What was the purchasing power of the money borrowed as measured in dollars at the price index of 60?
(2) On the current balance sheet, the debt is shown at $7,200,000. Adjust the debt to dollars at the price index of 60.
(3) Compute the purchasing power gain or loss from having outstanding debt during the period of the price level change.

6. Overseas Enterprises, Inc., conducts business in a country where the price level has increased rapidly in a very short period of time. As a result, the company is reluctant to extend credit in this country's currency. A 25 percent charge is added to all sales with payment due in three months. A sale was made to a customer for 180,000 units of the foreign currency. When the sale was made the price index was at 120. At the time of collection three months later, the price index was at 150.

Required: Did Overseas Enterprises, Inc. have a price level gain or loss during the collection period? Show computations.

7. The president of Hastings Company reports that the company has been earning a rate of return on the sales dollar that is slightly higher than the 20 percent rate for the industry. A summary income statement for the past year follows:

Net sales		$12,000,000
Cost of goods sold	$6,000,000	
Operating expenses	1,100,000	
Income taxes	2,300,000	9,400,000
Net income		$ 2,600,000

Inventories are accounted for by the lifo method, and in the past year the company liquidated old inventories. Inventories that cost $2,400,000 when the price index was at 100 are included in the cost of goods sold. Also, depreciation of $750,000 was deducted on plant assets that were acquired when the price index was at 60. Depreciation is included in operating expenses. All other revenues and expenses are on a current price basis with the index at 120.

Required: Prepare an income statement in dollars at the 120 price index. Compute a revised rate of return on net sales.

8. A summary balance sheet for Andover Design Company appears below:

Cash and accounts receivable	$1,300,000
Plant and equipment, net of depreciation	1,400,000
Total assets	$2,700,000
Current debt	$ 600,000
Long-term debt	1,000,000
Owners' equity	1,100,000
Total equities	$2,700,000

The price index is 140. The plant and equipment and the long-term debt were acquired when the price index was at 80.

Required: Revise the summary balance sheet to restate all assets and equities in dollars at the 140 price index.

Problems

4–1. Over the past few years, Ben Marcus invested savings as follows:

Total Amount Invested	Type of Investment		Price Index at Time of Investment
	Common Stock	Bonds	
$ 4,500	$4,500	—	100
6,000	6,000	—	120
7,000	3,000	4,000	140
9,500	4,500	5,000	150
12,000	4,000	8,000	180
$39,000			

At the present time, the price index is at 200. The bonds are redeemable at the amounts shown above, and the common stock can be sold as follows:

Price Index at Time of Investment	Common Stock	
	Cost	Present Market Value
100	$4,500	$6,000
120	6,000	7,500
140	3,000	2,500
150	4,500	2,500
180	4,000	2,000

Required: (1) Restate the costs of the investments in dollars at the price index of 200.

(2) Compute the loss in purchasing power by holding the bonds.

(3) Compare the present market values of the investments in common stocks with the costs stated in dollars having a purchasing power of 200.

116

4-2. An income statement for Traub Bearings Company for the year ended June 30, 19X2 follows:

Traub Bearings Company
Income Statement
For the Year Ended June 30, 19X2

Net sales	$2,400,000
Cost of goods sold	$1,500,000
Operating expenses, excluding depreciation	410,000
Depreciation	10,000
Total expenses	$1,920,000
Net income	$ 480,000

Sales of $960,000 were made when the price index was at 150. The balance of the sales was made when the price index was at 200. Cost of goods sold of $1,200,000 was at the price index of 150, and the balance of the cost of goods sold was at the price index of 200.

Operating expenses of $240,000 were incurred at a price index of 150, and $170,000 was incurred at a price index of 200.

Depreciation was deducted on plant assets that were acquired at a price index of 100.

Required: Prepare an income statement in uniform dollars of purchasing power at a price index of 200, the price index at the end of 19X2.

4-3. An income statement for Gibson Machine Company for the fiscal year ended September 30, 1972, is given below in summary form.

Gibson Machine Company
Income Statement
For the Fiscal Year Ended September 30, 1972

Net sales	$1,300,000
Cost of goods sold	$ 830,000
Depreciation	140,000
Other operating expenses, including income taxes	255,000
	$1,225,000
Net income	$ 75,000

During the fiscal year, the company sold 170,000 units of product. Inventory costs are accounted for on a first-in, first-out basis. A summary of the costs entering into inventory and cost of goods sold is given below:

	No. of Units	Unit Cost
Inventory at the beginning of the fiscal year	15,000	$4.00
First half of fiscal year	70,000	4.50
Third quarter of fiscal year	55,000	5.00
Fourth quarter of fiscal year	50,000	6.00

At the end of the fiscal year, the president of the company estimated that it would cost $7.00 a unit to replace the inventory sold.

Equipment used in operations had an original cost of $800,000, an estimated useful life of 5 years, and an estimated residual salvage value of $100,000 at the end of 5 years. The equipment has been in operation for exactly two years, and depreciation has been deducted by the straight-line method. It is estimated that it would cost $1,200,000 to replace this equipment today. Based on this estimate the residual salvage value at the end of 5 years would amount to $200,000.

Required: (1) The president of the company asks you to prepare an income statement that shows current costs matched against revenue. Use the lifo method in accounting for cost of goods sold and the double-rate method of depreciation (second year) for the equipment.

(2) Also show an income statement with current replacement costs matched against revenue. Use straight-line depreciation for equipment.

4-4. A group of businessmen invested $300,000 to form a new corporation designated as Webster Hall Company. The investment was made when the price index was at 150. Equipment costing $120,000 was acquired at the price index of 150 with $60,000 of the cost being financed by notes due in 5 years. An inventory of merchandise costing $90,000 was purchased when the price index was at 180, and additional purchases of $120,000 were made when the index was at 200. Inventory costs are determined by the fifo method. Expenses of $48,000 were incurred at a price index of 240, and all sales were made at a price index of 240. At the end of the year, the price index was 240.

Condensed financial statements are given below:

Webster Hall Company
Condensed Income Statement
For the Year 19A

Net sales	$350,000
Cost of goods sold	$180,000
Other expenses, excluding depreciation	48,000
Depreciation	15,000
	$243,000
Net income	$107,000

Webster Hall Company
Condensed Balance Sheet
December 31, 19A

Assets

Cash and receivables	$370,000
Inventory	30,000
Plant assets, net of depreciation	105,000
Total assets	$505,000

Equities

Accounts payable	$ 38,000
Long-term notes payable	60,000
Capital stock	300,000
Retained earnings	107,000
Total equities	$505,000

Required: (1) Compute the purchasing power gain or loss on monetary items.

(2) Prepare a condensed income statement in dollars of purchasing power at the price index of 240.

(3) Prepare a condensed balance sheet in dollars of purchasing power at the price index of 240.

4–5. A balance sheet for Celestial Electric, Inc., at December 31, 19X1 follows:

Celestial Electric, Inc.
Balance Sheet
December 31, 19X1

Assets

Cash	$ 80,000
Accounts receivable	55,000
Inventory	30,000
Plant equipment, net of depreciation	45,000
Total assets	$210,000

Equities

Accounts payable and other current liabilities	$ 30,000
Capital stock	90,000
Retained earnings	90,000
Total equities	$210,000

The price index at the end of 19X1 was 100, and all assets and equities on the balance sheet are stated in common dollars of purchasing power at the index of 100. The inventory consists of 15,000 units at a unit cost of $2.00. Inventory is accounted for on a first-in, first-out basis.

Transactions for 19X2 are summarized below:

(1) Merchandise costing $156,000 was purchased when the price index was at 120.

(2) Depreciation of $8,000 was charged to operations during the year.

(3) The company sold 75,000 units of product for $375,000 when the price index was at 140.

(4) The inventory at the end of 19X2 of 15,000 units of product was assigned a cost of $52,000.

(5) Selling and administrative expenses amounting to $13,000 were incurred when the price index was at 130. (Depreciation has been excluded.)

(6) The outstanding accounts receivable at the beginning of the year were collected when the price index was 120, and $300,000 was collected on current sales when the price index was 150.

(7) Current liabilities at the beginning of the year were paid when the price index was at 100.

(8) Payments of $160,000 were made on materials purchased and for various other costs incurred during the year. The price index was at 130 when $80,000 of these payments were made and was at 150 for the other payments of $80,000.

(9) Income taxes are estimated at 50 percent of net income before income taxes. (Include the liability with other current liabilities.)

The price index at December 31, 19X2 was 150.

The board of directors believes that cash reserves are more than adequate at the end of the year and is considering a distribution of the total net income after income taxes as a dividend. The board recognizes, however, that the net income was measured in mixed dollars of purchasing power and that dividends should be limited to the net income measured in common current dollars of purchasing power.

Required: (1) Prepare an income statement for 19X2 and a balance sheet at December 31, 19X2 in both mixed dollars of purchasing power and in dollars of purchasing power at a price index of 150.

(2) Can the board of directors distribute the net income for the year as a dividend without an involuntary distribution in excess of this amount because of measurements made in mixed dollars of purchasing power? What is the maximum dividend distribution that can be made without distributing more than the amount of the net income as measured in common current dollars of purchasing power?

4–6. Transactions for Blue Rock Vista, Inc., are given for 19A, the first year of operations.

(1) Stockholders invested $850,000 when the price index was at 100.

(2) Equipment costing $560,000 was purchased and paid for when the price index was at 120.

(3) Merchandise was purchased as follows:

$480,000 at a price index of 120.
370,000 at a price index of 150.

At the end of the year there was an inventory of merchandise on hand that cost $70,000 when the price index was at 150. The accounts payable for merchandise purchased was $40,000 at the end of the year.

(4) Depreciation of $80,000 was recorded on the equipment.

(5) Other operating expenses of $270,000 were incurred and paid at a price index of 150.

(6) Sales of $1,400,000 were made at a price index of 150. All sales were on a cash basis.

(7) Dividends of $80,000 were declared and paid when the price index was at 150.

(8) Income taxes of $130,000 were incurred and paid when the price index was at 150.

The price index at the end of the year was 150.

Required: (1) Prepare an income statement for 19A and a balance sheet at the end of the year. The statements are not to be adjusted for changes in the purchasing power of the dollar.

(2) Compute the gain or loss in purchasing power during the year.

(3) Prepare an income statement for 19A and a balance sheet at the end of the year in dollars of purchasing power at a price index of 150.

4–7. During the past year the general price index increased from 100 to 120. Walter Payson, the president of W. F. Payson, Inc., hopes that the company has been able to keep up with the price level changes and has maintained the original purchasing power of its assets. The assets of the firm in mixed dollars of purchasing power have been taken from the balance sheet at the end of the year.

Cash		$ 212,000
Marketable securities		163,000
Accounts receivable		238,000
Inventory		316,000
Land		23,000
Buildings	$1,280,000	
Accumulated depreciation	223,000	1,057,000
Machinery and equipment	$1,835,000	
Accumulated depreciation	438,000	1,397,000
Total assets		$3,406,000

The president of the company tells you that the assets, aside from cash and the accounts receivable, have been acquired at different times and, of course, at different price conditions. He goes on to state that the amount of $3,406,000 shown for total assets has no real significance as a measurement of the assets or as a basis for rate of return computations. For the most part, however, the income statement is on a current dollar basis. Last year the company earned a net income after income taxes of $380,000 or a rate of return on total assets at the end of the year of 11.2 percent.

$$\frac{\$\ 380,000 \text{ net income}}{\$3,406,000 \text{ total assets}} = 11.2\%$$

The marketable securities consist of common stocks acquired at the price index of 100. The securities had a market value of $186,000 at the end of the year.

The inventory was acquired at the price index of 100, and at the end of the year it could have been replaced at a cost of $382,000.

Land was acquired at an index of 80 and has a present market value of $37,000. The buildings, which were recorded at an index of 80, have an appraised value as set forth below:

Buildings	$1,630,000
Accumulated depreciation	262,000
Net appraised value	$1,368,000

The machinery and equipment were recorded at an index of 80 and have appraised values as follows:

Machinery and equipment	$2,160,000
Accumulated depreciation	542,000
Net appraised value	$1,618,000

Required: (1) Prepare a statement of the assets on a uniform dollar basis at an index of 120.

(2) Prepare a statement of the assets at the current values given.

(3) Compare the current values with the amounts at an index of 120. Show the individual differences and the total difference.

(4) Compute a revised rate of return on the total assets at the end of the year, using the current values as determined in (2) above.

4–8. James Graham, the president of Tartan Products Company, recognizes that the company has been affected by the increase in the price level. He also recognizes that the financial statements on a mixed dollar basis do not give a complete account of what has taken place. At the end of 19A, the price index was 80; and at the end of 19B, the price index was 120.

Balance sheets in mixed dollars of purchasing power are given below:

Tartan Products Company
Balance Sheets
December 31

	_19A_	_19B_
Assets		
Current assets:		
Cash	$ 93,000	$ 118,000
Accounts receivable	112,000	116,000
Inventory	147,000	144,000
Total current assets	$352,000	$ 378,000
Investment in stock of other companies ..	300,000	480,000
Land	40,000	40,000
Buildings and equipment, net of		
depreciation	220,000	200,000
Total assets	$912,000	$1,098,000
Equities		
Current liabilities:		
Accounts payable	$ 56,000	$ 90,000
Other current liabilities	86,000	78,000
Total current liabilities................	$142,000	$ 168,000
Long-term debt	260,000	260,000
Capital stock	300,000	300,000
Retained earnings	210,000	370,000
Total equities	$912,000	$1,098,000

The inventory on the balance sheet at the end of 19A was acquired when the price index was 80, and the inventory on the balance sheet at the end of 19B was acquired when the price index was 120. An investment of $300,000 in the stock of other companies was made when the price index was at 60. Another investment of $180,000 was made when the price index was at 120. The land and the buildings and equipment were acquired at a price index of 60. Capital stock was issued, and long-term debt was incurred when the price index was 60.

The retained earnings at the end of 19A as stated in uniform dollars at an index of 150 amounted to $315,000, and the retained earnings at the end of 19B as stated in uniform dollars at an index of 150 amounted to $610,000.

Required: Prepare balance sheets in dollars having a uniform purchasing power at a price index of 120. Show only one amount for retained earnings on each adjusted balance sheet.

4–9. For several years prices have been relatively stable, but within the past three years they have increased substantially. Price indices at the end of each of the last three years are given below:

$$19X1 - 100$$
$$19X2 - 120$$
$$19X3 - 150$$

During each of these years, the price index has been approximately equal to the index at the end of the year.

Henri LaSalle and Son, Inc., plan to replace the present building with a larger and more modern structure. The last of the mortgage notes on the present building and the machinery and equipment were paid by the end of 19X2.

The company has acquired marketable securities (included with cash) that will be used in part to finance the cost of the new building. The securities held at the end of each of the three years cost $640,000 when the index was at 80. In 19X3, additional securities costing $200,000 were acquired.

Insofar as possible, the building program is to be financed with resources obtained from profitable operations, with loans or long-term debt being held to a minimum.

The balance sheets for the company at the end of each of the past three years are given below:

Henri LaSalle and Son, Inc.
Balance Sheets—December 31
(In Thousands of Dollars)

Assets	19X1	19X2	19X3
Cash and marketable securities	$1,840	$1,920	$ 2,160
Accounts receivable	1,570	1,680	1,630
Inventory (fifo)	1,620	1,650	1,620
Investments in bonds of Castle Developers, Inc.	2,500	1,250	1,250
Plant and equipment:			
Land	140	260	260
Buildings, net of accumulated depreciation	860	810	760
Equipment, net of accumulated depreciation	1,080	2,350	3,180
Total assets	$9,610	$9,920	$10,860

Equities	19X1	19X2	19X3
Accounts and notes payable	$ 740	$ 830	$ 850
Accrued expenses payable	520	570	580
Mortgage notes payable	600	—	—
Capital stock	5,000	5,000	5,000
Retained earnings	2,750	3,520	4,430
Total equities	$9,610	$9,920	$10,860

The investment in bonds, land, buildings, and equipment on the 19X1 balance sheet were acquired at an index of 80. The mortgage note and capital stock were also recorded when the index was 80.

Equipment costing $1,500,000 was purchased in 19X2, and equipment costing $1,000,000 was purchased in 19X3. The undepreciated cost of equipment on the 19X2 and 19X3 balance sheets can be broken down as follows:

Index at Acquisition Date	19X2	19X3
80	850	800
120	1,500	1,380
150	—	1,000

All other assets and equities, aside from the ones described and with the exception of retained earnings, came into the records during the year as listed.

Required: (1) Prepare balance sheets in uniform dollars at the price index of 150. Round computations to the nearest thousand dollars.

(2) What changes in the assets and equities are revealed over the two years when the unadjusted statements are compared with the statements on a uniform dollar basis?

4-10. For several years Helgo Pressed Products Company has converted its financial statements to a common dollar basis by use of a published price index series. At the end of last year, the price index was 150, and the summary balance sheet given below is prepared in dollars of purchasing power at the 150 index.

Helgo Pressed Products Company
Balance Sheet
(Uniform Dollars of Purchasing Power)
December 31, 19X1

Assets

Cash	$1,840,000
Accounts receivable	1,670,000
Inventory	1,280,000
Plant, net of accumulated depreciation	3,600,000
Total assets	$8,390,000

Equities

Accounts payable and other current liabilities	$2,160,000
Notes due in 19X8	1,500,000
Capital stock	2,000,000
Retained earnings:	
Operations	2,400,000
Accumulated purchasing power gains	330,000
Total equities	$8,390,000

A summary of transactions for 19X2 at various price index levels follows:

(1) Purchases of merchandise:

Index	Amount
150	$3,200,000
180	1,650,000
200	1,700,000

(2) Inventories are costed on a first-in, first-out basis.

(3) Sales and cost of goods sold:

Index	Sales	Cost
150	$2,700,000	$4,480,000
180	3,800,000	1,650,000
200	3,700,000	320,000

(4) Operating expenses incurred:

Index	Amount
180	$800,000
200	550,000

Depreciation of $150,000 has been taken on plant assets acquired at the price index of 100.

(5) Income taxes of $1,180,000 have been recorded at the price index of 200.

(6) At the end of 19X2, the price index was 200.

The income statement given in summary form below is stated in mixed dollars of purchasing power.

Helgo Pressed Products Company
Income Statement
For the Year, 19X2

Net sales	$10,200,000
Cost of goods sold	6,450,000
Gross margin	$ 3,750,000
Operating expenses, including depreciation of $150,000	1,500,000
Net operating income	$ 2,250,000
Income taxes	1,180,000
Net income after income taxes	$ 1,070,000

Transactions for 19X2 in mixed dollars of purchasing power have been combined with the balance sheet amounts at December 31, 19X1, as stated in uniform dollars at an index of 150. The balance sheet at December 31, 19X2, is reproduced on the next page.

Required: Round all answers to the nearest thousand dollars.

(1) From the information provided, compute the net purchasing power gain or loss from holding monetary items during 19X2.

(2) Prepare an income statement converted to uniform dollars of purchasing power at an index of 200.

(3) Prepare a balance sheet at December 31, 19X2, in uniform dollars of purchasing power at an index of 200. Show the accumulated purchasing power gains or losses as a separate part of retained earnings.

Helgo Pressed Products Company
Balance Sheet
December 31, 19X2

Assets

Cash	$2,410,000
Accounts receivable	2,040,000
Inventory	1,380,000
Plant assets, net of accumulated depreciation	3,450,000
Total assets	$9,280,000

Equities

Accounts payable and other current liabilities	$1,980,000
Notes due in 19X8	1,500,000
Capital stock	2,000,000
Retained earnings:	
Operations	3,470,000
Accumulated purchasing power gains	330,000
Total equities	$9,280,000

Chapter 5

FINANCIAL STATEMENT ANALYSIS—RATE OF RETURN

Business management is evaluated to a large extent on the basis of earning power. The resources of business enterprise are to be used to earn as large a rate of return for the owners as possible after taking into account other business objectives, the type of business, prevailing business conditions, and the relative risk. A rate of return can be computed not only on the owners' equity but also on sales, total assets, total equities, or any particular segment of the assets or the equities.

In striving for higher profits and greater rates of return, the risk factor cannot be ignored. If the investment is inadequate in relation to sales volume, debt will tend to increase, with the owners assuming more risk of loss from business reversals. A certain amount of debt is expected in the operation of the business enterprise; but if the proportion of debt becomes too great, there is a risk that the owners will lose control. A balance will have to be maintained between rate of return on sales, rate of return on investment, the size of the investment in relation to sales volume, and the safety of the owners' investment. Conditions that exist within any industry will influence this interrelationship.

APPLICATIONS OF THE RATE-OF-RETURN CONCEPT

The various rates of return that can be computed serve as a guide to management in its efforts to maximize the rate of return on the owners' investment with risk being taken into account. Some of the applications of the rate-of-return concept are listed below:

(1) Rate of return measures the overall profitability of the company.

(2) Rate of return also measures the profitability of any division or segment of the business.

(3) Rate of return can be used in planning and controlling business operations.

(4) Rate of return may be used in planning the asset and equity structure of the firm.

(5) Rate of return may be employed in selecting plant assets or other types of investments.

(6) Rate of return can be helpful where choices are to be made between alternative courses of action.

(7) Rate of return may also be used to arrive at selling prices for the product lines.

Financial analysts and potential investors will evaluate a company and its management by looking at the profits that are earned in relation to the assets employed and in relation to the stockholders' equity. A company that can earn a better-than-average rate of return without taking unwarranted risks will ordinarily be able to attract more investment funds and to obtain them at a lower cost than its less fortunate competitors.

Management will use the rate-of-return concept to control business operations and to plan for the future. Rates of return may be calculated for individual segments of the business. If the rate appears to be too low in a given situation, an investigation can be made to determine the cause. Perhaps the assets are not being used effectively, or it may be that more sales volume is needed. Or possibly the spread between the selling prices and the costs should be widened either by increasing prices or by reducing costs or both.

Top management not only assumes responsibility for operations but also assumes responsibility for the asset and equity structure, seeking a proper balance wherever possible. Ordinarily a certain amount of debt should appear in the equity structure. Contacts with credit sources should be maintained so that additional resources can be borrowed whenever needed. When the owners furnish all or nearly all of the assets, there may be less risk; but there is also the possibility that the company will be out of touch with useful sources of credit. In addition, the company will lose the benefits that can be obtained from leverage. The assets, likewise, must be held in proper proportions. Assets that should turn over in the normal course of business operation must not be allowed to remain idle. There may be substantial investments in inventories, accounts receivable, or plant assets. These assets are included in the asset base, but they may be contributing little to profits, with the result being a depressed rate of return.

RATE OF RETURN—ASSETS

The rate of return on assets is one of the most important measurements to be obtained from an analysis of financial statements. This rate of return is computed as follows at the top of the next page.

$$\frac{\text{Net income}}{\text{Average assets}} = \text{Rate of return on assets.}$$

Both the net income and the assets must be defined carefully not only to obtain a proper rate of return but to obtain a rate of return that is appropriate for a given purpose.

Net income. The net income to be used in calculating the rate of return may be the net income before the deduction of interest expense, the net income after the deduction of interest expense, or the net income before or after income taxes. The net income figure to be selected depends upon how the rate of return is to be used.

First of all, the income statement should be adjusted to remove items that are of an unusual nature and that are not expected to recur with regularity. The income statement then shows the results of normal operations, results that can be used in the measurement of operating performance and as a predictor of future profits. For example, a material gain on the sale of an asset not dealt with in the normal course of trade should be deducted from net income. If the gain is not deducted, the rate of return may be distorted. Furthermore, if unusual items are allowed to remain in the income statement, comparisons cannot be made with other years.

The dividends and the interest earned on investments are included in net income if the investments are also included in the asset base, but the dividends and the interest should be excluded if the investments have been removed from the assets. If different years are to be compared, both the net incomes and the assets should be adjusted so that they are stated on the same basis. A true comparison cannot be made if investments and investment income are included in one year and not in another.

The net income *before* the deduction of interest expense should be used if the intention is to measure operational performance. A manager may be responsible for how an asset is used, but he may have nothing to do with the acquisition of the asset. Resources are often borrowed to finance the purchase of assets; and interest expense, the cost of borrowing resources, should not be charged to personnel who have no part in making financial arrangements. Furthermore, comparisons between companies may be distorted by differences in financing. To test the effectiveness of operations as opposed to financing, interest expense should not be deducted on the income statement.

Top management, on the other hand, is responsible not only for how the assets are used but also for how they are acquired. Therefore, it is proper to use the net income *after* the deduction of interest to evaluate the total managerial effort. The rate of return is then a rate of return to the owners on the total asset investment inasmuch as the net income has already been reduced for amounts due to other equity holders.

Likewise, income taxes may or may not be deducted depending upon circumstances. Management at the operating level has no control over the computation of income taxes or the tax planning activities; consequently, net income before the income tax deduction would be a more appropriate measurement of its efficiency. From the owners' viewpoint, however, there can be no return until all expenses, including income taxes, have been deducted. The income taxes are as much an expense of doing business as any other expense and should be considered as such in rating the total business performance.

If charges and credits are to be added back to or deducted from net income *after* taxes, they will have to be adjusted for the income taxes. Each item added to or subtracted from net income should be stated on an after-tax basis, otherwise the net income will not be the net income after taxes as intended. To illustrate, assume that the loss on the sale of a plant asset of $20,000 is to be removed from the income statement given below:

Net sales	$800,000
Cost of goods sold	500,000
Gross margin	$300,000
Operating expenses and other deductions, including loss of $20,000 on sale of plant asset	240,000
Net income before income taxes	$ 60,000
Income taxes	30,000
Net income after income taxes	$ 30,000

Assuming an income tax rate of 50 percent, the net income will be adjusted by adding back the loss as adjusted by the income taxes. In other words, with a 50 percent tax rate only one half of the loss will be added back.

Net income after income taxes		$30,000
Add: Loss on sale of plant asset	$20,000	
Deduct income tax benefit of loss deduction	10,000	10,000
Net income after income taxes with loss on sale of plant asset excluded		$40,000

The asset base. Assets as shown on the balance sheet may also have to be adjusted in making rate-of-return computations. The nature of the adjustments will depend upon the definition of the rate of return. Assets will increase or decrease during the year, and the rate of return on the assets will obviously be affected by the asset base selected. For example, a rate of return may be calculated on the assets held at the beginning of the year. But this rate-of-return calculation does not take into account the changes in assets during the year. On the other hand, a rate of return on the assets at the end of the year is also misleading for the same reason. Perhaps, a better measurement can be made by averaging the assets at the beginning and at the end of the year or by averaging monthly balances. In the discussion and in the examples that follow it is assumed, when reference is made to either total assets or to total owners' equity, that the data have been properly averaged or are representative data for rate-of-return computation.

Assets that are not available for productive use should be excluded from the asset base in the calculation of a rate of return on assets that are actively employed in profit-making activity. The cost of idle facilities, for example, and the cost of construction in process produce nothing in the way of current profits. Presumably these assets are expected to yield profits at a later date. At the present time, however, there is no profit yield, and the cost should be subtracted from the asset base so that the return will be related to the assets that produced it. An additional rate of return calculation may be made with the cost of standby and idle facilities included in the asset base. This rate of return can be compared with the rate of return on the productive assets and may reveal that the management is holding on to more nonproductive assets than it should under the circumstances.

If management at the operating level is to be evaluated, investments in the securities of other companies should also be eliminated. Operating management cannot take credit for the dividends or interest earned on investments, nor can it be held responsible for the cost of the investments.

Asset turnover and rate of return. In seeking a given rate of return, management recognizes that various factors interlock. These factors are:

(1) The rate of profit on the sales dollar.
(2) The volume of sales.
(3) The investment in assets.
(4) The ratio of sales to the asset investment.

The rate of return on total assets depends upon the ratio of net income to sales and the ratio of sales to total assets. Often these relationships are expressed in equation form as follows:

$$\frac{\text{Net income}}{\text{Total assets}} = \frac{\text{Net income}}{\text{Sales}} \times \frac{\text{Sales}}{\text{Total assets}}$$

or

$$\text{Rate of return on total assets} = \text{Rate of return on sales} \times \text{Asset turnover}$$

Assume that two companies each with assets of $400,000 earn a 10 percent return on the assets, or $40,000 in net income. Company A with net sales of $400,000 turns its assets over only once but earns a 10 percent return on sales. Company B turns its assets over ten times but earns only 1 percent on the sales dollar.

Rate of Return on Assets

	Company A	Company B
Net sales	$400,000	$4,000,000
Total assets	400,000	400,000
Net income	40,000	40,000
Percentage of net income to net sales	10%	1%
Asset turnover	1	10
Rate of return on total assets	10%	10%

Company A relies upon its profit margin to obtain a 10 percent return on assets, while Company B depends upon turnover. By doubling asset turnover, Company A can double the rate of return on assets with the same volume of sales and profit percentage. If Company B can increase its margin of profit

Rate of Return on Assets

	Company A	Company B
Net sales	$400,000	$4,000,000
Total assets	200,000	400,000
Net income	40,000	80,000
Percentage of net income to net sales	10%	2%
Asset turnover	2	10
Rate of return on total assets	20%	20%

to 2 percent of net sales, it can also double the rate of return on assets with the same sales volume and turnover.

Various combinations of turnovers and profit percentages can be computed to arrive at a combination that will most likely be realized in seeking a certain rate of return. The combination can be tabulated or, if desired, plotted on a graph. The line on the graph shown on the next page represents a given rate of return on assets for different combinations of turnovers and profit percentages.[1]

By examining these relationships, management can sometimes detect weak points and seek ways to overcome them. In some circumstances, however, little can be done to change the factors. The rate of net income to net sales is relatively small in some industries and there is little opportunity to raise prices or to cut costs. The asset turnover may be as good as can be expected, in which case the rate of return on assets is virtually at a maximum. Conversely, a company may earn as high a rate of profit on sales as

---

[1] *Return on Capital as a Guide to Managerial Decisions,* NAA Research Report 35, pp. 33-37.

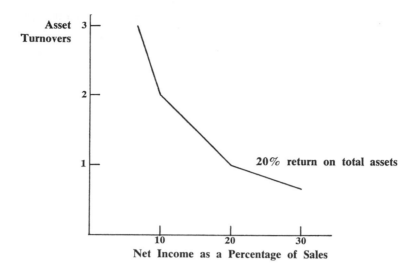

Net Income as a Percentage of Sales

can be expected, but a large investment in assets may be required to support the sales. Once again, the rate of return on assets cannot be improved to any great extent.

Net plant assets. Assets subject to depreciation or amortization are particularly troublesome in rate of return computations. Depreciation is a peculiar type of expense because, unlike many of the other business expenses, it does not result in a reduction of current assets or in an addition to current liabilities. For example, when merchandise is delivered to customers, inventory, which is a current asset, is reduced. Or rent expense results in either a reduction in current assets or an increase in current liabilities. In contrast, plant assets may be used in operations over a period of many years with a portion of the cost being charged to depreciation expense each year. Any particular plant asset will be shown on the balance sheet at a lower amount as a result of the annual depreciation deductions.

The asset base will become smaller each year, even though the same assets are being used. The shrinkage in the asset base would be caused by recording depreciation. If revenues are constant over the life of the assets with no appreciable increase in the cost of operation, the rate of return will rise. The management and the investors may be misled into thinking that an increase in the rate of return is an indication of improvement, when in reality the increase has resulted from the reduction of the asset base.

This effect is illustrated by assuming that depreciable assets costing $500,000 were purchased. It is also assumed that the income earned each period can be identified with these particular assets. These assets were estimated to have a useful life of five years with no residual salvage value. Straight-line depreciation was recorded, and revenue for each of the five years amounted to $200,000 with annual expenses other than depreciation amounting to $84,500.

Depreciation—Straight-Line Method

Years	1	2	3	4	5
Cost of assets	$500,000	$500,000	$500,000	$500,000	$500,000
Accumulated depreciation	100,000	200,000	300,000	400,000	500,000
Assets, net of depreciation	$400,000	$300,000	$200,000	$100,000	–0–
Revenue	$200,000	$200,000	$200,000	$200,000	$200,000
Expenses, other than depreciation	84,500	84,500	84,500	84,500	84,500
Depreciation	100,000	100,000	100,000	100,000	100,000
Net income	$ 15,500	$ 15,500	$ 15,500	$ 15,500	$ 15,500
Rate of return on gross investment	3.1%	3.1%	3.1%	3.1%	3.1%
Rate of return on net investment at beginning of the year	3.1%	3.9%	5.2%	7.8%	15.5%

Looking at this particular segment of the assets, one might conclude that the company made considerable progress over the five years. But the company earned the same net income each year on the same assets with the rate being only 3.1 percent each year as shown by the rate of return calculated on the gross investment.

Gross plant assets. It may appear that the problem of an artificially increasing rate of return can be avoided by including plant assets at original cost without reduction for depreciation. As stated earlier, plant assets are shown on the balance sheet net of accumulated depreciation. The recording of depreciation expense does not result in the reduction of current assets or in an increase in current liabilities. The offsetting credit to depreciation expense is to accumulated depreciation which is subtracted from plant assets. If operations are profitable with the entire profit being distributed to the stockholders as dividends, other assets will be held in the business that are equal to the depreciation charge. Therefore, if gross assets are used to compute the rate of return, there would seem to be double counting. The portion of the plant asset recovered through depreciation charges is counted once as a part of the cost of the plant asset and again as an asset that has been retained.

For example, assume that depreciation of $50,000 has been taken on assets costing $200,000. This will result in the retention of assets equal to the depreciation of $50,000 if operations are profitable and an amount equal to the profit is paid in dividends.

Assets at the Beginning of the Year

Gross investment in plant assets	$200,000

Assets at the End of the Year

Assets retained by depreciation	$ 50,000
Gross investment in plant assets	200,000
Total assets	$250,000

There may be some question as to whether the total assets have increased or not. The company has already received service from its plant assets, and this has been recognized by matching part of the cost against revenue in the income determination process. Other assets have been retained as a result of recording depreciation, but the total investment remains the same as it was at the beginning of the year.

Assets at the Beginning of the Year

Gross investment in plant assets	$200,000

Assets at the End of the Year

Assets retained by depreciation		$ 50,000
Gross investment in plant assets	$200,000	
Less: Accumulated depreciation	50,000	150,000
Total assets		$200,000

According to this argument, the total asset base remains unchanged; and if the revenue from using the asset is constant over the years, it would seem logical that the rate of return should also remain the same. In a physical sense, the company still has the same use from the plant assets and may earn the same net income from the plant assets each year. But, in addition, the assets retained should be reinvested to earn a return. Therefore, the total net income should increase and the rate of return should be calculated on a higher asset base. If the total net income does remain the same over the years in spite of reinvesting the capital, then there is a decrease in the rate of return that should be revealed. However, a better approach to the problem may be to change the method of depreciation and to use the net plant asset base.

Annuity method of depreciation. Distortion in the rate of return as shown above may be avoided by using the annuity method of depreciation. If the cash returns from using plant assets are constant and if the interest rate used in the annuity method of depreciation is the same as the rate of return earned by the asset, the rate of return calculated on a net asset base will not increase over a period of time. Furthermore, there can be no confusion with respect to double counting of assets if net assets are used as a base.

The depreciation charge under the annuity method of depreciation can be broken into two parts:

(1) The depreciation charge itself, that is, the amortization of the cost of the asset.

(2) The theoretical interest that could have been earned if resources had been invested elsewhere.

Operations are charged not only with the cost of the asset subject to depreciation, but they are also charged with the interest return that has been sacrificed by investing in a plant asset.

The theoretical interest that could have been earned by an alternative employment of resources is included in depreciation expense and is also recorded as interest earned. The plant asset is reduced by accumulated depreciation equal to the difference between the total depreciation charge and the theoretical interest earned.

Net income is unaffected by the inclusion of the theoretical interest earned. Depreciation is higher by the amount of the interest, and the theoretical interest is offset by the excessive depreciation with no effect on the net result.

This method of recording depreciation is illustrated by using data from the previous example:

Cost of assets	$500,000
Less: Present value of residual value of zero	—0—
Present value of investment	$500,000
Assumed rate of interest	5%

$$\frac{\text{Present value of investment of } \$500,000}{\text{Present value of annuity of } \$1 \text{ at } 5\% \text{ for 5 years—} 4.330} = \$115,500 \text{ annual depreciation expense}$$

Annual depreciation expense	$115,500
Theoretical interest earned in the first year (5% of $500,000)	25,000
Credit to accumulated depreciation, first year	$ 90,500

The depreciation entry for the first year is as follows:

Depreciation Expense	115,500	
Interest Earned		25,000
Accumulated Depreciation		90,500
To record depreciation for the first year.		

In subsequent years the depreciation expense would remain the same, but the interest would be reduced each year by 5 percent of the investment recovered in the preceding year. Stated in another way, the interest each year is equal to 5 percent of the unrecovered investment at the beginning of the year. Accumulated depreciation is increased by an amount equal to the interest reduction. A tabulation showing computations for the five years is given below.

Annuity method and rate of return. The rate of return does not increase over a period of time when the calculation is based on net plant assets under the annuity method if the actual cash inflow each year is equal to the estimated cash inflow used to determine the interest rate. This will be true because the net income each year is reduced by an amount equal to the

Years (Col. 1)	Unrecovered Investment —Beginning of the Year (Col. 2)	Deprecia- tion Expense (Col. 3)	Interest Earned (5% of Col. 2) (Col. 4)	Accumulated Depreciation Increase (Col. 5)
1	$500,000	$115,500	$25,000	$ 90,500
2	409,500	115,500	20,475	95,025
3	314,475	115,500	15,724	99,776
4	214,699	115,500	10,735	104,765
5 *	109,934	115,500	5,497	110,003

* Difference due to rounding.

rate of interest applied to the reduction in the asset base and does not remain constant in relation to a declining base.

The rate of return on the assets costing $500,000 is calculated on the net investment under the annuity method, using the original data presented, at the top of the next page.

It should be observed that the net income each year is adjusted downwards by 5 percent of the reduction in the asset base; or in other words, the interest earned is calculated at 5 percent of the amount of unrecovered capital.

In general, then, the straight-line method of depreciation has a tendency toward an increasing rate of return over a period of time. However, if the plant assets are well distributed according to age, perhaps the errors will

Depreciation—Annuity Method

Years	1	2	3	4	5*
Cost of assets	$500,000	$500,000	$500,000	$500,000	$500,000
Accumulated depreciation	90,500	185,525	285,301	390,066	500,069
Assets, net of depreciation	$409,500	$314,475	$214,699	$109,934	($ 69)
Revenue	$200,000	$200,000	$200,000	$200,000	$200,000
Expenses other than depreciation	84,500	84,500	84,500	84,500	84,500
Depreciation	115,500	115,500	115,500	115,500	115,500
Interest earned	25,000	20,475	15,724	10,735	5,497
Net income	$ 25,000	$ 20,475	$ 15,724	$ 10,735	$ 5,497
Rate of return on net investment at beginning of the year	5%	5%	5%	5%	5%

* Difference due to rounding.

average out; that is, for new assets the rate of return is understated, but for older assets the rate will be overstated. If plant assets of all ages are being used, the understatements and the overstatements may tend to offset each other.

The annuity method, because it considers the time value of money and because it imputes an interest income based on the size of the unrecovered investment, does not have a tendency toward an increasing rate of return over a period of time as does the straight-line method. In a firm where the plant assets are well distributed and there is no marked tendency to expand or contract plant asset investment, the two methods will give almost the same results. However, the straight-line method will give some distortion in the rate of return on net plant assets if:

(1) The firm is primarily a "one-asset" firm (the rate of return will increase over time).

(2) The firm is young or has predominantly new assets (the rate of return will be understated relative to later years).

(3) The firm has predominantly old assets (the rate of return will be overstated relative to the early years).

There is no easy solution to this problem. Depreciation cannot be determined precisely, and it may be difficult to arrive at an interest rate which should be used in the calculation of depreciation according to the annuity method. Nevertheless, the analyst should be aware of the problem and should recognize that distortions in the rate of return on the asset investment can be caused by the timing of investments and methods used in computing depreciation.

LEVERAGE

Both management and outsiders will be interested in the rate of return on the owners' equity. This rate of return depends upon decisions made with respect to the financial structure and also upon profits that in turn depend upon the effective employment of available resources.

Property acquisitions can be financed in various ways. Resources or capital may be furnished directly by the owners through the sale of capital stock if the business is incorporated or may be furnished indirectly by the owners through the reinvestment of profits that have been retained. Capital may also be furnished by outsiders either in the form of short-term credit or long-term credit. Ordinarily, a business will employ resources that have been furnished by both owners and outsiders; and a balance will be maintained between debt and owners' equity.

The equity of the common stockholders is the residual equity—the equity remaining after provision has been made for the claims of all other equity holders. The retained earnings to be included as a part of common stockholders' equity, for example, is reduced by any dividend requirements on preferred stock. Similarly, net income must be reduced by the dividend claims of preferred stockholders.

The rate of return on the common stockholders' equity is computed as follows:

$$\frac{\text{Net income less dividends on preferred stock}}{\text{Average common stockholders' equity}} = \text{Rate of return on common stockholders' equity.}$$

If there is only one class of stock outstanding, the rate of return is net income as a percentage of the average owners' equity with the average being computed as a simple average of the balances at the beginning and at the end of the year or, if desired, an average of monthly balances.

Seemingly, debt is undesirable because it imposes an obligation, and it would appear that management would avoid debt financing wherever possible. But this is not necessarily true. Management will sometimes try to increase the rate of return on the owners' equity by using resources furnished by outsiders. If borrowed assets can be put to work to earn a return in excess of the interest cost, the owners will benefit. Suppose that $100,000 can be borrowed at 8 percent and put to work to earn 16 percent. The owners receive an $8,000 return without any investment on their part. Using borrowed assets to enhance the return to the owners is spoken of as *leverage* or as *trading on the equity*.

Leverage is frequently employed by finance companies, savings and loan institutions, and by public utilities. The finance company, for example, may lend money at 8 percent interest. Without a fresh source of funds, a finance company would have to wait until payments were made on the loans before it could make additional loans. Instead of doing this, the company will borrow money at, perhaps, 6 percent interest and pledge loans as security. The money obtained at 6 percent interest cost will be loaned at 8 percent with the owners of the finance company receiving the advantage of the interest differential.

The effect of leverage is illustrated by the following example. The Bay Company and the Weller Company each possesses assets in the total amount of $1,000,000. Each company has current liabilities of $100,000. The Bay Company has no long-term debt and has an owners' equity of $900,000. The Weller Company, on the other hand, has $400,000 of 6 percent bonds payable and an owners' equity of $500,000. Summary balance sheets as of December 31, 1972, for each company are as follows:

Bay Company
Summary Balance Sheet
December 31, 1972

Total assets	$1,000,000
Equities:	
Current liabilities	$ 100,000
Owners' equity	900,000
Total equities	$1,000,000

Weller Company
Summary Balance Sheet
December 31, 1972

Total assets	$1,000,000
Equities:	
Current liabilities	$ 100,000
Bonds payable, 6%	400,000
Owners' equity	500,000
Total equities	$1,000,000

Each company earns net income before interest and income taxes of $150,000, or, in other words, earns a 15 percent return on the assets before interest and income taxes.

The Bay Company only obtains the leverage benefit from the current liabilities of $100,000. All other assets have been furnished by the owners.

With an income tax rate of 40 percent, the Bay Company earns a net income after income taxes of $90,000 as computed below:

	Bay Company
Net income before income taxes	$ 150,000
Income taxes, 40%	60,000
Net income after income taxes	$ 90,000
Total assets	$1,000,000
Owners' equity	$ 900,000
Rate of return on total assets (90,000/1,000,000)	9%
Rate of return on owners' equity (90,000/900,000)	10%

The owners have furnished almost all of the assets employed, and the rate of return on the owners' equity is only slightly higher than the rate of return on the total assets. The leverage from the current liabilities accounts for this differential. The owners receive a 10 percent yield on their investment, and the rate of return on the total assets is 9 percent.

The Weller Company, however, pays 6 percent for $400,000 that it has borrowed. The $400,000 is employed to earn more than 6 percent, and the owners receive not only the earnings on their own invested capital but also the benefit of the difference between the amount earned on the $400,000 borrowed and the interest cost to the bondholders. Of course, like the Bay Company, it obtains the use of $100,000 furnished by the current creditors at no interest cost. A summary income statement is given below:

	Weller Company
Net income before interest and income taxes	$ 150,000
Interest (6% of $400,000)	24,000
Net income before income taxes	$ 126,000
Income taxes, 40%	50,400
Net income after income taxes	$ 75,600
Total assets	$1,000,000
Owners' equity	$ 500,000
Rate of return on total assets (75,600/1,000,000)	7.56%
Rate of return on owners' equity (75,600/500,000)	15.12%

The Weller Company earns a lower rate of return after interest and income taxes than the Bay Company because of the interest on the bonds. But the rate of return to the owners is much higher. The owners' investment is $400,000 less than in Bay Company, and the resources obtained from the bond issue earn more than the interest cost as shown on the next page.

Earnings on $400,000 furnished by the bond-
holders:

Net income before interest and income taxes (15% of $400,000)		$60,000
Less: Income taxes, 40%		24,000
Net income before interest, *after* income taxes ..		$36,000
Cost of $400,000 furnished by the bondholders: Interest (6% of $400,000)	$24,000	
Less: Income taxes, 40%	9,600	
Interest after income taxes		14,400
Net return for the owners		$21,600

The rate of return on the owners' equity is, of course, higher. The investment base is lower, and the proceeds from the sale of the bonds earn more than the interest cost.

Without Bond Leverage

$$\frac{\$90,000 \text{ return}}{\$900,000 \text{ owners' investment}} = 10\% \text{ rate of return on the owners' investment}$$

With Bond Leverage

$$\frac{\$75,600 \text{ return}}{\$500,000 \text{ owners' investment}} = 15.12\% \text{ rate of return on the owners' investment}$$

Although there are advantages in leverage, there are also disadvantages. With leverage there is greater risk. Possibly the borrowed assets will not even earn the interest cost or may earn so little that the additional expected return is not worth the risk.

Using the same example as before, assume that each company earns only $40,000 before interest and income taxes—a very small net income in relation to the total amount invested. The results are as follows:

	Bay Company	Weller Company
Net income before interest and income taxes	$ 40,000	$ 40,000
Interest, 6% of $400,000	—	24,000
Net income before income taxes	$ 40,000	$ 16,000
Income taxes, 40%	16,000	6,400
Net income after income taxes	$ 24,000	$ 9,600
Total assets	$1,000,000	$1,000,000
Owners' equity	$ 900,000	$ 500,000

	Bay Company	Weller Company
Rate of return on total assets:		
(24,000/1,000,000)	2.4%	
(9,600/1,000,000)		.96%
Rate of return on owners' equity:		
(24,000/900,000)	2.7%	
(9,600/500,000)		1.92%

Neither company earned a satisfactory rate of return for the owners, but the Weller Company was in a worse position because of its debt commitment. When conditions are unfavorable, the owners of the leveraged company will not benefit from debt. In extreme cases, the company may not be able to meet its obligations, and the owners may find that creditors have taken over the company.

EARNINGS AND MARKET VALUE OF STOCK

The rate of return as computed on the owners' equity depends upon the earnings in relation to the total investment and the ways in which the total investment is financed. This rate of return as computed from data appearing on past financial statements may not necessarily be in agreement with the rate of return used by investors to determine the market price of the stock.

The market price of a stock depends upon many factors; one of the most important is anticipated future earnings. The market price of a stock should be approximately equal to the present value of the expected future earnings per share. The rate used to discount the future earnings is the rate desired by investors as determined by market conditions and conditions within the industry and within the company itself. Past earnings may serve as a guide as to what may be expected in the future, but the value of a stock depends upon future earnings rather than earnings in the past.

The net income for any one year may be stated on a unit basis as the earnings per share of outstanding stock. For example, a company with 1,000,000 shares of capital stock outstanding may report a net income after income taxes for the year of $2,500,000. Assuming that there is no dividend requirement on preferred stock, the earnings per share are $2.50 ($2,500,000 net income/1,000,000 shares outstanding).

Some of the complexities related to the computation of the earnings per share were discussed in Chapter 3. In an attempt to improve the reporting to investors, the American Institute of Certified Public Accountants has made a study of the problem; and recommendations have been made in Accounting Principles Board Opinion Number 15.

Price earnings ratio. A ratio between the price of the stock on the market and the earnings per share is often computed and referred to as the price earnings ratio. A stock selling for $25 a share with earnings of $2.50 a share has a price earnings ratio of 10.

$$\frac{\text{Price of stock}}{\text{Earnings per share}} \quad \frac{\$25}{\$2.50} = 10 \text{ price earnings ratio}$$

This rule of thumb measurement is quite popular in the investment market, serving as a general guideline in the evaluation of stock prices.

Companies with a steady record of earnings over the years but with little prospects for growth tend to sell at lower price earnings ratios than stocks with growth potential. Assume that the company in the example has reported earnings of approximately $2,500,000 each year and pays all of the earnings to the stockholders in dividends. With a price of $25 a share, the market expects a 10 percent return on the investment.

Market rate of return on the investment:

$$10\% = \frac{\$\ 2.50 \text{ earnings per share.}}{\$25.00 \text{ market price per share.}}$$

The market rate of return on the investment is the reciprocal of the price earnings ratio.

Future expected earnings may also be capitalized to establish an approximate value of the company in the market. Capitalized earnings are future expected earnings frozen into the form of an asset—an asset representing the value of the company to the owners. The capitalized earnings are the estimated annual earnings, divided by the market rate of return. In the example given, the capitalized earnings or the value of the owners' interest is $25,000,000.

$$\frac{\$2.50 \text{ earnings per share} \times 1,000,000 \text{ shares}}{.10 \text{ market rate of return on investment}} = \$25,000,000 \text{ capitalized earnings.}$$

Companies with prospects for growth will generally sell at higher price earnings multiples. For example, a stock earning $2.50 a share may sell for $50 or be selling at a price earnings ratio of 20. Whether or not this price earnings ratio of 20 is justified depends upon future events. If the earnings are reinvested and not paid out in dividends, it may be possible to increase the earnings in subsequent years. Next year the earnings may be $3.75 a share, and if the market expects the rate of growth to continue the stock may sell at 20 times earnings or at $75 per share. The original purchaser who paid $50 for the stock can sell his stock for $75 and realize a gain on the sale.

Book value and market value. The price of a stock is sensitive to the prospects for future earnings, and investors establish the price on the basis of their estimates of the future and the rate of return that they expect on investments. The rate of return in the market may be considerably different than the rate of return computed from data appearing on the financial statements. This difference can be readily understood when it is recognized that the owners' equity on the balance sheet has resulted from past investments by the owners and reinvested past earnings. The market rate of return, on the other hand, is not determined as a relationship between the net earnings of the past year and the owners' equity as it appears in the accounting records. Rather, it is a relationship between expected future earnings and the market value of the stock.

Sometimes a book value per share of stock is computed. The book value per share of stock is equal to the owners' equity identified with that class of stock divided by the number of shares outstanding. Assume that a company with one class of stock outstanding has an owners' equity of $35,000,000 with 1,000,000 shares of stock outstanding. The book value per share is then $35.

$$\frac{\text{Owners' equity}}{\text{Number of shares outstanding}} \quad \frac{\$35,000,000}{1,000,000} = \$35 \text{ book value per share.}$$

The book value per share and the market price per share may differ widely, as would be expected, considering that the market price is determined by future anticipations while book value is determined by amounts recorded in the past. Normally the stock of a company with prospects for growth will sell for a price that is considerably higher than book value. On the other hand, a company in a declining industry may sell for a price that is even less than book value.

Earnings and dividends. Some of the differences among companies can be explained by the peculiarities of the industry in which the company operates and the various policies of management. Certain companies tend to have a stable pattern of earnings, and a large portion of the earnings may be paid out each year to the stockholders as dividends. Other companies may operate in cyclical industries with earnings fluctuating from year to year and dividends also varying from year to year. Still other companies may be in growth industries with earnings increasing over the years. Often the dividend payout in growth industries will be relatively modest with a large portion of the earnings being retained for further growth.

1. State the various ways in which a rate of return can be computed.

2. Should a rate of return be computed on the asset investment at the beginning of the year? at the end of the year?

3. What is asset turnover? What effect does a higher asset turnover tend to have on the rate of return on assets? Give a logical explanation for this effect on the rate of return on assets.

4. If the asset turnover cannot be increased, how can management improve the rate of return on assets?

5. In making a rate of return computation, what adjustments should be made to net income? to the asset investment?

6. How is the rate of return affected if plant assets are included net of depreciation?

7. When depreciation is deducted by the annuity method, operations are charged with both the cost of the asset and the interest that could be earned by an alternative investment of funds. If theoretical interest is charged to operations, it appears that the operating costs are overstated. Explain.

8. Explain why the rate of return on assets does not tend to increase because of reductions in the plant asset base when depreciation is deducted by the annuity method.

9. Garcia Foods, Inc., earns 3 percent on net sales. The rate of return on assets, however, amounts to 15 percent. Explain.

10. Explain how the rate of return for the owners can be increased by borrowing resources from outsiders.

11. Are there circumstances in which debt financing can be disadvantageous? Explain.

12. Does the market price of a stock depend upon past earnings? Explain.

13. What is the price earnings ratio?

14. Explain how future expected earnings can be capitalized to establish a value for a company.

15. Is the market value of a stock the same as the book value? Explain.

Exercises

1. In the situations outlined below, compute the rate of return on net sales, the rate of return on assets, the asset turnover, or the net sales as requested.

(1) Net income is equal to 30 percent of net sales, and the net sales are equal to 40 percent of the assets. What is the rate of return on assets?

(2) Net income is 5 percent of net sales. What asset turnover is required to earn 20 percent on the assets?

(3) With an asset turnover of 3.2, what must the rate of return be on net sales if the rate of return on the assets is to be 16 percent?

(4) Assets are turned over 1.4 times in earning 7 percent on net sales. What is the rate of return on the assets?

(5) If the total costs of operation excluding income taxes amount to $1,520,000 for the year, what must net sales be if the net income after income taxes is 12 percent of net sales? Assume a 50 percent income tax rate.

(6) Net sales amount to $8,800,000. Average assets used in operations amount to $13,200,000. If the cost of goods sold and operating expenses including income taxes amount to $7,040,000, what is the rate of return on net sales? On assets?

(7) If the rate of return on the net sales decreases from 15 percent to 8 percent, what must the asset turnover be to maintain a rate of return of 20 percent on the assets?

(8) The rate of return on assets decreased from 20 percent to 15 percent, although net income remained at 6 percent of net sales. Compute the decrease in the asset turnover.

2. Debut Arts Company is planning its operations for 1973. Materials and labor costs for the year are estimated at $320,000. All other operating costs are estimated at $66,000. Customers are billed for 140 percent of materials and labor costs. The income taxes are estimated at 50 percent of net income before taxes. On January 1, 1973, total assets amount to $540,000. At December 31, 1973, it is estimated that the total assets will be $560,000.

Required: (1) Compute the estimated rate of return on sales.
(2) Compute the expected asset turnover. (Use average assets.)
(3) Compute the estimated rate of return on average total assets.

3. Old Home Products Company purchased equipment costing $149,220 on January 1, 1972. The equipment was estimated to have a useful life of three years with a nominal salvage value at the end of three years. Aside from the equipment, the company had other assets of $100,000 on January 1, 1972. At the beginning of 1973 the other assets amounted to $200,000, and at the beginning of 1974 they amounted to $300,000. Revenues and expenses other than depreciation for 1972, 1973, and 1974 were as follows:

	Revenues	Expenses Other Than Depreciation
1972	$350,000	$280,000
1973	370,000	290,000
1974	430,000	340,000

Required: What rate of return was earned each year on assets held at the beginning of the year? Compute the rate of return on net assets using the annuity method of depreciation. Make the same calculations using straight-line depreciation. (Use a 10 percent rate for annuity depreciation.)

4. Roy Mansfield has invested $200,000 in a franchise for the distribution of food products in industrial plants located in Virginia and North Carolina. The company granting the franchise has loaned him an additional $400,000 at an interest cost of 6 percent per year. He has obtained another $600,000 from his bank at an interest cost of 7 percent per year. According to estimates made, the net income before deducting interest and income taxes should amount to $280,000 in the first year of operation. Income taxes are estimated at 50 percent of net income before income taxes.

Required: (1) Compute the rate of return on assets invested at the beginning of the year. Deduct interest and income taxes.

(2) Compute the rate of return on the owner's initial investment.

5. In 1972, Janis Tools, Inc., earned $1,470,000 after income taxes on an average investment in assets of $9,200,000. At the beginning of 1973, the company plans to borrow $3,000,000 to finance plant expansion. Interest of 7 percent must be paid on the loan, and the interest is deductible in computing income taxes. The average investment in assets during 1973 is estimated at $14,000,000, and the company expects to earn the same rate of return after income taxes that was earned in 1972 on the average investment in assets. However, no provision has been made for the interest on the debt to be incurred at the beginning of 1973. The average owners' equity in 1973 is estimated at $10,000,000. Income taxes are estimated at 40 percent of net income before taxes.

Required: (1) Compute the estimated net income after taxes in 1973. Interest is to be deducted.

(2) Compute the estimated rate of return after interest and income taxes on the average owners' equity in 1973.

(3) Compute the estimated rate of return after interest and income taxes on the average total investment in 1973.

(4) Explain why the rate of return on the average owners' equity is greater than the rate of return on the average investment in assets.

6. Thomas Reid is the principal stockholder in Barton and Reid, Inc. Another company has been interested in buying the stock of his company. Mr. Reid, in attempting to set a value for the company, believes that the earnings should be capitalized at 5 percent. The officers of the purchasing company disagree and believe that a 10 percent rate is more appropriate. The earnings per share last year of $3.40 are accepted by both parties as being realistic. The owners' equity at June 30, 1972, amounted to $7,560,000, and there were 180,000 shares of stock outstanding.

Required: (1) Compute the book value per share at June 30, 1972.

(2) Compute the value of the company as determined both by Mr. Reid and by the purchasing company.

(3) Explain why the value of a company as determined by capitalized earnings may differ from the book value of the stock.

Problems

5–1. Thebes Supply Company, Inc., is an old established company in a declining industry. In recent years almost all of the net earnings have been paid out in dividends or applied to the retirement of preferred stock. The annual report shows that the rate of return on assets has increased during the past few years.

Data used in making the rate of return computations are given at the top of the next page.

	Fiscal Years		
	1973	1972	1971
Current assets	$1,000,000	$1,000,000	$1,000,000
Plant assets, net	400,000	700,000	1,000,000
Total assets	$1,400,000	$1,700,000	$2,000,000
Net sales	$2,500,000	$2,800,000	$3,000,000
Net income	$ 200,000	$ 220,000	$ 240,000

Gross plant assets have remained constant at $2,000,000 over the three years.

Required: (1) Explain the increase in rate of return on assets in light of the decreased sales and net income.

(2) Calculate a rate of return on assets with all assets being shown at gross amounts. (Do not average assets.)

5–2. Summarized financial data for DeAngelis Instruments, Inc., at June 30, 1971, follow:

Total assets	$27,300,000
Total liabilities	10,000,000
Net income for the fiscal year ended June 30, 1971	2,320,000
Number of shares of common stock outstanding	1,000,000

At the beginning of July, 1971, a product line that proved to be unprofitable was dropped. Assets used to support this product line having a net book value of $3,600,000 were sold for $400,000. The loss can be deducted in computing income taxes.

A new product line has been added to replace the old line. It is estimated that the average asset investment to support this line will amount to $2,200,000. Bank credit of $1,500,000 at 6 percent interest per year will finance a large part of the cost. The new product line is expected to contribute $520,000 to net earnings before interest and income taxes during the fiscal year that will end June 30, 1972. Sales are estimated at $3,600,000.

Income taxes are at the rate of 50 percent of net income before income taxes.

During the fiscal year ended June 30, 1972, the company estimates that the net income after income taxes without including the new product line will amount to $2,730,000 on net sales of $28,500,000. The liabilities, not including the liability for the new product line, will remain at $10,000,000.

Required: (1) Compare the estimated rate of return on sales, the asset turnover, and the rate of return on the asset investment for the new product line with the estimated results without the new product line. (Use assets at June 30, 1972.)

(2) Compute the estimated rate of return on sales, the asset turnover, and the rate of return on the asset investment for the total operation for the fiscal year ended June 30, 1972. (Use assets at the end of the year.)

(3) Compute the estimated net income per share for the fiscal year ended June 30, 1972.

(4) Compute the percentage of increase or decrease in net income per share expected for the fiscal year ended June 30, 1972.

5–3. Kramer and Detweiler, Inc., manufacture various medical instruments and supplies. Mr. Kramer, the president of the company, obtained his experience with a large company engaged in this line of business before he left to establish his own company.

In 1971 the company earned $402,000 after income taxes. A summary of operating results follows:

Revenues	$4,170,000
Cost of goods sold and other operating expenses	3,320,000
Net operating income	$ 850,000
Interest expense	180,000
Net income before income taxes	$ 670,000
Income taxes—40%	268,000
Net income after income taxes	$ 402,000

The equity section of the balance sheet at the end of 1971 follows:

Accounts payable and other non-interest bearing liabilities	$ 500,000
Notes payable—6% interest	3,000,000
Owners' equity	1,500,000
Total equities	$5,000,000

At the beginning of 1972 Mr. Kramer arranged for the company to borrow $1,500,000 at 7 percent interest. An additional $500,000 was obtained by the issuance of capital stock. With the proceeds received, the company introduced a new product line.

Results for 1972 were disappointing. The new product line did not produce the expected sales, and increased competition cut into the sales of other product lines. The company reported a net income before interest and income taxes in 1972 of $370,000. Income taxes are at the rate of 40 percent of net income before income taxes.

Required: (1) Compute the rate of return on the total assets at the end of 1971, and on the owners' equity at the end of 1971.

(2) Compute the rate of return on the total assets at the end of 1972, and on the owners' equity at the end of 1972. (Assume that total assets in 1972 increased by the amount of the net income for the year as well as the amounts obtained from borrowing and issuing stock.)

(3) What should the net income after taxes have been in 1972 to earn the same rate of return on the owners' equity that was earned in 1971?

5–4. A summary statement of financial position for Umber Products Company, Inc., as of September 30, 1972, appears below:

Current assets	$1,840,000
Investments	780,000
Plant assets, net of depreciation	1,520,000
Total assets	$4,140,000
Current liabilities	$ 830,000
Long-term debt	1,000,000
Owners' equity	2,310,000
Total equities	$4,140,000

During the fiscal year, it has been estimated that 100,000 product units having a unit selling price of $62 can be sold. The cost of goods sold should amount to 60 percent of sales revenue, and expenses of operation should be $960,000. Income taxes have been estimated at 50 percent of net income before taxes.

According to the plans for the next fiscal year, the total equities should be $600,000 higher than they are at the present time with the owners' equity being $400,000 higher.

The sales manager believes that the price of the product can be increased by 10 percent next year with no adverse effect on sales volume. Demand for the product is relatively inelastic, and conditions in the industry are such that a price increase would have little or no effect at this time. Half of the increased profits resulting from the price increase will be retained by the owners in the form of increased assets with the other half being distributed as dividends.

Required: (1) Calculate the rate of return on sales, the asset turnover, the rate of return on total assets, and the rate of return on the owners' equity under the original budget estimate. (Average the data at the beginning of the fiscal year with the estimates for the end of the fiscal year.)

(2) Make the same calculations assuming that the selling price is increased by 10 percent with no change in the budgeted costs.

5–5. Yeager Cabinet Company, Inc., has been successful in reducing operating costs while building up sales volume and revenue. However, the president of the company is disappointed to find that the rate of return on the sales dollar is still less than 5 percent.

Summary financial statements for 1972 follow:

Yeager Cabinet Company, Inc.
Income Statement
For the Year Ended December 31, 1972

Net sales	$230,000,000
Cost of good sold and expense	220,000,000
Net income	$ 10,000,000

Yeager Cabinet Company, Inc.
Balance Sheet
December 31, 1972

Current assets	$108,000,000
Plant assets	42,000,000
Total assets	$150,000,000
Current liabilities	$ 70,000,000
Owners' equity	80,000,000
Total equities	$150,000,000

The president of Yeager Cabinet Company, Inc., has received a copy of the annual report of Mountain Gas and Electric Company and has observed that this company had revenues that were equal to half of the revenues of his company but had twice as much net income. Although he recognized that the two companies are faced with different problems, he could not help but be impressed with the relatively large percentage of net income to net sales revenue earned by the gas and electric company.

Summary financial statments taken from the 1972 annual report of Mountain Gas and Electric Company follow:

Mountain Gas and Electric Company
Income Statement
For the Year Ended December 31, 1972

Revenues	$ 90,000,000
Direct cost of operations and other expenses	75,000,000
Net income	$ 15,000,000

Mountain Gas and Electric Company
Balance Sheet
December 31, 1972

Plant assets	$245,000,000
Current assets	55,000,000
Total assets	$300,000,000
Owners' equity	$100,000,000
Long-term debt	170,000,000
Current liabilities	30,000,000
Total equities	$300,000,000

Required: (1) Compare the two companies by computing the following percentages and ratios:

(a) Net income to sales revenue.
(b) Net income as a percentage of total assets.
(c) Net income as a percentage of owners' equity.
(d) Asset turnover.

(2) Which company earns a better rate of return for the owners? Point out factors that help to enhance the rate of return for the owners.

5–6. Two companies in a growing industry are being investigated by Frank Auretto as potential investment candidates. Mr. Auretto has a summary of data on the two companies for 1970 to 1973, inclusive, as follows:

Albertus Magnetics, Inc.

	Net Income	Interest Charges After Taxes	Total Assets	Total Owners' Equity
1973	$1,240,000	$ 6,000	$6,505,000	$4,490,000
1972	680,000	2,000	5,400,000	3,250,000
1971	730,000	5,000	4,871,000	2,570,000
1970	514,000	6,000	4,293,000	1,840,000

Hume Electroproducts, Inc.

	Net Income	Interest Charges After Taxes	Total Assets	Total Owners' Equity
1973	$ 797,000	$62,000	$7,513,000	$4,700,000
1972	762,000	58,000	7,217,000	4,283,000
1971	724,000	57,000	6,742,000	3,764,000
1970	608,000	55,000	6,035,000	3,326,000

Balance sheets in summary form are given below for the two companies at the end of 1973 and 1972. The income statements for the intervening year are given at the top of the next page.

Albertus Magnetics, Inc.
Balance Sheets (Summary)
December 31
(In Thousands of Dollars)

Assets	1973	1972
Current assets	$3,842	$3,160
Plant and equipment, net of depreciation	2,663	2,240
Total assets	$6,505	$5,400

Equities		
Current liabilities	$2,015	$2,150
Capital stock	1,600	1,600
Retained earnings	2,890	1,650
Total equities	$6,505	$5,400

Hume Electroproducts, Inc.
Balance Sheets (Summary)
December 31
(In Thousands of Dollars)

Assets	1973	1972
Current assets	$3,480	$3,399
Investment in stock of Byers, Inc.	1,772	1,772
Plant and equipment, net of depreciation	2,261	2,046
Total assets	$7,513	$7,217

Equities		
Current liabilities	$1,062	$1,183
Promissory notes, due 6/1/80	1,751	1,751
Capital stock	630	630
Retained earnings	4,070	3,653
Total equities	$7,513	$7,217

Required: Mr. Auretto has asked you to compute some percentages and relationships from the financial data presented.

(1) Compute the percentage of net operating income after income taxes to sales for each company for 1973.

Income Statements
For the Year Ended December 31, 1973
(In Thousands of Dollars)

	Albertus Magnetics, Inc.	Hume Electroproducts, Inc.
Sales	$6,342	$7,306
Cost of goods sold	$3,827	$4,055
Operating expenses	1,306	1,658
Income taxes	817	672
* Interest expense	12	124
Gain on sale of equipment (tax on the gain is included in income taxes at $215,000)	860	—
Net income	$1,240	$ 797

* The reduction in income taxes resulting from interest amounts to 50 percent of the interest expense.

(2) Compute the asset turnover for each company for 1973. Use average assets.

(3) Determine the percentage of net operating income after income taxes to average total assets for both companies for 1971, 1972, and 1973.

(4) Determine the percentage of net operating income after income taxes to average owners' equity for both companies for 1971, 1972, and 1973.

(5) Which company earns the larger rate of return on owners' equity? Which of the companies makes the greater use of leverage?

5–7. The president of Conway Metals, Inc., has been looking at various candidates for acquisition and at the present time is interested in Norbert Products Company.

Norbert Products Company obtained plant assets costing $4,000,000 on January 1, 1969. These assets were estimated to have a useful life of five years with a negligible salvage value at the end of five years. Depreciation has been deducted by the straight-line method.

Data with respect to the assets of Norbert Products Company are given below:

Investment in Assets

	Gross Plant Assets	Accumulated Deprecia- tion	Net Plant Assets	Other Assets	Total Assets
Jan. 1, 1969 ..	$4,000,000	—0—	$4,000,000	$3,800,000	$7,800,000
Dec. 31, 1969 .	4,000,000	$ 800,000	3,200,000	4,500,000	7,700,000
Dec. 31, 1970 .	4,000,000	1,600,000	2,400,000	5,100,000	7,500,000
Dec. 31, 1971 .	4,000,000	2,400,000	1,600,000	6,000,000	7,600,000
Dec. 31, 1972 .	4,000,000	3,200,000	800,000	7,000,000	7,800,000
Dec. 31, 1973 .	4,000,000	4,000,000	—0—	8,000,000	8,000,000

Summarized income statements for five years follow:

Summary Income Statements

	1973	1972	1971	1970	1969
Net sales	$8,400,000	$8,200,000	$7,900,000	$7,600,000	$7,300,000
Cost of goods sold and operating expenses, excluding depreciation .	$6,750,000	$6,580,000	$6,300,000	$6,010,000	$5,740,000
Depreciation	800,000	800,000	800,000	800,000	800,000
Total expenses	$7,550,000	$7,380,000	$7,100,000	$6,810,000	$6,540,000
Net income after income taxes ...	$ 850,000	$ 820,000	$ 800,000	$ 790,000	$ 760,000
Rate of return on the assets at the beginning of the year	10.9%	10.8%	10.7%	10.3%	9.7%

Required: (1) Compute the rate of return on the assets for each of the five years with depreciation deducted by the annuity method. Use a 10 percent rate for annuity depreciation and compute the rate of return on the assets at the beginning of each year. (Round computations to the nearest dollar.)

(2) Compare the rates of return computed in (1) with the rates of return computed by the company.

5–8. Oleander and Glass, Inc., has drawn up plans for the investment of $10,000,000 in an expansion program. Three alternatives are being considered to finance the expansion.

(1) Borrow the entire $10,000,000 on long-term notes bearing interest at 8 percent.

(2) Issue 200,000 shares of stock at $50 per share.

(3) Pay $2,000,000 immediately, obtain $4,000,000 on long-term notes bearing interest at 6 percent, and obtain the balance of the $10,000,000 required by the issuance of 80,000 shares of stock at $50 per share.

In 1972 the company earned a net income after income taxes of $1,620,000 and distributed dividends of $2.00 per share. It is estimated that the net income before interest and income taxes will amount to $3,800,000 in 1973 if the plant is expanded. Income taxes are estimated at 50 percent of net income before income taxes. All interest accrued within the year will be paid during the year, and current liabilities at December 31, 1973, will be approximately equal to the current liabilities at December 31, 1972.

A balance sheet for Oleander and Glass, Inc., at December 31, 1972, is given at the top of the following page.

Required: (1) Assuming that the investment is made at January 1, 1973, compute the rate of return on total assets and on the owners' equity at December 31, 1973, under each of the proposals. (Assume no dividend distributions and do not average assets or owners' equity.)

(2) What would the earnings per share amount to under each of the proposals?

Oleander and Glass, Inc.
Balance Sheet
December 31, 1972

Assets

Current assets:

Cash	$1,768,400	
United States Treasury bills	2,870,500	
Accounts receivable, net	1,830,600	
Inventory	3,170,700	
Total current assets		$ 9,640,200

Plant assets:

Land	$ 144,000	
Building and equipment, net of depreciation	4,215,800	4,359,800
Goodwill		1,500,000
Total assets		$15,500,000

Equities

Current liabilities:

Accounts payable	$1,318,600	
Wages and salaries payable	176,800	
Estimated income taxes payable	542,000	
Other current operating costs payable	137,700	
Total current liabilities		$ 2,175,100

Owners' equity:

Capital stock, $10 par value	$5,000,000	
Premium on stock	4,500,000	
Retained earnings	3,824,900	
Total owners' equity		13,324,900
Total equities		$15,500,000

5–9. Income statements and balance sheets are given for two competing companies for 1972.

Income Statements
For the Year Ended December 31, 1972

	Phillips, Inc.	Crater Company
Net sales	$5,000,000	$5,000,000
Cost of goods sold	2,700,000	2,900,000
Gross margin	$2,300,000	$2,100,000
Operating expenses	1,080,000	1,240,000
Net operating income	$1,220,000	$ 860,000
Interest expense	—	80,000
Net income before income taxes	$1,220,000	$ 780,000
Income taxes	610,000	390,000
Net income after income taxes	$ 610,000	$ 390,000

Balance Sheets
December 31, 1972

Assets	Phillips, Inc.	Crater Company
Current assets:		
Cash	$ 530,000	$ 580,000
Accounts receivable, net	880,000	860,000
Inventory	730,000	540,000
Total current assets	$2,140,000	$1,980,000
Property and equipment	$1,960,000	$2,350,000
Less: Accumulated depreciation	630,000	190,000
Net plant assets	$1,330,000	$2,160,000
Total assets	$3,470,000	$4,140,000
Equities		
Current and long-term debt	$ 810,000	$2,170,000
Owners' equity	2,660,000	1,970,000
Total equities	$3,470,000	$4,140,000

The two companies handle the same line of product and had the same sales volume, prices, and costs of products in 1972.

Phillips, Inc., accounts for its inventory costs on the first-in, first-out basis, while Crater Company uses the last-in, first-out method. Only one product is handled by both companies. Neither company had any units in inventory at the beginning of the year.

Both companies purchase the product from one manufacturer who in each case shares the cost of product service warranties with the dealers on the same basis. It is estimated that the average service cost to the dealer amounts to about 2 percent of net sales each year. Crater Company has included expense on this basis in its operating expenses. Phillips, Inc., on the other hand, recognizes the expense only when service is given to the customers. During 1972, it recorded product service expenses of $78,000.

Phillips, Inc., has used its building and equipment for several years and has recorded depreciation expense of $50,000 in 1972. Crater Company recently acquired its plant assets and has taken depreciation of $90,000 in 1972.

Required: (1) Compute the following percentages for each company:

(a) Net income to net sales.
(b) Net income to total assets.
(c) Net income to owners' equity.

(2) Point out factors that would cause the percentages to differ as between the two companies.

Chapter 8

FINANCIAL STATEMENT ANALYSIS—STATEMENT RELATIONSHIPS

Much can be learned about a business from a careful examination of its financial statements. Some of the significant facts and important relationships may be overlooked, however, if the statements are not properly interpreted and analyzed. Statement analysis, as the term would seem to imply, is not entirely a probing for more detail behind the account classifications. Instead, it may be better described as being a process of synthesis and summarization, and a study of relationships. For example, large dollar amounts may be expressed in percentages, and several items under one classification may be combined. Data from both the income statement and the balance sheet will be brought together in the form of ratios to reveal important relationships. In short, statement analysis calls attention to the significant relationships that would otherwise be buried in a maze of detail.

THE IMPORTANCE OF STATEMENT ANALYSIS

Anyone who is interested in a particular company will want answers to the following questions:

(1) Does the company earn adequate profits?
(2) Can the company meet its obligations promptly? In other words, does it have sufficient liquidity?
(3) Is an investment in the company a safe investment?

Exact answers cannot be given to these questions; the answers depend upon what will happen in an uncertain future. But statement analysis can reveal what has taken place in the past and will give some indication of what can be expected.

Stockholders, creditors, employees, prospective investors, and the public at large judge a company, in part at least, by financial measurements that are revealed through statement analysis. Business management recognizing that the statements are a report on the company and on their managerial skill will see in statement analysis a means for self-evaluation. Knowledge derived from analysis can be combined with other information in planning and controlling various aspects of the business. The expected rate of return on the sales dollar and on the assets, for example, can be applied in pricing and in controlling costs. A guide to the adequacy of the inventory level is furnished by relating inventories to cost of goods sold. Credit and collection policy can be evaluated in general by referring to the accounts receivable turnover. And there are many other policies that will be influenced to some extent by what the ratios reveal.

THE ELEMENT OF RISK

It will not be possible to predict the future performance of a company and its future financial position with complete certainty. There are too many variable factors that cannot be controlled or cannot be estimated precisely. Conditions in the world economy, technological change, and other factors increase the element of uncertainty or risk.

The element of risk as it pertains to any particular industry, however, may be relatively high or low. There is more risk, for example, if a company operates in a cyclical industry. Manufacturers of heavy equipment used in construction will generally perform better in an expansion phase of the business cycle. In contrast, a business that furnishes perishable staples required for everyday living will not be affected as much by changes in the business cycle.

A record of fluctuating profits from year to year is a sign of greater risk. Two companies may report the same profits in a given year. However, if one company has a steady record of earnings over the years with increases in line with the general growth of the economy while the other company has high profits in some years and low profits or even losses in others, there is a difference in risk. The more volatile performer is in a less certain position. It is not as easy to predict what is likely to happen to this company in the future. It is too erratic.

The equity structure also reveals risk. A large proportion of debt places a burden upon the company. Interest must be paid on the debt and the debt must be retired on schedule. As pointed out earlier, obligations to make fixed payments in addition to interest must also be considered. No rule can be given that will fit every company in deciding upon a safe proportion of debt. In general, a company that operates in a cyclical industry should have a smaller proportion of debt in its equity structure. Profits are too uncertain, and there is a greater risk that the company will be unable to meet its obligations. On the other hand, an electric power company has a relatively stable market and can safely operate with a high proportion of debt.

INTERLOCKING DATA

On the surface it may appear that each financial statement stands alone. This is not true. The statements are very closely related. Everything fits into a pattern, with no one piece of financial information being isolated from the others. Financial statement analysis is valuable, if for no other reason, because it shows how financial data interlock in the fabric of an accounting system, thereby giving the reader a better understanding of business operations and the related financial effects.

The assets and the equities as they appear on the balance sheet can be tied in with the revenues and the expenses on the income statement. Any one item of financial data means little in itself. For example, to say that the net income for the year amounted to $500,000 is not enough. There are other questions that come to mind immediately. Does the net income appear to be adequate when compared with sales revenue? What does this net income represent in the way of a return on the total assets used in operations? What rate of return is being earned on the owners' equity? Can the sales be translated into cash within a short time? Is the company financially sound? All of these questions and many more are answered, at least in part, by an intelligent analysis of the financial statements.

COMPARABILITY

Like the data themselves, however, the ratios pertaining to any given year cannot stand alone. There should be a basis for comparison between years and between companies. Ordinarily, the statements and the ratios for the current year are presented along with the statements and the ratios for one or two preceding years so that the improvements or the deteriorations can be detected. A ratio for the most recent year in itself may appear to be satisfactory; but if it is found that even better results were obtained in the past, there is reason for concern. On the other hand, a favorable trend is encouraging even if present conditions are not all that they should be. Sometimes a pattern is revealed by comparison, and it may be possible to make a reasonable prediction of what can normally be expected in the future. On the other hand, there is more uncertainty and greater risk if no discernible pattern is evident or if there is significant variation with some years being favorable and other years being unfavorable.

Comparisons should be made not only with the company's own past performance but also with the average performance of the industry. Usually a business unit will tend to follow the trends of the industry or business group to which it belongs. The peculiarities and the limitations of a certain type of business are reflected in the statements and in the ratios. For example, a manufacturer of heavy equipment would be expected to have a larger proportionate investment in plant assets than a retailer or a manufacturer engaged in some other line of business. The investment in inventory in relation to sales, for example, would likely be high in an industry where long periods of time are required in processing inventories. In each case, the statement relationships have to be examined against the backdrop of the industry. If the ratio of net income to net sales is low, it does not necessarily mean that the company is not doing well. Conditions throughout the industry may be such that only a small margin can be made on the sales dollar. In fact, the business unit may be doing quite well considering the average for the industry.

Variations in accounting methods. It is difficult enough to compare different years for the same company, but it is more difficult to make a comparison between companies. Each company even within a given industry will be different from others because of variations in policies, practices, and accounting methods. Two companies of similar size may handle the same product lines and yet have entirely different items and amounts appearing on their financial statements. These differences are not necessarily an indication of the superiority of one company over the other. One company may be following a different accounting policy, or it may be using some equally acceptable but different accounting method.

Significant variations between companies are often caused by the methods used in matching costs against revenues. For example, one company may capitalize a cost and write it off against revenues in future years while another company will elect to write off a similar cost in the year that it is incurred. Under existing circumstances, each company may be following accepted accounting practice. But the financial statements for the two companies will be entirely different.

Company A, for example, elects to write off research and development costs during the year in which they are incurred. During the 3-year period the costs were as follows:

1971	$150,000
1972	400,000
1973	600,000

The income statements of Company A and Company B for 1971, 1972, and 1973 are presented in summary form at the top of the next page. Company B has exactly the same revenues and costs as Company A but amortizes the costs referred to above over a period of five years. On the balance sheets of Company A there would be no costs to be carried

	Company A		
	1973	*1972*	*1971*
Net revenues	$3,100,000	$2,400,000	$2,000,000
* Operating and other costs ...	2,300,000	2,100,000	1,850,000
Net income before income taxes	$ 800,000	$ 300,000	$ 150,000

* Including write-off of costs indicated above.

	Company B		
	1973	*1972*	*1971*
Net revenues	$3,100,000	$2,400,000	$2,000,000
Operating and other costs ...	1,930,000	1,810,000	1,730,000
Net income before income taxes	$1,170,000	$ 590,000	$ 270,000

forward, but on the balance sheets of Company B there would be costs still to be matched against future revenues.

Unamortized costs:	*1973*	*1972*	*1971*
Company A	—0—	—0—	—0—
Company B	$780,000	$410,000	$120,000

While both companies have the same net revenues and costs, there are wide differences in the net incomes reported each year and in the assets shown on the balance sheets. To some extent, at least, these differences are attributable to the choice of accounting method used.

Methods used in accounting for inventory costs and in the valuation of inventories are often responsible for significant variations between the statements of one company and those of another. One company may consistently value its inventory at cost regardless of fluctuations in market value, while another company may just as consistently follow the practice of valuing inventory at the lower of cost or market. If market values are below cost, the statements of the two companies will not be on a comparable basis. In Chapter 1 it was pointed out that inventory costs can be accounted for on a first-in, first-out (fifo) basis, a last-in, first-out (lifo) basis, an average cost basis, or some variation of these methods. The choice of the costing method will obviously affect the amounts to be reported on the statements.

Variations in estimates and changes in accounting methods. It is also possible to have different results when the same methods of accounting are employed but when estimates vary. For example, two companies may each purchase plant assets costing $250,000. One company estimates the residual salvage value at $50,000 and records depreciation over a 10-year period at $20,000 a year. The other company may decide that the residual salvage value should be $25,000 and that depreciation should be taken on a straight-line basis over eight years. There is a difference in the annual depreciation expense of $8,125 merely because of a difference in estimates.

Even statements for a series of years for one company will not be comparable if there have been changes in the methods of accountability. Aside from the problem of differences in the price level, there are other factors that make comparison difficult. For example, the company may have accounted for inventories in past years according to the fifo method; but in more recent years, inventories may be accounted for on a lifo basis. Estimates of depreciation and estimates of various costs to be matched against revenues may be revised over the years.

NEED FOR USE OF AVERAGES

Ratios can be affected by the timing of transactions. Before passing judgment as to whether a ratio is too high or too low, it is necessary to define a meaningful average. If the average is really not a "measure of central tendency," it should not be used in analysis. For example, it may appear that a company is earning only a 3 percent return if the net income for the year is $24,000 and the total assets amount to $800,000. Suppose, however, that the assets were increased by $560,000 by a large bank loan just before the end of the year. This means that $24,000 was earned on assets of $240,000 that were used throughout the entire year, and the rate of return was really 10 percent.

It is necessary to average data. In the example given above, the rate of return should have been calculated on the average assets employed during the year. As another example, a relationship between the outstanding balances due from customers and credit sales may show how rapidly collections are being made from customers. The amount shown for accounts receivable at the end of the year, however, may be abnormally high or low because of seasonality. The accounts receivable balances should perhaps be averaged for the year. Inventories, plant assets, accounts payable, and other classifications may also be averaged so that they can be properly used in ratio analysis. But averages are not always representative, and care must be exercised in the selection of an average amount.

A ratio can be changed drastically by only one transaction. The ratio of current assets to current liabilities, for example, can be improved merely by paying off some of the current debt. Near the end of the fiscal year the current assets and the current liabilities may appear in total as follows:

Current assets	$60,000
Current liabilities	40,000
Ratio of current assets to current liabilities	1.5 to 1

But if a $30,000 payment can be made on the current liabilities before the year closes, the ratio will increase, as follows:

Current assets	$30,000
Current liabilities	10,000
Ratio of current assets to current liabilities	3 to 1

SHORTCOMINGS OF FINANCIAL DATA

Financial statement analysis is further complicated by inherent weaknesses in the data themselves. In Chapter 4 it was pointed out that dollars do not have the same purchasing power at all times and that, as a result, financial statements may include a mixture of dollar valuations. Relationships can easily be distorted if dollars of current purchasing power are compared with dollars having some other purchasing power.

For the purposes of statement analysis, it may be necessary to adjust the data so that they can be used properly. For example, the current assets as reported on conventional financial statements may not be a good measure of current debt-paying ability. If marketable securities and inventories are reported at cost, the total current assets do not show what may be applied to the payment of current indebtedness. Perhaps, to measure debt-paying ability, the current assets should be converted to present market valuations.

While there are many limitations to statement analysis and many pitfalls to guard against, the problem is not so hopeless as it would appear. Statements can be placed upon a comparable basis by making conversions, and data can be chosen selectively according to how they are to be used. Furthermore, it must be remembered that the analysis is only intended to call attention to areas that require further investigation and that in itself it does not give final answers.

COMMON-SIZE STATEMENTS

The financial statements can be reduced to simpler terms by expressing the dollar amounts in even thousands of dollars or by reducing the dollar amounts to percentages. The relative importance of each classification or of each individual account in the total stands out when expressed as a percentage of the total. For example, on the income statement net sales are shown at 100 percent with each item of expense and the net income being shown as a percentage of net sales. On the balance sheet each individual asset classification is shown as a percentage of the total assets, and each individual equity classification is shown as a percentage of the total equities. Statements reduced in this way are called *common-size statements*. Often the percentages are given beside the actual dollar amounts on the statements.

Financial statements and common-size statements for Brewster Manufacturing Company are presented below and on pages 166 and 167.

The unconverted statements show that net sales have increased substantially since 1971 and that profits, the assets, and the owners' equity have also increased. But this is only part of the story. The statements alone do not indicate what effect the changes have on rate of return and safety of operations.

The common-size statements, however, go beyond the absolute dollar amounts to reveal percentage relationships. For example, in 1973 the net income was only 4.4 percent of net sales in contrast to 5.4 percent in 1971. The operating expenses have increased as a percent of net sales since 1971. The company earned a greater number of dollars in 1973, but the rate of return on the sales dollar was lower.

Brewster Manufacturing Company
Income Statements
For the Years Ended December 31

	1973	1972	1971
Net sales	$12,740,100	$8,920,600	$5,740,300
Cost of goods sold	9,080,600	6,140,300	4,180,700
Gross margin	$ 3,659,500	$2,780,300	$1,559,600
Operating expenses	2,407,300	1,608,100	942,200
Net operating income	$ 1,252,200	$1,172,200	$ 617,400
Interest expense	123,000	75,000	8,000
Net income before income taxes	$ 1,129,200	$1,097,200	$ 609,400
Provision for income taxes .	564,600	548,600	304,700
Net income after income taxes	$ 564,600	$ 548,600	$ 304,700
Depreciation included in cost of goods sold and operating expenses	$ 367,200	$ 232,100	$ 115,700

Brewster Manufacturing Company
Income Statements (Common Size)
For the Years Ended December 31

	1973	1972	1971
Net sales	100.0%	100.0%	100.0%
Cost of goods sold	71.3	68.8	72.8
Gross margin	28.7	31.2	27.2
Operating expenses	18.9	18.1	16.4
Net operating income	9.8	13.1	10.8
Interest expense	1.0	.8	.1
Net income before income taxes	8.8	12.3	10.7
Provision for income taxes	4.4	6.1	5.3
Net income after income taxes	4.4%	6.2%	5.4%

Brewster Manufacturing Company
Balance Sheets
December 31

	1973	1972	1971
Assets			
Current assets:			
Cash	$ 361,400	$ 673,100	$ 824,500
Accounts receivable, net of uncollectibles	2,835,300	1,730,800	985,700
Inventories:			
Raw materials	1,220,500	912,300	582,400
Finished goods	2,584,500	1,904,900	1,612,600
Prepaid expenses	28,700	39,300	42,100
Total current assets	$ 7,030,400	$5,260,400	$4,047,300
Plant assets, net of accumulated depreciation	5,930,100	3,880,300	2,370,900
Total assets	$12,960,500	$9,140,700	$6,418,200
Equities			
Current liabilities:			
Accounts payable	$ 2,409,600	$1,465,000	$ 973,100
Notes payable	100,000	50,000	—0—
Other current liabilities ..	2,680,300	1,169,700	287,700
Total current liabilities	$ 5,189,900	$2,684,700	$1,260,800
Long-term notes payable ...	2,000,000	1,000,000	—0—
Owners' equity:			
Capital stock, $10 par ...	500,000	500,000	500,000
Paid-in capital in excess of par value	3,500,000	3,500,000	3,500,000
Retained earnings	1,770,600	1,456,000	1,157,400
Total equities	$12,960,500	$9,140,700	$6,418,200

Brewster Manufacturing Company
Balance Sheets (Common Size)
December 31

	1973	1972	1971
Assets			
Current assets:			
Cash	2.8%	7.4%	12.8%
Accounts receivable, net of uncollectibles	21.9	18.9	15.4
Inventories:			
Raw materials ..:...........	9.4	10.0	9.1
Finished goods .:...........	19.9	20.8	25.1
Prepaid expenses	.2	.4	.7
Total current assets	54.2	57.5	63.1
Plant assets, net of accumulated depreciation	45.8	42.5	36.9
Total assets	100.0%	100.0%	100.0%

	1973	1972	1971
Equities			
Current liabilities:			
Accounts payable	18.6%	16.0%	15.2%
Notes payable	.8	.5	—0—
Other current liabilities	20.7	12.8	4.5
Total current liabilities	40.1	29.3	19.7
Long-term notes payable	15.4	10.9	—0—
Owners' equity:			
Capital stock, $10 par	3.9	5.5	7.8
Paid-in capital in excess of par value	27.0	38.4	54.5
Retained earnings	13.6	15.9	18.0
Total equities	100.0%	100.0%	100.0%

The common-size balance sheets show that accounts receivable and inventories have increased as a percentage of the total assets and that cash has decreased. In other words, the company was less liquid at the end of 1973 than it was at the end of 1971. Current liabilities were also larger in relation to the total equities at the end of 1973. Long-term debt was first incurred in 1972 and increased to a point where it was equal to over 15 percent of the total equity at the end of 1973. The stockholders' percentage of ownership has decreased steadily since 1971.

ANALYSIS OF TRENDS

A trend can be detected or a significant change from one year to another will stand out if percentages of increase or decrease are computed. The income statements for Brewster Manufacturing Company are now given on the following pages with the percentage of increase or decrease of each item over the base year, 1971, given beside the dollar amounts.

The trend percentages are helpful in that they call attention to large proportionate changes, but they can be misleading if used improperly. The percentages of increase computed on a small base may be large, but the dollar amount involved may be relatively insignificant. For example, on the statements for Brewster Manufacturing Company, an increase in interest expense from $8,000 to $75,000 appears as a 1,437 percent increase. The percentage of increase is tremendous, but the dollar increase is not large when compared with the dollar amounts shown. On the other hand, a dollar increase of almost two million dollars in cost of goods sold from 1971 to 1972 is shown as an increase of only about 47 percent. The percentage of change depends upon the size of the change in relation to the base. Percentages will tend to be smaller when measured from a large base.

A common base year should be used consistently in making the computations. Comparison is more difficult if base years are changed. For Brewster

	1973	1972	1971	Percentages Increase or (Decrease) 1973 over 1971	1972 over 1971
Net sales	$12,740,100	$8,920,600	$5,740,300	121.9%	55.4%
Cost of goods sold	9,080,600	6,140,300	4,180,700	117.2	46.9
Gross margin....	$ 3,659,500	$2,780,300	$1,559,600	134.6	78.3
Operating expenses	2,407,300	1,608,100	942,200	155.5	70.7
Net operating income	$ 1,252,200	$1,172,200	$ 617,400	102.8	89.9
Interest expense .	123,000	75,000	8,000	1,437.5	837.5
Net income before income taxes ..	$ 1,129,200	$1,097,200	$ 609,400	85.3	80.0
Provision for income taxes ..	564,600	548,600	304,700	85.3	80.0
Net income after income taxes ..	$ 564,600	$ 548,600	$ 304,700	80.0	80.0
Depreciation included in cost of goods sold and operating expenses	$ 367,200	$ 232,100	$ 115,700	217.4	100.6

Manufacturing Company, 1971 was used as the base year, and the results for 1972 and 1973 were both related to that year. Normally, the earliest year in a series is used as a base. A percentage of change can be computed only if there is a positive amount for the base year.

Common-size statements and trend percentages make it easier to sift significant information from the raw dollar data appearing on the statements. Analysis can be carried further with certain peculiarities being brought to attention. If the results of the analysis are unfavorable, perhaps some steps can be taken to improve the situation.

A REVIEW OF EARNING POWER

In the preceding chapter earning power and rates of return were discussed at length; in this chapter the various income statement relationships and rates of return are computed using data for Brewster Manufacturing Company. For purposes of illustration, it is assumed that the average amounts of the assets and the equities for the year are equivalent to the balances at the end of the year. It is also assumed that the dollar amounts are on the same price level basis and that they can be compared in other respects. Dividends of $5.00 a share, a total amount of $250,000, were declared and paid in each of the three years.

Earning Power Relationships

Percentages, Net Income, and Dividend per Share	1973	1972	1971
(1) Net income * to net sales .	4.4%	6.2%	5.4%
(2) Gross margin rate	28.7	31.2	27.2
(3) Percentage of operating expense to net sales	18.9	18.1	16.4
(4) Net income * to total assets	4.4	6.0	4.7
(5) Net income * to owners' equity	9.8	10.1	5.9
(6) Net income per share .... $	11.292 $	10.972 $	6.094
(7) Dividends per share	5.00	5.00	5.00
(8) Net income *	564,600	548,600	304,700
(9) Total assets	12,960,500	9,140,700	6,418,200
(10) Total owners' equity	5,770,600	5,456,000	5,157,400
(11) Number of shares of stock outstanding	50,000	50,000	50,000

* After income taxes.

Income statement relationships. In absolute terms, net sales and net income have increased in each of the three years, yet the percentage of net income to net sales has decreased. This means that the costs in total have been increasing at a faster rate than sales revenue. The net income to sales increased from 5.4 percent in 1971 to 6.2 percent in 1972 and then declined to 4.4 percent in 1973.

The gross margin rate has increased from 27.2 percent in 1971 to 28.7 percent in 1973. The cost to purchase materials from suppliers, factory labor cost, and other manufacturing costs have apparently increased at about the same rate as the increase in sales revenue. A difference in the gross margin rate may require further explanation, particularly if the amount of change is significant. Perhaps, the mix of products sold may have changed, with a greater proportion of less profitable product lines being sold. Or, a greater volume may be handled at lower selling prices with a resulting lower gross margin percentage. Various factors may account for changes in the rate of gross margin, and investigation may reveal possibilities for corrections.

Operating expenses are often shown as a percentage of net sales, and in this case the operating expenses have increased relative to net sales. Perhaps, some of this increase could not be avoided in handling a higher volume of sales. On the other hand, cost control may have been neglected. Each item included under the operating expenses should be examined in relation to net sales and in relation to past years. Information developed can then be applied in cost control.

Return on assets and equities. The net income has also decreased as a percentage of total assets. The percentage in 1973 is equal to the percentage of net income to net sales, indicating that the assets turned over only once during the year.

$$\frac{\$12,740,100 \text{ net sales}}{\$12,960,500 \text{ total assets}} = 1.0 \text{ turnover}$$

The rate of return on total assets is then equal to 1.0 times the rate of return on net sales. The calculation is made as follows:

4.4% return on net sales $\times$ 1.0 turnover $=$ 4.4% return on total assets.

The rate of return on the owners' equity each year is greater than the rate of return on the total assets, and the difference is greater in 1973 than it was in 1971. This indicates that the company is making greater use of leverage. In 1971, only 19.6 ($1,260,800 $\div$ $6,418,200) percent of the total assets were furnished by outsiders; but in 1973, outsiders furnished 55.5 ($7,189,900 $\div$ $12,960,500) percent of the total assets. The owners gain an advantage if the rate of interest is less than the rate of return that can be earned on the borrowed assets. On the basis of the information given, no judgment can be made as to whether or not leverage is justified. If the company is in a cyclical industry, debt can be a handicap. With business reverses, it may become difficult to pay the interest and to retire the debt according to schedule.

The company has been able to increase its net income per share and has maintained its dividends at the same rate. While business operations have been expanded since 1971, the expansion in plant assets has been financed to a considerable extent by long-term debt. If anything, it appears that debt may be too large in relation to the total equity. Perhaps further expansion should be financed without incurring additional debt. That is, additional stock may be issued and earnings may be retained for reinvestment. A final decision will rest upon an evaluation of the type of business, expected returns, and the nature of the industry and its future prospects.

CIRCULATION OF CURRENT ASSETS AND CURRENT LIABILITIES

The current assets of a business are put to active use in conducting operations and are sometimes spoken of as *working capital*. The term "working capital" is also applied to the excess of the current assets over the current liabilities. To avoid any misunderstanding, the excess of current assets over current liabilities will be referred to in this text as *net working capital*.

There is a very close relationship between the income statement and the current assets and current liabilities on the balance sheet. For example, materials and services may be purchased on credit terms with the liability being shown as a current liability. Costs identified with the products will appear under the caption of inventories in the current asset classification. When the inventories are sold to customers, the accounts receivable will be increased by the amounts billed, and the inventory costs will be reduced by the cost of the goods delivered. Ultimately, cash will be realized upon the accounts receivable and applied to the reduction of the current liabilities arising out of operating transactions. If the business is successful, it should generate more cash than it uses in operations. This cash may be used to acquire plant assets or investments, to retire long-term debt, to increase net working capital, or to make payments of dividends to the owners.

Within certain limits, the operating cycle should be repeated as frequently as possible. The inventories should be converted rapidly into accounts receivable and cash, current obligations should be paid, and the cycle should be started again. Limitations are imposed, however, by the nature of the business and by the investment required to support business volume. In some lines of business, rapid turnover cannot be expected. In the shipbuilding industry, for example, materials cannot be converted quickly into a finished product. The nature of the product, the time required for its production, and the demand for the product according to the season will have an effect upon the rapidity of the conversion of current assets.

A company that earns a relatively low return on sales may be able to maintain a satisfactory rate of return on its investment by a rapid turnover of that investment. On the other hand, if the return on sales is fairly high, the rate earned on the investment can be maintained with a lower turnover.

Current asset turnover. Sometimes the ratio of cost of goods sold and expenses to current assets (the current asset turnover) is computed. In computing current asset turnover, depreciation should be eliminated from the cost of goods sold and expenses inasmuch as the depreciation charge for the year is not dependent upon current assets.

If a company can turn over its investment in current assets rapidly, it is an indication that the current assets are more liquid than if large balances are being accumulated needlessly. Other things being equal, increased turnover should result in a better rate of return on current assets and on total assets. This is true, however, only if profit per turnover can be maintained.

Turnover in itself does not give the complete answer. Turnover may increase; but if the rate of return per turnover decreases, there may be a smaller rate of return on total assets. In fact, an increase in the current asset turnover may indicate that the company is trying to support too large a volume of business on its current investment.

The current asset turnover analysis for Brewster Manufacturing Company is given below:

Current Asset Turnover and Rate of Return

	1973	1972	1971
Cost of goods sold and operating expenses, less depreciation	$11,120,700	$7,516,300	$5,007,200
Current assets	7,030,400	5,260,400	4,047,300
Net income after income taxes	564,600	548,600	304,700
Current asset turnover	1.58 times	1.43 times	1.24 times
Rate of return on current assets	8.0%	10.4%	7.5%
Rate of return per turnover	5.1%	7.3%	6.0%

The turnover has increased since 1971. The rate of return on the current assets increased in 1972 but decreased in 1973 relative to 1972. In 1973 the rate of return per turnover is less than it was in 1971. This indicates that the current assets are being worked harder, but they are earning less.

Current ratio. The general ability of a company to meet its short-term indebtedness is measured by the current ratio. The current ratio is the ratio of current assets to current liabilities. Although a ratio of 2 to 1 has often been singled out as the desirable one, this rule of thumb is not necessarily valid. Ratios will vary in different industries. In fact, some companies may operate quite satisfactorily with ratios of only slightly over 1 to 1. Much depends upon the customary practice in the industry.

The current ratio for Brewster Manufacturing Company was more than 3 to 1 at the end of 1971 and has decreased to less than 2 to 1 at the end of 1973. The current assets have increased, but the current liabilities have increased by an even greater rate.

Current Ratio

	1973	1972	1971
Current assets	$7,030,400	$5,260,400	$4,047,300
Current liabilities	5,189,900	2,684,700	1,260,800
Current ratio	1.35	1.96	3.21

Acid test ratio. A more rigorous measurement of the company's ability to service short-term debt is made by excluding inventories and prepaid expenses from current assets in computing the ratio. The so-called *quick assets* consisting of cash, marketable securities, and accounts receivable are divided by the current liabilities in the computation of the *acid test ratio*. It is generally considered that a dollar in quick assets should lie behind each dollar of current debt.

Acid Test Ratio

	1973	1972	1971
Quick assets	$3,196,700	$2,403,900	$1,810,200
Current liabilities	5,189,900	2,684,700	1,260,800
Acid test ratio	.62	.90	1.44

The substantial decrease of the acid test ratio since 1971 indicates that the company is much less liquid at the end of 1973 than it was at the end of 1971.

Accounts receivable turnover. Analysis of the working capital can be extended further to determine how long it takes for inventories and accounts receivable to translate themselves into cash.

When the customers' accounts are collected promptly with little loss or collection expense, it will be much easier to meet obligations when they become due. But if there is a severe time lag in the collection of accounts receivable, this may have an adverse effect upon a company's ability to pay its debts. Conversely, higher turnovers may offset a lower current ratio. An approximation of the average time required to collect accounts receivable can be calculated by dividing the net credit sales by the average balances of accounts receivable that are outstanding. The turnover, referred to as the accounts receivable turnover, can be converted into a number of days by dividing the turnover into 365, the number of days in a year.

It is assumed that Brewster Manufacturing Company made all of its sales on credit and that the ending accounts receivable can be considered to be typical of the balances throughout the year. It would not be proper to use the year-end balances, however, if the accounts receivable balances varied to any extent during the year. For example, if the balances were relatively high during a large part of the year as a result of seasonal sales, the turnovers would be incorrectly computed by using the lower balances at the end of the year.

Accounts receivable in 1973 were outstanding on the average for 81 days, but in 1971 the customers settled their bills in 63 days from the date of the sale. A slowdown in the rate of collection tends to make it more difficult to meet payments for materials and the various costs of operation. Computations are shown on the following page.

	1973	1972	1971
Net credit sales	$12,740,100	$8,920,600	$5,740,300
Accounts receivable	2,835,300	1,730,800	985,700
Accounts receivable turnover	4.49 times	5.15 times	5.82 times
Number of days per turnover	81 days	71 days	63 days

Inventory turnovers. Turnovers can also be computed for the inventory investments. A turnover of the average investment in materials is calculated by dividing the cost of materials used during the year by the average investment in materials. Too high a ratio may indicate that the inventory balance is too low. Orders will then have to be placed more frequently, and there is a risk of production slowdowns because of insufficient materials. Conversely, a low ratio may call attention to an investment that is too high in relation to the production requirements. Funds may be needlessly tied up in the form of materials inventory.

The turnover is a measurement of relative liquidity. With a decreasing rate of turnover, there is a greater investment in inventory relative to sales; and in all likelihood, inventory is a large percentage of current assets, leaving a small proportionate investment in relatively liquid assets.

In the example given, it is assumed that the year-end balances of raw materials inventory are equal to the average investment. The cost of materials used over the three years is given below:

1971	$2,530,400
1972	3,050,700
1973	4,370,500

The turnover of raw materials has decreased. It seems that larger amounts of raw materials are being maintained in inventories in relation to the amounts consumed in production. The turnover rates are translated into days to show the average number of days that have elapsed between the time that the inventories were acquired and the time that they were put to use in production.

Raw Materials Turnover

	1973	1972	1971
Cost of raw materials used ..	$4,370,500	$3,050,700	$2,530,400
Average inventory of raw materials	1,220,500	912,300	582,400
Inventory turnover	3.6 times	3.3 times	4.3 times
Conversion period	101 days	111 days	85 days

Gross margin per inventory turnover may be computed as an indication of profitability in relation to inventory movement. This computation is made in the following tabulation showing the turnover of the average investment in finished goods. The finished goods turnover is calculated by dividing the cost of goods sold by the average finished goods inventory. The average number of days required to convert finished goods into cost of goods sold has also been calculated.

Finished Goods Turnover

	1973	1972	1971
Cost of goods	$9,080,600	$6,140,300	$4,180,700
Average inventory of finished goods	2,584,500	1,904,900	1,612,600
Inventory turnover	3.5 times	3.2 times	2.6 times
Conversion period	104 days	114 days	140 days
Gross margin	$3,659,500	$2,780,300	$1,559,600
Gross margin per turnover ..	$1,045,571	$ 868,844	$ 599,846

The ratios show that Brewster has not increased its investment in finished goods in relation to sales. In fact, inventory turnover has improved.

The inventory turnover is significant, but in addition it is important to find out how much profit is being earned per turnover. A company may be moving its inventories more rapidly and be more liquid, but the profit for each turnover or even the profit in total may be less. An advantage to be derived from rapid inventory turnover can be lost in part if the profit per turnover decreases. The inventories move more rapidly with less profit on each movement. Hence, inventory turnover is probably a better measure of liquidity than of profitability. Brewster Manufacturing Company, however, has not only increased its turnover of inventory, but it has also earned a greater amount of gross margin on each turnover.

THE EQUITY RELATIONSHIPS

Ordinarily, as a company progresses, the owners' proportionate share in the total equity should increase or at least should be maintained at some established level. When the relative interest of outsiders is increased, there is an advantage to the owners in that they get the benefit of a return on assets furnished by others; yet in gaining this advantage there is increased risk. The relative interests of the various equity holders in Brewster Manufacturing Company are given at the end of each of the three years:

	1973	1972	1971
Current liabilities	40.1%	29.3%	19.7%
Long-term liabilities	15.4	10.9	—0—
Owners' interest	44.5	59.8	80.3
	100.0%	100.0%	100.0%

The proportionate interest of the owners has declined substantially since 1971. In 1971, however, the company had very little debt in its equity structure and was not getting much benefit from leverage. On the other hand, there may be too much debt in the equity structure at the end of 1973. Justification of greater risk depends on the level and stability of future earnings.

NET INCOME AND FIXED CHARGES

The rate of return on total assets and the rate of return on owners' equity give the prospective investor some idea of the *size* of profits relative to his investment. However, the investor is also interested in the *risk* involved.

Risk has many aspects, but one important aspect has to do with the fixed charges imposed against earnings. Resources obtained from outsiders can be used to produce increased profits for the shareholders. However, a fixed charge is imposed for the use of these resources. Interest, for example, is charged for the use of borrowed money. If the level of revenue drops enough, the company may not be able to meet its fixed interest charge or other fixed charges; and both the creditors and shareholders may lose.

Therefore, both the bondholders and the shareholders will be interested in the number of times the company is able to earn its fixed charges. The shareholders are interested because of the possible risk to their investment, and the bondholders are interested because the bond interest may be only one of many costs that are fixed by contract.

In the past, the popular and most widely used test was the number of times that interest was earned. Interest was the fixed charge of most importance and consequently received most of the attention. This charge was fixed by contract; failure to meet the charge constituted a breach of contract.

More recently it has been recognized that other contractual obligations also impose a fixed charge against earnings. For example, buildings or equipment may be leased for long periods of time; and the lessee may be required to make rental payments regularly. Or there may be a requirement to pay dividends on preferred stock. The number of times that interest is earned may not be a complete evaluation of risk. Seemingly, it would be better to find out how many times *all* fixed charges are earned.

The interest charges against Brewster Manufacturing Company are well covered, but the charges were earned fewer times in 1973 than in 1971.

Times Interest Earned

	1973	1972	1971
Net operating income	$1,252,200	$1,172,200	$617,400
Times interest earned	10.2	15.6	77.2
Interest	$ 123,000	$ 75,000	$ 8,000

The number of times that fixed charges are earned is computed by dividing the net income, *before* the charges are deducted, by the fixed charges.

Assume, for example, that Brewster Manufacturing Company had the use of equipment in 1973 under a long-term equipment lease requiring that an annual rental of $400,000 be paid each year. The total fixed charges (rent and interest) are then earned only 3.16 times.

Net operating income before deduction of rent	$1,652,200
Rent and interest	523,000
Times fixed charges earned	3.16

With the rent in addition to the interest, the risk is much greater. With a lower ratio, there is always the risk that business reverses will make it difficult to meet the terms of fixed obligation agreements.

AN EVALUATION OF THE COMPANY

One particular percentage or relationship may not be too significant in itself. Taken together, however, the results of analysis will help to point out unfavorable characteristics that require attention.

Brewster Manufacturing Company has grown considerably since 1971 and there are many favorable points, but there are also some weak spots. Operating expenses are taking a larger share of the sales dollar in 1973 than in 1971. Sales volume has increased, but a larger investment in assets is required to produce the increased sales and profits. For the most part, the increased investment in assets has been financed by additional debt. Ratios clearly show that the company is less liquid than it was in 1971, but it does not appear to be in serious trouble.

Statement analysis, however, does suggest that Brewster Manufacturing Company should try to make improvements in the following areas:

(1) Examine possibilities for cost reduction to improve rate of return on sales.

(2) Pay close attention to collections on customer accounts to reduce the time required to convert accounts receivable to cash.

(3) Investigate needs for raw materials. It may be possible to meet production schedules with a smaller investment in inventory.

(4) Examine dividend policy. The dividend in 1973 is well covered; if dividends are not increased as earnings per share increase, the company can retain a greater proportion of its earnings for the retirement of debt and for financing further expansion.

(5) Future growth may also be financed by the issuance of stock or by a combination of stock and debt.

SHORT-TERM CREDIT PLANNING

Financial statement analysis not only helps to point out weak points, but it can also be used as an aid in other types of planning. For example, it may be used to test the validity of cash budgets that have already been prepared. The cash budget, for example, is often used in planning short-term credit needs. This budget can perhaps be checked for reasonable accuracy by comparing budgeted amounts with amounts that can be expected from using typical ratios or financial statement relationships.

A cash budget for 60 days is given below for the Phoenix Company.

Cash Budget for 60 Days

Beginning cash balance	$ 460,000
Add:	
Estimated collections on accounts receivable	600,000
Estimated cash sales	300,000
	$1,360,000
Deduct:	
Estimated payment on accounts payable	$ 500,000
Estimated cash payments	220,000
Contractual payments on long-term debt	150,000
	$ 870,000
Estimated ending cash balance	$ 490,000

Analysis of the financial statements of The Phoenix Company shows that the accounts receivable remain at about $300,000 throughout the year; that is, there is no seasonal factor in sales. Net credit sales for the year amount to approximately $3,600,000. Hence, the accounts receivable turns over 12 times a year, or once in every 30 days ($3,600,000 ÷ $300,000). The inventory throughout the year remains at about $900,000 and turns over every 90 days. The accounts payable remains at about $500,000 and turns over six times a year, or once about every 60 days.

With an accounts receivable collection period of 30 days and an average balance outstanding of $300,000, it appears that $600,000 is the amount that should be collected on the receivables in 60 days. Cash sales should amount to about $300,000 if the inventory of $900,000 valued at cost turns over once in 90 days and if the markup is about $450,000 on the average. In other words, if an inventory of $1,350,000 at retail turns over once every 90 days and $600,000 flows through accounts receivable every 60 days ($900,000 in 90 days), then approximately $300,000 must be sold in 60 days on a cash basis.

Total sales, 90 days	$1,350,000
Total sales, 60 days (⅔ of $1,350,000)	$ 900,000
Less collections on accounts receivable, 60 days	600,000
Cash sales, 60 days	$ 300,000

Cash payments for expenses are estimated to be $220,000 in the next 60 days. This figure can be roughly checked by referring to the expenses on the income statement. A measure of the cash expenses can perhaps be obtained by using the operating expenses less any noncash expenses such as depreciation. If there is no seasonal factor, the total amount divided by six should be an approximate check on the amount budgeted for the next 60 days.

The tests used above will serve as a rule-of-thumb guide in checking the reasonableness of the budget. If it appears that the budgeted amounts will differ substantially from ratios and relationships taken from past statements, then further attention should be given to the budget. Perhaps some factors were overlooked in budgeting; or it may be possible that the past statement relationships are no longer applicable because of some changes that should be recognized.

Questions

1. What other factors aside from earning power must be evaluated in statement analysis?

2. What important factors may be overlooked by a management that places too much emphasis on sales volume?

3. What are common-size statements? How can they be used in statement analysis?

4. Trend percentages can be helpful, but they can be misleading if used improperly. Explain.

5. Describe how the current assets circulate in the normal profit-making activities of a company.

6. What is net working capital?

7. How is the current asset turnover computed? What is measured by current asset turnover? Is an increase in the turnover favorable or unfavorable? Explain.

8. Summarized data taken from the financial statements of Hilary Retail Stores, Inc., are given below. Discuss the favorable and unfavorable aspects of the increase in the current asset turnover.

(Thousands of Dollars)

	1973	1972	1971
Net sales	$800	$650	$500
* Cost of goods sold and expenses	580	450	350
Net income	$220	$200	$150
Current assets	$100	$100	$100
Current liabilities	80	60	40

* Includes depreciation of $50,000 each year.

9. Why is depreciation eliminated from cost of goods sold and expenses in the computation of the current asset turnover?

10. How does the acid test ratio differ from the current ratio?

11. What does a decrease in the accounts receivable turnover tell you about credit and collection policy?

12. The inventory turnover is a measurement of relative liquidity. Explain.

13. What difficulties may be encountered if the inventory turnover is too high? too low?

14. What is the significance of gross margin per inventory turnover?

15. The controller of Highway Stores, Inc., states that promotional expenses have increased 3 percent this year. Is this significant? What other information would you need in appraising the increase in promotional expense?

16. Operating expense data are given below for a department of Pine Grove Products Company.

	1973	1972
Salaries and wages	$28,000	$25,000
Supplies used	9,800	9,600
Heat and light	2,100	2,000
Telephone	1,000	800
Taxes	2,200	2,400
Insurance	500	600
Repairs and maintenance	5,400	3,600
Depreciation	4,500	4,500

Point out significant changes on a percentage basis; on an absolute dollar basis; on both a percentage and an absolute dollar basis.

Exercises

1. Two companies, Bock Bros., Inc., and Dill City, Inc., are engaged in the same line of business and are identical in almost every respect. Differences in their financial reports are attributable to differences in accounting practice. Without considering *any* transactions responsible for the differences, each company reported average total assets of $7,000,000 during 1972, net sales of $8,000,000, and cost of goods sold and various expenses of $6,500,000 for the year. Transactions responsible for differences are listed below.

(1) Bock Bros., Inc., paid $600,000 during the year for research and development costs and charged the cost to operations. Dill City, Inc., paid the same amount but elected to spread the cost over five years. The payments were not included in the average asset computations.

(2) Bock Bros., Inc., estimates the cost of warranties at 2 percent of net sales each year and charges operations accordingly. Each company actually paid $95,000 on warranties during 1972. The payments were not included in the average asset computations. Dill City, Inc., charges these payments as expenses.

(3) Depreciation of $300,000 was deducted by Bock Bros., Inc., in contrast to $100,000 deducted by Dill City, Inc. The depreciation deductions were not included in the average asset computations.

Required: (1) Adjust the average total assets and the net income for the year to give effect to the differences.

(2) Using the adjusted data, compute the following relationships for each company:

> (a) Rate of return on net sales.
> (b) Asset turnover.
> (c) Rate of return on average total assets.

2. John W. Waycross became president of Rhinesmith Stores, Inc., early in 1971. In his opinion, the investment in inventory was too large in relation to sales volume. Accordingly, he decided to reduce the inventory investment by making a careful analysis of the minimum stock required. At the same time, he worked to increase sales volume, revenue, and profits. Sales and inventory data are given below.

	1973	*1972*	*1971*
Net sales	$6,080,000	$5,230,000	$4,380,000
Cost of goods sold	4,120,000	3,137,000	2,570,000
Average inventory investment for the year	630,000	685,000	825,000

Required: (1) Compute the inventory turnovers for each fiscal year and the number of days for inventory conversion. (Use a 360-day year.)

(2) Did the company earn more profit per turnover in 1973 or in 1972 than it earned in 1971? Show calculations. Comment on your findings.

3. In 1972, Sea Foam Stores, Inc., reported sales revenue of $15,000,000. Sales revenue in 1973 will probably be the same, and the gross margin will also remain at 30 percent of sales revenue. There are some opportunities for cost savings that are expected to increase net profits. For example, the average inventory in 1972 of $1,600,000 is to be reduced to $1,200,000 in 1973. This reduction is not expected to interfere with customer service, but it will reduce the losses from spoilage and obsolescence and the interest costs required to finance inventories. Studies have been made that show losses of inventory and financing costs for the year are equal to approximately 20 percent of the total average inventory cost.

Required: (1) Compute the inventory turnover for 1972 and the turnover expected for 1973.

(2) Determine the gross margin per turnover for each year.

(3) What effect should the inventory reduction have on net income after income taxes assuming an income tax rate of 50 percent?

4. Summarized financial data are given at the top of the next page for Winch Fashions, Inc., in thousands of dollars.

The board of directors is greatly disappointed to find that net income did not increase in proportion to the increase in sales volume. Furthermore, they suspect that any advantage gained from the increased use of leverage may be offset by increased risk and the difficulty in obtaining additional funds at a reasonable cost.

	1972	1971
Net sales	$24,000	$10,000
Cost of goods sold	16,000	6,000
Operating expenses	4,000	1,500
Interest expense	400	100
Income taxes	1,800	1,200
Average total asset investment for the year	20,000	12,000
Average owners' equity for the year	10,000	7,200

Required: (1) Prepare common-size income statements. Call attention to significant changes in the proportions on the 1972 statement.

(2) Compute the following relationships for both years:

    (a) Rate of return on net sales.
    (b) Rate of return on average total assets.
    (c) Asset turnover.
    (d) Rate of return on average owners' equity.

5. The high interest charges on bank loans has made it necessary for Judd Processing Co., Inc., to operate with a minimum of short-term loans. Ordinarily, inventories are financed at an interest cost of 8 percent per year, and the loans are paid with interest when collections are made from the customers. In the past, sales revenue amounted to approximately $1,500,000 each year with cost of goods sold of about $1,000,000. The investment in inventory each year averaged about $250,000, and accounts receivable averaged about $375,000. Next year the company plans to operate with an average inventory investment of $200,000 and will pay more attention to credit and collections in an attempt to reduce average accounts receivable to $300,000. No changes are expected in sales revenue and cost of goods sold.

Required: (1) In the past, how long did it take to convert inventory to cash? (Use a 360-day year.)

(2) How long should it take to convert inventory to cash under the new plan? (Use a 360-day year.)

(3) Compute the anticipated saving in interest cost by reducing the turnover periods and the inventory investment.

6. The current assets and current liabilities of Cort Supply Company are given in summary form at June 30, 1971 and 1972.

	June 30	
	1972	1971
Current assets:		
Cash	$ 50,000	$ 40,000
Accounts receivable	60,000	80,000
Inventories	180,000	120,000
Prepayments	10,000	—
Total current assets	$300,000	$240,000
Current liabilities:		
Accounts payable	$ 90,000	$ 60,000
Notes payable	10,000	—
Estimated income taxes payable	50,000	20,000
Other current liabilities	50,000	20,000
Total current liabilities	$200,000	$100,000

Net sales were $600,000 in 1972 and $400,000 in 1971. Cost of goods sold was $360,000 in 1972 and $240,000 in 1971.

Required: (1) Prepare common-size statements of current assets and current liabilities.

(2) Determine the net working capital at the end of each year.

(3) Compute the current ratio and the acid test ratio at the end of each year.

(4) Compute the inventory turnover and the accounts receivable turnover for each year. (Do not average data.)

(5) Was the company in a more liquid position at the end of 1972 than it was at the end of 1971?

7. Data from the income statements for Borger Mills, Inc., are shown along with trend percentages depicting changes during the past three years.

Borger Mills, Inc.
Sales and Expense Trends
Percentages of Increase and (Decrease)
For the Years Ended June 30

	1973	1972	1971	1970
Sales revenue	$1,000,000	$900,000	$850,000	$800,000
Cost of goods sold ...	720,000	600,000	520,000	500,000
Wages and salaries ..	75,000	60,000	60,000	50,000
Supplies	25,000	25,000	20,000	10,000
Advertising	80,000	75,000	70,000	60,000
Cost of occupancy ..	40,000	40,000	30,000	30,000

	1973	1972	1971
Sales revenue	25.0	12.5	6.3
Cost of goods sold	44.0	20.0	4.0
Wages and salaries	50.0	20.0	20.0
Supplies	150.0	150.0	100.0
Advertising	33.3	25.0	16.7
Cost of occupancy	33.3	33.3	—0—

Required: (1) Which of the expense classifications increased by the largest absolute dollar amount?

(2) Which of the expense classifications increased by the largest percentage?

(3) Compute the gross margin percentages for 1971 and 1973.

(4) Point out the most significant areas of change in profitability when 1973 is compared with 1971.

8. Relatively large investments must be held in inventories by Hines Processing Company because of the long production cycle. As a result, storage costs are high. Loans must be made to finance the inventories with interest cost being an important factor. Production costs for the past three years are given below:

	1973	1972	1971
Raw materials used	$ 6,520,000	$4,800,000	$3,200,000
Labor	3,210,000	2,230,000	1,360,000
Other production costs	1,450,000	1,050,000	580,000
Total production costs	$11,180,000	$8,080,000	$5,140,000

There was no work in process on hand at any time during the three years. Other inventories are listed at cost.

	1973	1972	1971
Inventory of raw materials beginning of year	$ 710,000	$ 670,000	$ 630,000
Inventory of raw materials, end of year	730,000	710,000	670,000
Inventory of finished goods, beginning of year	1,530,000	1,450,000	1,250,000
Inventory of finished goods, end of year	1,610,000	1,530,000	1,450,000

Improved methods of handling inventories and careful inventory control procedures have made it possible to reduce the amount of inventory on hand.

Required: (1) Compute inventory turnovers.

(2) How many days are required each year on the average to process materials and sell the finished products to customers?

(3) Assuming that the collection period on accounts receivable remains the same for the three years, calculate the net time advantage (fewer days per turnover) in financing by reducing the inventory turnover periods. Compare 1973 and 1972 with 1971. (Use a 360-day year.)

9. The charter of Eastern Power and Light Company restricts dividends on common stock to 25 percent of net earnings for the year if the ratio of common stock and retained earnings falls below or is equal to 25 percent of the total equity. This restriction is not permanent and can be removed by increasing the percentage of owners' equity to total equity above the limitation. For several years, the company has distributed approximately ⅔ of its net earnings as dividends. Summarized financial data are given:

Equity at December 31, 1972 (Balance Sheet)

Capital stock	$ 19,000,000
Retained earnings	102,000,000
Long-term debt, 7% interest	277,000,000
Current liabilities	37,000,000
Total equities	$435,000,000
Net income for the year, 1972	$ 34,800,000
Dividends paid, 1972	$ 23,000,000

Required: (1) Did the company meet the terms of the charter restriction at the end of 1972?

(2) How much can the company borrow without being affected by the restriction or, if it is currently applicable, how much must be retained before the restriction can be removed?

(3) What was the rate of return on total assets in 1972? On owners' equity? (Use year-end dollar amounts.)

(4) Assuming that interest applies only to the long-term notes and that the income tax rate is 50 percent, compute the number of times that interest is earned.

10. A summary cash budget prepared for Lister Shops, Inc., for the fiscal year ended August 31, 1972, is as follows:

Cash balance, September 1, 1971	$ 1,816,000	
Estimated collections on accounts		
receivable	13,500,000	
Estimated receipts from cash sales	1,100,000	
Total estimated cash available		$16,416,000
Less:		
Estimated payments for merchandise .	$ 9,120,000	
Estimated payments for operating		
expenses	2,280,000	
Income tax payments	1,900,000	
Payments on debenture notes including		
interest	800,000	
Dividends	600,000	
Total estimated cash disbursements		14,700,000
Cash balance estimated at August 31, 1972		$ 1,716,000

Financial statement relationships are used to test the validity of the cash budget. No significant changes are expected in these relationships in the fiscal year 1972. The company has very little difficulty in the collection of its accounts and has few returns or customer allowances. Accounts receivable of $2,350,000 usually turn over in 60 days. The gross margin is normally 40 percent of net sales, and operating expenses, excluding depreciation, are about 15 percent of net sales. The accounts payable for merchandise and the inventory turn over in approximately 72 days. The average inventory at cost amounts to $1,824,000. The liability for operating expenses is expected to remain at about $180,000 throughout the year. Past experience and recent trends show that cash sales should amount to $1,100,000 in the fiscal year 1972.

Required: Review the cash budget and statement relationships and point out any discrepancy that you find. (Use a 360-day year.)

Problems

6–1. Incomplete financial data are given for Parr Brothers for 1972. Net sales have been reported for the year at $3,850,000 with cost of merchandise sold to the customers amounting to $1,800,000. All sales were credit sales, and both sales and purchases were made evenly throughout the year.

Current assets at the end of the year were as follows:

Cash	$ 268,000
Accounts receivable	622,000
Inventory	400,000
Total current assets	$1,290,000

The accounts receivable and inventory are the same in amount as they were at the beginning of the year. Parr Brothers maintains a sufficient cash balance to pay for merchandise purchases and operating expenses for one month.

Depreciation of $90,000 was deducted in the computation of net income last year.

At the end of the year, the current ratio was 3 to 1, and the current liabilities are 20 percent of the total equity. There were no long-term investments or debts.

Required: (1) What was the net investment in plant assets at the end of the year?

(2) Compute the accounts receivable turnover and the inventory turnover.

(3) What rate of return did Parr Brothers earn on its net sales? on total assets? on owners' equity? (Use asset and equity balances at the end of the year.)

(4) What was the current asset turnover?

(5) What was the rate of net income per current asset turnover?

6–2. Charles Slocum plans to release some of his capital that is presently held in the form of accounts receivable and inventory. By closely enforcing credit terms, he hopes to collect customers' accounts in 30 days instead of 90 days. Also, he believes that he can operate effectively with a 20-day supply of goods in inventory instead of a 60-day supply. He will maintain the same cash balance and will apply the capital released to the acquisition of new facilities.

A summary income statement for the year ended April 30, 1973, is given below, along with a statement of the current assets at April 30, 1973:

Net sales	$960,000
Cost of goods sold	630,000
Gross margin	$330,000
* Operating expenses	193,000
Net income	$137,000
Current assets:	
Cash	$132,000
Accounts receivable	240,000
Inventory	105,000
Total current assets	$477,000

* Includes depreciation of $52,000.

Current asset balances at April 30, 1973, are typical of the balances held throughout the fiscal year.

Required: (1) How much capital can Charles Slocum release, assuming that he will operate in the same way during the next fiscal year with volume of sales, prices, and costs remaining about the same? (Use a 360-day year.)

(2) What was the current asset turnover for the fiscal year ended April 30, 1973?

(3) What will the current asset turnover be if the stated objectives are realized?

6–3. Harold Matson has been looking at potential investment situations, hoping to be able to buy a stock that appears to be underpriced with a potential for price appreciation. At the present time, he is interested in Waner Products, Inc. The company has had a relatively stable earnings record over a period of many years, and the stock is currently selling at a price of $60 a share.

Financial statements covering the past three fiscal years are given on the next page.

Required: (1) Compute the following ratios, amounts, and percentages for each year:

    (a) Net income to net sales.
    (b) Net income to total assets at the end of the year.
    (c) Net income to owners' equity at the end of the year.
    (d) The book value per share of stock.

(2) Give your opinion of Waner Products, Inc., as a potential investment candidate.

Waner Products, Inc.
Comparative Balance Sheets
September 30
(In Thousands of Dollars)

	1973	1972	1971
Assets			
Current assets:			
Cash	$1,715	$1,582	$1,444
Marketable securities	386	312	255
Accounts receivable	1,390	1,370	1,240
Inventories	900	880	850
Total current assets	$4,391	$4,144	$3,789
Plant and machinery	$1,482	$1,450	$1,450
Less: Accumulated depreciation	944	882	832
Net plant and machinery	$ 538	$ 568	$ 618
Total assets	$4,929	$4,712	$4,407
Equities			
Current liabilities:			
Accounts payable	$ 614	$ 618	$ 592
Other amounts currently due	318	287	228
Total current liabilities	$ 932	$ 905	$ 820
Capital stock, $10 par value	500	500	500
Amount paid in excess of par	1,630	1,630	1,630
* Retained earnings	1,867	1,677	1,457
Total equities	$4,929	$4,712	$4,407

* Changes attributable only to profits and dividends.

Waner Products, Inc.
Comparative Income Statements
For the Fiscal Years Ended September 30
(In Thousands of Dollars)

	1973	1972	1971
Net sales	$4,750	$4,680	$4,620
Cost of goods sold	3,260	3,230	3,210
Gross margin	$1,490	$1,450	$1,410
Operating expenses	850	850	830
Net income before income taxes	$ 640	$ 600	$ 580
Income taxes	320	300	290
Net income after income taxes	$ 320	$ 300	$ 290

6–4. In 1972 Ventura-Badinger, Inc., added new product lines and changed the nature of its general operation. A review of the financial statements is being made in 1974 to appraise the results and to make corrections wherever necessary. Comparative balance sheets in summary form are given on page 188.

Ventura-Badinger, Inc.
Balance Sheets
December 31
(In Thousands of Dollars)

	1973	1972	1971
Assets			
Current assets:			
Cash	$ 316	$ 281	$ 463
Accounts receivable	452	338	286
Inventories	624	582	247
Prepaid expenses	23	21	18
Total current assets	$1,415	$1,222	$1,014
Plant assets:			
Land	$ 146	$ 146	$ 82
Buildings, net of depreciation	917	923	386
Machinery and equipment, net of depreciation	1,347	1,355	435
Net plant assets	$2,410	$2,424	$ 903
Total assets	$3,825	$3,646	$1,917
Equities			
Current liabilities:			
Accounts payable	$ 248	$ 190	$ 137
Notes payable	200	350	100
Accrued expenses	80	31	28
Income taxes	312	270	218
Total current liabilities	$ 840	$ 841	$ 483
Long-term notes payable	1,100	1,100	—0—
Stockholders' equity:			
Capital stock	$ 300	$ 300	$ 300
Paid-in capital in excess of stated value	540	540	540
Retained earnings	1,045	865	594
Total stockholders' equity	$1,885	$1,705	$1,434
Total equities	$3,825	$3,646	$1,917

Summary income statements for 1972 and 1973 are given on page 189.

Required: (1) Compute the rate of return on net sales for 1972 and 1973.

(2) Compute the rate of return on the total assets at the end of 1972 and 1973.

(3) Compute the rate of return on the owners' equity at the end of 1972 and 1973.

(4) Compute the percentage of current assets to total assets at the end of each of the three years.

(5) Compute the percentage of owners' equity to total equity at the end of each of the three years.

(6) Point out favorable and unfavorable relationships revealed by your analysis.

Ventura-Badinger, Inc.
Income Statements
For the Years Ended December 31
(In Thousands of Dollars)

	1973	1972
Sales	$4,730	$3,840
Cost of goods sold	2,666	2,235
Gross margin	$2,064	$1,605
Operating expenses, including depreciation in 1972 and in 1973	$1,186	$1,022
Interest charges	77	31
	$1,263	$1,053
Net income before income taxes	$ 801	$ 552
Income taxes	286	217
Net income after income taxes	$ 515	$ 335

6–5. One line of product is manufactured by Abbott Mills, Inc., Production is carried on uniformly throughout the year, which consists of 250 working days, and it takes ten days to convert raw materials into a finished form.

Production statistics for the year ended June 30, 1972, are given below:

Cost of materials used $6,800,000
The average inventory of materials on hand is equal to 30 days production. The stock of finished products is maintained at an average of 20 days production.
Labor cost ...... 50 percent of materials cost
Overhead .... 50 percent of materials cost

The inventories were not increased or decreased during the fiscal year.

Required: (1) What was the materials turnover in the year ended June 30, 1972? The turnover of work in process and finished goods?

(2) How many production days elapsed between the time that materials were purchased and the time that they were sold in the year ended June 30, 1972?

6–6. Bayard Hathaway has made some changes in accounting for Hathaway Styles, Inc., in 1973. In his opinion these changes will improve financial reporting by giving a more realistic picture of the company's financial condition.

In 1971, Bayard Hathaway borrowed $100,000 from the company and gave the company a note as evidence of the debt. This note has been shown on the balance sheets for 1971 and 1972 as a noncurrent asset. In 1973, it is shown under current assets.

Marketable securities were stated at cost at June 30, 1971 and 1972 and at current market value at June 30, 1973.

The inventories were valued at cost by the last-in, first-out method at June 30, 1971, and 1972. The method of assigning costs to inventories was changed in July, 1972, and at June 30, 1973, the inventories are shown at cost as determined by the first-in, first-out method. If the last-in, first-out method had been continued, inventories would have been shown at a cost of $482,000 on June 30, 1973.

Checks written in June, 1973, in the amount of $55,000 were recorded as payments of accounts payable. These were mailed during July, 1973.

The current assets and current liabilities of Hathaway Styles, Inc., as of June 30, 1971, 1972, and 1973, as taken from the annual statements are given below:

| | June 30 | | |
	1973	1972	1971
Current assets:			
Cash	$ 22,000	$ 67,000	$ 123,000
Marketable securities	320,000	240,000	240,000
Accounts receivable	986,000	914,000	826,000
Notes receivable	285,000	185,000	185,000
Inventory	591,000	482,000	471,000
Prepaid expenses	16,000	27,000	26,000
Total current assets	$2,220,000	$1,915,000	$1,871,000
Current liabilities:			
Accounts payable	$ 733,000	$ 851,000	$ 512,000
Wages, taxes, and other operating expenses payable	316,000	283,000	235,000
Notes payable	420,000	350,000	200,000
Estimated liability for income taxes	—0—	42,000	96,000
Total current liabilities ...	$1,469,000	$1,526,000	$1,043,000

Required: (1) Calculate the net working capital, the current ratio, and the acid test ratio from the statement data given for each year without making any adjustment.

(2) Make adjustments that you believe to be necessary to make the data comparable. Calculate the revised net working capital, the revised current ratio, and the revised acid test ratio for fiscal year 1973.

(3) Is the company in a better position to meet its obligations at June 30, 1973, than it was in the earlier years? Explain.

6–7. A balance sheet for Carter Container Company at December 31, 1972, appears at the top of the next page.

Operations for the year 1973 have been planned, and an estimated income statement for the year follows:

Carter Container Company
Estimated Income Statement
For the Year Ended December 31, 1973

Net sales		$904,500
Expenses:		
Cost of goods sold	$620,000	
Wages	132,150	
Advertising	62,300	
Taxes and insurance	4,800	
Maintenance and repairs	5,600	
Utilities	3,700	
Rent	15,000	
Depreciation	8,600	
Interest	1,130	853,280
Net income		$ 51,220

Carter Container Company
Balance Sheet
December 31, 1972

Assets

Current assets:

Cash		$ 28,420
Accounts receivable		60,300
Inventory		77,500
Total current assets		$166,220
Machinery and equipment	$135,400	
Less: Accumulated depreciation	38,100	97,300
Total assets		$263,520

Equities

Current liabilities:

Accounts payable		$ 38,750
Accrued operating expenses		23,100
Installment due on notes payable		6,000
Total current liabilities		$ 67,850
Notes payable		12,000
Jon Carter, capital		183,670
Total equities		$263,520

The business is not seasonal, and, with the exception of cash and the installment due on notes payable, the amounts shown on the balance sheet for assets and liabilities at December 31, 1972, are typical of what can be expected at any time during 1973.

Jon Carter plans to withdraw $1,000 each month for personal living expenses and plans to pay $6,000 in the first quarter for the installment due on notes payable.

Required: (1) Calculate the accounts receivable turnover assuming that all sales are made on credit terms.

(2) Calculate the inventory turnover.

(3) Prepare a budget of estimated cash receipts and disbursements for the first quarter of 1973 from an analysis of statement relationships and the information given.

6–8. One product line is sold by Dryden and Henry, Inc. The summary financial statements given below and on page 192 are considered to be typical.

Dryden and Henry, Inc.
Income Statement
For the Year Ended April 30, 1972

Net sales	$740,000
Cost of goods sold	450,000
Gross margin	$290,000
Operating expenses, including depreciation of $28,000	118,000
Net operating income	$172,000
Income taxes	86,000
Net income after income taxes	$ 86,000

Dryden and Henry, Inc.
Balance Sheet
April 30, 1972

Assets

Cash	$110,000
Accounts receivable	143,000
Inventory	112,000
Machinery and equipment, net of accumulated depreciation	273,000
Total assets	$638,000

Equities

Accounts payable	$ 74,000
Wages and payroll taxes payable	12,000
Other operating expenses payable	28,000
Capital stock	150,000
Retained earnings	374,000
Total equities	$638,000

The business is not seasonal, and the balances for accounts receivable and inventory do not vary to any extent during the year. A new product line is being considered and, if accepted, will be sold along with the present product line. It is estimated that 20,000 units of the new line can be sold in a year at a unit price of $25. Each unit will cost $18. Operating expenses will increase by $85,000 a year, and income taxes will be equal to 50 percent of the profit before taxes.

Current assets to support the product line will be financed by the sale of stock. The additional asset investment has been estimated as follows:

Cash	$ 43,000
Accounts receivable	32,000
Inventory	50,000
Total additional asset investment	$125,000

Required: (1) Using the 1972 statements, calculate the following:

        (a) Accounts receivable turnover.
        (b) Inventory turnover.
        (c) Current asset turnover.
        (d) Rate of return on current assets.
        (e) Rate of return per current asset turnover.
        (f) Rate of return on net sales.
        (g) Rate of return on owners' equity.

(2) Calculate the turnovers and rates of return listed in (1) for the combined operation with the new product line included.

(3) From your analysis, do you believe that the new product line should be accepted?

(Do not average assets or owners' equity.)

6–9. The management of Sloan and Gifford, Inc., plans to expand operations by building a new plant or by acquiring another company in the industry. Sloan and Gifford, Inc., is well established in the industry and will not have to depend upon technical assistance from the acquired company's management. However, it will gain an advantage if it can acquire an operating plant and avoid the delays and difficulties of building a new plant.

A survey shows that Baldwin Processing Company has been quite successful, earning more than the normal 10 percent rate of return on assets that can be expected in the industry. The management of Baldwin Processing Company is willing to discuss plans for the sale of the business.

In 1971, Baldwin Processing Company earned a net income of $148,000 after income taxes on assets of $1,040,600. The average assets during the year were approximately $1,000,000 and the company earned a 14.8 percent rate of return on the average assets.

A balance sheet at December 31, 1972 follows:

Baldwin Processing Company
Balance Sheet
December 31, 1972

Assets

Current assets:

Cash	$218,600	
Marketable securities	115,200	
Accounts receivable, net of estimated returns, allowances, and collectibles ..	243,000	
Inventories	181,400	
Total current assets		$ 758,200

Plant and equipment:

Land		27,600
Building	$288,100	
Machinery and equipment	153,800	
Automotive equipment	19,100	
Furniture and fixtures	28,400	
	$489,400	
Less: Accumulated depreciation	234,600	254,800
Total plant and equipment		$ 282,400
Total assets		$1,040,600

Equities

Current liabilities:

Accounts payable	$ 66,400	
Bank loans	16,800	
Income taxes payable	130,200	
Accrued payables	143,300	
Total current liabilities		$ 356,700

Owners' equity:

Capital stock	$ 40,400	
Premium on stock	33,400	
Retained earnings	610,100	
Total owners' equity		683,900
Total equities		$1,040,600

The management of Baldwin Processing Company suggests that goodwill should be equal to approximately 5 times annual earnings in excess of 10 percent of the average assets for the fiscal year 1972. According to their calculations, goodwill should amount to $240,000. The plant and equipment have been written off rapidly in the early years of company operation, and the costs to acquire similar plant facilities would be considerably higher at the present time. It has been agreed that the plant and equipment should be valued at $950,000. Inventories appreciated in value, and the total current assets have been appraised at $820,000. The purchaser of Baldwin Processing Company is to assume the current liabilities.

If Sloan and Gifford, Inc., builds its own plant, it will probably have to pay $950,000 for plant assets and will require supporting current assets of $820,000.

Required: (1) Assuming that the net income after income taxes for 1972 is stated on a current dollar basis, compute the rate of return on total assets at December 31, 1972 stated at current valuations.

(2) What rate of return was earned on the owners' equity shown on the balance sheet at December 31, 1972? If current valuations are used, what would be the rate of return on the owners' equity?

(3) If a 10 percent rate of return on assets is considered to be normal in the industry, how much premium would Sloan and Gifford, Inc., be paying for the advantages of purchasing a going business as compared with a direct investment in a new plant?

6–10. David Albertson became president of Kenwood and Durant, Inc., in September, 1972. The company has earned small profits and has sustained losses in recent years. Because some of the investments made in the past have not worked out satisfactorily, plans are made to discontinue some of the former policies and practices.

Mr. Albertson has been trying to reduce costs and pay off old obligations before embarking on new programs that will be financed largely through the sale of capital stock.

Financial statements for the company are given below and at the top of the next page.

Kenwood and Durant, Inc.
Income Statements
For the Years Ended December 31
(In Thousands of Dollars)

	1973	1972
Sales	$10,318	$11,521
Cost of goods sold	$ 7,645	$ 9,234
Operating expenses	2,194	1,872
	$ 9,839	$11,106
Net operating income	$ 479	$ 415
Interest charges	138	152
Net income before income taxes	$ 341	$ 263
Income taxes	182	142
Net income after income taxes	$ 159	$ 121

Required: (1) Compute the following using a 360-day year:

(a) Percentage of net income to sales (1972 and 1973).
(b) Number of times interest earned (1972 and 1973).

Kenwood and Durant, Inc.
Balance Sheets
December 31
(In Thousands of Dollars)

	1973	1972	1971
Assets			
Current assets:			
Cash and marketable securities	$ 756	$ 632	$ 687
Accounts receivable, net	1,210	1,238	1,212
Inventories	863	917	933
Prepaid expenses	47	58	53
Total current assets	$2,876	$2,845	$2,885
Plant assets:			
Land	78	78	78
Buildings, net	1,356	1,396	1,436
Machinery and equipment, net	1,905	2,077	1,921
Total assets	$6,215	$6,396	$6,320
Equities			
Current liabilities:			
Accounts payable	$ 687	$ 730	$ 726
Notes payable	700	700	800
Wages and salaries payable	176	192	187
Interest payable	37	51	49
Income taxes payable	68	83	75
Other current liabilities	414	416	450
Total current liabilities	$2,082	$2,172	$2,287
Notes payable, due May 1, 1980	1,900	2,150	2,080
Owners' equity:			
Capital stock	1,750	1,750	1,750
Retained earnings	483	324	203
Total equities	$6,215	$6,396	$6,320

(c) Common-size balance sheets (1971, 1972, and 1973). Show major classifications only. A breakdown by item within a classification is not required.

(d) Percentage of each current asset to total current assets (1971, 1972, and 1973).

(e) How many days did it take on the average to collect accounts receivable in 1972? in 1973?

(f) Compute the current ratio at the end of 1971, 1972, and 1973.

(2) Does the company appear to be in a better financial position at the end of 1973 than it was at the end of 1972 and 1971?

Chapter 7

CHANGES IN NET WORKING CAPITAL AND FINANCIAL POSITION

In the course of business operation, there are many changes in the assets, equities, revenues, and expenses. The increase or the decrease in an asset or equity account or in a group of related accounts over a period of time may be measured and presented in a flow statement. A flow statement may be prepared, if desired, to show how the materials inventory account was increased during the year by purchases and decreased by withdrawals from stores and returns to vendors. For that matter, a flow statement can be prepared to explain the increases and decreases in any account classification. A flow statement may also explain increases and decreases that can be attributed to certain types of transactions. For example, an income statement shows how the owners' equity is increased by the transactions with customers that are measured in revenue accounts and how it is decreased by the costs of serving customers as measured in expense accounts.

FLOW STATEMENTS

In accounting, four basic flow statements can be prepared from the accumulated financial data:

(1) The income statement.
(2) The statement of changes in financial position.
(3) The statement of sources and uses of net working capital.
(4) The statement of cash receipts and disbursements.

The income statement measures the inflows and outflows of net assets resulting from the rendering of goods or services to customers over a certain period of time. A net inflow is designated as net income, and a net outflow is designated as a net loss. The income statement does not measure the changes with respect to any particular account. Instead, a measurement is made of the *total* net asset inflow and the *total* net asset outflow that results from a particular activity, that is, rendering goods or services to customers.

The statement of changes in financial position presents changes in the noncurrent asset and equity structure as well as in the changes in net working capital. For example, a company may issue capital stock in exchange for cash; or capital stock may be issued for machinery and equipment. This type of transaction is not a result of rendering goods and services to customers and would not be reported on an income statement. However, it does change the financial position and should be reported on a statement of changes in financial position.

The American Institute of Certified Public Accountants in Accounting Principles Board Opinion No. 19 recommends that a statement of changes in financial position be presented as a basic financial statement for each period for which an income statement is presented.[1] This recommendation governs financial reporting, but it does not bind management in the preparation of reports and data that are to be used for internal purposes. Management is expected to follow certain standards of disclosure in the preparation of reports to stockholders and the public, but has independence in the selection of information to be used in controlling and planning business activities.

The other two flow statements, in contrast to the income statement and the statement of changes in financial position, are not necessarily included in the published annual reports but are quite useful in internal management. The statement of sources and uses of net working capital and the statement of cash receipts and disbursements measure the inflows and outflows of net working capital and of cash respectively. All of the changes in net working capital and cash are included on these flow statements and not just the changes that have come about as a result of rendering goods or services to customers. Management will have to consider the inflow of net working capital that can be expected over the years in planning the acquisition of properties and in deciding how these properties shall be financed. The statement of cash receipts and disbursements is particularly useful in planning the cash requirements over a fairly short interval of time, such as a year.

Both the statement of sources and uses of net working capital and the statement of cash receipts and disbursements may be referred to in general either as funds flow statements or as cash flow statements. Unfortunately, this terminology is not always precise. In this chapter, primary attention will be focused on the flow of net working capital, and the flow statement will

---

[1] See *Reporting Changes in Financial Position,* Accounting Principles Board Opinion No. 19 (New York: American Institute of Certified Public Accountants, 1971).

be specifically designated as a *statement of sources and uses of net working capital.* Net working capital, it will be recalled, was defined in Chapter 6 as the difference between current assets and current liabilities.

A statement of changes in financial position is essentially an extension of the statement of sources and uses of net working capital. It includes not only the changes that result in increases or decreases in net working capital but also the changes in the noncurrent asset and equity structure that do not affect net working capital. The methods of analysis used in the preparation of a statement of sources and uses of net working capital can also be applied in the preparation of a statement of changes in financial position.

A more thorough discussion of the flow of cash and a more detailed statement of cash receipts and disbursements are presented in Chapter 8.

Comparative balance sheets and other data are presented for Warren Service Company, Inc., to illustrate the differences in the four flow statements. In 1973, Warren Service Company, Inc., billed customers $75,000 for services rendered. Wages, rent, and other costs of operation excluding depreciation amounted to $41,000. Depreciation of equipment used in operations amounted to $10,000. During the year, a long-term note becoming due on March 1, 1980 in the amount of $20,000 was converted to capital stock. The company also borrowed $5,000 on a long-term note that will become due on June 1, 1977. New equipment was acquired for cash at a cost of $25,000. Collections from customers during the year amounted to $66,000, and operating expenses of $43,000 were paid during the year.

Warren Service Company, Inc.
Comparative Balance Sheets
December 31

	1973	1972
Assets		
Cash	$ 12,000	$ 9,000
Accounts receivable	19,000	10,000
Equipment, net of accumulated depreciation	72,000	57,000
Total assets	$103,000	$76,000
Equities		
Accounts payable	$ 6,000	$ 8,000
Note payable, due March 1, 1980	—	20,000
Note payable, due June 1, 1977	5,000	—
Capital received from stockholders	50,000	30,000
Retained earnings	42,000	18,000
Total equities	$103,000	$76,000

The flow statements follow:

(1) *Income Statement*

Revenue	$ 75,000
Operating expenses, excluding depreciation	$ 41,000
Depreciation	10,000
Total expenses	$ 51,000
Net income	$ 24,000

(2) *Statement of Sources and Uses of Net Working Capital* [2]

Net income	$ 24,000
Add: Depreciation	10,000
Net inflow of net working capital from operations	$ 34,000
Add: Proceeds from note due June 1, 1977	5,000
	$ 39,000
Less: Payment for new equipment	25,000
Net increase in net working capital	$ 14,000

(3) *Statement of Changes in Financial Position*

Net income	$ 24,000
Add: Depreciation	10,000
Net inflow of net working capital from operations	$ 34,000
Add: Proceeds from note due June 1, 1977	5,000
	$ 39,000
Less: Payment for new equipment	25,000
Net increase in net working capital	$ 14,000
Capital stock issued in exchange for note due March 1, 1980	20,000
	$ 34,000
Less: Note maturing on March 1, 1980, that was exchanged for capital stock	20,000
Net increase in net working capital and net changes in financial position	$ 14,000

(4) *Statement of Cash Receipts and Disbursements*

Cash receipts:

Collections from customers	$ 66,000
Proceeds from note due in 1977	5,000
	$ 71,000

Cash disbursements:

Payment of operating expenses	$ 43,000
Payment for new equipment	25,000
	$ 68,000
Net increase in cash balance	$ 3,000

---

[2] The net inflow of net working capital from operations can also be computed by starting with sales revenue and deducting the expenses that require an outflow of net working capital. In this example, operating expenses, excluding depreciation, amount to $41,000 and would be deducted from revenue of $75,000 to show net working capital provided by operation in the amount of $34,000.

The income statement shows that the net assets of the business were increased by $24,000 as a result of rendering services to the customers. The income statement only reports the results of revenue-producing operations. It does not show other increases or decreases in the assets or equities; nor does it reveal the increases or decreases in net working capital, cash, or any other specific asset or equity.

The statement of sources and uses of net working capital explains how the net working capital has increased by $14,000. All inflows and outflows of net working capital are set forth, not just the inflows and outflows related to revenue-producing operations. As stated in Chapter 5, the net working capital is not affected by depreciation expense. Therefore, the net working capital provided by operations can be computed by adding depreciation to net income. Additional net working capital was provided by long-term borrowing, and net working capital was used to acquire equipment. Note that the increase in net working capital of $14,000 as shown by the statement is also in agreement with the increase shown on the comparative balance sheets.

	1973	1972
Current assets:		
Cash	$12,000	$ 9,000
Accounts receivable	19,000	10,000
Total current assets	$31,000	$19,000
Less: Current liability of accounts payable	6,000	8,000
Net working capital.........................	$25,000	$11,000
Less: Net working capital at December 31, 1972	11,000	
Increase in net working capital	$14,000	

The statement of changes in financial position goes beyond the statement of changes in net working capital and reveals changes in the non-current asset and equity structure that have no effect on net working capital. For example, the conversion of the long-term note to capital stock has no effect on net working capital. However, the disclosure of this information in published financial reports may be useful to outside readers in evaluating decisions made by management. Management will also find this statement useful although in many cases decisions relative to the financing of long-term investments will depend upon the anticipated flow of net working capital, especially the expected inflow from operations.

The statement of cash receipts and disbursements is more specific than the statement of sources and uses of net working capital in that it shows the increases and decreases in cash itself. In the example given, information for the statement could be developed from the data in the comparative balance sheets and the income statement. The accounts recivable, for example, have increased by $9,000 during the year, indicating that cash receipts were $9,000 less than the $75,000 in revenue billed to the customers, or $66,000. The accounts payable decreased by $2,000. Thus, payments for operating expenses were $2,000 more than the amount shown for those expenses on the income statement. The company paid an amount equal to the current charges of $41,000 plus an additional $2,000 to reduce accounts payable, thus paying a total of $43,000. If the new equipment had not been acquired, the equipment net of accumulated depreciation on the 1973 balance sheet would be shown at $47,000—reduced $10,000 as a result of the depreciation expense for the year. The equipment, however, is shown at $72,000, an amount that is higher than the expected balance of $47,000. With no information to the contrary, the cash payment for equipment of $25,000 can be determined by analysis. The long-term note account has a net increase of $5,000 on the balance sheet indicating that a loan of $5,000 was taken during the year.

The statement of sources and uses of net working capital is particularly useful in long-range planning where projections of available liquid resources are to be made on an approximate basis. For example, management will want to know if sufficient net working capital can be provided by operations to meet repayment schedules on a long-term debt. Or management may plan for a business expansion and estimate the net working capital that will be required and make plans to obtain it as needed. In making projections of this sort, it is not necessary to estimate an exact flow of cash; but it is important to know that resources that can be converted into cash in a relatively short period of time will be available after making allowance for short-term debt commitments.

A statement of cash receipts and disbursements, in contrast to a statement of sources and uses of net working capital, tends to be more useful in short-run analysis. Cash itself is needed to pay off debts that mature in the near future or to pay dividends to the shareholders in the next fiscal quarter. The statement of cash receipts and disbursements tells how cash enters and leaves the business and in what amounts. Reliable projections can generally be made for the immediate future but not for years in advance. Often cash receipts and disbursements projections are used in planning short-term credit and in planning operations over a budget period of a fiscal quarter or a fiscal year.

THE SIGNIFICANCE OF NET WORKING CAPITAL FLOWS

An analysis of how net working capital is provided and used can be applied in many ways. Some of the more important applications are listed on the next page.

(1) It may suggest ways in which the net working capital position can be improved.

(2) It focuses attention on what resources are available for the acquisition of plant assets or other investments.

(3) It can help in the selection of the best investment alternative.

(4) It can be used in deciding how to finance the acquisition of plant assets and other long-term investments.

(5) It can be used in planning for the retirement of long-term debt.

(6) It can also serve in the planning of a sound dividend policy.

A statement of the sources and uses of net working capital tells management where net working capital was obtained in the past and how it was put to use. With this background, management can then make plans for the future. Estimates can be made of future net working capital flows that can be applied to the retirement of long-term debt, to the expansion or replacement of plant facilities, or to the payment of dividends.

Profits are very important, but there are other elements to be considered in a successful business operation. For example, a company may earn an adequate return on investment but at the same time the net working capital position may deteriorate, allowing the company to run into serious difficulties. With a large proportion of the resources frozen in the form of plant assets or other long-term investments, the company will be restricted in its freedom of movement. To obtain liquid resources, the company may increase its debt, possibly more than it can handle properly.

Often a company that is growing rapidly will be faced with a shortage of net working capital. Profits may be increasing, but the company may not have the liquid resources that are required to expand plant facilities to meet the increased sales demand. To obtain liquid resources, the company may borrow heavily. As a result, the interest of the owners is proportionately smaller with increased risk in the event of business reverses.

A STATEMENT OF CHANGES IN NET WORKING CAPITAL

Often a statement of changes in net working capital is prepared as a preliminary step before making an analysis to show *how* net working capital was provided and used. A statement of the changes in net working capital during the year ended December 31, 1972, is given on the next page for Manning Supply Company.

The net working capital is increased by increases in the current assets and is decreased by decreases in the current assets. The rule is the opposite for changes in current liabilities. The current liabilities are a negative

Manning Supply Company
Statement of Changes in Net Working Capital
For the Year Ended December 31, 1972

	Dec. 31, 1972	Dec. 31, 1971	Net Working Capital	
			Increase	Decrease
Current assets:				
Cash	$21,400	$19,300	$2,100	
Accounts receivable	23,100	23,300		$ 200
Inventories	32,500	30,600	1,900	
Total current assets	$77,000	$73,200		
Current liabilities:				
Accounts payable	$17,800	$15,500		2,300
Other current liabilities	12,700	13,200	500	
Total current liabilities	$30,500	$28,700		
Net working capital	$46,500	$44,500		
Increase in net working capital				2,000
Totals			$4,500	$4,500

factor in the computation of net working capital. Therefore, an increase in a current liability decreases net working capital, and a decrease in a current liability increases net working capital.

A statement of changes in net working capital shows the increase or decrease in net working capital for the fiscal period and the fluctuations of the various current asset and liability accounts. In this illustration, net working capital has increased by $2,000. Cash has increased by $2,100 and the inventories have increased by $1,900. The other current liabilities have been reduced by $500. Offsetting these increases to net working capital, however, is a reduction in accounts receivable of $200 and an increase in accounts payable of $2,300.

The statement of changes in net working capital shows that the net working capital has increased by $2,000, but it does not tell *how* net working capital was provided nor *how* it was put to use during the year.

NET WORKING CAPITAL FLOWS

A statement of sources and uses of net working capital tells how net working capital is acquired and where it goes. A company in the normal course of events will have transactions that change net working capital. And there will be transactions that have no effect on net working capital. The transactions may be classified in the following manner:

(1) Transactions that result in an increase or a decrease in the net current balance sheet accounts.

(2) Transactions that do not increase or decrease the net current balance sheet accounts.

    (a) Shifts within the current balance sheet structure that have no effect on the net balance.

    (b) Transactions that affect only the noncurrent balance sheet accounts.

Transactions that result in a *net* increase or decrease in current balance sheet accounts change net working capital. For example, accounts receivable (a part of net working capital) increase as a result of a sale to a customer. Many expenses such as salaries, rent, insurance, and taxes either decrease current assets or increase current liabilities. Hence, they reduce net working capital.

Both current and noncurrent balance sheet classifications may be affected by a transaction. Cash (a part of net working capital) may be increased as a result of borrowing on a long-term note (noncurrent balance sheet account). Or net working capital may be reduced by the retirement of long-term debt or by the acquisition of treasury stock. Any change in a noncurrent classification that has an effect on net working capital must be included in a statement of sources and uses of net working captial.

Some transactions have no effect on the net working capital balance. For example, cash may be collected on accounts receivable, or accounts payable may be converted to short-term notes payable. These transactions cause shifts within the net working capital structure but do not increase or decrease the net balance.

There are transactions that affect only the noncurrent balance sheet accounts. Depreciation expense, for example, reduces plant assets. Net working capital is neither increased or decreased. Hence, in determining the net inflow of net working capital from operations, depreciation expense is added to net income to reverse the effect of the expense deduction.

Shifts may also be made in the noncurrent area. Long-term notes payable may be exchanged for capital stock or a long-term investment may be acquired by issuing capital stock. These transactions do not increase or decrease net working capital. As mentioned earlier, the effect of these transactions must be reported on a statement of changes in financial position. This statement goes beyond the statement of sources and uses of net working capital and reports *all* significant changes in the asset and the equity structure during the fiscal period.

Sources of net working capital. Some of the most common sources of net working capital are:

(1) Operations.
(2) Investment by the owners.
(3) Issuance of long-term debt.
(4) Sale of long-term investments.
(5) Sale of plant assets.

Changes in all noncurrent balance sheet accounts are analyzed to determine their effect on the net working capital balance. Net working capital is normally increased as a result of transactions that (1) decrease noncurrent assets or (2) increase noncurrent equities. For example, long-term investments or plant assets can be sold to provide additional net working capital. Net working capital can also be increased by making long-term loans, or by issuing additional shares of stock in return for cash, other current assets, or in return for cancellation of short-term debt. In any given fiscal period a company will obtain its net working capital from many different sources.

Ordinarily, profitable operation is expected to be the main source of net working capital. In the long run a successful business will acquire plant assets and investments, pay long-term debt, and distribute dividends to the owners from the net working capital generated as a result of rendering goods and services to customers.

In the normal course of operations, sales are made to customers and expenses are deducted in the computation of net income or net loss. Ordinarily, net working capital is provided by the customer in the sales transaction. Sales are typically recorded as follows:

```
Cash ............................. XXXXX
Accounts Receivable ................. XXXXXX
    Sales ............................    XXXXXX
        To record cash sales and sales to cus-
    tomers on credit terms.
```

Cash and accounts receivable are increased. Cash and accounts receivable are included in net working capital, and the increases in these assets therefore increase net working capital.

In making the sales, however, net working capital will also be reduced. The inventory of products will be reduced, for example, when delivery is made to the customer.

```
Cost of Goods Sold ................... XXXXXX
    Inventory ........................    XXXXXX
        To record the cost of goods sold.
```

Various operating expenses must also be deducted from revenue. When expenses such as rent, wages, taxes, and insurance are recorded, a corresponding credit is made to cash, a prepaid expense, or to a current liability.

```
Wages, Rent, Taxes, or Insurance Expense ... XXXXX
    Cash, Prepaid Expenses, or Liability for
    Operating Expenses ...................            XXXXX
        To record operating expenses.
```

Note that the credit is made either to a current asset or to a current liability account. These expenses reduce current assets or increase current liabilities or, in other words, decrease net working capital.

Depreciation expense results in a reduction of the amount shown for plant assets, but it has no effect upon either the current assets or the current liabilities. The entry for depreciation would appear as follows:

```
Depreciation Expense ...................... XXXX
    Accumulated Depreciation ................            XXXX
        Depreciation adjustment for the year.
```

There are other expenses that are similar to depreciation in that they are not related to changes in net working capital. Depletion and the amortization of patents, for example, are offset against revenues in the determination of net income or loss, but are in no way related to net working capital. Net income is closed to the owners' equity at the end of the fiscal period and is lower than it would be if depreciation had not been deducted. Therefore, depreciation has reduced a noncurrent equity (the owners' equity) and has reduced a noncurrent asset (the plant asset) with no effect on net working capital. Similarly, a patent may be written off or goodwill may be written off. The owners' equity is reduced, and the noncurrent asset is reduced, but the net working capital is unaffected.

Sometimes it is said that depreciation provides net working capital that may be used for expansion or for the replacement of plant assets. This is not true. The net working capital is provided by the revenues from sales, not from depreciation. Depreciation, unlike many operating expenses, does not require the *use* of net working capital. The net increase or decrease in net working capital from operations is generally computed by adding depreciation to the net income or subtracting it from the net loss. Similarly, other expenses not requiring the use of net working capital, such as depletion or patent amortization, are added to net income or subtracted from a net loss to determine the net increase or decrease in net working capital from operations.

Uses of net working capital. Some of the more common ways in which net working capital is put to use are:

(1) Acquisition of investments, plant assets, or other noncurrent assets.

(2) The retirement of long-term debt or the redemption of an issue of capital stock.

(3) The acquisition of treasury stock.

(4) The payment of dividends.

(5) Involuntary losses on operations.

As previously mentioned, changes in noncurrent balance sheet accounts are analyzed to determine their effect on the net working capital balance. Net working capital is normally decreased as a result of transactions that (1) increase noncurrent assets or (2) decrease noncurrent equities. For example, if cash is used to purchase (increase) plant assets, net working capital will be decreased. The noncurrent asset is increased and net working capital is reduced. Or long-term debt may be retired, and if this retirement is financed by using available cash, net working capital is reduced.

Operations are not always conducted on a profitable basis. In fact, a net operating loss may be of such a magnitude there may even be a decrease in net working capital from operating activity after the depreciation and other items that have no effect on net working capital have been applied in computing the net working capital flow from operations. A short example is given below:

Net loss on operations	($115,000)
Add: Depreciation	21,000
Net working capital reduction from operations	($ 94,000)

In still other circumstances a net loss may be reported; yet when depreciation or other charges not requiring net working capital are considered, there may be a net inflow of net working capital from operations as shown below:

Net loss on operations	($ 8,000)
Add: Depreciation	21,000
Net working capital provided by operations	$13,000

A COMPREHENSIVE ILLUSTRATION—SOURCES AND USES OF NET WORKING CAPITAL

A statement of the sources and uses of net working capital can often be prepared quite easily from comparative balance sheets. However, if there are several changes in any one noncurrent account classification, the analysis may be somewhat more complicated. Since this analysis often requires an income statement for the year and data not directly obtainable from the accounts, some reasonable assumption may have to be made.

The analytical procedures are illustrated by using the balance sheets below for Baines Fixtures, Inc., at December 31, 1972, and 1973; the income statement on the next page for the year 1973; and additional data.

Baines Fixtures, Inc.
Comparative Balance Sheets
December 31

	1973	1972	Changes Debit	Changes Credit
Current assets:				
Cash	$ 92,700	$ 86,400		
Accounts receivable	71,300	70,800		
Inventories	94,600	93,300		
Total current assets	$258,600	$250,500		
Current liabilities:				
Accounts payable	$ 36,800	$ 35,300		
Wages payable	9,100	9,500		
Estimated income taxes payable	74,300	78,600		
Dividends payable	8,000	8,000		
Total current liabilities	$128,200	$131,400		
Net working capital	$130,400	$119,100	$ 11,300	
Investment in Raven Metals, Inc. ..	85,000	—0—	85,000	
Plant assets, net of depreciation ..	140,900	128,400	12,500	
	$356,300	$247,500		
Less: Long-term notes	$ 98,000	$ 47,000		$ 51,000
Bonds payable	—0—	25,000	25,000	
	$ 98,000	$ 72,000		
Owners' equity	$258,300	$175,500		
Detail of owners' equity:				
Capital received from				
stockholders	$ 90,000	$ 45,000		45,000
Retained earnings	168,300	130,500		37,800
Total owners' equity	$258,300	$175,500		
			$133,800	$133,800

Additional data:
(1) Baines Fixtures, Inc., paid $85,000 in 1973 for an investment in the stock of Raven Metals, Inc.
(2) Detail on the plant assets follows:

	1973	1972
Plant assets	$169,000	$160,000
Accumulated depreciation	28,100	31,600
Plant assets, net of depreciation	$140,900	$128,400

During the year plant assets costing $34,000 with accumulated depreciation of $21,000 were sold.

208

Baines Fixtures, Inc.
Income Statement
For the Year Ended December 31, 1973

Sales	$836,600
Cost of goods sold	473,100
Gross margin	$363,500
Operating expenses, including depreciation of $17,500 ...	$173,200
Interest expense	8,700
Gain on sale of plant assets	15,000
	$196,900
Net income before income taxes	$166,600
Income taxes	98,800
Net income after income taxes	$ 67,800

(3) No payments were made on the long-term notes in 1973.

(4) The bonds payable were converted to capital stock.

(5) Additional shares of stock were issued to the stockholders in 1973 as a dividend. The stock dividend amounted to $20,000. Cash dividends amounting to $10,000 were also declared.

(6) A statement of the changes in retained earnings is summarized below:

Balance of retained earnings, beginning of 1973	$130,500
Net income, 1973	67,800
	$198,300
Less:	
Dividends, stock	$ 20,000
Dividends, payable in cash	10,000
	$ 30,000
Balance of retained earnings, end of 1973	$168,300

The sources and uses of net working capital analysis can be made in a 3-step operation as follows:

(1) Compute the increase or decrease in net working capital.

(2) Determine the net working capital provided by operations.

(3) Analyze the changes in the noncurrent assets and equities for the effect of the changes on net working capital.

The net working capital increase for 1973 has already been computed at $11,300. What caused the net working capital to increase by this amount? This question is answered by carrying out the last two steps listed above.

The net income after income taxes for 1973 amounted to $67,800. This amount includes depreciation of $17,500 which has to be added to net income after income taxes to compute the net working capital flow from operations.

The gain on the sale of plant assets does represent an inflow of net working capital, but it is deducted from net income in the computation of the net inflow of net working capital from operations. The *total* amount received from the sale of the plant assets (the recovery of the net book value of the asset and the gain) will be reported as one item on the sources and uses of net working capital statement. If the gain is included in the net working capital flow from operations *and* is included as the net working capital received from the sale of the asset, there would be double counting. Also, such a gain does not result from an *ordinary* business transaction and therefore to be properly classified should not be included as an inflow resulting from *operations*. The double counting and improper classification is avoided by deducting the gain in computing the net working capital flow from operations.

Net income after income taxes	$67,800
Add: Depreciation	17,500
	$85,300
Less: Gain on sale of plant assets	15,000
Net inflow of net working capital from operations	$70,300

If there is a loss on the sale of a noncurrent asset, the loss is added to net income in calculating the net working capital flow from operations. The loss does not reduce net working capital, but it is, of course, a deduction in computing net income. The total amount received from the sale of the asset is reported as one item on the statement of sources and uses of net working capital.

At this point, each change in the noncurrent assets and equities can be examined in order to determine the net working capital effect.

    (1) Investment in Raven Metals, Inc.

        The investment was increased by $85,000 in 1973. With no information to indicate otherwise, it can be assumed that net working capital of $85,000 was used to acquire this investment.

    (2) Plant assets

        The plant assets net of depreciation increased by a net amount of $12,500. It is known that depreciation reduced net plant assets by $17,500 and that a further reduction of $13,000 was caused by the sale of plant assets having a net book value of $34,000 minus accumulated depreciation of $21,000. In spite of these decreases totaling $30,500 ($17,500 + $13,000), the net amount increased by $12,500. Apparently, plant assets were acquired; and the investment must have been large enough to compensate for the decreases and to provide for a net increase of $12,500. Therefore, the net working capital used to acquire plant assets must have amounted to $43,000.

210

Decreases in net plant assets:

Depreciation	$17,500
Sale of assets	13,000
Total decreases	$30,500
Net increase in net plant assets	12,500
Increase in plant assets, by additional investment	$43,000

In this particular illustration, enough information has been given for a more direct computation of the net working capital used for the acquisition of plant assets. The gross plant assets have increased by $9,000 ($169,000 — $160,000). This increase came about in spite of the fact that plant assets costing $34,000 were sold. The company not only compensated for the reduction caused by the sale of assets but added $9,000 more. The company must have used net working capital of $43,000 to acquire plant assets.

Net increase in gross plant assets	$ 9,000
Reduction caused by sale of plant assets	34,000
Net working capital used to increase plant assets	$43,000

The net book value of the plant assets sold was $13,000 ($34,000 — $21,000). A gain of $15,000 was recognized on the sale. Hence, net working capital was increased $28,000 by the sale of plant assets ($13,000 + $15,000).

(3) Long-term notes payable

The long-term notes payable increased by $51,000. No payments were made during the year. Net working capital of $51,000 was then obtained from long-term borrowing during 1973.

(4) Bonds payable

The bonds payable were converted to common stock with no effect on net working capital.

(5) Capital received from stockholders

The capital received from stockholders has increased by $45,000. This increase did not result from an additional investment by the stockholders. Instead, bonds payable of $25,000 were converted to capital stock, and additional shares of stock were issued as a stock dividend. The retained earnings were reduced by the stock dividend $20,000 and capital stock was increased by $20,000. Neither the bond conversion nor the stock dividend had any effect on net working capital.

(6) Retained earnings

The statement of changes in retained earnings shows that cash dividends of $10,000 were declared. These dividends reduced net working capital.

The results of the analysis of the sources and uses of net working capital are presented on the following page along with a statement of changes in financial position. The statement of changes in financial position was obtained by extending the analysis of net working capital to include all significant changes in the financial position. The conversion of bonds payable to shares of stock did not change the net working capital, but it is an important change

Baines Fixtures, Inc.

Statement of Sources and Uses of Net Working Capital

For the Year, 1973

Sources of net working capital:
    Operating activity:

Net income	$67,800	
Add: Depreciation	17,500	
	$85,300	
Less: Gain on sale of plant assets	15,000	
Net working capital provided by operations ..		$ 70,300
Sale of plant assets		28,000
Additional long-term notes		51,000
Total net working capital provided		$149,300

Uses of net working capital:

Investment in Raven Metals, Inc.		$ 85,000
Acquisition of plant assets		43,000
Dividends		10,000
Total net working capital used		$138,000
Net increase in net working capital		$ 11,300

Baines Fixtures, Inc.

Statement of Changes in Financial Position

For the Year, 1973

Sources of net working capital:
    Operating activity:

Net income	$67,800	
Add: Depreciation	17,500	
	$85,300	
Less: Gain on sale of plant assets	15,000	
Net working capital provided by operations		$ 70,300
Sale of plant assets		28,000
Additional long-term notes		51,000
Total net working capital provided		$149,300

Uses of net working capital:

Investment in Raven Metals, Inc.		$ 85,000
Acquisition of plant assets		43,000
Dividends		10,000
Total net working capital used		$138,000
Net increase in net working capital		$ 11,300
Changes in financial position not affecting net working capital:		
Bonds payable converted to capital stock ..	$25,000	
Capital stock issued in exchange for bonds payable	25,000	—0—
Net increase in net working capital and net changes in financial position		$ 11,300

in the financial position. The stock dividend, however, does not have to be included inasmuch as there has been no change in the basic equity structure. Retained earnings have been converted to capital stock, and the interest of the stockholders remains the same.

THE DEMAND FOR NET WORKING CAPITAL

The techniques of net working capital analysis can also be applied in the preparation of estimates of future sources and uses of net working capital. Planning net working capital flows is an important part of budgeting and is applied in making decisions as to whether or not certain investments should be made.

Ordinarily financial resources are scarce. Net working capital must be obtained and applied to the retirement of debt, to the payment of dividends, and to the acquisition of plant assets and investments. Approved and contemplated projects will compete with each other for net working capital allocations. Priorities will have to be assigned to the projects that will be activated according to relative urgency, the rates of return earned on the projects, and the expected net working capital that can be obtained to finance the cost.

A statement of estimated flow of net working capital can be prepared for future years and rearranged to show what net working capital should be available after all of the required commitments have been met. The available net working capital can then be related to the various demands as shown in the projected statement reproduced on page 214.

The statement shows that operations are expected to provide most of the additional net working capital. Dividends to be paid to the stockholders are deducted in computing the $1,538,000 of additional net working capital from operations that will be available for other purposes. The sale of investments and plant assets will provide more net working capital. Scheduled payments on long-term debt and a planned increase in net working capital are deducted to leave a balance of net working capital that may be used for various purposes. Some projects have already been approved for the year, and other projects are still to be considered. In addition, the company plans to increase its payments on debt.

In long-term planning, it is not necessary to estimate the cash receipts and disbursements. The management does not need to know exactly when cash will be received in certain amounts as would be the case in planning the receipts and disbursements by the month. It is sufficient to know that the company will have enough net working capital available to undertake certain projects and to meet its general commitments.

The Ott Company
Statement of Estimated Sources and Uses of
Net Working Capital
For the Year Ended June 30, 1973

Net income	$1,860,000
Add: Depreciation and other charges not requiring the use of net working capital	218,000
	$2,078,000
Less: Dividends	540,000
Estimated net working capital to be provided from operations after dividends	$1,538,000
Add: Proceeds from sale of investments and plant assets	70,000
	$1,608,000
Less: Payments on debt	180,000
	$1,428,000
Planned increase (decrease) in net working capital	150,000
Net working capital available	$1,278,000
Demand for net working capital:	
Approved projects	$ 830,000
Unapproved projects	380,000
Increased payments on debt	50,000
Total demand for net working capital	$1,260,000
Excess (or deficiency) of net working capital	$ 18,000

Questions

1. Give the names of four important flow statements.

2. What is net working capital?

3. What type of flow is measured by an income statement? How does this flow differ from a flow of net working capital?

4. Distinguish between a statement of sources and uses of net working capital and a statement of cash receipts and disbursements.

5. How can a statement of sources and uses of net working capital be used by management? Where is a cash receipts and disbursements statement more appropriate?

6. Point out how the net working capital provided by operations is sometimes confused with net income.

7. Can the net working capital provided by operations be looked upon as a form of income measurement? Explain.

8. Is there an increase or decrease in net working capital from all transactions that affect only the current balance sheet accounts? Explain.

9. Can a business increase its net working capital and yet have net losses from operations? Explain.

10. Name some major sources of net working capital.

11. Does depreciation provide net working capital for a business? Explain.

12. List some ways in which net working capital may be used.

13. Capital stock has been issued in exchange for patents. Has net working capital been provided or applied? Discuss.

14. If dividends have been declared but not paid, is there any effect upon the flow of net working capital? Why?

15. How do statements of estimated sources and uses of net working capital assist management in planning?

16. During a period of heavy construction expenditures, would you expect net working capital outflow to exceed the inflow? What steps could management take to obtain additional net working capital?

Exercises

1. Summarized balance sheet data as of September 30, 1972 and 1973 are given below for Oliver Stores, Inc.

	1973	1972
Cash	$ 62,140	$ 59,320
Marketable securities	25,000	27,000
Accounts receivable	42,380	44,220
Merchandise inventory	47,670	45,230
Prepaid insurance	1,850	1,690
Equipment, net of depreciation	78,200	80,100
Total assets	$257,240	$257,560
Accounts payable	$ 23,190	$ 24,860
Bank loans	12,400	10,600
Accrued payroll taxes	1,480	1,360
Estimated income tax payable	26,500	27,800
Equipment loan, due June 1, 1980	20,000	20,000
Capital stock	60,000	60,000
Retained earnings	113,670	112,940
Total equities	$257,240	$257,560

Required: (1) Calculate the increase or decrease in net working capital from October 1, 1972 to September 30, 1973.

(2) Prepare a schedule showing the increases or decreases in the individual accounts included in the net working capital area.

2. Data taken from the records of Holverstott Windings, Inc., for the year 1973 appear below and at the top of the next page.

Rent	$ 14,000
Supplies expense	8,420
Wages and salaries	21,600

Required: Prepare an income statement for 1973 and calculate the net inflow of net working capital from operations.

Advertising	$ 17,250	
Depreciation	7,300	
Heat and light	11,830	
Cost of goods sold	121,750	
Net sales	401,200	
Property taxes	3,540	
Payroll taxes	1,940	
Insurance	1,360	
Amortization of patents	1,500	
Travel and entertainment	4,820	
Income taxes	93,200	

3. An income statement for Harold Lohrman for the year ended March 31, 1973, follows:

Harold Lohrman
Income Statement
For the Year Ended March 31, 1973

Net sales		$136,350
Cost of goods sold	$78,140	
Wages and salaries	16,360	
Payroll taxes	1,030	
Advertising	21,440	
Property taxes	2,170	
Heat and light	4,350	
Insurance	1,260	
Amortization of goodwill	8,000	
Amortization of patents	1,200	
Depreciation	14,300	
Loss on sale of equipment	15,200	163,450
Net loss		($ 27,100)

Required: Determine the net increase or decrease in net working capital from operating activity.

4. A summary of the furniture and fixtures owned by Chonko Fashions, Inc., at December 31, 1972, and at December 31, 1973, are listed below:

	December 31, 1973	December 31, 1972
Furniture and fixtures	$84,800	$81,800
Accumulated depreciation	32,400	32,500

During 1973 furniture was sold for a gain of $2,100. New furniture was purchased at a cost of $23,000. Fixtures costing $3,000 with accumulated depreciation of $1,800 were destroyed by fire and written off during the year. Depreciation expense for the year amounted to $11,500.

Required: From the information furnished, calculate the proceeds received from the sale of the furniture.

5. Net income after income taxes of $163,800 was reported by Pederson Brothers, Inc., in 1973. On the income statement, depreciation of $31,200 was deducted. A loss of $14,500 from the retirement of equipment having a net book value of $53,200 was also included on the income statement. Goodwill in the amount of $15,000 was written off against retained earnings. Dividends of $12,000 were declared but not paid by the end of the year. Marketable securities carried at a cost of $47,000 were sold for $49,200 with the gain being shown on the income statement.

Required: Prepare a statement of the sources and uses of net working capital for Pederson Brothers, Inc., for 1973.

6. The president of Yermo Products, Inc., expected an increase in net working capital during 1973. The company reported net income of $83,200 that year, yet a comparison of the 1972 and 1973 balance sheets shows that net working capital decreased by $23,700. During the year, the company paid $47,000 for new equipment purchased. Depreciation of $10,600 was deducted on the income statement. Dividends of $22,000 were declared and paid to the stockholders. Capital stock of the company was reacquired at a cost of $48,500.

Required: Prepare a statement that will show the president why net working capital decreased during the year.

7. On January 1, 1973, Midway Oil Company had net working capital of $323,500. During the year, revenue of $2,642,200 was reported. Operating expenses for the year, including depletion of $421,700 and depreciation of $193,400, amounted to $2,803,600. Long-term notes in the amount of $800,000 were issued near the end of the year to finance anticipated exploration activity. If possible, the company would like to spend $1,100,000 on exploration without reducing net working capital or resorting to loans or stock issues.

Required: Prepare a brief statement that will show whether or not the company can meet the cost of exploration under the terms indicated.

8. The chairman of the board of Rolf Industries, Inc., is greatly concerned about the bonds in the amount of $1,500,000 that must be retired next year. The net working capital at the present time (not including the provision for bond retirement) is $480,000 and should not be reduced. During the year, it is estimated that the company will earn a net income after taxes of only $670,000. Depreciation of $520,000 is to be deducted in the computation of net income. Equipment having a net book value of $218,000 will be sold at a gain of $36,000. The gain is included in the computation of net income after taxes.

Required: Prepare a statement that will show whether the bonds can be retired without reducing net working capital.

Problems

7–1. David Klein is the owner and manager of Klein Store. Balance sheets for Klein Store are given as of December 31, 1972, and 1973, along with the income statement for the year 1973. These statements are on page 218.

Required: Based upon the information given, prepare a schedule of changes in net working capital and a statement of sources and uses of net working capital for the year ended December 31, 1973.

Klein Store
Balance Sheet
December 31

	1973	1972
Assets		
Current assets:		
Cash	$ 53,720	$ 49,860
Marketable securities	26,500	28,900
Accounts receivable	71,230	73,380
Inventory	84,620	81,730
Prepaid insurance	2,040	1,250
Total current assets	$238,110	$235,120
Plant assets:		
Furniture and fixtures	$112,700	$ 81,300
Less: Accumulated depreciation	27,100	18,600
Total plant assets	$ 85,600	$ 62,700
Total assets	$323,710	$297,820
Equities		
Current liabilities:		
Accounts payable	$ 48,940	$ 46,260
Notes payable	15,000	21,500
Accrued wages and taxes	7,820	7,440
Total current liabilities	$ 71,760	$ 75,200
Bank loan, due November 30, 1981	25,000	—
Owners' equity:		
David Klein, capital	226,950	222,620
Total equities	$323,710	$297,820

Klein Store
Income Statement
For the Year Ended December 31, 1973

Net sales	$586,330
Cost of goods sold	372,140
Gross margin	$214,190
Operating expenses:	
Supplies expense	$ 3,840
Wages	105,620
Taxes	2,080
Advertising	27,400
Insurance	3,860
Utilities	1,760
Rent	18,000
Depreciation	8,500
Total operating expenses	$171,060
Net operating income	$ 43,130
Less: Interest expense	2,170
Net income	$ 40,960

7-2. An income statement is given for Laboratory Research, Inc.

Laboratory Research, Inc.
Income Statement
For the Year Ended December 31, 1973

Net sales		$1,312,000
Materials and supplies expense	$988,300	
Wages and salaries	247,500	
Advertising	22,600	
Insurance	4,200	
Taxes	5,100	
Repairs and maintenance	8,600	
Utilities	11,300	
Depreciation of buildings	7,400	
Depreciation of equipment	24,300	
Amortization of patent cost	5,300	
Amortization of research and development costs	19,500	1,344,100
Net loss		($ 32,100)

The company has capitalized research and development costs. During 1973, research and development costs amounting to $87,000 were incurred and were capitalized. The research and development costs were financed by short-term bank loans.

Required: From the information given, compute the increase or decrease in net working capital for 1973.

7-3. The president of Reis Tool Supply, Inc., in reviewing the financial statements for 1972, has expressed surprise at the decrease in net working capital for the year. He expected the dividends of $200,000 that were paid during the year to be covered by the resources retained through depreciation charges, and he had planned to finance new plant acquisitions by the long-term debt increase and profits for the year with net working capital remaining at about the 1971 level. The balance sheet is shown on the next page.

Reis Tool Supply, Inc.
Income Statement
For the Year Ended December 31, 1972

Net sales	$3,950,000
Cost of goods sold including depreciation of $90,000	2,783,500
Gross margin	$1,166,500
Operating expenses including depreciation of $50,000	673,500
Net income before income taxes	$ 493,000
Income taxes	212,000
Net income after income taxes	$ 281,000

Required: Prepare a statement of the flow of net working capital for the year ended December 31, 1972. Explain to the president why his expectations were not realized.

Reis Tool Supply, Inc.
Balance Sheet
December 31

	1972	1971
Assets		
Current assets:		
Cash	$ 591,000	$ 640,000
Accounts receivable	770,000	765,000
Inventories	1,080,000	1,200,000
Prepaid expenses	85,000	80,000
Total current assets	$2,526,000	$2,685,000
Plant assets:		
Plant and equipment	$2,100,000	$1,420,000
Less: Accumulated depreciation	480,000	340,000
Plant and equipment, net of depreciation	$1,620,000	$1,080,000
Total assets	$4,146,000	$3,765,000
Equities		
Current liabilities:		
Bank loans	$ 422,000	$ 355,000
Accounts payable	637,000	586,000
Accrued operating expenses	96,000	112,000
Estimated income taxes payable	212,000	174,000
Total current liabilities	$1,367,000	$1,227,000
Long-term debt	760,000	600,000
Owners' equity:		
Capital stock, $10 par value	800,000	800,000
Premium on stock	550,000	550,000
Retained earnings	669,000	588,000
Total equities	$4,146,000	$3,765,000

7–4. The board of directors of National Products, Inc., has approved the following plans for the next fiscal year:

(1) Expenditures for machinery and equipment, $232,000.

(2) Retirement of all of the preferred stock outstanding at a redemption premium of $30,000.

(3) Dividends to be paid on the preferred stock before redemption, $15,000.

(4) Cash dividends on common stock, $45,000.

(5) The net working capital should be no less than $300,000 by the end of the year.

A balance sheet at December 31, 1972, along with a statement of budgeted operations for the year 1973 are shown on the following page.

Required: (1) Does it appear that the objectives of the board of directors will be realized?

(2) Prepare a statement that will support your position.

National Products, Inc.
Estimated Income Statement
For the Year Ended December 31, 1973
(In Thousands of Dollars)

Net sales	$1,733
* Cost of goods sold	948
Gross margin	$ 785
* Selling, administrative, and other expenses	314
Net income before income taxes	$ 471
Income taxes	230
Net income after income taxes	$ 241

* Depreciation of $83,000 is included in cost of goods sold and in the operating expenses.

National Products, Inc.
Balance Sheet
December 31, 1972
(In Thousands of Dollars)

Assets

Current assets:		
Cash	$196	
Marketable securities	225	
Net receivables	232	
Inventories	217	
Total current assets		$ 870
Plant properties:		
Land	$ 21	
Buildings, net of depreciation	387	
Machinery and equipment, net of depreciation	468	
Net plant properties		876
Total assets		$1,746

Equities

Current liabilities:		
Accounts payable	$129	
Notes payable	70	
Accrued operating expense	63	
Income taxes payable......................	135	
Total current liabilities		$ 397
Stockholders' equity:		
Preferred stock	$150	
Common stock	250	
Premium on common stock	635	
Retained earnings	314	
Total stockholders' equity		1,349
Total equities		$1,746

7–5. The president of Mobile Fittings, Inc., has been looking at the financial statements of his competitor, Basin Industries, Inc. He was surprised to find that Basin Industries, Inc., had invested over $3,000,000 in new plant and equipment in 1970 and 1971 without the incurrence of debt or the issuance of stock. Furthermore, dividend payments to stockholders were not reduced. The president of Mobile Fittings, Inc., wondered how his competitor was able to finance the additions.

In 1971 equipment having a net book value of $342,000 was sold at a loss of $37,000. The loss was included in the computation of net income for the year. No other plant assets were sold in the three years. New plant and equipment additions in 1970 cost $1,200,000 and additions in 1971 cost $2,300,000. Financial data for the 3-year period follow:

(In Thousands of Dollars)
Year Ended

	1971	1970	1969
Net income after income taxes	$671	$587	$521
Depreciation deducted for the year	576	522	501
Dividends declared and paid	250	250	250

Balance sheets for Basin Industries, Inc., are as follows:

Basin Industries, Inc.
Balance Sheets
December 31
(In Thousands of Dollars)

	1971	1970	1969
Assets			
Cash	$ 1,201	$ 1,189	$ 790
Marketable securities	700	1,600	2,400
Accounts receivable	925	909	865
Inventory	1,042	983	976
Plant and equipment, net of depreciation	8,213	6,831	6,153
Total assets	$12,081	$11,512	$11,184
Equities			
Accounts payable	$ 742	$ 613	$ 634
Other current payables.............	546	527	515
Capital stock	5,000	5,000	5,000
Amount paid in excess of par value of stock	3,800	3,800	3,800
Retained earnings	1,993	1,572	1,235
Total equities	$12,081	$11,512	$11,184

Required: (1) Explain to the president how net working capital was acquired for the plant additions made by Basin Industries, Inc.

(2) Prepare statements for 1970 and 1971 that will show how net working capital was obtained and put to use.

7–6. A balance sheet for Castle Rim Products, Inc., at June 30, 1971, is found on the next page.

Castle Rim Products, Inc.
Balance Sheet
June 30, 1971

Assets

Cash	$ 1,743,000
Accounts receivable	1,962,000
Inventories	3,816,000
Land	385,000
Plant, net of accumulated depreciation of $1,050,000	3,230,000
Machinery and equipment, net of accumulated depreciation of $1,154,000	3,676,000
Total assets	$14,812,000

Equities

Accounts payable	$ 1,645,000
Accrued operating expenses	732,000
Income taxes payable	1,285,000
Notes payable, 4½ percent (long-term)	2,000,000
Notes payable, 5½ percent (long-term)	2,500,000
Capital stock, $5 par	3,000,000
Capital in excess of par	2,000,000
Retained earnings	1,650,000
Total equities	$14,812,000

The board of directors is interested in a project that will require new capital of $3,200,000. This project is expected to add $580,000 to net working capital each year. Depreciation of $315,000 will be deducted each year on the plant and equipment acquired as a part of this project.

The board plans to finance the project by issuing 160,000 shares of stock at $20 a share. Approximately $3,000,000 will be used for plant and equipment, and the balance of the proceeds will be held as net working capital.

Before undertaking the project, the board wants to know whether or not the project can be expected to increase the net income per share of stock. The board also wants to know the *total* inflow and outflow of net working capital that can be expected during the next fiscal year and the net working capital that should be available at June 30, 1972.

In the fiscal year ended June 30, 1971, the company earned $1,320,000 after income taxes with a net inflow of net working capital from operations of $1,890,000. It is estimated that operations (not including the new project) will provide the same net income and net working capital in the fiscal year ended June 30, 1972. The difference between the net income after income taxes and the net working capital inflow was caused by depreciation.

The company will have to pay $460,000 to replace plant equipment and $500,000 to retire some of the outstanding notes in the fiscal year ended June 30, 1972. For several years, the company has paid dividends of $1.00 a share and plans to continue this policy.

Required: (1) Compute the net income per share on present operations and the net income per share that can be expected after the new project is installed.

(2) Prepare an estimated statement of the sources and uses of net working capital for the year ended June 30, 1972.

(3) Compute the balance of net working capital that should be available on June 30, 1972.

7–7. An equipment appropriation in the amount of $4,500,000 is being considered by R. G. Taylor, Inc. This equipment is required for the production of a new line of product which the company is planning to introduce. The equipment is expected to have a useful life of 10 years with a residual salvage value of $500,000 at the end of its useful life.

The equipment can be financed by equipment notes of $4,000,000 bearing 6 percent interest per year. Installments of $500,000 must be paid on the principal at the end of each year. Upon acquisition of the equipment, R. G. Taylor, Inc., will make a down payment of $500,000.

In computing income taxes, the company plans to deduct depreciation of $900,000 in the first year, $720,000 in the second year, and $576,000 in the third year. This is in accordance with the double-rate method of depreciation. Income taxes are estimated at 50 percent of net income before income taxes.

An estimated income statement for this new line of product has been prepared showing only the revenues and costs directly attributable to the project. The income statement follows:

R. G. Taylor, Inc.
Estimated Income Statement for Project
First Year

Net sales	$4,480,000
Cost of goods sold including depreciation of $600,000	2,000,000
Gross margin	$2,480,000
Wages and salaries	$ 315,000
Employee fringe benefits	42,000
Advertising and promotion	163,000
Insurance and taxes	38,000
Utilities	22,000
Depreciation	300,000
Interest	240,000
	$1,120,000
Net income before income taxes	$1,360,000
Income taxes	680,000
Net income after income taxes	$ 680,000

The equipment for this project can also be obtained on a lease requiring annual payments of $960,000 a year, payable in monthly installments of $80,000. Assume that the payments can be deducted for income taxes. With the exception of depreciation and interest, there will be no effect on other costs shown on the income statement.

The president of the company believes that this new product line has great future potential, but he also recognizes the risk of increasing competition and changes in consumer preferences. Before making a decision, he would like to see a projection of the net working capital flows that can be expected in connection with the project over the next three years. If the project will increase net working capital by at least $2,000,000 over the first three years after providing for all costs, the president will vote for authorization of the project.

Required: (1) Determine the net inflows of net working capital that can be expected from the project over each of the first three years taking into consideration both the alternative of purchase and lease. (Show computations.)

(2) Does it appear that the president of the company will accept the project?

7–8. Ionic Motors, Inc., has approved a project for the manufacture of essential parts to be used in a revolutionary type of automobile vehicle. Preliminary research costs of $1,600,000 were incurred in 1969, and additional research costs of $1,200,000 were incurred in 1970. These costs reduced net working capital in the years incurred and were deducted in the computation of income taxes in 1969 and 1970.

In 1970, the company issued 400,000 additional shares of common stock and received $15 per share from the issue. Funds of $6,000,000 were paid to contractors in 1970 for plant construction, and additional funds of $3,400,000 were paid for construction in 1971.

Debenture notes bearing 5 percent interest each year were issued in return for $12,000,000 at the beginning of 1971. Proceeds from the issue in the amount of $8,000,000 were invested to yield a 6 percent return for the last six months of 1971.

The company paid $4,500,000 to install equipment early in 1972. Materials and labor costs of $800,000 used to start plant operations in 1972 were experimental costs and were deducted in the computation of income taxes.

Operational budgets for 1972 to 1975, inclusive, are given below:

	Product Sales Revenue	Cost of Sales, Excluding Depreciation	Selling and Administrative Expenses, Excluding Depreciation
1972	$ 1,300,000	$ 900,000	$ 185,000
1973	4,800,000	3,200,000	560,000
1974	8,500,000	5,500,000	780,000
1975	11,000,000	7,200,000	1,100,000

Depreciation is to be deducted as follows:

1972	$ 800,000
1973	2,000,000
1974	1,500,000
1975	1,000,000

In addition to the above revenues and expenses, the company plans to spend $1,200,000 in 1972 on advertising to introduce the new product. This advertising cost will be deducted on the income tax return in 1972.

Income taxes are estimated at 40 percent of net income before income taxes. Net losses in any one year will be offset against profits from other divisions of the company's operation. Hence, the income tax savings on losses will be realized in the years the losses are incurred.

Required: (1) From the information given, estimate the effect of the new product project, including financing on net working capital for each year from 1969 to 1975 inclusive. The income tax effect must be recognized. Also include the effect of interest cost on any debt incurred.

(2) Summarize the effect of the project activity on net working capital flows from 1969 to 1975 including the effect of financing.

7–9. Harry Jordan and his son own 55 percent of the outstanding stock of Jordan Industries, Inc. A group of minority stockholders own 10 percent of the stock and has recently been trying to acquire more shares. The balance of the stock is widely dispersed among many holders.

The company has expanded rapidly and has incurred a long-term debt of $3,000,000 to finance growth. This debt becomes due in 1973. The market for the products has been somewhat slow, but the prospects for 1972 are favorable. Mr. Jordan has attempted to extend the time for payment of the $3,000,000 debt but has been unsuccessful. However, he has made an arrangement to borrow $1,500,000 in 1972 at interest of 8 percent a year.

An additional issue of stock has been considered, but Mr. Jordan and his son have only $360,000 available for investment. They fear that equity financing will take control of the company out of their hands. If stock is issued, they would want to issue it under conditions where they would have no less than 55 percent control. There is no possibility of raising funds by the issuance of preferred stock or non-voting stock. Common stock can be sold to realize $16 a share for the company, but it will have to be issued to maintain at least the net working capital that was available at the end of 1971.

Comparative balance sheets are given for December 31, 1970 and 1971:

Jordan Industries
Comparative Balance Sheets
December 31

	1971	1970
Assets		
Current assets:		
Cash	$ 696,000	$ 853,000
Accounts receivable, net of estimated returns and uncollectibles	1,097,000	1,156,000
Inventories	1,183,000	1,042,000
Prepayments	94,000	85,000
Total current assets	$3,070,000	$3,136,000
Plant assets, net of accumulated depreciation	4,565,000	4,650,000
Total assets	$7,635,000	$7,786,000
Equities		
Current liabilities:		
Accounts payable	$ 531,000	$ 486,000
Notes payable	760,000	650,000
Other current liabilities	223,000	189,000
Total current liabilities	$1,514,000	$1,325,000
Notes payable, due March 31, 1973	3,000,000	3,000,000
Owners' equity:		
Capital stock, $1 par value	600,000	600,000
Premium paid on capital stock	900,000	900,000
Retained earnings	1,621,000	1,961,000
Total equities	$7,635,000	$7,786,000

An income statement for 1971 is at the top of the next page.

Jordan Industries, Inc.
Income Statement
For the Year Ended December 31, 1971

Net sales	$8,241,000
Cost of goods sold	$6,587,000
Operating expenses	1,778,000
Interest	216,000
	$8,581,000
Net loss	($ 340,000)

Included in the income statement is depreciation of $335,000. No plant assets were retired during 1971.

Budget estimates for 1972 indicate a much better situation. Net sales have been forecast at $9,800,000. Cost of goods sold should amount to $6,900,000 and operating expenses should amount to $1,940,000. Interest expense will be the same as it was in 1971. Depreciation of $275,000 which is included in the cost of goods sold and operating expenses, will be deducted.

During 1972, the company must acquire new equipment estimated to cost $220,000.

Required: (1) Prepare a statement of net working capital flow for 1971.

(2) Prepare an estimated statement of net working capital flow for 1972, based on information given.

(3) Does it appear that Mr. Jordan and his son can retain 55 percent control of the company?

7–10. Comparative balance sheets at June 30, 1972, and at June 30, 1973, are given below and at the top of the next page.

Wister and Mayberry, Inc.
Comparative Balance Sheets
June 30

	1973	1972
Assets		
Current assets:		
Cash	$ 193,000	$ 162,000
Marketable securities	224,000	116,000
Accounts and notes receivable	273,000	224,000
Inventory	212,000	178,000
Accrued interest receivable	4,000	4,000
Prepaid insurance	2,000	1,000
Total current assets	$ 908,000	$ 685,000
Investment in Pike Metals, Inc.	960,000	—0—
Property, plant and equipment:		
Land	37,000	37,000
Buildings, net of accumulated depreciation	1,024,000	1,047,000
Equipment, net of accumulated depreciation	1,346,000	1,380,000
Total assets	$4,275,000	$3,149,000

Equities

Current liabilities:	1973	1972
Accounts payable	$ 140,000	$ 158,000
Accrued wages and payroll taxes	42,000	45,000
Estimated income taxes payable	173,000	154,000
Other current obligations payable	51,000	53,000
Total current liabilities	$ 406,000	$ 410,000
Bonds payable, net of unamortized bond discount	696,000	688,000
Stockholders' equity:		
Capital stock, $10 par value	1,930,000	1,500,000
Amount of capital invested in excess of par value........................	740,000	300,000
Retained earnings	518,000	296,000
Less: Cost of shares in treasury	(15,000)	(45,000)
Total equities	$4,275,000	$3,149,000

An income statement for the fiscal year ended June 30, 1973, follows:

Wister and Mayberry, Inc.
Income Statement
For the Year Ended June 30, 1973

Net sales	$2,326,000
Cost of goods sold and operating expenses, including depreciation of buildings and equipment in the amount of $135,000	1,695,000
Net operating income	$ 631,000
Add: Gain on sale of marketable securities	11,000
Gain on sale of equipment	15,000
	$ 657,000
Less: Interest on bonds payable	52,000
Net income before income taxes	$ 605,000
Income taxes	223,000
Net income after income taxes	$ 382,000

Additional information is given to explain certain transactions.

(1) Marketable securities costing $42,000 were sold during the fiscal year for $53,000.

(2) The investment in Pike Metals, Inc., was financed in part by the issuance of 35,000 shares of capital stock at a market price of $20 a share.

(3) There were no acquisitions or retirements of buildings.

(4) New equipment was acquired during the fiscal year at a cost of $138,000.

(5) On June 30, 1972, the company held 3,000 shares of its stock at a cost of $15 per share. During the fiscal year, 2,000 shares of the treasury stock were sold.

(6) Capital stock was issued during the year as a dividend by a transfer from retained earnings to capital stock and to the amount of capital invested in excess of par value. The dividend consisted of 8,000 shares of stock at a value of $20 a share.

(7) Aside from the credit for net income and the charge for the stock dividend, there were no other entries to retained earnings for the fiscal year.

Required: Prepare a statement showing the sources and uses of net working capital for the fiscal year ended June 30, 1973.

7–11. The consolidated balance sheets for The Bunker-Ramo Corporation and Subsidiaries at December 31, 1968 and 1969 are given in summary form below:

The Bunker-Ramo Corporation
Summary Balance Sheets
December 31

	1969	1968
Assets		
Current assets:	$ 95,619,651	$ 90,319,687
Property at cost:		
Land	$ 6,304,786	$ 5,956,947
Buildings and improvements	37,761,129	29,146,697
Service equipment	99,347,723	79,294,489
Machinery and equipment	56,905,487	54,034,491
Total	$200,319,125	$168,432,624
Less: Accumulated depreciation and amortization	88,995,166	79,937,606
Property—net	$111,323,959	$ 88,495,018
Other assets	$ 4,018,503	$ 6,972,643
Total assets	$210,962,113	$185,787,348
Equities		
Liabilities:		
Current liabilities	$ 48,483,760	$ 37,085,240
Long-term debt	23,354,549	23,785,929
Total liabilities	$ 71,838,309	$ 60,871,169
Stockholders' Equity:		
Preferred stock	$ 45,128,375	$ 46,085,775
Common stock	3,603,445	3,511,898
Paid-in capital in excess of par or stated value	49,198,494	45,498,090
Retained earnings	41,193,490	29,820,416
Total stockholders' equity	$139,123,804	$124,916,179
Total equities	$210,962,113	$185,787,348

Other data:

(1) Included in other assets on the balance sheets are investments in other companies. Assume that the investments were $4,957,971 at December 31, 1968 and were $2,364,705 at December 31, 1969. These investments were disposed of during 1969 at a loss of $1,482,000.

(2) Also included in other assets are patents and license agreements net of accumulated amortization. Assume that there were no additions to patents or license agreements during 1969.

(3) Assume that the cost of service equipment retired during 1969 amounted to $7,687,733 and that the accumulated depreciation on this equipment amounted to $6,776,366. There were no other retirements of plant assets during the year.

(4) During 1969, a portion of the preferred stock was converted to common stock under the terms of a conversion option extended to the preferred stockholders. The preferred stockholders exchanged their shares of stock and paid an additional $2,834,551 for the common shares. Assume that there were no other transactions in capital stock during the year.

(5) Dividends of $2,733,347 were paid in 1969. Aside from the dividends and net income, assume that no other entries were made to retained earnings.

A summarized income statement for 1969 is given below:

The Bunker-Ramo Corporation
Summary Income Statement
For the Year, 1969

Net revenues	$254,660,393
Costs and expenses (including depreciation of $15,833,926 and amortization of patents and licenses in the amount of $360,874)	$190,050,925
Selling, general and administrative expenses	39,501,518
	$229,552,443
Income from operations	$ 25,107,950
Other expense (income):	
Interest expense	$ 1,865,085
Other income—net	(1,108,066)
Total	$ 757,019
Income before income taxes and extraordinary items	$ 24,350,931
Provision for income taxes	11,800,000
Income before extraordinary items	$ 12,550,931
Extraordinary items:	
Gain on retirement of service equipment	$ 3,037,490
Loss on sale of investments in other companies	(1,482,000)
	$ 1,555,490
Net income	$ 14,106,421

Required: (1) From the information furnished, prepare a statement of sources and uses of net working capital for 1969.

(2) Extend the statement of sources and uses of net working capital to include *all* changes in the financial position of the company.

Chapter 8

A STATEMENT OF CASH RECEIPTS AND DISBURSEMENTS

In the last chapter it was pointed out that a statement of the sources and uses of net working capital can be quite helpful in long-range planning where an approximation of the increases and decreases in net working capital will be sufficient. It is difficult at best to estimate the cash receipts and disbursements, and this will be particularly true if projections are to be made well into the future. Furthermore, it will not be necessary to estimate the flow of cash itself in long-range planning.

In making plans for the more immediate future, however, management will want to know how much cash will be available to meet obligations to trade creditors, to pay bank loans, and to pay dividends to stockholders. Also, interest must be paid and payments must be made on long-term debt as it matures. In some months, cash disbursements may be greater than cash receipts, in which case it may be necessary to sell short-term investments or to arrange for bank loans. In other months when receipts are greater than disbursements, bank loans will be repaid and short-term securities will be purchased. With careful planning, there should be enough cash available for the payment of obligations on schedule; but the cash balance should not be too large. Cash in itself is not productive and, if not immediately needed, should be employed to earn a return. Ordinarily, excess cash will be invested in short-term securities that can be easily liquidated.

An analysis dealing with the inflow and outflow of cash can be referred to as a cash flow analysis. But the term cash flow is often used in a very broad sense and may or may not apply to a literal flow of cash. In popular financial publications, cash flow may be another name for a flow of net working capital or for a flow of the more liquid current assets as reduced by current liabilities. In this chapter, however, the literal flow of cash will be discussed; and a statement of this flow will be designated as a *statement of cash receipts and disbursements*.

A statement of cash receipts and disbursements can be prepared from the accounting records of receipts and disbursements. But the accounting records include details of receipts from specific customers, payments to specific vendors, and other data that are not essential in general cash planning. In many cases, sufficient information can be obtained from an analysis of the financial statements.

CASH FLOW ANALYSIS AND NET WORKING CAPITAL ANALYSIS COMPARED

In Chapter 7, an analysis was made to determine the sources and uses of net working capital by relating the increases and decreases in noncurrent assets and equities to the net working capital. These relationships are briefly summarized in T-account form below:

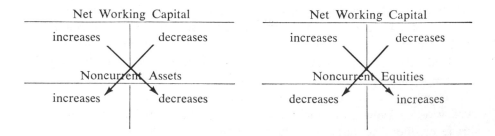

The T-account presentation shows that net working capital is ordinarily decreased to acquire noncurrent assets and that it is ordinarily increased when noncurrent assets are sold or retired. Increases in net working capital may also be explained by increases in noncurrent equities, and decreases may be related to decreases in noncurrent equities. These are general rules, and there are exceptions. For example, a plant asset may be discarded with the net book value being charged against the owners' equity. The noncurrent assets and equities are reduced in this case with no effect on the net working capital.

The logic that is employed in net working capital analysis is also employed in an analysis of the changes in cash, but the analysis must be extended further. Cash is only one of the current assets and is part of the net working capital. Therefore, the changes in all of the other current assets and in the current liabilities must be analyzed in relation to their effect on cash. Also, the changes in the noncurrent assets and noncurrent equities must be analyzed by following the same procedures that are used in net working capital analysis.

A T-account summary is given to show how the changes in cash can be related to the changes in other balance sheet classifications.

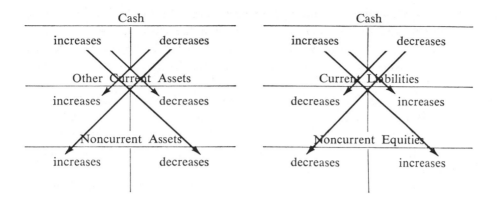

CASH AND OPERATIONS

There is a close relationship between the revenues and expenses and the current assets and liabilities. This relationship is set forth below in a diagram of an operating cycle.

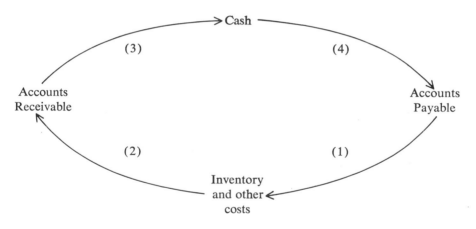

(1) Buy inventory and incur costs (credit accounts payable)
(2) Sell inventory to customers (debit accounts receivable)
(3) Collect accounts receivable
(4) Pay accounts payable

An operating cycle begins with the acquisition of materials or merchandise and the incurrence of costs that are necessary in processing a product or service salable to customers. The costs are recorded in inventory or in some other appropriately labeled current asset account until matched against sales in the income determination process. At the same time, accounts payable or some other current liability account is increased to record the obligation to make eventual payment for these materials and services. Products and services when completed are sold to customers. At this point, revenue is recognized, and the accounts receivable from the customers are recorded. The costs to obtain this revenue are offset against the revenue as expenses. Cash collections are made from the customers, the creditors are paid, and the cycle repeats itself.

In the income determination process, attention is usually directed to only one part of this cycle. Revenues are generally recognized when sales are made to customers, and the expenses of making these sales are offset against the revenues to determine net income or loss. These measurements are made over a designated fiscal period, usually a year.

Cash flows that result from operating activity are also measured over a fiscal period. But the cash flows are not exclusively related to the revenues and expenses of that period. Collections, for example, may be made not only on current sales but also on sales billed in past years or even on sales to be billed in the future. These collections are the cash inflows for the year from sales activity. Similarly, payments made for materials and services, whether expensed in the current year or not, are shown as cash outflows for expense activity.

A summary analysis. In computing the flow of net working capital from operations, additions and deductions are made to the net income or net loss reported on the income statement in order to remove items that do not affect this flow. Similarly, a flow of cash from operations can be determined by making additions and deductions to the net income or net loss. The flow of net working capital from operations will be computed first, and then the changes during the fiscal period in current assets other than cash and the current liabilities will be added or deducted in order to determine the net increase or decrease in cash from operations.

Rules for relating the changes in current assets and current liabilities to the income statement in the computation of a flow of cash from operations are summarized below:

Changes in Assets and Liabilities	Cash Effect	Procedure
Increases in current assets other than cash	Decrease cash	Deduct from net income in computation
Decreases in current assets other than cash	Increase cash	Add to net income in computation
Increases in current liabilities	Increase cash	Add to net income in computation
Decrease in current liabilities	Decrease cash	Deduct from net income in computation

Increases in current assets that result from operating activity have a negative effect on cash. For example, accounts receivable increase because sales are greater than the cash collections from customers. Inventories are increased when the cost of merchandise purchased is greater than the cost of the merchandise sold. Or prepaid rent, prepaid insurance, and other prepayments are increased by paying for more services than are currently used.

Decreases in current assets that result from operating activity tend to increase the cash balance. When the accounts receivable are reduced, the collections from the customers are greater than the sales reported on the income statement. Decreases in inventory indicate that the cost of goods sold is greater than the cost of goods purchased during the fiscal period. Reductions in prepaid expenses reveal that the payments for these services are not equal to the cost of the services used.

When current liabilities that are related to operating activity are increased, the company has used more goods or services than it has paid for. The increases are added to net income to compute the inflow or outflow of cash from operations. Conversely, reductions in the current liabilities related to operating activity show that cash payments are greater than the expenses deducted on the income statement. The decreases are deducted from net income in computing the flow of cash from operations.

A computation of the net increase in cash from operations may be made in the following manner:

Net income for the fiscal period			$XXX
Add: Depreciation	$XXX		
Loss on sale of plant assets	XXX	XXX	
Net working capital provided by operations .			$XXX
Add: Decreases in current assets (list individually)	$XXX		
Increases in current liabilities (list individually)	XXX		
Total additions		$XXX	
Deduct: Increases in current assets (list individually)	$XXX		
Decreases in current liabilities (list individually)	XXX		
Total deductions		XXX	
Net changes			XXX
Net increases in cash from operations			$XXX

In Chapter 7, an illustration was given to show that operations may provide net working capital even when a company is operating at a net loss. Cash may also be increased by operations when there is a net loss. If depreciation and other charges not requiring the use of net working capital or cash are greater than the reported net loss, there will be a net inflow of net working capital and cash, everything else being equal.

A detailed analysis. A computation of the net amount of cash received from operations may not always be sufficient. Management may want more detail that will show how much cash was provided by customers and how much was used to pay for certain costs of operation. As an alternate approach in computing the cash flow from operations, each item of revenue and expense on the income statement can be related to the individual current assets and liabilities. For example, the cash collected from customers can be determined by relating sales to the changes in the accounts and notes receivable from customers. The cash paid for merchandise can be computed by relating cost of goods sold to the changes in the inventory and the changes in accounts payable. Or the cash disbursements for wages can be computed by relating wages expense to the change in the wages payable liability.

Current asset and liability account balances are related to revenue and expense account balances as summarized below:

Current Assets	*Related To*
Cash	
Accounts receivable	Sales
Inventory	Cost of goods sold
Prepaid expenses	Operating and other expenses, excluding depreciation and the amortization of other noncurrent items
Current Liabilities	
Accounts payable	Cost of goods sold
Operating costs payable	Operating and other expenses, excluding depreciation and the amortization of other noncurrent items

In analysis, the changes in accounts receivable are related to sales. The changes in the inventory and accounts payable are related to cost of goods sold. The changes in prepaid expenses and operating costs payable are related to the corresponding operating expenses. Depreciation and the amortization of noncurrent items have no effect on cash and are eliminated in a computation of the flow of cash from operations. Note that the cash effect of changes in current assets and current liabilities as explained above is consistent with the T-account presentation given on page 233.

The rules for restating revenues and expenses on a cash basis as given on the next page are merely an elaboration of the rules given for a summary computation.

A COMPREHENSIVE ILLUSTRATION

Up to this point, attention has been directed to the cash flow from operations. In most cases, however, the analysis will have to be extended

Changes in Assets and Liabilities	Cash Effect	Procedure
Increases in current assets	Decrease cash	Deduct an increase from related revenues and add it to related expenses
Decreases in current assets	Increase cash	Add a decrease to related revenues and deduct it from related expenses
Increases in current liabilities	Increase cash	Add an increase to related revenues and deduct it from related expenses
Decreases in current liabilities	Decrease cash	Deduct a decrease from related revenues and add it to related expenses

beyond the income statement and the related current assets and liabilities. Changes in other current balance sheet items that cannot be related to revenues and expenses must be considered along with the changes in noncurrent balance sheet items. In short, the changes in all of the accounts with the exception of cash must be analyzed in relation to their effect on the flow of cash.

The procedures used in the analysis of the other current balance sheet items and the noncurrent items will be exactly the same as those that were employed in the analysis of the sources and uses of net working capital. The logic is the same, but the analysis is extended further so that the flow of cash can be determined instead of the flow of net working capital.

A working paper will also be used in this illustration to organize the cash receipts and disbursements from operations, but the remaining cash receipts and disbursements can be derived without difficulty by direct reference to the balance sheet changes and the additional data furnished.

Financial statements for Highland Stores, Inc., are given below and on the next page.

Highland Stores, Inc.
Income Statement
For the Year Ended December 31, 1972

Net sales	$1,345,000
Cost of goods sold	$ 763,000
Operating and other expenses, including depreciation of $18,000 and uncollectible accounts expense of $27,000	358,000
Total cost of goods sold and expenses	$1,121,000
Net income	$ 224,000

Additional data:

(1) Marketable securities were not sold during the year, and there were no retirements of plant and equipment.

Highland Stores, Inc.
Comparative Balance Sheets
December 31

	1972		1971		Increases (Decreases)
Assets					
Current assets:					
Cash		$ 182,000		$152,000	$ 30,000
Marketable securities..		150,000		118,000	32,000
Accounts receivable ..	$283,000		$239,000		44,000
Less: Allowance for					
doubtful accounts ..	19,000		15,000		(4,000)
		264,000		224,000	
Inventory		192,000		201,000	(9,000)
Prepaid expenses		12,000		9,000	3,000
Total current assets		$ 800,000		$704,000	
Plant and equipment ...	$407,000		$273,000		134,000
Less: Accumulated					
depreciation	79,000		61,000		(18,000)
		328,000		212,000	
Total assets		$1,128,000		$916,000	$212,000
Equities					
Current liabilities:					
Accounts payable		$ 82,000		$ 88,000	($ 6,000)
Bank loans payable ...		30,000		15,000	15,000
Accrued expenses					
payable		27,000		33,000	(6,000)
Dividends payable		30,000		15,000	15,000
Total current liabilities ..		$ 169,000		$151,000	
Notes payable, due June					
1, 1980		90,000		—0—	90,000
Capital stock		500,000		500,000	—0—
Retained earnings		369,000		265,000	104,000
Total equities		$1,128,000		$916,000	$212,000

(2) Accounts receivable of $23,000 were determined to be worthless and were written off against the allowance for doubtful accounts.

(3) The board of directors declared dividends of $120,000.

The cash receipts and disbursements flow from operating activity is computed and set forth on the working paper shown on the next page.

The accounts receivable have increased by $44,000, indicating that the sales billed to customers were greater than the cash collections. The increase in the accounts receivable is deducted from sales in computing the cash inflow from sales activity. In this example, another factor has been introduced. Accounts receivable in the amount of $23,000 have been written off as uncollectible. The accounts receivable were reduced by the write-offs, but

	Income Statement	Cash Effect Add	Cash Effect Subtract	Flow of Cash
Net sales	$1,345,000		$67,000	$1,278,000
Cost of goods sold	$ 763,000	$6,000	9,000	$ 760,000
Operating and other expenses including depreciation of $18,000 and uncollectible accounts expense of $27,000	358,000	9,000	45,000	322,000
	$1,121,000			$1,082,000
Net income	$ 224,000			
Net inflow of cash from operations				$ 196,000

no cash was received. Therefore, both the increase of $44,000 in accounts receivable and the $23,000 decrease that did not produce cash are combined and deducted from sales to determine the cash inflow from sales activity. The cash inflow is computed below from a T-account analysis.

Cash

Cash collections (a) 1,278,000	

Accounts Receivable

Beginning balance 239,000	Write-off of uncollectible
Sales 1,345,000	accounts 23,000
	Cash collections (a) 1,278,000
	Ending balance 283,000
1,584,000	1,584,000

The same results can also be computed as follows:

Accounts receivable, beginning balance		$ 239,000
Sales		1,345,000
Potential cash collections		$1,584,000
Less:		
Write-off of uncollectible accounts	$ 23,000	
Ending balance of accounts receivable (to be collected)	283,000	306,000
Current collections		$1,278,000

The estimated uncollectible accounts expense is recorded with a credit being made to the allowance for doubtful accounts. The net accounts receivable are reduced as a result of this entry, but there is no effect on the flow of cash. The estimated uncollectible accounts expense, like depreciation, is not deducted in computing the net inflow of cash from operations.

The cash paid for merchandise is computed from cost of goods sold in two steps.

(1) Purchases during the year are computed by relating cost of goods sold to the change in the inventory.

(2) Cash payments for merchandise are computed by relating purchases to the change in the accounts payable.

In the illustration, inventory has decreased by $9,000. This means that the cost of goods sold was greater than the cost of goods purchased.

Cost of goods sold	$763,000
Less: Decrease in the inventory	9,000
Cost of purchases	$754,000

In the next step, cash payments are calculated by relating the purchases to the changes in the accounts payable. The accounts payable have been decreased by $6,000. The accounts payable were reduced because payments were greater than purchases.

Cost of purchases	$754,000
Add: Decrease in accounts payable	6,000
Cash payments for merchandise	$760,000

The analysis is repeated in T-account form:

Cash

	Cash payments (c) 760,000

Accounts Payable

Cash payments (c) 760,000	Beginning balance 88,000
Ending balance 82,000	Purchases (b) 754,000
842,000	842,000

Inventory

Beginning balance 201,000	Cost of goods sold (a) 763,000
Purchases (b) 754,000	Ending balance 192,000
955,000	955,000

Cost of Goods Sold

Cost of goods sold (a) 763,000	

Cash was disbursed to pay operating and other expenses, to increase the related prepaid expenses, and to reduce the related liability for accrued expenses. Depreciation and uncollectible accounts expense, of course, are operating expenses not requiring a cash disbursement and are subtracted to compute the cash disbursed for operating and other expenses.

Operating and other expenses, including depreciation of $18,000 and uncollectible accounts expense of $27,000		$358,000
Add: Increase in prepaid expenses	$ 3,000	
Decrease in accrued expenses payable ..	6,000	9,000
		$367,000
Less: Depreciation	18,000	
Uncollectible accounts expense	27,000	45,000
Cash payments		$322,000

This analysis can also be made from T-accounts.

Cash

	Cash payments (a) 322,000

Prepaid Expenses and Accrued Expenses Payable (Combined)

Beginning balance of prepaid expenses	9,000	Beginning balance of accrued expenses payable	33,000
Ending balance of accrued expenses payable	27,000	Ending balance of prepaid expenses	12,000
Cash payments (a)	322,000	Operating expenses reduced by depreciation of $18,000 and uncollectible accounts expense of $27,000	313,000
	358,000		358,000

The cash flow from operations can also be computed in summary form by making the adjustments to net income.

Net income		$224,000
Add: Decrease in the inventory		9,000
Uncollectible accounts expense		27,000
Depreciation		18,000
		$278,000
Less: Increase in accounts receivable		$ 44,000
Write-off of uncollectible accounts		23,000
Decrease in accounts payable		6,000
Increase in prepaid expenses		3,000
Decrease in accrued expenses payable		6,000
		$82,000
Net inflow of cash from operations		$196,000

Some current assets and current liabilities are not related to revenues and expenses and will have to be considered separately along with the non-current balance sheet items. In this example, the marketable securities, the bank loans payable, and the dividends payable are not related to income statement accounts.

The changes in the balance sheet accounts that must still be considered in terms of their effect on cash receipts and disbursements are listed below:

	Increases (Decreases)
Marketable securities	$ 32,000
Plant and equipment (gross)	134,000
Accumulated depreciation	18,000
Bank loans payable	15,000
Dividends payable	15,000
Notes payable, due June 1, 1980	90,000
Retained earnings	104,000

The marketable securities have increased by $32,000. Investments were not sold during the year. Therefore, cash of $32,000 was disbursed to purchase securities.

The plant and equipment at the gross amount increased by $134,000. There were no retirements during the year, and analysis indicates that $134,000 was disbursed to acquire additional plant assets. The related accumulated depreciation account has increased by the amount of the depreciation for the year, as would be expected, if there were no retirements.

The increase in the bank loans payable of $15,000 and the increase in the notes payable due on June 1, 1980, of $90,000 provided cash.

The liability for dividends payable has increased by $15,000 because the company paid out less dividends than it declared. Dividends of $120,000 were declared, but the dividends paid amounted to $105,000 ($120,000 minus $15,000).

The increase in retained earnings of $104,000 can be explained by the net income for the year of $224,000 and the dividends declared of $120,000. The flow of cash as affected by both operations and the dividend declaration was considered previously.

The changes in all of the balance sheet accounts have been explained in relation to their effect on the flow of cash, with particular attention being given to the income statement and the changes in corresponding current balance sheet accounts. A statement of cash receipts and disbursements prepared from this analysis is found at the top of the next page.

THE VALUE OF CASH ANALYSIS

Management, in particular, is interested in the flow of cash and will estimate cash receipts and disbursements for future months. The future needs for cash will be anticipated and related to the budgeted cash inflow from regular operating activities. When the demands for cash are expected

Highland Stores, Inc.
Statement of Cash Receipts and Disbursements
For the Year Ended December 31, 1972

Cash balance, January 1, 1972		$152,000
Add:		
Net receipts from operations:		
Collections from customers	$1,278,000	
Less:		
Payments for merchandise	760,000	
Payments for operating and other expenses	322,000	
	$1,082,000	
Net receipts from operations		196,000
Receipts from bank loan		15,000
Receipts from long-term notes		90,000
		$453,000
Less:		
Disbursements for marketable securities ..		$ 32,000
Disbursements for plant and equipment ..		134,000
Disbursements for dividends		105,000
		$271,000
Cash balance, December 31, 1972		$182,000

to exceed the inflow, plans will be made to convert short-term investments into cash or to obtain short-term credit. Later on when the cash inflow is expected to exceed the cash outflow, the plans will provide for the reduction of short-term debt and for increases in the marketable securities.

Frequently operations are conducted on a seasonal basis. During certain months, sales volume may be particularly heavy. At other times the level of activity will be relatively low. Cash planning will be built around the seasonal fluctuations. There will be some degree of variation in the cash receipts and disbursements throughout the year, even in a nonseasonal type of business or in a business that has minimized the seasonal effect by having many product lines which sell in different seasons.

Operating activity, as reported in monthly or quarterly income statements, does not necessarily correspond with the cash activity. In some months, materials may be purchased in large quantities in anticipation of future sales. During those months, the cash receipts may not be sufficient for payments that must be made to the suppliers of goods and services. Short-term credit will be needed. At a later date the sales volume may be high, but the inflow of cash may still be relatively small. Finally, the sales volume may decline, but collections will be coming in from customers to whom sales were made in earlier months. Variations in the pattern of the flow of cash will have to be allowed for in planning a schedule of cash payments and in planning short-term credit and investment policy.

It may be helpful to build the cash plans around the normal operating cycle of the business without the arbitrary time restrictions imposed by conventional months and fiscal quarters.[1] Typically, a manufacturing enterprise acquires inventories that are converted into products that are sold to customers on account. Cash is collected from customers and payments are made to the suppliers of materials and services. Tracing the flow of cash over a complete operating cycle may call attention to some weaknesses that can be corrected. Perhaps too much time is being taken in converting inventories to receivables to cash, or cash balances may be held in excess of current needs. A business entity will not necessarily have sharply defined operating cycles. Most likely, operating cycles will overlap to some extent. A penetrating review of cash movements over an operating cycle, however, may provide management with more information for use in the general cash planning problem.

Questions

1. Point out the difference between a statement of sources and uses of net working capital and a statement of cash receipts and disbursements.

2. Explain how cash receipts and disbursements analysis can be applied in short-term planning.

3. How is the income statement related to current assets and current liabilities in the calculation of sources and uses of net working capital? of cash receipts and disbursements?

4. Explain how sales reported on the income statement can be converted to cash collected from customers.

5. Is the cash result of cost of goods sold equal to the cash disbursed for materials and services sold during the period? Explain.

6. How is the cost of goods sold adjusted in the computation of the cost of goods purchased?

7. How can the cost of goods purchased be adjusted in the computation of the cash outflow for goods acquired?

8. Ionacco, Inc., has decreased its inventory during the year. (1) Would this decrease be added to or deducted from cost of goods sold in the flow of cash computation? (2) The accounts payable for merchandise purchased has also decreased. What effect would this have in the adjustment of cost of goods sold to a flow of cash basis?

---

[1] Colin Park and John W. Gladson, *Working Capital* (New York: The Macmillan Company, 1963).

9. Is it possible for a company to have a net inflow of cash from operations while operating at a net loss? Explain.

10. Can a company be operating at a profit yet show a net outflow of cash from operations? Explain.

11. Explain how a company can operate at a profit and have a net inflow of cash from operations, yet have a decrease in its cash balance.

12. Accounts receivable are shown on the comparative balance sheets of Willis Wyatt net of the allowance for doubtful accounts. If the uncollectible accounts expense reported on the income statement amounted to $16,000, what effect would this have on the allowance for doubtful accounts? on the amount reported as receivables net of allowance for doubtful accounts? on the gross amount reported as accounts receivable? How does uncollectible accounts expense on the income statement affect the cash receipts or disbursements from operations? How does uncollectible accounts expense affect the flow of net working capital from operations?

13. What is the effect on net working capital when marketable securities are purchased? on the flow of cash? Explain.

14. In a seasonal type of business explain why there might be large variations in the flow of cash between months?

15. What steps can be taken to maintain a relatively uniform cash balance when cash inflows and outflows vary between months?

Exercises

1. The owner of Delta Specialties Company estimates that net sales for the first quarter of 1973 will amount to $287,000. A gross margin of 30 percent should be realized. At the beginning of the quarter, the accounts receivable were $63,700. The collection manager plans to reduce the amounts owed by customers and expects the accounts receivable balance to amount to $48,000 at the end of the quarter. The inventory of merchandise will be decreased by $8,000 in the first quarter, and the amounts owed to merchandise creditors will be decreased by $5,500.

Required: Calculate the *net* amount of cash to be realized in the first quarter of 1973 from merchandising activity.

2. Lavender Sales Company has budgeted sales for the fourth quarter of 1973 at 85,000 units of product with a unit selling price of $24. The gross margin is estimated at one third of the sales revenue. The inventory will be increased during the quarter by $128,000 in anticipation of increased sales early in the next year. Amounts owed to trade creditors are expected to increase by about $48,000.

Required: Calculate the payments to be made during the quarter for merchandise.

3. A fire at the Benton Appliance Company destroyed equipment carried on the records at a net book value of $283,000. The equipment was insured, and the company collected $176,000 in insurance. Proceeds were also received from salvage in the amount of $33,000. Cash payments were made in the amount of $17,500 to clean away debris left by the fire. Other equipment not damaged by the fire was sold at a loss of $16,000. This equipment had a net book value of $87,000. It is estimated that new equipment costing $425,000 will be needed to replace equipment destroyed or sold.

Required: Compute the additional amount required to replace the equipment after offsetting the net proceeds from the insurance and the sale of other equipment.

4. An estimated income statement for Dahl Implement Company for October, 1972, is given below in summary form.

Net sales	$173,000
Cost of goods sold	96,700
Gross margin	$ 76,300
Wages and payroll taxes	$ 29,400
Advertising	17,200
Insurance	1,500
Depreciation	3,200
Other operating expenses	8,800
Total expenses	$ 60,100
Net income	$ 16,200

Changes in current assets and liabilities have been estimated as follows:

Increases:

Accounts receivable	$11,200
Accounts payable	7,500
Prepaid insurance	400
Accrued wages and payroll taxes	2,100

Decreases:

Inventory	3,800
Accrued liability for advertising	1,600
Accrued liability for other operating expenses	700

Required: (1) Convert the income statement to a net cash flow from operations by applying the increases and decreases in current assets and liabilities to the net income.

(2) Convert each item on the income statement to a cash flow basis by relating it to the increases or decreases in corresponding current assets or liabilities.

5. The treasurer of Jacobs Patterns, Inc., has estimated the cash position of the company at November 30, 1973. Data used in making the estimate is given below:

Collections from customers	$246,600
Payments for merchandise purchased	115,800
Payments for various operating expenses	31,200
Cash to be received on the retirement of equipment	11,800
Payments on equipment purchased	5,900
Dividend payments	6,000
Cash to be received in exchange for investments costing $18,700	21,400

In November a payment of $45,000 is to be made on a long-term note. Interest amounting to $3,600 is to be paid in addition to the payment on the note. The cash balance at November 1 is $112,600.

Required: Prepare an estimated statement of cash receipts and disbursements for the month of November, 1973.

6. George Fehnel has budgeted operations for the next year as follows:

Revenue	$117,000
Operating costs:	
Materials and supplies used	$ 14,800
Wages and payroll taxes	39,200
Advertising	17,500
Insurance	2,700
Depreciation	4,300
Other expenses	3,800
Total operating costs	$ 82,300
Net income	$ 34,700

Service is given to customers on a cash basis. Prepaid advertising will be increased by $1,600 during the year, and prepaid insurance will be decreased by $800. Accrued wages and payroll taxes will be reduced by $2,500. Accounts payable for materials and supplies and other expenses are expected to increase by $2,100. Mr. Fehnel plans to withdraw $1,500 each month for living expenses.

Required: Calculate the expected increase or decrease in the cash balance.

7. A receiver in bankruptcy has been appointed for Peak Industries, Inc. The receiver plans to continue operations in the hope that more assets will be available for eventual distribution to the creditors. The cash balance at June 1, 1973, amounted to $3,250. Obsolete and fully depreciated equipment is to be sold at the beginning of June for $8,600. Obsolete inventory on hand at a cost of $17,800 is to be sold for $4,520. Cash of $7,360 is to be paid for materials. Additional payments of $6,470 are to be made for wages. The products manufactured during the month are to be sold for cash in the amount of $19,430. Payments for the costs of administration and overhead are estimated at $12,650.

Required: Prepare an estimated statement of cash receipts and disbursements for the month of June, 1973.

8. Donna Martinez sells gifts and antiques with most of the sales being made during the summer months. Her income statement budget for the summer season of 1973 shows the following:

	May	June	July	August	Sept.	Oct.
Net sales	$18,500	$19,600	$37,000	$39,000	$21,500	$16,400
Cost of goods sold	$12,400	$13,200	$20,200	$20,600	$14,800	$12,100
Wages	900	900	1,500	1,500	900	900
Advertising	650	750	600	500	400	400
Insurance and taxes	200	200	200	200	200	200
Utilities	120	120	150	180	120	120
Depreciation	500	500	500	500	500	500
Total expenses	$14,770	$15,670	$23,150	$23,480	$16,920	$14,220
Net income	$ 3,730	$ 3,930	$13,850	$15,520	$ 4,580	$ 2,180

During the 6-month period, Donna anticipates the following changes in certain balance sheet accounts.

	May	June	July	August	Sept.	Oct.
Accounts receivable	—0—	—0—	$ 8,000	$ 5,000	($9,000)	($3,000)
Inventory	2,000	3,000	1,000	(3,000)	(3,000)	—0—
Accounts payable .	—0—	—0—	—0—	—0—	(6,000)	—0—

In June, new store fixtures costing $3,000 are to be purchased for cash. The cash balance at May 1 amounted to $16,000. Each month Donna Martinez plans to withdraw $1,000 for her personal use.

Required: Donna hopes to have a cash balance of no less than $15,000 at all times. Can this be accomplished without making a bank loan or obtaining cash from other sources?

Problems

8–1. Ott Machine Company does not expect to earn enough during the next quarter to cover the regular dividend of 80 cents a share. The board of directors will grant the dividend on the basis of past performance and expectations for future quarters, provided that the net reduction in the cash balance is not in excess of $50,000.

An estimated income statement for the quarter is given below:

Ott Machine Company
Estimated Income Statement
For the Current Quarter

Net sales	$3,465,100
Cost of goods sold, including depreciation of $138,300 ..	$2,542,800
Selling and administrative expenses	534,000
Interest expense	22,600
Income taxes	173,700
Total expenses	$3,273,100
Net income	$ 192,000
Number of shares of stock outstanding	300,000
Earnings per share (estimated)	$ .64

Further estimates have been made showing that accounts receivable will be reduced during the quarter by about $78,000 as a result of collections made on current and past sales. Payments for manufacturing costs should exceed the cost of goods sold, excluding depreciation, by about $33,000. Payments to be made for selling and administrative costs are expected to amount to $558,000. Interest of $12,000 is to be paid during the quarter, and a payment of $25,000 must be made on outstanding notes payable. The income tax payment during the quarter has been estimated at $180,000. Payments to be made for new equipment to be acquired in the quarter will probably amount to $75,000.

Required: On the basis of the information given, does it appear that the quarterly dividend of 80 cents a share will be paid? Support your conclusion by a statement showing the estimated flow of cash for the quarter.

8–2. Current assets and current liabilities as of June 30, 1973, and 1972 are listed below for Thomas Cuttings, Inc.:

	June 30, 1973	June 30, 1972
Current assets:		
Cash	$ 43,500	$ 47,800
Marketable securities	43,800	35,000
Accounts receivable, net	109,000	118,700
Inventory	93,400	78,200
Prepaid insurance	3,400	2,600
Prepaid rent	2,100	2,700
Total current assets	$295,200	$285,000
Current liabilities:		
Accounts payable	$ 47,300	$ 47,800
Wages and salaries payable	16,200	15,700
Estimated income taxes payable	62,100	58,800
Other operating expenses payable	19,700	21,200
Total current liabilities	$145,300	$143,500

No marketable securities were sold during the fiscal year. An income statement for the year ended June 30, 1973, is given below:

Thomas Cuttings, Inc.
Income Statement
For the Year Ended June 30, 1973

Sales	$565,300
Cost of goods sold	308,900
Gross margin	$256,400
Operating expenses:	
Wages and salaries	$ 71,300
Advertising	21,500
Rent	9,000
Supplies expense	5,600
Insurance	4,000
Utilities	3,100
Uncollectible accounts expense	6,200
Depreciation of equipment	11,500
Total operating expenses	$132,200
Net income before income taxes	$124,200
Income taxes	62,100
Net income after income taxes	$ 62,100

Dividends amounting to $30,200 were declared and paid during the fiscal year. The company purchased equipment costing $175,000 and financed 80 percent of the cost by long-term notes.

Required: (1) Prepare a statement of sources and uses of net working capital for the fiscal year ended June 30, 1973.

(2) Prepare a statement of cash receipts and disbursements for the fiscal year ended June 30, 1973. (Convert each item on the income statement to a cash basis. Assume that the liability for utilities is shown as other operating expenses payable.)

8–3. Data taken from the accounting records of Ben Adamson at September 30, 1972, are given below:

Cash	$ 24,600
Marketable securities	33,000
Accounts receivable	42,500
Inventory	35,400
Prepaid insurance	2,200
Prepaid rent	3,700
Equipment	78,600
Patents	11,400
Accounts payable	17,800
Accrued wages and payroll taxes	3,800
Allowance for doubtful accounts	4,500
Accumulated depreciation	19,300
Ben Adamson, capital	186,000

At September 30, 1973, the ledger showed the following balances before closing the accounts for the fiscal year:

Cash	$ 69,800
Marketable securities	16,000
Sales	245,000
Accounts receivable	78,300
Cost of goods sold	133,500
Accounts payable	21,300
Prepaid rent	3,000
Insurance expense	3,600
Rent expense	9,000
Amortization of patents	1,200
Depreciation expense	7,900
Accumulated depreciation	14,300
Inventory	34,300
Prepaid insurance	2,000
Accrued wages and payroll taxes	4,700
Wages and payroll tax expense	26,300
Uncollectible accounts expense	2,500
Ben Adamson, personal withdrawals	32,000
Ben Adamson, capital	186,000
Gain on sale of equipment	8,000
Loss on sale of marketable securities	3,500
Equipment	49,600
Patents	10,200
Allowance for doubtful accounts	3,400

There were no purchases of marketable securities or equipment during the fiscal year. Accounts receivable of $3,600 were written off against the allowance account as uncollectible. All the accounts listed have normal debit or credit balances.

Required: From the information given, prepare:

(1) an income statement.

(2) a statement of sources and uses of net working capital.

(3) a statement of cash receipts and disbursements. (Show the details of cash receipts and disbursements from operations.)

8–4. A creditors' committee has assumed responsibility for the operations of Thomas Manufacturing Co., Inc. During the fiscal year, the committee hopes to be able to pay off the following obligations:

Outstanding loans	$ 5,000
Interest accrued on loans	900
Mortgage installment	3,000
Interest on mortgage	600
Various debts incurred in past years	11,400

New equipment costing $6,000 must be acquired to carry on business operations. Payment is required upon purchase. Old equipment having a net book value of $23,600 will be sold.

The cash balance at the beginning of the fiscal year is $16,200.

Operating activity for the year has been estimated, and it is believed that the estimates are realistic. The estimated income statement follows:

Thomas Manufacturing Co., Inc.
Estimated Income Statement
For the Year Ended June 30, 1973

Net sales	$132,200
Cost of goods sold, including depreciation of $23,820 ..	$ 72,140
Wages and salaries	43,610
Advertising	9,270
Office supplies expense	3,140
Taxes, other than income tax......................	5,880
Insurance	1,230
Utilities	2,920
Depreciation	2,600
Patent amortization	3,000
Goodwill write-off	2,700
Loss on sale of plant assets	12,800
	$159,290
Net loss	($ 27,090)

Required: From the information furnished by the creditors' committee, does it appear that it can accomplish its objective without reducing the cash balance? Support your answer with a statement of cash receipts and disbursements.

8–5. Harry Danner owns and operates a hardware and lawn supply company. By the end of the next fiscal quarter, he hopes to be able to pay off a bank loan in the amount of $10,000. The cash balance at July 1, 1973 is $32,000. Transactions and various business events for the next quarter that ends on September 30, 1973, have been estimated as shown below and on the next page.

Sales to customers	$100,700
Collections on accounts receivable:	
Customer balances at gross amount (discount of 2% to be allowed)	65,000
Customer balances at gross amount (no discounts allowable)	19,000
Cash sales (included in sales to customers)	12,000
Sales returns and allowances (includes the 2% mentioned above)	4,700

Purchases	$63,800
Inventory increase	6,100
Accounts payable at the beginning of the quarter	21,700
Accounts payable at the end of the quarter	19,300
Personal withdrawals by Harry Danner	5,400
Payments to employees for wages	6,800
Increase in liability for net wages payable	600
Payroll taxes and income taxes withheld from employees' pay during the quarter	1,400
Payment of payroll taxes and taxes withheld from wages	1,100
Employer's share of payroll taxes for the quarter	500
Interest expense for the quarter	350
Liability for interest at the beginning of the quarter	200
Payment of insurance premium on a policy giving coverage from July 1, 1973, to June 30, 1976	1,200
Prepaid advertising allocated to the quarter as expense (payment made in May, 1973)	150
Depreciation for the quarter	800
Estimated liability for interest at the end of the quarter	100
Various other operating expenses (equal to the payments made)	2,640

Required: (1) Prepare an estimated income statement for the quarter ended September 30, 1973.

(2) Prepare an estimated statement of cash receipts and disbursements for the quarter and state whether or not the loan can be repaid without reducing the cash balance below the amount available at July 1, 1973.

8–6. On August 1, 1973, the cash balance of Fountain Stores, Inc., amounted to $742,600. Operating activity for the month of August has been planned, and an estimated income statement for the month follows:

Fountain Stores, Inc.

Estimated Income Statement

For the Month of August, 1973

Net sales	$638,700
Expenses:	
Cost of goods sold	$314,300
Materials and supplies used	19,100
Wages and salaries	58,700
Advertising	28,800
Taxes, other than income taxes	6,200
Insurance	3,100
Heat and light	1,100
Repairs and maintenance	1,300
Telephone	700
Depreciation	4,600
Interest	1,700
Income taxes	95,600
Total expenses	$535,200
Net income	$103,500

The treasurer of the company would like to have a cash balance of at least $600,000 at August 31. If the balance falls below $600,000, additional funds will be borrowed.

Disbursements during the month of August have been planned as follows:

Quarterly dividend declared and paid	$132,000
Payment on notes	50,000
Payment on equipment loan	8,000

Estimates of changes in current assets and liabilities follow:

Accounts receivable increase	$ 73,000
Inventory of merchandise decrease	17,000
Accounts payable decrease	11,000
Prepaid insurance increase	1,500
Income tax liability increase	13,000
Inventory of materials and supplies decrease	2,500
Interest liability decrease	1,600

Required: From the estimates made, does it appear that the cash balance will amount to at least $600,000 on August 31? Support your answer with a statement of cash receipts and disbursements. (A detailed analysis of operations is not required.)

8–7. The financial statements of Bethel Furnishings, Inc., as taken from the financial report for 1972 are given below and on the next page. Alvin Meyer, the president of the company, is disappointed to find that the cash balance has decreased by over $50,000 during the year. He had hoped that the cash balance would increase by $40,000. Dividends of $20,000 were declared and paid during the year, and Mr. Meyer planned plant asset additions of an amount approximately equal to the depreciation charges. With a net income of $60,000 and dividends paid in the amount of $20,000, he expected an increase of $40,000 in cash from operations net of the dividend payments.

Bethel Furnishings, Inc.

Comparative Balance Sheets

December 31

	1972	1971
Assets		
Current assets:		
Cash	$ 41,800	$ 92,300
Marketable securities	18,000	16,000
Accounts receivable	124,500	93,600
Inventory	138,700	115,100
Prepaid expenses	5,300	3,100
Total current assets	$328,300	$320,100
Plant assets:		
Land	$ 39,000	$ 22,000
Buildings and equipment	212,000	197,000
Accumulated depreciation	(88,200)	(73,500)
Net plant assets	$162,800	$145,500
Goodwill	28,000	28,000
Total assets	$519,100	$493,600

	1972	1971
Equities		
Current liabilities:		
Accounts payable	$ 31,200	$ 44,600
Notes payable—bank loans	5,000	15,000
Estimated liability for income taxes	62,000	54,000
Other current liabilities	9,100	8,200
Total current liabilities	$107,300	$121,800
Owners' equity:		
Capital stock	$200,000	$200,000
Retained earnings	211,800	171,800
Total equities	$519,100	$493,600

Bethel Furnishings, Inc.

Income Statement

For the Year Ended December 31, 1972

Net sales	$744,200
Cost of goods sold	486,200
Gross margin	$258,000
* Operating and other expenses	138,000
Net income before income taxes	$120,000
Income taxes	60,000
Net income after income taxes	$ 60,000

* Includes depreciation of $14,700.

Required: Prepare statements that will show Mr. Meyer why the cash balance decreased by $50,500. (Show the detail of cash receipts and disbursements from operations.)

8–8. Jessel Fixtures Company had considerable difficulty in the year ended June 30, 1973. A long strike and rising costs were largely responsible for the net loss for the year. Although operations were conducted at a loss, the cash balance increased by a substantial amount.

An income statement is given for the year ended June 30, 1973, along with balance sheets as of June 30, 1972 and 1973. These statements are shown on page 255.

The bank notes and accounts payable arose out of transactions involving the purchase of merchandise for resale. Depreciation of $164,000 is included in the operating expenses along with uncollectible account losses of $7,800. Accounts receivable amounting to $6,500 were written off during the fiscal year against the allowance account. Plant assets were not retired, and there were no purchases of marketable securities.

Required: Recast the income statement to show cash receipts and disbursements from operations and prepare a statement showing how the cash balance increased in spite of the net loss.

Jessel Fixtures Company

Balance Sheets

June 30

	1973	1972
Assets		
Current assets:		
Cash	$1,246,160	$ 973,240
Marketable securities	143,700	171,800
Accrued interest receivable	3,840	3,920
Accounts receivable, net of allowance for		
doubtful accounts	831,320	911,770
Inventory	1,199,200	1,302,900
Prepaid operating expenses	51,750	49,220
Total current assets	$3,475,970	$3,412,850
Plant assets:		
Store equipment, net of accumulated		
depreciation	1,842,500	1,850,500
Total assets	$5,318,470	$5,263,350
Equities		
Current liabilities:		
Accounts payable	$ 710,830	$ 587,310
Notes payable—bank	305,000	240,000
Wages and salaries payable	132,350	135,140
Taxes payable other than income taxes	143,100	142,350
Accrued interest payable	12,100	11,300
Total current liabilities	$1,303,380	$1,116,100
Owners' equity:		
Capital stock, $1 par value	1,500,000	1,500,000
Paid-in capital in excess of par	1,750,000	1,750,000
Retained earnings	765,090	897,250
Total equities	$5,318,470	$5,263,350

Jessel Fixtures Company

Income Statement

For the Year Ended June 30, 1973

Net sales	$6,282,740
Cost of goods sold	4,732,200
Gross margin	$1,550,540
Operating expenses	1,675,000
Net operating loss	($ 124,460)
Interest expense	14,700
	($ 139,160)
Interest and dividends earned	4,250
Gain on sale of marketable securities	2,750
Net loss	($ 132,160)

8–9. The directors of Northern Products Company are planning cash flows for the next year. The company has made some poor investment decisions in the past with the result being that the liabilities are relatively large and that substantial losses will be taken on both accounts receivable and inventories. However, operations for the next year are expected to be profitable, and the directors are confident that the company will be able to make progress again if past debts can be discharged.

A balance sheet at December 31, 1972, appears below:

Northern Products Company
Balance Sheet
December 31, 1972

Assets

Cash	$ 36,300
Accounts receivable	141,200
Inventories	137,400
Prepayments	3,500
Land	35,000
Buildings, net of depreciation of $87,000	308,000
Equipment, net of depreciation of $63,000	184,000
Total assets	$845,400

Equities

Accounts payable	$ 92,200
Bank loans	78,000
Current installment due on notes	25,000
Accrued liabilities	36,400
Serial notes payable	300,000
Capital stock	245,000
Retained earnings	68,800
Total equities	$845,400

An estimated income statement for 1973 follows:

Northern Products Company
Estimated Income Statement
For the Year, 1973

Net sales	$873,500
Cost of goods sold, including depreciation of $33,000	662,900
Gross margin	$210,600
Operating expenses, including depreciation of $4,800	167,200
Net operating income	$ 43,400
Loss on sale of equipment	2,300
Net income before income taxes	$ 41,100
Income taxes	16,300
Net income after income taxes	$ 24,800

The company cannot borrow additional funds until it reduces its present debt substantially. Planned debt reductions for 1973 are listed on the next page.

Accounts payable	$ 40,000
Bank loans	50,000
Current installment due on loans	25,000
Accrued liabilities	15,000
Total	$130,000

During the year, uncollectible accounts will be written off against retained earnings in the amount of $44,000. At the end of the year, accounts receivable should amount to $94,500.

Inventories will be reduced to $71,000 with losses on obsolete and damaged materials being absorbed in operations for the year.

If the company is to continue operations, it must obtain new equipment at a cost of $16,000. Old equipment having a net book value of $12,400 will be sold during the year.

One of the directors believes that additional investment by the stockholders will be required to reduce the debt and maintain a cash balance that is at least as much as it was at December 31, 1972. Another director claims that this may not be necessary. If the losses on accounts receivable are not written off to retained earnings, he reasons that the retained earnings accumulated in the past plus the net income anticipated for 1973 and depreciation should be sufficient for the planned reduction in debt.

Required: (1) Prepare an estimated statement of cash flow for 1973 from the information available.

(2) How much must be invested by stockholders, if any, to meet the objectives?

(3) Point out why the director, who believes no additional resources from stockholders will be needed, is correct or incorrect.

PART TWO
OPERATIONS PLANNING
AND CONTROL

Chapter 9

COST CONCEPTS OF
PLANNING AND CONTROL

The work of management, as explained in the Introduction, can be summarized as (1) planning, which includes determining objectives and budgets to meet these objectives, and (2) control, which includes directing the activity required to achieve the objectives. During the course of operations, many factors may alter the original plan: objectives may have to be redefined, the plan revised, or control strengthened. The planning and control functions are continuous and interrelated. Each provides feedback to improve the management process.

Although management relies heavily on information developed in financial accounting, more detailed information provided in cost accounting is eventually required. The first eight chapters emphasized the ways in which financial accounting can be used by management. An analysis of statements and different methods used in financial reporting, an understanding of the price level problem, or information on the sources and uses of net working capital may reveal to management areas that require more attention in planning and control. In the chapters that follow, cost accounting will be given close attention, to show how more detailed information on costs are also vital to planning and control by management.

COSTS

There are many different types of costs, and the costs can be classified in various ways according to the needs of management. There are many complexities in the cost area, which arise either because of the nature of the costs themselves or the ways in which the costs are used. The problem of working with costs can be simplified if one considers carefully how the costs are to be used and *selectively chooses cost data that will serve that purpose.*

Management, stockholders, employees, and other groups will be interested in summarized cost data. Management will want to know, for example, how much it costs to operate a given plant for a year or the total cost of the various products sold during the year. But management will also want more detail. For example, to manage an enterprise effectively, it will be necessary to know how much it costs to operate a given segment of the business such as a division or a department, how much it costs to produce and sell a given quantity of a certain product line, and how much it costs to produce and sell each unit of the various lines handled. Detailed cost information is furnished by a system of cost accounting and can be used to control business activities, plan operations, and make decisions.

The use of the term "cost accounting" implies that cost accounting is an entirely different system of accountability. As mentioned in Chapter One cost accounting is only an extension of general accounting. Costs are accounted for in any event. In general financial accounting the costs are reported in aggregate, but in cost accounting they are broken down on a *unit* basis. The unit may be a plant, department, product line, function, or other item to which costs can be assigned.

Period costs. Some costs that are referred to as *period* costs are identified with measured time intervals and not with goods or services. Office rent, for example, may be at the rate of $250 a month. Each month the rental cost is $250 without regard to the amount of business transacted. The cost is matched against revenue as expense according to the time interval that has elapsed. An income statement for the year will show rent expense of $3,000. For managerial purposes, of course, rent and other period costs may be identified with some given part of the business or with some product line or unit of product even though they are charged as expenses on a period basis. In general financial accounting, costs are recorded by natural classifications such as wages, taxes, insurance, etc. They may also be classified according to the functions served. For example, costs may be classified as manufacturing costs, selling costs, or costs of administration. Often the costs are related to a period of time and not to a product or an activity. This is particularly true of selling and administrative costs that are often difficult to identify according to product or service.

Product costs. Costs cannot always be properly matched against revenues on a period-of-time basis. In the income determination process, costs incurred to produce revenues should be offset as expenses against the resulting revenues. The period in which the benefit is received is the period in which the costs should be deducted as expenses. For example, rent on a factory building for a certain year should not be charged off as rent expense for that year if the products that were manufactured then are not sold until the next year. The rent cost should follow the products and should be matched against the revenue from their sale as expense. The costs incurred to manufacture products should become a part of the product cost and should become expense only when the products to which they are attached are sold. Usually manufacturing costs are treated as product costs and not as period costs. Factory rent, while accruing on a time basis, is generally considered to be a part of the cost of the goods produced. If the goods produced during a year are the only goods sold in that year with no inventory remaining at the end of the year, the resulting net income would be the same under either a time basis or a product basis of accountability. But if completed or partially completed goods are on hand at the end of the fiscal year, some of the rent would be attached to them and would be carried over to the following fiscal year.

Cost accounting beyond the manufacturing area. The principles of cost accounting do not have to be restricted to manufacturing operations. Within recent years, much attention has been given to the determination of costs by units in service industries. For example, automobile insurance companies have calculated the costs of servicing customers by age classification, marital status, accident record, location, etc. Banks also make use of cost analysis in arriving at service charges and amounts to be charged for handling special checking accounts.

Even in a manufacturing enterprise, the principles of cost accounting can be extended to include the selling and administrative areas. Usually the formal accounting records will show selling and administrative costs as period costs and not as a part of product cost. But for managerial purposes, supplemental analysis may be made to show what it costs to serve certain customers, or what it costs to sell certain product lines, or the costs to sell in particular geographical areas. This breakdown of costs provides a means for control over sales and administration in much the same way as manufacturing cost accounting provides a means for control over production.

Cost transitions. That part of cost accounting which supports financial accounting is based upon the premise that assets which are acquired are transformed within the enterprise and ultimately become a part of the inventory of products to be sold. Eventually the products are sold, and the costs of the various assets that have been transformed into product cost are released as expense.

This process of transformation is illustrated by using a simple example. Fuel is purchased to give power to a certain machine in Department 5. The machine is used to turn out products. The following table shows the process of transformation:

Transaction	Asset Conversion	Account	Type of Account
1. Purchase of fuel	Acquisition of potential energy	Fuel	Asset
2. Consumption of fuel by machine in Department 5	Potential energy becomes active energy	Manufacturing Cost in Department 5	Asset
3. Costs of Department 5 applied to products	Active energy identified with products	Work in Process	Asset
4. Products completed and transferred to finished stock	Products are completely manufactured	Finished Goods	Asset
5. Products removed from finished stock and sold	Products sold	Cost of Goods Sold	Expense

The consumption of the fuel does not constitute expense. The fuel has merely changed form. It has been converted into energy, which becomes a part of the cost of the products that have been manufactured. The fuel cost becomes expense when the products leave the business as a result of sales transactions. Fuel cost, along with other costs, then becomes a part of the cost of goods sold.

The cost elements. The manufactured cost of any product consists of three elements:

(1) Direct materials.
(2) Direct labor.
(3) Manufacturing overhead.

Direct materials cost is the cost of materials incorporated in the product and measurable as such. Obviously the steel used in manufacturing socket wrenches would be a part of the product, and its cost could be measured as direct materials cost. A galvanizing solution used to coat the tools, while a part of the product, may not be easy to measure as a cost of any particular unit processed. The cost per unit may be too insignificant to measure as direct materials cost and may be classified under manufacturing overhead as an indirect materials cost. Similarly, the cost of other materials that are not even a part of the product, such as abrasives and polishes, are classified under manufacturing overhead.

Direct labor cost is the labor cost directly traceable to the creation of the products. Some workers, frequently designated as production workers, will spend most of their time in turning out products. The labor cost attached to this time is called the direct labor cost. The idle time of the production workers, which is not related to any group of products under production, may be wasted, or may be used in cleaning the factory and repairing the equipment, or may be put to use in some other way. Labor cost that cannot be traced to the products is included as a part of manufacturing overhead under the general heading of indirect labor. The wages or salaries of the factory foremen, engineers, maintenance men, and others who do not work on the product itself but who assist in the manufacturing operation are likewise classified under manufacturing overhead as indirect labor.

Manufacturing overhead cost consists of all manufacturing costs with the exception of direct materials and direct labor. Included under the heading of manufacturing overhead are the cost of indirect materials, supplies used, indirect labor, repairs and maintenance, heat and light, taxes, insurance, depreciation, and other costs to operate the manufacturing division.

The costing procedure. The costs of manufacturing, regardless of their various characteristics, are accumulated by cost element and are gathered together into an inventory account designated as Work in Process. This account is an asset account and is also a focal account into which all product costs are funneled. After the products have been completed and placed in finished stock, the costs are transferred to another asset account designated as Finished Goods. When the products are sold, the cost becomes Cost of Goods Sold, as shown in the following diagram:

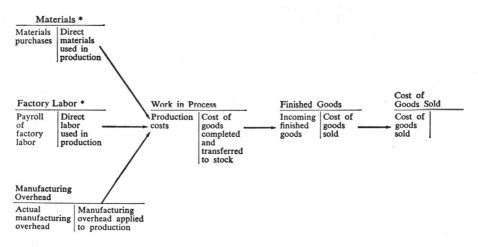

* The indirect materials and indirect labor costs are transferred from Materials and Factory Labor to Manufacturing Overhead.

Fixed and variable costs. Costs are often distinguished as being either fixed costs or variable costs. This distinction is important not only in cost accounting but throughout managerial accounting. Obviously, if costs are to be estimated and controlled properly, it will be necessary to know whether or not the cost can be expected to change under given conditions and, if so, by what amount.

As used in accounting, *fixed costs* refer to costs that do not change in total amount *with changes in volume of output or activity*. Such items as salary of a plant superintendent, depreciation, insurance, taxes, and rent, usually remain the same regardless of whether the plant is above or below its normal capacity level. However, a fixed cost, like any cost, is subject to certain variations. Rent may increase, or insurance rates go up, but these changes are caused by factors independent of the firm's output or activity.

Fixed costs are sometimes classified as being either *committed costs* or *programmed costs*. Management, in making long-range decisions, may commit a company to a cost pattern that will extend several years into the future. For example, when a building is acquired, future years will have to absorb the depreciation cost and the related property taxes, insurance, repairs, and maintenance. These fixed costs are committed costs. Other costs, referred to either as programmed costs, managed costs, or discretionary costs are determined as a part of general management policy. A budget for product research and development, for example, may be established each year, or supervisory salaries are set each year by management decision. These costs are established at a certain fixed amount, but the amount is determined by management.

Variable costs, in the strict sense, are costs that vary in *direct proportion*, or in a one-to-one relationship, to changes in productive output or activity. For example, direct materials cost is usually a variable cost with each unit manufactured requiring a certain quantity of material. Thus, the materials cost will change in direct proportion to the number of units manufactured.

Many costs, however, are semivariable. The cost may change, but not in direct proportion to the changes in output or activity. Often *semivariable costs,* which have the attributes of both variable and fixed costs, are falsely designated as variable costs. Repairs, for example, will not be fixed in amount but will probably increase as hours of activity increase. Among costs that are semivariable are indirect materials, supplies, indirect labor, maintenance, fuel, and payroll taxes. Semivariable costs may be broken down into fixed and variable components, thus making it easier to budget and control costs, and to apply cost data for decision-making purposes.

The troublesome fixed costs. The fixed costs are often responsible for difficulties in accounting for costs. By definition, the *total* fixed cost remains constant over a specified range of activity or output. This means that the fixed cost per unit of product will vary. When a greater number of units is produced, the fixed cost per unit will decrease. Conversely, when a smaller number of units is produced, the fixed cost per unit will increase. This variability with respect to unit costs creates problems in product costing. The cost per unit will depend upon the number of units being manufactured.

This problem of product costing can be illustrated by assuming that variable manufacturing overhead costs vary at a rate of $4 per unit of product manufactured and that the total fixed manufacturing overhead amounts to $150,000 for the year. Cost budgets show the following:

Number of units of product manufactured	30,000	50,000	60,000
Variable manufacturing overhead ..	$120,000	$200,000	$240,000
Fixed manufacturing overhead	150,000	150,000	150,000
Total manufacturing overhead	$270,000	$350,000	$390,000
Unit manufacturing overhead cost:			
Variable	$4.00	$4.00	$4.00
Fixed	5.00	3.00	2.50
Total	$9.00	$7.00	$6.50

The variable manufacturing overhead cost in total will be higher when more units are manufactured, but the cost per unit will remain at $4. The fixed manufacturing overhead costs in total are the same at any output level, but the cost per unit is less when more units are manufactured. If the company makes only 30,000 units, the fixed manufacturing overhead cost of $150,000 will be spread over 30,000 units, and the fixed manufacturing overhead cost per unit will be $5. With the production of 60,000 units, the fixed manufacturing overhead cost per unit will be reduced to $2.50.

It is obvious that the unit cost of a manufactured product will depend upon the number of units that are to be produced during the year. But the products must be assigned a cost before the number of units that will be produced during the year can be determined. Ordinarily, this problem is resolved by assigning fixed manufacturing overhead cost to each unit of product from a predetermined normal budget of costs and units to be manufactured.

For example, assume that the company in the illustration can normally be expected to manufacture and sell 50,000 units a year with its facilities. In this case, each product would bear $3 of fixed manufacturing overhead. At the end of the year, it may be found that only 30,000 units were actually manufactured. Therefore, only $90,000 of the total fixed manufacturing overhead of $150,000 has been costed to the products. The remaining $60,000 that was unabsorbed can be measured in the accounts as a *capacity variance.* It is the variance that was caused by not using the manufacturing facilities according to the plan incorporated in the normal budget of operations. This type of problem is quite common in cost accounting and will be discussed at greater length in later chapters.

COSTS AND CONTROL

The costs used for control are not necessarily the costs that are reported on conventional accounting statements. Much of the disagreement about how costs should be accounted for arises because of a misunderstanding of how the cost data will be used. It may be quite proper, for example, to say that the costs to operate a given plant for a year were $260,000 in total and that the costs to operate the two departments in the plant were $152,000 and $108,000 respectively. Yet, in evaluating the effectiveness of the two departments, this information is inadequate. Suppose that the depreciation of the plant, the plant superintendent's salary, and the other costs of operating the plant that are not directly related to departmental operation were $160,000 and were included in the total cost of $260,000. Assume further that the costs of $160,000 were allocated equally to each of the departments. Should the supervisor of the first department be held responsible for the total costs of $152,000 assigned to his department? Included in this cost is $80,000 of allocated cost, 50% of $160,000. Hence, the costs that can be directly traced to the department are $72,000 ($152,000 — $80,000). The allocation of costs tends to blur areas of responsibility. In evaluating the supervisors of the departments, it would be more useful to charge them with only the costs for which they are responsible. Their particular areas can be controlled more effectively by comparing the costs over which they have jurisdiction with budgets or standards prepared on the same basis.

In arriving at a decision as to whether or not operations have been conducted efficiently, management will depend upon some basis of measurement such as a budget or a cost standard. The budget or the standard serves as a point of reference. Differences between the actual costs incurred and the budgeted or standard costs can be calculated and put to use in evaluating performance. If further investigation reveals that budget differences were caused by unsatisfactory conditions, positive steps can be taken to correct the situation. In other words, budget comparisons produce information that can be used to control the business at various levels of operation.

Direct and indirect costs. Costs are sometimes spoken of as being direct or indirect with respect to an activity, a department, or a product. For example, the materials and the labor that are easily identified as a part of the product cost are the direct materials and the direct labor cost of the product. The manufacturing overhead costs are not directly identifiable with any particular product and are thus indirect costs with respect to the product.

The distinction between a direct cost and an indirect cost depends upon the unit under consideration. A cost such as the plant superintendent's salary is a direct cost of the plant, but it is an indirect cost of any department within the plant or of any line of product manufactured. Or the cost of supplies used may be identified directly as a cost of a particular department, yet not be a direct cost of the products manufactured. If a cost can be directly attached to the unit under consideration, it is a direct cost with respect to that unit. If it is a cost of a unit only through allocation, it is an indirect cost.

Controllable and noncontrollable costs. This cost classification also depends upon a point of reference. All costs are controllable at one level or another of management. Top management has the authority to dispose of facilities, increase or decrease executive salaries, and control any cost as it sees fit. Only at intermediate or at lower management levels can a cost be said to be uncontrollable. The lower levels of management have no authority over certain costs, which are uncontrollable insofar as they are concerned. Costs that can be authorized at a certain managerial level are said to be controllable at that level. A departmental supervisor may have control over the supplies used by his department, but he has no control over the plant depreciation cost allocated to his department.

Direct costs and controllable costs are not necessarily the same. A cost may be a direct cost of a given department but may not be controlled by the departmental supervisor. For example, the salary of a departmental supervisor, which is a direct cost of the department, is controlled at a higher level of management rather than by the supervisor.

Nor can a cost be looked upon as being uncontrollable because it is a fixed cost. Often there is a tendency to view a cost as either controllable or uncontrollable because it is either variable or fixed. It is incorrect, however, to confuse cost behavior characteristics with controllability. While a fixed cost such as property insurance may be uncontrollable at a given managerial level, it is nevertheless subject to control by a manager who has the authority to obtain insurance coverage for the firm.

Time also plays a part in controllability. A cost that can be controlled in the long run may not be controllable over a short period of time. For example, a sales manager may have committed the company to a contract for advertising and while the contract is in force has no control over the cost. However, when the contract has expired, the sales manager is free to renegotiate and thus has control over the cost in the long run.

RESPONSIBILITY ACCOUNTING

In *responsibility accounting* costs are identified with the person responsible for their incurrence. Because responsibility is localized, it is possible to rate individual managers on a cost basis by comparing the *controllable* costs of his department or division with a budget prepared on the same basis. Budgets will be discussed at length in Chapters 20 and 21.

Each manager is expected to prepare a budget of the costs that he controls and he is expected to operate within the limits of this budget. Periodic cost reports prepared on this basis of cost responsibility are compared with the budgets and are used by each manager as a basis for self evaluation. Managers at higher levels may rate subordinate managers by using this information. Responsibility can be a most useful concept in controlling costs.

Cost reports. Costs that have been authorized by the plant manager of the Edgewood Plant of Baker Enterprises, Inc., for the administration of his own office are reported below for illustration. The costs that have been incurred by his subordinates, the departmental foremen, are not included on this particular report.

Baker Enterprises, Inc.
Cost Report—Plant Administration
Plant Manager—Edgewood Plant
For the Month of May, 1973

	Year to Date			May, 1973		
	Budget	Actual	Actual Over (Under)	Budget	Actual	Actual Over (Under)
Materials and supplies ...	$ 3,450	$ 3,950	$500	$ 620	$ 870	$250
Wages and payroll taxes	14,700	14,950	250	2,800	2,900	100
Labor fringe benefits ...	1,830	1,970	140	380	360	(20)
Travel and entertainment	1,100	1,030	(70)	250	220	(30)
Insurance	500	500	—	100	100	—
Telephone	750	770	20	140	130	(10)
Miscellaneous	120	80	(40)	30	—	(30)
Totals	$22,450	$23,250	$800	$4,320	$4,580	$260

This report can help the plant manager to control the costs that he is *personally* responsible for in the administration of the plant. Costs that appear to be out of line with the budget by a material amount may be given closer attention. Information developed from the report may be helpful in budget revisions or in the preparation of future budgets.

If more detail is needed, supplemental reports may be issued. For example, a computer report may be given to show the voucher numbers and the names of payees for individual items of cost under each natural cost classification. From basic input information, computer programs can be designed to reclassify and accumulate information in various ways to serve the needs of management. Suppose in this case that the plant manager wants to know the composition of the materials and supplies cost for the month of May. A report showing the vouchers approved for materials and supplies during the month will provide basic information on the charges to this classification.

The plant manager, in addition to being responsible for the administration of his own office, is also responsible for the activities of his subordinates. Hence, he will receive a report showing in summary form the costs incurred by himself and by his departmental foremen. A report for the month of May is given below:

Baker Enterprises, Inc.
Cost Report—Departmental Costs
Edgewood Plant
For the Month of May, 1973

	Year to Date			May, 1973		
	Budget	Actual	Actual Over (Under)	Budget	Actual	Actual Over (Under)
Plant adminis-tration	$ 22,450	$ 23,250	$ 800	$ 4,320	$ 4,580	$260
Department 1	173,600	172,480	(1,120)	34,170	33,240	(930)
Department 2	121,300	121,740	440	28,220	28,510	290
Department 3	89,750	91,260	1,510	18,330	18,780	450
Totals	$407,100	$408,730	$1,630	$85,040	$85,110	$ 70

Each foreman will receive a cost report on his own operation similar to the one prepared for the plant manager. He may also receive a detailed report showing the individual vouchers charged under each cost classification.

All of the costs that are controllable at the plant level may also be reported to the plant manager by natural classification as shown in the report given at the top of the next page.

Responsibility cost reports can be designed in various ways to suit individual preferences. In general, a manager will expect to receive a report on the costs that he personally incurs, a summary report on the controllable costs for each manager within his jurisdiction, and a report of these controllable costs broken down by natural classification. In some cases, it will be more meaningful to receive a report on costs for particular projects or jobs that are in process. A network of reports showing a comparison of controllable costs with budgets extends all the way from the president's office to the lowest level of management.

Baker Enterprises, Inc.
Cost Report—Natural Classification
Edgewood Plant
For the Month of May, 1973

	Year to Date			May, 1973		
	Budget	Actual	Actual Over (Under)	Budget	Actual	Actual Over (Under)
Materials and supplies	$241,650	$242,820	$1,170	$49,330	$49,230	($100)
Wages and pay- roll taxes	135,820	135,930	110	29,750	29,800	50
Labor fringe benefits	14,230	14,380	150	2,790	2,820	30
Travel and entertainment ...	3,800	3,850	50	780	820	40
Insurance	7,300	7,300	—	1,470	1,470	—
Telephone	3,100	3,190	90	640	670	30
Miscellaneous	1,200	1,260	60	280	300	20
Totals	$407,100	$408,730	$1,630	$85,040	$85,110	$ 70

It might seem that costs can be budgeted and reported quite easily on the basis of controllability, but such is not the case. Costs may be authorized by one responsible individual, and in that sense are controlled by him, but other persons within the organization may influence the amount of the cost. Thus, control by one individual is not absolute.

Often a service department, such as a repair and maintenance department, will render services to other departments. The other departments have no direct control over the costs of the service department; yet by requesting the service, they are implicitly accepting the cost of the service.

Sometimes the problem is solved by allocating the service department costs to the other departments on the basis of (1) the investment in machinery and equipment in other departments or (2) hours of service given. This will not always be satisfactory because the service department might not control its costs properly. Also, an increase in the service department costs due to a request by one department for rush service should not be allocated to other departments or to the service department.

One solution is to establish an hourly billing rate for the service department, based on a normal service department budget. Each department will be billed as if it were an outside customer, thus absorbing the penalty cost for rush work. If the managers are charged only for the costs that they control directly, they may operate more efficiently and minimize friction over cost responsibility between the service department and other departments.

In some cases it is believed that costs should be allocated even though they are not controlled directly by the departments receiving the service. The argument for cost allocation is that all managers should be conscious of the full cost of operating their departments and as a result they will be more careful in requesting services. This is a departure from pure responsibility accounting. Whether or not it will produce results depends upon the attitudes of the individuals within the organization. Full allocation may result in tighter cost control.

Control features. The responsibility cost reports provide a basis for control. They identify specific responsibility centers and costs within the centers that may require further attention. An identification of trouble areas, however, is only the beginning of the control process. Questions must be asked. Is the difference between the budgeted cost and the actual cost material enough to justify further investigation? What caused the variation? Is it likely that a variation from the budget will be repeated in the future if action isn't taken? It may be found that measures can be taken that will reduce variations in the future or that the variation was a normal variation from the average and didn't warrant investigation. In some cases it will be found that the budget was unrealistic and should be revised. The responsibility reports are somewhat like switchboards that flash warning lights when there is trouble. They furnish the initial information that serves as a basis for corrections.

A responsibility cost system can be a subtle means of enforcing company policy. Decisions are made at the top management level in regard to which costs will be controlled at the lower management levels. At all levels of management, supervisory personnel are conscious of cost and will be most careful when costs are charged against them. Top management will not have to spell out policy in a directive. The lower levels of management will be guided according to how the costs are charged to their responsibility areas.

Costs that would normally be included in the reports of subordinates may be excluded if top management believes that the company will benefit from a more liberal policy. On the other hand, costs that are to be controlled more rigorously will be given more attention if they are authorized by the manager and charged to his area.

For example, a company may provide a copying service to expedite the preparation of many copies of forms and reports. The services may be given to all departments with no charge, thus encouraging the departmental supervisors to make use of this service with no cost appearing on their cost reports. However, if top management believes that the service is being drawn upon too freely, a charge may be made to the departments for this service. A manager, knowing that he will be charged for the service, will tend to use the service more sparingly.

The successful operation of a responsibility accounting system depends to a large extent upon the attitudes of company personnel. Some research has been done in the area of human behavior within organizaitons, but there is still much to be done. The central objective is to assign cost responsibility in such a way that the individuals affected will be motivated to act in the best interests of the company to achieve the established goals. A policy that may work in one organization will not necessarily work in another because of the differences in the attitudes and behavior of the personnel involved.

Often it is believed that the only goal of business enterprise is to maximize profits. This is not necessarily true. Ordinarily, there are a combination of goals. In addition to profits, the company may seek to provide a superior product or service and may be concerned with the welfare of the employees and the community at large.

The various goals of the organization should be co-ordinated. If one goal is inconsistent with another, management will be confused and will need direction as to how much attention is to be given to one objective as compared with another. For example, a company may seek to train employees on the job in an effort to develop skilled personnel. However, this can interfere with efficient performance and may reduce profits. Guidelines should be established that will spell out how much cost and supervisory effort is to be expended on job training, and a balance must be struck that is clearly understood by the personnel affected.

COSTS AND PLANNING

Budgets have already been discussed to some extent in relation to responsibility accounting, but this is only one application of the budget principle. In cost accounting, for example, budgets and standards are used in determining how much it costs to operate a department or to manufacture a certain line of product or even to manufacture one unit of a product line. In budgeting, a thorough study of operations is combined with past experience and estimates of future possibilities. Individual budgets prepared for each function, department, and product line are related to each other and are interlocked in a master budget plan. For example, the estimated production for the next fiscal year is broken down by product line. From this figure it is possible to estimate the activity level and draw up cost budgets for the manufacturing department. In turn, the budgets of costs for the departments, when related to the number of units of various product lines to be manufactured, yield budgeted costs per unit for each line of product. Budgets are prepared in the same way for other functions of the business, such as sales and administration.

Cost data can be combined and analyzed in the process of either budgeting or reporting costs. Some costs, such as past or historical costs, may serve as a basis for estimating what costs will be in the future, yet these costs are not accounted for in a conventional manner in decisional analysis. The costs measured in the accounting records are not necessarily costs used in decision making. If past performance is to be measured, historical costs will be relevant, but if plans are to be made for the future, estimated *changes* in costs and revenues will be more significant.

Various cost concepts are appropriate (1) for controlling operations, (2) for conventional product costing, or (3) for planning future operations. Some of the cost concepts that have particular value in planning are identified and discussed in the following paragraphs.

Differential costs. Management is expected to make decisions and in doing so will compare alternatives. Perhaps a choice must be made between two types of equipment that can be used to perform the same work, or the choice may involve the selection of a plant location. There are various business situations where alternatives must be compared with one alternative being accepted to the exclusion of the others.

In making a decision, management will compare the costs of the alternatives. The costs that will remain the same in any case can be disregarded, but the difference in cost between one alternative and another is very important in decision making. A difference in cost between one course of action and another is spoken of as a *differential cost*. If a decision will result in an increased cost, the differential cost may be more specifically referred to as an *incremental cost*. If the cost will be decreased, the differential cost may be referred to as a *decremental cost*.

Differential cost is a broad concept. For example, it may cost $6 to produce one unit of product and $11 to produce two units. The difference in cost or the differential cost is $5. Often the additional cost to produce one more unit of product is spoken of as the *marginal cost* of producing that unit. But it is also the differential cost or the incremental cost. The additional cost of producing a unit of product over a given range of productive output is ordinarily spoken of as the *variable cost per unit*. (Within a given range of production, the marginal cost per unit will be equal to the variable cost per unit. Marginal costs and variable costs are discussed at length in Chapter 17.) The variable cost can also be designated as the differential cost or the incremental cost of producing and selling one more unit. In the situations mentioned above, the cost differentials are usually designated specifically as marginal costs or as variable costs as the case might be.

A decision may result in changes in costs that are ordinarily fixed. As stated before, costs are said to be fixed if they are not altered by changes in output or activity. But a fixed cost may be changed by some decision made by management. Assume that the production superintendent plans to change a certain production process. Some of the costs will be higher, and some will be lower. Costs that are ordinarily considered to be variable costs or fixed costs may be increased or decreased if the new production process is accepted. In this situation, the production superintendent estimates that the total manufacturing costs will be decreased by $17,000 a year under the new process. In other words, the differential cost which in this case is also a decremental cost is estimated at $17,000. The differential cost is the difference in cost between operating under one alternative as compared with another. The term is not reserved for specific applications. Instead, it may be used whenever there is a difference in cost between alternatives.

Sunk costs. A *sunk cost* is a cost that will not be changed by a decision. Costs that will not be affected are irrelevant to the decision and may be disregarded in the decision-making process. A sunk cost may be a variable cost or a fixed cost. The important point is that the cost will not be changed by the decision that is to be made. If the decision involves the production of more units of product, variable costs will be increased and will not be sunk costs. On the other hand, if no change in productive output is contemplated by the decision, the variable costs may not be affected, in which case they will be sunk costs with respect to the decision.

In the example given above, the production costs are expected to decrease by $17,000 a year if the new production process is used. Costs for each alternative have been estimated as shown below:

	Present Process	New Process
Materials and labor	$ 75,000	$ 75,000
Manufacturing overhead	50,000	33,000
Total costs	$125,000	$108,000

The materials and labor costs are estimated at $75,000 under either alternative. They are the sunk costs in this situation. Manufacturing overhead, however, is expected to change with the result being that the differential cost in favor of the new process amounts to $17,000.

In many cases, the sunk cost will be a cost that has already been incurred. After a cost has been incurred, it cannot be changed by any decision to be made at the present time or in the future. An individual may regret having made a purchase; but after he has made the purchase, he cannot avoid the cost by any action that he may take. Perhaps he can sell the property that he purchased in which case the cost of the property will be matched against the proceeds from the sale in the determination of gain or loss. Or he may decide to keep the property, in which case the cost will be matched against revenues over the time that it is used in operations. In any event, the cost has been incurred and cannot be avoided. It is a sunk cost with respect to present and future decisions.

To illustrate, it is assumed that Weller Products Company purchased a drying rack for $15,000. The drying rack can be used in operations for five years and is not expected to have any residual salvage value. Shortly after making the purchase, the management of the company recognized that the investment should not have been made. The drying rack cannot yield the operating advantages that were originally planned, and it is estimated that its use will provide only an $8,000 cost saving over the 5-year period. However, the company is committed to the purchase and cannot avoid the $15,000 cost. The company is considering whether to use the drying rack or to sell it.

	Alternative No. 1 Use	Alternative No. 2 Sell
Saving in cost over 5 years by using the drying rack	$ 8,000	
Proceeds from immediate sale of the drying rack		$12,000
Less: Cost of the drying rack:		
Depreciation over 5 years ..	15,000	
Cost of the drying rack		15,000
Net loss over 5 years	($ 7,000)	
Net loss on the sale		($ 3,000)

The relevant amounts for decision making are the $8,000 in cost saving over five years as compared with the $12,000 that can be received from the sale of the property. The $15,000 invested in the property is not relevant; it is the same in both cases. Weller Products Company should sell the property for $12,000. The decision was obvious in this situation. Ordinarily, future dollar amounts should be reduced to present values when a comparison is to be made. (The present value concept is discussed in Appendix D.)

Opportunity costs. Costs are generally looked upon as being outlays or expenditures that must be made either in the present or in the future to obtain goods and services. But the concept of cost can be extended to include *sacrifices that are made when incoming benefits or returns are refused.* In choosing between alternatives, management will try to select the best alternative but in doing so will have to give up the returns that could have been derived from the rejected alternatives. The sacrifice of a return or benefit from a rejected alternative is spoken of as being the *opportunity cost* of the alternative accepted.

The opportunity costs are not entered in the accounting records, of course, but they are used in decision making.

Often management will be confronted with alternatives, each of which has its advantages. For example, there may be an opportunity to make one of two different product lines, but both product lines cannot be manufactured with the present facilities. It may be estimated that Product A will contribute $16,000 a year to profits and that Product B will contribute $21,000 a year to profits. Product B should be selected, and the opportunity cost of selecting Product B is the sacrifice of the $16,000 that could be earned by Product A.

Estimated increase in annual profits from Product B $21,000
Less: Opportunity cost (sacrifice of estimated annual profits
     from Product A) 16,000
Advantage of Product B .... $ 5,000

An illustration of decision-making costs. The distinctions that have been made between direct and indirect costs, controllable and noncontrollable costs, and fixed and variable costs are important in product costing and are important in the control of operations. In costing products and in controlling operations, management will want to know which costs can be identified directly with a function or operation and will want to know which costs can be controlled at a certain management level. In addition, cost behavior is important. A distinction must be made between costs that can be expected to vary with changes in activity or output and the costs that will remain fixed over a given range of changes in activity or output. These cost distinctions are important in product costing and in controlling operations and when used properly are most helpful in planning and in decision making.

Differential costs and opportunity costs have little or no value in costing products or in controlling costs, but these cost concepts are most valuable in decision making. Decisions influence the future course of events, and the emphasis is on what lies ahead and not on what has already taken place.

Changes in costs and the sacrifice of returns that can be expected from the decision deserve the most attention.

Assume that Bridger and Sons, Inc., are presently using a unit of equipment to manufacture a certain line of product. The results of operation each year are approximately as follows:

Revenue from product sales	$50,000
Cost of products sold and operating expenses excluding depreciation	$30,000
Depreciation of equipment	8,000
	$38,000
Net income	$12,000

The present operation can be continued, or the company can use the equipment to manufacture another line of product that should produce revenue of $60,000 each year. The cost to manufacture this product and the operating expenses excluding depreciation of the equipment are estimated at $35,000.

The new product line adds $10,000 to revenue, and the differential cost is $5,000. There is a net advantage of $5,000 a year in accepting the new product line. The depreciation of the equipment is a sunk cost and can be ignored in making the decision. Perhaps sunk costs are included in the cost of the products sold and in the operating costs, but if they are included in both of the alternatives, they will not affect the analysis. The differentials are the relevant factors in making the decision.

Additional revenue from new product line ($60,000 — $50,000)	$10,000
Additional costs of new product line ($35,000 — $30,000)	5,000
Net advantage of new product line	$ 5,000

The problem can be examined in still another way. The present operation contributes $20,000 each year to net working capital. (Add depreciation of $8,000 to the net income of $12,000.) Any alternative use of the equipment must produce net working capital of at least $20,000 if it is to be equally acceptable. Stated in another way, the opportunity cost of any other alternative is the $20,000 increase in net working capital that must be sacrificed if another alternative is selected.

The new product line is expected to add $25,000 to net working capital each year: the $60,000 revenue minus the cost of goods sold and the operating expenses of $35,000.

Net working capital to be contributed by new product line each year	$25,000
Less: Opportunity cost (the sacrifice of the net working capital contributed each year by the present product line)	20,000
Net advantage of new product line each year	$ 5,000

Questions

1. How do period costs differ from product costs?

2. Can the general principles of cost accounting be applied in nonmanufacturing activities? Explain.

3. When an asset is consumed in manufacturing operations, is the cost measured as expense? Explain.

4. Name the three cost elements. Can all three cost elements be identified directly with the product? Explain.

5. Distinguish between fixed costs and variable costs.

6. Why is it difficult to account for fixed costs on a unit-of-product basis?

7. Distinguish between direct and indirect costs.

8. Distinguish between controllable and noncontrollable costs.

9. What is responsibility accounting?

10. How can responsibility accounting serve as an important tool in cost control?

11. Should a manager be held responsible for costs that he does not directly control? Discuss.

12. How does a responsibility accounting system serve as a subtle means of enforcing company policy?

13. What are differential costs?

14. Can a fixed cost ever be a differential cost? Explain.

15. Why aren't sunk costs relevant in decision making?

16. What are opportunity costs? Are opportunity costs important in decision making? Explain.

17. What are committed costs; programmed costs?

Exercises

1. Some typical cost classifications are listed below:

> Sales commissions
> Factory power and light
> Supplies used, general office
> Salaries of factory foremen
> Depreciation, office equipment
> Telephone, sales office
> Travel expense, salesmen
> Indirect materials used, factory
> Advertising, newspaper and radio
> Insurance, factory equipment
> Insurance, general office
> Office salaries

Required: Identify the costs that would be matched against revenues on a period-of-time basis. Which costs are identified with the products? Classify the costs by function: manufacturing, selling, or general and administrative.

2. The general foreman at Machine Shop #8 has the authority to purchase supplies, requisition repairs and maintenance services, and hire labor for his department. During May, 1972, the manufacturing overhead cost report for Machine Shop #8 showed the following costs:

Supplies	$ 1,120
Indirect labor—shop #8	3,500
Foreman's salary	1,500
Factory superintendence	1,750
Repairs and maintenance—shop #8	920
Depreciation of equipment—shop #8	780
Factory heat, light, and power	640
Depreciation, building	500
Assigned costs of plant personnel and medical departments	830
Total	$11,540

Required: (1) List the overhead costs that can be controlled by the foreman.
(2) List the overhead costs that can be directly identified with the department.
(3) List the overhead costs that have been allocated to Machine Shop #8.

3. During July, 1972, Henri, Inc., purchased paint at a cost of $1,200. Paint costing $900 was withdrawn from inventory during July. One-third of the paint was used in painting signs used for sales promotion. The balance of the paint withdrawn was used in painting the products. Seventy-five percent of the products painted during the month were completed and transferred to finished stock. Two-thirds of the stock completed during the month was sold in July. There were no inventories of any kind on hand at July 1.

Required: From the information given, estimate the cost of paint included in the following accounts at July 31:

(1) Materials
(2) Work in process
(3) Finished goods
(4) Cost of goods sold
(5) Selling expense

4. Mr. Hastings is responsible for the operation of a division of Rover Mills, Inc. The company has a responsibility accounting system, and each supervisor is authorized to incur all costs of operating his division. The machinery and equipment, however, is not purchased at the divisional level; it is purchased by management at the plant level.

Mr. Hastings authorizes the acquisition of certain materials that are used not only in his division but in other divisions as well. In order to get better prices, the company has centralized the purchase function and has assigned the responsibility for buying in large lots to Mr. Hastings. He has the technical knowledge required for the purchase of these particular materials and is in a better position than anyone else to obtain the best quality at the lowest prices.

He questions some of the costs that are listed on his responsibility cost report. He recognizes that he should be held accountable for the purchase function, but he states that his materials cost is often distorted when other departments use these materials extravagantly. He has no control over how other divisions use the materials and does not believe that his division should be burdened with the total cost of materials consumed.

In addition, he states that fixed costs are not controllable. Yet, he is assigned a portion of liability insurance cost on policies that he had renewed almost 3 years ago. His reports also show depreciation on machinery and equipment.

Required: Answer the questions raised by Mr. Hastings, pointing out why the costs should or should not be charged to his division. Consider more acceptable alternatives if you agree with Mr. Hastings.

5. The vice president in charge of operations at Mountain State Power Company has been asked to give his opinion with respect to how the cost responsibility should be assigned to each cost area in the following situations:

(a) The construction department plans to erect towers and run a 220 KV line through the Bluefield, Red Creek, and Highland districts. This will result in better service for these districts.

(b) Construction department employees were called out to help the employees at Red Creek restore service that was disrupted by an early spring storm.

(c) Guests of the district sales manager at Westport visited a power station at Braden Dam and were invited to lunch by the power station superintendent.

(d) Gasoline is purchased by the Bluefield district for the vehicles used on district business. Sometimes vehicles on business from other districts will stop at the Bluefield district for gasoline.

Required: Which cost area, if any, should be held responsible for the cost in each of the situations outlined? Explain.

6. The general foreman of Department #9 supervises work in producing parts required by other departments. He would like to have a cost report showing the costs by function (operations), by natural classification, and by departments requesting the work. Prepare 3 separate reports. The overhead costs cannot be directly identified by operations or by department. They are assigned at 80 percent of the direct labor cost to the operations and to the other departments.

Cost data for January, 1972, are given below:

Operations	Direct Materials	Direct Labor
Cutting	$46,300	$40,000
Machining	23,100	30,000
Boring	—	25,000
Polishing	—	15,000
Coating	—	10,000

Forty percent of the cost is to be identified with Department #5, and the balance of the cost is to be divided equally between Departments #3 and #4.

Actual overhead costs incurred are shown on the next page.

Required: Prepare the three cost reports requested by the general foreman of Department #9.

Supplies	$30,800
Indirect labor	51,100
Payroll taxes	2,800
Rent	8,000
Insurance	1,050
Electric	850
Heat	700
Water	300
Telephone	150
Miscellaneous	250
Total	$96,000

7. A few years ago the plant manager at Cole Products Company acquired equipment to be used in shaping metal parts. This equipment has not been very satisfactory. Occasionally parts are spoiled, and the equipment breaks down resulting in a loss of time to make necessary repairs.

Another type of equipment on the market costing $47,000 can be obtained for this work, and one of the foremen in the plant states that he has seen this equipment operate and that it could handle the work more efficiently and would reduce spoilage losses.

The plant manager agrees with the foreman that the new type of equipment could do a better job. He goes on to say, however, that the foreman does not recognize the economics of the situation. The equipment in operation at the present time had an original cost of $38,000. Accumulated depreciation to date amounts to $14,000. If this equipment were sold or traded, it would bring only $9,000. Obviously, the company cannot stand a $15,000 loss, he goes on to explain. Hence, the present equipment must be retained in service.

Required: Point out the errors in the plant manager's logic. List the factors that are relevant in making a decision as to whether or not the new equipment should be obtained.

8. John Dougherty has retired and plans to open a store selling photographic supplies and art materials. He has made a down payment on a lease for a store for one year. The down payment was $1,500. An additional payment of $3,000 must be made during the year. If the lease is canceled by Mr. Dougherty, the down payment of $1,500 is forfeited. Operating results for the year have been estimated as follows:

Net sales		$85,000
Cost of goods sold	$48,000	
Wages	15,000	
Rent	4,500	
Utilities	2,000	
Miscellaneous	900	70,400
Net income		$14,600

Mr. Dougherty has made no provision for the cost of his own time, considering the business to be an extension of his hobby. A business friend offers him $6,000 for the use of the store for the year.

Required: (1) Identify the sunk cost in this decisional situation. Also identify the opportunity cost.

(2) What decision should Mr. Dougherty make based upon the information given?

9. Morrison Specialties, Inc., is considering the production of a new product line. This product line can be manufactured with the present equipment, and the only effect that this product line will have on manufacturing overhead is to increase the cost of supplies and indirect materials by $18,000. If this product line is not produced, it is estimated that another line can be manufactured and sold. The other line should contribute additional profits each year of $12,000.

The new product line under consideration should produce the following results each year:

Net sales	$92,000
Direct materials	$23,000
Direct labor	16,000
Supplies and indirect materials	18,000
Heat and light	7,000
Repairs and maintenance	11,000
Factory rent	6,000
Insurance and taxes	3,000
Depreciation, equipment	2,000
Total costs	$86,000
Net income	$ 6,000

Required: (1) Identify the sunk costs.

(2) Should Morrison Specialties, Inc., produce the new product line under consideration? Show computations. Identify the opportunity cost.

10. Three different product lines can be produced by Dowling Supply Company with the present equipment in one of the divisions. The annual depreciation of the equipment is $8,000 and the annual cost of equipment operation is $3,000. These costs will not be affected by the choice of product lines.

Product A is expected to yield sales revenue of $46,000 a year with increased costs of production amounting to $28,000. Product B should yield sales revenue of $34,000 a year with increased costs of $11,000. Product C should yield sales revenue of $39,000 with increased costs of $24,000.

Required: (1) Which of the three product lines seems to offer the best profit potential based on the information given? Show computations.

(2) Identify the sunk costs.

(3) What is the opportunity cost of selecting only the best product line?

Problems

9–1. Actual costs for the year are compared with the budget for one of the producing departments of Axel-Porter, Inc. The departmental foremen have the authority to incur various costs for their departments including the right to purchase equipment. However, the salaries of the foremen are listed under supervision and are controlled at a higher management level. The comparison is found on page 282.

During the year the department manufactured 20,000 units as budgeted.

Required: (1) Compute the budgeted unit cost of the product and the actual unit cost.

(2) Prepare a revised cost report, showing only the costs that can be controlled by the foreman. Show actual cost variations from the budget on this report.

	Budget	Actual
Direct materials	$180,000	$181,200
Direct labor	64,000	64,800
Department costs:		
Supervision	18,000	18,000
Indirect labor	17,400	17,000
Indirect materials	42,300	41,500
Repairs and maintenance	14,500	13,200
Depreciation	3,000	3,000
Allocated plant costs:		
Superintendence	46,000	46,000
Heat, light and power	12,500	16,000
Taxes and insurance	8,500	9,500
Repairs and maintenance	23,600	28,700
Depreciation	11,000	11,000
Total costs	$440,800	$449,900

(3) Does it appear that the foreman was responsible for a large part of the variation between total actual costs and budgeted costs?

9–2. Plans have been made to process a holiday gift package of luxury foods at the Silver Run plant of Mayberry Foods, Inc.

Cost estimates show that the direct materials for each unit of product will cost about $3.00. Direct labor cost on a unit-of-product basis is estimated at $.80. Indirect materials costing $1.50 per unit are also expected to vary with the number of units produced.

The manager of the department in which this product is to be produced has control over the materials and labor costs with the exception of his own salary included in indirect labor at $17,000.

Costs that can be identified with the department without allocation have been estimated for the year as follows:

Indirect labor	$28,000
Repairs and maintenance of equipment	8,000
Depreciation of equipment	6,000
Total	$42,000

Costs of the plant for the year have also been estimated as shown below:

Heat, light and power	$ 37,000
Taxes and insurance	9,000
Repairs and maintenance of plant	44,000
Superintendence	65,000
Depreciation of plant	25,000
Total	$180,000

The cost of the plant operation is allocated to the departments, and the department in which this product line is to be processed is expected to share 20 percent of the cost.

The plant superintendent believes that 50,000 units of this holiday package can be manufactured and sold each year. With favorable customer response, production could be increased to 60,000 units without difficulty. On the other hand, if holiday trade is slow, demand may be down to 40,000 units.

Required: (1) Determine the estimated variable costs per unit of product.

(2) What is the total estimated unit product cost if 50,000 units are processed? 60,000 units? 40,000 units?

(3) List the costs that are to be controlled by the department manager with the variable costs being shown in total based on the assumption that 50,000 units are to be processed.

9–3. Cost data pertaining to the operations of the plant maintenance department of Thomasville Windings Company for the month of June, 1972, follow:

Maintenance materials used	$1,470
Wages and salaries	9,000
Telephone	160
Taxes and insurance	550
Heat and light	280
Outside contracted services	860
Vehicle use	420
Depreciation	300
Miscellaneous expense	130

The departmental supervisor is responsible for the various costs of operation with the exception of his own salary and the allocated costs of building occupancy and depreciation.

The supervisor's salary of $1,500 is included in wages and salaries. The salaries of clerical workers in the department amount to $3,000, and the balance of the wage and salary cost is for the maintenance workers.

The taxes and insurance and the heat and light are costs of the plant that have been allocated to the maintenance department.

Occasionally, the supervisor must contract for services outside the company, and the cost of this service is classified under Outside Contracted Service.

A motor pool is available for authorized company personnel. Each department is billed on a mileage basis for the use of these vehicles.

Required: Prepare a responsibility accounting report for the plant maintenance department for June, 1972.

9–4. Madison Kravitz is the foreman of a heat treatment department at the Pennington plant of Coyne Metals, Inc. His responsibility accounting report for June, 1972, follows:

	Budget	Actual	Variance
Materials	$ 4,400	$ 6,600	$ 2,200
Salaries and wages	7,600	10,290	2,690
Employee benefits	765	1,074	309
Payroll taxes	762	1,043	281
Power	678	625	(26)
Telephone	75	83	8
Repairs	165	383	218
Maintenance	95	126	31
Miscellaneous	48	46	(2)
Total	$14,588	$20,297	$ 5,709

At the time the budget was prepared, materials could be purchased for 80 cents a pound. During June the quantity of materials used was in agreement with the budget at 5,500 pounds, but the purchasing department could no longer obtain the materials at the 80 cent price. The price had increased to $1.20 a pound.

Labor was paid at a rate of $3.80 an hour when the budget was prepared. A new union contract was signed in May that increased the rate to $4.20 an hour. Overtime was not anticipated in the budget, but 300 hours of overtime were authorized during the month. The total labor rate for the overtime hours was $6.30 an hour. Regular hours of 2,000, as budgeted, were paid at the new labor rate of $4.20 an hour.

Employee benefits and payroll taxes are each at approximately 10 percent of the labor cost.

Mr. Kravitz states that his responsibility accounting report is not a fair report of the costs for which he is responsible. Increases in materials and labor prices are not subject to his control. Hence, he believes that variances resulting from the price differences should not be chargeable to him. Also, he points out that the overtime was required because his department had to assist another department in an emergency. The repair costs are higher than the budget, he points out, because he must work with older equipment. His request for new equipment has been approved, but the new equipment has not been received.

Required: (1) Prepare an adjusted report showing variances chargeable to Mr. Kravitz and variances that may be beyond his control.

(2) Comment on the points raised by Mr. Kravitz.

9–5. Each cost area of Warlock Energy Products, Inc., is expected to prepare a responsibility cost budget for the year showing the number of employees and the costs by natural classification. In addition, provision is to be made for the cost of services received from other cost areas with each cost area being identified.

Cost area 683 produces components used by other production cost areas. Budgets for other cost areas serve as a basis for estimating labor hours in cost area 683.

Labor hours estimated for cost area 683 have been prepared for the services requested by the other cost areas.

Cost Area	Hours Required
512	9,600
514	8,500
521	8,400
526	7,200

Past experience reveals that cost area 521 overestimates its requirements with the result that the budget for hours is usually 20 percent higher than the hours that will eventually be required. Cost area 512 will not be able to move ahead on a project that would require 500 hours. These adjustments must be made to the original estimates given.

Labor rates are estimated at $4.50 an hour. Payroll taxes and fringe benefits are to be estimated at 15 percent of the labor cost. Production workers are each estimated to work an average of 1,800 hours a year and are each paid for 2,000 hours. There are three salaried employees in the department (to be included in the count of total employees), and these employees are collectively to receive salaries of $40,000 for the year.

Materials requirements for the year have been estimated as follows:

Material A	210,000 lbs.	@ $.25
Material B	80,000 yds.	@ $.15
Material C	4,000 tons	@ $200

Other costs have been estimated as follows:

Lubricants	$ 800
Repairs and maintenance	5,300
Telephone	600
Electric	8,700
Outside services	3,100
Miscellaneous	300

In addition, cost area 683 plans to request 300 hours of service from cost area 716 to be billed at $20 an hour and 8,000 miles from the motor pool (cost area 746) at 12 cents a mile.

Required: From the information given, prepare a responsibility cost budget for cost area 683. Estimate the number of employees required.

9–6. The Glades Service Company has recently installed a system of responsibility accounting. The supervisor of cost area 373 was charged with the following costs in his report for September, 1972:

Materials	$ 81,270
Wages	63,900
Payroll taxes	2,860
Advertising	4,600
Rent	500
Insurance	150
Utilities	430
Gasoline and oil	2,700
Other costs	6,830
Depreciation	400
Miscellaneous	110
Total	$163,750

Included in wages is $1,870 for wages to employees borrowed on a temporary basis from cost area 412. Payroll taxes on this labor were $115. Advertising costs incurred by the home office in the amount of $2,800 was allocated to cost area 373. Rent for the building is allocated to the cost areas. Insurance for the year in the amount of $1,800 was paid in July. The cost has been allocated to each month. Utility expenses authorized and paid amounted to $320. The additional utility expense reported represents an accrual. Gasoline and oil cost $2,700, but other cost areas withdrew gasoline and oil for their own work. The cost of the gasoline and oil withdrawn by these areas amounted to $950. Each cost area is expected to handle its own gasoline and oil cost. Other costs are the costs of an exhibit for the company at a state fair held in the city served by cost area 373. The costs are authorized by the home office.

Required: (1) Comment on the costs included in the report for cost area 373.
(2) Prepare a revised report, as you believe it should be prepared, for September, 1972.

9–7. Last year Basso Creations, Inc., manufactured and sold 160,000 units of a product at a unit selling price of $25. The unit manufacturing cost was $20, computed as follows:

	Unit Cost
Direct materials	$ 9
Direct labor	6
Variable overhead	3
* Fixed overhead	2
Total unit cost	$20

* Total fixed overhead of $320,000 divided by 160,000 units.

During the next year, it is estimated that 160,000 units can be again sold with no change in the selling price or the cost structure. However, 40,000 additional units can be manufactured and sold in another market for $20 apiece. The president of the company is not receptive to this idea, stating that he sees no point in producing additional units that will be sold at cost.

Another option is available. The same facilities can be used not only to produce 160,000 units of the regular line but to produce a slightly different type of product that can be sold for $15 apiece. Sales volume has been estimated at 60,000 units, and variable costs per unit are given below. Fixed costs are not expected to change.

	Unit Cost
Direct materials	$7
Direct labor	4
Variable overhead	2

Required: (1) Should the company produce additional units to be sold in another market or should the slightly different type of product be manufactured? Show computations.

(2) Identify the sunk cost in this situation.

(3) What is the opportunity cost of the decision?

9–8. Harbor Construction Company builds piers and breakwaters along the Atlantic coastline. One unit of equipment costing $340,000 is required for certain jobs. In the spring of 1972, Harbor Construction Company has an opportunity to use this equipment on either of two different projects but not both.

The controller of the company has been asked to prepare an estimate showing the contract prices and a cost comparison for the two projects, including only the costs that can be identified with the projects. The estimate is given below and on the following page.

Project No. 1

Contract price	$180,000
Materials	$ 58,500
Labor	41,600
Supplies	3,700
Power and lubrication	3,400
Repairs and maintenance	2,300
Insurance	3,000
Depreciation	30,000

Project No. 2

Contract price	$140,000
Materials to be furnished	—0—
Labor	$ 51,000
Supplies	4,100
Power and lubrication	2,000
Repairs and maintenance	2,300
Insurance	500
Depreciation	30,000

The insurance cost on Project No. 1 is higher because of the higher risk of damage claims. Both projects are charged with depreciation on the equipment.

Harbor Construction Company can reject both projects and receive $70,000 rent for the equipment by leasing it to Cardwell and Hauser. If the equipment is leased, Cardwell and Hauser will be responsible for all materials and labor, insurance, power and lubrication, and repairs and maintenance.

Required: (1) Identify the sunk costs in this decisional situation.

(2) Which alternative is the best? Prepare a report showing revenue and cost differentials to support your conclusion.

(3) What is the opportunity cost of the best alternative?

Chapter 10

ESTIMATING AND CONTROLLING COSTS

In a business enterprise there are many different costs such as materials, wages, insurance, and taxes, and each has its own peculiar characteristics. Even within a company, a particular type of cost will behave differently depending upon the way a particular service or material is used by a division or a department. A knowledge of how costs are affected by operations is essential in the budgeting process and the control of costs.

TECHNIQUE OF COST ESTIMATION

Cost studies are made continuously inasmuch as cost behavior may change over time as conditions change. Management is constantly examining cost behavior in an effort to prepare better budgets through more accurate cost prediction. The costs of projects or departments may be estimated or predicted by a combination of two approaches:

(1) Engineering estimates of materials and work requirements.
(2) An examination of past cost behavior.

Engineers who are familiar with the technical requirements will estimate the quantities of materials that are needed for production and the labor or machine hours required for various operations. Prices and rates are applied to the physical measurements to obtain cost estimates. In the preparation of budgets, the effect of changes in critical factors such as materials prices, labor rates, or machine hours of operation must be considered in the prediction process and controlled to the extent possible in actual operations.

Past cost behavior is also studied as a guide in predicting costs. The future is seldom a duplication of the past, yet a study of past cost behavior can be effectively utilized in the overall problem of cost prediction.

It may appear that costs that have already been incurred can be determined precisely. This isn't always true. For example, the cost of repairs may have been $600 at a time when a department operated at 300 hours and may have been $700 in another period of similar length. The rate of cost variability per hour may not be determinable at a precise amount. As a general rule, the problem is estimating cost behavior, that is, determining the *average* rate of cost variability.

COST SEGREGATION

Costs are segregated for the purpose of determining the rate of *past* cost variability. After the variable cost is determined, the estimated fixed cost can be established.

Two general methods are often employed in cost segregation:

(1) The high-low point.
(2) The line of regression.

The high-low point method. In the high-low point method, the observed costs for various hours of activity are listed in order from the highest number of hours in the range to the lowest. The difference in hours between the highest level of activity and the lowest is divided into the difference in cost for the corresponding hours to arrive at a rate of variable cost per hour. For example, repair costs for various hours of operation have been incurred in the past as follows:

	Hours of Activity	Repair Cost
(High)	80,000	$246,000
	70,000	216,000
	60,000	186,000
	50,000	156,000
	40,000	126,000
(Low)	30,000	96,000

The difference in hours is 50,000 (80,000 — 30,000), and the difference in cost is $150,000 ($246,000 — $96,000). The variable repair cost is computed below:

$$\frac{\text{Difference in cost}}{\text{Difference in hours}} = \frac{\$150,000}{50,000} = \$3.00 \text{ variable cost per hour.}$$

The fixed cost can be estimated at any level (assuming a uniform rate of variability) by subtracting the variable cost portion from the total cost. At 80,000 hours, for example, the total cost is $246,000; and the total variable cost is $240,000 (80,000 hours × $3.00 variable cost per hour). Hence, the fixed cost is $6,000 ($246,000 — $240,000). In this example, it was assumed that a constant rate of variability existed over the entire range. For every increase of 10,000 hours, there was a $30,000 increase in cost. In some cases, however, the rate of variability may change, and this possibility must be considered in cost analysis.

The line of regression. When cost characteristics are such that they do not always vary at a constant rate for each hour of activity, the most frequently used alternative to the high-low point method is the line of regression method wherein an *average* rate of variability is computed. The costs for the various numbers of hours may be plotted on a graph, and by visual inspection a line of average that represents the costs for the various hours can be fitted to the data. The line of average for costs that are influenced by a factor such as hours of activity is called the *line of regression*. The variable cost per hour is indicated by the slope of the line, and the fixed cost is measured where the line begins at zero hours of activity.

For purposes of illustration, it is assumed that a record of maintenance cost has been kept for various hours of operation as follows:

Hours	Maintenance Cost
50	$120
30	110
10	60
50	150
40	100
30	80
20	70
60	150
40	110
20	50

The maintenance costs have been plotted on the following graph, and a line of regression has been fitted to the data. The line is drawn so that the sum of the distances from the line to all points above the line is equal to the sum of the distances from the line to all points below it. The average (defined as an arithmetic mean) is the point at which the sum of the deviations above that point is equal to the sum of the deviations below that point. The line of regression represents a continuous series of average points and thus is a line of averages.

The line of regression illustrated on the next page, begins at $30 and rises $20 for each increase of 10 hours. Therefore the estimated fixed cost is $30, and the variable cost is an average rate of $2 per hour ($20 ÷ 10 hours).

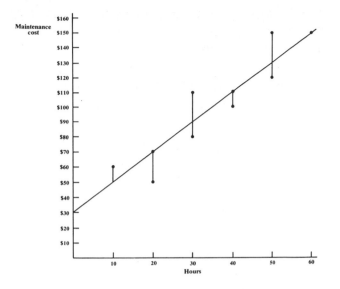

Least squares. A line of regression can be fitted to a large quantity of data more precisely by the least squares method. The line of regression is derived by simultaneous equations, with the equation for a straight line serving as a foundation for the computations.[1]

The equation for the determination of a *point* on a line is given below:

$$Y = a + bX.$$

This equation states that the value of Y is equal to a point (a) plus a percentage (b) of the change in X. In the last example, a was the $30 of fixed cost. The percentage (b) was the change in Y in relation to the change in X. In the example, Y increased by $20 for each increase of 10 hours. Hence, the percentage of change was 200 percent (20/10).

Then,

$$Y = \$30 + 200\% \ X.$$

If X is assigned a value of 10, Y is equal to 50.

$$Y = \$30 + 2(10).$$
$$Y = \$50.$$

By substituting various values for X, a line is formed on a graph.

---

[1] It is assumed that the costs vary at a uniform rate and can be represented by a straight line of average.

The equation for a *point* on a line is $Y = a + bX$, and the equation for a *line* is the equation·for a set of connected points, $\Sigma Y = Na + b\Sigma X$. N represents the number of items of data.

Assume that maintenance costs for various hours of operation have been recorded and that computations have been made as shown below:

Hours X	Maintenance Cost Y	X^2	XY
20	$ 200	400	$ 4,000
50	500	2,500	25,000
30	450	900	13,500
20	250	400	5,000
10	150	100	1,500
60	650	3,600	39,000
30	250	900	7,500
40	500	1,600	20,000
60	550	3,600	33,000
50	600	2,500	30,000
40	200	1,600	8,000
10	200	100	2,000
$\Sigma X = 420$	$\Sigma Y = \$4,500$	$\Sigma X^2 = 18,200$	$\Sigma XY = \$188,500$

The first step in obtaining a line of regression is to set up an equation for a line that will represent all of the data.

$$\text{Equation (1)} \quad \Sigma Y = Na + b\Sigma X.$$

Another equation [Equation (2)] is formed by multiplying *each point* that constitutes Equation (1) by ΣX. Note that Equation (1) is not merely multiplied by ΣX. Instead, each point ($Y = a + bX$) is multiplied by ΣX.

$$\text{Equation (2)} \quad \Sigma XY = \Sigma Xa + b\Sigma X^2.$$

Referring to the data listed above, substitute values and by simultaneous equations solve for either a or b.

$$\text{Equation (1)} \quad 4,500 = 12a + 420b.$$
$$\text{Equation (2)} \quad 188,500 = 420a + 18,200b.$$

To solve for b multiply Equation (1) by 35 (420 ÷ 12) to provide:

$$\text{Equation (3)} \quad 157,500 = 420a + 14,700b.$$

Subtract Equation (3) from Equation (2); the a values will cancel out to yield:

$$31,000 = 3,500b$$
$$\text{or } b = \$8.857$$

the rate of variable maintenance cost per hour.

Substitute the value of *b* in Equation (1) and solve for *a*.

$$4,500 = 12a + 3,719.94.$$
$$12a = 780.06.$$

or a = $65 estimated fixed maintenance cost (approx.).

A line of regression for the data given on page 292 is shown on the graph below.

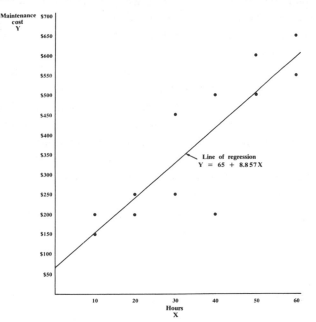

Control limits. From the data given in the example, it has been estimated that the fixed maintenance cost should amount to $65 and that the variable maintenance cost should vary at the rate of $8.857 per hour. For 20 hours of operation the total cost is estimated to be approximately $242. This is an *average* cost, however, and it is unlikely that the actual cost will be precisely $242.

Because some variation in cost can be expected, management should establish an acceptable range of tolerance. Costs that lie within the limits of variation can be accepted. Costs beyond the limits, however, are identified and may be investigated. Before investigating a cost variance, management should recognize that there is a cost attached to investigation. A certain amount of time and money must be spent to find out why the variance occurred. Management must balance the benefits to be derived from the investigation against the costs of the investigation. Time itself has a cost and thus, time that has been taken for the analysis of insignificant variations or the analysis of variations that are not likely to occur again could have been used to better advantage. There is an opportunity cost of investigating one variation in preference to another.

In dealing with cost variances, or variances in any type of data, it is necessary to consider the way that the data are distributed. Statistical data may form a pattern of distribution designated as a normal distribution. In a *normal distribution,* data can be plotted on a smooth, continuous, symmetrical, bell-shaped curve with a single peak in the center of distribution. Surveys have revealed, for example, that the height of persons or the length of steel bars manufactured in a production process can be described by a normal distribution.

Management may find that cost data are normally distributed and, in deciding upon an acceptable range of cost variability, may employ the standard deviation concept that is commonly used in statistics. The *standard deviation* measures the extent of variation that may be expected in a distribution of data, and in this chapter it will be assumed that cost data are normally distributed. Published tables show what proportion of the data may be expected to lie within plus and minus a given number of standard deviations from the mean (average).

The equation for the computation of the standard deviation is given below:

$$\text{Standard Deviation} = \sqrt{\frac{(X - \overline{X})^2}{N - 1}}$$

X = item of data (i.e., actual maintenance cost)
$\overline{X}$ = average (i.e., average maintenance cost)
N = number of items of data

Expressed in words, the standard deviation is equal to the square root of the sum of the squares of the deviations from the mean (average) divided by the number of items reduced by one.

Assume that an average cost has been estimated to be $180 and that the standard deviation has been computed to be $10. A table of probabilities for a normal distribution shows that about ⅔ of the data (more precisely, 68.27%) lie within plus and minus one standard deviation from the mean. Hence, there is a 68.27% probability that the cost will be between $170 and $190, that is, $180 minus $10 and $180 plus $10.

If more confidence in the prediction is desired, the limit of variation must be extended. For example, there is a 95 percent probability that a cost in a normal distribution will lie within plus and minus 1.96 standard deviations. From the data given above, there is a 95 percent probability that the cost will be between $160.40 and $199.60 [$180 plus and minus

$19.60 (1.96 × $10)]. Management will have to make a decision **by** balancing two alternatives:

(1) A relatively narrow range of cost variation with a low probability of being correct.

(2) A relatively wide range of cost variation with a high probability of being correct.

A standard deviation is computed from the 12 items of data given **in** the maintenance cost illustration.

Hours	Actual Cost X	* Average Cost $\overline{X}$	Deviations $(X - \overline{X})$	Deviations Squared $(X - \overline{X})^2$
20	$200	$242.14	$ 42.14	$ 1,775.78
50	500	507.85	7.85	61.62
30	450	330.71	119.29	14,230.10
20	250	242.14	7.86	61.78
10	150	153.57	3.57	12.74
60	650	596.42	53.58	2,870.82
30	250	330.71	80.71	6,514.10
40	500	419.28	80.72	6,515.72
60	550	596.42	46.42	2,154.82
50	600	507.85	92.15	8,491.62
40	200	419.28	219.28	48,083.72
10	200	153.57	46.43	2,155.74
			$\Sigma (X - \overline{X})^2 =$	$92,928.56

* Line of regression values (Hours multiplied by $8.857 plus $65).

The standard deviation (SD) is calculated as follows:

$$SD = \sqrt{\frac{\$92,928.56}{12 - 1}}$$
$$SD = \$92 \text{ (Approx.)}$$

With a standard deviation of $92, there is a probability of 68.27 percent that the cost will lie within a range extending from $92 above the line of regression to $92 below the line of regression.

At 40 hours of operation, for example, the cost can be expected to **lie** between $327.28 and $511.28 about ⅔ of the time.

	Standard Deviation Plus One	Minus One
Average cost	$419.28	$419.28
Standard deviation	+92.00	—92.00
Limits	$511.28	$327.28

Graphic presentation. The data can be visualized when plotted on a graph as shown below. A line of regression is drawn on the graph. In addition, parallel lines are drawn to lie above and below the line of regression at a distance of approximately plus one and minus one standard deviation.

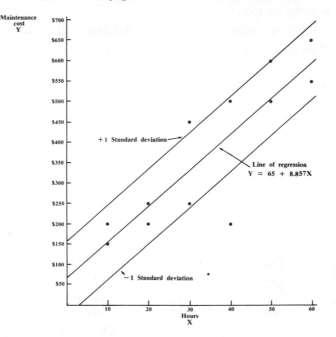

Note that the cost of $450 at 30 hours lies more than one standard deviation above the line of regression and that the cost of $200 at 40 hours lies more than one standard deviation below the line. These costs are identified for investigation because they have probably been influenced by some factor other than hours of operation. Perhaps, time was wasted or machine operation was inefficient. Allowing a range of acceptable cost variability enables management to concentrate on extreme situations and to use the information derived in the preparation of more accurate budgets and in better cost control.

CORRELATION

In the process of estimating and controlling costs management must determine whether the factor selected for estimating cost behavior is suitable for that purpose. Costs may or may not vary with changes in hours of operation or with changes in the factor selected for cost analysis. In making a study of cost behavior, management will be constantly looking for positive relationships between the costs and various factors in the operation, such as pounds of materials used, hours of operation, labor cost, etc.

Sometimes it may be found that the costs are randomly distributed and are not at all related to the factor selected as illustrated below:

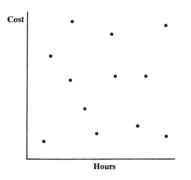

Cost Behavior—Negative Correlation

At the other extreme, the relationship may be so close that the data can almost be plotted on a line as shown below:

Cost Behavior—Positive Correlation

Between these extremes the correlation may not be so evident. A high degree of correlation exists when the standard deviation from the line of regression is relatively small when compared with the standard deviation from the average, determined without respect to changes in the factor selected. Thus, a relatively small standard deviation around the line of regression indicates that the cost tends to follow the hours of operation or other factor selected for measurement purposes.

The degree of correlation is measured by the *coefficient of determination,* most frequently designated as r^2. The equation is given below:

$$r^2 = 1 - \frac{(\text{Standard deviation measured from the line of regression})^2}{(\text{Standard deviation measured from the average of the data})^2}$$

If the standard deviation from the line of regression is small when compared with the standard deviation measured from the average, the value of the fraction in the equation will be small. When this fraction is subtracted from one, the value of r^2 expressed as a percentage will be relatively large and the correlation will be good. On the other hand, a large standard deviation from the line of regression in relation to the standard deviation from the average results in a low r^2. Hence, the costs do not closely follow the factor selected, and the correlation is poor.

A value for r^2 is computed using data from the previous illustration. The standard deviation from the line of regression has already been computed at $92. The average for the data is computed by dividing the sum of the costs by the number of items ($4,500 $\div$ 12). The average is $375. The variations from this average are computed, squared, and totaled.

Maintenance Cost	Average	Variations	Variations Squared
$ 200	$375	$175	$ 30,625
500	375	125	15,625
450	375	75	5,625
250	375	125	15,625
150	375	225	50,625
650	375	275	75,625
250	375	125	15,625
500	375	125	15,625
550	375	175	30,625
600	375	225	50,625
200	375	175	30,625
200	375	175	30,625
$4,500			$367,500

The standard deviation is equal to the square root of the sum of the squared variations divided by 11 (N — 1 or 12 — 1).

$$SD = \sqrt{\frac{\$367,500}{11}}$$

$$SD = \$182.78.$$

The r^2 is computed by substituting values in the equation:

$$r^2 = 1 - \frac{(92)^2}{(182.78)^2}$$

$$r^2 = 1 - \frac{8,464}{33,409}$$

$$r^2 = 1 - .253$$

$$r^2 = .747 \text{ or } 74.7\%$$

In the illustration given, there is a fairly high degree of correlation between hours of operation and maintenance cost. The correlation is not extremely high, but it is high enough to indicate that the hours of operation must be considered as an important factor in predicting and controlling maintenance costs.

MULTIPLE REGRESSION

Usually it will be found that more than one factor will be related to cost behavior. Hours of operation, for example, may not be the only factor to be considered. A certain cost may vary not only with changes in the hours of operation but also with the weight of product produced, temperature changes, or other factors. In simple regression only one factor is considered, but in multiple regression several factors are considered in combination. Insofar as possible, all factors that are related to cost behavior should be brought into the analysis. With a penetrating analysis, costs can be predicted and controlled more effectively.

The equation for simple regression can be expanded to include more than one variable factor. Two variable factors are given in the equation below:

$$Y = a + bX + cZ.$$

The b is the percentage of variability applied to the factor X as it was before. The c is the percentage of variability applied to the new factor designated as Z. The cost relationship can no longer be depicted on a two-dimensional graph. The value of Y (cost), however, can be determined by using simultaneous equations. The arithmetic computations become more complex as other factors are introduced, but the principle is the same as it is in simple regression. However, with the use of computer library programs, the complexity of the computations is reduced insofar as the numerical manipulations are concerned.

AN OPTIMUM SOLUTION

Usually various factors such as labor, materials, and machinery are used in combination to attain a given objective. In attaining this objective, management will seek an *optimum solution,* that is, a solution that will minimize costs. In addition, the factors entering into the solution should be tested to determine the effect of changes or errors. Assume that a company has been operating equipment with a combined cost of repairs and maintenance amounting to $1,100. Management believes that the combined cost can be reduced by increasing preventive maintenance and thus reduce repairs. It is assumed that it is not possible to move in the opposite direction and increase repairs while decreasing maintenance. If a unit of maintenance is added, a unit of repairs will be deducted. A *unit* is defined so that a certain quantity of materials and labor used for maintenance can be substituted for a given quantity of materials and labor defined as a unit of repairs. Hence, for each unit of maintenance added, there will be a reduction of a unit of repairs.

A study of maintenance cost gives the following cost function:

$$Y = M^2 + 300.$$
$$Y = \text{maintenance cost.}$$
$$M = \text{number of maintenance units added.}$$

Maintenance cost is now $300. If an additional unit of this service is added, the total maintenance cost will be $301. For two units, the cost will be $304, etc.

Repair cost is now $800. With each decrease of a unit of repair service, it is assumed that the cost can be reduced by $8. The total repair cost for any number of reduced units is expressed in equation form below:

$$Z = 800 - 8R.$$
$$Z = \text{repair cost.}$$
$$R = \text{number of repair units subtracted.}$$

According to the assumption, the units are defined so that an increase of one unit in maintenance is balanced by a decrease of one unit in repairs. Hence, the number of units of maintenance to be added (M) equals the number of units of repair to be subtracted (R). Let $X = M$ or R. The combined costs are determined by adding the individual equations and substituting X for M and R.

$$Y = M^2 + 300.$$
$$Z = 800 - 8R.$$
$$C = \text{combined costs.}$$
$$C = Y + Z.$$
$$C = M^2 - 8R + 1100.$$
Substitute X for M and R.
$$C = X^2 - 8X + 1100.$$

The number of units to be interchanged to minimize total cost can be computed by using a basic principle of differential calculus. As the units are changed, the costs will change. The ratio of a small change in cost to a small change in units can be expressed as:

$$\frac{dC}{dX}.$$

The *d* indicates difference. The objective is to compute this ratio when both the cost difference (dC) and the unit difference (dX) are very small.

According to the rules of differential calculus, an algebraic equation is differentiated (expressed in terms of $\frac{dC}{dX}$) as follows:

(1) Multiply the exponent of the factor by the coefficient of the factor to obtain a new coefficient.

(2) Reduce the exponent of the factor by one.

For example, $6X^3$ when differentiated becomes $18X^2$. The exponent has been multiplied by the coefficient to obtain a new coefficient. The exponent has been reduced by one. With a factor of $2X$, the differential is 2. The exponent of one when multiplied by two yields a coefficient of two. The new exponent is zero. Any factor with an exponent of zero is equal to one. Hence, the X disappears. A fixed constant such as 1,100 is not a variable and is eliminated in differentiation.

The equation given in the previous illustration follows:

$$C = X^2 - 8X + 1100.$$

Following the rules of differentiation,

$$\frac{dC}{dX} = 2X - 8.$$

The next step is to set the differential equal to zero.

$$\frac{dC}{dX} = 0.$$

At this point the difference in C in relation to X is zero. It is a turning point at which the cost is minimized. The combined cost decreases in relation to unit changes, it is at a point of rest with no change, and then it increases in relation to unit changes.

If 4 units are interchanged, the combined cost is minimized at $1,084. This can be solved by the equation:

$$\frac{dC}{dX} = 2X - 8.$$

$$\text{Set } \frac{dC}{dX} = 0.$$

Then,
$$2X - 8 = 0.$$
$$X = 4.$$

A graph is given below showing combined costs for different values of X.

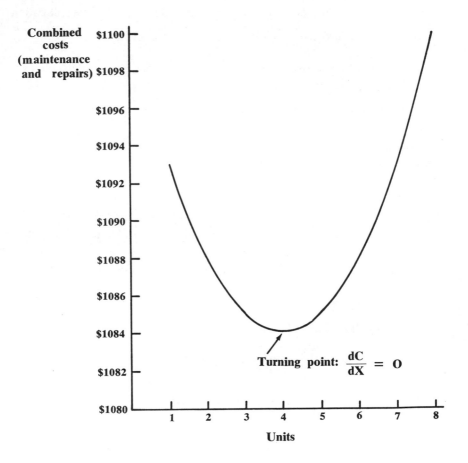

Combined Cost Curve C = X² − 8X + 1,100

Units (X = M or R)	Maintenance (Y = M² + 300)	Repairs (Z = 800 − 8R)	Combined Cost (C = M² − 8R + 1100)
1	$301	$792	$1,093
2	304	784	1,088
3	309	776	1,085
* 4	316	768	1,084
5	325	760	1,085
6	336	752	1,088
7	349	744	1,093
8	364	736	1,100

* Optimum point (minimum cost).

SENSITIVITY ANALYSIS

An estimation of a future cost is an approximation at best. The actual cost will in most cases be larger or smaller than the predicted cost. Part of the cost estimation problem is to find out how variations from cost predictions will affect the results. *Sensitivity analysis* is a technique that can be used to determine how the costs of an operation will be influenced by changes or errors in the input data.

Assume, from the last example, that the repair cost can only be reduced by $5 for every unit removed. How will this change affect the optimum solution? The original cost equation was:

$$C = X^2 - 8X + 1100.$$

Substitute the new value for the repair cost reduction in the combined cost equation and solve for the point of minimum cost.

$$C = X^2 - 5X + 1100.$$

$$\frac{dC}{dX} = 2X - 5.$$

$$\frac{dC}{dX} = 0.$$

$$2X - 5 = 0.$$

$$X = 2.5 \text{ units.}$$

Assuming that the units can be divided, a minimum cost is reached when 2.5 units of maintenance are added with a reduction of 2.5 units of repair. The combined minimum cost will then be:

$$C = X^2 - 5X + 1100.$$
$$C = 6.25 - 12.5 + 1100.$$
$$C = \$1,093.75.$$

The minimum cost is $9.75 more than the original estimated cost of $1,084.

Various changes in the values of the variables can be tested separately or in combination to determine the effect on the optimum solution. Hence, the more critical elements can be identified and can be given closer attention in the estimation and control process. Sometimes it will be found that the solution will be affected about as much by a change in one variable as by the change in another, in which case a point of indifference is reached. This important information can be applied in planning and control. The amounts used in the illustration given were relatively insignificant, but in practice it may be found that the amounts are rather large and that sensitivity testing can direct attention to the most significant factors.

There are a variety of ways in which sensitivity analysis can be used to determine how a solution to a problem will be influenced by errors in estimating amounts or by changes in the data. In complex situations, a computer may be helpful in testing the effects of the many possible changes in a large number of variables.

Questions

1. Describe the high-low point method of cost segregation.

2. When costs are plotted on a graph, a line can be drawn to represent the average costs. What is this line called?

3. How can the average rate of cost variability be determined from the line?

4. How can a standard deviation measurement be used in cost control?

5. In a normal distribution of data, what proportion of the data should lie within plus and minus one standard deviation of the line of regression?

6. Costs may tend to vary with hours of operation. How can the degree of correlation between costs and hours of operation be measured?

7. What is meant by multiple regression?

8. Explain in general what is meant by sensitivity analysis.

9. What is an optimum solution?

10. In certain situations a point of minimum cost is reached when the slope of the cost curve is equal to zero. Why would this be a point of minimum cost?

11. How can sensitivity analysis be used to predict the effect of an error in cost estimates or the effect of a change in cost behavior?

12. Can the effect of various changes be tested in combination?

Exercises

1. The costs of electric power have been recorded for various hours of operation as follows:

Hours	Cost
5,500	$5,000
4,200	3,960
4,000	3,800
5,300	4,840
6,500	5,800
6,000	5,400
5,400	4,920
5,700	5,160

Required: Determine the average rate of cost variability per hour and the fixed cost.

2. A study of office expense shows that the cost is semivariable. A record of the past hours of operation with corresponding costs is given below:

Hours	Cost	Hours	Cost
4,200	$40,200	5,000	$45,000
4,000	39,000	5,300	46,800
5,800	49,800	7,000	57,000
6,500	54,000	3,000	33,000
3,500	36,000	4,500	42,000
3,800	37,800	6,200	52,200
		4,800	43,800

Required: Determine the variable cost rate and the fixed cost.

3. The cost of a certain indirect material has characteristics of a fixed cost and of a variable cost. The average rate of cost variability is to be predicted from a past record of costs. Hours of operation and costs are listed below:

Hours	Costs	Hours	Costs
200	$2,800	400	$5,600
400	5,000	300	3,900
100	2,200	200	3,000
100	2,300	500	5,700
300	3,600	600	7,100
500	5,800	600	7,000

Required: Plot the costs on a graph and fit a line of regression to the cost data. Prove that the line of regression is the line of average cost.

4. Supplies used in a certain operation at Chambot Industries, Inc., are semivariable costs. By making a study of past cost behavior, management hopes to be able to establish the estimated amount of fixed cost and the rate of cost variability per hour. Costs for various hours of operation are listed below:

Hours	Costs	Hours	Costs
2,000	$7,200	2,500	$8,100
2,500	8,200	1,000	4,900
2,000	7,000	1,500	5,600
1,000	5,400	3,500	10,000
3,500	9,800	1,500	6,300
3,000	8,600	3,000	8,900

Required: Plot the costs on a graph and fit a line of regression to the cost data. Prove that the line of regression is the line of average cost.

5. A distribution of a certain cost shows that the average cost of 10 items is $800. The sum of the squares of the deviations from the mean (average) is equal to $4,000.

Required: (1) What is the standard deviation?
(2) Within what range can the cost be expected to lie about ⅔ of the time?
(3) What range of costs can be expected 95 percent of the time?

6. At 200 hours of operation the average cost has been computed at $1,600. The standard deviation is $50. During the month of November the company operated at 200 hours and incurred a cost of $1,672.

Required: (1) Does a cost of $1,672 fall within a range of acceptability if control limits are established at ± 1.96 standard deviations from the mean?

(2) Give the range within which the cost should lie 95 percent of the time.

Problems

10-1. Wayne Uhler is estimating the behavior of the cost of a certain indirect material in relation to hours of operation for Cambria Equipment Company. From this study he hopes to have a basis for the prediction of future costs and a tool for improved cost control.

Cost data for various hours of operation are given below:

Hours	Costs	Hours	Costs
100	$150	400	$310
100	160	400	320
200	220	500	340
200	180	500	340
300	230	600	400
300	240	600	410

Sum of the hours (ΣX) = 4,200
Sum of the costs (ΣY) = $3,300
Sum of hours multiplied by costs (ΣXY) = $1,330,000
Sum of hours squared (ΣX^2) = 1,820,000

Required: From the data given compute the estimated variable cost per hour and the amount of the fixed cost. (Round answers to third decimal place.)

10-2. The foreman of the finishing department believes that the cost of a certain buffing operation tends to vary with hours of operation. Part of the cost is fixed. Cost data taken from past records are given below:

Hours	Costs	Hours	Costs
400	$3,600	600	$5,500
400	3,800	700	6,000
500	4,600	700	5,900
500	4,500	800	7,100
600	5,300	800	6,600

Sum of the hours (ΣX) = 6,000
Sum of the costs (ΣY) = $52,900
Sum of hours multiplied by costs (ΣXY) = $33,280,000
Sum of hours squared (ΣX^2) = 3,800,000

Required: (1) From the data given compute the estimated variable cost per hour and the amount of the fixed cost. (Round answers to third decimal place.)

(2) Compute a standard deviation and predict a cost range for 600 hours of operation so that the cost should be included within this range about ⅔ of the time.

10-3. James Cantor notes that the cost of abrasive polishing materials, while fixed to an extent, tend to vary with hours of machine operation. Past cost data are collected and plotted on a graph with a line of regression being fitted to the data. Mr. Cantor wants to know whether or not the costs are correlated with hours of operation so that he can use estimates of past cost behavior as a basis for the prediction of future costs.

In making this cost study, Mr. Cantor has used 200 items of past cost data. He finds that the sum of the squared standard deviations from the line of regression is 1,800 and that the sum of the squared standard deviations from the average of all data is 80,000.

Required: (1) Compute r², the coefficient of determination. Does it appear that there is a valid correlation between machine hours and cost?

(2) Assume that the sum of the squared standard deviations from the average of all data was 5,400. What would your answer be in this case?

10–4. A cost report for one of the divisions of Bliss Products, Inc., shows that the cost of an indirect material used during March was $17,860. During the month, 4,000 units of product were manufactured. Cost studies have been made to relate this cost to the number of units produced. When 4,000 units are manufactured, the average cost has been estimated at $17,450 with a standard deviation of $230 on a line of regression. The standard deviation from the average computed without respect to the variation in the number of units produced, amounts to $340.

A cost analyst identified the indirect materials cost for March as excessive since it fell more than one standard deviation above the line of regression value for 4,000 units. Yet, subsequent investigation revealed that there was no discernable waste in the operation.

Required: (1) From the information given, explain how the cost could be reasonable even though it was above the one standard deviation limit established.

(2) Compute the r². Does there appear to be a good correlation between number of units produced and the indirect materials cost?

10–5. The foreman of one of the production departments of Ivory Molding Company questions the validity of using labor hours as a basis for the prediction and control of machine maintenance cost. He states that the cost does not tend to vary with labor hours and an attempt to control the cost on that basis is incorrect. It is his opinion that other factors are more relevant.

During the month of June, the cost was $4,100. For the number of labor hours that month, the cost was expected to ranged from $3,520 to $3,680 with a probability that the cost would lie within this range approximately ⅔ of the time. The standard deviation from the average of the data has been computed at $90.

Required: (1) Do you agree with the foreman? Compute the coefficient of determination to support your position.

(2) If the cost is related to several factors, how can the control problem be approached?

10–6. The controller of Moretz Products Company makes a continuous study of cost behavior in relation to hours of operation and various other measurable factors. When a high degree of cost correlation is found, he has a tool for better cost estimation and a basis for improved cost control.

Early in the year the company operated at approximately the same number of machine hours each month in a certain department. The cost of indirect materials used in this department has been within one standard deviation from the average for the machine hours of operation, which is $1,600. A standard deviation from the line of regression has been measured at $80, and the standard deviation from the general average is $500.

Changes were made in this operation later in the year, and the controller notes that, for the past few months, the cost of indirect materials for the same number of hours has been running over one standard deviation from the mean. The controller suspects that factors other than machine hours may now be more closely related to cost behavior. Accordingly, another study of cost behavior is made. The standard deviation from the new line of regression is $60, and the standard deviation from the general average is $75.

Required: (1) Determine the range of indirect materials cost early in the year between plus and minus one standard deviation from the mean.
(2) Compute the coefficient of determination during the early months of the year.
(3) Compute the coefficient of determination after the operation has been changed. Does it appear that the controller is correct in his assumption that factors other than machine hours may be more closely related to indirect materials cost?

10-7. Wainright Towers, Inc., estimates that the cost of a supply varies on the basis of the number of units of product manufactured with a certain portion of the cost being fixed. The production manager would like to test the degree of correlation between the cost and the number of units of product manufactured. Cost data and units of product for past months are given below:

Units	Costs	Units	Costs
1,000	$12,000	2,000	$23,000
1,000	15,000	2,000	18,000
1,000	11,000	2,500	24,000
1,500	12,000	2,500	26,000
1,500	17,000	2,500	25,000
1,500	16,000	3,000	25,000
2,000	18,000	3,000	29,000
2,000	17,000	3,000	32,000

Sum of the hours $(\Sigma X) = 32,000$
Sum of the costs $(\Sigma Y) = \$320,000$
Sum of hours multiplied by costs $(\Sigma XY) = \$703,000,000$
Sum of hours squared $(\Sigma X^2) = 71,500,000$
Standard deviation from the line of regression $= \$2,366.44$
Standard deviation from the average $= \$12,143.58$

Required: (1) Compute the average rate of cost variability per unit of product. (Round answers to the nearest dollar.)
(2) Compute the coefficient of determination (r^2). Does it appear that there is a good correlation between costs and units of product manufactured?

10-8. In processing a certain product line, Owens Mills, Inc., can use various combinations of labor and machine time. At the present time, the combined cost is $2,300 with the labor cost amounting to $500 and the balance of the cost being the cost of machine operation. As units of machine time are added, the costs of machine operation are estimated as follows:

Units of Machine Time	Cost
1	$1,801
2	1,804
3	1,809

For each addition of a unit of machine time, there will be a decrease of a unit of labor time. As units of labor decrease, the costs are expected to decrease as follows:

Units of Labor Time	Cost
1	$490
2	480
3	470

Required: (1) Determine the number of units of machine time to be added (this is also the number of units of labor time to be deducted) in order to minimize the combined machine and labor cost.

(2) Prepare a tabulation to show how combined costs decrease to a minimum and how they begin to increase again.

10-9. Albert Nelson has estimated that two labor operations in his department are interchangeable. As one type of labor service is increased, the other type can be decreased. At the present time, the combined cost of this labor is $800. By substituting one type of labor for another, he believes that this cost can be reduced.

According to his estimates, if he adds one type of labor the cost will increase as follows:

$$\text{Predicted cost increase} = X^3.$$

$$X = \text{number of labor units added.}$$

At the same time, another type of labor will be reduced with the following cost effect:

$$\text{Predicted cost decrease} = 10X^2.$$

$$X = \text{number of labor units deducted.}$$

As one unit of labor is added, a unit of another type of labor is subtracted.

Mr. Nelson is not certain with respect to the pattern of expected labor cost decreases. It is possible, he admits, that the labor cost may only be reduced by $8X^2$.

Mr. Nelson's supervisor is inclined to believe that the cost situation is changing and that the combined costs in this suitation are more likely to follow the pattern given below.

$$Y = 2X^3 - 5X^2 + \$800.$$

$$Y = \text{cost.}$$

$$X = \text{units.}$$

Required: (1) Using Mr. Nelson's original estimates, compute the minimum cost and the number of units to be interchanged. (Round your answer to the nearest unit.)

(2) If Mr. Nelson believes that costs can only be reduced by $8X^2$, what effect will this have on the minimum cost and the number of units to be interchanged? (Round your answer to the nearest unit.)

(3) Compute the minimum cost according to the estimate made by Mr. Nelson's supervisor. Also compute the number of units to be interchanged. (Round your answer to the nearest unit.)

10–10. Dresden Company manufactures a pharmaceutical product in one of its divisions, and strict temperature and humidity controls must be maintained during the processing operation. To a large extent, these controls are automated. However, under certain operating conditions, these controls can only be maintained by incurring substantially higher costs.

Joseph Sutton, the superintendent of this division, believes that a variation in the production process can accomplish the desired results at a reduced cost. For each unit of the variation added, a unit of the old operation can be deducted. He admits that there are risks and that the variation, if not handled properly, can increase costs by more than the expected savings.

He estimates that the variation will add to total cost as follows, with X being equal to the number of processing units added:

$$10 (4X^2 + 20).$$

At the same time, a unit of the old operation can be deducted for every unit of the new method added. This is estimated to reduce costs as follows:

$$10 (40X + 25).$$

The manager of this particular processing operation is not so sure that this innovation will reduce costs. He believes that Mr. Sutton is too optimistic. With the new operation, he believes that costs will be increased as follows:

$$10 (6X^2 + 30).$$

In his opinion, costs of the new process will increase too rapidly in relation to the cost savings expected by switching over from the present method. He agrees with Mr. Sutton's estimate of cost reductions by reducing units of the old operation.

Mr. Sutton explains that there will still be cost savings even if the costs increase according to the manager's estimates. With careful vigilance, he believes that the cost pattern can be detected while the operation is in process and that substitutions of productive factors can be made accordingly to attain optimum cost savings.

Required: (1) Compute the point of maximum cost saving using Mr. Sutton's estimates.

(2) Give computations to show what can be expected if the manager's estimates are correct. (Round computations to nearest unit.)

Chapter 11

ACCOUNTING FOR PRODUCT COSTS

Manufacturing costs are accumulated and assigned to the products through the use of one of two basic cost accounting systems:

(1) The job order cost system.
(2) The process cost system.

The system used depends upon the type of manufacturing operation.

THE JOB ORDER COST SYSTEM

The *job order cost system* can be used when the products are manufactured in identifiable lots or groups or when the products are manufactured according to customer specifications. A printer, for example, may receive an order from a university to print 5,000 copies of a summer school bulletin. This bulletin will be prepared as directed by the university, and it will differ in form and content from the printing work done for other customers. The printer's costs are accumulated by customer order. Manufacturers and contractors, like the printer, may work on a project or order basis and identify costs by project or order.

In a job order cost system the costs are assigned to the jobs passing through the plant and accumulated on forms referred to as job or production orders. Each order is usually divided into three *basic* sections—materials, labor, and overhead—thus, the three cost elements can be accounted for separately. A section is usually provided in which a summary of the costs is shown and a unit cost determined. This section is completed when the job is finished.

A separate production order is kept for each job going through the plant, and the file of production orders in process constitutes a subsidiary ledger in support of the Work in Process account in the general ledger. A production order is shown on page 317.

Costing direct materials and direct labor. The direct materials and direct labor cost can usually be attached to the products by measuring the costs of materials and labor that have been used for particular orders. When materials are purchased, an entry is made to debit Materials and to credit Accounts Payable. A factory payroll may be recorded by a debit to Factory Labor with offsetting credits to Income Tax Withheld, Social Security Tax Withheld, other liability accounts for payroll deductions, and Accrued Wages Payable. As direct materials are used in production, requisition tickets are prepared to show the cost of materials used on specific production orders. Similarly, as direct labor is used in production, labor time tickets measure the labor hours and cost identified with particular orders.

Assume that requisition tickets show that direct materials costing $80,000 have been transferred from the materials inventory to production. This is recorded by a journal entry as shown below:

Work in Process	80,000	
Materials		80,000

Direct materials requisitioned for production. Entries are also made on the individual production orders supporting the work in process account.

Direct labor time tickets show that 10,000 hours of labor at $5 an hour were used in producing various orders. This is also recorded by a journal entry as shown below:

Work in Process	50,000	
Factory Labor		50,000

Direct labor costed to production. Entries are also made on the individual production orders supporting the work in process account.

Costing the manufacturing overhead. Manufacturing overhead, unlike direct materials and direct labor, cannot be requisitioned or measured directly as a cost of any particular production order. Manufacturing overhead consists of a variety of costs such as indirect materials, indirect labor, insurance, and taxes, all of which are indirectly related to the products.

Manufacturing overhead is attached to the products indirectly by means of a factor that *can* be directly related to the products. This factor serves as a bridge between manufacturing overhead and the products. Often the factor chosen for overhead allocation is direct labor hours, machine hours, or direct labor cost. Manufacturing overhead is budgeted for the year, and the factor selected for bridging the gap between overhead and the product is also budgeted. The budgeted factor is then divided into the budgeted overhead in the determination of what is called an *overhead rate*. Products then are assigned overhead costs by multiplying the actual quantities of the factor by the rate calculated.

The factor chosen as a basis for overhead allocation should be related logically to both the overhead and the product. If machinery plays an important role in the manufacturing operation, the overhead costs will likely consist largely of power cost, lubrication, maintenance, repairs, depreciation, and other costs closely related to machine operation. These costs are necessary in the manufacturing process and assist in the creation of the products. The benefits received by the products can probably be best measured by the machine hours used in their production. Therefore, overhead costs will be allocated to the products on a machine hour basis. For other departments in the plant where machinery does not play such an important part in the manufacturing process, direct labor cost, direct labor hours, or some other basis may be more appropriate for overhead allocation.

The calculation of an overhead rate is illustrated by assuming that a manufacturing overhead budget has been prepared for the following year as shown below:

Budget of Manufacturing Overhead

Indirect materials	$ 82,000
Indirect labor and supervision	93,600
Payroll taxes	3,650
Repairs and maintenance	6,830
Depreciation of equipment	2,000
Rent	6,000
Heat and light	2,520
Fuel	3,400
Total budgeted manufacturing overhead	$200,000

In this case, it is assumed that manufacturing overhead will be allocated to the products on the basis of direct labor hours. Direct labor hours are budgeted for the next year at 100,000. The overhead rate is then calculated at $2 per hour.

$$\frac{\text{Budgeted manufacturing overhead}}{\text{Budgeted direct labor hours}} \quad \frac{\$200,000}{100,000} = \$2 \text{ per direct labor hour}$$

During the year, the products passing through the plant were charged with *budgeted* manufacturing overhead. Assume that 96,000 hours of direct labor were used during the year. While the manufacturing operation was going on, various entries were made to cost the products. In aggregate, it would be as if one summary entry were made as follows:

Work in Process	192,000	
Applied Manufacturing Overhead		192,000
Allocation of manufacturing overhead cost to the orders, 96,000 hours at $2 each.		

Each order is charged with a portion of this overhead as it goes through production at the rate of $2 for each direct labor hour charged to the order.

At this point, a question may be raised as to why the accountant goes to so much trouble in assigning manufacturing overhead costs to the products. If the accountant would only wait until the end of the year when all of the actual manufacturing overhead has been collected and when the actual direct labor hours of operation have been determined, he could calculate an actual overhead rate and could allocate the actual costs to the orders that were manufactured during the year. Why bother with a budget and a budget rate?

When a budget rate is used, product costs can be determined quickly. There is no need to wait until the end of a month or other fiscal period of measurement to determine the cost of making a certain order or batch of product units. Costs are available while production is in process, thus making it easier to control operations while they are in progress.

Furthermore, the product costs will not fluctuate as they would if actual overhead rates were used in computing monthly costs. Seasonal variations throughout the year would cause the overhead cost per unit to be higher or lower depending upon the volume produced. Interim financial reports might show various unit product costs, total costs, and profits depending upon the seasonal operation. These variations can be leveled out by using a budget rate.

Returning to the illustration, assume that total actual manufacturing overhead for the year amounting to $203,500 is recorded as a debit to the control account Manufacturing Overhead. Supporting the control account is a subsidiary ledger in which the detailed costs of manufacturing overhead are accumulated. The subsidiary ledger shows the following debit balances at the end of the year:

Actual Manufacturing Overhead (Subsidiary Account Balances)

Indirect materials	$ 82,800
Indirect labor and supervision	94,200
Payroll taxes	3,720
Repairs and maintenance	7,950
Depreciation of equipment	2,000
Rent	6,000
Heat and light	3,130
Fuel	3,700
Total actual manufacturing overhead	$203,500

While the products were being costed, with budgeted manufacturing overhead, actual manufacturing overhead costs were being collected and recorded as debits to Manufacturing Overhead. At the end of the year, after all adjusting entries had been made, the manufacturing overhead accounts would have balances as shown on the next page.

	Debit	Credit
Manufacturing Overhead	$203,500	
Applied Manufacturing Overhead		$192,000

Not all of the actual manufacturing overhead was charged to products by means of the budget. There was a difference or variance of $11,500. This difference can be closed out at the end of the year to Cost of Goods Sold or, if desired, can be allocated to Cost of Goods Sold, Finished Goods, and Work in Process on the basis of relative costs. If too little overhead has been costed to the products, the variance is called an underapplied, unabsorbed, or unfavorable variance. On the other hand, if too much overhead has been costed to the products, the variance is called an overabsorbed, overapplied, or favorable variance.

The entry to close out the actual overhead, the applied overhead, and the variance is given below:

Applied Manufacturing Overhead	192,000	
Cost of Goods Sold	11,500	
Manufacturing Overhead		203,500

To close out applied and actual overhead accounts, with the variance being charged to Cost of Goods Sold.

If the overhead had been overabsorbed in the example given, the variance would have been credited to Cost of Goods Sold.

Normal capacity. The products are usually costed by using an overhead rate calculated at the level of normal activity or normal capacity. The reason for having to choose a certain level of capacity is that the fixed cost per unit will depend on the number of units produced. This practice of assigning fixed overhead cost to units is necessary as long as full cost is to be used in the income determination process. Hence, the prime emphasis on the costing procedure comes from the need for data to calculate profit.

Normal capacity is not easy to define. The term has been used in many different ways partly because there is no real agreement as to what is meant by "normal." In a good many cases, normal capacity is looked upon as an average use of facilities over a sufficiently long period of time so that minor variations in production costs because of seasonal and cyclical influences can be evened out. Sometimes plant capacity is considered to be a theoretical maximum capacity without regard for sales demand and for delays and inefficiencies in production. This concept of maximum output may be useful in evaluating what the plant could conceivably produce, but it cannot be looked upon as being a normal condition. Practical capacity may be a more useful concept in costing products for profit determination.

Certain interruptions and inefficiencies in production can be expected. Perfection cannot be achieved. For example, production may be slowed down or stopped at times because of breakdowns, shortages of labor and materials, retooling, etc. These possibilities should be taken into account in arriving at practical plant capacity. Sales demand is also a factor. If there is insufficient demand for the product, then there is little point in striving to produce at practical plant capacity. Normal capacity is often a compromise between practical plant capacity and sales demand over the long run.

Seemingly, a normal overhead rate should not be used if the company does not plan to operate at normal capacity during the next year. For profit reporting, if all the overhead is to be attached to the products, it would appear that the costing rate should be calculated from a budget at the expected level of operation.

A JOB ORDER COST ILLUSTRATION

Summarized cost data for the year ended April 30, 1972, are presented below in aggregate form for Kelso Machine Company to illustrate job order cost procedures using historical costs.

Historical costs are the actual costs that have been incurred, and in this chapter it will be assumed that the actual or historical costs are to be assigned to the products to the extent that this is possible. In Chapters 12 and 13, a standard cost accounting system will be discussed. Standards of cost and performance will be established, and standard costs will be identified with the products. Actual costs are measured and compared with the standards. Differences are identified and serve as a basis for better control and for better planning.

It should be borne in mind that the entries given are in composite form and that in practice there are many repetitious entries to record individual transactions that take place during the fiscal year.

The sequential order of the cost transactions should also be understood. For example, the budget of manufacturing overhead and the overhead rate calculation were made before the beginning of the fiscal year. The overhead rate must be calculated from a budget of manufacturing overhead so that the products being manufactured during the year can be assigned the proper overhead cost, as nearly as it can be determined. Only at the end of the year did the company know that 185,000 direct labor hours were used and that the actual manufacturing overhead cost was $980,000. Throughout the year, the manufacturer purchased materials and incurred labor and manufacturing overhead costs, as products were continually being worked on, completed, and sold. At the same time, costs were being attached to the products and released as expenses when deliveries were made against sales.

Kelso Machine Company
Transactional Data
For the Year Ended April 30, 1972

(1) Materials were purchased during the fiscal year at a cost of $712,000.

(2) Direct materials requisitioned for production cost $586,700. Included in this amount are the material costs for Job 318 of $2,380. Indirect materials costing $73,000 were also requisitioned.

(3) Factory payrolls in total amounted to $828,000. The income taxes withheld from the employees' wages totaled $157,500, and the deduction for social security taxes withheld amounted to $39,200.

(4) A distribution of the factory labor cost of $828,000 shows that $715,000 was direct labor while the remaining $113,000 was indirect labor. The portion of the direct labor cost that pertained to Job 318 was $1,170.

(5) Manufacturing overhead at the normal operating level of 200,000 direct labor hours has been budgeted at $1,000,000. An overhead rate based on direct labor hours has been calculated at $5.00 an hour. During the year, 185,000 direct labor hours were used.

(6) The manufacturing overhead, in addition to the indirect materials and the indirect labor referred to above, amounted to $794,000. Included in this amount was depreciation of $80,000. The balance of the overhead was acquired through accounts payable. Job 318 was completed with 220 direct labor hours. The production order for Job 318 is shown below.

PRODUCTION ORDER

Customer __Ohio Company__   Job Order __318__

Description __Products Code #816__   Date Started __2/10/72__

Quantity __1,000__   Date Completed __2/14/72__

Materials			Labor			Overhead	
Date	Code	Amount	Date	Hours	Amount		
Feb.10	183	$1,630	Feb.10 to 12	150	$ 750	Direct Labor Hours	220
						Overhead Rate	$5.00
						Overhead Applied	$1,100
11	215	750	Feb.13 to 14	70	420		
						Summary	
						Direct Materials	$2,380
						Direct Labor	1,170
						Manufacturing Overhead	1,100
						Total cost	$4,650
						Unit cost	$4.65
	Total	$2,380	Totals	220	$1,170		

---

(7) Other jobs costing $1,872,500 were completed and transferred to stock during the year.

(8) The cost of orders sold during the year was $1,346,300.

(9) Applied Manufacturing Overhead and Manufacturing Overhead were closed out at the end of the fiscal year with the variance being closed to Cost of Goods Sold.

The transactions given in summary form above were entered in the accounts as follows:

(1) Materials purchased:

Materials	712,000	
Accounts Payable		712,000
Purchase of materials		

(The cost of each type of material was also entered on the appropriate materials inventory ledger cards.)

(2) Materials requisitioned:

Work in Process	586,700	
Manufacturing Overhead	73,000	
Materials		659,700
Materials issued to production.		

(Requisition forms were the basis for entries reducing the materials inventory ledger cards and for posting direct materials costs to each job order and the indirect materials costs to the manufacturing overhead subsidiary ledger.)

(3) Factory payrolls:

Factory Labor	828,000	
Income Tax Withheld		157,500
Social Security Tax Withheld		39,200
Wages Payable		631,300
Aggregate factory payrolls.		

(4) Distribution of labor cost:

Work in Process	715,000	
Manufacturing Overhead	113,000	
Factory Labor		828,000
Payroll distribution for the year.		

(A classification of labor time by jobs as shown by labor time tickets was a basis for distribution of direct labor cost to individual job orders and for posting indirect labor cost to the manufacturing overhead subsidiary ledger.)

(5) Manufacturing overhead applied:

Work in Process	925,000	
Applied Manufacturing Overhead		925,000
Manufacturing overhead applied to products on direct labor hour basis. 185,000 hours $\times$ $5.00 rate = 925,000.		

(6) Actual manufacturing overhead (in addition to indirect materials and indirect labor):

Manufacturing Overhead	794,000	
Accumulated Depreciation		80,000
Accounts Payable		714,000

        Actual manufacturing overhead recorded.

(Entries were made to record the costs in the manufacturing overhead ledger.)

(7) Work completed during the year and transferred to stock:

Finished Goods	1,872,500	
Work in Process		1,872,500

        Transfer of cost of completed orders to Finished Goods.

(Completed job orders were removed from the file of job orders in process and held as a subsidiary ledger supporting the finished goods inventory. Separate ledger cards may be kept for the finished goods inventory if sales are not made on a strict order basis.)

(8) The cost of products sold:

Cost of Goods Sold	1,346,300	
Finished Goods		1,346,300

        To record the cost of products sold to the customers.

(Deductions were recorded in the finished goods inventory ledger cards. Entries were also made to bill the customers for the sales.)

(9) Applied Manufacturing Overhead and Manufacturing Overhead closed:

Applied Manufacturing Overhead	925,000	
Cost of Goods Sold	55,000	
Manufacturing Overhead		980,000

To close manufacturing overhead accounts. Actual overhead not absorbed during the year as part of the product cost is closed to Cost of Goods Sold.

THE PROCESS COST SYSTEM

In many cases costs cannot be identified readily with any particular batch of products. For example, in the candy industry all chocolate of a given type will be the same. When all of the units of product are much alike, a *process cost system* can be used. The costs are directly or indirectly assigned for an interval of time to the departments in which the products are made, rather than identified by product groups or orders. Unit cost is computed by dividing the number of units completed in the department into the corresponding departmental cost.

The unit costs are applied to the number of units transferred in the manufacturing process and ultimately identified with the units completed and sold. Before a product is completely manufactured, it may be transferred from one department to another in a series of processing operations. Each unit of product will carry costs that have been assigned to it from the various departments in which it is processed.

The departmental production report. Both the number of units manufactured and the costs are accounted for on a departmental basis. Monthly production reports are prepared for each producing department showing the quantities of product, the total cost, and the unit cost. The production report is the focal point in process cost accounting, whereas in job order costing, it is the production order. The production report may provide departmental cost and quantity data either separately or combined in one report with each section showing (1) what responsibility is charged to the department, and (2) how that responsibility is discharged.

The number of units accounted for is always equal to the number of units charged to the department. Lost units must be accounted for as such. Costs are similarly charged to a department and must be accounted for.

A production report for both quantities and costs is given below:

DEPARTMENTAL PRODUCTION REPORT
Department I
For the Month of June, 1972

Quantities:
  Charged to the department:
    In process, beginning .... 3,000 units
    Transferred in 50,000
    Total units charged to department 53,000

  Units accounted for:
    Transferred out .... 53,000 units
    In process, ending .... —0—
    Total units accounted for 53,000

Costs:
  Charged to the department:
    In process, beginning .... $ 4,000
    During the period 71,000
    Total cost charged to department $75,000

  Costs accounted for:
    Transferred out $75,000
    In process, ending .... —0—
    Total cost accounted for $75,000

A process cost flow. Often the units of product go through several manufacturing operations (departments) before they are finally completed. In the first operation, for example, impurities may be removed from the basic raw materials. In subsequent operations, the materials may be refined and treated in various ways before the product units are completed.

A simple flow of costs through only two departments is illustrated using the cost data given below:

| | *Departments* | |
	I	*II*
Materials	$38,000	—0—
Labor	21,000	$32,000
Manufacturing overhead	12,000	14,000
Total costs	$71,000	$46,000

Work in process in Department I at the beginning of the month amounted to $4,000, but there was no work in process in either department at the end of the month. All units of product were sold during the month.

The cost elements for each department were entered in the respective work in process accounts. As the units moved through the departments on their way to completion, the related costs were transferred to the next departmental work in process account and were combined with the costs of that department. Eventually, the goods were completed and were transferred to the finished goods inventory. When they were sold, the costs were transferred to the cost of goods sold account and the customers were billed for the sales. A diagram of the cost flow is given on page 322.

Journal entries to record the flow of costs follow:

(1)

Work in Process—Department I	71,000	
Materials		38,000
Factory Labor		21,000
Applied Manufacturing Overhead		12,000
Manufacturing costs of Department I.		

(2)

Work in Process—Department II	75,000	
Work in Process—Department I		75,000
Transfer of costs from Department I to Department II.		

(3)

Work in Process—Department II	46,000	
Factory Labor		32,000
Applied Manufacturing Overhead		14,000
Manufacturing costs of Department II.		

A diagram of the cost flow is given below:

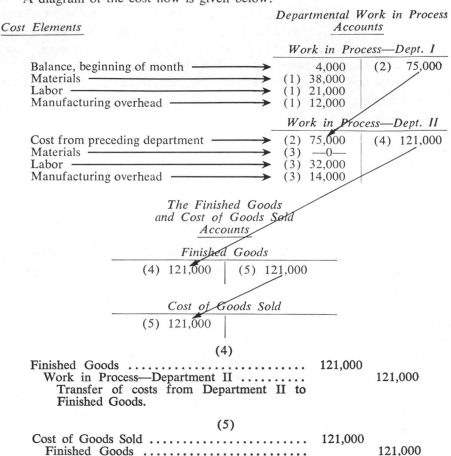

Cost Elements | Departmental Work in Process Accounts

Work in Process—Dept. I

Balance, beginning of month	→	4,000	(2) 75,000
Materials	→	(1) 38,000	
Labor	→	(1) 21,000	
Manufacturing overhead	→	(1) 12,000	

Work in Process—Dept. II

Cost from preceding department	→	(2) 75,000	(4) 121,000
Materials	→	(3) —0—	
Labor	→	(3) 32,000	
Manufacturing overhead	→	(3) 14,000	

The Finished Goods and Cost of Goods Sold Accounts

Finished Goods

| (4) 121,000 | (5) 121,000 |

Cost of Goods Sold

| (5) 121,000 | |

(4)

Finished Goods	121,000	
Work in Process—Department II		121,000
Transfer of costs from Department II to Finished Goods.		

(5)

Cost of Goods Sold	121,000	
Finished Goods		121,000
Cost of goods sold during the month.		

The equivalent unit concept. In the preceding illustration all of the work was completed in each department, and the entire production for the month was sold. In many cases, however, not all of the work will be completed and sold within the month. Usually there will be units and costs remaining in process and in finished goods at the end of the month. Costs are attached to the units transferred out of a department and to the remaining work in process by means of a unit cost.

In process cost accounting, the problem of determining unit costs is resolved by using *equivalent units*. The equivalent units, as defined under the average cost method, are the units completed during the month (regardless of when the work was done) plus the equivalent units of work done on the work in process at the end of the month. They are not the equivalent units of work done during a given month. The objective is to obtain an average cost by adding the cost of work done in previous months to the cost of work done during the current month.

Assume that equivalent units and unit costs are to be computed for Department A. Quantity and cost data follow:

	Number of Product Units	Total Cost
Charged to department:		
Inventory in process at the beginning of the month	4,000	$ 4,000
Placed in production during the month	30,000	26,000
Total units and costs charged to the department	34,000	$30,000
Accountability:		
Completed and transferred to Department B ..	19,000	?
Inventory in process at the end of the month (40% completed)	15,000	?
Total units accounted for	34,000	

At this point, the costs to be assigned to the units transferred to Department B and to the ending inventory of work in process have not been determined. However, they can be computed as shown below:

Equivalent Units Computation

Units completed during the month	19,000
Equivalent units of work done on the ending work in process (15,000 units $\times$ 40%)	6,000
Equivalent units	25,000

Average Unit Cost Computation

$$\text{Average unit cost} = \frac{\text{Costs of Dept. A}}{\text{Equivalent units}} \quad \text{or} \quad \frac{\$30,000}{25,000} = \$1.20.$$

Accountability—Costs of Department A

Cost of units completed and transferred to Department B (19,000 units $\times$ $1.20 average unit cost)	$22,800
Cost of work in process at the end of the month (6,000 units $\times$ $1.20)	7,200
Total costs accounted for	$30,000

The cost elements. In a process cost accounting system, no distinction is made between direct materials and indirect materials with respect to the product. The materials are not requisitioned for particular orders. Instead, both the direct materials and the indirect materials are identified only with the department in which they are used. A measurement is taken of the material consumption in a department over a stated time interval, but requisition forms do not show how much material was used in the manufacture of any particular group of products.

Labor costs are also accumulated by department with no distinction being made between direct and indirect labor. The wages of the workers are not identified by order but by department.

The various manufacturing overhead costs are assigned to departments directly or by allocation. If manufacturing overhead costs are evenly distributed throughout the year and production is carried on at a fairly uniform level, this method may result in reasonably accurate product costs. However, if production is seasonal or if overhead costs are unequally distributed throughout the year, more accurate product costs can be obtained by using a predetermined annual overhead rate calculated from a budget. Departmental overhead rates can be computed in the same way as they are in job order cost accounting. When a predetermined overhead rate is used, all products processed during the year bear their share of the overhead cost.

PROCESS COST ILLUSTRATED

Barton Chemical Co., Inc., manufactures one line of product in two processing operations. All materials are added in Department I at the beginning of the processing operation. No units have been lost in production, and costs are accounted for on an average cost basis.

A quantity report. A quantity production report has been prepared for the two departments for the month of October, 1972. It is shown on the next page.

Since all materials were added at the beginning of the total operation, the equivalent units of materials and the actual units of product in Department I are the same.

The ending work in process has been partially completed with respect to labor and overhead. In Department I, one-fifth of the labor and overhead work has been completed on 10,000 units; and if the work had been concentrated, 2,000 of these units would have been finished. In Department I during October, 32,000 equivalent units of labor and overhead were completed (30,000 + 2,000).

In Department II, the units are complete with respect to the work done in Department I. The unit cost of work done in Department I can be computed by dividing the total of 50,000 units available into the accumulated total cost of work that has been done in Department I.

The work in process in Department II is three-eighths completed with respect to labor and overhead in that department. The 45,000 equivalent

```
                    Barton Chemical Co., Inc.
                    Production Report—Quantities
                          October, 1972
```

	Dept. I	Dept. II
Quantities charged to departments:		
Units in process, beginning	—0—	20,000
Units started in production	40,000	
Units received from Department I		30,000
Total units charged to departments	40,000	50,000
Quantities accounted for:		
Units transferred to Department II	30,000	
Units completed	—0—	42,000
Units in process, ending (all materials, but only 1/5 complete as to labor and overhead)	10,000	
Units in process, ending (all materials, but only 3/8 complete as to labor and overhead)		8,000
	40,000	50,000
Equivalent units (average cost method):		
Materials (30,000 + 10,000)	40,000	
(42,000 + 8,000) *		50,000
Labor and overhead (30,000 + 2,000)	32,000	
(42,000 + 3,000)		45,000

```
     * All materials in Dept. II were received from Dept. I.
```

units are equal to the sum of the 42,000 units completed and three-eighths of the 8,000 units in ending inventory.

The unit costs. After the equivalent units have been computed, the important unit cost calculations can be made. The unit costs are used in tracing the total cost through the accounts.

The costs charged to the departments are as follows:

	Dept. I	Dept. II
In process, beginning:		
Costs from previous departments		$ 25,000
Costs of department		20,000
October costs:		
Costs from previous departments		45,000
Costs of department:		
Materials	$30,000	
Labor and overhead	16,000	70,000
Total costs charged to departments	$46,000	$160,000

A unit cost computation is presented below. Note that a separate unit cost has been computed in Department II for work done in Department I. Another unit cost has been computed for the work done in Department II.

	Total Cost	Equivalent Units	Unit Cost
Department I:			
Materials	$30,000 ÷	40,000 =	$ .75
Labor and overhead .	16,000 ÷	32,000 =	.50
Total	$46,000		$1.25
Department II:			
Combined costs and units from Department I:			
In Process, beginning	$25,000		
Current period	45,000		
Total	$70,000 ÷	50,000 =	$1.40
Combined labor and overhead of Department II:			
In process, beginning	$20,000		
Current period	70,000		
Total	$90,000 ÷	45,000 =	$2.00

A cost report. The cost section of the production report can be completed when the unit costs have been determined. Costs can be attached to the work that is still in process at the end of the month. A cost report for Barton Chemical Co., Inc., for October, 1972, is given on the next page.

It may seem strange that the unit cost of Department I was $1.25 in October, yet the unit cost for Department I as computed in Department II amounted to $1.40. However, in Department II the cost of the work done in an *earlier month* has been included as a part of the beginning work in process cost. Apparently, the cost of work done in Department I was higher in September. The *average* cost of the work done in Department I in both months amounts to $1.40.

PROCESS COST ACCOUNTING PROBLEMS

Two important problems that are often encountered in a process type of manufacturing operation are:

(1) Joint product costing.
(2) The product mix decision.

These problems arise because several product lines may be produced in combination. How should costs be allocated to the individual product lines, and what costs are relevant in making decisions as to what quantities of the various lines should be produced?

Barton Chemical Co., Inc.
Production Report—Costs
October, 1972

	Dept. I		Dept. II	
	Total Cost	Unit Cost	Total Cost	Unit Cost
Costs charged to departments:				
In process, beginning:				
Costs from Department I	—0—	—0—	$ 25,000	
Costs from Department II ...			20,000	
October costs:				
Costs from Department I			45,000	$1.40
Materials	$30,000	$ .75	—0—	
Labor and overhead	16,000	.50	70,000	2.00
Total costs charged to				
departments	$46,000	$1.25	$160,000	$3.40
Costs accounted for:				
Transferred out of Department I				
(30,000 × $1.25)	$37,500			
Transferred out of Department II				
Department I cost				
(42,000 × $1.40)			$ 58,800	
Department II cost				
(42,000 × $2.00)			84,000	
Total cost transferred out of				
Department II			$142,800	
In process, ending:				
Department I				
Materials				
(10,000 × $.75)	$ 7,500			
Labor and overhead				
(2,000 × $.50)	1,000			
Total, Department I	$ 8,500			
Department II				
Cost of Department I				
(8,000 × $1.40)			$ 11,200	
Labor and overhead				
(3,000 × $2.00)			6,000	
Total, Department II			$ 17,200	
Total costs accounted for	$46,000		$160,000	

Joint product costing. Often more than one line of a product is derived from some basic material. The cost of the basic material and the costs of processing it to a point where the end products can be identified are usually allocated to the end products for income determination purposes. These costs, which are common to all of the resulting products, are called *joint costs*, and the products are called joint products. Joint products often result from processing some basic material found in nature. For example, timber may be converted into various grades of lumber. Coal may be broken down into coke, gas, tar, etc.; or crude oil when refined becomes gasoline, kerosene, burning oil, asphalt, etc.; or a meat packer may get various cuts of meat from one animal.

If the resulting products are on an approximately equal footing with respect to relative values, they are often referred to as *coproducts*. If each of the coproducts is to share the joint costs, it is not always easy to decide how the costs should be allocated. Costs may be apportioned according to weight, the assumption being that the weight of the basic material is distributed over the end products. Other characteristics, such as chemical content, specific gravity, or energy potential, may be selected as a basis for allocation. Sometimes joint costs are apportioned according to the relative market values of the end products or according to the costs that must be incurred to process the products after the point of split-off from the basic material. The costs determined for the coproducts may serve as a basis for the transfer of costs to other company divisions; or if the allocation appears to be too arbitrary, transfers may be made at market values.

In a manufacturing process, incidental products may be produced which are not necessarily desired, but result automatically from the operation. These products are known as *by-products*. Usually the by-products will not be assigned any original costs but will bear only the costs required to process them after split-off from the basic material. The proceeds that can be derived from the sale of by-products will reveal whether or not additional processing costs are justified. In some cases it may be better to scrap the by-product. On the other hand, a by-product may grow in importance until it becomes one of the major products.

The product mix decision. Assume, for example, that a basic chemical substance is put through a manufacturing process which will yield three product lines designated as Product A, Product B, and Product C. Joint costs of $500,000 are incurred in processing the basic material into 1,000,000 pounds of finished products during the year. These costs are allocated to the product lines on a relative weight basis. An allocation of joint costs must be made if full costs are to be attached to the products and used in income determination and in reporting inventory costs. This allocation is shown in the table on the next page.

	Product Lines			
	Total	A	B	C
Pounds produced	1,000,000	500,000	300,000	200,000
Joint costs:				
Direct materials	$200,000			
Direct labor	180,000			
Manufacturing overhead	120,000			
Total	$500,000	$250,000	$150,000	$100,000
Costs after split-off:				
Direct labor		100,000	55,000	70,000
Manufacturing overhead		50,000	20,000	30,000
Total cost		$400,000	$225,000	$200,000
Total cost per pound .		$ .80	$ .75	$1.00
Unit selling price		1.20	.70	1.50

The costs after split-off can be easily identified with the product lines and are combined with the allocated joint costs in the computation of the total cost for each line of product.

According to the selling prices given, it would seem that Product B should not be manufactured. For each pound sold there is a loss of 5 cents. In this manufacturing process, however, Product B may be involuntarily produced along with Products A and C. To get 500,000 pounds of Product A and 200,000 pounds of Product C, there may be an automatic production of 300,000 pounds of Product B.

Even so, why should the company incur a cost of 75 cents a pound to get a return of 70 cents a pound? It would appear that the product should be disposed of and that the additional processing costs of $75,000 should not be incurred. Yet, by incurring the additional cost the company will have a better total profit than it would have otherwise. By selling 300,000 pounds at a unit price of 70 cents, there is additional revenue of $210,000. This covers the additional processing cost and provides $135,000 toward the recovery of the joint costs.

Additional revenue from the sale of 300,000 pounds of Product B	$210,000
Additional cost to obtain Product B	75,000
Contribution to joint costs	$135,000

The additional costs to process Product B after point of split-off and the revenues to be derived from Product B are compared in making the decision. The joint costs, however, are ignored in decision making. They are sunk costs with respect to Product B and cannot be changed or eliminated by any decision with respect to Product B. The joint costs of $500,000 are incurred for the total operation, and $150,000 of this cost has been allocated to Product B. But the joint costs will not be affected by decisions as to what should be done with Product B.

Using the same data as before, assume that it is possible to continue processing Product C to get a new product called Product D that will sell for $2.40 a pound. From 200,000 pounds of Product C, 150,000 pounds of Product D can be derived at an additional processing cost of $75,000. The $100,000 in costs to process Product C after split-off must still be incurred to obtain Product D. *Neither the joint costs nor the cost of $100,000 after split-off is relevant to the decision.* These costs will be incurred in any event and are sunk costs with respect to the decision of producing or not producing Product D. But the *changes* in costs, and revenues, that is, the differential costs and revenues, are important. From the information given, it appears that the company should not process and sell Product D.

Revenues to be derived from the sale of Product D (150,000 pounds × $2.40)	$360,000
Less:	
Additional processing cost to obtain 150,000 pounds of Product D	$ 75,000
Opportunity cost (the loss of revenue that could be obtained by selling 200,000 pounds of Product C at $1.50 a pound)	300,000
Total incremental cost	$375,000
Net disadvantage in processing and selling Product D ...	($ 15,000)

The loss of revenue from the sale of Product C is not an incurred cost, but it represents a sacrifice and is an *opportunity cost* attached to the production and sale of Product D. The sacrifice of a benefit to be derived from some course of action is designated as the opportunity cost of any other action under consideration. This cost is not an incurred cost to be entered in the accounting records, but it has significance in decision making. The opportunity cost attached to the decision to make Product D is the sacrifice of the $300,000 in revenue that can be obtained from the sale of Product C.

To obtain the full cost of the various product lines manufactured jointly, the costs that are indirectly related to the products are usually allocated for financial reporting purposes. But a preoccupation with cost allocations may prevent the company from making the most of its opportunities. As shown by the example, allocation of joint cost is not relevant for product mix decisions.

Questions

1. What are the characteristics of a manufacturing operation when a job order cost system is used? When a process cost system is used?

2. What are job or production orders?

3. Why is it difficult to identify manufacturing overhead with the products manufactured?

4. Explain why a budget is used in costing manufacturing overhead and why actual overhead costs are not assigned to the products after the end of the year.

5. What is the basis for selecting a factor to be used in costing manufacturing overhead?

6. What is normal capacity?

7. If the company does not expect to operate at normal capacity during the next year, why should the products be costed by using an overhead rate determined at normal capacity?

8. What account is credited when manufacturing overhead cost is assigned to work in process?

9. How is the difference between the actual manufacturing overhead and the overhead assigned to the products handled at the end of the year?

10. In a job order cost system, how are the costs of direct materials and direct labor identified with the production orders?

11. Identify the two basic sections of the production report used in process cost accounting. Explain how the data are presented in each of these two sections.

12. Give a brief explanation of how costs flow through various departments in the processing operation.

13. Explain how equivalent units are computed by an average cost method.

14. Are the equivalent units the equivalent units of work done in a given month under the average cost method or are they the number of units completed during the month plus the equivalent units of work in process at the end of the month? Explain.

15. Explain how a predetermined overhead rate can be helpful in costing products in a process cost system.

16. What are joint costs? How can the joint costs be allocated to the products?

17. What are by-products?

18. Why are joint costs ignored in decision making?

19. Are the costs that are incurred after the split-off point relevant in decision making?

20. Can the loss of revenue from a decision alternative be looked upon as being a cost? Explain.

Exercises

1. Frantz Machine Company has a normal operating capacity of 60,000 machine hours a year. Manufacturing overhead costs budgeted at this level of operations follow:

Indirect materials and supplies	$220,300
Indirect labor	216,400
Holiday and vacation pay	38,900
Fuel	11,200
Lubrication	7,900
Repairs and maintenance	27,700
Property taxes	2,200
Insurance	3,300
Heat and light	6,800
Depreciation	14,300

Required: (1) Compute the manufacturing overhead cost per machine hour.

(2) If the company actually operates at 57,000 machine hours during the year, how much overhead will be assigned to the products by using the rate calculated in (1) above.

(3) Compute the over or underabsorbed overhead (the manufacturing overhead variance) if the company operates at 57,000 machine hours and incurs overhead costs of $519,600.

2. Summary cost data for 1972 are given for Gaylord Tube, Inc. Materials were purchased during the year at a cost of $306,000. Direct materials costing $233,000 were requisitioned for production, and indirect materials costing $42,000 were used in manufacturing. Factory payrolls for the year amounted to $150,000. Income taxes of $31,000 were withheld from wages, and social security taxes of $7,800 were withheld. Included in the factory payrolls was direct labor of $112,500 for 25,000 hours of labor identified with production. The balance of the labor cost is chargeable to indirect labor. Other manufacturing overhead costs of $143,000 were incurred with credits to accounts payable. Manufacturing overhead is applied to production at a rate of $8.40 per direct labor hour.

Required: Prepare journal entries to record the information given.

3. Bryson Lock Company manufactured 50,000 clasp devices on a government contract. Materials costing $21,960 were requisitioned for use on this contract, and 1,800 direct labor hours at $4.30 per hour were used in production. Manufacturing overhead at normal capacity has been budgeted at $720,000. Direct labor hours are used as a basis for costing overhead, and at normal capacity the company should operate at 120,000 direct labor hours.

Required: (1) Determine the overhead rate at normal capacity.

(2) Compute the total cost of the government contract and the cost per unit.

4. A soft drink marketed under the trade name of Whiz is made by Logan Bottling Company in three processing operations. In July, 1972, the company made 4,000,000 gallons of this drink. Materials costing $287,000 were started in Process 1. Labor and overhead costs of that process amounted to $63,400. Other costs for the month of July are given below:

	Process 2	Process 3
Materials	—0—	$55,000
Labor and overhead	$41,000	48,600

Required: (1) Prepare journal entries to trace the manufacturing costs through the three processes and into finished goods. (There were no inventories of work in process at the beginning or at the end of the month.)

(2) Compute the cost per gallon.

5. Redgrave Mills, Inc., uses a process cost accounting system and traces costs through the records on an average cost basis. Compute the number of equivalent units manufactured in the following situations (each situation is independent of the other):

(1) Department A started 80,000 pounds of product in production in August, 1972; at the end of the month, 12,000 pounds were in process, ⅔ completed. There was no work in process at the beginning of the month.

(2) At October 1, 1972, Department A had 10,000 pounds of product in process, 30 percent completed. The department started and completed 60,000 pounds during the month, completed the work in process at October 1, and had an inventory in process of 8,000 pounds at the end of the month, 25 percent completed.

(3) Department C had 7,000 pounds in process on June 1, 1973. During June, 65,000 pounds of product were received from Department B. Department C transferred 72,000 pounds to Department D in June.

(4) On December 1, Department C had an inventory of 15,000 pounds, 60 percent complete with respect to operations in Department C. During the month, 120,000 pounds were received from Department B. Department C transferred 123,000 pounds to Department D. The work in process in Department C at December 31 was 90 percent complete with respect to work in Department C.

6. Landino Plastics, Inc., places materials in process as labor and overhead are incurred in the manufacturing operation. Cost data for September, 1973, follow:

	Units	Costs
Work in process, September 1	18,000	$14,400
September data	46,000	61,000

In September, 49,000 units were completed and transferred to finished stock. The 15,000 units in process at September 30 were 60 percent completed.

Required: (1) Compute the number of equivalent units.

(2) Compute the unit cost.

(3) Compute the cost of the completed units and the cost of the work in process at September 30.

7. Data for the month of August, 1972, are given on the next page for the first processing operation of Lenhardt Purification Company. At the end of August, there were 9,000 units in process ⅓ completed as to labor and overhead. All materials are placed in production at the beginning of the operation. All of the other units were completed and transferred to the second operation.

Work in process, August 1:	Units	Costs
Materials		$ 19,440
Labor and overhead		5,800
Total	8,000	$ 25,240
August costs:		
Materials		$164,800
Labor and overhead		210,400
Total	90,000	$375,200

Required: (1) Compute the equivalent units of materials and of labor and overhead by the average cost method.

(2) Compute the unit costs of materials and of labor and overhead.

(3) Determine the total cost of the units transferred out of the first operation and the total cost of the units still in process at the end of the month.

8. Krueger Mills, Inc., normally manufactures 60,000 units of Product A and 80,000 units of Product B in a year. These product lines can be identified after they are put through a basic process having a fixed cost of $280,000. The variable costs amount to $84,000 when the company operates at normal capacity.

Product A is sold for $9 a unit after it goes through an additional processing operation. The fixed cost of the additional operation amounts to $60,000 a year, and the variable costs per unit of Product A in this operation amount to $2.50.

The material used to manufacture Product A can be taken after point of split-off and can be manufactured into Product C with no loss of units. This work can be done in the same department where Product A is processed. The variable costs to manufacture Product A after point of split-off can be eliminated if Product C is made. The variable costs to make Product C, however, amount to $1.80 a unit. Each unit of Product C can be sold for $8.75.

Required: Should Krueger Mills, Inc., continue to manufacture Product A or should it manufacture Product C? Show computations.

9. Two product lines identified as K-84 and M-21 are manufactured by Laventhal Chemical Company from a basic material, and a residue having little value is produced as a by-product. Joint costs are allocated to the two product lines on a relative weight basis, but no cost is assigned to the residue. Normally, 700,000 pounds of a basic material costing 30 cents a pound are used to manufacture 500,000 pounds of K-84 and 100,000 pounds of M-21 with 100,000 pounds of the by-product. Labor and overhead costs for the basic manufacturing operation amount to $420,000 a year.

The by-product is sold for 40 cents a pound with no further processing cost and is hauled away by the customers in their trucks.

Additional labor and overhead costs of $200,000 are incurred to refine K-84, and additional labor and overhead costs of $70,000 are incurred to refine M-21.

It is estimated that with the expenditure of an additional $45,000 a year, the by-product could be sold for $1.20 a pound. Costs of delivery to the customers and administrative costs, however, would probably increase by $20,000 a year.

Required: (1) Compute the total cost to manufacture a pound of K-84 and M-21 under the system of costing used.

(2) Compute the total cost to manufacture a pound of K-84, M-21, and the by-product, assuming that the basic processing cost is assigned to all three product lines.

(3) Should Laventhal Chemical Company refine the by-product? Show calculations.

10. Mayberry Farms, Inc., raises and packages various health food products. One particular jelly is being sold below cost at 49 cents a jar. Each year 300,000 jars are sold. A basic processing cost of $60,000 has been assigned to this particular product line. This will be incurred whether this type of jelly is manufactured or not. The separate costs of processing this food product amount to $75,000 a year. Costs of packaging and distributing amount to 6 cents a jar.

A national food chain has offered to buy the entire output of this jelly after it has gone through only the basic processing operation and will pay $42,000 for the yearly production. The food chain will pay all costs of packaging and shipment.

Required: (1) Compute the total unit cost per jar.
(2) If the food chain had not offered to buy the output, should the company continue to produce and sell the product? Show computations.

Problems

11-1. A summary of manufacturing cost transactions for Klein Products Company for 1972 follows:

(1) Materials costing $430,000 were purchased from suppliers on account.
(2) Materials were requisitioned during the year as follows:

Direct materials	$338,000
Indirect materials	87,000

Included among the requisitions were requisitions for $4,200 of direct materials for Order 884.
(3) Factory labor for the year amounted to $280,000. Social security taxes withheld amounted to $13,800. Income taxes withheld amounted to $57,000, and the net amount paid to the employees amounted to $209,200.
(4) The factory labor was utilized as follows:

Direct labor	$212,000
Indirect labor	68,000

Direct labor costing $3,400 included in the total direct labor, was identified by labor time tickets with Order 884.
(5) Manufacturing overhead was applied to production at 150 percent of the direct labor cost.
(6) Manufacturing overhead costs during the year, in addition to the cost of indirect materials and indirect labor referred to above, amounted to $171,000. Included in the $171,000 is depreciation of $36,000. Credit the balance of the cost to Accounts Payable.
(7) Orders costing $646,000 were completed during the year. Order 884 is included among the completed orders.
(8) Goods costing $576,000 were sold to customers on credit terms for $820,000.

Required: (1) Journalize the transactions.
(2) Set up T-accounts, and post the journal entries to the T-accounts. No beginning balances are to be entered in the T-accounts.
(3) Compute the cost of Order 884 and the cost per unit of product assuming that 4,000 units were produced on that order.

11–2. Fargo Castings, Inc., budgeted manufacturing overhead at a normal operating capacity of 400,000 machine hours a year as follows:

Variable overhead:

Indirect materials	$316,300
Supplies	144,600
Power	18,600
Repairs and maintenance	43,400
Lubrication	13,100

Fixed overhead:

Indirect materials	284,000
Supervision	167,500
Indirect labor	342,600
Repairs and maintenance	47,000
Rent	63,000
Heat and light	19,400
Taxes and insurance	24,500
Depreciation	20,000

In 1973, the fixed manufacturing overhead costs with the exception of taxes and insurance were in agreement with the budget. The taxes and insurance cost amounted to $27,300.

Variable manufacturing overhead in 1973 was recorded as follows:

Indirect materials	$292,800
Supplies	130,200
Power	16,900
Repairs and maintenance	41,300
Lubrication	11,900

Fargo Castings, Inc., identified manufacturing overhead with the products on a machine hour basis using a machine hour rate for variable overhead and a machine hour rate for fixed overhead as determined from the budget at normal operating capacity. The company operated at 360,000 machine hours in 1973.

Required: (1) Determine the machine hour rate for costing variable overhead and the machine hour rate for costing fixed overhead.

(2) Compute the over or underabsorbed manufacturing overhead.

11–3. Continental Precision Tools, Inc., has been awarded a contract to produce 135,000 devices that can be used to manipulate small objects by remote control. The company expects to realize $1,755,000 when all deliveries are made on the contract.

This device is similar to a standard item normally manufactured and sold for $16 a unit. The cost of the materials used for the standard item amounts to $1.93 per unit, and it is estimated that the materials used for the contract will cost $1.75 per unit.

Hourly labor rates and the time required to make a unit of the standard item in each operation are listed below.

Operation	Hourly Rate	Time per Unit
Cutting	$3.00	5 min.
Shaping	3.60	12 min.
Assembly	3.70	12 min.
Finishing	3.30	10 min.
Inspection	3.00	6 min.

The time required for the shaping operation can be reduced by 2 minutes per unit on the contract production. In all other respects, the labor costs will not be affected by the contract.

Manufacturing overhead is applied to the products at the rate of $7.80 per direct labor hour.

Required: (1) Compute the total cost to produce each unit on the contract and the total cost of the contract.

(2) Compare the profit that can be earned by selling 135,000 units of the standard item with the profit that can be expected from the contract.

11-4. The quantities and costs of production chargeable to Department A of Vaughn Products, Inc., in October, 1972, are summarized as follows:

Quantities

Units in process on October 1	6,000
Units started in production, October	45,000
Units in process on October 31	5,000

All materials are added at the time the units are started in production. The work in process at October 31 was 40 percent completed as to labor and overhead.

Costs

	Work in Process, October 1	October Costs
Materials	$40,800	$316,200
Labor	31,800	217,800
Overhead	27,600	193,200

Required: Prepare a production report for Department A for October showing an accounting for both the quantities and costs.

11-5. Parts to be used on a government contract are being produced by Roath and Heller, Inc. Roath and Heller is a subcontractor and has almost completed the first production run for 25,000 units.

The parts are processed in five operations. The company estimated that it could manufacture these parts at a cost of $30 per unit. The costs may be over $30 per unit on the initial batch; but with experience and tight control, it is believed that the cost will average $30 per unit for the total contract requirement.

Data for Department V for April, 1973, are given below.

	Units	Cost
Work in process, April 1:		
Costs from earlier operations		$200,000
Costs of Department V		48,000
Total	8,000	$248,000
Current costs, April:		
Costs from earlier operations		$400,000
Costs of Department V		136,000
Total	17,000	$536,000

In April, 20,000 units were completed; and 5,000 units were in process at the end of the month, 60 percent completed in Department V.

Required: (1) Compute the unit cost of the parts.

(2) Compare the unit cost with the $30 estimated cost, and determine the difference between the actual unit cost and the estimated unit cost.

(3) Prepare a production report for Department V.

11–6. A metal tool used in building construction is manufactured by Ontario Metals, Inc. In 1972, the company made and sold 400,000 units of this tool and incurred the following costs:

Direct materials, a variable cost	$1,120,000
Direct labor, a fixed cost	380,000
Manufacturing overhead:	
Variable	200,000
Fixed	100,000
Total manufacturing costs	$1,800,000

The tool is sold at a price of $8 a unit. A commission of 15 percent of sales is granted to sales representatives. The selling and administrative expenses, excluding the sales commissions, are $160,000.

In 1973, the company plans to produce and sell 600,000 units. The fixed manufacturing overhead will probably amount to $140,000, and the selling and administrative expenses other than commissions are estimated to be $175,000. By purchasing larger quantities of materials, the company will save 20 percent on materials prices. The direct labor cost is expected to remain the same, and variable overhead will vary at the same rate per unit of product.

Required: (1) Compute the unit cost of manufacturing in 1972; in 1973.

(2) In 1973, the company plans to reduce the price to $7.75 a unit. Prepare an income statement for 1972 and an estimated income statement for 1973 and compare the results. Assume an income tax rate of 40 percent.

11–7. Andover Mills, Inc., makes a solvent used by one of its manufacturing divisions. The costs of processing 1,000,000 gallons are summarized below:

	Operations		
	1	*2*	*3*
Materials	$120,000	—0—	—0—
Labor	64,000	$45,000	$47,000
Overhead:			
Variable	17,000	41,000	43,000
Fixed	34,000	38,000	31,000

This solvent can be purchased from an outside supplier for 40 cents a gallon. The company also has an opportunity to sell this solvent after it has been passed through operation 1 at a price of 25 cents a gallon. The cost of materials, labor, and variable overhead can be eliminated in any of the three operations if that operation is discontinued. The fixed overhead costs have been allocated to the departments and will be incurred in any event.

Required: Should the company continue to make the solvent, should the solvent be purchased, or should the solvent be partially processed and sold with company needs being taken care of by purchase? (Show computations.)

11–8. Pharmaceutical products are manufactured in various processing plants by Flint Drugs, Inc. At one of the plants, a particular type of therapeutic product designated as FD8701 is manufactured exclusively. Operating at normal capacity, the plant should produce 10,000,000 units of FD8701 in a year.

On July 1, 1972, at the beginning of the fiscal year, the plant had an inventory of 500,000 units in process. The cost of this inventory is given below:

Direct materials	$150,000
Direct labor	200,000
Variable manufacturing overhead	150,000
Total cost	$500,000

During the fiscal year ended June 30, 1973, production costs were incurred as follows:

Direct materials	$3,378,000
Direct labor	1,096,000
Variable manufacturing overhead	1,065,000

The plant completed and shipped out 8,000,000 units of FD8701 during the fiscal year and had on hand an inventory of 400,000 units in process at June 30, 1973, that were completed as to materials but only 25 percent complete as to direct labor and variable manufacturing overhead.

Fixed manufacturing overhead costs are not assigned to the product as a part of product cost.

Unit costs are determined by an average cost method on an equivalent unit basis, and are computed to six places to the right of the decimal point.

Management is quite concerned with the problem of increasing costs and is finding it increasingly difficult to pass these increases along to customers in the form of higher prices. Next year it is estimated that the plant will incur production costs as follows:

Direct materials	$3,640,000
Direct labor	1,350,000
Variable manufacturing overhead	1,280,000

The plant will again complete and ship out 8,000,000 units of product and have 400,000 units in process at the same stage in production as the inventory at the beginning of the year.

Required: (1) For the fiscal year 1972-73, compute the average unit cost of production, the total cost of the units completed and shipped, and the total cost of the work in process at the end of the fiscal year.

(2) Make the same computations on the basis of the estimates for the next fiscal year.

(3) What effect will the anticipated cost increases have on the total unit cost of the product?

11-9. Santos Mills, Inc., produces a dairy feed, putting it through three operations: grinding, mixing, and finishing.

The costs to process 100,000 cwt. (100,000 units at 100 lbs. per unit) of a basic feed have been determined as shown on the next page.

This particular feed is sold for $4.25 per cwt.

By adding different materials and changing the process slightly, an enriched feed can be produced and sold for $5.30 per cwt.

The superintendent of the mill estimates that he can either produce and sell 100,000 cwt. of the basic feed or 60,000 cwt. of the basic feed and 40,000 cwt. of the enriched feed.

	Grinding	Mixing	Finishing
Materials	$ 77,400	$57,800	$ 7,000
Labor	26,200	28,600	18,500
Supplies	1,600	—0—	—0—
Power	1,400	1,200	—0—
Repairs and maintenance	800	600	—0—
Heat and light	2,000	1,900	1,500
Taxes and insurance	1,300	1,100	1,100
Depreciation	1,500	1,500	1,000
Total costs	$112,200	$92,700	$29,100

The enriched feed will have to go through the grinding department along with the other feed. However, 40 percent of the total cost of the materials added to the basic feed in the mixing operation can be eliminated, but other materials costing 65 cents per cwt. will have to be added for the enriched feed. The total labor cost is fixed, but another man will be needed in the mixing department if the enriched feed is to be produced. It is estimated that the additional labor cost will be $10,000. No changes are expected in heat and light, taxes and insurance, and depreciation costs that have been allocated to the department. There will also be no change in the cost of supplies used. Power cost can be reduced in the mixing department by $300, while repairs and maintenance cost in the same department will increase by 100 percent.

Costs in the finishing department will remain the same with the exception of materials used in packaging the product. These costs will be increased by 1 cent per cwt. for the enriched feed.

Required: (1) Can Santos Mills, Inc., increase its profits by producing and selling the enriched feed under the conditions stated? Prepare an analysis to support your conclusion.

(2) What is the lowest price at which the enriched feed can be sold if it is to contribute additional profits?

(3) If the enriched feed is produced and sold at this lowest price, what will the total manufacturing profit be on processing 100,000 cwt? How does this compare with the profit earned on the present operation?

11–10. Three grades of a chemical used for water purification are refined from a basic ingredient by Masters Controls, Inc. At the major processing plant located near Cleveland, Tenn., 3,000,000 gallons of the basic material are processed each year into the three grades as follows:

Cost to Process 1,500,000 Gallons of the Basic Material

Variable costs:

Direct materials (vary by gallons of input)	$450,000
Direct labor	645,000
Variable manufacturing overhead	360,000

Fixed costs:

Fixed manufacturing overhead	525,000

The plant can process 3,600,000 gallons of the basic material each year without increasing the fixed overhead costs, but the domestic market can only absorb the output from 3,000,000 gallons. There is a foreign market for the partially processed output from 3,600,000 gallons started in process. The partially processed material can be sold in this market at a price of $.80 a gallon. These sales will have no effect on domestic sales.

During the first six months of the year, the company processes 1,500,000 gallons of the basic material into ingredients that are further processed into the three final grades of product.

Grades of Product	Quantities of Ingredients Used in Final Processing (Gallons)	Selling Price per Gallon	Total Cost of Additional Processing
M-Hi	600,000	$2.50	$253,000
M-Standard	300,000	2.20	129,500
M-Economy	300,000	1.80	63,000

In the second six months of the year, 1,500,000 gallons are processed in the same way with the same results. The joint product costs are allocated to the final products on the basis of their relative weights.

The marketing situation is such that the demand for the products is different during the second six months, and the selling price of M-Hi must be reduced.

Grade of Product	Product Demand (Gallons)	Selling Price per Gallon
M-Hi	200,000	$2.30
M-Standard	700,000	2.20
M-Economy	300,000	1.80

The additional gallons of M-Standard are obtained by converting M-Hi to M-Standard with no loss of product on the conversion but with an additional cost of $.08 per gallon converted.

There is no loss of materials in the additional processing stage, and the additional processing costs in the second six months are the same as in the first six months without regard to differences in the quantities of final product produced. All work must be done on M-Hi before it can be converted to M-Standard.

Required: (1) Compute the *total* cost of processing each of the three grades of product for sale in the domestic market assuming an input of 1,500,000 gallons of the basic material for each six months. Compute the unit costs for each six months and compare these unit costs with the unit selling prices to determine the unit net profit or loss expected. (Carry computations to three decimal places.)

(2) Compute the total profit or loss for each six-month period.

(3) If any of the three product lines is sold for a loss, should the company continue to produce the final products for sale in the domestic market? Or should the ingredient used in its production be sold in the foreign market?

(4) Should the company put 3,600,000 gallons through the basic operation and sell the surplus output in a foreign market? Show calculations.

11–11. A summary of manufacturing operations for the past fiscal year is given for the Meadow Spring Plant of Clydeford Processing Company. A part component used by the aircraft industry is manufactured at this plant, and the parts are costed by the process cost method. Each part is sold for $28.50.

At the beginning of the fiscal year, there were 12,000 parts in process with costs broken down as follows:

Direct materials	$86,400
Direct labor	36,000
Manufacturing overhead	31,500

All direct materials are placed in production at the beginning of the manufacturing operation.

During the fiscal year, enough direct materials were placed in production to make 394,000 parts; and no materials were spoiled or lost in production. The direct materials and direct labor cost for the fiscal year are given below:

Direct materials $2,955,000
Direct labor 2,382,000

The manufacturing overhead is applied to production on the basis of the number of equivalent units manufactured during the year at the rate of $5.25 per equivalent unit.

The company sold 380,000 part units during the fiscal year and had 16,000 finished units in stock at the end of the year. There was no inventory of finished parts at the beginning of the fiscal year. There were 10,000 units in process at the end of the fiscal year, 40 percent complete as to direct labor and manufacturing overhead. The equivalent units of production are computed by the average cost method.

The actual manufacturing overhead cost for the fiscal year is summarized below:

Indirect materials and supplies .... $ 324,000
Indirect labor 435,000
Supervision 233,000
Repairs and maintenance 203,000
Utilities 119,000
Taxes 154,000
Insurance 62,000
Depreciation 582,000
    Total $2,112,000

All over or underapplied manufacturing overhead is closed into cost of goods sold at the end of the fiscal year.

Selling and administrative costs for the plant sales division amounted to $931,600 for the year including $175,000 of depreciation.

Income taxes for the year are estimated at 50 percent of net income before taxes.

The company is obligated to repay loans on the plant and equipment in the amount of $1,600,000. There are also interest payments of $260,000 that must be made on loans made to finance the plant and equipment.

Required: (1) How many equivalent units as to direct labor and manufacturing overhead were manufactured during the fiscal year?

(2) Compute the manufactured cost per unit. (Carry computations to three decimal places.)

(3) Prepare an income statement from the data given.

(4) Did plant operations provide sufficient net working capital to meet the loan obligation including the interest?

Chapter 12

CONTROL: MATERIALS AND LABOR

In many cases, the cost of materials and labor is substantial and a great deal of effort is made to control the cost. Often an apparently insignificant cost saving on a unit basis or on an operation performed can add many dollars to profit. Although this chapter will consider materials and labor as direct costs, many of the control measures apply to both direct and indirect materials and labor.

THE ACQUISITION OF MATERIALS

Control over materials begins with procurement. The purchasing department will seek a reliable supplier whose material meets the quality standard in the desired quantity at the lowest price. After receiving a purchase requisition from individual departments the purchasing department places the order for the material. When the materials are received they are counted, inspected, and turned over to the storekeeper.

The storekeeper is the only person with access to the physical materials, which are stored in an enclosed area to prevent theft or loss. An accounting record of the quantities of materials received and withdrawn is maintained by a stores ledger clerk. Incoming items are entered from receiving reports on the inventory cards, which constitute the inventory subsidiary ledger. The requisition forms for materials to be withdrawn for production support the entries for inventory withdrawals. The physical inventory kept by the storekeeper should be in substantial agreement with the book record revealed by independent counts. The separation of the duties acts as a check on both the storekeeper, who realizes that a book record of the inventory is being maintained, and the stores ledger clerk, who has no access to the physical inventory and thus no reason to falsify the record. This separation of physical custodianship of a property and the responsibility for accountability follows a general principle of internal control: that one person should control the physical asset while another person maintains the accounting record. This is true not only in inventory accounting but also in accounting for cash, securities, and other business properties.

Invoices received for materials purchased are compared against purchase orders and receiving reports to determine whether or not the company was properly billed for materials ordered and received. Arithmetic computations on the invoices are checked, and the verified invoices are filed by the dates when payments must be made.

Purchase discounts. Materials are frequently purchased under terms permitting the purchaser to deduct cash discounts if payments are made promptly. The true cost of the materials is the net cost after the allowable discounts have been deducted. It is important that a company pay all obligations within the discount period. This will be true even if funds must be borrowed for that purpose. Substantial profits can be lost by careless management in this area. Purchases discounts lost may be treated as finance charges or penalties assessed against purchasers who do not make payments within the stipulated discount period. If this is the case, purchase discounts are not part of materials cost and logically should be excluded from inventory.

Materials may be purchased on cash terms of 2/10, n/30. This means that a 2 percent cash discount may be deducted if payment is made within ten days. In any event, the bill is to be paid within 30 days. A purchase billed at $2,000 under these terms may be recorded as shown below.

```
Materials ....................................... 1,960
    Accounts Payable ...........................          1,960
        To record materials billed at $2,000 with a dis-
    count of 2% allowable.
```

If payment is made within the discount period, Accounts Payable and Cash will be reduced by $1,960. But if the discount is lost, the loss is recorded separately as follows:

```
Accounts Payable ............................. 1,960
Purchases Discounts Lost ........................   40
    Cash ......................................          2,000
        Payment after lapse of discount.
```

The discounts lost are reported and serve as a control over the disbursement function. A large amount shown as purchases discounts lost may indicate needless waste and laxity in the disbursements area.

Additions to materials costs. The invoice cost of materials purchased is not necessarily the total materials cost. The transportation costs on incoming materials, the purchasing and receiving department costs, the costs of materials handling, and the storage costs are all part of the cost of the materials. These costs should accompany the invoice cost of materials through the records. In many cases it will be difficult to identify these costs with specific items of materials. An apportionment of the costs to materials may be made in much the same way that manufacturing overhead is apportioned to the products.

A budget of the various costs that should be attached to materials can be related to a budget of the invoiced materials cost. A percentage is computed, and on this basis the costs related to materials are added to the invoiced materials costs. Any difference between the actual costs and the amounts applied to materials by the budgeted rate can be closed out as an addition to or as a deduction from cost of goods sold at the end of the year.

The following is an example of the computation and the application of a budget rate to apply costs related to materials.

Budgeted Costs Related to Materials

Transportation in	$ 9,600
Purchasing Department cost	27,500
Receiving Department cost	16,400
Inspection Department cost	8,200
Storage costs	8,300
Total	$ 70.000
Budgeted materials costs (as invoiced by suppliers)	$875,000

$$\frac{\text{Costs related to materials}}{\text{Invoiced cost of materials}} = \frac{\$ 70,000}{\$875,000} = 8\%$$

During the year the actual cost of materials purchased amounted to $915,000. Transportation costs and other costs of handling and storing materials in aggregate amounted to $76,000. By using the predetermined rate of 8 percent, $73,200 was added to materials cost. The unabsorbed portion was then closed out to Cost of Goods Sold, as shown on the next page.

A more accurate apportionment can be made by calculating a separate rate for each item included under materials and handling costs. The dollar basis of apportionment used in the last example may not be realistic in many cases. For example, an item with a high cost but low bulk may cost little to handle and store in comparison with a cheaper but bulkier item, yet on a dollar basis it will carry a larger proportion of the handling and storage costs. Freight charges, for example, would be more logically allocated according to weight and shipping distance factors.

By allocating the related costs to materials, it is possible to obtain better materials costs for financial reporting and possibly to have more information

Materials

Invoice cost of materials .. 915,000	
Applied materials handling and storage costs 73,200	

Materials Handling and Storage Costs

Actual costs transferred from detailed accounts .. 76,000	Applied to materials by using rate 73,200
	Unabsorbed portion closed out to Cost of Goods Sold 2,800

Cost of Goods Sold

Unabsorbed materials handling and storage costs... 2,800	

for control purposes. A material that apparently costs very little may be revealed to be quite high in cost when the costs of purchasing it, transporting it, and handling it are taken into account. A study of the relationships between the various material-related costs and the billed cost of the materials may show that the relationship is changing. Perhaps the costs related to materials are becoming excessive, and investigation may show that better service can be obtained at less cost. Transportation costs, for example, may possibly be reduced by selecting other shipping routes or by choosing some other type of carrier.

The inventory level. Included as a very important part of materials control is control over inventory balances. Excessive amounts should not be kept on hand, nor should the inventories be allowed to become dangerously low. An unnecessarily large investment in inventory ties up resources that could be put to better use in some other way. The rate of return that is sacrificed by holding resources idle is an implicit cost to the business. Therefore, if the company has too much invested in inventory, it has sacrificed a return that could be earned if the excessive investment were available and actively employed to earn a return. In short, there is a cost attached to the inventory investment. For the same reason, storage space may also be costly. When large quantities of materials are held, either warehouse space must be rented or valuable plant space must be sacrificed. The return from alternate uses of the plant space becomes a cost of inventory storage. In addition, the insurance cost will probably be higher and there is a greater risk of loss or damage that may or may not be completely covered by insurance. Obviously, a certain inventory level must be maintained if operations are to be continued efficiently and without interruption. Under normal circumstances, customers will not excuse delays in shipments resulting from a manufacturer's failure to produce because of material shortages.

Ordinarily maximum and minimum quantity limits are set for each item in the inventory. These limitations can be computed from information showing what quantities will probably be used during the period of time required to obtain delivery on an order, that is, a *procurement period*. Assume that a certain material can be acquired 30 days after an order has been placed and that usage experience has been as follows:

Average use during a 30-day procurement period ...... 1,000 units
Minimum use during a 30-day procurement period   700
Maximum use during a 30-day procurement period 1,500

An order should be placed when the inventory is at 1,500 units; otherwise, there is a risk that with maximum use the inventory will become depleted before materials are received. This inventory level is sometimes called the *order point*. This is a simplified example because the costs of carrying inventory and the ill will cost of not being able to satisfy a customer's order have not been taken into consideration.

Balancing order and storage costs. There is a cost to order materials, and there is a cost to store materials. As mentioned above, when materials are stored the company has to use space that has a rental value, there may be higher insurance costs, and funds that are invested in inventories are committed so that they are not available for other purposes. On the other hand, when materials are ordered more frequently but in smaller quantities, the freight charges, the costs of processing the increased number of orders, and the costs to receive and handle the materials may be higher. Too, it may be necessary to increase the number of personnel in the purchasing and materials handling departments, thereby adding to labor cost. In some industries the materials are bulky and are difficult to handle at best, which only aggravates the problem. By placing frequent orders, the company may be losing quantity discounts that could be obtained by purchasing in bulk. Perhaps the saving to be obtained from placing large orders will more than compensate for the increased storage costs.

Various factors must be considered, and these factors should be quantified, if possible. The costs to order and store materials will be minimized in many cases, when the costs of storage are equal to the costs of ordering. Normally the costs of ordering will increase as orders are placed more frequently, but the costs of storage will decrease. The total cost may be at a minimum when the two costs are approximately equal.

The order and storage costs can be tabulated under different assumptions as to the number of orders placed and the inventory investment. Assume that a company predicts that 3,000 units of a certain material will be needed next year. Each unit costs $6. Past experience indicates that the storage costs are approximately equal to 10 percent of the inventory investment. The cost to place an order amounts to $9. If only one order were placed for the year, it would be for 3,000 units, and the average number of units held in the inventory during the year would be 1,500 (3,000 ÷ 2) assuming a uniform rate of withdrawal. With two orders, 1,500 units would be purchased on each order, and the average inventory would be only 750 units. The costs to order and store the inventory are computed and set forth on page 349 under different assumptions as to the number of orders and the investment in inventory. The company should place ten orders each for 300 units. The storage costs of $90 are equal to the total ordering costs at this point, and the combined costs are at a minimum.

This same result can be computed by use of the following formula: [1]

$$Q = \sqrt{\frac{2\ DO}{S}}$$

When
$Q =$ Optimum quantity per order (unknown)
$D =$ Annual demand for materials expressed in units of material—3,000 units
$O =$ Cost per order placed—$9
$S =$ Storage cost—60¢ (10% of material cost, $6)

---

[1] This formula was derived as follows:

$$\text{Cost to order} = \frac{\text{Annual demand}}{\text{Optimum quantity per order}} \times \text{Cost per order} \quad \text{or} \quad \frac{DO}{Q}$$

$$\text{Cost to store} = \frac{\text{Optimum quantity per order}}{2\ *} \times \text{Storage cost} \quad \text{or} \quad \frac{QS}{2\ *}$$

* Divide by 2 to get an average.

$$\frac{DO}{Q} = \frac{QS}{2}$$

$$DO = \frac{Q^2 S}{2}$$

$$Q^2 S = 2\ DO$$

$$Q^2 = \frac{2\ DO}{S}$$

$$Q = \sqrt{\frac{2\ DO}{S}}$$

348

Number of Orders	Number of Units per Order	Average Inventory	Storage Cost — Cost of Average Inventory	10% Storage Cost	Order Cost — $9 Each Order
1	3,000	1,500	$9,000	$900	$ 9
2	1,500	750	4,500	450	18
3	1,000	500	3,000	300	27
4	750	375	2,250	225	36
5	600	300	1,800	180	45
6	500	250	1,500	150	54
7	429	215	1,290	129	63
8	375	188	1,128	113	72
9	333	167	1,002	100	81
10	300	150	900	90	90
11	273	137	822	82	99
12	250	125	750	75	108

The optimum order quantity can be computed directly from the formula by inserting the inventory data developed.

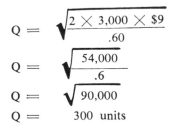

$$Q = \sqrt{\frac{2 \times 3,000 \times \$9}{.60}}$$

$$Q = \sqrt{\frac{54,000}{.6}}$$

$$Q = \sqrt{90,000}$$

$$Q = 300 \text{ units}$$

The annual requirement of 3,000 units purchased on the basis of 300 units per order would require the placing of ten (3,000 units/300 units) orders.

Shipping routes. Often a problem arises when materials or merchandise can be obtained from various sources for shipment to various locations. With proper planning a program can be designed that will minimize the total cost of shipping. Routes are chosen so that all units can be delivered as scheduled with the least total cost. For example, assume that 3 units of a material are required at Destination 1 and that 3 units of this material are also required at Destination 2. There are 2 units available at Warehouse I and 4 units available at Warehouse II. The costs to ship each unit from each warehouse to each destination are shown in the matrix given on the next page.

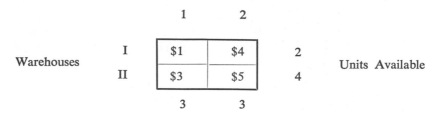

Destinations

		1	2		
Warehouses	I	$1	$4	2	Units Available
	II	$3	$5	4	
		3	3		

Units Needed

At present, the units are being shipped along the routes given below at a total cost of $21.

No. Units	From Warehouse	To Destination	Unit Cost	Total Cost
1	I	1	$1	$ 1
2	II	1	3	6
1	I	2	4	4
2	II	2	5	10
Total shipping cost				$21

By changing the route structure, the total shipping cost can be reduced to $20. Ship one more unit from Warehouse I to Destination 1 and one less unit from Warehouse II to Destination 1. The total effect on cost in this example is trivial; but in actual practice with many units and various shipping costs, the total costs may be substantial.

Cost Effect of Route Change from Destination 1:

Reduced cost:

  1 less unit from Warehouse II $3

Added cost:

  1 more unit from Warehouse I 1

Net advantage of this change $2

However, this route change will make it necessary to ship one less unit from Warehouse I to Destination 2 and to ship one more unit from Warehouse II to Destination 2.

Cost Effect of Route Change for Destination 2:

Added cost:

  1 more unit from Warehouse II $5

Reduced cost:

  1 less unit from Warehouse I 4

Net disadvantage of this change $1

The net effect of the entire change is a net reduction in total cost of $1 as shown on the revised route schedule.

No. Units	From Warehouse	To Destination	Unit Cost	Total Cost
2	I	1	$1	$ 2
1	II	1	3	3
3	II	2	5	15
Total shipping cost				$20

An optimum shipping schedule is obtained when no further cost reductions can be made by shifting the routes. The schedule given above is the optimum schedule.

In linear programming, this type of problem is called the *transportation model*. With many points of origin and destination, the problem becomes more complicated; and a computer may be used in testing for route changes that will result in the lowest possible cost. The principle, however, remains the same. Each change in the route structure is tested for its effect on the total cost. The opportunity cost of shipping by other routes is compared with the cost of the present plan, and the lowest cost routes are chosen until no further cost reductions can be made.

Materials in production. Materials control, of course, extends into the production area. A certain amount of materials loss in manufacturing may be unavoidable, but this loss should be held to a minimum. Some companies distribute reports on materials consumption to their production foremen. These reports show the actual yield from the materials used and compare this yield with a predetermined standard.

Scrap materials are often a residue of a manufacturing operation. For example, when metal parts are stamped out of a sheet of metal, the stamped-out sheet of metal will remain as scrap. Or spirals or chips of metal may be left over from a machining operation. Sometimes the scrap can be reheated and worked over with little loss. In other cases, the scrap may be collected and sold. A study of operations may reveal that scrap can be reduced if materials are used more economically in production.

The proceeds from the sale of scrap may be credited against the cost of the products manufactured, or they may be reported separately as incidental revenue. In any event, the scrap itself should be controlled. The value of scrap may be considerable; and if no control is established over the quantity that should be turned in and accounted for, there is a possibility that the company will not receive the proceeds to which it is otherwise entitled.

Sometimes products are spoiled in the manufacturing operation and must be sold for less than cost. A certain amount of spoilage may be normal (as determined by the engineering department, for example), but spoilage in excess of normal should be reported and brought under control. The losses from spoilage may be charged to manufacturing overhead if spoilage is to be expected on various orders. On the other hand, if an order because of its peculiarities causes added spoilage costs, it should bear the loss. Ordinarily, the loss is attached to an order by crediting the order with the cost recovered by the sale of spoiled units. The remaining unrecovered cost is still on the order, and the good units on the order must absorb this cost.

Certain defects on the products can, perhaps, be removed by additional work. Control must be exercised here also; otherwise, the time and cost required for rework may become excessive. When rework is a normal part of the operation, the cost of rework may be charged to manufacturing overhead. But if the requirements of a particular order were responsible for the rework, the cost should be identified directly with the order.

Standard costs. Standards may be established for the cost of obtaining materials and for the quantities to be used in production. Actual costs can be compared against these standards, and variances can be measured. Basically there are two types of variances: (1) price, and (2) quantity. Several different variances may be developed for specialized purposes, but they always can be classified as being variations in the price of materials, the quantities used, or a combination of price and quantity. If the actual cost is greater than the standard used in comparison, the variance is *unfavorable*; if actual is less than the standard, the variance is *favorable*.

Materials price variance. A standard price is set for each class of material to be purchased. If the purchasing function is being carried out properly, the standard price should be attainable. When lower prices are paid, a favorable materials price variance is recorded, indicating that the purchasing department was under the standard. On the other hand, higher prices are reflected in an unfavorable materials price variance, showing that the purchasing department did not meet the standard. Quality standards have to be watched, of course, as otherwise the purchasing department in its zeal to surpass the standard may acquire poor quality materials that will be costly on the production floor.

A *materials price variance* measures the difference between the prices at which materials were purchased and the prices at which they should have been obtained according to the established standards. Production management is responsible for how materials are used, but it may have no control over the prices that are paid. A factory may be operated efficiently; but if materials are not purchased at reasonable prices, potential profits will be lost before the manufacturing operation begins.

Periodic reports show how actual prices compare with standard prices for the various types of materials purchased. The total cost effect is, of course, equal to the quantities purchased multiplied by the price differentials. Reports on price variances may be made monthly to the purchasing agent and to the executive who is responsible for the purchasing function. They reveal which materials, if any, are responsible for a large part of any total price variation and can help the purchasing department in its search for more economical sources of supply and better terms.

Standard costs are not always incorporated in the accounting records. The price variance, for example, can be measured even though both the materials and the liability to the supplier are accounted for on an actual cost basis. In this chapter, however, the operation of a standard cost system is illustrated by tracing the standard costs through the accounting records. At different points in the accounting operation, variations can be measured in the accounts quite easily; and a knowledge of the flow of actual and standard costs helps in understanding how the variances are determined.

A materials price variance can be isolated at the time materials are purchased. The actual quantity of materials purchased can be recorded in the materials inventory at *standard prices,* but the liability to the supplier must be recorded by using actual quantities and *actual prices.* The difference between the debit to Materials and the credit to Accounts Payable is caused by the difference in price and is recorded as a price variance.

To illustrate, it is assumed that the purchasing department did better than the standard by buying 1,000 units of a certain material at a price of 70 cents when the standard price was 80 cents. This is recorded by a journal entry as:

Materials	800	
Materials Price Variance		100
Accounts Payable		700
Purchases at below standard price, favorable variance.		

Materials quantity variance. Materials are withdrawn and used in production, but more or less materials may be used than specified by the standards. The variations in the use of materials are called *materials usage* or *materials quantity variances.* The differences can be calculated by comparing the record of materials withdrawn with consumption standards, or the differences may be directly recorded in a materials quantity variance account at the time materials are transferred into production.

Reports on the quantities of materials used are made to responsible production personnel. A production foreman, for example, may receive daily or weekly summaries showing how the quantities used in this department compared with the standards. At the operating level, the use of materials can be controlled directly. The foreman should have daily or weekly reports on their operations so that corrections can be made before losses become too great. Summary reports of actual and standard materials consumption given in dollars, with variances and percentages of variances to the standards, can be presented to the general foreman or to the plant superintendent on a monthly basis. If the variances in any department are too large, this will be revealed so that the superintendent can localize the differences and take steps to reduce them in future months. During the month, of course, the operating foremen are expected to watch materials use; and if they have been doing their jobs properly, the accumulated variances for the month should be relatively small.

Ordinarily, materials quantity variances are chargeable to the production departments. They often arise as a result of wasteful practices in working with materials, or they arise because of products that must be scrapped through faulty production. For example, it should be possible to get a certain number of stamped parts from a metal sheet of a given size. But if the stamping operation is not performed properly, more sheets will be used in getting the desired number of parts. Or some part may be machined improperly, with the result that the part will have to be discarded.

Not all excessive materials consumption can be charged to inefficient factory operation. The purchasing department may have to share the blame. Perhaps poor quality materials were acquired in order to obtain a price saving. An inferior grade of material may contribute to losses that are detected in the factory. Any measured variance will reveal a condition, but it will not tell why that condition exists. Management is given the basic information, which it can apply in looking for the underlying causes.

Returning to the last example, assume that 600 units of material are withdrawn from the inventory for use in the factory. The standard calls for only 500 units. The 100-unit difference between actual and standard use is multiplied by the standard unit cost of 80 cents to arrive at an unfavorable quantity variance of $80. If standard costs are recorded in the accounts, Work in Process is charged with *standard quantities* priced at standard unit costs. In other words, the work in process inventory is carried at standard cost. The materials inventory, however, is credited with *actual quantities used* as multiplied by the standard unit costs. The journal entry is shown on the next page.

Work in Process	400	
Materials Quantity Variance	80	
Materials		480
Materials charged to production at standard cost.		

When indirect materials are used, the actual quantities are recorded at standard prices as manufacturing overhead. No variances are measured at this point. Assuming that 100 units of material are transferred to the factory for use as indirect materials, the following entry is made:

Manufacturing Overhead	80	
Materials		80
Withdrawal of 100 units of material having a standard unit cost of 80 cents for indirect use in factory operations.		

LABOR COST CONTROL

The cost of labor, like the cost of materials, is controlled from its inception to its release in the form of the cost of products sold. Personnel records will be kept on each employee as a basic control over the persons to be reported on the payrolls. The total time for which wages are to be paid is controlled by time clock cards, and the distribution of that time within the plant is measured by labor time cards or time reports that show how much time was used on various orders that were in production.

Additions to labor costs. There are additional related costs in connection with labor much the same as there are related costs in connection with materials. An employee, in addition to being paid a straight hourly rate, may receive bonuses, vacation payments, sick leave payments, supplemental unemployment benefits, pensions, overtime pay, and shift differential adjustments. The extras are often referred to as *fringe benefits*.

The proper accounting for these costs in the income determination process can be rather complicated. The estimated cost of providing pensions, for example, may be broken down by years and related to the active work force. A supplemental hourly rate can then be calculated and added to the regular hourly rate in attaching the cost to the products. Similarly, the vacation pay for the year can be reduced to an hourly rate basis for costing products. In many cases, however, the extra pay is charged to manufacturing overhead and is apportioned to all jobs accordingly. If manufacturing overhead is allocated on a direct labor hour basis, the results will be the same under either method. Additional or premium pay for overtime work or for work on a less desirable shift may be charged to manufacturing overhead and allocated to all jobs. A job should not be penalized with extra cost just because it happened to be worked on during an overtime period or during a night shift. On the other hand, a special job that causes overtime work should be charged with the additional cost.

Incentives. Additional pay may also be given for superior work performance. When employees produce more units of product in a given time period, the company gains advantages. There is increased revenue from the sale of the additional units produced, and there is an increase in the variable costs of production. But the increase in revenue should be greater than the increase in the variable costs of production. As a result, the profits will be increased.

Some of the costs of production are fixed. Direct labor, for example, may be paid an hourly rate, and the total direct labor cost over an interval of time will be the same regardless of the number of units produced. There are also fixed manufacturing overhead costs that will not be increased by an increase in production. The direct labor cost and the fixed manufacturing overhead cost are spread over a greater number of units. As a result, the cost per unit of product is lower.

To increase productivity, a company may install superior machinery and equipment, search for better work methods, and reward the employees for superior work performance. There is a variety of incentive pay plans that may be used to encourage the employees to increase production. Employees may be given bonus pay for the time saved in production or may receive higher rates of pay when they exceed standard rates of production for sustained periods of time.

The advantage of increased labor productivity is illustrated by assuming that five men are employed by Hexagon Company during the year to produce a certain line of product that should be manufactured at the rate of five units per man per labor hour. Each man works 2,000 hours during the year and is paid a regular wage rate of $3 an hour. The standard direct labor cost per unit of product is then 60 cents. If an employee can exceed this standard, he will be paid a bonus equal to one half of the pay for the time saved. Each unit of product can be sold for $6. The direct materials cost per unit is $2, and the variable manufacturing overhead cost per unit is 50 cents. The fixed manufacturing overhead cost for the year is $50,000 or $1 a unit when 50,000 units are manufactured.

An income statement is shown at the top of the next page for the manufacturing operation assuming that standard quantities are produced and sold.

If a worker can increase his productivity from five units an hour to six units an hour, he will save 12 minutes on the standard. He will produce in one hour what would normally be produced in one hour and 12 minutes. His bonus would be equal to one half of the pay for 12 minutes or would be equal to the regular pay for six minutes. Six minutes is one tenth of an hour, and the pay for one tenth of an hour is 30 cents (1/10 of $3). The total pay per hour including the bonus would be $3.30.

Assume that all of the employees produced consistently during the year at the rate of six units per hour and produced a total of 60,000 units (5 men × 2,000 hours per man × 6 units per hour). According

Hexagon Company
Income Statement
(Manufacturing Operation)
For the Year Ended December 31, 1972

Standard production of 50,000 units of product
(5 men × 2,000 hours per year × 5 units per hour = 50,000 units)

	Per Unit	Total
Sales (50,000 units)	$6.00	$300,000
Standard cost of units manufactured and sold:		
Direct materials	$2.00	$100,000
Direct labor	.60	30,000
Variable overhead	.50	25,000
Fixed overhead	1.00	50,000
	$4.10	$205,000
Net income (manufacturing)	$1.90	$ 95,000

to the standard, 60,000 units should be manufactured in 12,000 hours (60,000 units ÷ 5 units per hour). The employees saved 2,000 hours and should receive a bonus equal to the pay for one half of the time saved, or the bonus should amount to $3,000 (2,000 hours saved × ½ × $3 labor rate per hour). The total labor cost for the year including the bonus is $33,000, and the labor cost per unit of product is 55 cents ($33,000 labor cost ÷ 60,000 units). The fixed overhead cost of $50,000 is spread over a greater number of units and is 83⅓ cents per unit ($50,000 ÷ 60,000 units).

An income statement for the manufacture and sale of 60,000 units is shown on the next page.

The increased productivity of labor has made it possible to increase the net income by $32,000. The increase of $32,000 is explained on the next page.

Hexagon Company
Income Statement
(Manufacturing Operation)
For the Year Ended December 31, 1972

Production of 60,000 units of product
(5 men × 2,000 × 6 units per hour = 60,000 units)

	Per Unit	Total
Sales (60,000 units)	$6.00	$360,000
Standard cost of units manufactured and sold:		
Direct materials	$2.00	$120,000
Direct labor	.55	33,000
Variable overhead	.50	30,000
Fixed overhead	.833	50,000
	$3.883	$233,000
Net income (manufacturing)	$2.117	$127,000

Additional revenue from the sale of 10,000 more product units (10,000 units × $6)	$60,000
Additional cost of producing 10,000 more units:	
Direct materials (10,000 units × $2)	$20,000
Direct labor bonus	3,000
Variable overhead (10,000 units × 50¢)	5,000
Total increased cost	$28,000
Increased net income	$32,000

THE USE OF STANDARDS

Standards are recognized and are applied in many different areas of activity as a basis of measurement and comparison. A school, for example, sets standards of academic achievement and measures the performance of the students against these standards. Or a manufacturing plant inspects finished products and accepts or rejects them according to how they compare with established standards. A standard is usually looked upon as being a criterion by which something can be judged, or in other words it is a basis for the measurement of the adequacy or inadequacy of the results from a particular operation or undertaking.

The process of arriving at standards is more or less scientific in that work measurement techniques are usually used. A thorough study is made of plant operations, general economic conditions, and the effect of economic conditions on the costs that must be incurred for materials and services. Engineers measure the length of time required to complete various manufacturing operations and establish standards of performance. Cost standards are also set and, when related to performance standards, may be referred to as the standard costs of the operations to which they apply. Often a standard cost is expressed on a unit basis. There will be a standard price for a unit of materials and a standard quantity of materials to be used for a unit of product, and there will be a standard labor rate and a standard time to perform a certain amount of work. The standards will remain unchanged as long as there is no change in the method of operation or in the unit prices of materials or services.

ADVANTAGES OF STANDARD COST ACCOUNTING

Standards are particularly useful in accounting as a basis for evaluating various operations. Within a standard cost accounting system, there are checkpoints so that variations from the standards can be detected and brought under control. While operations are in progress, comparisons of actual results with the standards can be made and unfavorable conditions can be brought to attention and corrected before losses accumulate.

Standard cost accounting follows the principle of *management by exception*. Actual results that correspond with the standards require little attention. The exceptions, however, are emphasized. In actual or historical cost accounting, it is sometimes difficult to separate the exceptions from the flow of data being processed. Furthermore, many of the measurements may not be made until after it is too late to take corrective action.

When reasonable standards are used, there is normally a desirable secondary effect. The employees become cost conscious, watching the standards and seeking ways to improve their work. This tendency can, of course, be encouraged by having an incentive system that is tied in with the standards.

For purposes of income determination as well, a standard cost system may be more economical and less complicated than a historical cost accounting system. Standard cost cards are set up for each job or process showing what quantities of materials, labor, and overhead should be used according to the standards. These cards are printed in advance, with the standard quantities and costs being listed. When a job is started in production, the standard cost card shows the complete costs that should apply to it. Materials, for example, are issued on a standard requisition according to the standard quantities required for the order. If more materials are needed than are called for by the standard, a supplemental requisition having a distinctive color may be prepared to call attention to a quantity variance on the order. Many of the transactions follow the preestablished standard pattern. Any variations from the standards receive extra attention.

When operations are automated, standard conditions can be built into the computer program that controls the manufacturing process. Any deviation from the standards can be detected immediately, and corrections can be made while the work is going on. Losses can be reduced or eliminated entirely in a system that provides for an immediate reaction to any tendency to stray from a predetermined standard. Automatic control devices are used to redirect space vehicles in mid-flight when the vehicle strays off the prescribed course. Similarly, a manufacturing operation can be controlled automatically by an on-line, real-time system. An on-line, real-time system is a system that provides immediate feedback of actual conditions so that corrections can be made at the time the event itself is taking place.

In an automated production system, management will not be as concerned with the problem of controlling the actual operations as it will be with the planning of controls. Considerable attention will be given to the development of standards and to the development of programs that will provide checkpoints to keep the operation in line with the standards. Variations from the standards may measure, in part, inadequacies of the program, unrealiability of the equipment, or conditions that were not provided for in the program of instructions. Control by means of standards and a comparison of results with standards will be employed in any case and will be applied by management to fit the circumstances.

THE QUALITY OF STANDARDS

The term *standard* has no meaning unless it is known what type of standard is being used. A standard may be very strict, or it may be very loose. Standards may be broadly classified as follows:

(1) Strict or tight standards.
(2) Attainable standards.
(3) Loose or lax standards.

There is no easy solution to the problem of how standards should be set. The objective, of course, is to obtain the best possible results at the lowest possible cost. Often this problem will involve human behavior. A very high standard may motivate the employees and may produce the best results. On the other hand, it may discourage them to such an extent that they will not even meet fairly modest standards of achievement. In setting a level of standards, management must consider the employees, their abilities, their aspirations, and the degree of control that they exercise over the results of operations.

The *strict standards* are set at a maximum level of efficiency, representing conditions that can seldom if ever be attained. This type of standard is more a standard of perfection than a standard for the measurement of practical or attainable efficiency. It would appear that a standard should be set at a high level rather than at a level that is below maximum attainment. Idealistically, a person should reach for the stars. Yet, there are serious objections to this approach. As mentioned above, strict standards may discourage employees who might otherwise be motivated if the standards were set within their limits of capability. The variations from ideal standards will probably be large, but they cannot be looked upon entirely as measurements of poor performance. Variance accounts will not only measure shortcomings in performance, but will also measure reasonable deviations from the ideal. When standards are too strict, the unfavorable variances may be abnormally large. As a result, the variations that deserve attention will be hidden within the large variances that include deviations from an absolute perfection that cannot be expected.

The *attainable standards* can be achieved with reasonable effort. There will be variations, of course, but these variations may be more accurate measurements of superior or subnormal performance. There is always the possibility, of course, that the standards aren't high enough to stimulate the superior type of employee, or that they are too high for the less skilled individual.

With *loose standards*, there may be a tendency to indulge in self-con-gratulation. If standards are easily attained, actual performance may be better than standard but still not as good as it should be. For example, 500 labor hours at $4.50 each hour may be established as the standard time required to manufacture 1,000 units of product. This standard may be too liberal if the employees can easily make 1,000 units in 400 hours. If the employees know that they are expected to produce the 1,000 units in 500 hours, they may tend to slow down. If they are paid a bonus for exceeding the standard, they may receive a bonus for performance that deserves no additional reward. If the standards are too loose, certain variations from efficiency will not be revealed but, instead, will be incorporated as a part of the standards. As a result, management will not receive the most useful information for the control of operations.

The variations from the standards will be relatively large or small depending upon how the standards are set. Suppose, for example, that the standard cost to manufacture a unit of a certain product has been calculated in three ways as shown below:

		Types of Standards	
Cost Elements	Strict	Attainable	Loose
Materials	$10.00	$10.00	$10.00
Labor	2.00	2.50	3.00
Overhead	1.00	1.25	1.50
Total unit cost	$13.00	$13.75	$14.50

During the year, this product was manufactured at a total unit cost of $14.30, as shown in the following comparative summary:

Cost Elements	Actual Cost	Types of Standards			Actual Over (Under)		
		Strict	Attainable	Loose	Strict	Attainable	Loose
Materials	$10.00	$10.00	$10.00	$10.00	–0–	–0–	–0–
Labor	2.80	2.00	2.50	3.00	$ .80	$.30	($.20)
Overhead	1.50	1.00	1.25	1.50	.50	.25	–0–
Total	$14.30	$13.00	$13.75	$14.50	$1.30	$.55	($.20)

Materials prices and quantities were in agreement with the standards, which provide in each case for a unit materials cost of $10. The labor and the overhead variances are relatively high when the ideal standard is used. But this total variance of $1.30 per unit is not necessarily a measurement of excessive costs or of poor performance. A portion of the variance may be looked upon as a normal deviation from perfection and hence not controllable. The more significant difference, which management has the ability to control, is not revealed but instead is buried within the total variation of $1.30. At the other extreme, when comparison is made with expected operations, it appears that the company has done very well in trimming 20 cents off the standard unit labor cost. This also may be misleading. The budget standards may be too lax. Assuming that the normal or attainable standards are reasonably tight and are realistic, the controllable variance of 55 cents will be more useful in evaluating costs and performance.

REVISING THE STANDARDS

Standards may be set with the intention that such standards will be retained over long periods of time, barring any substantial changes in the methods of production. Standards of this type are often called *bulletin standards, basic standards,* or *bogies.* When conditions change so that the standard is out-of-date, an adjustment is made by using index numbers in much the same way that index numbers are used in making adjustments for the effect of price level changes. Often the standards are not entered in the accounting records but are used as statistical supplements in arriving at information for control purposes. On the other hand, both the actual data and the standard cost data may be entered in the accounts by dual recording.

In many cases standards are established for relatively short periods of time with revisions being made whenever necessary. For example, a standard price for a material may be relevant for a certain period of time but will have no meaning after there has been an increase in the price level of that material. A variation of the actual price from the standard price will not measure purchasing department inefficiency if an outdated standard price is used for the measurement. Therefore, standards have to be changed from time to time so that they will correspond to current conditions. Similarly, labor standards will have to be revised if the rate structure is changed or if some changes have been made in the methods of production.

Labor price variance. Labor, like materials, must be controlled on a price and quantity basis. With proper work scheduling, employees will be paid regular wage rates for the work that is to be done. Deviations from the standard pattern can be measured and brought under control. Labor performance is also measured by comparing the actual time for production with the standard time. Cost differences attributable to labor efficiency differences can be measured and identified for control purposes. The *labor price variance* measures the difference between the actual hours worked multiplied by the actual labor rates (actual labor cost) and the actual hours worked multiplied by the standard labor rates. Labor price variances are often created by transferring men with high pay rates to jobs that call for low standard rates or by authorizing overtime work at premium pay. These labor cost differences are caused by *rate* differences rather than by changes in performance. The cost effect of unfavorable transfers or of premium pay for overtime should be called to management's attention as a price variance.

In labor accounting, the payrolls are accounted for in the usual manner, with gross wages earned being recorded in a payroll account pending distribution to the production accounts. The direct labor cost as determined is not recorded directly in Work in Process but instead passes through an intermediate account entitled Direct Labor.

Assume, for example, that a payroll for direct production workers shows a gross wage cost of $90,000 for a payroll period. A journal entry to record the payroll follows:

Factory Labor	90,000	
Social Security Tax Withheld		5,000
Income Tax Withheld		18,000
Wages Payable		67,000

To record direct labor payroll for the payroll period.

When the payroll is distributed to Direct Labor, an entry is made to charge Direct Labor with actual hours, multiplied by *standard labor rates*. The factory labor account is reduced by an amount equal to the product of the actual hours and the *actual labor rates*. The difference between the debit to Direct Labor and the credit to Factory Labor is the *labor price variance*.

In the entry given below, the payroll for direct labor amounted to $90,000. There were 20,000 direct labor hours at the rate of $4.50 an hour. The standard labor rate is $4.25 an hour.

Direct Labor	85,000	
Labor Price Variance	5,000	
Factory Labor		90,000

Transfer of factory labor costs to direct labor account with price variance separated.

A payroll for indirect labor would be recorded either directly in Manufacturing Overhead or would be transferred out of Factory Labor to Manufacturing Overhead when information is available for a distribution of the labor cost.

Labor efficiency or quantity variance. Labor productivity is also measured. When labor is used more effectively, not only is the labor cost per unit of product lower, but the overhead per unit of product is also lower. It is not hard to understand why management will strive to increase the productivity of its labor force by introducing better work methods and more modern equipment. There can be a double advantage in that both labor and overhead cost per unit can be reduced.

Labor performance, or labor efficiency as it is sometimes called, is compared by department and by job with established standards. Daily or weekly reports to the foremen and the plant superintendent help to locate and solve difficulties on a particular job or in a department. The vice-president in charge of production or the plant superintendent receives a report relating labor efficiency to labor costs on a weekly or monthly basis. Differences between jobs and departments may show that a job cannot be handled at standard labor costs or that a department is not being managed properly.

When the direct labor cost is transferred to the work in process inventory, the products are charged with standard costs obtained by multiplying the standard hours by the standard labor rates. The direct labor account is relieved of the costs originally charged to it by multiplying the *actual hours* by the standard rates. The *labor efficiency* or *quantity variance* is then the difference between the actual and the standard hours multiplied by the standard rate. Using the data from the preceding example, suppose that 20,000 direct labor hours were used to complete work that should have been done in 21,000 hours. This is recorded by the following journal entry:

Work in Process	89,250	
Labor Efficiency Variance		4,250
Direct Labor		85,000

Direct labor transferred to the products.

In this case, there is a favorable variance because the work was done in less than the standard time.

SUMMARY OF VARIANCES

Attention should be called to how the variances are developed in the journal entry presentation. The price variance and the quantity or efficiency variance are separately identified in the accounts by holding either the price or the quantity factor constant in both halves of the entry while permitting the other factor to vary. This same principle can be applied in variance determination when standard costs are not entered in the accounting records.

The price and quantity or efficiency variances can be segregated quite easily in tracing the cost flows. The general approach is summarized in the diagram given below:

		Accounts Used	
	Basis of Recording	Materials	Labor
(1) Initial acquisition	Actual quantities at actual prices *	Accounts Payable	Payroll
	↓		
	Difference is a price variance ↑	Materials Price Variance	Labor Price Variance
(2) Distribution to intermediate accounts	Actual quantities at standard prices **	Materials	Direct Labor
	↓		
	Difference is a quantity variance ↑	Materials Quantity Variance	Labor Efficiency Variance
(3) Transferred to product cost	Standard quantities at standard prices	Work in Process	Work in Process

 * Initial entries will be made to Materials and to Direct Labor by debits. These accounts will be credited when distribution is made to Work In Process.
 ** The actual quantities of materials purchased during a fiscal period will not necessarily be equal to the actual quantities withdrawn for use in production.

Materials and Direct Labor described above as intermediate accounts provide a means for separating the difference between the actual costs and the standard costs into price and quantity variances. The principle of inserting an intermediate account as a separator between two different costs is often used in breaking down a total variance into two portions (i.e., a price variance and a quantity or efficiency variance).

An identification of variances by type is a step in the determination of the causes of the variance. The variances are broken down further by functional area or department. Then, if a variance is judged to be significant, an investigation may be made to find out why the variance occurred. Perhaps, with better control, the variance can be reduced or eliminated in the future. Or, it may be found that the standards are unrealistic and should be revised.

Questions

1. Why should the accounting records with respect to an asset such as inventory be kept by someone other than the storekeeper? Wouldn't it be more efficient to have the storekeeper keep the inventory records as well as the physical inventory?

2. What advantage is there in borrowing money at 8 percent annual interest to obtain 2 percent cash discounts on payments to suppliers?

3. What are purchases discounts? How can management know that discounts are not being lost?

4. Can freight on incoming materials and the costs of receiving and handling materials be identified as a part of materials cost? Explain.

5. The freight costs of Lark Products, Inc., are applied to the materials by a predetermined rate calculated from a budget of estimated freight costs and weights. In 1972, the freight cost has increased relative to the invoice cost of materials. What factors might be responsible for this increase in relation to invoice cost?

6. The controller of Newport Patterns, Inc., states that the inventories of materials are held at a high level to prevent the risk of production shutdowns that would result if a supplier could not make deliveries. Furthermore, he explains that the materials are difficult to handle and that it is more convenient to purchase large lots infrequently. Comment on this policy.

7. A certain amount of materials loss can be expected in some types of manufacturing operations. What type of report can be given to the foremen to help them control the loss?

8. What is the transportation model? How can opportunity costs be applied in selecting the least expensive shipping routes?

9. How is the increased productivity of labor related to manufacturing overhead?

10. What are labor fringe benefits? Can these costs be related to the hourly wage costs? How?

11. How does the problem of employee motivation relate to the problem of setting standards?

12. What are price and quantity or efficiency variances?

13. How are materials price variance and materials quantity variance computed?

14. An examination of the cost records of Magill Products Company reveals that the materials price variance is favorable but that the materials quantity variance is unfavorable by a relatively large amount. What might this indicate?

15. Describe briefly the way in which the variances are isolated in standard cost accounting.

16. What is a labor efficiency variance?

17. How can variances be used to control operations?

18. What is meant by management by exception?

Exercises

1. Lopez Medical Supplies, Inc., observes the following practices in purchasing materials and in processing claims for payment:

(a) Orders are placed for standard quantities of materials when the materials inventory records indicate that the quantities are down to certain minimum levels.

(b) The orders are placed with established suppliers whenever possible. If the orders cannot be filled by established suppliers, bids are requested from competing suppliers. The bids are opened in the presence of two individuals, and the purchase order is awarded to the lowest bidder.

(c) The materials are tested for purity when received with the quantity and results of the test entered on a receiving report.

(d) The purchase order, the receiving report, and the supplier's invoice are compared in the accounting department; and a voucher is prepared.

(e) The voucher is filed so that it will be paid within the discount period.

(f) The voucher is approved for payment, and a check is drawn. The check is signed by two individuals, each of whom examines the underlying voucher.

(g) The amount is recorded on the check in perforations by a check protector.

Required: Explain the control features behind each practice described.

2. Last year Neil Furnishings, Inc., purchased merchandise having a gross cost of $1,350,000. Two percent cash discounts were allowed on all payments made within 10 days. The company took discounts on merchandise having a gross cost of $700,000, but discounts were not taken on the other purchases. The manager explained that the company was short of cash and that in order to take all discounts he would have had to increase the cash balance by $80,000, and this could only be done by borrowing money at the bank at an annual rate of 9 percent for the entire year.

Required: Comment on the manager's policy. Compute the net advantage or disadvantage of borrowing to obtain the cash discounts.

3. Direct labor at Twin City Motors, Inc., is paid a regular wage of $4.50 per hour. Fifteen units of product should be manufactured each labor hour, and the production employees are paid a bonus for time saved in production. The bonus is equal to 80 percent of the regular pay for the time saved. According to the budget, variable manufacturing overhead should vary at the rate of 50 cents per unit of product, and the fixed manufacturing overhead should amount to $300,000 a year. Ordinarily the company operates at 50,000 direct labor hours a year. In 1973 the company produced 810,000 units of product by working 50,000 direct labor hours. Actual overhead costs conformed to the budget estimates.

Required: (1) Compute the labor cost and the overhead cost per unit of product for standard production.

(2) Compute the labor cost and the overhead cost per unit of product in 1973.

(3) Explain why the unit costs are lower in spite of the labor bonus.

4. Steel beams and bars are purchased by Hellertown Steel Company for use in production. Overhead cranes are employed to transport the materials to and from the storage area. Costs for 1973 have been estimated as follows:

Freight on incoming materials	$ 1,520,000
Materials handling costs	138,000
Receiving department costs	142,000
Cost of materials purchased	36,000,000

The weight of the material to be received has been estimated at 180,000 tons. The costs related to the materials are to be applied to the materials by a predetermined rate. In 1973, the company actually purchased 168,000 tons of steel at a total cost of $40,320,000. The freight on incoming materials was $1,542,000, the materials handling costs were $127,000, and the receiving department costs were $144,000.

Required: (1) Compute the predetermined rate that can be used to assign the materials-related costs to the materials. (One rate is to be used for all costs.)

(2) Determine the over or underapplied cost for 1973.

5. Rolf Fittings, Inc., has two plants: one located at Rockport and the other at Clearview. Shipments are made from both plants to three regional warehouses. Next month the Rockport plant is expected to produce 6 units. Four of these units will be shipped to Warehouse B, and the remaining units will be shipped to Warehouse C. The Clearview plant is expected to produce 4 units and will ship all four units to Warehouse A. Unit shipping costs from each plant to each warehouse are given below:

Plants	*Warehouses*		
	A	*B*	*C*
Rockport	$4	$6	$10
Clearview	3	8	8

Required: (1) Compute the expected shipping costs next month under the existing plan.

(2) Prepare a shipping plan for the next month that will meet the stated conditions and will minimize the costs of shipment.

6. Standard costs have been established by Solomon Bros., Inc., for the production of a certain machine part. The production workers receive $4.20 an hour and are expected to produce six units of this part each hour. The direct materials that are used on a unit of product cost $1.80. Cost studies reveal that the variable manufacturing overhead varies at the rate of $8.40 an hour. By revising the production process slightly, management believes that it will be possible to produce seven units of this part each hour.

Required: (1) Determine the standard unit variable cost of the product at the present time.

(2) Determine the standard unit variable cost of the product under the revised production plan.

7. A cutter for trimming trees and shrubs is manufactured by Harmon-Smith, Inc. Standard quantities and costs of the parts used to make each cutter are as follows:

	Cost Per Unit of Part
1 Metal pole	$.50
5 Bracing parts	.10
2 Cutting parts	.35
8 Rivets	.005
6 Screws	.005
2 Springs	.05
1 Handle	.40
8 Feet of wire	.08

In 1972, the company made 10,000 of these cutters. No materials were on hand at either the beginning or end of the year. The quantities purchased and used in production are given below at actual costs:

11,000 Metal poles	$6,050
51,500 Bracing parts	5,150
20,300 Cutting parts	7,105
87,000 Rivets	696
93,000 Screws	837
23,400 Springs	1,170
10,150 Handles	5,075
92,000 Feet of wire	7,360

Required: Determine the total materials cost variance and analyze it as to the materials price variance and the materials quantity variance.

8. Redfern Valley, Inc., has established standards for the production of a small household item. Summary data on standard costs are given:

Labor time per unit of product	10 minutes
Labor hour rate	$3.60

Variable manufacturing overhead is expected to vary at the rate of $6.00 an hour. In 1973, the company produced 516,000 of these items in 84,000 direct labor hours. The direct labor cost amounted to $327,600. The variable overhead varied as budgeted at the rate of $6.00 an hour and amounted to $504,000.

Required: (1) Determine the labor cost variance and split it into a price variance and an efficiency variance.

(2) Determine the effect of labor efficiency on the variable overhead cost.

Problems

12–1. The plant superintendent of Dawson Lines, Inc., has been experimenting with standards of productivity in an attempt to determine whether relatively tight or relatively loose standards motivate employees to better performance. Time studies show that a fast worker can produce 60 units of product an hour, but he cannot work at this rate for any sustained period of time. In general, 40 units of product can be produced each hour on a sustained basis. All trained employees without undue effort can produce at the rate of 30 units per hour.

During one three-month period, the standard was set at the rate of 60 units an hour. Highly skilled employees were assigned this work and were paid $5.60 an hour. In this period, the company manufactured 197,400 units of product in 4,700 labor hours.

In another three-month period the standard was set at the rate of 40 units an hour. Regular employees were assigned this work and were paid $4.20 an hour. In this period, the company manufactured 204,000 units of product in 5,100 labor hours.

In still another three-month period the standard was set at the rate of 30 units an hour. Regular employees were assigned this work and were paid $4.20 an hour. In this period, the company manufactured 193,500 units of product in 4,300 labor hours.

Required: (1) Which of the three standards produces the best results?
(2) Compute the labor cost per unit of product under each of the three plans.

12–2. At the close of 1972, the variance accounts on the records of Padfield Instruments Company showed the following information:

	Dr.
Materials price variance	$39,200
Materials quantity variance	1,240
Labor price variance	19,200
Labor efficiency variance	66,600

Jon Grady, the president of the company, cannot understand why the variances are so large. During the year, the company operated at 48,000 direct labor hours and manufactured 240,000 units of product.

The standard materials and labor cost per unit of product are given below:

Direct materials	$1.24
Direct labor	.4625

Two units of material are to be used for each unit of product, and the standard labor rate is $3.70 an hour.

The type of material used in this product can no longer be purchased at 62 cents a unit. The purchasing department had to pay 70 cents a unit for the 490,000 material units purchased during the year. There were 482,000 units of material used in production.

A new union wage scale at the beginning of the year provides for hourly wages of $4.10. A review of labor performance standards reveals that only five units of product can be manufactured per direct labor hour.

Required: (1) Set up a more realistic schedule of standard unit costs for materials and labor.
(2) Recompute the variances according to the new schedule.
(3) Explain why the original variances were so high and identify the more realistic variances that should be given attention.

12–3. A decorative light fixture is assembled by one of the divisions of Hebner Furnishings, Inc. In 1972, this division started 450,000 of these fixtures in production. Cost data are summarized below:

(1) Three basic types of materials were purchased for production. Price and quantity data follow:

Type of Material	Quantity	Prices Standard	Prices Actual
A	465,000	$4.50	$4.70
B	960,000	.60	.56
C	1,420,000	.80	.85

(2) During the year, 450,000 units of Material A were used, 915,000 units of Material B were used, and 1,360,000 units of Material C were used. All materials are added at the beginning of the manufacturing operation. According to the standards, one unit of Material A is to be used for each fixture, two units of Material B, and three units of Material C.

(3) Direct labor payrolls are summarized below:

Gross Wages	$1,827,000
Income Taxes Withheld	370,000
Social Security Taxes Withheld	92,000
City Wage Tax Withheld	18,270

The labor rate was $4.20 per hour.

(4) The standard time required for the assembly of each fixture is one hour, and the standard labor cost per hour is $4.00.

(5) In 1972, the company manufactured 400,000 of these fixtures and transferred them to finished goods. There was no inventory of work in process at the beginning of the year. The 50,000 units in process at the end of the year were complete as to materials but only one-half complete as to direct labor and overhead.

Required: Prepare journal entries to trace the costs through the records. Transfer the direct materials and direct labor cost of the completed units to finished goods inventory. Isolate the price and quantity or efficiency variances in the journal entries.

12–4. A relatively high-cost material is used by Sachiko Instruments, Inc., in the production of a device used in industrial photography. This material costs $50 a unit, and it is estimated that approximately 10,000 units will be purchased next year to meet production requirements. The costs to process each order have been estimated as follows:

Freight and shipping	$125
Receiving department	80
Inspection	30
Purchasing department	10
Total	$245

The material does not weigh much, and freight and shipping charges do not vary to any great extent because of the number of units ordered.

Space that is used for storage can be used for other purposes. Management estimates that the opportunity cost of using space for storage of these materials plus financing costs are approximately equal to 20 percent of the cost of the materials.

Required: (1) Determine the optimum number of orders that should be placed each year to minimize the total annual cost of placing orders and storage. Prove your answer by showing the combined costs for 10 orders, 12 orders, etc., until a maximum of 20 orders is reached.

(2) The company plans to apply the ordering costs to the materials inventory cost, using a predetermined rate. (Storage costs are not to be applied. A large portion of the storage costs are opportunity costs and not incurred costs.) Compute the predetermined rate for applying order costs to the materials inventory. Use the optimum number of orders to determine the rate.

(3) Assume that the costs of ordering amounted to $3,542 in the next year and that the company actually purchased materials costing $490,000. Determine

the difference between the actual cost and the amount applied by using the predetermined rate. How should this difference be handled in the accounting records?

12–5. Shipments are to be made from three regional plants of Huff Brothers, Inc., to a customer who wants deliveries made at three different locations. The number of units available at each plant and the customer demand schedule are given along with the unit costs of shipment from each plant to each location.

Customer Locations

		1	2	3		
	East	$5	$12	$8	6	
Plants	South	$4	$10	$7	5	*Units Available at the Plants*
	West	$6	$15	$5	9	
		4	12	4		

Units required

Required: Plan a shipping schedule that will minimize the total cost of delivery to the customer.

12–6. An insecticide is manufactured at the Aberdeen plant of Pope Chemicals, Inc. Standards have been established for variable costs.

A certain amount of shrinkage and loss of materials can be expected in production. If a better grade of material (Grade A) is used in production, the product output should amount to 90 percent of materials input. An inferior grade of material, designated as Grade B, can be substituted for Grade A. If this inferior material is used, the product yield should be equal to 80 percent of the materials input.

Standard unit costs of the two grades of material are as follows:

Grade A—$.22   *Grade B—$.17*

During the following year, it is estimated that 360,000 pounds of product will be manufactured.

The plant production manager recommends that Grade B material be used. He points out that the total cost will be lower in spite of the relatively poor yield.

According to the standards, 6,000 hours of labor each at $3.80 are required for an output of 360,000 pounds of product when Grade A material is used. If Grade B material is used, 8,000 hours of labor each at $4.50 are required for the same output. Labor hours vary with pounds of output.

The variable manufacturing overhead should vary at the rate of $6.50 per labor hour.

During the following year, the plant used Grade B materials and manufactured 340,000 pounds of product. The yield rate was better than anticipated, amounting to 85 percent of input. The materials, however, were higher in price, costing $.19 a pound instead of $.17 as expected. The higher cost labor was employed in production, and 7,800 hours were utilized at the rate of $4.50 an hour. Variable manufacturing overhead amounted to $54,600.

Required: (1) To obtain lower product costs, which materials should be used according to the standards set for 360,000 pounds of production? Show computations.

(2) Compute the material and labor cost variances for the year based on the standards established for Grade B material. Both the price and quantity or efficiency variances should be computed.

12–7. Weaver Chemical Products, Inc., assigns standard variable costs to the pharmaceutical products processed in its plant at Woodbury, New Jersey. Last week the labor rate and efficiency variances were unfavorable by substantial amounts.

An investigation was made, and the variances were traced to operations in Department 6. In that department 1,200 hours of labor paid at the regular rate of $4.80 were used to process 50,000 pounds of product that should be produced according to the standards in 900 hours with labor paid at the regular rate of $4.20 an hour. The department not only used labor having a higher hourly rate but also had to pay overtime rates at one and one-half times the $4.80 rate for all of the 1,200 hours. Hours were in excess of the standard only because of the emergency condition. Under normal conditions, this batch could be processed in 900 hours with labor paid at the rate of $4.20 an hour. The standard variable overhead amounts to $8.00 per direct labor hour.

The foreman of Department 6 states that he authorized overtime because of an emergency situation. If the 50,000 pounds of product were not processed immediately, 80 percent of the batch would have been completely spoiled. The standard cost of this material received by his department is 8 cents a pound. However, the present cost of this material is 12 cents a pound, and the cost standards are in the process of revision. To replace any losses it would now cost 12 cents a pound.

Required: (1) Did the foreman make the correct decision in avoiding the loss of product through delay in processing? Show the dollar advantage or disadvantage.

(2) Compute the standard variable cost for 50,000 pounds; for one pound. (Use $.12 per pound as the new materials cost standard.)

(3) Based on the production data for that week, compute the actual variable cost for 50,000 pounds; for one pound. Assume that the materials were received at the old standard cost of $.08 per pound. Break down the labor variance into a labor rate variance and a labor efficiency variance.

12–8. Standards are being established for the production of a chemical product manufactured by Sanford Processing Company. Preliminary studies have been made on trial production runs, similar operations have been examined, and cost data have been obtained.

Data relevant to the manufacturing process are summarized below:

1. *Direct materials*—The company may use either of two grades of a certain type of material. The Grade A material costs $24 per ton and the Grade B material costs $16 per ton. (A ton is defined as 2,000 pounds.)

2. *Direct labor*—A crew of six men working as a team is required on the production line. The productive working time for each man for a year is estimated at 1,500 hours, and the direct labor cost for each man per hour amounts to $4.20. The product yield is equal to 80 percent of material input when Grade A material is used and is 75 percent of input when Grade B material is used.

As an alternative, higher cost labor may be employed. A crew of six men, each earning $4.80 for each productive hour may be utilized. Productive working time for each man for a year is estimated at 1,500 hours. The higher skilled labor is able to obtain an 85 percent yield when Grade A material is used and an 80 percent yield when Grade B material is used.

   3. *Variable manufacturing overhead*—The company plans to produce 6,000,000 pounds of product each year. The variable manufacturing costs have been estimated for the 9,000 productive labor hours that should be employed during the year to obtain the normal output of 6,000,000 pounds of product. The costs per labor hour, using either high or low cost labor, are set forth below:

	High-Cost Labor	Low-Cost Labor
Employee benefits	$ .80	$ .60
Other materials	2.00	2.40
Lubrication	.50	.50
Maintenance	1.20	1.50
Repairs	.80	1.00
Utilities	.40	.40

   Required: (1) Calculate the standard cost per hundredweight of product for each of the alternatives given. (Compute materials input to the nearest ton. Carry answer to four decimal places.)

   (2) Which alternative should yield the lowest product cost?

   (3) Compute the combined standard cost of direct labor and variable manufacturing overhead per direct labor hour using both types of labor. Is there a significant difference in the cost per hour? Explain.

Chapter 13

CONTROL: OVERHEAD

As explained earlier, manufacturing overhead consists of many different types of costs, and these costs, unlike the costs of direct materials and direct labor, are indirectly related to the products. Manufacturing overhead is applied to the products by means of an overhead rate that is calculated by dividing a budgeted measurable factor that is related both to the products and to the overhead into a budget of manufacturing overhead at normal capacity. The factor selected may be direct labor cost, direct labor hours, machine hours, or some other basis of measurement that is appropriate for the particular manufacturing operation.

THE MANUFACTURING OVERHEAD BUDGET

Manufacturing overhead cost standards can be incorporated in a manufacturing overhead budget. As stated in Chapter 9, some of the overhead costs will vary with the amount of productive activity while other costs will be fixed with respect to changes in the amount of productive activity. Often overhead budgets are prepared for several activity levels. An overhead budget consisting of separate budgets for different levels of activity is called a *flexible budget.*

A flexible budget for Avalon Products Company is given at the top of the next page.

Assume that the company has a normal operating capacity of 100,000 machine hours and standards show that five units of product should be manufactured each hour. The total overhead at normal operating capacity has been budgeted at $305,000.

In 1972, it is assumed that (1) the company produced 350,000 units of product, (2) used 80,000 machine hours, and (3) incurred overhead costs as shown below the flexible budget on the next page.

Avalon Products Company
Flexible Budget (Standard Costs)

	Overhead Budgets at Various Hours of Operation			
Standard number of product units	500,000	450,000	400,000	350,000
Machine hours of operation	100,000	90,000	80,000	70,000
Variable overhead:				
Indirect materials	$ 90,000	$ 81,000	$ 72,000	$ 63,000
Repairs and maintenance	42,000	37,800	33,600	29,400
Lubrication	8,000	7,200	6,400	5,600
Power	15,000	13,500	12,000	10,500
Total variable costs	$155,000	$139,500	$124,000	$108,500
Variable overhead rate	$1.55			
Fixed overhead:				
Supervision	$ 80,000	$ 80,000	$ 80,000	$ 80,000
Taxes and insurance	31,000	31,000	31,000	31,000
Heat and light	12,000	12,000	12,000	12,000
Depreciation	27,000	27,000	27,000	27,000
Total fixed costs	$150,000	$150,000	$150,000	$150,000
Fixed overhead rate	$1.50			
Total overhead	$305,000	$289,500	$274,000	$258,500
Overhead rate per machine hour .	$3.05			

	Actual Overhead Incurred
Indirect materials	$ 76,000
Repairs and maintenance	33,200
Lubrication	6,100
Power	12,800
Supervision	80,000
Taxes and insurance	32,000
Heat and light	12,400
Depreciation	27,000
Total overhead	$279,500

The company should have used only 70,000 machine hours (350,000 units at 5 units per hour) to produce 350,000 product units, and the overhead should have been only $258,500. (See the flexible budget.) Hence, the overhead cost variance is $21,000 as calculated below:

Actual manufacturing overhead	$279,500
Budget of manufacturing overhead for 70,000 machine hours that are *required* to produce 350,000 units of product	258,500
Unfavorable overhead variance	$ 21,000

THE OVERHEAD VARIANCE AND COST CONTROL

The overhead variance can be used for cost control and can be refined further by:

(1) An analysis of the causes of the variance.

(2) A breakdown of the total variance by cost classifications.

The total overhead variance can be analyzed into a *budget* or *spending variance* and an *efficiency variance*. The two variances may be combined and called the *controllable variance*.

The budget or spending variance. The budget or spending variance is the difference between the actual cost and the budget for the *actual* hours of operation. If a spending variance is to be measured properly, both the actual costs and the budget used for comparison must be for the same interval of time.

The budget or spending variance in manufacturing overhead is comparable to the price and quantity or efficiency variances developed for direct materials and direct labor. It measures (1) the differences between the actual and standard costs of manufacturing overhead materials and services and (2) differences between the actual and standard quantities used.

In the example given, the company operated at 80,000 machine hours. The budget of overhead for the 80,000 *actual hours of operation* shows a total cost of $274,000. This budget amount is compared with the actual overhead costs to isolate the *budget or spending variance* of $5,500 (unfavorable).

Actual manufacturing overhead	$279,500
Budget of manufacturing overhead for 80,000 machine hours (actual hours of operation)	274,000
Unfavorable spending variance	$ 5,500

The company spent $5,500 more for overhead at the 80,000 machine hour level than was called for in the budget.

The efficiency variance. The spending variance is only part of the total variance. In the example, with a standard of five units of product for each machine hour, the company should have manufactured the 350,000 units of product in 70,000 machine hours. Instead, 80,000 hours were used to manufacture the output of 350,000 units of product. The difference in budgeted cost between the 80,000 hours actually used and the 70,000 hours that should have been used is called the *efficiency variance*. It is caused by the inefficient use of machine hours. The efficiency variance is computed as follows on the next page.

Budget of manufacturing overhead for 80,000 machine
hours (actual) $274,000
Budget of manufacturing overhead for 70,000 machine
hours (required) 258,500
Unfavorable efficiency variance .... $ 15,500

The variance can also be calculated by multiplying the difference between the standard and actual hours by the variable rate per hour as shown below:

$$(80,000 \text{ actual hours} - 70,000 \text{ standard hours}) \times \$1.55$$
$$= \$15,500 \text{ unfavorable efficiency variance.}$$

The efficiency variance does not measure efficiency in the *use* of overhead. Instead, it measures efficiency in the use of the factor that is employed in costing overhead to the products. If, for example, machine hours are used in costing overhead and if more machine hours are used than required, the variable overhead cost will be higher. Note that the efficiency variance includes only the variable costs. Fixed costs by definition remain the same over the range of hours and are not affected by the efficient or inefficient use of machine time.

In this example, the spending variance would have been favorable if actual overhead cost for the attained level of activity had been less than budgeted. There would have been a favorable efficiency variance if the company had used fewer machine hours than budgeted for the production level attained.

A variance report by cost classification. More detailed information can be given in a cost report by showing the spending and efficiency variances for each cost classification. This type of report as illustrated on the next page can be used by management to identify specific costs that may require further attention.

The fixed costs should not be included in the efficiency variance. Note that the variable costs are the only costs that contribute to the efficiency variance. That is to be expected. It is impossible to reduce the fixed costs by operating at less machine hours.

A STANDARD COST SYSTEM FOR PRODUCT COSTING

If the standard cost system is used only for control purposes, the analysis given above will serve the purpose. To control costs, the manager will usually want to know, for example, if the foreman is (1) spending too much for overhead (spending variance) or if he is (2) using too many hours in production (efficiency variance). To answer these questions, it is not necessary to reduce total fixed cost to a *unit* cost. The important point in

	(1) Total Overhead Incurred	(2) Budgeted Cost (80,000 Hours)	(3) Budgeted Cost (70,000 Hours)	(4) Spending Variance (1) — (2)	(5) Efficiency Variance (2) — (3)
Variable overhead:					
Indirect materials ...	$ 76,000	$ 72,000	$ 63,000	$4,000 *	$9,000 *
Repairs and					
maintenance	33,200	33,600	29,400	400	4,200 *
Lubrication	6,100	6,400	5,600	300	800 *
Power	12,800	12,000	10,500	800 *	1,500 *
Fixed overhead:					
Supervision	80,000	80,000	80,000		
Taxes and insurance .	32,000	31,000	31,000	1,000 *	
Heat, light, and power	12,400	12,000	12,000	400 *	
Depreciation	27,000	27,000	27,000		
Total variable and fixed					
overhead	$279,500	$274,000	$258,500	$5,500 *	$15,500 *

* Denotes unfavorable variance.

cost control is to control the *total* cost, and information for cost control is given by the above analysis.

However, it may be too costly to design an accounting system to serve only one purpose. Certainly, the firm will want a system that gives information that can be used to calculate profit. This being the case, if the firm chooses to use full cost as a basis for calculating profit, then the standard cost system must be modified to arrive at the fixed cost per unit.

The capacity variance. A third variance called the *capacity (or volume) variance* may arise when fixed overhead costs are expressed as unit costs. The fixed overhead for Avalon Products Company is $150,000 for the volume range of 70,000 to 100,000 machine hours. In order to reduce the total fixed overhead to a cost per unit of product, it will be necessary to choose a volume level. The fixed overhead per machine hour for various machine hours of operation is computed below:

Fixed Overhead	÷	Machine Hours	=	Fixed Overhead per Hour
$150,000		70,000		$2.143
150,000		80,000		1.875
150,000		90,000		1.667
150,000		100,000		1.500

For cost accounting purposes, the fixed overhead rate is usually set in advance. The company will not want to wait until the end of the accounting period to cost out the product. Hence, the fixed cost per hour must be calculated in advance of actual operations.

The volume on which the fixed cost per unit is based is called the *normal volume*. In order to prevent large fluctuations in unit cost from one accounting period to the next, due only to differences in volume from period to period, normal volume is usually considered to be an average for several years and is not necessarily changed each year.

The normal volume for Avalon Products Company is 100,000 machine hours a year. The standard overhead cost per machine hour is then:

Variable overhead cost per hour	$1.55
Fixed overhead cost per hour	1.50
Total overhead cost per hour	$3.05

A unit of product should be manufactured each 12 minutes (rate of 5 units per hour). Hence, the standard overhead cost per unit of product is $.61 (1/5 of $3.05). The fixed overhead rate per unit of product is $.30 (1/5 of $1.50).

The products are assigned the standard overhead cost, or in this illustration, $213,500 of the overhead cost is assigned to the 350,000 units.

350,000 units × $.61 standard overhead cost per unit of product = $213,500.

The flexible budget shows that overhead cost of $258,500 has been budgeted for the production of 350,000 units. The difference between the overhead budget for 350,000 units and the overhead costed to the products is designated as a *capacity* or *volume variance*.

Flexible budget for 350,000 units of product (70,000 machine hours)	$258,500
Standard overhead cost applied to the products (350,000 units × $.61 standard overhead cost per unit of product)	213,500
Unfavorable capacity (volume) variance	$ 45,000

The capacity variance measures the over or underabsorption of fixed overhead. Variable overhead does not become a part of the capacity variance. The fixed overhead per unit of product is budgeted at $.30 for 500,000 units of product ($150,000 fixed overhead ÷ 500,000 units of product). But the company made only 350,000 units of product and did not absorb all of the fixed overhead in product cost by using the rate for 500,000 units.

Fixed overhead budgeted	$150,000
Fixed overhead absorbed (350,000 units of product $\times$ $.30 fixed overhead rate per unit of product)	105,000
Unfavorable capacity variance	$ 45,000

The same result can be obtained by working with either the difference in machine hours or product units and using the appropriate fixed overhead rate.

150,000 product units $\times$ $.30 fixed overhead $=$ $45,000 capacity variance.
    below normal   per unit of
    capacity   product
(500,000 — 350,000)

30,000 machine hours $\times$ $1.50 fixed overhead $=$ $45,000 capacity variance.
    below normal   rate per machine
    capacity   hour
(100,000 — 70,000)

Summary of overhead variances. The diagram given below shows how the overhead variance can be broken down into three segments where the system is used for both product costing and control.

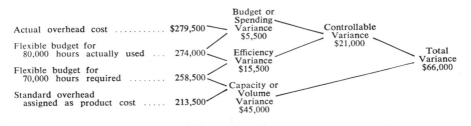

Actual overhead cost $279,500

Flexible budget for
  80,000 hours actually used ... 274,000

Flexible budget for
  70,000 hours required 258,500

Standard overhead
  assigned as product cost 213,500

Budget or Spending Variance $5,500

Efficiency Variance $15,500

Capacity or Volume Variance $45,000

Controllable Variance $21,000

Total Variance $66,000

PLANT UTILIZATION

The capacity variance developed in the product costing operation arises only when fixed manufacturing costs are assigned to the products and when the fixed overhead absorbed by using a rate computed at normal capacity is more or less than the fixed overhead budget.

Outside of the conventional accounting records, capacity may be measured in physical units such as hours or units of product. Statistics on plant capacity may help to place responsibility for the failure to use the plant facilities to the extent possible.

In the preceding example, normal capacity was defined at 100,000 machine hours or 500,000 units of product. Normal capacity, as defined earlier, is an average concept representing the average level of plant operation over the years considering variations from year to year.

Practical plant capacity, on the other hand, is the level at which the plant can operate if all facilities are used to the full extent. Some allowance must be made for expected delays because of changes in machine setups, necessary maintenance time, and other interruptions. Hence, practical capacity is less than the theoretical maximum capacity that could be obtained only under ideal conditions.

A comparison of the actual output with the output for practical plant capacity broadly measures the failure of the plant to operate at the level for which the plant was designed. Assume, for example, that Avalon Products Company has a plant that could reasonably be expected to produce 600,000 units a year. Yet, only 350,000 units were produced.

Practical capacity	600,000 units
Actual production	350,000
Total idle capacity	250,000 units

The idle capacity, as expressed in product units, can be analyzed further to determine why the plant was not used as intended. Assume that the sales budget shows that 500,000 units were to be sold during the year but that orders for only 450,000 units were received.

Practical capacity	600,000		
		100,000	(1)
Sales budget	500,000		
		50,000	(2)
Sales orders received	450,000		
		100,000	(3)
Actual production	350,000		

(1) Practical capacity minus sales budget

The difference between the practical plant capacity and the sales budget for the year requires further investigation. Perhaps, the company was overly optimistic and provided too much plant capacity. Or the sales department may not be obtaining potential available sales. Additional analysis may reveal the true nature· of the problem and provide a foundation for improvements.

(2) Sales budget minus sales orders received

The difference between the sales budget for the year and the sales orders received is a measuremnt of the inability of the sales department to meet the budget quota. Perhaps the sales quota was too high. On the other hand, the sales department may not have taken the proper steps to obtain sales.

(3) Sales orders received minus actual production

The difference between the sales orders received and actual production results in a mixture of idle capacity and inefficiency. Avalon Products Company used enough machine time to produce 400,000 units of product but only produced 350,000 units. Hence, 50,000 units included under idle capacity really indicate wastefulness rather than nonutilization. The difference between the sales orders received and the expected production from the time used

(450,000 — 400,000) is a measurement of idle capacity. The idle capacity may be chargeable to poor production scheduling or to some other lapse in production management that caused production to fall below scheduled customer deliveries.

In the example given for Avalon Products Company, no allowance was made for inventories at either the beginning or the end of the period in order to simplify the example. In practice, adjustments must be made for units carried over into the year as inventory or for units remaining on hand at the end of the year.

The significance of the variances may be emphasized by considering the dollar effect. If the sales department fails to meet the sales quota, there is an opportunity loss of profits that should be realized. For example, assume that 50,000 units of product may be expected to bring in $600,000 in revenue. Additional costs to manufacture and deliver these units are estimated at $400,000. The $400,000 consists of the direct material, direct labor, and variable overhead cost as well as the cost to deliver the units. The opportunity cost of not meeting the sales budget (sales budget of 500,000 units minus sales orders received of 450,000 units = 50,000 units) is then estimated at $200,000. At best, this is an approximation. Arguments can be made that the additional units could only be sold by reducing prices or that the cost estimates are not entirely accurate. Nevertheless, this approach to the problem can be helpful in that it points out how dollars of profit may be sacrificed by not using the facilities as intended.

A STANDARD COST ILLUSTRATION

Cost transactions for Reichard Supply Company are traced through the records for the year in a summary form. Only one product line is manufactured, with a standard unit cost shown on the standard cost card below:

Reichard Supply Company
Standard Cost—Product A

Materials: 10 units of material × $3 standard price .... $ 30.00
Labor: 15 hours × $4.20 standard labor rate 63.00
Overhead: 15 hours × $5.00 standard overhead rate 75.00
Standard production cost per unit $168.00

The total manufacturing overhead at normal operating capacity has been budgeted at $600,000, and 120,000 direct labor hours have been budgeted at normal capacity. The overhead rate per direct labor hour is $5.00.

Summary transactions and cost data pertaining to the year are as follows:

(1) Materials purchases, 62,000 units at a unit cost of $3.20.

(2) Direct materials issued to production, 61,000 units. The standards require only 60,000 units of materials.

(3) Factory payrolls, $537,200; income taxes withheld, $108,000; social security taxes withheld, $27,000.

(4) Labor distribution:

Direct labor, 84,000 hours @ $4.80
Indirect labor, $134,000

(5) Manufacturing overhead other than indirect labor:

Indirect materials	$126,500
Reduction of supplies	14,000
Reduction of prepaid insurance	3,000
Accrued expenses	152,500
Depreciation	118,000

(6) There were no units in process at either the beginning or at the end of the year. During the year 6,000 units were manufactured, and 5,500 units were sold on account for $250 apiece.

(7) A portion of the flexible manufacturing overhead budget is given in summary form below:

Percentages of Normal Operating Capacity	70%	75%	80%	100%
Standard production in units of product ...	5,600	6,000	6,400	8,000
Variable overhead	$140,000	$150,000	$160,000	$200,000
Fixed overhead	400,000	400,000	400,000	400,000
Total overhead	$540,000	$550,000	$560,000	$600,000
Budgeted direct labor hours	84,000	90,000	96,000	120,000
Overhead rate per hour				$5.00

The flow of the transactional data through the accounts is shown in summary journal entry form below and on the next three pages.

(1) Materials purchased during the year:

Materials	186,000	
Materials Price Variance	12,400	
Accounts Payable		198,400

Acquisition of materials:

Standard—62,000 units × $3 = 186,000
Actual—62,000 units × $3.20 = 198,400

(2) Direct materials issued to production at various times:

(a) On standard requisitions:

Work in Process	180,000	
Materials		180,000

       Standard quantities issued. (10 material units $\times$ 6,000 product units = 60,000 standard units of material $\times$ \$3 standard unit cost = \$180,000)

(b) On supplemental requisition:

Materials Quantity Variance	3,000	
Materials		3,000

       Requisition of 1,000 (61,000 issued minus 60,000 standard) units in excess of standard at \$3 standard unit cost.

(3) Factory payrolls for the year:

Factory Labor	537,200	
Income Taxes Withheld		108,000
Social Security Taxes Withheld		27,000
Wages Payable		402,200

       Summary of factory payrolls.

(4) Labor distribution for the year:

(a) Preliminary step:

Direct Labor	352,800	
Manufacturing Overhead	134,000	
Labor Price Variance	50,400	
Factory Labor		537,200

       Distribution of payrolls:

          Direct labor: 84,000 hours $\times$ \$4.20 standard hourly rate = \$352,800. Price variance = \$.60 (\$4.80 actual minus \$4.20 standard) per hour $\times$ 84,000 hours = \$50,400.

(b) Final distribution:

Work in Process	378,000	
Labor Efficiency Variance		25,200
Direct Labor		352,800

       Standard hours per unit of product of 15 $\times$ 6,000 product units = 90,000 standard hours $\times$ \$4.20 standard rate = \$378,000 product cost. Actual hours of 84,000 $\times$ standard rate cleared out of Direct Labor.

(5) Actual manufacturing overhead for the year, excluding indirect labor.

Manufacturing Overhead	414,000	
Materials		126,500
Supplies		14,000
Prepaid Insurance		3,000
Accrued Expenses Payable		152,500
Accumulated Depreciation		118,000

       Summary of manufacturing overhead including result of adjusting entries made at end of year.

(6) Manufacturing overhead applied to production during the year:

Work in Process	450,000	
Applied Manufacturing Overhead ...		450,000

Standard hours required for production (15 standard hours per unit × 6,000 units = 90,000 total standard hours. 90,000 standard hours × $5 rate = $450,000 standard overhead cost)

(7) Completed units transferred to finished goods inventory:

Finished Goods	1,008,000	
Work in Process		1,008,000

Transfer of 6,000 units to stock at a standard cost of $168 apiece.

(8) Total sales of 5,500 units:

Accounts Receivable	1,375,000	
Sales		1,375,000

Sale of 5,500 units at $250 per unit.

Cost of Goods Sold	924,000	
Finished Goods		924,000

The standard cost of 5,500 units sold is charged to Cost of Goods Sold (5,500 units × $168 per unit).

(9) Actual and applied manufacturing overhead accounts closed and variance recorded:

Applied Manufacturing Overhead	450,000	
Manufacturing Overhead Variance	98,000	
Manufacturing Overhead		548,000

To close actual and applied overhead accounts. The unfavorable variance is recorded. (Indirect Labor, $134,000 + other manufacturing overhead, $414,000 = $548,000)

Analysis of Manufacturing Overhead Variance

Budget (spending):

Actual overhead incurred	$548,000	
Flexible budget for 84,000 hours of operation	540,000	
Budget variance (unfavorable)		($ 8,000)

Efficiency:

Flexible budget for 84,000 hours of operation	$540,000	
Flexible budget for 90,000 standard hours required	550,000	
Efficiency variance (favorable)		10,000

(handwritten: 400,000 Fixed 148,000 Variable 400,000 Fixed 140,000 Variable)

Capacity variance:

Flexible budget for 90,000 standard hours required	$550,000	
Standard overhead applied (90,000 standard hours × $5 rate)	450,000	
Capacity variance (unfavorable)		(100,000)
Total variance (unfavorable)		($ 98,000)

(10) Variances closed to Cost of Goods Sold at the end of the year:

Cost of Goods Sold	138,600	
Labor Efficiency Variance	25,200	
Materials Price Variance		12,400
Materials Quantity Variance		3,000
Labor Price Variance		50,400
Manufacturing Overhead Variance ..		98,000
To close out all variances for the year.		

NONMANUFACTURING COSTS

Manufacturing costs are often used to illustrate how differences between actual and standard costs can be analyzed as a basis for cost control. These same concepts can be applied, however, in dealing with selling and administrative costs and can be applied by entities that do not manufacture and sell products but instead render services. Outside of the manufacturing area, standard costs and variances are usually not incorporated in the accounts but are determined by supplemental analysis.

Banks, insurance companies, finance companies, and other companies that sell services instead of products can determine how much it should cost to render their service under different conditions to various customer groups. Work measurement techniques can be used to measure the standard output expected in a unit of time from a given activity or function. The time standards are then combined with cost standards to establish a standard cost for a service.

To illustrate, it is assumed that 2 hours of clerical time are required to process a certain type of insurance claim. The standard variable cost per hour is $5.00. The fixed cost of operating the claims division has been budgeted at $4,000 a month; normally 400 claims are to be processed each month. The standard cost to process a claim is:

Variable cost (2 hours × $5)	$10.00
Fixed cost ($4,000 ÷ 400 claims)	10.00
Standard cost per claim	$20.00

In a given month, assume that 360 claims were processed in 750 hours with actual fixed costs as budgeted and actual variable costs of $3,840.

Variations from the standards can be identified for control purposes by the following analysis:

Actual variable cost	$3,840	
Budget of variable cost for 750 actual hours (750 hours × $5 rate)	3,750	
Spending variance		$ 90
Budget of variable cost for 750 actual hours	$3,750	
Budget of variable cost for 720 standard hours required (360 claims × 2 hours per claim = 720 standard hours × $5 rate)	3,600	
Efficiency variance		150
Fixed overhead	$4,000	
Overhead absorbed by 360 claims (360 claims × $10 rate)	3,600	
Capacity variance		400
Total variance		$640

For any function or activity that can be performed in a measured unit of time, standard costs can be developed. The general principles of variance analysis can be employed as an aid in cost control.

Questions

1. Why are variable overhead costs higher when the actual hours of operation are in excess of the standard hours allowed?

2. What is a capacity or volume variance?

3. Name three manufacturing overhead variances that are often developed in standard cost accounting.

4. Which two of the three variances are called the controllable variance?

5. What is a flexible budget?

6. How is a budget or spending variance determined in the analysis of a manufacturing overhead variance?

7. Does an overhead efficiency variance measure efficiency in the use of overhead? Explain.

8. The fixed manufacturing overhead will not be completely applied to the products if the company does not operate at a normal level of capacity. Explain why this is true.

9. How can variances be used to control operations?

10. Can a capacity variance be controlled?

11. How are the variances handled at the end of the fiscal year?

12. Explain briefly how the total manufacturing overhead variance can be analyzed into a spending variance, an efficiency variance, and a capacity variance.

13. Can the principles of standard cost accounting be applied by nonmanufacturing companies? Explain.

Exercises

1. Summary flexible overhead budgets are to be prepared for two departments of Shaw Machine Company. Budget data follow:

Dept. 1

Manufacturing overhead varies at the rate of $6.50 for each machine hour, and the fixed manufacturing overhead is budgeted for the year at $300,000. At normal capacity, the department should operate at 200,000 machine hours.

Dept. 2

Manufacturing overhead varies at the rate of $7.00 for each direct labor hour, and the fixed manufacturing overhead is budgeted for the year at $500,000. At normal capacity the department should operate at 400,000 machine hours. One direct labor hour is equal to two machine hours.

Required: Prepare in summary form a flexible budget for each department showing costs at normal capacity and at 90, 80, 70, and 60 percent of normal capacity.

2. The Williams Company has prepared a flexible budget of manufacturing overhead for the year, a portion of which is given below:

Percentage of Normal Capacity:	80%	90%	100%
Variable costs:			
Indirect materials	$ 4,000	$ 4,500	$ 5,000
Supplies	2,800	3,150	3,500
Repairs	1,600	1,800	2,000
Maintenance	1,360	1,530	1,700
Heat and light	640	720	800
Total variable costs	$10,400	$11,700	$13,000
Fixed costs:			
Indirect labor	$ 8,000	$ 8,000	$ 8,000
Repairs	4,500	4,500	4,500
Maintenance	2,800	2,800	2,800
Taxes and insurance	1,600	1,600	1,600
Depreciation	1,900	1,900	1,900
Total fixed costs	$18,800	$18,800	$18,800
Total overhead	$29,200	$30,500	$31,800

The company has budgeted 5,000 machine hours at the normal capacity level. Five units of product should be manufactured each machine hour. The company actually produced 20,000 units of product during the year in 4,500 hours.

Required: (1) Compute a variable overhead costing rate and a rate for costing fixed overhead to the products.
(2) How much variable overhead was costed to the products?
(3) Determine the overhead efficiency variance.
(4) How much fixed overhead was costed to the products?

(5) Determine the capacity variance.

(6) If the actual overhead amounted to $31,600, what was the budget or spending variance?

3. One of the divisions of Samolis Fastener Company manufactures two types of product. The standard time required to manufacture one unit of Product A is 30 minutes, and the standard time of Product B is 20 minutes. During the year the company is expected to operate at a normal capacity of 100,000 machine hours with variable manufacturing overhead costs of $650,000 and fixed manufacturing overhead costs of $800,000. Variable manufacturing overhead costs vary proportionately with machine hours. In 1972, the company produced 82,000 units of Product A in 48,000 hours and 90,000 units of Product B in 32,000 hours. Actual variable manufacturing overhead amounted to $524,500, and the actual fixed manufacturing overhead was $814,000.

Required: (1) Determine the standard manufacturing overhead cost assigned to each of the two product lines.

(2) How much of the overhead variance was caused by an efficient or inefficient use of machine hours?

(3) Which product line was responsible for most of the efficiency variance?

(4) Determine the budget or spending variance.

(5) Determine the capacity variance.

4. A flexible budget of manufacturing overhead for Winston Products is summarized below:

Percentages of Normal Operating Capacity

	70%	80%	90%	100%	110%
Variable overhead	$126,000	$144,000	$162,000	$180,000	$198,000
Fixed overhead	300,000	300,000	300,000	300,000	300,000
Total overhead	$426,000	$444,000	$462,000	$480,000	$498,000

Standard costs are used to measure managerial performance. According to the standards established, eight units of product should be manufactured in an hour, and 480,000 units of product should be produced when the company operates at its normal capacity of 60,000 machine hours a year. Last year the company produced 432,000 units of product in 57,000 machine hours. The total variable manufacturing overhead for the year amounted to $173,000, and the total fixed overhead amounted to $312,000.

Required: Compute the manufacturing overhead variance for the year. Analyze the variance into a budget variance, an efficiency variance, and a capacity variance.

5. Quantum Parts Company has been operating below normal capacity for several years. Part of the problem is excess capacity in the industry, but management has found that part of the problem can be attributed to faulty lines of communication between the sales manager and the field representatives. At normal operating capacity the company should be able to produce 1,000,000 units of product in 200,000 machine hours with variable manufacturing overhead at $300,000 and fixed manufacturing overhead at $1,500,000. During the last year 700,000 units of product were manufactured in 140,000 machine hours with actual manufacturing overhead being equal to approximately the amount budgeted for 140,000 hours. With better coordination between the sales managers and field representatives, the company should have produced and sold 820,000 units of product.

Required: Determine the total capacity variance. How much of this variance can be charged to the sales division?

6. Marigold Parcel Service delivers package in the city area and hires drivers to make deliveries. Variable costs have been budgeted, and an average standard time has been established to make a delivery. According to the standards, one delivery should be made each hour. The office is located in the center of the business area, and it takes as much time to deliver to one location as it does to another. Fixed costs have also been budgeted and should amount to $22,500 each month. The variable costs are expected to amount to $3.90 per delivery per hour. Last month the company made 2,700 deliveries in 2,550 hours and incurred variable costs of $10,120 and fixed costs as budgeted. Under normal operating conditions, 3,000 deliveries should be made each month.

Required: (1) Compute the standard cost of making a delivery.
(2) Determine the budget variance and the efficiency variance.
(3) How much of the total variance can be considered to be a capacity variance?

7. Greenfield Mixing Company has established standard costs for a unit of product manufactured as follows:

Materials (8 pounds @ $1.30 per pound)	$10.40
Labor (1 hour @ $4)	4.00
Variable overhead ($6 per labor hour)	6.00
Fixed overhead ($10 per labor hour)	10.00
Total standard unit cost	$30.40

At normal operating capacity, 15,000 units of product should be manufactured in a year.

Cost data pertaining to the operations of 1972 are summarized below:

Materials purchased (114,000 pounds)	$142,500
Materials used in production	108,000 pounds
Labor hours	12,600 hours
	@ $4.20

Manufacturing overhead:

Variable	$ 78,200
Fixed	150,000

During the year, 12,000 units of product were put into production and were completed. There were no units in process at the beginning of the year or at the end of the year.

Required: (1) Prepare journal entries to record the flow of cost data from the time the materials are purchased until the products are completed. (Ignore withholdings from the wages of employees and credit accounts payable for all manufacturing overhead costs incurred.) Variances from standard costs are to be segregated in the accounts.
(2) Which variances were unfavorable? Which one was the most unfavorable?

8. At a normal operating capacity, Brandywine Container Company operates at 400,000 direct labor hours with a standard labor rate of $4.50. Variable manufacturing overhead is applied at the rate of $8.00 per direct labor hour, and fixed overhead is applied at the rate of $7.00 per direct labor hour. Five units of product should be manufactured in an hour. In 1972, 1,400,000 units of product were manufactured in 300,000 direct labor hours. Included in the direct labor hours are 50,000 overtime hours at $6.75 an hour. All other hours were paid at the regular standard labor rate. Actual manufacturing overhead for the year was as follows:

Variable $2,320,000
Fixed 2,840,000

Required: (1) Prepare an analysis of direct labor cost showing a labor price variance and a labor efficiency variance.

(2) Prepare an analysis of manufacturing overhead cost showing a controllable variance and a capacity variance.

(3) Analyze the controllable overhead variance with regard to a budget variance and an efficiency variance.

Problems

13–1. The superintendent of the Waynesboro plant of Hawley-Ford, Inc., is in the process of preparing a fixed manufacturing overhead budget for the year.

Property taxes for the year have been increased to $16,200. Insurance premiums for protection of the property are estimated at $1,950.

Salaries of the plant foremen and other supervisors in the plant are established at $318,000. The salary of the plant superintendent, not included in salaries given above, is $46,500. Product engineering and development costs are budgeted for the year at $116,000.

Plant maintenance and repairs are handled by a maintenance department, and the costs of operating this department are estimated at $128,000 for the year. The fixed portion of the heat and light cost is governed by the size of the plant and its facilities and is estimated at $48,000 for the year. Depreciation of the plant and equipment is expected to amount to $33,000.

The plant superintendent, in attempting to reduce product cost, is considering the possibility of decreasing the budgeted product engineering and development costs by $20,000 and the plant maintenance and repair costs by $35,000.

At normal operating capacity, the plant should yield 500,000 units of product by operating at 200,000 machine hours.

Required: (1) Prepare a fixed manufacturing overhead budget.

(2) Identify the committed costs and the programmed costs.

(3) Determine the fixed overhead costs per unit of product. What would the fixed overhead costs be on a unit-of-product basis if the budget is reduced.

(4) Can the company obtain benefits from the budget reductions? Explain.

13–2. Kreitzer Flexible Tubing Company manufactures various types of plastic and rubber-coated tubing products for various industries and for direct sale to the retail trade. A standard cost accounting system is used.

In one of the plants a particular type of tubing is manufactured in a continuous process, and the standard output has been set at 1,000 feet per hour. During the last year, this division produced 45,000,000 feet of tubing in 48,000 machine hours.

At a normal operating capacity of 60,000 machine hours, the manufacturing overhead budget shows variable costs of $318,000 and fixed costs of $480,000.

Actual manufacturing overhead costs for the year were as follows:

Variable overhead $243,000
Fixed overhead 478,000

Required: (1) Calculate the total manufacturing overhead variance.

(2) Analyze the variance. Show how much of it was controllable and how much of it was attributable to a difference in operating capacity.

(3) Analyze the controllable variance into a spending variance and an efficiency variance.

13–3. Abbot Pattern Company produced 40,000 units of product during the month of May, 1972.

Two units of material each having a standard cost of $3.50 are required for each unit of product. The actual materials purchased and used had a unit cost of $3.70. The total cost of materials purchased and used was $351,500.

Each unit of product requires two hours of labor time. The standard labor rate is $4.40 an hour. The actual hourly rate was $4.80. Enough labor time was utilized for the manufacture of 41,500 units of product.

The company has a normal operating capacity of 90,000 hours per month. A portion of a flexible overhead budget is given below:

Hours of operation	80,000	90,000
Variable costs	$ 560,000	$ 630,000
Fixed costs	1,260,000	1,260,000
Total overhead	$1,820,000	$1,890,000

Actual overhead for the month amounted to $1,844,000. Included in this amount was $1,260,000 in fixed manufacturing overhead.

Required: Calculate price and quantity variances for direct materials and price and efficiency variances for direct labor. Split the manufacturing overhead variance into a budget variance, an efficiency variance, and a capacity variance.

13–4. Standard costs have been established for Payne Industries, Inc. At a normal operating capacity of 120,000 machine hours, the company should produce 6,000,000 pounds of an industrial chemical in a year. Standard costs have been established at this level of operation and rate of output. The manufacturing overhead costs incurred in 1972 are given below along with standard manufacturing overhead budgets for 90,000 and 120,000 machine hours of operation.

Controllable at plant operating level:

	Actual Costs	90,000-Hour Budget	120,000-Hour Budget
Supplies	$ 81,500	$ 63,000	$ 84,000
Indirect materials	72,400	46,800	62,400
Indirect labor	135,000	135,000	135,000
Maintenance	71,000	67,500	90,000
Repairs	86,200	73,800	98,400
	$446,100	$386,100	$469,800

Not controllable at plant operating level:

Supervision	$182,000	$182,000	$182,000
Depreciation	27,000	27,000	27,000
Heat and light	14,000	14,000	14,000
Taxes and insurance	23,000	23,000	23,000
	$246,000	$246,000	$246,000
	$692,100	$632,100	$715,800

In 1972, the company manufactured 5,500,000 pounds of product in 100,000 machine hours of operation.

Required: (1) Prepare a report that will show the budget or spending variance for each item of overhead that is controllable at the plant operating level.

(2) Prepare another report that will show the efficiency variance.

(3) Identify the costs with relatively large budget or spending variances and explain these variances.

(4) Determine the capacity variance.

13–5. Vanderslice Processing Company uses standard costs in a plant where an industrial solvent is manufactured. Operating at normal capacity, the plant should produce 8,100,000 pounds of this solvent with fixed manufacturing overhead of $648,000.

In 1972, the plant used 8,200,000 pounds of raw material in manufacturing 7,200,000 pounds of product. According to the standards established, the company should obtain a 90 percent product yield from raw material inputs. The standard price of the raw material per pound is 18 cents. During 1972, the company purchased 6,500,000 pounds of the raw material at the standard price and 1,900,000 at 16 cents a pound. Materials price variances are computed on the pounds purchased.

Ordinarily, 100 pounds of product should be manufactured per labor hour. In 1972, the plant used 78,000 labor hours in production of which 69,000 were paid for at the standard labor rate of $4.00 an hour. The balance of the hours were paid for at the overtime rate of $6.00 an hour.

A budget of variable manufacturing overhead shows that the variable overhead should vary at the rate of $3.00 per labor hour. The total variable overhead in 1972 amounted to $232,000.

There were 120,000 pounds of finished product on hand at the beginning of 1972 and 130,000 pounds of finished product on hand at the end of the year. The product is sold for $.52 a pound.

Required: Prepare an income statement for the manufacturing division for 1972 using standard costs. Show variances at the end of the statement. The manufacturing overhead variance should be shown as a controllable variance and a capacity variance.

13–6. One of the divisions of Kool-Air, Inc., assembles electric fans. Two models are assembled: Model KA38 and Model KA65.

Comparative manufacturing costs for 1972 and 1973 are listed below:

	1973	1972	*Increase (Decrease)*
Direct materials	$4,150,000	$5,480,000	($1,330,000)
Direct labor	1,460,000	2,496,000	(1,036,000)
Supervision	220,000	220,000	—
Indirect labor	895,000	870,000	25,000
Repairs and maintenance .	131,000	112,000	19,000
Depreciation—equipment .	26,000	26,000	—
General manufacturing overhead	372,000	372,000	—
Totals	$7,254,000	$9,576,000	($2,322,000)

Standards in effect in 1972 on a unit of product basis are given below:

Materials:	Motors		Assemblies	
	Units	Unit Cost	Units	Unit Cost
Model KA38 1		$ 8.00	1	$2.00
Model KA65 1		15.00	1	7.00

Labor:	Hours	Rate per Hour
Model KA38	1	$4.00
Model KA65	3	4.00

All of the manufacturing overhead costs are fixed costs and are not controllable at the division level. The manufacturing overhead budget is given below:

Supervision	$220,000
Indirect labor	870,000
Repairs and maintenance	112,000
Depreciation—equipment	26,000
General manufacturing overhead	372,000

At normal operating capacity the division should be operating at 800,000 direct labor hours each year.

In 1972, the company used 140,000 motors each at a cost of $12 for KA38; and 160,000 motors each at a cost of $15 for KA65. Also used in production were 140,000 assemblies each costing $2 for KA38 and 160,000 assemblies each costing $7 for KA65. Direct labor hours were in agreement with the standard with the exception that 4,000 more hours were used in the production of KA38. Actual and standard labor rates were the same.

In 1973, a new production method was introduced that can reduce the time required to produce a unit of KA65 from 3 hours to 2 hours.

During 1973, 126,000 motors each costing $10 were used for KA38; and 120,000 motors each costing $15 were used for KA65. Also used in production were 125,000 assemblies each costing $2 for KA38 and 120,000 assemblies each costing $7 for KA65. Direct labor hours and rates were in agreement with the standards as revised.

The two models were produced in the two years as follows:

Model	Units Manufactured	
Number	1973	1972
KA38	125,000	140,000
KA65	120,000	160,000

Required: (1) Compare actual results with the standards for 1972. Compute price and quantity or efficiency variances for direct materials and direct labor.

(2) Compare actual results with the standards for 1973. Compute price and quantity or efficiency variances for direct materials and direct labor.

(3) Determine the capacity variance each year.

(4) Did the division operate as efficiently in 1973 as in 1972? Explain.

13–7. Leith Fittings, Inc., manufactures three product lines in three producing departments. Results for the month of November, 1972, are summarized on the next page.

	A	B	C
Materials:			
Product 1	$24,000	—0—	—0—
Product 2	16,940	—0—	—0—
Product 3	—0—	$3,600	—0—

	A		B		C	
Labor:	Hours	Cost	Hours	Cost	Hours	Cost
Product 1	2,400	$9,600	7,300	$29,200	—0—	—0—
Product 2	2,400	9,600	5,000	20,000	—0—	—0—
Product 3	—0—	—0—	2,100	8,400	2,750	$13,750

	A	B	C
Overhead:			
Controllable variable overhead	$ 9,800	$32,300	$13,800
Direct and controllable fixed overhead	40,000	40,000	12,000
Allocated fixed overhead .	60,000	60,000	16,000

All materials were purchased at standard unit prices.

In November, 1972, the company manufactured the following quantities of products:

Product 1 .... 4,700 units
Product 2 .... 2,400 units
Product 3 ....   900 units

Standard cost data are given for the three departments and product lines:

Department A

		Labor	
Materials per Product Unit		Time per Product Unit	Rate per Hour
Product 1	$5.00	½ hour	$4.00
Product 2	$7.00	1 hour	4.00

Department B

		Labor	
Materials per Product Unit		Time per Product Unit	Rate per Hour
Product 1	—0—	1½ hours	$4.00
Product 2	—0—	2 hours	4.00
Product 3	$3.00	2 hours	4.00

Department C

	Labor	
	Time per Product Unit	Rate per Hour
Product 3	3 hours	$5.00

Overhead standards for Departments A and B are based on machine hours. There are two machine hours for each hour of labor time. The overhead standard for Department C is based on labor hours.

Normal operating activity for a month has been established as follows:

Department A .... 20,000 machine hours
Department B .... 40,000 machine hours
Department C .... 4,000 labor hours

The overhead rate for each department has been broken down into a variable overhead rate, a fixed overhead rate for costs directly chargeable and controllable at the department level, and a fixed overhead rate for fixed costs allocated to the departments. All variable overhead costs are controllable at the department level. Overhead rates follow:

	Departments		
	A	B	C
Variable rate	$1.00	$1.00	$ 5.00
Fixed rate, direct	2.00	1.00	3.00
Fixed rate, allocated	3.00	1.50	4.00
	$6.00	$3.50	$12.00

Required: (1) Prepare a total overhead budget at normal capacity for each department.

(2) Calculate the total variances from standard costs for each cost element by department.

(3) Determine the controllable overhead variances by department.

(4) Which department shows the poorest performance record?

13-8. In the Parkersburg plant of Hydro Processing Company, an industrial chemical is manufactured. Standard costs are used for control and for product costing, and each departmental supervisor is held accountable for the costs that he controls. Because of the nature of the manufacturing process, losses of the product can be expected during the process cycle. Provision is made for normal losses.

Actual controllable costs are compared against a budget of controllable costs for each departmental supervisor each month. The department is also charged with abnormal losses by computing the product of the standard variable unit cost of work received from other departments and the excess of units lost over the normal allowance.

In June, 1972, Department #4 received 1,500,000 units of material from Department #3. The standard unit cost of the material received amounted to $.06 including standard unit variable cost of $.04.

Department #4 was expected to produce 1,200,000 units from this input but succeeded in producing only 1,000,000 units acceptable for delivery to the warehouses for sale to customers. The selling price per unit of product is $.15.

A budget of costs for Department #4 for the 100,000 machine hours required to produce 1,200,000 units is given below and on the next page.

Direct labor (fixed cost) $21,000
Indirect labor (fixed cost) 17,500
* Lubrication 1,500
* Power 1,200
* Supplies 13,000

* Maintenance, material and labor	$ 4,600
* Repairs, materials and labor	3,700
Equipment repairs and maintenance (fixed cost)	6,500
Depreciation—equipment (fixed cost)	2,200
Building occupancy cost (fixed cost)	10,800
Total	$82,000

* Costs vary with machine hours.

All costs are controllable by departmental supervision with the exception of depreciation and building occupancy cost. If only 1,000,000 units of product were to be produced, this production could have been obtained by 83,000 machine hours of operation in Department #4.

Actual manufacturing costs for Department #4 in June follow:

Direct labor	$21,000
Indirect labor	17,500
Lubrication	1,500
Power	1,200
Supplies	12,800
Maintenance, materials and labor	4,900
Repairs, maintenance and labor	3,500
Equipment repairs and maintenance	6,500
Depreciation—equipment	2,200
Building occupancy cost	12,000

Required: (1) Compute the controllable cost variance for the costs incurred by Department #4 in June.

(2) Analyze this variance into a portion measuring the variation in the prices and quantities of materials and services used and a portion representing the cost of inefficient operation.

(3) Determine the responsibility of Department #4 for the cost of work performed in earlier operations but lost in Department #4.

13–9. A standard cost accounting system is employed by Davis and Mangum, Inc. One line of product is manufactured exclusively at the Millersville plant. A summary of standard cost data and the costs of operation during the year, 1972, are set forth below.

Standard Cost Data

The direct materials cost per unit of product, according to the standards, should amount to $6.00.

Direct labor is to be paid at the rate of $4.50 an hour, and two units of product are to be produced each labor hour.

At a normal operating capacity of 85,000 machine hours, the plant should produce 340,000 units of product.

The manufacturing overhead costs have been segregated. The variable portion of the costs varies with machine hours.

A budget of manufacturing overhead costs at a normal level of operations is given below and on the next page.

	Cost per Machine Hour	Fixed Cost
Indirect materials and supplies	$1.50	—0—
Indirect labor	—	$ 56,000
Repairs	.80	28,800

	Cost per Machine Hour	Fixed Cost
Maintenance	$ .50	$ 18,700
Taxes	—	9,000
Insurance	—	5,200
Utilities	1.80	15,300
Depreciation	—	37,000
Total fixed cost		$170,000

Actual Cost Data

During 1972 the plant operated at 76,500 machine hours and produced 289,000 units of product.

In the manufacturing operation, enough materials were used to manufacture 293,000 units of product. Materials used to manufacture 210,000 units cost $5.50 per unit. The rest of the materials cost $6.00 per unit.

The plant operated at 153,000 direct labor hours. All of the hours with the exception of 18,000 hours were paid for at the standard rate. The 18,000 hours were paid for at the rate of $4.80 an hour.

Actual overhead costs for the year are given below:

	Variable	Fixed	Total
Indirect materials and supplies ...	$115,200	—	$115,200
Indirect labor	—	$ 58,500	58,500
Repairs	61,500	30,600	92,100
Maintenance	37,600	18,700	56,300
Taxes	—	15,000	15,000
Insurance	—	5,200	5,200
Utilities	138,100	15,300	153,400
Depreciation	—	37,000	37,000
Totals	$352,400	$180,300	$532,700

Required: (1) Prepare a report showing the variations between standard costs and actual costs for the year 1972. Break down the direct materials and direct labor costs into price and quantity or efficiency variances. Show a controllable variance and a capacity variance for manufacturing overhead. Divide the overhead variance to show how much of the variance was caused by spending variations and how much of it was caused by efficiency variations.

(2) Assuming that labor is responsible for machine efficiency, how much of the *total* variation in costs can be attributable to labor efficiency?

Chapter 14

VARIABLE COSTING

According to the generally accepted cost accounting theory underlying income determination, all of the manufacturing costs are to be attached to the products either directly or indirectly by allocation. The cost of any manufactured article then includes the cost of the direct materials, the cost of the direct labor used in its creation, and an apportioned share of the other manufacturing costs. These other manufacturing costs, collectively referred to as manufacturing overhead, differ from each other greatly. Some of the costs, such as the salary of the plant manager, depreciation, and insurance on the plant, tend to remain fixed over various ranges of output; other costs, such as the cost of supplies used, fuel, and electric power, may increase or decrease with changes in output. All of these costs, however, are to be identified with the manufactured products. This conventional theory of product costing is sometimes called an *absorption costing* or a *full costing method*, the terms being derived from the fact that the full or total manufacturing costs are to be absorbed by the products.

It is not a simple matter, however, to identify all costs with the products. It has been pointed out that allocation is one of the more difficult problems in cost accounting. The costs that cannot be directly identified with any particular department, function, or product may be apportioned; but then there is always some doubt as to whether or not the apportionment has been made properly. In fact, it may even be said that the costs should not be apportioned at all.

The total fixed costs, for example, are not affected to any extent by differences in the volume of productive output that fall within an established range. Therefore, when only a few units of product are made, the fixed cost per unit is high. The unit cost decreases as more units are produced. The cost of a unit of product then depends on how many other units are being manufactured at the same time. This in turn means that the profits for the year are influenced not only by the volume of sales, the sales price, and the costs of production, but also by the quantity of units manufactured during the year.

As explained in the earlier chapters, the manufacturing overhead is applied to the products by using a predetermined rate. The fixed manufacturing overhead, for example, is budgeted along with the hours of operation at a normal level of production. The budgeted cost is divided by the budgeted hours to obtain a rate per hour that can be used in costing the products. The products then are assigned a normal or a standard charge for fixed overhead. Variable manufacturing overhead costs are, of course, assigned to the products in the same way. If the plant operates above or below its normal capacity, the fixed overhead will be over or underabsorbed. The over or underabsorbed overhead is designated as the capacity variance and is written off to operations for the year.

THE CONCEPT OF VARIABLE COSTING

In cost accounting there will always be the problem of cost apportionment. This cannot be avoided. The real issue is whether or not certain costs should be assigned to the products. According to the *variable costing concept,* only the variable manufacturing costs should be assigned to the products. The fixed manufacturing costs should not be costed to the products but should be written off each year as period costs. An investment in facilities and other productive factors is required before any products can be manufactured. There are fixed costs such as depreciation, insurance, taxes, heat and light, and salaries of plant management that must be incurred each year in the manufacturing business. Hence, the fixed costs of manufacturing are not product costs but are the annual costs incurred to have a manufacturing establishment. The fixed manufacturing costs, like the selling and administrative costs, are too remotely related to the product to be attached as a part of its cost. Following this theory, the fixed costs of manufacturing should be expensed each year and not carried as a part of the cost of an inventory of product.

Variable costing is more widely known as direct costing. This is unfortunate. It is not correct to say that the "direct costs" are attached to the products. Rather, the variable costs are assigned. A direct cost, it will be recalled, is a cost that can be identified readily with a department, a function, a unit of product, or some other relevant unit. Manufacturing overhead cost is an indirect cost with respect to the products, yet the variable manufacturing overhead is included in product cost when the direct costing method is used! Direct costs can be either fixed or variable. For example, a machine operator's salary may be the direct cost and may be fixed under a guaranteed annual wage agreement. The salary is a fixed cost, and although it may be directly identified with a product line, it would not be considered to be a part of the product cost in direct costing. Variable costs that may or may not be directly identified with the products become part of the product cost in direct costing; hence, direct costing is more appropriately called *variable costing*. Both terms should be recognized, but the term "variable costing" is to be preferred because it is a more accurate designation.

ABSORPTION AND VARIABLE COSTING COMPARED

The differences between the two costing concepts can be brought out by showing how an income statement prepared by the absorption costing method compares with an income statement prepared by the variable costing method. To illustrate, income statements are presented for Ross Machine Company using the data that follow:

	Per Unit of Product
Selling price	$14
Variable manufacturing costs	2
Variable selling and administrative expense	1

	Total Cost
Fixed manufacturing costs for the year	$1,600,000
Fixed selling and administrative expenses for the year	100,000

When products are costed by the absorption costing method, the fixed manufacturing cost is allocated to the products. Assume that the company produces 200,000 units of product at its normal capacity. The fixed overhead cost per unit is then $8 ($1,600,000 ÷ 200,000 units). The total manufacturing cost per unit of product is $10.

Variable manufacturing cost per unit	$ 2
Fixed manufacturing cost per unit	8
Total manufacturing cost per unit	$10

If the variable costing method is used, however, only the variable manufacturing costs of $2 a unit will be assigned to the products.

Assume that 200,000 units of product were manufactured and sold in 1971 and that there were no units in inventory at the beginning of the year. Income statements have been prepared using both the absorption costing method and the variable costing method.

Ross Machine Company
Income Statements
For the Year Ended December 31, 1971

	Absorption Costing	Variable Costing
Number of units manufactured and sold ..	200,000	200,000
Sales (200,000 units @ $14)	$2,800,000	$2,800,000
Cost of goods manufactured and sold:		
Variable manufacturing costs (200,000 units @ $2)	$ 400,000	$ 400,000
Fixed manufacturing costs (200,000 units @ $8)	1,600,000	—0—
Cost of goods manufactured and sold	$2,000,000	$ 400,000
Gross margin	$ 800,000	
Contribution margin (manufacturing)		$2,400,000
Selling and administrative expenses:		
Variable selling and administrative expenses (200,000 units @ $1)	$ 200,000	200,000
Fixed selling and administrative expenses	100,000	—0—
Total selling and administrative expenses	$ 300,000	
Contribution margin (final)		$2,200,000
Fixed costs:		
Manufacturing		$1,600,000
Selling and administrative		100,000
Total fixed costs		$1,700,000
Net income before income taxes	$ 500,000	$ 500,000
Income taxes (40% rate)	200,000	200,000
Net income after income taxes.........	$ 300,000	$ 300,000

The net income, in this case, is the same under either costing method. All of the fixed costs for the year have been matched against revenue on both statements. Fixed manufacturing costs have not been carried over from an earlier year as a part of beginning inventory cost, nor have fixed manufacturing costs been included in an inventory at the end of the year. On the absorption costing statement, the fixed manufacturing cost was deducted as a part of the cost of goods sold. On the variable costing statement, the fixed manufacturing cost was deducted at the bottom of the statement as a period cost.

The excess of the revenue over the variable manufacturing cost of goods sold is designated as *contribution margin (manufacturing)*. It is the amount contributed to the recovery of fixed manufacturing costs, operating expenses, and profits. The difference between the revenue and all of the variable costs is the *contribution margin* (*final*). It is equal to the revenue minus all variable costs and is the net contribution to fixed costs and profits. The contribution margin concept is most important and can be applied by management in planning profits and in making certain types of decisions. The contribution margin concept and applications will be discussed later in this chapter and will be given even more attention in Chapter 15.

A BALANCE OF SALES AND PRODUCTION

When sales and production are in balance at any level of operation, the results tend to be the same under either absorption or variable costing. If standard costs are assigned to the products, each unit of product will bear the same amount of cost. Therefore, when sales and production are in balance, the number of units in the beginning inventory will be equal to the number of units in the ending inventory, and the cost of the beginning and ending inventory will be the same. As a result, fixed manufacturing costs equal in amount to the fixed manufacturing costs for the year will be deducted against revenue by either costing method. If the absorption costing method is used, the fixed costs will be deducted as cost of goods sold. If the variable costing method is used, the fixed costs will be deducted as an expense of the fiscal period.

For example, assume that Ross Machine Company had an inventory of 20,000 units of product on hand at the beginning of a certain year and that 200,000 units were manufactured and sold during the year. The selling price and cost data are the same for beginning inventory and current production. Partial income statements showing results of the manufacturing operation by the two costing methods are given on the next page.

Fixed costs of $1,600,000 have been deducted on both statements. The cost of production (the cost of goods manufactured in this case) is equal to the cost of the goods sold, and on the absorption costing statement fixed costs of $1,600,000 have been deducted (included in $2,000,000) as cost of goods sold. On the variable costing statement, the same amount has been deducted as a period cost.

If the company operates above or below its normal operating capacity, part of the fixed manufacturing cost will be deducted as product cost on an absorption costing statement, and the balance of the fixed manufacturing cost will be shown as a capacity variance. An amount equal to the fixed manufacturing cost for the year will be deducted from revenue assuming a standard cost system and assuming that inventories are not increased or decreased during the year.

In 1972, Ross Machine Company began the year with no inventory, operated at 90 percent of its normal capacity, and manufactured and sold

Ross Machine Company
Partial Income Statements
(Manufacturing Operations)
For the Year

	Absorption Costing	Variable Costing
Number of units manufactured and sold ..	200,000	200,000
Sales (200,000 units @ $14)	$2,800,000	$2,800,000
Cost of goods sold:		
Inventory, beginning of year:		
(20,000 units @ $2 + $8)	$ 200,000	
(20,000 units @ $2)		$ 40,000
Cost of production:		
(200,000 units @ $2 + $8)	2,000,000	
(200,000 units @ $2)		400,000
Cost of merchandise available for sale	$2,200,000	$ 440,000
Less: Inventory, end of year:		
(20,000 units @ $2 + $8)	200,000	
(20,000 units @ $2)		40,000
Cost of goods sold	$2,000,000	$ 400,000
Gross margin	$ 800,000	
Contribution margin (manufacturing)		$2,400,000
Less: Fixed manufacturing costs		1,600,000
Net income (manufacturing operation) ...	$ 800,000	$ 800,000

180,000 units of product. There were no changes in the selling price or the costs. Income statements prepared by the absorption costing method and the variable costing method are illustrated on the following page.

Once again, note that the net income as reported by both costing methods is the same. This will be true whether the company operates at normal capacity or not, as long as there is a balance between sales and production.

SALES AND PRODUCTION OUT OF BALANCE

Differences between the two costing methods appear when the sales for the year are more or less than the production. When absorption costing is employed, the fixed manufacturing costs are shifted from one year to another as a part of the inventory cost. If a company produces more than it sells in a given year, not all of the current fixed manufacturing cost will be deducted against revenue, part of it will be held as inventory. This fixed

Ross Machine Company
Income Statements
For the Year Ended December 31, 1972

	Absorption Costing	Variable Costing
Number of units manufactured and sold ..	180,000	180,000
Sales (180,000 units @ $14)	$2,520,000	$2,520,000
Cost of goods manufactured and sold:		
Variable manufacturing costs (180,000 units @ $2)	$ 360,000	$ 360,000
Fixed manufacturing costs (180,000 units @ $8)	1,440,000	—0—
Cost of goods manufactured and sold at standard cost	$1,800,000	$ 360,000
Capacity variance (20,000 units @ $8) ..	160,000	
Total	$1,960,000	
Gross margin	$ 560,000	
Contribution margin (manufacturing)		$2,160,000
Selling and administrative expenses:		
Variable selling and administrative expenses (180,000 units @ $1)	$ 180,000	$ 180,000
Fixed selling and administrative expenses	100,000	—0—
	$ 280,000	$ 180,000
Contribution margin (final)		$1,980,000
Fixed costs:		
Manufacturing		$1,600,000
Selling and administrative		100,000
Total fixed costs		$1,700,000
Net income before income taxes	$ 280,000	$ 280,000
Income taxes (40% rate)	112,000	112,000
Net income after income taxes	$ 168,000	$ 168,000

cost will be released as part of goods sold in a later year, perhaps in a year when sales are in excess of production.

Hence, profits will not necessarily increase with increases in sales revenue. In fact, the profits will decrease if the effect of shifting fixed costs from one year to another as a part of inventory cost is more than the increased contribution margin to be derived from the increased sales.

Management may find it difficult to understand how profits can decrease with increased sales volume and no changes in selling prices and costs. Seemingly, profits should increase when sales revenue increases. The shift of fixed manufacturing costs from one year to another must be recognized when an absorption costing system is used.

The peculiarity in profit behavior is illustrated by income statements for 1972 and 1973. The selling price and the cost data remain the same. Sales and production data follow:

1972—Produced	....	200,000 units
Sold	....	180,000 units
1973—Produced	....	180,000 units
Sold	....	200,000 units

Income statements prepared by the absorption costing method for 1972 and 1973 are illustrated below:

Ross Machine Company
Income Statements
For the Years Ended December 31, 1972, and 1973
(Absorption Costing)

	1973	1972
Number of units manufactured	180,000	200,000
Number of units sold	200,000	180,000
Sales	$2,800,000	$2,520,000
Cost of goods sold:		
Inventory, beginning of year	$ 200,000	—0—
Current production cost:		
Variable costs	360,000	$ 400,000
Fixed costs	1,440,000	1,600,000
Total merchandise available for sale	$2,000,000	$2,000,000
Less: Inventory, end of year	—0—	200,000
Cost of goods sold	$2,000,000	$1,800,000
Capacity variance	160,000	—0—
Total	$2,160,000	$1,800,000
Gross margin	$ 640,000	$ 720,000
Selling and administrative expenses:		
Variable costs	$ 200,000	$ 180,000
Fixed costs	100,000	100,000
Total selling and administrative expenses .	$ 300,000	$ 280,000
Net income before income taxes	$ 340,000	$ 440,000
Income taxes (40% rate)	136,000	176,000
Net income after income taxes	$ 204,000	$ 264,000

The income statements show that Ross Machine Company earned less in 1973 than it did in 1972, and yet more units were sold in 1973 with no change in the selling price or the cost structure. Ordinarily, profits are expected to increase with increases in sales volume.

The income statements prepared by the absorption costing method tend to conceal the fact that fixed manufacturing costs from 1972 in the amount of $160,000 (20,000 × $8) have been shifted to 1973 as a part of the inventory carry-over to 1973. The reduction in net income before income taxes of $100,000 can be explained as follows:

Increased revenue (20,000 more units @ $14)	$280,000
Increased variable costs ($40,000 variable costs in beginning inventory and $20,000 in variable selling and administrative expenses)	60,000
Increased contribution margin	$220,000
Less:	
Fixed costs of 1972 shifted to 1973 (decreases 1972 costs)	$160,000
Fixed costs of 1972 shifted to 1973 (increases 1973 costs)	160,000
Increase caused by shift in fixed costs	$320,000
Decrease in net income before income taxes	$100,000

Income statements on a variable costing basis show that the final contribution margin has increased in 1973 as a result of selling 20,000 more units of product. The fixed manufacturing costs are not transferred from one year to another as part of the inventory cost. The income statements can be understood without additional interpretation. Income statements on a variable costing basis for 1972 and 1973 are reproduced on the next page.

The income statements as prepared by the variable costing method show that the net income was greater in 1973 when more units were sold. The net income before income taxes in 1973 was $220,000 greater than it was in 1972. This would be expected, considering that 20,000 more units were sold with each unit making a contribution of $11 to fixed costs and profits (selling price of $14 minus variable unit manufacturing costs of $2 and variable selling and administrative expenses of $1). The profits tend to vary with sales volume when the variable costing method is used. However, differences attributable to a lack of balance between sales and production are not revealed by variable costing. Sales activity may be overemphasized at the expense of production. In reality, profits depend upon *both* sales and production.

EMPHASIS ON PRODUCTION OR SALES

In absorption costing the effects of sales and production are combined. Particular emphasis is placed upon plant utilization. The cost of idle facilities either is added to product cost or is shown separately as a capacity variance.

Ross Machine Company
Income Statements
For the Years 1972 and 1973
(Variable Costing)

	1973	1972
Number of units manufactured	180,000	200,000
Number of units sold	200,000	180,000
Sales	$2,800,000	$2,520,000
Cost of goods sold:		
Inventory, beginning of year	$ 40,000	—0—
Current production costs, variable	360,000	$ 400,000
Total merchandise available for sale	$ 400,000	$ 400,000
Less: Inventory, end of year	—0—	40,000
Cost of goods sold	$ 400,000	$ 360,000
Contribution margin (manufacturing)	$2,400,000	$2,160,000
Less: Variable selling and administrative expenses	200,000	180,000
Contribution margin (final)	$2,200,000	$1,980,000
Less fixed costs:		
Manufacturing	$1,600,000	$1,600,000
Selling and administrative	100,000	100,000
Total fixed costs	$1,700,000	$1,700,000
Net income before income taxes	$ 500,000	$ 280,000
Income taxes (40% rate)	200,000	112,000
Net income after income taxes	$ 300,000	$ 168,000

In variable costing the emphasis is placed on sales. The cost of each unit of product manufactured is not affected because of changes in the level of activity. Unit variable cost is assumed to remain the same over certain ranges of output. Of course, both unit variable cost and total fixed cost may change at certain production levels. However, the data used for variable costing apply to a range of output at which unit variable costs and total fixed costs are relatively constant. Variable costing serves a useful purpose in bringing out the relationships between prices, costs, and volume.

But if management relies too heavily on variable cost analysis, it may be deluded into thinking that the company can operate profitably at low contribution margin rates only to find that volume does not come up to expectations. Selling at less than normal prices may be helpful in short-term situations, but in the long run this policy may result in margins that are not adequate in relation to invested resources. Short-term expediency should be recognized for what it is and should not be allowed to become a part of long-term strategy. Both costing methods can be useful when applied in appropriate circumstances.

THE ADVANTAGES OF VARIABLE COSTING

Variable costing is particularly useful to management in applications where the relative profitability of product lines is to be determined or where the effect of changes in volume, prices, or costs is to be calculated. When fixed costs are allocated to the products, analysis by product line becomes more difficult.

The advantages to be derived from variable costing are listed below as summarized in NA(C)A Bulletin, Research Series No. 23: [1]

1. Cost-volume-profit relationship data wanted for profit planning purposes is readily obtained from the regular accounting statements. Hence management does not have to work with two separate sets of data to relate one to the other.
2. The profit for a period is not affected by changes in absorption of fixed expenses resulting from building or reducing inventory. Other things remaining equal (e.g. selling prices, costs, sales mix) profits move in the same direction as sales when direct costing is in use.
3. Manufacturing cost and income statements in the direct cost form follow management's thinking more closely than does the absorption cost form for these statements. For this reason, management finds it easier to understand and to use direct cost reports.
4. The impact of fixed costs on profits is emphasized because the total amount of such cost for the period appears in the income statement.
5. Marginal income figures facilitate relative appraisal of products, territories, classes of customers, and other segments of the business without having the results obscured by allocation of joint fixed costs.
6. Direct costing ties in with such effective plans for cost control as standard costs and flexible budgets. In fact, the flexible budget is an aspect of direct costing and many companies thus use direct costing methods for this purpose without recognizing them as such.
7. Direct cost constitutes a concept of inventory cost which corresponds closely with the current out-of-pocket expenditure necessary to manufacture the goods.

The data produced by variable costing are easily understood by management. By considering the troublesome fixed costs as period cost rather than product cost, sales revenue can be directly related to the variable costs. The difference between the sales revenue and the variable costs is the contribution of the products to the recovery of fixed costs and to profits.

---

[1] *Direct Costing*, Research Series No. 23 (New York: National Association of Accountants, 1953), p. 1127.

THE DISADVANTAGES OF VARIABLE COSTING

Variable costing may encourage a short-sighted approach to profit planning at the expense of the long-run situation. Over a short period of time there may be an advantage in selling products at prices that are below the total unit costs. Profits will be made so long as the fixed costs are covered by the sales from regular operations and so long as the selling price is in excess of the unit variable cost. Or in other cases, fixed costs that would not be covered otherwise may be recovered through making sales at a price below the total unit cost. Products may also be sold in another market at less than the full cost to absorb idle plant capacity. This approach should be recognized, however, for what it is, a short-term expediency.

In the final analysis, *all* costs must be recovered along with an adequate return on investment. The product lines that cannot carry their share of the fixed costs are reducing the overall profits. A low-profit line may be carried to round out the other product lines or as a customer service. But unless there is some compelling reason for continuing with low-profit products, these products should be replaced with more profitable items.

Variable costing tends to give the impression that variable costs are recovered first, that fixed costs are recovered later, and that finally profits are realized. Actually the revenue from the sale of each unit of product contains a portion of variable cost, fixed cost, and profit. No one cost has priority over another, and each unit of product earns a share of the profit.

The acceptability or the nonacceptability of variable costing for general reporting purposes or for income tax is not a valid argument for or against the use of the method in reporting to management. There are various cost concepts and techniques like variable costing that are useful to management but that are not acceptable in reporting to outsiders. If they can be put to use by management, they should not be discarded.

VARIABLE COSTING IN PLANNING AND DECISION MAKING

The concept of variable costing may be applied in the measurement of income, but in any event, it is most important in planning and decision making. For example, a certain line of product selling for $10 a unit with variable costs of $7 contributes $3 per unit to fixed costs and profits. If the fixed costs amount to $300,000 a year, the company must sell 100,000 units to break even ($300,000 fixed costs ÷ $3 unit contribution margin). The *break-even point* is the point at which there is neither profit nor loss.

In this example, management knows that at least 100,000 units must be sold if there is to be no loss. In addition, management will plan profits on the basis of the expected contribution margin. Suppose that profits before income taxes are budgeted at $120,000. The contribution margin must then be equal to the fixed costs of $300,000 plus the budgeted profits of $120,000, or in other words must be $420,000. The company must sell 140,000 units of a product yielding a $3 contribution margin a unit to cover fixed costs of $300,000 and to earn a profit before income taxes of $120,000.

Management may also plan to sell a product at a regular price in one market and to sell the same product at a reduced price in another market. It is presumed, of course, that the additional sales can be made without disturbing the regular market or without violating fair price laws. The fixed costs will not have to be considered. The additional profits that can be obtained from selling at a lower price in another market can be calculated easily from variable cost information.

Kelly Forms, Inc., manufactures and sells 150,000 units of a product that sells for $20 a unit. The variable manufacturing costs amount to $12 per unit and the fixed manufacturing overhead amounts to $600,000. The results of the manufacturing operation would appear as follows:

Sales (150,000 units × $20)	$3,000,000
Cost of goods sold (150,000 units × $12 unit variable cost)	1,800,000
Contribution margin	$1,200,000
Fixed costs	600,000
Net income on manufacturing	$ 600,000

An opportunity presents itself to sell 50,000 additional units at a price of $14 per unit. Apparently the opportunity should be rejected because it costs $16 to manufacture each unit according to conventional or absorption costing with normal capacity defined at 150,000 units of product. There is a unit variable cost of $12 and a unit fixed cost of $4 ($600,000 ÷ 150,000 units). Even when 200,000 units are produced, the unit fixed cost would still seem too high at $3 a unit ($600,000 ÷ 200,000 units) to permit the sale of products at $14 per unit. Yet variable costing shows that Kelly Forms, Inc., can earn an additional profit of $100,000 by accepting this opportunity. The profit computation is shown below:

	Total	Regular Operations	Additional Sales
Sales	$3,700,000	$3,000,000	$700,000
Cost of goods sold	2,400,000	1,800,000	600,000
Contribution margin	$1,300,000	$1,200,000	$100,000
Fixed costs	600,000		
Net income on manufacturing	$ 700,000		

The sale of the additional units has no effect upon the fixed costs. In making this type of decision, only the additional revenues and the additional costs are important.

The distinction between the variable costs and the fixed costs can be helpful in planning profits and in making decisions with respect to the pricing and sale of the various product lines. For managerial purposes, it is not essential that variable costing be used for income measurement. But the data processing system should furnish information on variable costs and fixed costs for use in planning operations and in making decisions.

VARIABLE COSTING AND BUDGET VARIANCES

For cost control purposes, however, a distinction between variable and fixed costs may not be too important; nor will it make much difference whether products are costed with variable manufacturing costs or total manufacturing costs when the objective is to control the *total* costs of the manufacturing operation.

For example, assume that Baker Equipment Company has budgeted sales and manufacturing costs for 1972 as follows:

Estimated production .... 100,000 product units.
Estimated sales .... 90,000 product units.

	Per Unit of Product	Total
Sales revenue	$15	$1,350,000
Variable costs	9	810,000
Fixed costs (normal production of 100,000 product units)	1	100,000

There was no inventory on hand at the beginning of the year.

During the year, the company sold 90,000 units at $15 apiece and incurred variable manufacturing costs of $916,000 and fixed manufacturing costs of $107,000. The actual variable costs were $16,000 more than budgeted, and the actual fixed costs were $7,000 more than budgeted. The total unfavorable variance for the year was $23,000.

A comparison of the budgeted income statement with the actual income statement on a variable costing basis and on an absorption costing basis is shown on page 414.

A comparison of the statements shows that the net income reported by absorption costing is $10,000 greater than the net income reported by variable costing. A comparison of the budgeted statements shows the same difference. This difference arises because fixed overhead of $10,000 is included

Baker Equipment Company
Income Statement (Variable Costing)
Budget and Actual Comparison
For the Year Ended December 31, 1972

	Budget	Actual	Variance Over (Under) Budget
Sales	$1,350,000	$1,350,000	—0—
Cost of goods sold:			
Variable manufacturing costs	$ 900,000	$ 916,000	$16,000
Less: Ending inventory (10,000 units @ $9)	90,000	90,000	—0—
Cost of goods sold	$ 810,000	$ 826,000	$16,000
Contribution margin (manufacturing)	$ 540,000	$ 524,000	($16,000)
Less: Fixed manufacturing costs	100,000	107,000	7,000
Net income (manufacturing)	$ 440,000	$ 417,000	($23,000)

Baker Equipment Company
Income Statement (Absorption Costing)
Budget and Actual Comparison
For the Year Ended December 31, 1972

	Budget	Actual	Variance Over (Under) Budget
Sales	$1,350,000	$1,350,000	—0—
Cost of goods sold:			
Variable manufacturing costs	$ 900,000	$ 916,000	$16,000
Fixed manufacturing costs	100,000	107,000	7,000
Total manufacturing costs	$1,000,000	$1,023,000	$23,000
Less: Ending inventory (10,000 units @ $10 standard unit cost) ...	100,000	100,000	—0—
Cost of goods sold	$ 900,000	$ 923,000	$23,000
Net income (manufacturing)	$ 450,000	$ 427,000	($23,000)

in the ending inventory and will be carried over to 1973 under the absorption costing method. The budget variance is $23,000 in both cases.

A comparison of budgeted and actual costs is not affected by the costing method selected. The cost comparison is based on the *total* costs that are incurred and used in production. The method used to match costs against revenue is important in measuring net income but is of little importance when the objective is to control costs.

414

Questions

1. In conventional cost accounting practice, how are the fixed manufacturing overhead costs applied to the products?

2. When the variable costing concept is employed, how are the fixed manufacturing overhead costs applied to the products?

3. How does absorption costing differ from variable costing?

4. Fixed manufacturing overhead costs should be treated as period costs. Give arguments to support this statement. Give arguments against it.

5. Why is there no capacity variance under variable costing?

6. What is the contribution margin?

7. Why is the concept of a contribution margin important to management?

8. How are fixed manufacturing overhead costs shifted from one year to another in absorption costing?

9. When a company sells the same number of units that it produces, the profits as reported by absorption costing and by variable costing tend to be the same. Explain.

10. If a company sells more units than it produces, would the profits reported by absorption costing tend to be higher or lower than the profits reported by variable costing? Why?

11. Assume that a company is operating at a profit. Can the profits be increased by selling additional units at a price that is only slightly higher than the variable costs per unit?

12. The Kreider Stores expect to earn a net income before taxes of $410,000 in 1972. In addition, management plans to sell 50,000 units of a certain type of merchandise to other distributors at a unit price of $23. The variable cost of this merchandise per unit amounts to $22. How much will Kreider Stores add to its net income before income taxes by selling 50,000 units to other distributors?

13. Why might variable costing be looked upon as a short-sighted approach to profit planning?

14. Should management make use of techniques that are not accepted for use in the preparation of financial statements for the public? Explain.

Exercises

1. John Beale manufactured and sold 30,000 units of a certain product last year. Each unit was sold at a price of $25. The variable costs were $16 per unit of product, and the fixed costs were $126,000. John Beale operated at a normal level of capacity.

Required: (1) Prepare a summary income statement accounting for costs by the absorption costing method.
(2) Prepare a summary income statement accounting for costs by the variable costing method.

2. Coburn Supply Company manufactured 100,000 units of product in 1972 and operated at normal capacity. Variable costs per unit were $15. Total fixed costs for the year were $300,000. The company sold 80,000 units of product during the year at a unit price of $20.

Required: (1) Prepare a summary income statement accounting for costs by the absorption costing method.

(2) Prepare a summary income statement accounting for costs by the variable costing method.

3. Production and cost data are given for Best Stores, Inc.

	1973	1972
Number of units manufactured	10,000	15,000
Number of units sold	15,000	10,000
Unit selling price	$ 30	$ 30
Unit variable costs	$ 8	$ 8
Total fixed costs	$240,000	$240,000

In 1972, the company operated at a normal level of capacity.

Required: (1) Prepare income statements for the two years on an absorption costing basis.

(2) Explain the difference in net income, pointing out why the net income for 1973 was higher or lower than it was in 1972.

4. Fixed costs are applied at a rate of $4.00 per unit for every unit of product manufactured by Hastings Brake Company. At normal capacity the company is expected to manufacture 500,000 units of product. Sales and production data are given for three years.

	1973	1972	1971
Units manufactured	350,000	400,000	500,000
Units sold	500,000	450,000	300,000
Unit selling price	$ 16	$ 16	$ 16
Total variable manufacturing costs	$2,800,000	$3,200,000	$4,000,000
Total variable selling and administrative expense	500,000	450,000	300,000
Total fixed selling and administrative expense	300,000	300,000	300,000

Fixed manufacturing costs were in agreement with the budgeted costs each year. A capacity variance is shown on the income statement if production is either above or below the normal capacity level.

There was no inventory on hand at the beginning of 1971.

Required: (1) Prepare income statements for each of the three years by the absorption costing method.

(2) For each of the three years show the effect of shifting fixed costs from one year to another as a part of inventory cost. Explain why the gross margin has increased or decreased in 1972 and 1973.

5. A statement of income on the manufacturing operations for 1972 is given on the next page for Hayes and Webb, Inc. The fixed manufacturing costs have been applied to the products at a standard rate per unit of product. Included in the inventories and in the current costs of production are fixed costs that amount to 40 percent of the inventory cost and the costs of current production. All units in inventory at the end of the year were manufactured during the year.

Hayes and Webb, Inc.
Income Statement—Manufacturing
For the Year, 1972

Sales		$2,350,000
Cost of goods sold:		
Inventory, January 1	$ 350,000	
Current production cost	1,280,000	
	$1,630,000	
Less: Inventory, December 31	260,000	
Cost of goods sold		1,370,000
Net income, manufacturing, standard		$ 980,000
Less: Capacity variance		160,000
Net income, manufacturing, actual		$ 820,000

Required: Recast the statement on a variable costing basis. (For purposes of the problem, assume that fixed costs of past years have already been deducted.)

6. Donovan Fabrics, Inc., produced 8,000,000 yards of fabric during the fiscal year ended April 30, 1972, but sold only 7,000,000 yards at a price of 42 cents a yard. Variable manufacturing costs were 26 cents a yard. The fixed manufacturing costs are applied at a rate of 8 cents for every yard produced. Actual and budgeted fixed costs for the fiscal year amounted to $800,000. There was no inventory on hand at May 1, 1971.

Required: Prepare two income statements for the manufacturing operation for the fiscal year ended April 30, 1972. Use the absorption costing method for one statement and the variable costing method for the other statement.

7. Three major lines of product are sold by Verso Supply Company. Sales and cost data for 1972 are given below:

	A	B	C
Number of units sold	20,000	24,000	32,000
Unit selling price	$ 60	$ 35	$ 42
Unit purchase price	40	20	30

In addition to regular salaries, the sales employees receive a 10 percent commission on sales. The estimated cost to ship each unit of Product A to the customers amounts to 50 cents, and the store absorbs the cost.

Fixed costs of operation are listed below:

Sales salaries	$18,000
Administrative salaries	14,000
Advertising	9,000
Rent	5,200
Heat and light	1,700
Depreciation of fixtures	2,600
Other operating costs	3,300

Required: (1) Compute the estimated contribution margin from each unit of each product line.

(2) Compute the total contribution margin from each product line.

(3) Prepare an income statement for the total store operation using the variable costing method. (Ignore income taxes.)

8. Lowry Instruments Company plans to bid on a contract to manufacture 50,000 thermostatic control units. A careful study has been made to determine the costs of production.

Estimated cost of materials per unit	$3.80
Labor cost per unit	.90
Variable overhead per unit	.80
Fixed overhead per unit	1.40

In addition, there will be costs of shipping the units. These costs are estimated at 60 cents a unit.

In the normal commercial market, this unit is sold for a price of $9.80 a unit. If the contract is taken, it is estimated that there will be no interference with regular production.

Required: (1) What is the lowest bid price that can be submitted to earn additional profits from the contract?

(2) How much additional profit can be earned if the bid price is established at 110 percent of variable manufacturing cost?

Problems

14–1. Standard unit costs are given for the production of a spray attachment manufactured by Carson Products Company.

Direct materials	$1.60
Direct labor	1.50
Variable manufacturing overhead	1.20
Fixed manufacturing overhead	3.00

At normal operating capacity, 200,000 units of product should be manufactured. Variable selling and administrative expenses amount to 50 cents a unit, and the fixed selling and administrative expenses amount to $75,000 a year. Income taxes are estimated at 40% of net income before taxes.

Production and sales data for 1972 and 1973 follow:

Inventory on hand, January 1, 1972	28,000 units
Number of units produced, 1972	200,000
Number of units sold, 1972	160,000
Number of units produced, 1973	150,000
Number of units sold, 1973	180,000

In both years, each spray attachment was sold for $10.50.

Required: (1) Prepare income statements for the two years by the absorption costing method.

(2) Prepare income statements for the two years by the variable costing method.

14–2. A new product line is to be introduced by Quitel Metals, Inc., and it will be manufactured at a plant specifically designed for that purpose. When the plant is operating at normal capacity, it is estimated that 100,000 units of product can be produced in a year. A budget of costs for the production and sale of 100,000 units appears below and at the top of the next page.

Fixed costs:

Manufacturing overhead	$570,000
Selling and administrative costs	325,000

Variable costs:

Direct materials	$430,000
Direct labor	295,000
Manufacturing overhead	145,000
Shipping supplies	60,000
Sales commissions	280,000
Other selling and administrative costs	85,000

The product is to be sold for $28 a unit.

Assume that the number of units to be produced and sold for each of the next three years has been projected as follows:

Year	Number of Units Produced	Number of Units Sold
1	100,000	100,000
2	100,000	80,000
3	90,000	100,000

Income taxes are estimated at 50 percent of net income before taxes.

Required: (1) Prepare budgeted income statements for each of the next 3 years using the absorption costing method.

(2) Prepare budgeted income statements for each of the next 3 years using the variable costing method.

14–3. Summarized income statements are given for Campbell-Dunbar Company for 1971, 1972, and 1973.

Campbell-Dunbar Company
Income Statements

	1973	1972	1971
Sales	$1,050,000	$ 900,000	$1,050,000
Cost of goods sold:			
Inventory, January 1	$ 260,000	—0—	—0—
Cost of goods manufactured	780,000	$1,040,000	$ 910,000
Total merchandise available for sale	$1,040,000	$1,040,000	$ 910,000
Less: Inventory, December 31	130,000	260,000	—0—
Total cost of goods sold	$ 910,000	$ 780,000	$ 910,000
Add: Capacity variance	60,000	—0—	30,000
Total	$ 970,000	$ 780,000	$ 940,000
Gross margin	$ 80,000	$ 120,000	$ 110,000
Selling and administrative expenses	39,000	37,000	39,000
Net income before income taxes	$ 41,000	$ 83,000	$ 71,000
Income taxes (40% rate)	16,400	33,200	28,400
Net income after income taxes	$ 24,600	$ 49,800	$ 42,600

Sales and production data follow:

	1973	1972	1971
Number of units produced	60,000	80,000	70,000
Number of units sold	70,000	60,000	70,000

Fixed manufacturing overhead of $3 a unit is included in the cost of goods manufactured, and the total fixed manufacturing overhead was $240,000 for each of the three years. Variable selling and administrative expenses amount to 20 cents for each unit of product sold, and these expenses are included in the total selling and administrative expenses. The variable costs per unit were the same in all three years, and the fixed costs were the same in total for each of the three years.

Required: (1) If 70,000 units were sold in 1971 and in 1973, why was the net income before income taxes lower in 1973 than it was in 1971?

(2) How could the company earn more in 1972 than in 1971 with lower sales volume?

(3) Revise the income statements to show what the results would be for each year if the variable costing method had been used. Assume that income taxes are at the rate of 40 percent of net income before income taxes.

14–4. Income statements for the first and second quarters of 1972 are given below for Boulder Ridge, Inc.

Boulder Ridge, Inc.
Income Statements

	First Quarter, 1972	Second Quarter, 1972
Sales, number of units	6,000	8,000
Sales revenue	$240,000	$320,000
Cost of goods sold:		
Inventory, beginning	$ 17,000	$ 85,000
Cost of goods manufactured	272,000	204,000
Total merchandise available for sale	$289,000	$289,000
Less: Inventory, ending	85,000	17,000
Cost of goods sold	$204,000	$272,000
Capacity variance	—0—	48,000
Total	$204,000	$320,000
Gross margin	$ 36,000	$ —0—
Selling and administrative expenses	13,000	15,000
Net income before income taxes	$ 23,000	($ 15,000)
Income taxes (40% rate)	9,200	(6,000)
Net income after income taxes	$ 13,800	($ 9,000)

In the first quarter, Stephen Lawson, the president of the company, planned to increase inventory in anticipation of increased sales volume in the second quarter. The sales volume increased as expected, but Stephen Lawson was surprised to find that instead of having increased profit, the company operated at a loss. Inasmuch as selling price and costs did not change, he believes that there must be some mistake in the income statement.

The company operated at normal capacity and manufactured 8,000 units during the first quarter. Total manufacturing cost per unit amounts to $34 at normal capacity with the fixed costs per unit at $24. During the second quarter, 6,000 units were manufactured. Fixed selling and administrative expenses of $7,000 are included in the total selling and administrative expenses for each quarter.

Required: (1) How would you explain the profit difference to Stephen Lawson? Show why the net income before income taxes of $23,000 for the first quarter changed to a loss of $15,000 in the second quarter.

(2) Revise the statements for the two quarters to show the operating results on a variable costing basis. (Ignore income taxes in your solution.)

14–5. Microelectric Company manufactures a certain component that it sells for $21 a unit. Until recently a historical cost accounting system has been used. All manufacturing costs, including the manufacturing overhead costs, were assigned to the products produced on the basis of the equivalent units manufactured during the year.

Last year the company processed 55,000 units, completing and selling 50,000 units with 5,000 units in inventory at the end of the year that were complete as to direct materials but were only 50 percent complete as to direct labor and manufacturing overhead. There was no inventory of finished goods or work in process at the beginning of the last year.

Actual manufacturing costs for the last year are listed below:

Direct materials	$220,000
Direct labor	145,000
Indirect materials	55,000
Indirect labor	60,000
Power	12,000
Maintenance and repairs	42,000
Taxes and insurance	36,000
Heat and light	15,000
Depreciation	52,000
Total costs	$637,000

The fixed selling and administrative expenses amounted to $135,000, and the variable selling and administrative expenses amount to $.80 for each unit sold.

According to standards that have been established, the company should produce 60,000 units of product when operating at normal capacity. A flexible budget of standard manufacturing costs follows:

	Standard Costs		
Units manufactured	40,000	50,000	60,000
Direct materials	$160,000	$200,000	$240,000
Direct labor	110,000	130,000	150,000
Indirect materials and supplies	39,000	45,000	51,000
Indirect labor	60,000	60,000	60,000
Power	12,000	12,000	12,000
Maintenance and repairs	40,000	45,000	50,000
Taxes and insurance	36,000	36,000	36,000
Heat and light	15,000	15,000	15,000
Depreciation	52,000	52,000	52,000
Totals	$524,000	$595,000	$666,000

The actual selling and administrative expenses last year were in agreement with the standards established; and the actual fixed manufacturing costs were in agreement with the standard fixed costs.

Required: (1) Prepare income statements by the absorption costing method showing a comparison of the actual costs with the standard costs. (Disregard income taxes.)

(2) Prepare income statements by the variable costing method showing a comparison of the actual costs with the standard costs. (Disregard income taxes.)

14–6. Under normal operating conditions, Masterson Assemblies, Inc., manufactures two lines of product and operates at 400,000 labor hours each year.
Budget data for 1973 follow:

	Units to be Produced and Sold	Unit Selling Price	Time Required to Produce Each Unit
Product I	400,000	$12.00	30 minutes
Product II	300,000	10.00	20 minutes

The materials required to manufacture a unit of Product I cost $2.00, and the materials required to manufacture a unit of Product II cost $3.00. In addition, supplies used in finishing Product I cost 20 cents per unit of product.
The direct labor cost has been budgeted at $4.20 an hour.
A flexible budget of manufacturing overhead cost is given below:

Hours of operation in thousands	280	300	360	400
Cost in thousands:				
Supervisory salaries	$260	$260	$260	$260
Other indirect labor	115	115	115	115
Maintenance	81	85	97	105
Repairs	62	65	74	80
Heat and light...............	21	22	25	27
Lubrication	39	41	47	51
Telephone	4	4	4	4
Insurance	14	14	14	14
Taxes	17	17	17	17
Depreciation	28	28	28	28
Total cost	$641	$651	$681	$701

Fixed selling and administrative expense budgets are given below:

	Selling Expenses	Administrative Expenses
Executive salaries	$220,000	$240,000
Office salaries	150,000	190,000
Advertising	430,000	—
Rent	32,000	18,000
Heat and light	15,000	6,000
Telephone	6,000	3,000
Depreciation	9,000	7,000
Total fixed costs	$862,000	$464,000

In addition to the costs listed above, there are sales commissions amounting to 15 percent of sales revenue and fixed delivery costs of $23,000 a year plus additional delivery costs for Product I of 30 cents a unit.

Required: (1) Prepare a budgeted income statement for 1973 by product line and in total that will show the total contribution margin for each product line and for the total operation.

(2) Prepare a budgeted income statement for 1973 by product line and in total using the absorption costing method.

14-7. A condensed income statement for the manufacturing division of Kessman Products Company is given below:

Kessman Products Company
Manufacturing Division
Income Statement
For the Year Ended December 31, 1972

Sales revenue	$1,635,000
Variable costs (includes direct materials cost of $480,000)	1,200,000
Contribution margin	$ 435,000
Fixed costs absorbed by operations	$ 184,000
Unabsorbed fixed costs	46,000
Total fixed costs	$ 230,000
Net income—manufacturing	$ 205,000

Fixed manufacturing overhead is costed to production using a machine hour rate established for 100,000 machine hours at a normal operating level. Some of the unused capacity can be absorbed by the production of one of two new product lines that management plans to introduce. In the long run, additional capacity may be added if both of the lines appear desirable and market conditions are favorable. At the present time, however, the plan is to introduce only one new line, if any.

Market studies indicate that there is a potential market for 50,000 units of Product A at a unit selling price of $16. Each unit will require materials costing $8 and 15 minutes of production time. Fixed costs are expected to increase by $50,000 a year if this line is put into production, and it will cost 40 cents a unit to deliver the product to the sales division.

As an alternative, the company may produce and sell 150,000 units of Product B at a unit selling price of $5.50. Each unit will require materials costing $2.50 and 6 minutes of production time. Fixed costs are expected to increase by $80,000 a year if this line is put into production, and it will cost 30 cents a unit to deliver the production to the sales division.

No change is anticipated in the rate of variability of the labor and overhead costs. Labor and overhead included in the variable costs vary according to machine hours.

Required: (1) Prepare comparative statements that will show which of the two product lines will contribute more to the total profits of the company.

(2) Prepare an income statement for the total manufacturing division assuming that the better of the two product lines is accepted and that operations in other respects produce the same results as in 1971.

14-8. An income statement in summary form for Oliver Integrated Parts, Inc., for the year 1972 is given on the following page.

A standard cost accounting system is employed; with the exception of the fact that the company did not operate at normal capacity in 1972, the actual costs were in agreement with the standards.

Four lines of product are manufactured and sold. Data with respect to product lines and costs follow:

Oliver Integrated Parts, Inc.
Income Statement
For the Year Ended December 31, 1972

Net sales	$5,934,000
Cost of goods sold	$4,170,400
Overhead capacity variance	312,000
Selling and administrative expenses	552,000
Income taxes	427,400
Total expenses	$5,461,800
Net income	$ 472,200

	Product Lines			
	A	*B*	*C*	*D*
Number of units sold	56,000	108,000	100,000	336,000
Selling prices	$12.00	$6.50	$12.00	$10.00
Unit materials cost	$3.60	$4.30	$ 5.70	$ 2.30
Unit cost of factory supplies	.30	.20	.40	.20
Unit labor time	15 min.	10 min.	12 min.	5 min.
Unit shipping and delivery cost	$.70	$.70	$.70	$.70

The direct labor rate is $4.20 an hour, and variable overhead excluding factory supplies varies at the rate of $5.40 an hour.

Fixed manufacturing overhead is applied to the products on the basis of a rate established for 100,000 hours of production. During the year, the company operated at 80,000 hours and produced the standard output for 80,000 hours.

The fixed selling and administrative expenses amounted to $132,000.

The inventories did not increase or decrease during the year.

Required: (1) Prepare an income statement showing only the variable manufacturing costs as product costs and show the contribution made by each line of product to fixed costs and profits.

(2) Identify the product lines, if any, that are not contributing to the total operation.

Chapter 15

COST-VOLUME-PROFIT RELATIONSHIPS

The concept of variable costing discussed in the preceding chapter is applied extensively in profit planning. And profit planning is a vital part of the total budgeting process which will be discussed in Chapters 20 and 21. Before a budget can be prepared in detail for the various segments of the total operation, there must be a profit plan. Management establishes profit goals and prepares budget plans that will lead to the realization of these goals. In profit planning, management must know the selling price of a unit of product, the variable cost to make and sell it, and the difference between the selling price and the unit variable cost. In short, management must know what the contribution margin is for each unit of each product line that is handled.

Several factors affect profits. They are:

(1) Selling prices.
(2) The number of units sold (quantity).
(3) The unit variable costs.
(4) The total fixed costs.
(5) The combinations in which the various product lines are sold.

All these factors must be considered in profit planning. Cost-volume-profit analysis, the subject matter of this chapter, is a means of showing the relationships between these variables which form the basis for profit planning.

BREAK-EVEN ANALYSIS

This analysis, sometimes called cost-volume-profit analysis, stresses the relationships between the factors affecting profits. As stated in Chapter 14, the point at which there is no profit or loss is designated as the break-even point. The break-even point serves as a base indicating how many units of product must be sold if a company is to operate without loss.

Each unit of product sold is expected to yield revenues in excess of its variable costs and thus earn a contribution to fixed costs and profit. At the break-even point, the profit is zero; that is, the contribution margin is equal to the fixed costs. If the actual volume of sales is higher than the break-even volume, there will be profit.

Assume that a company manufactures and sells a single product line as follows:

Unit selling price	$ 20
Unit variable cost	10
Unit contribution margin	$ 10
Total fixed costs	$100,000

Each unit of product sold contributes $10 to cover fixed costs and profits. Based on these data, the company must sell 10,000 units of product to break even. The break-even volume is calculated by dividing the total fixed cost by the contribution per unit as shown below:

$$\frac{\$100,000 \text{ fixed costs}}{\$10 \text{ unit contribution margin}} = 10,000 \text{ units.}$$

If the company can sell more than 10,000 units, it will earn profits. If less than 10,000 units are sold, a loss will be incurred. The profits will be equal to the number of units sold in excess of 10,000 multiplied by the unit contribution margin. For example, if 22,000 units are sold, the company will be operating at 12,000 units above its break-even point and will earn a profit of $120,000 (12,000 units over break-even point × $10 unit contribution margin).

Sales (22,000 units @ $20)	$440,000
Less: Variable costs (22,000 units @ $10)	220,000
Contribution margin	$220,000
Less: Fixed costs	100,000
Net income	$120,000

The break-even chart. Total revenues and total costs at different sales volumes can be estimated and plotted on a break-even chart. The information shown on the break-even chart can also be given in conventional reports, but it is sometimes easier to grasp the fundamental facts when they are presented in graphic or pictorial form. Dollars are shown on the vertical scale of the charts, and the units of product sold (or produced) are shown on the horizontal scale. The total costs are plotted for the various quantities to be sold and are connected by a line. Total revenues are similarly entered on the chart. The break-even point lies at the intersection of the total revenue and the total cost line. Losses are measured to the left of the break-even point, the amount of the loss at any point being equal to the dollar difference between the total cost line and the total revenue line. Profits are measured to the right of the break-even point and at any point are equal to the dollar difference between the total revenue line and the total cost line.

The data from the last example are presented on the following break-even chart:

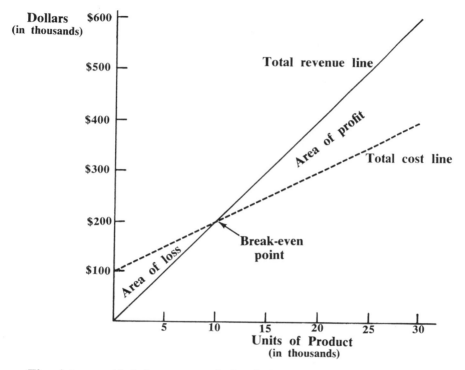

The data provided from an analysis of the chart is presented in tabular form as follows:

Units of products sold	5,000	10,000	15,000	20,000	25,000	30,000
Total revenue .	$100,000	$200,000	$300,000	$400,000	$500,000	$600,000
Total cost:						
Variable ...	$ 50,000	$100,000	$150,000	$200,000	$250,000	$300,000
Fixed	100,000	100,000	100,000	100,000	100,000	100,000
Total cost .	$150,000	$200,000	$250,000	$300,000	$350,000	$400,000
Profit (loss) ..	($ 50,000)	–0–	$ 50,000	$100,000	$150,000	$200,000

It is assumed, of course, that the selling price remains at $20 and that the variable cost per unit remains at $10 over the range of units sold. With only one product, there is no problem of sales mix. The sales mix or product combination problem will be discussed later.

Cost detail on the break-even chart. Additional information is sometimes shown on the break-even chart by drawing separate lines for the different cost classifications. A desired profit before taxes can also be added as if it were a fixed cost. Then, both the break-even point and the point of desired profit will be revealed on the chart. Using the same data as before, assume that the costs are broken down as follows:

Unit variable costs:		
Direct materials	$	4
Direct labor		2
Variable manufacturing overhead		2
Variable selling and administrative expenses		2
Total unit variable costs	$	10
Fixed manufacturing overhead		$ 80,000
Fixed selling and administrative expenses		20,000
Total fixed expenses		$100,000

The desired profit before income taxes is $100,000. The company must sell 10,000 units to recover the $100,000 in fixed costs (to break even) and must sell another 10,000 units to earn a $100,000 profit before taxes. In other words, the company must sell 20,000 units if it expects to earn a profit of $100,000 before income taxes. The break-even chart showing cost and profit details appears on the next page.

Curvature of revenue and cost lines. In some cases, revenues and costs cannot be represented by straight lines. If more units are to be sold, selling prices may have to be reduced. Under these conditions, the revenue function may be a curve rather than a line. Costs, on the other hand, may also be nonlinear. The curve may rise slowly at the start but may rise more steeply as volume is expanded. As more units are manufactured, variable costs per unit may become higher. Therefore, it may be possible to have two break-even points as shown below:

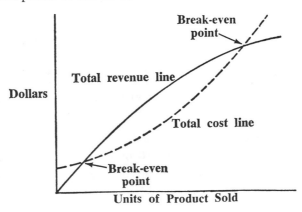

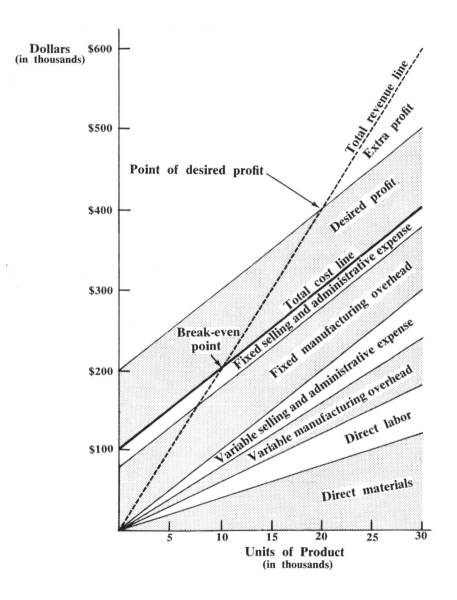

In many cases, however, revenues and costs can be represented by straight lines. Any given company probably operates within certain volume ranges where revenues and costs can usually be plotted without any noticeable curvature. If the revenue and the cost curves begin to converge, the company is not maximizing its profits. Total costs are increasing faster than total revenues; that is, each unit sold is adding more to costs than to revenues.

An alternative form of break-even analysis. Frequently, a break-even point is calculated in terms of the sales revenue that must be realized in order to break even. A break-even point is not necessarily expressed in units of product. The variable costs may be stated as a percentage of sales revenue and subtracted from 100 percent to arrive at the percentage of the contribution margin to sales revenue. For example, a company may sell one line of product for $15 a unit with unit variable costs of $9 and total fixed costs for a year of $60,000.

		Percentage
Unit selling price	$15	100%
Unit variable cost	9	60
Unit contribution margin	$ 6	40%

The break-even point can be calculated at 10,000 units by dividing the total fixed costs of $60,000 by the unit contribution margin of $6. But the break-even point can also be computed in dollars of sales. As shown above, 60 percent of the revenue is needed to cover the variable costs. This means that 40 percent of the sales revenue remains for the recovery of the fixed costs and for profits. When 40 percent of the sales revenue is equal to the fixed costs of $60,000 the company will break even. Therefore, divide $60,000 by 40 percent to arrive at a break-even revenue of $150,000. Hence, a break-even point in terms of sales dollars can be computed by using the simple equation given below:

$$\frac{\text{Fixed costs}}{\substack{\text{Contribution margin expressed} \\ \text{as a percentage of sales} \\ \text{revenue}}} = \text{Sales revenue required to break even}$$

$$\text{Therefore, } \frac{\$60,000}{40\%} = \$150,000 \text{ sales revenue required to break even}$$

	Amount	*Percentage*
Sales revenue	$150,000	100%
Variable costs	90,000	60
Contribution margin	$ 60,000	40%
Fixed costs	60,000	
Profit or (loss)	–0–	

By extending the break-even concept further, it is possible to set a profit goal and to calculate the required sales revenue necessary to produce a given or desired profit.

$$\frac{\text{Fixed costs} + \text{Desired profit}}{\text{Contribution margin expressed as a percentage of sales revenue}} = \begin{array}{l}\text{Sales revenue required to}\\\text{produce a desired profit}\end{array}$$

Using the data from the last example, assume that a net income before income taxes of $72,000 is budgeted. The sales revenue must then be $330,000 as computed below:

$$\frac{60,000 + 72,000}{40\%} = \$330,000 \text{ sales revenue required to earn a net income before income taxes of \$72,000}$$

In many cases, the profit objective may be stated as a net income *after income taxes,* in which case an additional computation must be made to solve for the net income before income taxes. Assume that the company wants a net income after income taxes of $60,000 and that the income tax rate is 40 percent. If the income tax is 40 percent of the net income before taxes, then the net income after taxes is 60 percent of the net income before taxes.

Net income before income taxes	100%
Less: Income taxes	40
Net income after income taxes	60%

To compute the net income before taxes, divide the after-tax net income by 60 percent, that is, by the complement of the tax rate or, in other words, by $(1 - \text{tax rate})$. The break-even equation is given below:

$$\frac{\text{Fixed costs} + \dfrac{\text{Desired after-tax profit}}{1 - \text{Tax rate}}}{\text{Contribution margin percentage}} = \begin{array}{l}\text{Sales revenue required to}\\\text{produce a desired after-}\\\text{tax profit}\end{array}$$

$$\frac{\$60,000 + \dfrac{\$60,000}{60\%}}{40\%} = \begin{array}{l}\text{Sales revenue required to produce an after-}\\\text{tax profit of \$60,000}\end{array}$$

$$\frac{\$60,000 + \$100,000}{40\%} = \$400,000 \begin{array}{l}\text{Sales revenue required to earn}\\\$60,000 \text{ after income taxes}\end{array}$$

A proof of the computation follows:

Sales revenue	$400,000
Variable costs (60% of revenue)	240,000
Contribution margin (40% of revenue)	$160,000
Fixed costs	60,000
Net income before income taxes	$100,000
Income taxes (40% rate)	40,000
Net income after income taxes	$ 60,000

THE PROFIT-VOLUME GRAPH

A profit-volume graph, or P/V graph, is sometimes used in place of or along with a break-even chart. Profits and losses are given on the vertical scale; and units of product, sales revenue, or percentage of activity are given on the horizontal scale. A horizontal line is drawn on the graph to separate profits from losses. The profits and losses at various sales levels are plotted and connected by the profit line. The break-even point is measured at the point where the profit line intersects the horizontal line. Dollars of profit are measured on a vertical scale above the line, and dollars of loss are measured below the line. The P/V graph may be preferred to the break-even chart because profits and losses at any point can be read directly from the vertical scale; but the P/V graph does not clearly show how costs vary with activity. Break-even charts and P/V graphs are often used together, thus obtaining the advantages that can be derived from each form of presentation.

Data used in the earlier illustration of a break-even chart given on pages 426 and 427 have been used in preparing the P/V graph given below:

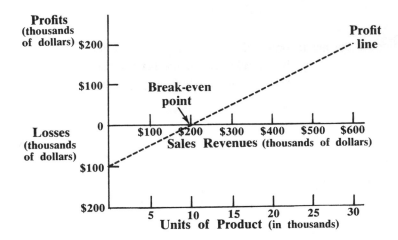

The profit-volume graph is a convenient device to show how profits are affected by changes in the factors that affect profit. For example, if unit selling prices, unit variable costs, and total fixed costs remain constant, how many more units must be sold in order to realize a greater profit? Or if the unit variable costs can be reduced, what additional profits can be expected at any given volume of sales? The effect of changes in sales volume, unit variable costs, unit selling prices, total fixed costs, and sales mix are discussed in the following paragraphs.

Sales volume. In some industries profits depend upon high sales volume. If each unit of product is sold at a relatively low contribution margin, profits can be made only by selling in large quantities. This will be all the more true when the fixed costs are high. For instance, a company may handle one product line that sells for $1 a unit. Assume that the variable costs per unit are 70 cents and that the fixed costs per year amount to $180,000. Each unit sold contributes 30 cents in excess of its variable costs to fixed costs and profits. Before any profit can be made, enough units must be sold at a 30-cent contribution per unit to recover the fixed costs. Therefore, 600,000 units must be sold just to break even. For every unit sold in excess of 600,000 there will be a 30 cent profit before taxes. Faced with such a situation, the company must be certain that it can sell more than 600,000 units and that it can sell enough more to earn a reasonable profit on the investment.

When the products sell for relatively high prices, the contribution margin per unit is often higher even though the rate of contribution may be fairly small. Fixed costs are recaptured with the sale of fewer units, and a profit can be made on a relatively low sales volume. Suppose that each unit of product sells for $1,000 and that the variable cost per unit is $900. The fixed costs for the year are $180,000. The percentage of contribution margin is only 10 percent, but the company receives a contribution of $100 from each unit sold for fixed costs and profits. Break-even point will be reached when 1,800 units are sold. The physical quantity handled is much lower than it was in the preceding example, but the same principle applies. More than 1,800 units must be sold if the company is to produce a profit.

The variable costs. The relationship between the selling price of a product and its variable cost is important in any line of business. Even small savings in variable costs can add significantly to profits. A reduction of a fraction of a dollar in the unit cost becomes a contribution to fixed costs and profits. If 50,000 units are sold in a year, a 10 cent decrease in the unit cost becomes a $5,000 increase in profit. Conversely, a 10 cent increase in unit cost takes $5,000 away from profits.

Management is continuously searching for opportunities to make even small cost savings. What appears to be a trivial saving may turn out to be the difference between profit or loss for the year. In manufacturing, it may be possible to save on material cost by using a cheaper material that is just as satisfactory. Savings can also come from buying more economically or by using the materials more effectively. With improved methods of production, labor and overhead costs per unit can be decreased.

A small saving in unit cost can give a company a competitive advantage. If prices must be reduced, the low-cost producer will usually suffer less. At any given price and fixed cost structure, the low-cost producer will move into the profit area faster as sales volume increases.

The comparison of the operating results of three companies given below shows how profits are influenced by changes in the variable cost pattern. Each of the three companies sells 100,000 units of one product line at a price of $5 per unit and has annual fixed costs of $150,000. Company A can manufacture and sell each unit at a variable cost of $2.50. Company B has found ways to save cost and can produce each unit for a variable cost of $2, while Company C has allowed its unit variable cost to creep up to $3.

	Company A	Company B	Company C
Number of units sold	100,000	100,000	100,000
Unit selling price	$ 5.00	$ 5.00	$ 5.00
Unit variable costs	2.50	2.00	3.00
Unit contribution margin	2.50	3.00	2.00
Percent of contribution margin	50%	60%	40%
Total sales revenue	$500,000	$500,000	$500,000
Total variable costs	250,000	200,000	300,000
Total contribution margin	$250,000	$300,000	$200,000
Fixed costs	150,000	150,000	150,000
Net profit before taxes	$100,000	$150,000	$ 50,000

A difference of 50 cents in unit variable costs between Company A and Company B or between Company A and Company C adds up to a $50,000 difference in profit when 100,000 units are sold. The low-cost producer has a $1 per unit profit advantage over the high-cost producer. If sales volume should fall to 60,000 units per company, Company B would have a profit of $30,000, Company A would break even, and Company C would suffer a loss of $30,000.

The profit picture at different operating levels for the three companies is shown on the P/V graph on the next page.

The profit line for each company starts at $150,000, the amount of the fixed costs. When 40,000 units are sold, there is a difference of $20,000 between each profit line. The lines diverge as greater quantities are sold, and at the 100,000-unit level the difference is $50,000. Company B can make a profit by selling any quantity in excess of 50,000 units, but Company C must sell 75,000 units to break even. With its present cost structure, Company C will have to sell in greater volume if it is to earn profits equal to those earned by Company A or Company B. Company C is the inefficient producer in the group and as such operates at a disadvantage. When there

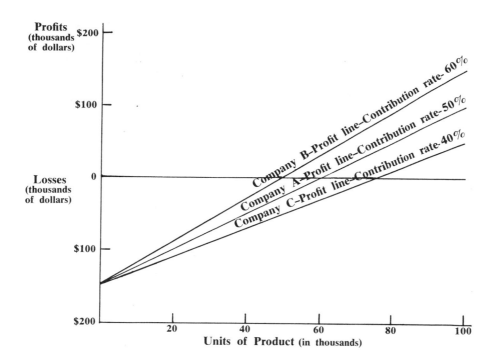

is enough business for everyone, Company C will earn profits but will most likely earn less than the others. When business conditions are poor, Company C will be more vulnerable.

Price policy. One of the ways to improve profits is to get more sales volume; and to stimulate sales volume, management may decide that prices should be reduced. But results may not work out as anticipated. It does not necessarily follow that sales volume will be increased by reducing prices. If the demand for the product is perfectly inelastic, volume will not respond to changes in price. The price reduction will result only in lower profits.

Suppose, however, that greater quantities can be sold at a lower price. The advantage, if there is one, will soon be eliminated if competitors retaliate by lowering their prices also. Eventually the market will be shared as it was before, and possibly with lower profits for all. Even assuming that competitors will not react to price reductions, there is still no guarantee that profits can be increased by increasing sales. In fact, profits may decline in the face of increased sales. It may turn out that more effort is being put forth to get a smaller return.

While sales volume may increase with reductions in price, it may not increase enough to overcome the handicap of selling at a lower price. This point is often overlooked by the optimistic businessman who believes that only a small increase in volume can compensate for a slight decrease in price.

Price cuts, like increases in variable unit costs, decrease the contribution margin. On a unit basis, price decreases may appear to be insignificant; but when the unit differential is multiplied by thousands of units, the total effect may be tremendous. Perhaps many more units must be sold to make up for the difference.

Company A, for example, hopes to increase its profits by selling more units; and to sell more, it plans to reduce its prices by 10 percent. The present price and cost structure and the one contemplated are given below:

	Present Price and Cost	Contemplated Price and Cost
Selling price	$5.00	$4.50
Variable cost	2.50	2.50
Contribution margin	$2.50	$2.00
Percentage of contribution margin	50%	44.4%

At present, one-half of each dollar in revenue can be applied to fixed costs and profits. When sales are twice the fixed costs, Company A will break even. This means that 60,000 units yielding a revenue of $300,000 must be sold if fixed costs are $150,000. But when the price is reduced, less than half of each dollar can be applied to fixed costs and profits. To recover $150,000 in fixed costs, sales revenue must amount to $337,500. Not only must the revenue be higher but with a lower price per unit more units must be sold to obtain that revenue. It will no longer be possible to get $337,500 in revenue by selling 67,500 units ($337,500 ÷ $5). Instead, 75,000 units must be sold just to break even.

To overcome the effect of the cut in price, sales volume in physical units must be increased by 25 percent:

> 75,000 units to be sold at lower price to break even
> 60,000 units to be sold at present price to break even
> 15,000 increase in number of units

$$\frac{15,000}{60,000} = \frac{1}{4} \text{ or } 25\%.$$

Sales revenue must be increased by 12½ percent:

> $337,500 sales revenue at new break-even point
> 300,000 sales revenue at present break-even point
> $ 37,500 increase in sales revenue

$$\frac{\$ 37,500}{\$300,000} = \frac{1}{8} \text{ or } 12\frac{1}{2}\%$$

The present profit before taxes of $100,000 can still be earned by selling 125,000 units for a total revenue of $562,500:

	Present Operation	Contemplated Operation
Number of units sold	100,000	125,000
Sales	$500,000	$562,500
Cost of goods sold	250,000	312,500
Contribution margin	$250,000	$250,000
Fixed costs	150,000	150,000
Net income before taxes	$100,000	$100,000

After 125,000 units are sold, the company can improve its profits, but at a slower rate than when it operated with a price of $5. For every $4,500 increase in revenue the profits will increase by $2,000. At present, a $4,500 increase in revenue beyond the break-even point yields $2,250 in profits.

The effect of the price reduction on profits can be depicted on a P/V graph as shown below:

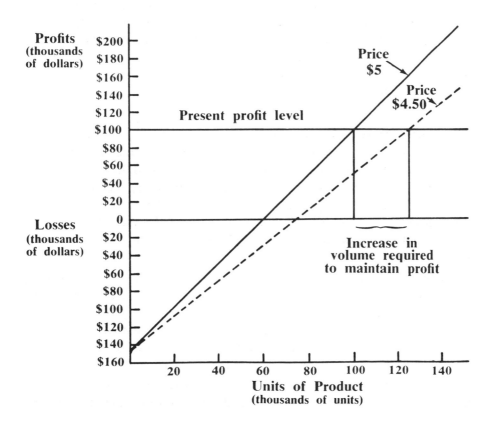

The increase in sales volume required to overcome the effect of a price reduction is proportionately greater when the rate of contribution margin is relatively low at the start. If each unit of product makes only a modest contribution, then a reduction in price makes it all the more difficult to recover the fixed costs and to earn profits.

Seemingly, prices should not be reduced. The handicap imposed by the decrease in price appears to be overwhelming; yet, in many circumstances, profits can be increased by lowering prices. A saving in variable cost, for example, can be passed along to the customer. The contribution margin remains the same; and if more units can be sold, profits can be increased. Even with no change in variable costs, increased profits may be realized by lowering prices, provided that sales volume can be increased by more than enough to make up for the effect of the decrease in price.

The policy with respect to price will depend upon the long-range and short-range objectives of management. In any event, it is important to know what will probably happen if a certain course of action is adopted. Prices may be cut with full knowledge that immediate profits will be reduced. The company accepts this disadvantage in the hope that it will be able to establish itself as a volume producer in the market. Another company, whose management is not informed with respect to cost-volume relationships, may cut prices in an attempt to gain immediate profits; then when the profits do not materialize, the management will be unpleasantly surprised. Price policy will be discussed more fully in Chapter 17.

The fixed costs. A change in fixed costs has no effect on the contribution margin. Each unit yields the same margin as before. Increases in fixed costs are recovered when the contribution margin from additional units sold is equal to the increase in fixed costs. On a P/V graph, the slope of the profit line is unaffected by changes in fixed costs. The new profit line is drawn parallel to the original line, and the distance between the two lines at any point on the horizontal scale will be equal to the increase or the decrease in cost.

In the P/V graph given on the next page, fixed costs have increased from $600,000 to $700,000. The product sells for $5 per unit, variable costs are $3 per unit, and the contribution per unit to fixed costs and profits is $2. Under the new fixed cost structure, the profit line has shifted to the right and at any point is $100,000 lower than it was originally. To maintain the same profit as before, 50,000 more units must be sold.

Increases in planned profits have the same effect as increases in fixed costs. For example, suppose that the fixed costs are to remain at $600,000

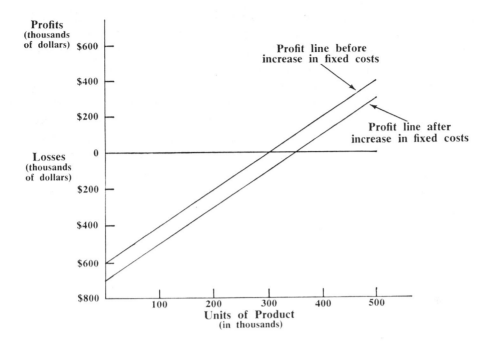

but that profits are to be increased from $200,000 to $300,000. Once again, 50,000 more units would have to be sold to provide $100,000, which in this case would be applied to increase profits.

Decreases in fixed costs will cause the profit line to shift to the left. The contribution to fixed overhead and profits can be reduced by the amount of the decrease in cost without affecting profits. The decrease in sales volume can be calculated by dividing the unit contribution into the decrease in fixed overhead. The new profit line is parallel to the original line at a distance equal to the decrease in fixed cost.

Fixed costs, like variable costs, are reduced whenever possible. Often it is necessary to handle a large volume of business merely to recover fixed costs. In some industries, fixed costs are relatively high. When expensive machinery and equipment are used in manufacturing, the fixed costs of necessity will be large. This makes it all the more imperative to look for ways of keeping the costs down. Fixed costs have a habit of creeping upward, and before long a company is confronted with a high fixed cost structure, the result being that a large volume must be sold even though the contribution margin per unit is adequate.

Changes in the sales mix. Usually more than one type of product is sold. Several different product lines may be handled, each of which makes a different contribution to fixed cost recovery and profits. The total profit depends to some extent upon the proportions in which the products are sold. If the more profitable products make up a relatively large part of the sales mix, the profits are greater than they would be if more of the low-margin contributors were sold instead.

Management sometimes concentrates on total sales volume, unit selling prices, unit variable costs, and total fixed costs but overlooks the importance of the sales mix. The total sales revenue, unit selling prices, unit variable costs, and total fixed costs may be in agreement with the budget, but the profits may be lower. A lower profit can result from a shift in the sales mix. For example, a larger quantity of less profitable product lines may be sold with a corresponding decrease in the sales of the more profitable product lines.

The effect of a change in sales mix is illustrated by assuming that a company plans to sell three product lines in the following proportions:

Product Lines	Quan-tities	Unit Sell-ing Price	Unit Vari-able Cost	Unit Contri-bution Margin	Total Contri-bution Margin	Total Revenue	Contri-bution Margin Percent-age
A	20,000	$50	$20	$30	$600,000	$1,000,000	60%
B	10,000	50	30	20	200,000	500,000	40
C	10,000	50	40	10	100,000	500,000	20
Totals					$900,000	$2,000,000	
Less: Fixed costs					500,000		
Budgeted net income before income taxes					$400,000		

During the next year, the company operated at the capacity budgeted with fixed overhead of $500,000. The unit selling prices and unit variable costs were in agreement with the budget. The results were as follows:

Product Lines	Quantities Sold	Unit Contribution Margin	Total Contribution Margin	Total Revenue
A	5,000	$30	$150,000	$ 250,000
B	20,000	20	400,000	1,000,000
C	15,000	10	150,000	750,000
Totals			$700,000	$2,000,000
Less: Fixed costs			500,000	
Actual net income before income taxes			$200,000	

Instead of earning $400,000 before income taxes, the company earned only $200,000. Sales of Products B and C, the less profitable lines, were much better than expected. At the same time, sales of the best product line, Product A, were less than expected.

440

When more than one product line is handled, profit data for all products combined may be shown on one line of a P/V graph, the sales mix being assumed, or a separate graph may be made for each product line. Sometimes the effect of each product as well as total products on profits is depicted by plotting several lines on one P/V graph. A solid line is drawn to represent the net income or loss for total products. Next a broken line is drawn to the point of net income or loss contributed by one product, and then the line is extended to the point of net income or loss contribution of two products combined and continued until all of the products and the net income or loss is accounted for. The broken line is drawn so that the most profitable product is depicted first and so on until all of the products are included. The products sell in a fixed proportion, and the broken line does not indicate that the most profitable product is sold first with a certain profit or loss and that the total profit or loss is increased or decreased by a certain amount as other product lines are sold. Instead, the broken line shows the sales volume for each product in the mix and the relative profitability of each product is revealed by the changes in the slope of the profit line. The total company profit for any combined sales volume must be read from the solid line. To illustrate, the budget data from the preceding example is entered on the first P/V graph illustrated below and the actual results are entered on the second graph.

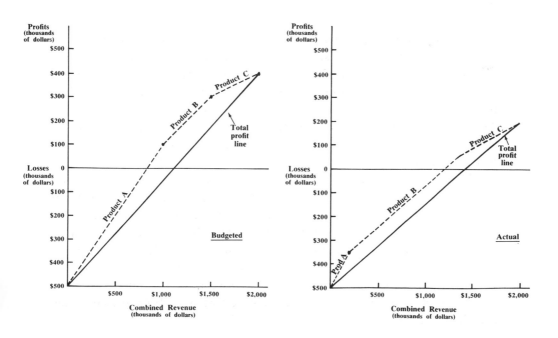

Break-even analysis is often used in short-term planning under the assumption that market prices are established and that moderate changes in the quantity offered for sale by the company will have little or no effect upon prices. Also, it is usually assumed that a fixed quantity of productive resources is available and, therefore, the company can manufacture only a limited quantity.

In the long run, the company can increase its productive capacity. The cost structure will then be different, and different break-even charts will be used. Sometimes a company will sacrifice immediate profits by producing beyond the point of maximum profit, the strategy being to secure markets that will yield greater profits when additional capacity is available. This, of course, is long-range planning.

Management is forced to look at both the immediate future and the more distant future. It would be foolish indeed to give up current profits for some remote advantage that may or may not materialize. Yet it would be equally foolish to maximize short-run profits at the expense of future development. By careful analysis, management can strike a balance that will tend to yield the best results for the company from either the short-run or the long-run viewpoint. Long-range planning will be discussed more fully in later chapters. In this chapter, the short-range outlook will be given more attention.

Sharing cost savings with customers. The principles of cost-volume-profit analysis can be put to use in a variety of circumstances. Perhaps savings in variable costs are anticipated. Should the savings be shared with the customers by reducing prices, or should the company hold prices at the present level and get the benefit of a better rate of contribution margin? The answer to this question will depend upon the long-run objective of the company, the estimate of the change in sales volume, and the possible reaction that is expected from competitors.

Suppose that the variable costs of manufacturing and selling each unit of a certain product can be reduced from $58 to $51. Reductions in material costs will account for $4 of this saving. Competitors will also gain this advantage and may or may not be able to obtain further savings in cost.

During the past year, 15,200 units of product were sold for $88 apiece. By holding the price at $88 next year, the company may lose sales to competitors if the competitors reduce their price to $84 a unit.

Estimates of sales volume at different prices have been prepared and are shown on the next page.

Sales Volume	Prices
9,000	$88
15,200	84
18,000	82
21,000	80

Contribution margins computed under these assumptions are given below:

Sales Volume	Prices	Unit Costs	Unit Contribution Margins	Estimated Total Contribution
9,000	$88	$51	$37	$333,000
15,200	84	51	33	501,600
18,000	82	51	31	558,000
21,000	80	51	29	609,000

According to the tabulation, prices will have to be reduced. When the price is reduced by the saving in material cost, the total market will be shared as it was before. But even greater profits can be made by reducing the price still further. The tremendous saving in variable cost coupled with the increased volume of sales make this possible. Eventually, competitors may be able to meet the new price, or they may reduce their prices and sacrifice profits. In either event, the increased profits will not be realized. Instead, there will be lower profits for all. In reaching a decision, management must be reasonably sure that its assumptions with respect to sales volume and costs are correct and that its evaluation of the competitive situation is sound.

Passing cost increases to customers. Sometimes cost increases may be anticipated, and a decision must be reached as to whether or not the additional costs should be absorbed. Rising costs will cut profits if higher costs cannot be passed along to the customer or if sales cannot be made in sufficient volume to overcome the effect. Analysis may show that certain customers will probably continue to buy about the same quantities even at higher prices, while in other cases sales volume will be reduced if prices are raised.

Hadden Springs Company deals in products where the contribution margin is relatively low and profits depend to a large extent on high sales volume. Next year the company must pay more to get some lines of merchandise from its suppliers, but the sales price on these lines cannot be increased in every case. To compensate for the increases in cost, prices will be raised on some other lines where there will be no increases in cost and relatively little effect on volume. In other words, the product lines will be priced according to what the traffic will bear.

Estimates of sales volume, prices, and costs for the next year are compared with the volume, prices, and costs of the current year in the analysis below. No additional sales volume is expected. In fact, Hadden Springs Company will be fortunate if it can retain its present position. During the current year the company sold five product lines yielding a total contribution margin of $395,000 as shown below:

Total Contribution Margin

Current Year

Product Lines	Sales Volume	Unit Prices	Unit Costs	Total Contribution Margin
1	12,000	$30	$25	$ 60,000
2	14,000	25	20	70,000
3	21,000	18	15	63,000
4	42,000	10	7	126,000
5	38,000	6	4	76,000
			Total contribution margin	$395,000

Costs on Products 1, 4, and 5 will increase next year, but prices cannot be increased on these product lines because of competition. It will be possible, however, to raise prices on Products 2 and 3 without reducing the sales volume below what it would be otherwise. Estimated results are given below for the next year assuming price and cost changes as shown:

Total Contribution Margin
Estimated for Next Year

Product Lines	Sales Volume	Unit Prices	Unit Costs	Total Contribution Margin
1	12,000	$30	$27	$ 36,000
2	14,000	27	20	98,000
3	21,000	21	15	126,000
4	42,000	10	8	84,000
5	38,000	6	5	38,000
			Total contribution margin	$382,000

While the total contribution margin will be reduced, it will be higher than it would be without the price changes. The estimated contribution for the next year with price revisions is computed and is compared with the contribution for the current year and with the estimated contribution for the next year with no price increases, as shown on the next page.

By increasing the prices of Products 2 and 3, the reduction in contribution margin will be less than it would be otherwise. Most of the decrease that could be expected will be salvaged by raising prices selectively.

Hadden Springs Company
Contribution Margin Comparison

Product Lines	Estimated Next Year with Price Revisions	Current Year	Estimated Next Year with No Price Revisions
1	$ 36,000	$ 60,000	$ 36,000
2	98,000	70,000	70,000
3	126,000	63,000	63,000
4	84,000	126,000	84,000
5	38,000	76,000	38,000
Totals	$382,000	$395,000	$291,000

PLANNING FUTURE PROFITS

Business is in a constant state of change. A formula for success that may have worked at one time will not necessarily work at a later date. Many companies that were successful in the past have faded from the scene because the products and the services that they provided are no longer in demand. These companies failed to adapt themselves to a changing environment. The progressive company, on the other hand, is always searching for new ideas and is looking toward the future.

Many interesting situations and ideas will come to those who are receptive to change, but only a very few of the many opportunities presented can be accepted. Some ideas will have to be rejected as impractical or as unacceptable when viewed as a part of the overall company plan for development. Still other possibilities, while holding promise, will have to be discarded in favor of even better alternatives.

Before any action is taken, careful plans and estimates will be made and used in building models that will show how future profits are likely to be affected. Different combinations are examined to see which one, if any, should be chosen. This look into the future enables management to test its ideas without committing itself to any course of action that may prove to be unprofitable or even disastrous. Projections into the future will depend upon estimates of sales volume, selling prices, costs, and product mix—the concepts that have been dealt with in this chapter.

Questions

1. How is the contribution margin per unit of product computed?

2. If the contribution margin per unit of product has been computed, how would you compute the contribution margin for the total number of product units sold?

3. When the total contribution margin is equal to the total fixed costs, is the company operating at a profit or at a loss?

4. What is meant by break-even point?

5. If the total fixed costs and the contribution margin per unit of product are given, is it possible to compute the number of units that must be sold in order to break even? Explain.

6. If the total fixed costs and the percentage of the contribution margin to sales revenue are given, is it possible to compute the sales revenue at the break-even point? Explain.

7. If the total fixed costs and the percentage of the variable costs to sales revenue are given, is it possible to compute the sales revenue at the break-even point? Explain.

8. How is a break-even chart prepared?

9. Is it possible to compute the number of units that must be sold to earn a certain amount of profit *before* income taxes? Explain.

10. Is it possible to compute the number of units that must be sold to earn a certain amount of profit *after* income taxes? Explain.

11. Can there be two break-even points? If there are two break-even points, how would the revenue and cost lines be drawn on the break-even chart?

12. In conventional practice, there is only one break-even point. Why?

13. (a) How does a P/V graph differ from a break-even chart?
(b) Which form of presentation is superior?

14. When the contribution margin is high in relation to sales revenue, is the slope of the profit line on the P/V chart relatively steep or flat?

15. If there is an increase in the variable costs per unit of product, is there any effect on the profit line on the P/V chart? Explain the effect.

16. If there is a decrease in the selling price per unit of product, is there any effect on the profit line on the P/V chart? Explain the effect.

17. A 10 percent decrease in the selling price of a product has the same effect on profits as a 10 percent increase in the unit variable costs of the product. Is this true? Explain.

18. Does the slope of the profit line on the P/V chart change when the total fixed costs are increased or decreased? How is the profit line affected by changes in the total fixed costs?

19. If more than one line of product is sold, can a P/V chart be prepared for the combined operation? How?

20. What is meant by sales mix?

21. If a company increases the volume of sales of a product line that contributes more to fixed costs and profits per unit and reduces the volume of sales of a product line that contributes less to fixed costs and profits per unit, what is the effect on total profits, assuming that the reduction in volume of one product line is balanced by an increase in volume of the other line?

22. Company R and Company S sell the same line of product at a unit selling price of $40. The variable cost per unit of product is $30 to both companies. Company R finds a way to reduce the variable cost per unit to $27 and passes some of the cost savings to the customers by reducing the selling price per unit to $38. Company S cannot reduce the variable costs per unit but is forced to adopt the price set by Company R. Each company sells 40,000 units of product. (a) What effect does this change have on the profits of Company R? (b) What effect does this change have on the profits of Company S?

Exercises

1. Compute the number of units of product that must be sold if the company is to break even in each of the following situations:

(1) The fixed costs amount to $64,000 a year. Each unit of product contributes $4 to the recovery of fixed costs and to profits.

(2) The fixed costs amount to $81,000 a year. Each unit of product is sold for $26. The variable costs per unit amount to $17.

(3) The contribution margin is 40 percent of the revenue, and the fixed costs are $56,000 a year. Each unit of product sells for $7.

(4) The variable costs to manufacture and sell a certain line of product amount to 70 percent of the revenue. The fixed costs for the year are $54,000, and each unit of product sells for $4.50.

(5) Two product lines are sold, Product A and Product B. Sales are in the fixed ratio of five units of Product A for every two units of Product B. The fixed costs are $168,000 a year. Product A is sold for $8 a unit, and the variable costs identified with the production and sale of each unit of Product A amount to $4. Product B is sold for $5 a unit, and the variable costs identified with the production and sale of each unit of Product B amount to $3.

2. Lawrence Kahn sells a popular brand of men's sport shirts at an average price of $9 each. He purchases the shirts from a supplier at a unit cost of $6. The costs of operating his shop are all fixed costs and amount to approximately $18,000 a year.

Required: (1) How many shirts must be sold in a year to break even?

(2) Compute the sales revenue at the break-even point.

(3) Compute the sales revenue required to earn a net income before income taxes of $15,000.

3. The Sutter Company earned a net income before income taxes last year of $92,000. The fixed costs of operation amounted to $132,000. The average contribution margin on sales was equal to 40 percent of the sales revenue.

Required: Compute the sales revenue last year.

4. Robbins Parts Company earned $75,000 after income taxes in 1971. Management is planning for a 20 percent increase in net income after taxes in 1972. The tax rate is 40 percent of net income before income taxes. The fixed costs for the year are estimated at $240,000, and the contribution margin is estimated at 25 percent of sales revenue.

Required: (1) Compute the sales revenue required to meet the stated profit objective for 1972.

(2) How much sales revenue will be required if the company can increase the contribution margin to 30 percent of sales revenue?

5. A popular household appliance is sold by Grayson Appliances, Inc., for $220 a unit. In the past years, this appliance could be purchased from a wholesale supplier at a cost of $185 a unit. This year the cost has increased to $195 a unit. The dealer is unable to pass this cost increase along to the customer because of the competition in the area. The fixed costs last year amounted to $70,000 and are expected to remain at that level. Income taxes are equal to 40 percent of net income before income taxes. The net income after income taxes last year was $21,000.

Required: (1) What was the sales revenue last year? How many units were sold?

(2) Compute the estimated sales revenue that will be required this year to earn $21,000 after income taxes. How many units must be sold this year to earn $21,000 after income taxes?

(3) Compute the percentage increase in the number of units to be sold.

6. Walter Best sells a special type of health food at a price of $16 per pound. Last year he was able to purchase this food from his supplier at a cost of $12 per pound. His supplier has informed him that his costs have increased and that this product will now be priced at $14 a pound. Over the years, Walter Best has established a steady market and intends to pass the cost increase along to his customers and also add a $1 per unit to the price for additional profit. Fixed costs for the year are not expected to change and will remain at $34,000. Income taxes amount to 40 percent of net income before income taxes. The net income after income taxes last year was $24,000.

Required: (1) If Walter Best can maintain sales volume at the same level as before with the new price and cost structure, how much profit can he expect after income taxes next year?

(2) If sales volume is reduced by 20 percent, how much profit can he expect after income taxes next year?

7. Sweihart Sales, Inc., ordinarily obtains a 15 percent rate of contribution margin on net sales. The fixed costs have amounted to $420,000 each year and are expected to remain at that level. Last year the company reported net sales of $4,750,000. Plans are being made to increase sales revenue to $5,250,000 next year by reducing selling prices. The contribution margin will then be reduced to 12½ percent of net sales.

Required: (1) What was the net income before income taxes last year?

(2) What will the net income before income taxes be next year if the plan is followed and if net sales amount to $5,250,000?

8. Under normal conditions, Bancroft Mills, Inc., sells 1,200,000 pounds of its principal product line at a price of $1.80 per pound. The variable costs associated with this quantity of the principal product line amount to $1,320,000. Another less profitable product line can be manufactured along with the regular line in an effort to utilize productive facilities more completely. This line will sell for $.70 a pound with variable costs per pound of $.60. It is anticipated that 800,000 pounds of this product line can be produced and sold each year. The total fixed costs each year for the company have amounted to $265,000. The new product line is expected to increase fixed costs by $34,000 a year.

Required: (1) How much net income before income taxes is realized on the sale of the principal product line?

(2) How much should the new product line contribute to net income before income taxes?

9. In 1972, Colbert Signs, Inc., sold products that contributed $3,415,000 to fixed costs and profits. As part of the profit improvement program, the company plans certain reductions in costs. Employees who are expected to retire in the next few months will not be replaced. As a result, salary costs for 1973 will be reduced by $38,000. Office expenses can be reduced by $17,000 as a result of economies in data processing. Various other fixed costs can be decreased by $23,000. Fixed costs in 1972 amounted to $2,140,000. In 1973, the contribution of products sold to fixed costs and profits is estimated at $3,240,000.

Required: (1) Compute the net income before income taxes for 1972.

(2) Considering the changes planned, what should the net income before income taxes be in 1973?

(3) What would the net income be in 1973 if the fixed costs could not be reduced?

10. Mary Cameron manufactures ceramic decorations that she sells to retailers at a price of $4.50 a unit. She has been able to obtain 8 units of product from one unit of material that she purchases at a cost of $12 a unit. Variable costs of manufacturing each unit are estimated at 70 cents. Shipping costs amount to 10 cents a unit. The annual fixed costs are $33,000. Mary Cameron has found a more economical way to use materials and can now obtain 10 units of product from one unit of material.

Required: (1) Compute the number of units that must be sold to break even when 8 units of product are obtained from one unit of material.

(2) Compute the number of units that must be sold to break even when 10 units of product are obtained from one unit of material.

(3) How much can Mary Cameron earn each year when she sells 30,000 units assuming that 10 units of product can be obtained from a unit of material?

(4) How much would she earn by selling 30,000 units with 8 units of product obtained from a unit of material?

Problems

15–1. Quay Novelties, Inc., sells a holiday ornament at a price of $10. The variable costs to produce and sell the ornament amount to $4. The fixed costs for the year were $40,000. Next year the fixed costs are estimated at $60,000.

Required: (1) Prepare a break-even chart with fixed costs at $40,000. On the same chart show what will happen if fixed costs increase to $60,000. Give intervals of 5,000 units varying from 5,000 units to 30,000 units.

(2) Prepare a profit-volume graph with fixed costs at $40,000. Draw another line on the graph to show what will happen if fixed costs increase to $60,000. Give intervals of 5,000 units varying from 5,000 units to 30,000 units.

15–2. Sound Engineering, Inc., produces and sells a television cassette unit at a price of $400 a unit. The variable costs to make and sell each unit amount to $300. Total fixed costs for the year are $12,000,000. A large potential market for this type of product is available if manufacturers can reduce the price. Sound Engineering, Inc., has changed production methods and has found a way to reduce the variable costs to $200 a unit. Plans are being made to sell this product next year for $250 a unit. The fixed costs will remain the same.

Required: (1) Prepare a break-even chart with the selling price at $400 and the variable costs at $300. Give intervals of 20,000 units varying from 100,000 to 200,000 units.

(2) Prepare a break-even chart with the selling price at $250 and the variable costs at $200. Give intervals of 20,000 units ranging from 200,000 to 300,000 units.

(3) Prepare a profit-volume graph with the selling price at $400 and the variable costs at $300. Give intervals of 20,000 units varying from 100,000 to 200,000 units.

(4) Prepare a profit-volume graph with the selling price at $250 and the variable costs at $200. Give intervals of 20,000 units ranging from 200,000 to 300,000 units.

15–3. Three different lines of product are produced and sold by Connors Machine Company. Selling prices and contribution margin data are given below:

Product Lines	Unit Selling Price	Unit Contribution Margin
A	$500	$300
B	200	100
C	100	20

Last year half of the total sales volume was accounted for by sales of Product C. Sales volume of Product A is 25% of the sales volume of Product B. The fixed costs are $160,000 a year.

During the coming year, the sales division anticipates that the sales volume will be divided among the three product lines in the proportion of 2:4:4. This shift in the sales mix is to be brought about by a revised allocation of the sales effort.

Required: Prepare a profit-volume graph for the sales mix last year. Show the combined units of sale in 1,000-unit intervals ranging from 1,000 to 6,000 units. On the same graph, draw another line for the sales mix estimated by the sales division.

15–4. In the year ended September 30, 1972, Tacoma Supply Company reported sales volume as follows on its four major product lines.

Product Lines	Number of Units Sold	Unit Selling Prices	Unit Variable Costs
A	4,000	$150	$100
B	6,000	200	160
C	3,000	250	100
D	7,000	120	90

During the year ended September 30, 1973, the same number of units will be sold in total, but 2,500 more units of Product C will be sold and 2,500 less units of Product D will be sold. Unit selling prices and variable costs are not expected to change. The fixed operating costs for the year ended September 30, 1972, were $280,000 and will probably increase to $412,000 in the year ended September 30, 1973, as a result of higher advertising and promotional costs.

Required: (1) Compute the net income before income taxes for the fiscal year ended September 30, 1972, and the net income before income taxes anticipated for the fiscal year ended September 30, 1973.

(2) Give a simple computation to show why the net income for the two fiscal years is different.

15–5. Aldrich Parts Company is continuously searching for operating economies. As costs are reduced, the benefits are passed along to the customers in the form of lower prices. By following this policy the company plans to increase its share of the market and as a result earn larger profits through increased sales volume.

One division of the company manufactures a part used in producing air compressors. In 1972, the division sold 2,500,000 of these parts at a price of $2 per unit. The variable costs of producing and selling the part were $1.30 per unit, and the fixed costs were $560,000.

The variable costs will be reduced to $1.10 a unit in 1973, and the selling price will be reduced to $1.75. Total fixed costs are estimated for 1973 at $520,000.

With the price reduction and the expected improvement in the market, the company plans to sell 4,000,000 units in 1973.

Required: Compute the profit on manufacturing for 1972 and the expected profit for 1973. Show the contribution margin for each year.

15–6. To stimulate sales volume, Regal Sales, Inc., plans to award prizes on the basis of a simple matching game. Parts of this game will be distributed to customers on the basis of 10 parts for each $5 sale. The parts will be given to the customers, but they are purchased by the company from a supplier at a cost of $5 per 1,000 parts.

Prizes totaling $100,000 will be awarded for winning combinations. The participating store dealers will receive 5 percent of the prize for the winning customer from his store. In addition, all dealers will receive a bonus of 5 percent of sales revenue on increases in sales volume. Advertising and promotional costs for this contest have been estimated at $300,000.

Last year the company sold 3,500,000 units of product at an average price of $5 per unit. Unit variable costs averaged $4.20 a unit, and the fixed costs amounted to $2,000,000.

Based on experience with past promotional ventures, it is estimated that sales volume can be increased by 40 percent during the year the contest is conducted.

Required: Compute the increase in net income before income taxes that can be expected during the year the contest is conducted.

15–7. A part used in the production of television sets is manufactured by Horne Electric Company. Walter Horne, the founder and president of the company, has been struggling along with low profit margins that have resulted from severe competition in the industry. Insofar as possible, he has held operating costs to a minimum to meet the low prices that he must charge to customers.

Mr. Horne hopes to get some government contracts that will help to cover fixed overhead costs until he can become better established in the commercial market.

A factory building is rented at a cost of $600 a month. The materials used to assemble each part cost $7.50. Labor is paid on a piece-rate basis at 60 cents per unit. Cartons used in shipping and various incidental supplies cost 20 cents per unit.

The fixed costs of operation, aside from factory rent, have been estimated on a monthly basis as shown below:

Salaries	$1,000
Office expense	150
Telephone	60
Electric	35
Advertising	145
Other costs	30
	$1,420

The fixed costs are expected to remain at this level without significant change from month to month.

During the past 6 months, the company sold 22,000 of these units for $9.75 apiece. The costs, both fixed and variable, were in agreement with the estimates.

Mr. Horne estimates that he can sell 30,000 units on the commercial market during the next six months at a price of $9.75 per unit. In addition, he believes that he has a good chance to be awarded a government contract for 10,000 units at a bid price of $84,000.

Required: (1) Compute the net profit or loss on operations for the last 6 months.

(2) Compute the estimated net profit or loss on operations for the year based on Mr. Horne's estimates for the last six months of the year.

(3) How much will the government contract contribute to the total operation?

15–8. Three different product lines are manufactured and sold by Paget Industries, Inc. Data with respect to the product lines for 1972 are given below:

	Product Lines		
	1	*2*	*3*
Number of units produced and sold	600,000	200,000	200,000
Production hours	300,000	50,000	50,000
Variable manufacturing cost per hour ...... $	6 $	12 $	8
Additional variable manufacturing cost per unit of product	2	40	4
Unit selling price	10	60	12
Traceable fixed manufacturing cost per product line	1,200,000	600,000	100,000
Supporting investment, each product line ..	3,000,000	6,000,000	2,500,000

Fixed manufacturing costs for the year in addition to the traceable costs amounted to $2,400,000. These costs are allocated to the product lines: 50 percent to Product 1 with the balance divided equally between Products 2 and 3.

The selling and administrative costs are fixed costs in the amount of $800,000 and are not identifiable with the product lines.

In addition to the assets specifically identified with the product lines, there is an investment of $3,000,000 in other assets employed for business operation. No attempt is made to allocate this investment to the product lines.

Income taxes are estimated at 50 percent of net income before income taxes.

Required: (1) Prepare an income statement for Paget Industries, Inc., for the year 1972. Show the contribution margin by product lines, the margin after traceable fixed manufacturing costs, the margin after the allocation of other fixed manufacturing costs, and the net income before and after income taxes.

(2) Compute the rate of return after income taxes for each product line on the fixed investment identifiable with that product line.

(3) Changes planned for 1973 are listed below. No other changes are expected.

(a) The variable costs for Product 2 are to be reduced by $3 a unit. No change in the variable hourly rate is anticipated.

(b) An additional 100,000 units of Product 3 can be sold on special contract at a unit price of $7.20. This contract will have no effect on regular sales.

(c) It is estimated that 100,000 more units of Product 1 can be sold if the price for all units sold is reduced to $8.00.

Which of these changes will have the most effect on net income after income taxes? (Show calculations.)

(4) What rate of return after income taxes did the company earn on its investment in 1972? What rate of return after income taxes can be expected in 1973 if all desirable changes described in (3) are put into effect?

15–9. Austin Drugs, Inc., processes and sells a variety of pharmaceutical products. At the Clearview plant, a product used for geriatric care is processed exclusively. In 1972, the company processed and sold 264,000 units of product, each unit having a weight of 4 ounces. The direct materials were purchased at a cost of $3.40 an ounce. In the manufacturing process there was a shrinkage of 20 percent in the weight of materials used. Direct labor is on a salary basis, and the salaries for 1972 were $135,000. Fixed costs, in addition to direct labor, amounted to $745,000. Variable costs in addition to materials cost were at the rate of $4.50 per each unit of product manufactured.

At the beginning of 1973, Austin Drugs, Inc., acquired another company engaged in the same line of business. With increased productive capacity, the company can now produce and sell 420,000 units of product a year. Also with more efficient equipment, the loss on materials shrinkage can be reduced to 10 percent of the materials started in production.

Materials will be purchased in large quantity lots and will now cost $3.15 per ounce. The direct labor cost for the year will increase to $216,000. Other fixed costs will increase to $970,000. Variable costs in addition to material cost are estimated at $5.00 for each unit of product manufactured.

The product is sold to distributors at total variable cost plus 40 percent of variable cost.

Required: (1) Compute the selling price per unit of product for 1972 and for 1973.

(2) Determine the net income before income taxes for 1972 and the estimated net income for 1973. Show computations.

15–10. Three different lines of product are manufactured and sold by Stehly Industries, Inc. For several years the company has operated at a loss, and a new management group plans to reverse the unfavorable trend. An income statement for the last year of operations under the old management is shown on page 454.

The fixed manufacturing overhead amounted to $4,320,000 and the fixed selling and administrative costs amounted to $900,000. The company should operate at a normal capacity of 720,000 machine hours, but in 1972 the company operated at only 432,000 machine hours.

The new management plans no immediate change in product lines, but some changes will be made to improve operations in 1973. Fixed manufacturing overhead is to be reduced to $3,200,000. The materials used in Product A will be obtained from another supplier at a cost per product unit of $23. With a more aggressive sales policy, it is estimated that the company can operate at

Stehly Industries, Inc.
Income Statement
For the Year Ended, December 31, 1972
(In Thousands)

		Product Lines		
	Total	A	B	C
Units sold	—	108	81	45
Net sales	$10,908	$5,400	$2,673	$2,835
Cost of goods manufac- tured and sold	12,078	6,372	2,511	3,195
Gross margin	($1,170)	($ 972)	$ 162	($ 360)
Selling and adminis- trative expenses	1,134	408	381	345
Net loss	($2,304)	($1,380)	($ 219)	($ 705)

Data with respect to each line of product appears below:

	A	B	C
Unit selling price	$50	$33	$63
Unit costs:			
Materials	25	14	20
Labor	8	4	12
Variable manufacturing overhead	6	3	9
Variable selling and administrative cost ..	1	1	1
Machine time required to manufacture each unit or product	2 hrs.	1 hr.	3 hrs.

600,000 machine hours in 1973 and can meet the production time schedule of 1972. The production time will be distributed as follows:

Product Lines	Machine Hours
A	230,000
B	130,000
C	240,000
Total	600,000

All of the production in 1973 will be sold during the year.

Required: Prepare an income statement for 1973 that will show the total contribution margin for each product line and for the total operation as well as the net income before income taxes on the total operation.

PART THREE

LONG-RANGE PLANNING

Chapter 16

COSTS AND MANAGERIAL DECISIONS

Business management is judged to a large extent by its ability to earn an adequate return on investment. Whether or not a return is "adequate" is decided by relating it to the industry and general business environment. In making plans for the future, management will be influenced by the minimum rate of return requirement. Various alternatives will be compared, future revenues and costs will be estimated and identified with the alternatives, and the alternative with the best return potential usually will be selected.

The decision-making process would be most accurate if *all* aspects of a decision could be quantified. This is not possible. Qualitative factors, e.g., company prestige or employee morale, often affect the final choice. However, the potential usefulness of quantitative analysis can be brought out by asking two questions (1) what is the general role of quantitative analysis in decision making, and (2) how *useful* is quantitative analysis to the manager?

In the next three chapters, the emphasis will be placed on the selection of quantitative data that can be used in making an evaluation of decision alternatives. (Qualitative factors will not be considered.) This chapter will center around methods for evaluating alternatives. Chapter 17 covers pricing decisions and Chapter 18 discusses capital investment decisions.

QUANTITATIVE ANALYSIS IN DECISION MAKING

Quantitative data and analysis play an important role in the phases of decision making which include:

(1) Identifying alternatives.
(2) Developing a method for evaluating the alternatives, sometimes called a *decision model*.
(3) Obtaining information, i.e., relevant data which would influence the decision, required by the decision model. The decision model chosen would decide, to an extent, what accounting data would be relevant.

The basis of quantitative analysis is the notion that if the problem at hand is too difficult to permit a solution, a simpler problem will be solved in its place; that is, if a complex problem is given to an analyst which he cannot solve, he may reply, "I can't solve this problem, but I can solve a simpler one." This may sound very amusing, but it is the basis of much of mathematics and quantitative analysis. The idea is to *abstract* (to withdraw) from the complex problem that cannot be solved to a simpler problem that can be solved. Then, having solved the simpler problem the analyst will try to proceed toward a solution to the complex problem. Sometimes the complex problem will defy solution and the best that can be done is to solve the problem subject to certain simplifying assumptions.

In the process of abstraction, the principal trick is to retain as much as possible of the complexity of the main problem. In so doing, the analyst, once he has solved the simpler problem, will have less of a "gap to bridge" to obtain a solution to the complex problem.

The process of abstraction is at its best when it is possible to abstract very little and yet still solve the abstracted problem more easily than the complex problem. This notion can be illustrated with a very simple example. Suppose that one must find the number of years in the period January 1, 1962 to December 31, 1975. It is usually difficult to remember whether the answer is 13 years, 14 years or 15 years. It is possible, of course, to count the years one at a time. However, it is also possible to abstract and ask how many years there are in the period January 1, 1962, to December 31, 1964, and then it is only necessary to count to three. Having done this it becomes clear that the general rule is to subtract the smaller number from the larger number and add one. Hence, there are 14 years in the actual time period given. This is an extremely simple problem, but the power of abstraction is well illustrated.

Decision making—a process of abstraction. Decision making is basically a process of abstraction—of first solving simpler problems than the ones presented. Except in the most trivial decisions, how many times do decision makers solve the problem *exactly* as it is given to them? This probably happens *very infrequently* indeed. The usual case is that decision problems are so complex that some abstraction from reality is necessary to even get started toward a solution. Having solved a simpler problem than the one given, the decision maker tries to move toward a solution for the real problem. Usually, the decision (solution) is based on some simplifying assumptions.

To illustrate the above discussion, assume that the decision problem is whether or not to introduce a new product. The decision maker may be fairly certain of the production and marketing costs. He estimates the variable cost per unit at $5 and the increase in fixed cost to be $100,000. Assume also that the facilities that would be used to produce the new product could be devoted to producing more of an existing product in which case a $200,000 profit per year would be earned. However, the decision maker is highly uncertain about what price to charge for the new product and how many units will be sold. Since he cannot solve the exact problem he is given—whether or not to introduce the new product—a useful starting place is to abstract from the complex problem and solve a simpler one, that is, it may not be possible to say whether the new product will be more or less profitable than the alternative use of the facilities but he can solve a simpler problem. *He can find the number of units that must be sold at each price in order for the new product to be equally as profitable as the old product;* that is, he may not be able to specify the market demand function that *does* exist for the new product, but he can solve for the demand curve that defines his indifference between the two alternatives. Thus, if a price of $10 is charged, then more than 60,000 units will have to be sold in order for the new product to be more profitable than the existing product $\left(\dfrac{\$100,000 + \$200,000}{\$10 - \$5} = 60,000 \text{ units} \right)$. Repeating this calculation for different prices, a "break-even" demand curve can be drawn as follows:

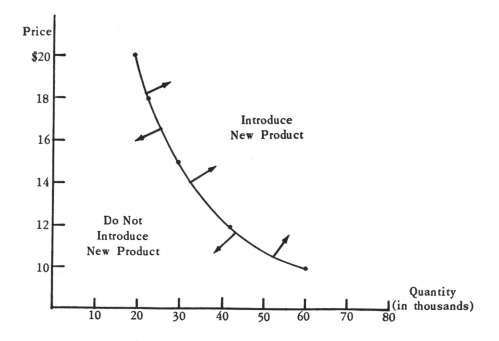

This break-even demand curve is really a line of equal profit. Any combination of price and quantity on the line will give a profit of $200,000. Hence, for any price-quantity combination to the right of the equal profit curve, the best decision is to introduce the new product; for any price-quantity combination to the left of the equal profit line, the best decision is to use the existing facilities to produce more of the old product.

Now the decision maker has not solved his real problem but he has solved a simple problem. This solution is based on certain assumptions:

(1) The variable cost of the new product,
(2) The increase in the fixed cost associated with the new product, and
(3) The alternative profit that can be earned from the facility.

Having solved a simpler problem than the one given, the next series of steps should be to move closer to the real problem. The decision maker may do this by asking his sales manager a question such as: "If we charge a price of $10 do you think we will sell more than (or less than) 60,000 units?" In this way, he may ultimately be able to solve the real problem. However, notice that the final solution will (1) have been reached through an initial process of abstraction, and (2) will be based on certain assumptions.

Relaxing the assumptions and changing the parameters—the power of experimentation. If it is true that abstraction is a basic feature of the decision process, as has been stated, then the decision maker should want to abstract in such a way that the importance of the assumptions can be tested. Abstraction typically involves the use of assumptions; hence, when the simpler, abstracted problem is solved, the decision maker may very well want to see the effect of relaxing or changing the assumption and parameters on the solution to the problem. Herein lies another advantage which quantitative analysis can bring to decision problems. The basis of the abstraction process in developing quantitative methods is a precise and rigorous statement of the assumptions that have been made. This rigor should permit the decision maker to experiment in order to determine how sensitive the solution is to changes in the assumptions of the model.

Returning to the new product decision problem given above, note that an assumption was made on the variable cost per unit; that is, the variable cost was estimated at $5 and it was assumed that this amount was constant per unit, no matter how many units were produced. Stated another way, the *total* variable cost was assumed to vary in direct proportion to changes in volume. Having made this assumption and having estimated the variable cost at $5 per unit, the decision maker calculated the equal profit curve given in the figure on page 457. Since quantity and price are highly uncertain, it may be useful to see how sensitive the equal profit line is to the assumption of cost proportionality as well as the variable cost estimate of $5. In this particular example, sensitivity analysis would probably be carried out by simply recalculating the equal profit line under different sets of conditions. For example, the graph illustrated below shows the effect of the equal line of an assumption that the unit variable cost of $5 decreases 20 cents for every 10,000-unit increase in volume over 20,000 units.

This type of analysis should aid the decision maker in deciding whether the proportionality assumption is of critical importance in the particular decision problem. In this particular case, the change in the cost proportionality assumption changes the correct decision very little; that is, the two equal profit lines are very close together. This fact is not obvious; hence, the analysis should be useful to the decision maker.

The process of experimentation described above is aimed at answering "what-if" type questions; that is, *what will happen* to the required volume *if* variable costs increase? Or how will the required volume change if selling prices change? Since the decision maker must abstract and since he can rarely solve the exact problem he faces, the answer to "what-if" type questions is a powerful method by which the decision maker can discover which variables are really critical to his decision. This type of analysis will rarely "make a decision," but it is a great help in considering the quantitative aspects of a decision.

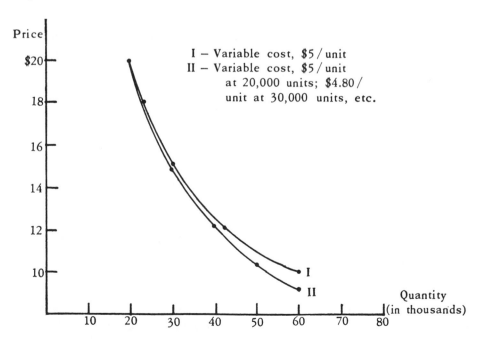

I — Variable cost, $5/unit
II — Variable cost, $5/unit
at 20,000 units; $4.80/
unit at 30,000 units, etc.

Quantitative processes such as described here are sometimes criticized for being too abstract. Yet, abstraction is the very power of the analysis. Certainly, in analyzing any complex problem, certain factors are either fixed by assumption or left out altogether. After doing an analysis, the decision maker should carefully consider the assumptions made and any qualitative factors which were excluded in the original analysis. In addition to helping the decision maker understand which variables are critical to his decision, quantitative analysis helps him predict the impact of his choices on profits.

RELEVANT COST DATA FOR DECISION MAKING

The costs that are relevant in making decisions are not necessarily the costs that are used in conventional accounting or in financial reporting. In fact, some of the costs to be used in decision making will not even be entered in the accounting records. Opportunity costs, for example, are important in decision making but are not entered as accounting costs.

An adjustment in thinking is required in planning for the future, and this adjustment may be particularly difficult for the person who has become accustomed to conventional accounting practices. In conventional accounting, for example, the cost of a depreciable asset is assigned to the fiscal periods as depreciation. But a cost that has been incurred in the past (a sunk cost) may play no role in making plans for the future, except for income tax effect. Income tax effects will be discussed in Chapter 18 on Capital Investment.

In decision making, the emphasis is on the *future*. The past is important only as a guide in predicting the future. When a choice is to be made between alternatives, the costs that will be increased or decreased as a result of a decision are the relevant costs. Costs that will be unaffected by a decision can be ignored. These ideas are illustrated in the following sections.

COSTS AND DECISIONS, AN ILLUSTRATION

The problem of selecting the appropriate costs for decision making is illustrated by a short example. Lane Products, Inc., has determined the total annual costs to operate one of its manufacturing departments. Only the costs that are directly identified with this department are listed. No costs have been allocated to this operation. An outside service contractor has agreed to furnish a repair and maintenance service, and the costs that can be expected if this alternative is selected are also listed in the same way as the costs of the present operation.

Some of the costs listed on the next page are not relevant to the decision. For example, the direct materials and direct labor costs will be the same in either case and, therefore, with respect to this decision, these costs are sunk.

460

	Present Operation	Alternative of Service Contract	Type of Cost
Direct materials	$15,000	$15,000	Unavoidable
Direct labor	25,000	25,000	Unavoidable
Supplies	6,000	7,000	Differential by $1,000
Indirect labor	15,000	10,000	Differential by $5,000
Repairs and maintenance	3,500	—0—	Differential by $3,500; also avoidable cost
Outside services	—0—	4,000	Differential by $4,000
Depreciation	2,000	2,000	Sunk cost

The sunk cost of $2,000 is a portion of the cost of a plant asset that will be assigned to a fiscal period in financial accounting. This cost was incurred in the past and can be excluded in the decision-making process. The *differential costs* are the relevant costs as shown below:

Lane Products, Inc.
Service Contract Decision

Estimated decreases in cost:		
Indirect labor	$5,000	
Repairs and maintenance	3,500	
Total estimated cost savings		$8,500
Estimated increases in cost:		
Supplies	$1,000	
Outside services	4,000	
Total expected cost increases		5,000
Anticipated cost advantage from service contract ..		$3,500

There will be a net saving of $3,500 a year if repair and maintenance work is done by an outside contractor, and, everything else being equal, the company should engage the contractor.

OPPORTUNITY COST

Opportunity costs play a vital role in decision making. As explained in Chapter 9, an opportunity cost is a benefit that would have been obtained from an alternative if it were not rejected. For example, a student may be able to earn $1,500 after taxes and other additional costs by working in the summer; but if he decides to go to summer school, he will not get the $1,500. The cost of his decision to attend summer school is not only the cost of tuition and books but is also the sacrifice of the $1,500 that he could earn after taxes and other additional costs. The net proceeds from summer work are the opportunity cost of attending summer school.

Returning to the examples given above, assume that another contractor presents a repair and maintenance service plan. To be acceptable, this new plan must yield cost savings each year of at least $3,500. In other words, to be acceptable any new proposal must be at least as advantageous as the plan that is now available. The opportunity cost of not accepting the alternative method is $3,500, the annual cost saving which will be produced by the proposal under consideration.

The concept of opportunity cost will be applied in Chapter 18 in evaluating investment alternatives. A potential investment is not accepted, as a rule, unless it appears that the rate of return will be at least equal to that which can be earned from other investment alternatives in the same risk category. The rate of return from a rejected alternative is the cost of accepting another alternative. For example, if there is an opportunity to make an investment that can be recovered with interest compounded at the rate of 10 percent, no other investment in this same risk category will appear attractive unless it too can produce at least that rate of return. The marginal rate of return established by other investment possibilities becomes the opportunity cost of the selection made.

COMBINATION DECISIONS

Management is constantly faced with the problem of how to make the best use of available facilities and the problem of how productive resources can be combined to minimize cost. Because all decision situations in which the manager might find himself cannot be anticipated, the following general types of combination decisions will be discussed:

(1) Process or sell,
(2) Product combination,
(3) Make or buy.

The combination problem has received a great deal of attention recently because of the increased availability of computers that can be programmed to solve complex problems having many variables.

Process or sell. An example of the opportunity cost concept applied to a combination decision is given below. Assume that a certain intermediate product can be produced and sold or can be processed further and sold as a completely processed product. In deciding upon which course of action to follow, the company compares the contribution margin from the sale of the partially processed product with the contribution margin from the sale of the completely processed product. The revenue to be derived from the sale of the partially processed product is the opportunity cost attached to the decision of further processing.

Assume, for example, that a product selling for $9 per unit partially processed is manufactured at a cost of $6. Further processing at a variable cost of $3 a unit will yield a product that can be sold at a unit price of $15. The firm can produce 10,000 units. The analysis is shown below.

There is a net advantage of $30,000 in processing the product further. Note that the market value of the partially processed product is considered

Decision Analysis

Revenue from sale of final product (10,000 units @ $15)		$150,000
Less:		
Additional processing costs (10,000 units @ $3)	$30,000	
Revenue from sale of intermediate product (10,000 units @ $9)	90,000	120,000
Net advantage in further processing		$ 30,000

to be the opportunity cost of further processing. Assuming that the company continues its processing operation and realizes profits as planned, the revenues and the costs will be accounted for in the usual manner as shown below:

Accountability

Revenue from sale of final product		$150,000
Less:		
Additional processing costs	$30,000	
Cost to process intermediate product	60,000	90,000
Net income		$ 60,000

Product combinations. The product combination problem arises when several product lines are manufactured and sold. A decision must be reached as to which product combination is most profitable. Oil refineries, for example, plan refinery production to meet the varying needs of the market. During some months of the year, larger quantities of heating oils will be produced, while in other months larger quantities of gasoline will be produced. In other industries, similar problems are encountered that involve a selection of the best combination of productive factors which will meet the limitations that are imposed by internal or external conditions. An increase in the production and sale of one line often means that the production and sale of another line will have to be reduced. There is only so much that can be done with a given set of productive factors. If at all possible, the product lines should be manufactured and sold in the most profitable combination.

Two products, no constraints. Assume that a firm produces two products, A and B, whose costs and selling prices are as follows:

	Product A	Product B
Selling price per unit	$10	$ 8
Variable costs per unit	5	6
Contribution margin per unit	$ 5	$ 2
Fixed cost per year	$50,000	

One of the decision problems faced by the manager is to decide which combination of Products A and B should be produced and sold. The decision rule that can be followed in this problem is to choose the combination of products that will maximize contribution margin. If fixed costs remain at $50,000, this decision rule will also maximize net income. This decision rule might be carried out by choosing the product that has the highest contribution margin per unit. If there are no constraints with respect to either production capacity or sales capacity, this method could give the desired result. However, this is a very unlikely situation. In most cases, the firm has a given plant facility, and if Product A is chosen, some units of Product B must be given up. Also, it is not unusual to find various market constraints that arise because the market will absorb only a limited number of units. In these cases, the break-even or cost-volume-profit information given above is useful but insufficient to arrive at a product-combination decision. In addition, management must have information on the *amount of scarce resources* used up in producing each product.

Two products, one constraint. Assume that the market for each product is unlimited and that the firm can therefore sell all units that can be produced. However, assume that the production facilities are limited to 200,000 labor hours. In this case the scarce production factor (scarce resource) facing the firm is the labor force. Further, assume that the labor requirement of each product is as follows:

	Product A	Product B
Labor hours required	10 hours	2 hours

Given the production constraint of 200,000 hours, it is possible to produce (and sell) 20,000 units of Product A $\left(\dfrac{200,000}{10 \text{ hours}}\right)$ or 100,000 units of Product B $\left(\dfrac{200,000}{2 \text{ hours}}\right)$. Actually the firm can produce Products A and B in any combination by giving up five units of Product B for one unit of Product A.

With this simple constraint, the firm should produce all Product B because this plan gives the greatest contribution margin. The situations are summarized in the following income statements:

Statements of Net Income

	If All A Is Produced	If All B Is Produced
Sales: (20,000 units at $10)	$200,000	
(100,000 units at $ 8)		$800,000
Variable cost:		
(20,000 units at $5)	100,000	
(100,000 units at $6)		600,000
Contribution margin	$100,000	$200,000
Fixed cost	50,000	50,000
Net profit	$ 50,000	$150,000

As can be seen, with one production constraint and two products, the solution to the product-combination problem is fairly simple. An alternate solution is to calculate a contribution margin per hour of production time and to choose the product with the highest rate. The calculation is as follows:

	Product A	Product B
Sales price	$10	$8
Variable cost	5	6
Contribution margin	$ 5	$2

	Product A	Product B
Hour requirement	10 hours	2 hours
Contribution margin per hour	$5/10 hrs.=$.50/hr.	$2/2 hrs.=$1/hr.

Since Product B returns $1 per hour in contrast with 50 cents per hour for Product A, Product B is the preferred product. As a matter of fact, the firm will continue to be a one-product firm producing all B and no A as long as there is no market limitation on Product B. It is the market limitation which creates a *product combination*. If the firm can sell its most profitable product (in this case, Product B) in an unlimited market, there would be no reason to produce any of Product A. However, as will be shown later, some of Product A will be produced if the market for Product B is limited to less units than can be produced.

This example, although simple, forms the basis for a linear programming problem. The firm is maximizing contribution margin subject to a single production constraint. The solution is simple since there are only two products and one constraint. In such a simple case, the concept of *a rate of return per the scarce factor* is a useful and effective concept. However, as the number of products and the number of constraints increases, this simple solution becomes inadequate and linear programming becomes necessary for the more complex cases.

Two products, many constraints. In the previous example, it was assumed that there were no market constraints. Assume that market conditions are of such a nature that only 80,000 units of Product B can be sold but that the market for Product A is unlimited. It would be possible to solve the problem by trial and error, but a more systematic solution and one that will generalize to the many-constraint case is a graphic linear programming solution.

The previous example, involving only one production constraint, the limitation of production facilities to 200,000 labor hours, has been plotted below.

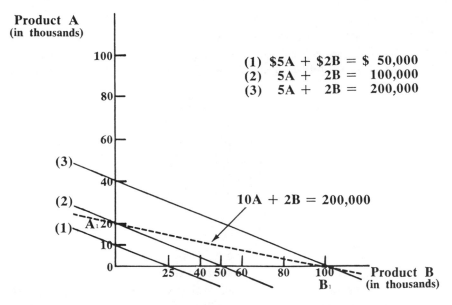

Product A
(in thousands)

(1) $\$5A + \$2B = \$\ 50,000$	
(2) $\ \ \ 5A + \ \ 2B = \ \ \ 100,000$	
(3) $\ \ \ 5A + \ \ 2B = \ \ \ 200,000$	

$10A + 2B = 200,000$

Product B
(in thousands)

The production constraint can be given by the line $10A + 2B = 200,000$. The set of possible solutions is given by the area O, A_1, B_1; that is, only 200,000 hours are available, so all possible solutions must use some number of hours less than or equal to 200,000. In symbols:

(1) $10A + 2B \leq 200,000$

This inequality states in symbol form the production constraint. If only Product B is produced, 100,000 units are possible; and if only Product A is produced, 20,000 units are possible. Other combinations that use all of the capacity (for example, 10,000 A and 50,000 B) will fall on the line $10A + 2B = 200,000$. The other possible solutions will fall somewhere in the area O, A_1, B_1, but these solutions will not use 100 percent of the hour capacity. These solutions will be feasible or possible but not optimal. An optimal solution will be somewhere on the boundary of the area O, A_1, B_1.

The problem is to maximize contribution margin subject to a single production constraint. In equation form:

(2) CM = $5A + $2B, where CM = contribution margin.

That is, for every unit of Product A that is sold, CM increases by $5, and for every unit of Product B, CM increases by $2. In the diagram above, three lines have been plotted showing contribution margins at three different levels, $50,000, $100,000, and $200,000. These lines are "equal contribution" lines in that they show different combinations of Products A and B that will give the same contribution margin. Since the objective is to maximize contribution margin, the CM lines should be moved upward and to the right until the CM line is at the boundary given by the production constraint equation. This occurs at the point A = O and B = 100,000 units. Higher levels of contribution margin are not feasible because of the hour constraint. This solution agrees with the one given earlier in the chapter.

The same example with the addition of the market constraint that only 80,000 units of Product B can be sold has been plotted below:

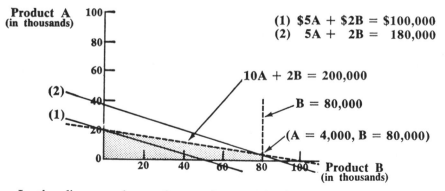

In the diagram above, the previous production constraint of 200,000 labor hours has been plotted. In addition, the line B = 80,000 will establish the constraint that the market will absorb a maximum of only 80,000 units of Product B. In inequality form, this constraint is:

(2) B ≤ 80,000

The set of possible or feasible solutions is therefore given by the shaded area. The objective function or contribution margin equation can be moved upward and to the right until the point A = 4,000, B = 80,000 is reached. At this point, contribution margin will be maximized at $180,000.

As can be seen, in the graphic linear programming solution the various production and marketing constraints can be plotted and, taken together, will define the set of possible or feasible solutions. The objective function or contribution margin line is then determined and a solution, giving the maximum contribution margin, can be found by moving the contribution margin line to higher and higher levels until the boundary formed by the restraint equations is reached. Note that this graphic technique will handle almost any number of restraints but only two products. If many products are involved, the graph would become multidimensional and would be impossible to work with.

Many products, many constraints. In the problem given above, there were only two products involved, and a graphic solution technique worked very well. This technique can handle almost any number of constraints because each constraint simply adds one more line on the graph. However, when many products and many constraints are involved, the full power of the linear programming techniques and the computer must be used.

The general linear programming problem can be formulated as follows:

$$\text{Maximize:} \quad CM = C_1 X_1 + C_2 X_2 + \ldots + C_n X_n$$
$$\text{Subject to:} \quad A_{11} X_1 + A_{12} X_2 + \ldots + A_{1n} X_n \leq B_1$$
$$A_{21} X_1 + A_{22} X_2 + \ldots + A_{2n} X_n \leq B_2$$
$$\cdot$$
$$\cdot$$
$$\cdot$$
$$A_{m1} X_1 + A_{m2} X_2 + \ldots + A_{mn} X_n \leq B_m$$

First the problem is to maximize some quantity, which in the previous examples was contribution margin (CM). This was done by choosing some combination of products, represented by the X's, that sell at a certain contribution margin per unit, represented by the C's. As can be seen, there are n products where n is a very large number.

In the preceding example, there were two products (n=2) that were designated A and B. The contribution margin per unit of A was $5 and per unit of B was $2. Hence, the objective function in this example reduced to:

Maximize: CM = $5A + $2B

In the general statement, there are m production and/or marketing constraints. The A's represent the amount of scarce resources used up by each product (each product being designated by an X). The B's represent the total amount of each scarce resource that is available.

In the example given, there were two constraints (m=2). One constraint was on the number of labor hours available. The other constraint was a market constraint and it limited the market for Product B to 80,000 units. Hence, the statement of the problem used in the illustration reduces to:

Maximize: $CM = \$5A + \$2B$
Subject to: $10A + 2B \leq 200,000$ (the constraint on labor hours)
$B \leq 80,000$ (the market constraint on B)

This problem was solved by using a graph, but if there had been many products to choose from, this simple approach would not have been possible.

It is possible to solve the set of equations given above by algebra. The problem requires a simultaneous solution to the three equations. Such a solution consists of finding values for A and B which will make the objective function (CM) as large as possible but which will not violate any of the constraints. This solution turned out to be A = 4,000 units and B = 80,000 units. This solution made CM = $5 (4,000) + $2 (80,000) = $180,000, and neither the labor hours nor the market constraint was violated.

A generalized algebraic solution called the simplex method is available for solving linear programming problems. This method has been programmed for most computers and it will solve problems with many products and many constraints. This technique consists of a set of rules which will systematically check out the amount of contribution margin associated with various product combinations.

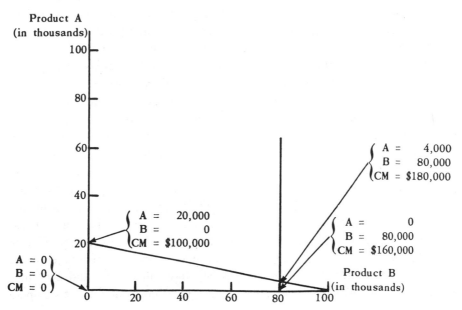

The diagram shows the two constraints used in the example. As indicated earlier, the optimal solution will be on the boundary formed by the constraints. As can be seen, there are four "corner points" which represent the following product combinations:

Product A	Product B
—0— units	—0— units
20,000	—0—
4,000	80,000
—0—	80,000

The simplex method will essentially check out each "corner point" and will stop when the product combination giving the highest contribution is found. In the example, the point represents A = 4,000, B = 80,000 and gives a contribution of $180,000. The simplex method is beyond the scope of this book but it is described in most books on linear programming.

Make or buy decision. Another important type of combination decision is whether to make or buy component parts. Often a company will expand by a vertical type of growth. In addition to carrying out its primary manufacturing function, it may produce its own parts or process its own basic materials; or moving in the other direction, it may extend the manufacturing process further or control its own market outlets.

The integrated company possesses certain advantages. For one thing, it is less dependent upon suppliers or distributors if it produces its own direct or indirect materials and has its own market outlets. A strike in the industry of a supplier, for example, may not handicap the manufacturer who makes his own materials. Furthermore, the integrated company not only realizes profits from its principal manufacturing process, but it may also realize profits from manufacturing parts—profits that would otherwise go to the suppliers. Or the manufacturer who moves into distribution sometimes has an opportunity to earn the profits resulting from sales to ultimate consumers.

Before deciding in favor of parts manufacture, some of the hazards should also be recognized. To begin with, the company must be sure that it can produce parts of the desired quality in sufficient quantity at a saving in cost. In effect, the company is entering into competition with its suppliers, and if it is unable to supply its own needs, it may find it difficult to make purchases from its former suppliers. Moving in the other direction, a manufacturer may compete with former customers. A large manufacturer of basic materials, for example, may have customers who are fabricators. If this company were to enter the fabricating business, it might lose out entirely. Its present customers would no longer buy basic materials, and the integrated company with its relatively high overhead costs might not compete effectively in the fabricating business against its low-cost competitors, the former customers.

The direct economic effect of a make or buy decision can be determined from an evaluation of differential costs. The purchase price of the parts will be compared with the estimated increased costs that will be attached to the parts manufacturing operation. The purchase price of a part is like the selling price for a product. As long as the incremental costs attached to making the parts are less than the outside purchase price, there is an advantage. The same concept is followed in normal business dealings. If a product can be sold for more than its cost, there is a profit.

To manufacture its parts, a company may need additional facilities. The plant may have to be enlarged, new equipment may be required, or capital investment for one reason or another may enter into the decision. The saving from parts production will be related to the investment to see whether or not the rate of return is adequate. The make or buy decision is then a capital investment decision also, and as mentioned before, this type of decision will be discussed in Chapter 18. In some instances, however, it may be possible to produce parts with little or no additional investment. Parts production may be accomplished with present facilities that would otherwise be idle.

For example, assume that a company can make a part that it has been purchasing at a unit cost of $3. The company can buy materials at a cost of $1.25 per part, direct labor cost has been estimated at 80 cents for each part, and variable manufacturing overhead has been estimated at 50 cents for each part. The company has been operating at 75 percent of normal capacity, and in the foreseeable future no use for the excess capacity is contemplated except for the possible production of the part. Production of this part will enable the company to operate at its normal capacity and will provide all parts needed for subsequent manufacturing operations. Fixed manufacturing overhead costs amount to $170,000 a year, whether the plant operates at 75 or 100 percent of capacity.

The cost to manufacture 50,000 units of the part that will be needed has been estimated as follows:

	Unit Cost	Total Cost
Direct materials	$1.25	$ 62,500
Direct labor	.80	40,000
Manufacturing overhead:		
Variable	.50	25,000
Fixed (25% of $170,000)	.85	42,500
Cost to manufacture	$3.40	$170,000

The management of the company reasons that the part should be purchased because the cost to manufacture it is $3.40, and this is greater than the purchase cost of $3. However, in the cost analysis, $42,500 of the total fixed overhead has been allocated to the parts manufacturing operation. The fixed overhead, in this example, is not affected by the decision, and the analysis is incorrect. Only the costs that will be increased or decreased as a result of making the part should be considered. In some cases, both the variable and fixed costs will be affected. The important point is that the costs that will be incurred in any event should not be allocated in decision making.

A correct analysis follows:

	Unit Cost	Total Cost
Direct materials	$1.25	$ 62,500
Direct labor	.80	40,000
Variable manufacturing overhead	.50	25,000
Total incremental costs	$2.55	$127,500
Cost to purchase part	3.00	150,000
Net advantage in parts production	$ .45	$ 22,500

If there is no better alternative for the use of the idle facilities, the part should be manufactured and not purchased.

CURTAILMENT DECISIONS

Not all managerial decisions will be based upon how various factors should be used in combination. Sometimes the choice will lie between operating as before on the one hand and on the other discontinuing a present activity or product line; or possibly operating at below capacity as opposed to a temporary shutdown. A product line, for example, may prove to be unprofitable. Instead of contributing to the total operation, it may be reducing the total profits by not contributing enough to cover its own costs.

The elimination of a product line. An income statement for Harris Department Store has been prepared for an average year, and the data have been rearranged to show which product lines should be retained or discontinued. The income statement is shown on the next page.

The variable costs identified with each product line and the fixed costs that are *specifically* incurred for each product line are subtracted from sales to determine whether or not the product line can cover its own costs. Note

472

Harris Department Store

Income Statement

Average Year

	Total	Product Lines			
		1	*2*	*3*	*4*
Net sales	$348,500	$86,200	$93,700	$81,200	$87,400
Direct costs:					
Variable costs:					
Cost of goods sold	$233,500	$51,800	$55,100	$68,700	$57,900
Supplies	13,800	3,300	2,800	3,900	3,800
Transportation	6,500	1,100	1,400	1,900	2,100
Total variable costs ...	$253,800	$56,200	$59,300	$74,500	$63,800
Contribution margin	$ 94,700	$30,000	$34,400	$ 6,700	$23,600
Fixed costs for the product line:					
Salaries	$ 35,000	$ 6,000	$11,000	$10,000	$ 8,000
Advertising	16,200	3,000	4,500	4,500	4,200
Total fixed costs for product line	$ 51,200	$ 9,000	$15,500	$14,500	$12,200
Margin over direct costs ...	$ 43,500	$21,000	$18,900	($ 7,800)	$11,400
Fixed costs of the total operation:					
Salaries	$ 16,000				
Rent	5,000				
Taxes	2,700				
Insurance	1,600				
Heat and light	1,700				
Total fixed costs of operation	$ 27,000				
Net income	$ 16,500				

that the analysis in this case does not depend entirely upon the variable costs. It is not a question of profit planning by planning selling prices, variable costs, or sales volume. Instead, the problem is extended further. The sales volume, the unit selling prices, and the variable costs per unit are assumed. The direct costs include the variable costs and the fixed costs that are incurred for each particular product line. These costs are the *avoidable costs*. They can be avoided if a product line is discontinued. The fixed costs for the total store should not be allocated. They are the *unavoidable costs*, the costs that will be incurred in any event.

Product 3 should be eliminated, unless it can be proved that the line helps to increase the sales of the profitable lines. It cannot cover its own costs. Without Product 3, the profit for the store would amount to $24,300 as shown below:

Profit Effect

Elimination of Product 3

Costs avoided by the elimination of Product 3:		
Variable costs	$74,500	
Fixed costs for the product line which can be		
eliminated	14,500	
Total costs eliminated		$89,000
Less: Revenue contributed by Product 3		81,200
Net advantage, elimination of Product 3		$ 7,800
Net income, including Product 3		16,500
Net income, without Product 3		$24,300

In this example, certain costs were identified with the product lines, but it cannot be assumed that these particular costs will be avoidable or unavoidable in all cases. Each situation should be evaluated on its own. The important point is that a distinction should be made between the costs that can be avoided and the costs that cannot be avoided by the decision. In this example, if the $14,500 fixed cost *could not* be eliminated with Product 3, then Product 3 should be retained.

Temporary shutdown. A curtailment decision is also illustrated by the consideration of a temporary shutdown. Frequently, plant operations are continued even when the demand for the products is low and when the plant is operating at a low level of capacity. A company may prefer to operate at below capacity on a temporary basis rather than to close down until demand picks up. It is expensive in many cases to shut down even for a short time. In the steel industry, the furnaces run continuously. If the heat is reduced, the brick linings will crack and will have to be replaced at considerable cost and inconvenience. When a plant is closed, preparations have to be made for storing idle machinery and equipment. Extra lubrication may be required to protect machinery while it is out of service. Furthermore, there are additional costs in starting up a plant that has been idle, not to mention the possibility of losing trained employees and faithful customers.

When operations are continued, however, the revenue from product sales may not be large enough to cover the fixed costs. While the plant is in operation, losses may be growing. These losses can perhaps be reduced but not eliminated entirely by discontinuing operations. There are certain fixed costs that can be avoided when the plant is idle. Indirect materials cost, indirect labor, and heat and light can sometimes be reduced substantially when the plant is closed, although such costs may be relatively fixed when the plant is running. Other costs such as property taxes, insurance, and costs to protect the building and equipment will tend to remain the same in any event.

The direct economic consequences of shutdown as compared with operating at below capacity can be computed. If the fixed costs that are not absorbed by product sales exceed the costs of shutdown, it would pay to close the plant until it can be operated at an economic advantage.

Suppose, for example, that a company when it is operating at normal capacity can produce and sell 300,000 units of product, each of which contributes $2 to fixed manufacturing overhead costs and to profits. The budget of fixed manufacturing overhead is given below along with the budget of fixed costs for the year when the plant is idle. Note that sunk costs, such as depreciation, are excluded. Taxes, insurance, and rent in this illustration can be included or excluded. They do not affect the decision, because they are the same in both cases.

Fixed Manufacturing Overhead Budgets

	Operating Plant	Shutdown Plant
Indirect materials	$ 84,000	$ 3,500
Indirect labor	147,000	23,000
Taxes	2,200	2,200
Insurance	1,500	1,500
Maintenance and repairs	15,500	600
Heat and light	3,800	400
Rent	6,000	6,000
Total fixed costs	$260,000	$37,200
Additional shutdown cost for a year:		
Cost of packing and storing equipment		12,800
Total shutdown costs for a year		$50,000

If the plant is closed for a year, the costs will amount to $50,000. If the plant continues to operate, the fixed costs will amount to $260,000. The plant should continue to operate if the contribution (sales revenue less variable costs) from product sales will be equal to or greater than the $210,000 difference in cost. However, if this differential cannot be recovered by product sales, the plant should be closed.

Each unit of product contributes $2 to fixed overhead and profits. The company can recover the $210,000 cost differential by making and selling 105,000 units of product ($210,000 ÷ $2). In other words, the company should continue to operate if it can produce and sell at 35 percent of its normal operating capacity (105,000 units as a percentage of 300,000 units). The point at which the losses from continued operation are equal to the shutdown costs is the *shutdown point*. If the company cannot produce and sell 105,000 units a year, it will lose more than $50,000 by operating, and the plant should be closed. This same type of analysis can be made, of course, for shorter intervals than a year if costs are estimated accordingly.

The shutdown analysis can be extended further to include the possibility of a permanent cessation of operations, that is, *plant abandonment*. The plant abandonment decision is also a capital investment decision. The proceeds to be received from the immediate sale of the plant are the opportunity cost of continued operation or are the capital investment.

Questions

1. Explain why the process of abstraction is usually necessary in decision-making.

2. Why is so much emphasis placed on the future in decision making? Does the past have any significance in decision making?

3. What are the relevant costs in decision making?

4. How can opportunity costs be used in deciding upon whether a product should be sold in a partially completed state or finished and sold as a completed product?

5. How can you find out whether or not a product line is making a contribution to the total operation?

6. Should fixed costs be considered in deciding upon whether or not a product line should be discontinued?

7. Distinguish between avoidable and unavoidable costs.

8. What is the shutdown point?

9. Costs can be reduced when a company is temporarily shut down, but some costs may remain the same or even increase. Name some costs that would probabily remain the same. Name some costs that would probably increase.

10. Explain what is meant by a make or buy decision.

11. How can there be a cost saving in parts manufacture when accounting records show the manufactured cost of a part to exceed the cost to purchase the part?

Exercises

1. Given the following data, choose the best combination of product.

	Products			
	A	*B*	*C*	*D*
Selling price	$10	$20	$5	$25
Variable cost	7	8	2	20
Hours required for each unit	3	10	1	4
Market limit	—0—	—0—	10,000 units	5,000 units
Total fixed cost $100,000				
Total hours available ... 100,000				

2. In Exercise 1, how would the solution change if there were no market limitation on any of the products? How much greater is the profit from this combination of products than the profit associated with the combination chosen in Exercise 1 above?

3. The Caughman Decorating Company has been selling a line of home furnishings to distributors at a price of $115 a unit and can expect to sell 15,000 units a year. The company plans to set up its own sales organization and will probably sell the same number of units but will sell directly to retailers at a unit price of $160. The annual costs that can be directly identified with the operation of a sales division have been estimated as follows:

Collection losses, allowances, and discounts are estimated at
5 percent of sales.
Salesmen are to receive 5 percent commissions on sales after
allowing for collection losses, allowances, and discounts.

Sales salaries	$65,000
Travel and entertainment	14,000
Advertising	87,000
Other selling expenses	95,000

Required: Can Caughman Decorating Company increase profits by having its own sales organization?

4. Lipsky Patterns, Inc., manufactures and sells three lines of product with contribution margins per unit as follows:

Product 1	$8
Product 2	1
Product 3	3

Each unit of product requires production time as follows:

Product 1	4 hours
Product 2	15 minutes
Product 3	1 hour

The market will absorb 16,000 units of Product 2 and 8,000 units of Product 3. The company can sell as many units of Product 1 as it can produce. The plant has a capacity of 16,000 hours a month.

Required: (1) What is the most profitable product line on the basis of contribution margin per unit of product?

(2) What is the most profitable product line on the basis of contribution margin per hour?

(3) Compute the maximum contribution margin for the month that will meet all conditions stated.

5. A regional association of home builders is planning a week-end conference. Pirates' Cove Inn offers accommodations for a banquet on Friday night and a luncheon on Saturday at a total cost of $4,000. The inn will be closed to normal trade for the weekend with an estimated loss of $2,200 in receipts from customers. To provide for the needs of the home builders association, additional waiters will be engaged at a cost of $400. Additional costs for food and decoration are estimated at $700.

Required: (1) What is the opportunity cost of closing the inn to normal trade?

(2) What additional advantage, if any, can be derived by accepting the conference group?

6. A firm needs two component parts, A and B, which can be manufactured or purchased. The economic information on each part is given below:

	Part	
	A	*B*
Number required	1,000	2,000
Variable cost	$5	$10
Outside price	$8	$14
Total fixed cost	←————$100,000————→	
Hours required per unit	1	2
Total hours available	←————2,000————→	

Any part of the requirement can be manufactured or purchased. Define the "contribution margin" as the difference between the outside purchase price and the variable cost.

Required: (1) Draw a graph with Part A on one axis and Part B on the other. Plot the constraints.

(2) Calculate the contribution margin and the numbers of A and B associated with each "corner point" on the graph.

(3) Choose the best solution.

7. Denver Construction Company plans to improve its facilities in 1973. The work can be done by another company at a cost of $140,000, but Denver Construction Company can do the work itself in an off-season with no interference with regular operations. The materials needed for the construction will probably cost $56,000. Labor and overhead costs will likely be increased by $38,000 and administrative costs will also be increased by $4,000 if the company does its own work. Fixed overhead costs to be allocated to the project will probably amount to $46,000.

Required: Prepare a cost comparison to show whether or not the company should construct its own facilities.

8. A summary statement of profits by operating divisions has been prepared for Schoeller Fastener Company showing the results for a typical year. Included in the costs are costs of the home office that have been allocated to the divisions in proportion to sales revenue. All costs with the exception of the home office

costs can be eliminated by elimination of a division. The home office costs in total amount to $700,000.

	Total	1	2	3	4
Sales	$3,000,000	$450,000	$1,200,000	$450,000	$ 900,000
Costs	2,830,000	260,000	950,000	580,000	1,040,000
Profits (Losses) .	$ 170,000	$190,000	$ 250,000	($130,000)	($ 140,000)

Required: Based on the information given, which division or divisions should be eliminated? Give reasons to support your answer.

9. Under normal operating conditions, Brookshire Tool Company manufactures 90,000 units of a particular product line in a 6-month period. Each unit of product contributes $8 to fixed overhead costs and to profits. The fixed overhead costs for six months amount to $320,000. Labor difficulties in other companies that buy this product have cut sales to a rate of 4,000 units a month. The company management plans to close the plant for six months, anticipating that the market will be back to normal in another six months. The fixed overhead costs can be reduced to $225,000 for six months if the plant is closed, but the additional costs to protect the facilities and to start up again have been estimated at $31,000.

Required: Should the plant be closed? What is the shutdown point in number of product units for six months?

Problems

16–1. The Lyons Company has a production facility which can be used to produce three products in any combination. The economic data are as follows:

	Products		
	1	2	3
Selling price	$10	$30	$6
Variable cost	9	15	2
Units of capacity required per unit .	1	10	2
Units of capacity available	←————————200,000————————→		
Fixed cost	←————————$180,000————————→		
Market limitation	none	4,000	40,000

Required: (1) Find the best combination of products.
(2) What is the profit associated with your solution?
(3) Will an increase in fixed cost to $280,000 affect your choice of products?
(4) Will the increase in fixed cost described in (3) affect the profit? If so, why won't the choice of products be affected?

16–2. The Iona Company produces two products using a single production process where the only production constraint is machine hours. The economic data are given on the next page.

Required: (1) What is the best combination of products?
(2) Assume that the company thinks the demand for both products will hold up. Also, additional machines can be rented for $12,000 per year which

	Products	
	X	Y
Selling price	$7	$9
Variable cost	4	5
Machine hours per unit	1	2
Market limitation	50,000	100,000
Total machine hours available	←——200,000——→	
Total fixed cost	←——$150,000——→	

will provide an additional 15,000 hours of capacity per machine. How many additional machines should be ordered? Show calculations.

(3) If the rental on a machine is $5,000 per year instead of $12,000, how many should be ordered? Show calculations.

16–3. Harry Kranepool and Son install new kitchens, bathrooms, and plumbing and heating systems. In addition, they excavate and install sewer service lines to homes. Inasmuch as the city has recently put in sewers in the rapidly expanding suburbs, there has been a relatively large volume of business from this source. However, it has been difficult to obtain the services of men for the excavation work and to rent the equipment necessary for this type of work.

Last year, revenues of $153,000 were obtained from the installation of sewer service lines and connections. Labor costs amounted to $52,500 and other costs including the costs of equipment rental directly attributable to this work amounted to $105,000.

The firm has been wanting to discontinue this type of work. If this activity is discontinued, more time can be devoted to another line of activity that should yield additional revenue of $53,000 a year with additional costs of $29,000 a year.

However, other business may be lost if the sewer service lines are no longer installed. Often customers for sewer installation will remodel kitchens and bathrooms and have other plumbing work done. An analysis of past results shows that approximately $86,000 in additional revenue each year results from sewer installations. The cost to perform this work, not including any allocated costs, amounts to $57,000.

There is also the possibility that the sewer projects can be sublet to another firm, and the additional business that can be derived from this activity will not be lost. However, the cost to handle the volume of work done last year, if done by an outside contractor, would amount to $160,000.

Required: Which alternative is most attractive? What is the second best alternative? Show computations.

16–4. The Lappen Company produces two products in two different production processes. The economic data are given on the next page.

Required: (1) Using a graph find the best product combination. What is the contribution margin associated with this solution?

(2) It is possible to add capacity in Process 1 by renting additional facilities. The annual rental cost is $5,000 for each 10,000-hour addition. If capacity can be added only in 10,000-hour units, how much should the process be expanded? What is the contribution margin associated with your solution?

		Products	
	_A_	_B_
Selling price	$13	$18
Variable cost	9	12
Market limitation	200,000	200,000
Time required per unit—Process 1	2 hours	2 hours
Time required per unit—Process 2	3 hours	6 hours
Time available in Process 1	←——300,000 hours——→	
Time available in Process 2	←——600,000 hours——→	
Total fixed cost—both processes	←——$400,000——→	

(3) Would your answer to (2) be different if the cost of each 10,000-hour addition were $12,000 instead of $5,000?

16–5. Three lines of product are manufactured at the Green Falls Plant of Zachary Specialty Products Company. An operating statement for the plant for the year 1972, is given below:

Zachary Specialty Products Company
Green Falls Plant
Operating Statement
For the Year, 1972

	Total	Product 1	Product 2	Product 3
Sales	$705,000	$375,000	$180,000	$150,000
Variable manufacturing costs.	508,000	300,000	108,000	100,000
Contribution margin	$197,000	$ 75,000	$ 72,000	$ 50,000
Fixed costs	84,000	42,000	21,000	21,000
Net income from manufacturing	$113,000	$ 33,000	$ 51,000	$ 29,000
Number of units sold	—	15,000	12,000	5,000

The fixed manufacturing costs are incurred for the plant as a whole and have been apportioned to the product lines on the basis of the floor space devoted to the production of each line.

There are 20,000 machine hours of unused capacity available in the plant each year that may be utilized as desired for any combination of the three product lines. The machine time required for the production of each unit of each product line is given below:

Product 1—20 minutes   _Product 2—30 minutes_   _Product 3—1 hour_

The plant manager believes that some of this excess capacity can be absorbed if an additional $33,000 is spent to promote Product 1. He estimates that sales volume of this line can be increased by 100 percent with the additional sales promotion.

Demand for Product 3 has been decreasing over the years, and management plans to discontinue production of this line. A new product, Product 4, will be substituted in its place. Estimates of the market indicate that 40,000 units of this product line can be sold each year. The machine time for each unit manufactured has been estimated at 30 minutes. Each unit will be sold for $8, and the variable costs per unit will be $3. If the new line is introduced, the fixed costs for the year will be increased to $156,000.

Required: How much additional profit can be expected each year from the substitution of Product 4 for Product 3 and from increased sales volume of Product 1?

16–6. Dunbar Displays, Inc., manufactures and sells devices that display information drawn from remote-access computer banks. The field is very competitive, and new improved models are being developed and introduced by both Dunbar Displays, Inc., and other manufacturers.

Dunbar Displays, Inc., is currently selling a model for $180 that is manufactured at a cost of $130. Soon the company plans to introduce an improved model that will sell for $210 with an estimated cost of $170.

Plans have been made to delay introduction of the new model until the inventory of old models, consisting of 15,000 units, can be sold. It is estimated that 12,000 of these old models can be sold in the next six months if the new model is delayed. All unsold old models will have to be sold at a reduced price of $120 a unit when the new model comes out.

A forecast of sales indicates that there is a market for 20,000 units of the new device in the next six months if it is available within the next few weeks. Sales volume in the following six-month period can be expected to increase to 25,000 units. If the new model is introduced after the old models are sold, 6 months later, the estimate of sales for that six-month period is 12,000 units.

Required: Based on the information furnished, when should Dunbar Displays, Inc., introduce the new model? Show computations. Point out other factors that may be relevant to this decision.

16–7. Lattimore Construction Company, Inc., plans to erect an office building. It will use part of the space for its own offices and lease the balance of the space to tenants. The company has three alternatives, (1) do its own construction, (2) use the services of a subsidiary, or (3) use an independent contractor.

Cost estimates have been prepared for the next year showing costs *to operate* if the entire project is handled by the independent contractor and the costs *to operate* if the company decides to do the work itself. These costs are listed below:

	Estimated Costs to Operate, Construction by Independent Contractors	*Estimated Costs to Operate, Construction by Lattimore Company*
Materials	$4,870,000	$6,320,000
Labor	2,062,000	3,115,000
Indirect materials and supplies.	317,000	405,000
Supervision	623,000	787,000
Taxes and insurance	38,000	41,000
Heat and light	27,000	27,000
Maintenance and repairs	76,000	76,000
Truck and equipment operation	131,000	131,000
Depreciation	62,000	62,000

	Estimated Costs to Operate, Construction by Independent Contractors	Estimated Costs to Operate, Construction by Lattimore Company
Travel	$22,000	$25,000
Telephone	9,000	9,000
Other utilities	23,000	23,000
Miscellaneous	6,000	6,000

If the company does its own construction work, it will not be able to handle outside contracts that will contribute $600,000 to profits after income taxes according to estimates made by management. The costs attributable to these outside contracts are excluded from the estimated costs of operation.

If the second alternative is decided upon, the construction can also be done by a company in which 80 percent of the capital stock is owned by Lattimore Construction Company, Inc. This company has some idle capacity and can do the work without sacrificing profits from other jobs. The subsidiary company has bid $3,600,000 on the office building project. Included in the bid price is a provision for $800,000 in profits.

The independent company has bid $3,500,000 for the job.

Required: Which of the three alternatives should be selected to obtain the lowest construction cost? Show calculations. (Ignore income taxes.)

16–8. An industrial chemical that is used by other companies is manufactured and sold by Creighton Mills, Inc. Impurities must be removed in the processing operation, and the company is considering alternatives that will accomplish this at low cost. Under normal operating conditions 522,000 gallons of this chemical product are manufactured and sold each year.

At the present time, the company is using a refinery cracking process similar to the process used in refining petroleum. This process has been satisfactory, but it is considered relatively expensive. Also, there is a 10 percent loss of materials input when this method is employed. The materials cost 38 cents per gallon of input. Included in the total costs are the costs that will be incurred whether the refinery process is used or not. These costs amount to $52,000.

The product may also be purified in an adjoining plant by a chemical processing method. If the chemical processing method is employed, the refinery process will be discontinued. The materials required for the chemical process, however, will cost 42 cents per gallon of input; and to produce 522,000 gallons, it is estimated that 48,000 gallons of these materials will be lost. There is sufficient capacity available in the chemical plant to permit the purification of 522,000 gallons without interference with other production. Included in the total cost of the chemical process is $21,000 of allocated costs that will be incurred regardless of the processing method selected.

Still another alternative is available. The chemical can be processed by an electrolytic method in another division. Losses of materials can be reduced to 18,000 gallons a year. The materials must be high quality materials that cost 45 cents per gallon of input. The electrolytic process is currently being used to process other product lines. If it is to be used for this operation, it is estimated that the company will sacrifice $35,000 in profits each year that are derived from other product lines. Included in the total cost of the electrolytic process is $54,500 of allocated costs that will be incurred regardless of the processing method selected. If this processing method is selected, it will be used exclusively.

The costs of processing by each of the three methods are summarized below.

	Refinery	Chemical	Electrolytic
Operation 1	$17,800	$15,000	$19,000
Operation 2	38,000	33,800	47,000
Operation 3	63,000	18,000	42,800
Operation 4	16,000	23,000	–0–

Required: (1) Compute the total cost to purify this chemical product and the cost per 1,000 gallons under each of the three alternatives. Follow conventional cost accounting procedures.

(2) Determine the most economical processing alternative. Show total relevant costs for each alternative.

16–9. A part used in the assembly of a final product is manufactured by Holmes Tool Company in two operations. Ordinarily 150,000 parts are manufactured each year with total manufacturing costs as follows:

Operation 1:

Direct materials	$ 84,000
Direct labor	78,000
Variable costs of supplies and indirect materials	18,000
Allocated costs of plant occupancy	36,000
Total Operation 1	$216,000

Operation 2:

Direct labor	23,000
Variable costs of supplies and indirect materials	11,000
Allocated costs of plant occupancy	27,000
Total Operations 1 and 2	$277,000

Operation 1 can be eliminated if these parts are purchased from an outside supplier at a price of $1.10 per unit. The space used for Operation 1 can be rented for $6,000 a year. The parts purchased from an outside supplier will still have to be put through Operation 2. If the parts are purchased, Helena Tool Company must absorb the freight charges estimated at $15,000 a year.

Required: Should the parts be manufactured, or should they be purchased? Give computations to support your conclusion.

16–10. When Joel Hendricks, Inc., operates at normal capacity it manufactures 200,000 units of product at the Castle Shannon plant per year. The unit cost of manufacturing at normal capacity follows:

Direct materials	$ 7.80
Direct labor	2.10
Variable overhead	2.50
Fixed overhead	4.00
Product cost (per unit)	$16.40

Each unit of product is sold for $21 with variable selling and administrative expenses of 60 cents per unit of product.

During the next three months, only 10,000 units can be produced and sold. Management plans to shut down the plant, estimating that the fixed manufacturing overhead can be reduced to $74,000 for the quarter. When the plant is operating, the fixed overhead costs are incurred at a uniform rate throughout the year. Additional costs of plant shutdown for the three months are estimated at $14,000.

Required: (1) Should the plant be shut down for three months? Show computations.

(2) What is the shutdown point for three months in units of product?

16–11. The Massey Company produces a line of iron and steel building products. Several subassemblies and parts enter into the line of products, and many of these parts and components can be either produced by Massey or purchased from outside suppliers. Several of these parts are listed below with related cost data:

	Iron Frames 10	*Steel Frames 11*	*Steel Housing 12*	*Assembly Unit 13*
Material cost per unit	$1.00	$2.00	$10.00	$4.00
Variable labor per unit	1.50	1.00	5.00	2.50
Overhead (100% of labor) per unit ...	1.50	1.00	5.00	2.50
Total cost	$4.00	$4.00	$20.00	$9.00
Hour requirement	½	1	4	½

The above four parts can be produced or purchased. The plant facility is flexible in that the particular department involved can produce these parts in any combination. However, the main product in this department is a steel shaft that cannot be purchased on the outside. This shaft is used in most of the company's products and consequently has first priority on capacity.

The company wishes to establish a make or buy policy for the four parts listed above. The materials and the labor are considered to be variable costs, but the overhead, in total, is fixed. The overhead is assigned to products at the rate of 100 percent of direct labor. This rate is a predetermined rate established from the factory overhead budget.

The purchase price of the parts varies somewhat from month to month, depending on the available capacity of the outside producers.

Required: The controller of the company asks you to prepare a policy statement on this make or buy problem. The policy is to set forth the calculations and the comparisons that should be made. The controller also requests you to be specific on the treatment of fixed costs. Should they be included in the analysis when the department is operating near capacity and excluded when the department has much excess capacity? You are to resolve questions such as this.

16–12. Assume the same situation as in Problem 16-11. In addition, the capacity of the producing department is 500,000 machine hours and 80 percent of the capacity is to be used for producing shafts. The forecasted requirements and outside price quotations on the parts for the coming period are as follows:

Part Number	*Units Required*	*Outside Prices*
10	100,000	$ 3.00
11	80,000	4.50
12	15,000	20.00
13	100,000	6.25

Required: Use the policy established in Problem 16-11 to decide which parts should be produced and which should be purchased. Assume that, for any part, a portion of the requirement could be purchased.

Chapter 17

THE PRICING DECISION

Perhaps the most difficult potential decision faced by the businessman is the pricing decision. In some situations there is no pricing decision. For example, a market price may prevail so that a higher price will not be accepted and there is no incentive for charging a lower price. Agricultural products provide a good example. In these situations, the major problem is how much to produce. However, in situations where the decision maker does have some control over the price to be charged, there is a need for information on demand for the product as well as the cost of producing and selling it. This is in contrast to a decision problem where price is already determined and where the decision may turn largely on cost data. This is not to say that cost is easy and simple to determine; however, these cost data are usually more certain and more easily determined than the demand for the product at various prices.

In previous chapters, the following decision classification was found useful:

(1) How to produce.
(2) How much to produce.
(3) What combination of products to produce.

The pricing decision fits best in the second classification, the quantity of production. If the firm faces a given market-demand situation, this question is really a dual problem consisting of price and quantity. In previous chapters, it was assumed that the price of the product was given. Subject to this assumption, such questions as make or buy, retain or drop a product, and buy a new machine or keep the old one were considered. The decision in almost every case turned on the comparable costs involved. If the problem is broadened to raise the question of price as well as the method of production or combination of products, the answer is not entirely determined by cost. However, it is now time to assume that the best methods of production and sales have been determined and to investigate the problem posed in the second decision classification; that is, what price should be charged and what quantity should be produced and sold.

In this chapter several approaches to the pricing problem will be discussed. The role of accounting data in this decision will be examined in some detail. There will be no attempt to set forth *the* correct method of establishing price. The discussion will be largely devoted to: (1) finding useful methods of examining the pricing problem; (2) setting forth some of the characteristics of a good price decision; and (3) showing the role of accounting data in the pricing decision.

THE ECONOMICS OF THE PRICE DECISION

A substantial part of microeconomic theory is devoted to the pricing problem. It will be useful to review some of these economic theory concepts to help establish the analytical framework for the price decision and also to show the relationship between the economic models and the accounting incremental analysis discussed in previous chapters.

The best price, according to economic theory, is that price which gives the greatest positive difference between total revenues and total costs. The sales revenue possibilities from selling different quantities of product at different prices are set forth in the *demand or average revenue* function, an example of which appears in the diagram below:

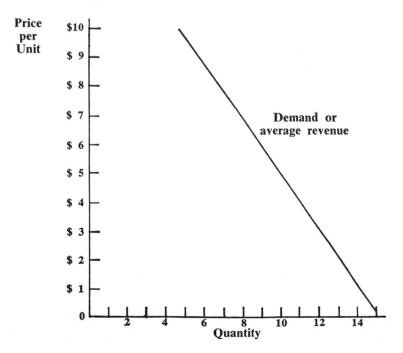

The selling price per unit is plotted on the vertical axis, and the quantity (in units) that can be sold at different prices is shown on the horizontal axis. The demand or average revenue line shows the functional relationship between price and the quantity that can be sold. For example, if a price of $3 is selected, 12 units can be sold at an average revenue of $3 per unit and a total revenue of $36. If a price of $5 is selected, ten units can be sold for a total revenue of $50. The price-quantity relationship given by this demand function is presented below in tabular form:

Price	Quantity	Total Revenue
$ 1	14 units	$14
2	13	26
3	12	36
4	11	44
5	10	50
6	9	54
7	8	56
8	7	56
9	6	54
10	5	50

In this example, the demand function is assumed to be linear (a straight line). This need not be the case. The demand function may be a curve. However, for simplicity, linear functions will be used throughout this chapter. The equation for the demand function used in the example is $Q = 15 - 1P$, where Q is quantity and P is price. When price is $10, the quantity demanded is five units. The slope of this demand function is constant and is equal to a -1, that is, quantity increases by one unit for every one-unit decrease in price. Again, it is not absolutely necessary that the quantity should vary inversely with price. However, for most goods and services this is the case and this relationship will be assumed throughout this chapter.

A demand function such as the one shown above is usually not easy to determine in a practical sense. Such a relationship can rarely, if ever, be estimated with certainty. However, it is really not a question of whether such an estimate is pertinent to the price decision; it is merely a question of how to make the required estimate so as to bring the demand considerations into proper focus. Even with data on product demand, the pricing decision is not completely solved. It can be seen that a price of $7 or $8 will maximize revenue; but usually the objective is to maximize total profits, not revenue. Consequently, it is necessary to consider the cost of the product as well as the revenue. The primary question involved here is to decide which cost is relevant and should be used.

Since fixed costs are fixed with respect to volume changes, net profits will be maximized when the contribution margin (excess of revenue over variable cost) is maximized. Therefore, the variable costs (costs that change as a result of volume changes) are the relevant costs insofar as the economic model is concerned. As a matter of fact, the point of maximum profit will occur where the cost of additional units is just equal to the additional revenue provided by the sale of these additional units. Beyond this point, when costs increase by more than the increase in revenue, there is a decrease in profits.

Price	Quantity	Total Revenue	Marginal Revenue
$10	5	$50	—
9	6	54	$ 4
8	7	56	2
7	8	56	0
6	9	54	— 2
5	10	50	— 4
4	11	44	— 6
3	12	36	— 8
2	13	26	—10
1	14	14	—12

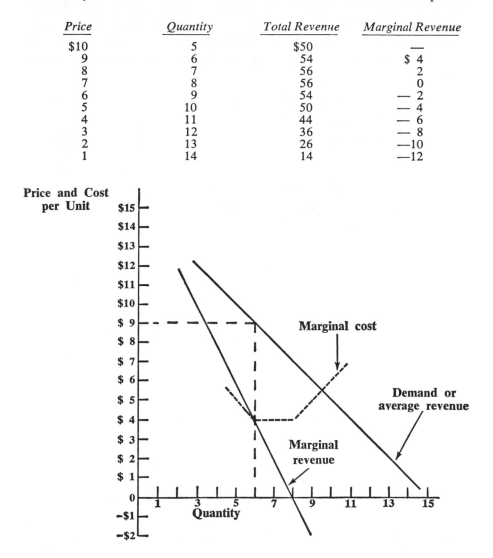

The last column of the above tabulation shows the additional revenue to be gained from selling one additional unit. This column is called the *marginal revenue*, which is defined as the increase in total revenue as a result of selling one additional unit of product. The term "marginal revenue" as used by the economist is not to be confused with "contribution margin" as used by the accountant. The former term means an increase in revenue, while the latter is the difference between revenue and variable cost. The contribution margin is a function of both revenue and cost, while marginal revenue is a function of revenue only. The marginal revenue relationship is plotted together with the demand function from which it was computed. Reading from either the diagram or the tabulation, it can be seen, for example, that selling six units instead of five will add $4 to total revenue. Hence, the marginal revenue of the sixth unit is $4. This calculation can be presented in another way as follows:

Selling price of the 6th unit	$9
Less: Decrease in revenue on the first 5 units:	
($10 — $9) × 5 units	5
Marginal revenue of the 6th unit	$4

Notice that the marginal revenue of the ninth unit is —$2. This is because the decrease in revenue on the first eight units is greater than the additional revenue of the ninth unit; that is:

Selling price of the 9th unit	$6
Less: Decrease in revenue on the first 8 units:	
($7 — $6) × 8	8
Marginal revenue of the 9th unit	—$2

Regardless of the cost situation, the firm should never push quantity to the point where marginal revenue is negative.

Assume that the cost situation facing the firm is as follows:

Units	Unit Marginal Cost
5	$5
6	4
7	4
8	4
9	5
10	6

The *marginal cost* is defined as the addition to total cost from producing one additional unit. Notice in the example that the unit marginal cost decreases from the fifth to the sixth unit, presumably because of increasing returns to scale or economies of mass production; that is, as output is increased, there is more opportunity for specialization of labor and other production factors, which results in cost economies. The marginal cost increases again with the ninth unit, presumably because of diminishing returns.

As shown in the following table, assuming the total cost of producing five units to be $30, maximum profit is achieved by selling six units:

Price	Quantity	Total Revenue	Unit Marginal Cost	Total Cost	Profit
$10	5	$50	$5	$30	$20
9	6	54	4	34	20
8	7	56	4	38	18
7	8	56	4	42	14
6	9	54	5	47	7
5	10	50	6	53	—3

The point of maximum profit is where marginal revenue and marginal cost are equal. As shown in the table, this occurs on the sixth unit, which adds $4 to total revenue and $4 to total cost. Actually, since marginal cost and marginal revenue of the sixth unit are *exactly* equal, this unit adds zero dollars to profit; hence, total profit would be just as great if five units are sold at $10 each as if six units are sold at $9 each. The seventh unit, however, adds only $2 to total revenue but $4 to total cost; hence, it should *not* be sold.

In accounting measurements, variable cost per unit is usually considered to be constant over the relevant volume range. This is in contrast to the economist's concept of marginal cost where marginal cost per unit is usually said to decrease because of increasing returns and then increase because of diminishing returns. In terms of a graph, this difference can be characterized by the difference between a curve and a horizontal line, as follows:

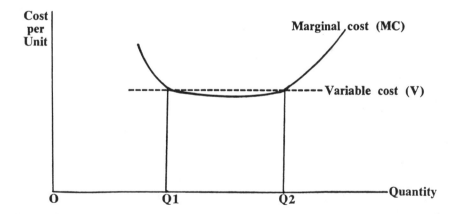

The MC curve shown above represents the marginal cost curve usually assumed by the economist. Over the volume range from O to Q1, the marginal cost per unit is assumed to decrease. The reason is that, as volume grows, the factory becomes more efficient costwise because of the opportunity to have specialization of labor and perhaps to adopt some mass production techniques. From Q1 to Q2, the marginal cost curve is fairly flat, indicating a constant marginal cost per unit. Eventually, however, if volume is expanded enough, the existing factory is no longer adequate; it becomes overcrowded and diminishing returns set in. At this point, marginal cost per unit begins to increase. Over the volume range from Q1 to Q2, it can be seen that the constant variable cost measurement (V) of the accountant is a good approximation of marginal costs. When these conditions exist, the same price and quantity decision will result from equating marginal costs and marginal revenue or variable costs and marginal revenue, as shown in the following graph:

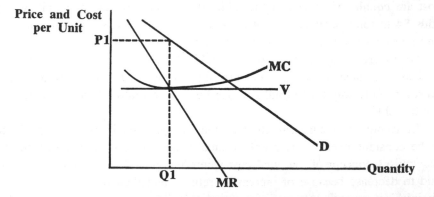

It can be seen that quantity Q1 and price P1 is the correct decision according to the marginal analysis model. This same result would be obtained by using variable costs V as an approximation of marginal costs, MC. This "flatness" characteristic of the marginal cost curve has been observed in several empirical industry and firm cost studies. Such studies lend support to the validity of the assumption of constant marginal or variable costs.

LIMITATIONS OF THE MARGINAL ANALYSIS MODEL

There are several obvious limitations and shortcomings to the marginal analysis pricing model. First of all, it is very difficult and costly to measure the variables required by the model. Estimates of demand and marginal revenue are usually filled with uncertainty. The necessary data for demand studies are difficult to isolate and frequently difficult to interpret. The measurement of marginal cost is perhaps not as difficult as demand because a fairly good approximation is usually available through accounting measurements of variable cost.

Another difficulty with the marginal analysis model (as it has been described) is that equating marginal cost and marginal revenue is a necessary but not a sufficient condition for maximizing profit. This problem is illustrated on the next page.

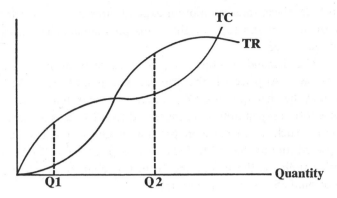

Total revenue and total cost have been plotted on the vertical axis. This is in contrast to the earlier examples where cost and price per unit were shown on the vertical axis. Since marginal revenue is the additional revenue (or change in revenue) from selling additional units, it can also be looked upon as the "slope" of the total revenue curve, TR. Likewise, marginal cost is the rate of change in total cost with respect to quantity and is the slope of the total cost curve, TC. To equate marginal cost and marginal revenue is to equate the slopes of the total revenue curve, TR, and the total cost curve, TC. These two slopes are equal at Q1 and Q2, but at Q1 total *loss* is maximized, and at Q2 total profit is maximized. Hence, for the economic marginal analysis model to give the desired results, it is necessary to be in that quantity range where the difference between total revenue and total cost is the largest in a positive sense. It is assumed in this chapter that this condition exists.

Another difficulty with the simplified model (as it has been presented) has to do with sales promotion effort such as advertising. Quantity is not simply a function of price alone. Quantity may be increased by additional sales promotion effort even though price is held constant. In order for this

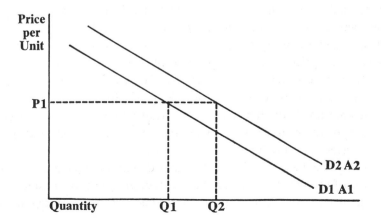

to take place, sales promotion expenditures must cause the demand curve to shift upward and to the right. This phenomenon is illustrated at the bottom of page 493.

The demand function, D1, assumes sales promotion expenditures are at level A1. At price P1, the firm can sell quantity Q1. At the same price, P1, it may be that quantity Q2, which is greater than Q1, can be sold if sales promotion expenditures are increased to A2 (A2 is assumed to be greater than A1). Such an increase in promotion effort might shift the demand curve upward and to the right (D2) so that price P1 will give quantity Q2. Since price policy is the main concern in this chapter it will be assumed that promotional efforts are held constant.

The simplified model also does not consider the possibility of retaliatory price actions by competitors. A price reduction in order to stimulate demand may result in further price reductions by competitors and lead to a price war. Such an occurrence may be quite undesirable even though the simple model indicated that the first price reduction was called for in order to equate marginal cost and marginal revenue. In this respect, the model is simply not complete enough to consider action by competitors.

In spite of these limitations, which any decision maker should be aware of, the model is useful because it does indicate some of the important ingredients in any price decision. Furthermore, the interaction of cost and revenue data is shown and some of the cost and revenue characteristics of a "good" price (that is, the maximum profit price) are set forth. The model is also useful in providing a standard by which to evaluate the role and the importance of various accounting cost analyses that may support the price decision.

PRICE BASED ON FULL COST

A method of pricing that is very widely used in business is the *markup* pricing method. In this method, the practice is to calculate a cost per unit and then to add a markup (which can be stated as a percentage of the cost) to arrive at the price. The basic purpose of the markup is to provide for a profit. It must be recognized that the term "cost" as used in this method is ambiguous until it is very carefully defined. In general, two different definitions are possible: the term could mean variable cost or full cost. In this section of the chapter full cost pricing will be discussed, and in a later section variable cost pricing will be discussed.

Probably the most widely used form of markup pricing is to base the markup on full cost; that is, the full cost of the unit is considered to be made up of the variable cost plus some allocated share of the fixed cost.

The full cost is then used as the basis for setting price, usually by adding some percentage markup.

The fixed cost problem. The proper treatment of fixed costs presents a problem in full cost pricing. Assume that the firm produces only one product and that the cost structure is as follows:

Variable raw materials cost $5
Variable direct labor cost 3
Total variable cost $8
Fixed annual overhead and other expenses $100,000

This information is highly simplified, but the problem of fixed cost in full cost pricing can be illustrated.

In order to determine the full cost of the unit, it is necessary to select a specific number of units over which to allocate the fixed cost. The relationship between unit fixed cost and volume is plotted below:

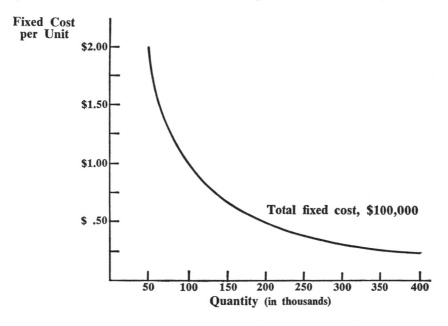

As can be seen, the fixed cost per unit decreases as the number of units increases. In an earlier discussion of job order and process cost accounting, it was pointed out that the number of units at normal volume is typically used as a basis upon which to spread the fixed cost. If the firm has a price policy of marking up 10 percent based on full cost, the following prices are possible depending on the decision as to volume:

	Number of Units (In Thousands)					
	50	100	150	200	250	300
Variable cost	$ 8.00	$8.00	$8.00	$8.00	$8.00	$8.00
Fixed cost per unit ...	2.00	1.00	.67	.50	.40	.33
Total full cost	$10.00	$9.00	$8.67	$8.50	$8.40	$8.33
10% markup	1.00	.90	.87	.85	.84	.83
Selling price	$11.00	$9.90	$9.54	$9.35	$9.24	$9.16

If the decision maker selects 200,000 units as the number of units over which to spread the fixed cost, the profit (markup) per unit is stated to be 85 cents. However, the profit will not be 85 cents per unit and it will not be $170,000 for the year (200,000 units × $.85) if some number of units other than 200,000 units is actually sold. For example, if only 100,000 units are sold, the profit will be only $35,000, as follows:

Revenue (100,000 × $9.35)		$935,000
Variable cost (100,000 × $8)	$800,000	
Fixed cost	100,000	900,000
Profit		$ 35,000

The difference in the profit per unit between 85 cents and 35 cents ($35,000 ÷ 100,000 units) is accounted for by the fact that the fixed cost per unit based on 100,000 units is $1 and not 50 cents as stated for 200,000 units.

It may be argued that the demand situation can be considered explicitly in choosing the number of units over which to spread the fixed cost. This may be a possibility, but this policy may also be in conflict with the selection of *normal* volume as it is used in job order and process cost accounting. It must be remembered that normal volume and expected volume for next year are not necessarily the same. Normal volume is usually looked upon as an average volume based on several years. If normal volume is used, the result should be a very stable price almost without regard for changes in the business cycle. Perhaps this is desirable; but, on the other hand, there is less chance that the price will be adapted to changes in business conditions.

Another difficulty with trying to use either expected volume or normal volume for spreading fixed cost is that the number of units to be sold depends on the price, and it is the price that is being determined. Hence, any attempt to consider the demand situation in establishing the full cost of the product is likely to involve circular reasoning. The demand situation must be considered in setting the price, but the fact remains that full cost pricing does not offer a very good means of considering this variable. In any particular situation, however, it may be that no other pricing method will give any better result than full cost pricing. It is usually easier to criticize a pricing method than to recommend one that is better.

The allocation problem. Another major problem is encountered in full cost pricing when two or more products are produced. How should the common costs be allocated? Although the allocation problem has been investigated in some detail in previous chapters, it will be reviewed here with respect to full cost pricing. The earlier discussions were primarily concerned with the cost allocation problem as it affects cost accounting systems where the data are used primarily for inventory valuation and income determination. However, the problem is much the same as that encountered in pricing. The reason for this is that the full cost data developed in cost accounting will probably be the same data used in full cost pricing. At the very least, the cost accounting data will furnish the starting point in calculating a full cost figure for pricing purposes.

Assume that the firm produces two products, A and B, and that the cost structure is as follows:

	Product A	Product B
Variable labor cost	$7	$3
Variable material cost	2	3
Overhead and other indirect annual		
expenses	$200,000	

This example is highly simplified so as to focus on the allocation problem. The $200,000 common cost will probably be made up of several different individual types of costs such as machine depreciation, indirect labor, insurance, and various selling and administrative expenses. In allocating these costs to the two products, perhaps the first step should be to separate and regroup those costs that are fairly homogeneous. For example, all indirect costs related to machine operations, such as machine depreciation and repairs, might be totaled. However, even after this type of regrouping, the individual cost items in any particular group will still not be entirely homogeneous and hence any method of allocation chosen is likely to be a compromise and will be open to criticism. Assume, for example, that the $200,000 indirect cost in the example is the cost incurred to operate the factory manager's office. Should this cost be allocated on the basis of direct labor hours, direct labor cost, raw materials cost, or some other base that might be chosen from a long list of allocation methods? The full cost and, therefore, the price will be affected by the allocation base chosen. For simplicity, assume that the volume of each product is equal. If labor cost is chosen, $140,000 (7/10 × $200,000) of the indirect cost will be assigned to Product A; whereas if materials cost is to be the base, only $80,000 (2/5 × $200,000) will be assigned to Product A. In addition to the problem of *how* to allocate the indirect costs, it must be remembered that the allocation process itself can involve a high clerical cost in cases where the cost and product structure is a complicated one.

The basis of allocation. In choosing the basis of allocation for inventory costing and income determination, it is possible to use the criterion of "benefit" received by the product; that is, the problem of allocating overhead costs to product is essentially the same as allocating depreciation or any long-term asset cost to time periods. In general, accountants try to allocate these common costs according to the benefit received by the unit of costing (in this case the products) from the incurrence of the cost. The argument is frequently made that machine-related overhead costs should be assigned to the product on the basis of machine time but that labor-related overhead should be assigned on the basis of labor hours. Why? Because the basis of allocation chosen in this fashion provides a fairly good means of allocating costs according to the benefit received by the various products. A product that uses more labor hours will bear a greater portion of the labor-related overhead, while a product that uses more machine time will bear a greater portion of the machine-related overhead.

The question arises, however, as to whether or not the benefit criterion provides a good basis of allocation if the cost data are to be used in setting prices. This is not an easy question to answer. It is sometimes argued that full cost pricing should give a *fair* price that will assure the firm of social approval of the pricing scheme. If this argument is valid, perhaps the allocation of common costs according to the benefit criterion is an acceptable basis for determining full cost and thus, price. It would seem that the businessman could publicly defend such a price, if required. However, in seeking a price that will provide the greatest positive difference between revenue and costs, it is difficult to see how the dual problems of cost allocation and choosing the volume over which to spread the fixed cost can be satisfactorily solved.

Adjusting the full cost. Even if the above-mentioned cost problems can be solved to the satisfaction of the decision maker, there are still some difficult decisions to be made before the full cost price can be established. First, there is the question of what markup to use. The markup may be stated as a percentage of the full cost or it may be based on the capital investment necessary to produce and sell the product. Perhaps the amount of the markup will be an expression of the businessman's feelings as to a fair or satisfactory profit to be earned on the sale of the product. More appropriately, it should be a reflection of the businessman's feelings of the markup necessary to give the maximum-profit price. Such a price does not imply cheating, profiteering, or other unethical business practices. It is simply an attempt to maximize long-run profits, which must be done within the bounds of public acceptance, government restrictions, and other sound ethical business practices.

Once the decision maker has solved the cost problems and has decided on a markup, the resulting price may still have to be adjusted. The first full cost price figure will generally be used as a first approximation. The price may be considered too high to meet competition. In such a case, some intuitive downward adjustment will take place. In other cases, the price may be adjusted up or down to fit into customary price lines that exist within the industry—for example, a $6.98 sport shirt.

The wide acceptance of full cost pricing. In spite of all of the above-mentioned difficulties, the full cost pricing method, which is filled with intuitive judgments, problems of cost allocation, and a general lack of rigor, is very widely used in modern-day business. What are some of the reasons for this widespread acceptance?

A set of reasons often given has to do with the inability of the businessman to quantify the variables called for by the marginal analysis model. If it is impossible to measure demand satisfactorily, perhaps the best way to price is to arrive at a full cost and then make an intuitive judgment as to markup in hopes that the resulting price will fit the decision maker's conception of the market. Also, it is probably easier to carry out a predetermined scheme of cost allocation than it is to feel comfortable with many measurements of variable or marginal cost. However, this sort of reasoning is like losing a dollar up the block but looking for it down the street where the street light provides better light! The real question is not whether full cost measurements are easier to make, but whether such measurements are relevant to the decision.

The full cost price has been referred to as a "safe" price. Perhaps there is a greater desire to prevent large losses than to achieve maximum profits. If businessmen are motivated toward a satisfactory profit that will minimize the chance of large losses, perhaps the full cost price will produce a more stable price and thus avoid the hazards of disastrous price wars. To the extent that full cost pricing is widely adopted in the industry and to the extent that industry-wide uniform cost accounting systems prevail, the desire for a stable price will probably become a reality. Also, it is true that all costs must be covered in the long run if the firm is to survive. There is no guarantee that full cost pricing will accomplish these objectives, but on the other hand it is difficult to construct a method of pricing that can be guaranteed.

VARIABLE COST PRICING

Another approach to cost-plus-a-markup pricing is to use the variable cost rather than the full cost as the cost base. One major advantage of this approach is that some of the difficult problems of indirect cost allocation and the spreading of fixed cost can be avoided. However, in order to exploit the advantages of the variable cost approach, it is necessary to have a reasonably accurate estimate of the demand situation. If such an estimate is available and if the variable cost approach is used, it may be possible to arrive at a price that will approach a maximum profit position. At the very least, such a procedure may consider more of the pertinent factors of a price decision than does the full cost approach.

Distress and special-order pricing. The argument has frequently been made that variable cost pricing should be used only in pricing a special order at a special price or in a distress situation. For example, assume that the firm has excess capacity and has the opportunity to sell additional units of product in a foreign market or in an isolated sector of a domestic market. Any price above the variable cost of these additional units will yield a contribution to fixed cost and hence will increase total profits.

The dumping or special-order situation can be illustrated as follows. Assume that the company, whose capacity is 100,000 units, is currently producing and selling only 90,000 units of product each year in the regular market at a price of $1 per unit. If the variable cost per unit is 50 cents and the annual fixed cost is $30,000, the income statement is as follows:

Income Statement

Sales (90,000 × $1)		$90,000
Cost:		
Variable cost (90,000 × $.50)	$45,000	
Fixed cost	30,000	75,000
Net income		$15,000

The full cost of the units is $.833 each ($75,000 ÷ 90,000 units). A foreign jobber approaches the company with an order for 10,000 units at 60 cents each. *If sales in the foreign market will not affect the regular market,* the company can add to total profit by accepting the special order even though the price is $.233 below the full cost ($.833 − $.60). At a price of 60 cents, the order will contribute 10 cents per unit toward fixed cost, and profit will increase by $1,000 (10,000 units × $.10). In such a case, the variable costs of 50 cents may provide a better guide to action than the full cost. This same result can be seen through the comparative income statements shown at the top of the next page.

500

	Income Statement Based on 90,000 Units	Income Statement Based on 100,000 Units
Sales (90,000 at $1.00) ..	$90,000	$90,000
(10,000 at .60) ..		6,000
	$90,000	$96,000
Costs:		
Variable cost at $.50 per unit	$45,000	$50,000
Fixed cost	30,000	30,000
	$75,000	$80,000
Net Income	$15,000	$16,000

The above example illustrates why some firms will make price concessions in periods of large excess capacity. However, the policy of accepting "special orders at special prices" is generally a good policy *only* when the special market can be kept separate from the regular market, and this is a marketing, not a cost, problem. For example, in the above illustration, assume that the foreign (special) market begins to affect the regular market to the extent that the price in the regular market drops from $1 per unit to 60 cents per unit. In this case, the firm's income statement for the next period would appear as follows:

Income Statement

Sales (100,000 × $.60)		$60,000
Cost:		
Variable cost (100,000 × $.50)	$50,000	
Fixed cost	$30,000	$80,000
Net loss		($20,000)

As can be seen, if the special market price takes over the regular market, the profit will decrease from $15,000 to a *loss* of $20,000 rather than increasing to $16,000. If the line of demarcation between the foreign and the domestic market cannot be maintained, then the lower price is bound to dominate, and the special order pricing policy would be a poor policy for the firm to follow. This problem has led some people to criticize the use of variable cost as a basis for establishing prices. Of course, any pricing policy can lead to poor results if the decision maker fails to properly assess the market considerations. The problem lies not in the fact that variable instead of full cost was used; rather, the root of the trouble is that the market conditions were not properly assessed.

Sometimes variable cost pricing is felt to be more appropriate when the sales are beyond the break-even point than when sales are below the break-even point.

For example, assume as in the previous illustration, that the selling price of the product is $1 per unit, the variable cost is 50 cents, the fixed cost is $30,000, and the capacity is 100,000 units. The break-even point is 60,000 units. It might be contended that only after a sales volume of 60,000 units is reached is it appropriate to use special order or variable cost pricing. This contention is, of course, a fallacy. First, special-order pricing is not wise unless there is unused capacity. Why lower the price if production is at full capacity? Assuming excess capacity does exist, the firm will be $1,000 better off by accepting 10,000 units of additional business at 60 cents per unit if current sales are 50,000 units (below the break-even point) just as if the current sales are 90,000 units (above the break-even point). In the former case, the loss will be reduced from $5,000 to $4,000, while in the latter case profits will increase from $15,000 to $16,000. Of course, if the special market price takes over the regular market, the firm will suffer a decrease in profit (or an increase in loss) regardless of what current volume is in relation to the break-even point. The appropriateness of variable cost pricing depends not so much on the volume position with respect to the break-even point, but rather on whether the regular market and the special market can be kept separate.

Even if the special market can be isolated from the regular market, and even if the special order is the most profitable use of the firm's excess capacity, there is an important legal consideration to be taken into account.

From a legal standpoint, the company must be careful not to violate the Robinson-Patman Act, a federal antitrust law that relates to price discrimination between customers. This law makes it essential that the firm be able to justify a discriminatory price between customers if the effect is to lessen competition. If these above-mentioned legal and economic conditions can be satisfied, then variable cost pricing is probably appropriate in a special-order or dumping situation.

Regular products. It is possible to build a pricing procedure for regular products using variable cost as a base. It is usually argued that variable cost is not appropriate in this situation. The use of variable cost pricing is frequently associated with a crisis situation. The presumed crisis in most cases is chronic overcapacity. Such an association is probably unfortunate, because a careful study of variable cost pricing will give additional insights into the pricing problem. The variable cost method is not a cure-all; but although not widely accepted in business circles, it has many features that should be given recognition in setting prices.

If variable cost is used, the markup that is added must be large enough to cover all fixed cost and also large enough to provide for a profit. There is always the danger that the variable cost may, in time, come to be looked upon as the full cost, and in such instances the results may be disastrous. The fear of this happening is probably the main reason for the low acceptance of variable cost pricing in modern-day business. This problem, however, should not arise if the operating management properly understands the kind of data they are working with. The misuse of cost data that stems from a lack of understanding is a problem throughout accounting and is not unique with variable cost pricing. Education in the proper use of cost data can do much to overcome such a defect.

Probably another reason why variable cost pricing is not widely accepted has to do with the inability of many conventional accounting systems to measure variable cost properly. Most systems are not geared for this type of measurement, and a careful review of job order and process costing will provide convincing evidence that this is the case. The historical reason for this situation is probably the overwhelming influence that inventory costing and income determination have had on cost systems. It was felt (and still is) that full cost is the most acceptable base for income determination. This follows from the postulate in accounting that requires revenue to be recognized only when it is realized. The realization postulate implies inventory valuation at cost. The benefit principle also reinforces the valuation of inventory at full cost. In years gone by, perhaps it was clerically impossible to measure both full cost and variable cost, and for that matter the measurement of variable or incremental cost presented some real difficulties. However, the computer and data processing people make the claim today that it is possible to measure almost any incremental quantity that is of use to management. To the extent that this is possible, variable cost pricing may be more operational now than it has been in the past.

One of the important advantages to be gained from a detailed investigation of variable cost pricing (for regular products) is a deeper knowledge of the relationship between the markup percentage and the market demand function. In pricing policy, even if cost (whether it be a full or variable cost) can be determined, it is still necessary to add the markup in order to establish a price. If the markup is too high, the price will be too high and the firm may price itself out of the market. If the markup is too low, the firm will charge too low a price and will forego profits. Hence, the proper markup is related to the market situation.

OUTSIDE INFLUENCES ON PRICE

Throughout this chapter the general assumption was made that the company had some control over its prices and that the object was to maximize profits. Frequently a company will be virtually forced to accept prices already established by its competitors or will find it necessary to adjust its prices because of the action of others. In some cases the price will not be set so that short-run profits will be maximized. It may be better strategy in the long run to accept more modest profits and not to attract attention that may result in the entry of others into the field. Such a strategy is an attempt to maximize long-run rather than short-run profits.

By making a study of its costs and the factors that influence the demand for its products, a company can establish prices more intelligently than if either of these factors is ignored. Outside forces may make it difficult to set prices that will tend to result in maximum profits; but with a knowledge of its price objectives, a company should be better prepared to take advantage of changing conditions.

Questions

1. What is a demand or average revenue function?

2. Graph the demand function, $Q = 10 - .5P$, where Q is quantity and P is price.

3. Why will net profit be maximized when contribution margin is maximized?

4. Define "marginal revenue." Calculate the marginal revenue for units two through seven in the demand function given in Question 2 above.

5. Briefly explain two of the limitations of the marginal analysis pricing model as it is discussed in the chapter.

6. "The proper treatment of fixed costs presents a problem in full cost pricing." Explain briefly.

7. Describe the "allocation" problem encountered in full cost pricing.

8. In what sense (if at all) is a full cost price a "safe" price?

9. What are the major considerations in deciding whether or not variable cost pricing is a good pricing procedure to use on *special* orders.

10. Assuming the decision maker has a good measure of cost (both fixed and variable), would pricing still be a difficult problem? Explain.

Exercises

1. Assume the demand function is $Q = 20 - 2P$ where Q is quantity and P is price. If marginal cost *per unit* is constant and is $5, what quantity will maximize profit? Show your calculation.

2. The Abel Company sells a product which has a total variable cost of $18 per unit and a selling price of $23. Fixed cost is $300,000. Show that if total contribution margin is maximized, profits will also be maximized. Assume volume levels of 80,000 and 100,000 units.

3. The Jon Company follows the policy of calculating selling price by adding a 10 percent markup to full cost. The variable cost is $15 per unit and the total fixed cost is $500,000. Calculate the selling price per unit for 50,000 units, 60,000 units, 80,000 units, and 100,000 units assuming that fixed costs are allocated to units based on the number produced.

4. The Classic Company produces Products A and B, whose costs and other production data are given below.

	A	B
Variable materials costs	$5	$10
Direct labor hours required	3	4
Hourly labor rate	$2	$ 2
Fixed overhead	←$360,000→	
Units produced	20,000	30,000

If the markup based on full cost is 25 percent, what prices would be charged if overhead is allocated based on (1) labor hours or (2) raw materials cost?

5. The Ryan Company estimates the demand function for a certain product to be $Q = 25 - 5P$ where Q is quantity and P is price. The variable cost of the product is uncertain and is estimated at either $1.50 or $2.

Advise the company of the appropriate prices to charge at each cost level. Also advise the company on the percentage markup based on variable cost which would give the appropriate price for each cost level.

6. The ABC Company markets a product which has a selling price of $25, a variable cost per unit of $15, and fixed costs associated with the operation of $200,000. At the $25 price, the current demand is 30,000 units. The sales manager estimates that if the price were reduced $2 per unit the company could sell 2,000 more units per year.

Required: (1) Should the company drop the price?
(2) How much would sales have to increase in order to make the price cut attractive?

7. The Brewer Company is currently selling 100,000 units of a product at $21 per unit. The variable cost of a unit is $17, and the annual fixed cost is $300,000. The company has been approached by a foreign buyer who will buy 50,000 units (Brewer Company's production capacity is 150,000 units), but will pay a price of only $18.50. Should the Brewer Company accept the order? How would your decision be affected if it became clear that the foreign and the domestic markets could not be kept separated?

8. The Lane Company markets a product which sells for $15 and has a variable cost of $13. The fixed cost is $100,000. The 1972 sales estimate was for 200,000 units. Based on this estimate, the controller calculates profit per unit as follows:

Selling price per unit		$15.00
Cost:		
Variable	$13.00	
Fixed $\dfrac{(\$100,000)}{(200,000 \text{ units})}$	.50	13.50
Profit per unit		$ 1.50

The actual sales for 1972 were 150,000 units, and the profit was $200,000.

The president of the Lane Company reasons that if profit per unit is $1.50 and sales are 150,000 units, the total profit should be $225,000 (i.e. $1.50 × 150,000).

Required: Explain to the president (show calculations) why the reported profit is $200,000 and not $225,000.

9. The May Company is currently selling 50,000 units of an electronic tube at a price of $20. The tube has a variable cost of $10, and the annual fixed costs are $200,000. The capacity of the factory is 50,000 units per year.

The opportunity exists for the company to phase out this tube and to produce an electronic subassembly which would use the same production facilities. Hence, the fixed costs will be the same regardless of which product is produced. The variable cost of the subassembly is estimated at $25 per unit. The company is uncertain about what price to charge and what the demand possibilities will be for the new product. The nature of the market is such that both products cannot be sold at the same time. Hence, the company must choose one or the other. A feasible range of price for the new subassembly is thought to be $50 to $70. No more than 20,000 subassemblies can be produced at full capacity.

Required: Calculate how many subassemblies would have to be sold at prices of $50, $55, $60, $65, and $70 per unit in order for the subassembly to be as profitable as the tube. How would this information aid the management in the decision?

10. The owner of a neighborhood grocery store is comparing notes with the manager of a supermarket. The neighborhood grocer observes that his "profit as a percentage of sales" is 20 percent. The supermarket manager, expressing amazement at the size of this percentage, observes that his profit percentage is only 5 percent. Further comparison reveals that the sales of the grocer are one tenth those of the supermarket (which are $2,000,000 per year).

Required: Do the two profit percentages necessarily indicate that the supermarket is less profitable than the neighborhood grocery? In your answer, assume that the owner's investment in the grocery store is $100,000, while the comparable investment in the supermarket is $200,000. In what sense is the profit percentage (based on sales) a reflection of the pricing policy chosen by each store?

Problems

17–1. The Russell Company produces a product sold by salesmen to retailers who in turn sell to the consumer. The present selling price is $20 per unit and the cost structure is as follows:

Variable Cost:	*Cost per Unit*
Materials	$ 6
Labor	4
Commissions (10%)	2
	$12

Total fixed cost	$600,000
Sales volume	300,000 units

Two alternative plans for increasing sales are being considered:

(1) Reduce the selling price by 10 percent, but keep commissions at $2.
(2) Increase the sales commission from 10 percent to 30 percent, but keep the same selling price.

Management believes that either plan would increase sales, but is uncertain how much the increase would be.

Required: Using profit-volume analysis and a profit-volume graph, help management decide what the implications of the two alternatives are on the profit picture. Try to structure your analysis to aid management in the decision.

17–2. The Stevens Company currently sells three products whose quantity, selling price, and variable costs are given below:

Product	Quantity	Selling Price	Variable Cost
110	5,000	$15	$14
111	10,000	16	10
112	15,000	25	18

The fixed costs for the operation are $120,000 and are allocated on the basis of the total units produced. The plant is currently at capacity and each unit requires the same production time. The cost report for Product 110, given below, shows that this product is a "loser."

Selling price		$15
Variable cost	$14	
Fixed cost	4	18
Loss		($ 3)

The fixed cost per unit is calculated by dividing the total fixed cost, $120,000, by the units produced, 30,000.

The above report causes the sales manager to argue that Product 110 should be dropped from the product line. He argues that it is difficult to "make up on volume what is lost on the individual unit."

Required: (1) If no alternative exists for the use of capacity, should Product 110 be dropped?

(2) If more of Product 111 can be sold at $16 per unit, should Product 110 be dropped?

(3) How much would the selling price of Product 110 have to be raised to make it as desirable as Product 111?

(4) Does the fixed cost have any relevance to any of the above questions?

17–3. Assume the same situation as in Problem 17–2 above, except that if Product 110 is dropped, no additional units of Products 111 or 112 can be sold.

The sales manager, in searching around, finds another product, 113, which can be sold for $10.00 and has a variable cost of $9.75 but it takes only one third the time to produce 113 as it does to produce 110.

The sales manager argues that 113 should be added and 110 should be dropped. He says, "It's true that the margin per unit is 75 cents less on 113 than on 110 (25 cents compared with $1), but since more units of 113 can be produced the fixed cost per unit will also go down. As a matter of fact, the fixed cost per unit on all units will drop by $1—from $4 ($120,000/30,000 units) to $3 ($120,000/40,000 units)—if we switch to Product 113."

Required: Is the sales manager right? How much would the price on 113 have to be increased before it would be as profitable as 110? Explain to the sales manager the error in his reasoning.

17–4. A company is currently producing and selling two products, X and Y. The date on costs, selling prices, and volume are given below:

	X	Y
Selling price	$10	$15
Variable costs—labor and materials	7	9
Fixed overhead costs allocated to products	4	4
Units sold	10,000	30,000

The total fixed overhead is $160,000 per year and is allocated equally since each product requires equal production time. Product Y requires a higher-priced raw material which explains why the variable cost of this product is higher than for Product X.

A major company in the industry is looked on as a price leader. Most of the smaller companies follow its actions on price setting. Recently this company has reduced the price on Product X to $9.00. The sales manager and president of the company are attempting to determine what to do in response to this action. The sales manager estimates that if the price on Product X is held at $10, sales will probably decline to 6,000 units. If the company follows the price decrease and reduces the price of X to $9, the sales manager estimates that volume can be maintained at 10,000 units. However, the sales manager notes that the loss on Product X is already $1.00 at the selling price of $10.00. He suggests to the president that the product be dropped entirely. Such an action would provide unused capacity since no more units of Y can be sold and there is no substitute product immediately available. Whatever is done, argues the sales manager, the price on Product X should not be reduced to $9 since the action will only increase the loss per unit from $1 to $2.

Required: Advise the president on what he should do. Show your calculations.

17–5. The Morgan Company produces a main product, Product M, and a by-product, Product B, from a common raw material which costs $30 per ton. Since the production process is fully automated, there is no direct labor cost. The fixed cost of the production facility is $120,000 per year, which includes indirect labor cost of $50,000. A ton of raw material will produce 2 units of M and 1 unit of B. It is possible to vary the proportions of M and B so as to produce no units of M and 3 units of B, but no other variations are possible.

The company has been operating at full capacity, processing 10,000 tons of raw material and producing 20,000 units of M and 10,000 units of B. Product M sells for $20 per unit. This selling price is set in a competitive market and the company can sell all the units it can produce. The price of B has been set at $15.40 per unit, as calculated on the next page. (Costs are allocated to all units equally.)

During the past two years, the company has been able to sell all units of M, but only 2,000 units per year of B. Hence, the inventories of B have been

	Product B
Raw material cost:	
$30 per ton ÷ 3 units	$10.00
Other cost—fixed:	
$120,000 ÷ 30,000 units	4.00
Total cost	$14.00
Markup 10%	1.40
Selling price	$15.40

building up. Since Product B deteriorates rapidly, units carried over from one year to the next are worthless.

The sales manager, in analyzing the situation, feels that the cost allocation system currently in use allocates too much cost to Product B. This, in turn, results in too high a price for Product B. He says that if the price of B is dropped to $10, the company could sell 10,000 units per year. Information he has gathered from major customers tends to confirm his estimate.

The sales manager recommends that the cost be allocated according to selling value and presents the following calculation:

	Product M	*Product B*
Raw material cost of $30:		
* 40% for unit of M	$12.00	
20% for unit of B		$6.00
Other costs of $120,000:		
Sales of M = 20,000 × $20		
= $400,000		
Sales of B = 10,000 × $10		
= $100,000		
Sales value $500,000		
$120,000/$500,000 = $.24 per dollar of sales		
Product M: $.24 × $20	4.80	
Product B: $.24 × $10		2.40
	$16.80	$8.40

* 80% of the $30 is allocated to Product M. Two units of M are produced for each unit of B produced, thus, *each* unit of M has 40% of the raw material cost allocated to it.

The sales manager contends that this calculation shows that Product B is profitable at a $10 selling price and that B is just as profitable as M since the markup on costs are equal, as shown below. He argues, therefore, that the company could be just as profitable producing all B as it would be producing 20,000 units of M and 10,000 units of B.

	Product M	*Product B*
Price	$20.00	$10.00
Cost	16.80	8.40
Profit	$ 3.20	$ 1.60
Markup on cost	3.20/16.80 = 19% *	1.60/8.40 = 19% *

* Rounded.

He indicates that the company could probably sell as many as 30,000 units of B at $10.

Required: (1) In order to sell product B before it becomes worthless, should the Morgan Company reduce the price to $10?

(2) Would the company be as profitable producing only product B as it is with its present product combination? (Show computations.) If not, what is wrong with the sales manager's analysis?

17-6. The Amos Company has been selling a product at $12. The selling price, based on cost, was arrived at as follows:

Variable materials and labor cost per unit	$ 6
Fixed general overhead allocated to product	4
Total cost	$10
Markup—20% of cost	2
Selling price	$12

The controller estimates that $1 of the $4 fixed overhead is the depreciation cost of the machine used to manufacture the product. This machine has now been fully depreciated on the books, and the controller suggests that the price be dropped to reflect this reduction in cost. His calculation is as follows:

Variable materials and labor cost per unit	$ 6.00
Fixed general overhead allocated to profit	3.00
Total cost	$ 9.00
Markup—20% of cost	1.80
Selling price	$10.80

At the $12 price, the company has been selling 10,000 units and at the lower price it is estimated that 11,000 units can be sold.

Required: (1) Should the price be reduced?

(2) Comment on the controller's argument for reducing the price since the machine is now fully depreciated.

17-7. The Corwin Company produces a limited line of metal containers that are used to store and ship certain chemical compounds. The capacity of the plant is 400,000 labor hours and it takes an average of four hours to produce one container. For the last few years, the company has been producing about 90,000 containers per year, but the prospects for the coming year look very bright. Several new industrial plants have recently located in the area, and the company management believes that the excess capacity can now be used. The average price of the standard container is $100 per unit and the cost structure is as follows:

	Cost per Unit
Materials	$50
Labor	30
Overhead	10
Total	$90

The materials and the labor are considered to be variable costs. The overhead in total is fixed and is allocated to product on the basis of hours. The rate is established as shown on the following page.

$$\frac{\text{Estimated overhead}}{\text{Hours of capacity}} \quad \frac{\$1,000,000}{400,000} = \$2.50 \text{ per hour}$$

The price of $100 per standard container is now fairly well established within the industry. The company set this price by adding to the full cost a profit of $10 per unit.

The company has been approached by a contracting officer for the government to build 10,000 special containers. The materials cost has been estimated to be about $5 lower per unit than on standard containers and the labor time will be about the same. The sales manager has calculated the following price for the contracting officer:

Materials	$45
Labor	30
Overhead	10
	$85
Markup (4 hours @ 2.50)	10
Price	$95

The contracting officer in reviewing the calculation, notices that the markup based on cost for the special container ($10/$85 = 11.8 percent) is higher than for the standard container ($10/$90 = 11.1 percent). He argues that the price on the special container should be reduced so as to make the special container no more profitable than the standard container.

Required: Assuming that the company wants to set the special container price to make it no more profitable than the standard container, is the $95 price appropriate? If not, what price should be charged? If so, explain to the contracting officer why his reasoning with respect to the markup percentage is incorrect.

17–8. The Spectre Company manufacturers a type of raw sheet metal that can be sold at this stage or that can be processed more and sold as a type of alloy used in manufacturing high-grade control systems of various types. The raw sheet metal market is such that the entire output can be sold at the market price, which at the present time is $100 per ton. The processed selling price has been about $180 per ton for several years, but recently the market has been weak and the price has dropped as low as $140 on several occasions. This has caused the sales manager to suggest that the alloy is no longer profitable and should be dropped. He feels that the entire capacity should be used to produce the raw metal. His suggestion is prompted by the data shown on the next page. The sales manager argues that, because of a $10 loss per unit on the alloy, the product should be dropped any time the price per ton falls below $150.

In the cost calculations, the raw materials and the labor costs are variable. The overhead rate per unit is calculated by estimating the total overhead for the coming year and dividing this total by the total hours of capacity available. Since the raw metal and the alloy require the same producing time, the rate per unit is the same. The total overhead is, for the most part, a fixed cost.

Required: (1) Should the alloy be dropped and the entire production facility be used to produce raw metal if the price per ton of alloy for the coming year is estimated to be $140? Support your conclusion with an appropriate analysis.

(2) Prepare an analysis to aid the sales manager in determining the lowest alloy price that would be acceptable to the company.

	Cost per Ton of Raw Sheet Metal	Cost per Ton of Alloy
Raw materials	$ 50	
Direct labor	10	
Overhead	30	
Cost per ton	$ 90	$ 90
Selling value	100	
Profit	$ 10	
Processing cost:		
Additional materials		20
Direct labor		10
Overhead		30
Cost per ton of alloy		$150
Selling value of alloy		140
Loss		($ 10)

(3) Assume that the total overhead for the company is about 50 percent fixed, 50 percent variable. Would you accept the $140 offer for alloy? Why? What would be the lowest acceptable price for the alloy?

17–9. The Able Company manufactures sheet metal that can be used in various types of metal products. In planning operations for the coming year, Mr. Able, the manager, is trying to decide between two different products that might be marketed. One of the products is a low quality metal that has a very broad market. It is used in several different types of construction. If this product is chosen, about 2,000,000 tons can be manufactured, and Mr. Able is certain that all the production can be sold at $10 per ton.

The other product is a high quality metal that is used in airplanes, automobiles, trucks, etc. The market for this product is quite uncertain because other materials can be used for many of the final products made from the high quality metal.

If the production facility is used for high quality metal about 1,500,000 tons can be produced. It is not possible to produce both types of metal at once and the company cannot change for a year once the choice is made.

The cost estimates are as follows:

	10% Capacity		100% Capacity	
	High Quality	Low Quality	High Quality	Low Quality
Materials and labor	$1,000,000	$1,200,000	$10,000,000	$12,000,000
Overhead	3,000,000	4,000,000	5,475,000	4,180,000
Other expenses	2,000,000	2,000,000	2,000,000	2,000,000

The accountant estimates that the cost increase between 10 percent and 100 percent of capacity on materials, labor, and overhead will be proportional to the changes in volume.

Required: Prepare an analysis that will aid Mr. Able in deciding which market to enter next year. Assume that a price range thought to be reasonable for the high quality product is between $15 and $25.

17–10. The Alexis Company has a production facility consisting of two producing departments and one service department which is currently being used to produce Product A.

The flexible budget relationships for labor and overhead for each of these departments are given below:

> Producing Department 1 $100,000 + $50 per hour
> Producing Department 2   50,000 +   75 per hour
> Service Department   X   20,000 +   15 per hour

The selling and administrative costs are estimated to be $100,000 per year fixed plus a 10 percent commission on products sold (based on selling price).

At the present time, 5,000 units of A are being produced and sold at a price of $500 per unit. A unit of Product A requires one-half hour in Department 1 and one hour in Department 2. One hour of time in Service Department X is required for *each* hour of operation in *each* of the two producing departments. The capacity of Departments 1 and 2 is 10,000 hours per year. The capacity in Department X is 12,000 hours per year.

The company is considering introducing Product B which would require one-quarter hour in Department 1 and one-half hour in Department 2. The selling price and quantity demanded are uncertain although the president would like to price the product to earn the same total contribution margin on B as is earned on A. He feels that the price on B should be no lower than $300 and no higher than $600.

Required: Prepare an analysis, showing the president the various prices (in the range given above) and quantities that would give a total contribution on Product B equal to Product A.

Chapter 18

THE CAPITAL INVESTMENT DECISION

A capital investment is an investment that yields returns during several future time periods in contrast to other types of investments that yield all of their returns in the current time period. The capital investment under consideration may be a new building, various plant assets, or stock in some other company. A special advertising program may be launched with present expenditures being made in anticipation of increased returns in the future. Or a new product line may be added, and new equipment and other facilities may be acquired to produce and sell this product.

The characteristic of all of these examples is that an investment is made now for returns in the future.

Decisions on capital investments are extremely important, and top management usually assumes direct responsibility for the authorization of the larger and more important expenditures. Capital investment decisions deserve the attention of top management for the following reasons:

(1) Ordinarily, substantial amounts of money are invested in capital projects.
(2) The resources that are invested in a project are often committed for a long period of time.
(3) It may be difficult to reverse the effects of a poor decision.
(4) In some cases, the success or failure of the company may depend upon a single investment decision.
(5) Plans must be made well into the future, a future that is uncertain at best.

THE INVESTMENT PROBLEM

Plans for capital investment are usually prepared for several years into the future. Projects are assigned priorities, costs are estimated for the various projects, and plans are made to obtain the resources required to finance the projects. This is the broad problem of capital investment planning.

In this chapter, however, the capital investment problem will be examined from a more limited point of view. It will be assumed that the project has received general approval and that it can be financed. The problem will be to select the specific investment candidate from among competing alternatives that will produce the best returns for the company. In other words, the investment alternatives are mutually exclusive. If one alternative is accepted, the others must be rejected. For example, a new building may be needed. The company may have a choice of sites and will have to decide which site is to be selected. Advantages and disadvantages will be identified with each location and quantified if possible. Comparison will be made to determine which site should be chosen. A similar type of problem faces the individual who needs a new home and has the means to finance it. Which home should he buy? If he selects one, he must reject the others.

FACTORS IN THE INVESTMENT DECISION

Three important factors are brought together in the evaluation of investment alternatives:

(1) The net amount of the investment.
(2) The returns expected from the investment.
(3) The lowest rate of return on the investment that will be acceptable to the company.

The returns that are expected from each investment alternative are discounted to a present value and are compared with the net amount invested. To be acceptable, an investment project must meet a minimum rate-of-return requirement. The most acceptable project, of course, is the one that shows the best return potential in relation to the amount invested and the minimum rate-of-return criterion.

The first step in the selection process is to estimate the net investment required for each investment alternative and to estimate the returns that it should produce over its useful life. However, the definitions for net investment and returns are somewhat different from those in conventional accounting practice.

The net investment. For decision-making purposes, the net investment is not necessarily the cost that would be entered in the accounting records. As stated in Chapter 9, the differential costs are important in decision making, and this also holds true for the capital investment decision. In many cases, the investment is the net *additional* outlay of cash that is required to obtain future returns. The net investment for decision purposes is generally the net outflow of cash to support a capital investment project.

In some cases, however, the net investment will be the sacrifice of an inflow of cash, that is, the opportunity cost that arises when a benefit is rejected. Assume, for example, that a building can be sold for $800,000. Should the building be sold or should it be held for use in future operations? This is an investment decision. If the building is sold, the cost of the building and the accumulated depreciation will be removed from the accounting records. The proceeds from the sale will be recorded along with any gain or loss on the transaction. If management refuses the sales offer and elects to use the building in operations, it has invested $800,000 in the future opera-tion of the building. Apparently, management has decided that the future returns justify the sacrifice of an immediate return of $800,000. Obviously, there is no cost to be recorded in the accounting records because of this decision. The company will continue to operate as it has before. The opportunity cost is relevant only when deciding whether or not to continue operations.

The net returns. The returns from an investment as defined for decision-making purposes are not the accounting profits. Instead, the returns are the inflows of cash expected from a project as reduced by the cash costs that can be directly attributed to the project. Some projects, however, are not expected to produce an inflow of cash, but they will yield returns in the form of cash savings. For example, a new type of machine may be operated at a lower labor cost; and there may be lower costs of machine maintenance, repairs, and so forth. The annual cash saving (as adjusted for income taxes) is the annual return on the investment.

The lowest acceptable rate of return. Relative to opportunities, funds are usually scarce and can be obtained only at a cost. If funds are borrowed, there is an interest charge for their use. The interest cost for the use of resources is present even when the funds are furnished by the owners either as capital investment or as retained earnings. An investor expects to receive a return on his investment—interest, dividends, or rent, as the case might be. Normally an investment will not be made unless it appears that it will earn more than the cost of the capital invested.

Funds for long-term investment are typically generated either from debt or equity sources. The cost of resources used for capital investment is thus a weighted average of these sources. In the case of bonds or debt capital, the cost is the after-tax interest rate. In the case of equity money, the cost can be determined by relating the estimated future return per share to the market price of the share. The cost of capital to the firm can then be looked upon as the weighted average of the cost of these two general sources of funds. The weights are chosen according to the proportion of each type of fund represented in the normal capital structure.

The cost of capital as defined above will depend on many factors. The element of risk associated with the company, the investors' appraisal of the future of the company, and the general economic outlook will affect the cost of capital to a company.

In general, it may be said that an investment should be made if it appears that the return will be greater than the cost of capital; that is, the investment will be worthwhile if it more than covers the cost of capital. Of course the risk inherent in a particular project may cause the company to reject the project even if the project rate exceeds the cost of capital. This situation arises because the cost of capital is usually calculated without regard for risks. Sometimes the company will increase the average cost of capital for a risk factor. A different risk factor may be used for different classes of investments.

Sometimes it is said that the cost of capital is not so much a limiting factor as is the scarcity of ideas. If the idea is profitable, management should feel confident that capital can be raised to support it. But this is only another way of saying that the investment opportunity is expected to earn more than the cost of capital. In any event, the cost of capital is usually looked upon as a cutoff point.

RATING THE INVESTMENT ALTERNATIVES

The net returns from each investment alternative are related to the net investment, and the results are compared using the lowest acceptable rate of return as a cutoff point. One of three methods is generally employed in rating investment alternatives:

(1) The payback method.
(2) The discounted rate-of-return method.
(3) The excess present value method.

The payback method. Investment alternatives are sometimes evaluated by relating the returns to the cost of the investment to determine how many years it will take to recover the investment. This method is simple to apply and in many cases will give answers approximately equivalent to those given by more sophisticated methods of analysis that will be described later on. It should be pointed out, however, that this method will be reliable only if the returns are evenly distributed over the years and if the investments to be compared are equal in amount and have the same life estimates with little or no residual salvage values.

An investment of $20,000 is expected to produce annual returns of $5,000 for ten years. No salvage recovery can be expected from the investment at the end of the ten years. The investment is recovered in four years, as calculated below:

$$\frac{\$20{,}000 \text{ investment}}{\$ 5{,}000 \text{ annual return}} = 4\text{-year payback period}$$

The ratio of the investment to the annual return is 4 to 1. Expressed in another way, the unadjusted rate of return is 25 percent, as follows:

$$\frac{\$ 5{,}000 \text{ annual return}}{\$20{,}000 \text{ investment}} = 25\%, \text{ rate of return}$$

The alternative with the shortest payback period or the highest unadjusted rate of return is the most acceptable, provided it meets the minimum standard that has been established.

The investment in the example above can be recovered in four years. If a payback period of four years satisfies the minimum standard that has been established and if no other alternative in this investment category has a shorter payback period, the investment will be accepted.

The discounted rate-of-return method. If returns are to be compared with a related investment, both the returns and the investment should be stated on a present value basis. Future dollar amounts are not equivalent to dollars in the present because of the difference in time. The problem of a difference in time can be resolved by converting future dollars to present values. The present value concept is explained in Appendix D.

A rate of return can be computed on an investment by discounting the estimated future returns at an interest (discount) rate that equates the present value of the returns with the investment. This rate of return is the discounted rate of return on the investment. To be acceptable, the discounted rate of return on an investment alternative must be at least equal to the minimum rate-of-return requirement. Ordinarily, the most acceptable investment alternative is the one that is expected to produce the highest discounted rate of return.

The discounted rate of return can be reached by trial and error. If the annual inflows are an equal amount for each year, the ratio of the investment to the annual return is calculated just as it is in the payback method. This ratio is then compared with the present values of annuities for the same number of years given in published tables. The discount rate for the present value of an annuity that most nearly corresponds with the ratio is selected as the rate of return.

In the last example, it was assumed that a $20,000 investment would yield returns of $5,000 each year with no terminal salvage recovery expected. The discounted rate of return can be computed as follows:

(1) Determine the payback period (the ratio of the investment to the annual return).

$$\frac{\$20,000 \text{ investment}}{\$\ 5,000 \text{ annual return}} = \text{4-year payback}$$

(2) Find the factor on the appropriate year line of a table of present values of $1 received annually that comes closest to the payback period.

> In the 22% column, 3.923 is closest to 4 on the 10-year line. (See Table II on page 701.) The investment is expected to have a 10-year life in this example. Therefore, the present value factor is taken from the 10-year line of the table.

(3) Use the interest rate identified with this factor to discount the future annual returns.

$$\begin{array}{c} \$5,000 \text{ annual} \\ \text{return} \end{array} \times \begin{array}{c} 3.923 \text{ present value} \\ \text{of } \$1 \text{ received} \\ \text{annually for} \\ 10 \text{ years at } 22\% \end{array} = \begin{array}{c} \$19,615 \text{ present value} \\ \text{of returns} \end{array}$$

If the present value of the returns is approximately equal to the present value of the investment, the discounted rate of return has been determined. In the example, the present value of the returns amounting to $19,615 is not quite equal to the investment of $20,000. The investment earns somewhat less than 22 percent. If the minimum rate-of-return requirement is 18 percent, this investment alternative would more than meet the minimum standard and would ordinarily be selected provided that no competing alternative promised an even better rate of return.

The returns for each year will not always be equal in amount. Returns for the early years may be relatively large when compared with returns for the later years. On the other hand, a project may develop slowly with returns increasing in the later years. Under these circumstances a discounted rate of return may have to be computed by trial and error. An average annual return may be calculated and used to find the ratio between the investment and the annual return. This ratio will be compared with the present value factors in the table for the appropriate number of years. If the returns for the early years are comparatively large, the first trial may be made by selecting a rate higher than the rate found in the table. If the returns for the early years are relatively low, a lower rate may be selected for the first trial. Using the discount rate selected, compute the present value for each year. Add the present values and compare the sum with the present value of the investment. An example of this procedure is given on page 697 of Appendix D.

The excess present value method. Investment alternatives can be evaluated without solving for the discounted rate of return. Future dollar amounts can be discounted at the lowest acceptable rate of return with the present value of the returns being compared with the present value of the investment. The alternative that produces the greatest excess of returns over the investment (on a present value basis) is the most acceptable. If the present value of the returns is less than the present value of the investment, the investment alternative does not meet the minimum rate-of-return requirement and should be rejected.

In the previous example, it was stated that the minimum rate-of-return requirement was 18 percent. The $5,000 annual returns that are expected for ten years are discounted at 18 percent and are compared with the investment of $20,000.

$5,000 annual return $\times$ 4.494 present value of $1 = $22,470
received each year
for 10 years at 18%

The excess present value of the returns is $2,470.

Present value of returns	$22,470
Investment	20,000
Excess present value	$ 2,470

The excess present values of the returns from competing alternatives would be computed; and if they were all less than $2,470, the alternative above would be the most acceptable.

REFINING THE INVESTMENT

An investment for decision-making purposes, as explained earlier, is a net outflow of cash, a commitment of cash, or the sacrifice of an inflow of cash. Sometimes adjustments must be made to determine the net investment. Three typical investment adjustments will be discussed at this point.

(1) The avoidable costs.
(2) Additional investment in current assets.
(3) The net proceeds from the sale of properties to be retired as a result of the investment.

The avoidable costs. By making an investment, an individual or company may be able to avoid some other cost. A cost that would otherwise be incurred will not be incurred if the investment is made. For example, an individual may plan to buy a new car costing $3,500 net of trade-in allowance granted by the dealer. He estimates that if he keeps his old car he will have to have it completely overhauled at an estimated cost of $600. The cost of overhaul can be avoided if he buys the new car. It is the *additional* cost that must be incurred that is relevant in decision making, in this case an additional cost of $2,900 ($3,500 — $600).

A company may also find that certain costs that would otherwise be incurred will not be incurred if an investment is made. For example, a company may be considering the purchase of new equipment costing $130,000. If this equipment is not purchased, extensive repairs will have to be made to the equipment now in service. The cost of the repairs is estimated at $15,000, and this cost is deductible in computing income taxes that are estimated at 40 percent of net income before income taxes. The tax deduction of $15,000 for repairs cost will reduce income taxes by $6,000 (40 percent of $15,000). The net cost of the repairs after income taxes is $9,000. The company receives a tax benefit of $6,000 from the deduction for repairs cost. Without the deduction, income taxes of $6,000 would have to be paid. Hence, if an investment is made in new equipment, the company will avoid the repair cost *net of income taxes* or will avoid a cost of $9,000 ($15,000 — $6,000). The net investment for decision-making purposes is computed below:

Investment in new equipment		$130,000
Less: Avoidable cost:		
Repairs cost to keep old equipment in operation	$15,000	
Less: Income tax of 40% on repairs deduction	6,000	
Net avoidable cost		9,000
Net investment		$121,000

The net investment of $121,000 will be compared with the estimated future returns discounted at the lowest acceptable rate of return (excess present value method) in making a decision. Or the estimated future returns may be discounted at a rate that will equate the present value of the returns with the investment (discounted rate of return method) to determine whether or not the investment meets the minimum rate of return requirement.

Additional investment in current assets. Sometimes a company will be considering an investment situation involving the introduction of a new product line or the expansion of facilities. If the project is to be under-taken, it may have to be supported by an additional investment in current assets. For example, a new line of product may be introduced. As a result, the investment in inventory will be higher, accounts receivable will go up, and the cash balance must be increased to provide for the additional costs of operation that must be paid. The required increment in current assets is part of the investment in the project. It seems strange to include an increase in a cash balance as an investment; but to the extent that cash and other current assets must be held to support a project, there is an investment that is frozen in the business, just like any other investment that is normally thought of as being long-term. When a project is eliminated, however, the supporting current assets are released.

Assume that a new project will require an investment of $500,000 in new equipment and additional current assets of $96,000 divided between cash, accounts receivable, and inventory as indicated below. The net invest-ment is computed as follows:

New equipment for project		$500,000
Add: Additional current assets:		
Cash	$18,000	
Accounts receivable	33,000	
Inventory	45,000	
Total additional current assets		96,000
Investment in new project		$596,000

The investment in the current assets as well as the salvage value of the equipment will be recovered at the termination of the project. The present value of the current assets released and of the net salvage value of the equipment can be included as a return from the investment in the last year of the life of the project.

For example, it may be estimated that the project will yield annual returns of $120,000 after income taxes for ten years. At the end of the project, it is estimated that the equipment will have a salvage value (net of income taxes) of $60,000. In addition, the current assets of $96,000 that were required for the operation of the project are released. The annual returns for the first nine years are then $120,000, but the return for the tenth year is $276,000 ($120,000 return from operation of the project plus $60,000 net salvage recovery plus $96,000 release of current assets). The returns are discounted to present values and are compared with the invest-ment following the procedures discussed earlier in the chapter.

The net proceeds from the sale of other properties. Properties may be retired as a result of an investment decision. If new equipment is obtained, for example, the equipment that is now in operation may be sold. The proceeds from the sale of the old equipment as adjusted for the income tax on any recognized gain or loss are deducted from the cost of the new equipment to arrive at the net investment. To illustrate, assume that equipment costing $50,000 is to be acquired. If this equipment is acquired, equipment having a net book value of $6,000 will be sold for $2,000. The loss of $4,000 on the sale is deductible in computing income taxes estimated at 40 percent of net income before taxes. The company can reduce its income taxes by $1,600 by selling the equipment at a loss of $4,000 (40 percent of $4,000 loss). The total benefit to be derived from selling this equipment amounts to $3,600; the $2,000 proceeds from the sale plus the income tax reduction of $1,600. The net investment is computed as follows:

Investment in new equipment		$50,000
Less: Proceeds from the sale of old equipment:		
Gross proceeds	$2,000	
Add: Reduction of income tax (40% of $4,000 loss deduction)	1,600	
Total proceeds		3,600
Net investment		$46,400

A gain may also be realized from the sale of equipment. Assume, in the last example, that the equipment having a net book value of $6,000 can be sold for $10,000 and that the gain of $4,000 will be taxed at a rate of 25 percent.[1] The net proceeds from the sale of the equipment will amount to $9,000 after subtracting the tax of $1,000 (25 percent of $4,000) from the $10,000 received from the sale of the equipment. The net investment in the new equipment is computed as follows:

Investment in new equipment		$50,000
Less: Net proceeds from the sale of old equipment:		
Gross proceeds	$10,000	
Less: Income tax on gain of $4,000 (25% of $4,000)	1,000	
Net proceeds		9,000
Net investment		$41,000

Often the old equipment will be traded in when new equipment is acquired. There is no income tax on a gain from a trade-in transaction, nor is any loss deduction allowed. Therefore, the net investment is equal to the cost of the new equipment minus the trade-in allowance.

---

[1] It is quite possible that a loss may be deductible at ordinary income rates (in our example, 40 percent) but that a gain would be treated as a capital gain with a maximum tax rate of 25 percent. Whether this is possible or not depends on the specific circumstances.

DEPRECIATION AND INCOME TAXES

Earlier in the chapter it was stated that the return from an investment is the cash flow return that is expected after income taxes. If the investment is expected to produce revenues, the excess of the cash inflow over the cash outflow will constitute the return. However, some investments are not expected to produce additional revenues. Instead, a saving in out-of-pocket costs is anticipated. The annual return from the investment then is the annual saving in out-of-pocket costs or, in other words, is the annual cash savings.

Depreciation must be considered in computing the annual cash returns after income taxes. As explained in Chapters 7 and 8, depreciation is a cost of operation to be deducted in computing net income, but there is no corresponding outflow of net working capital or cash. If depreciation is not an out-of-pocket expense, why must it be considered in computing the annual cash return after income taxes? Depreciation expense is an allowable deduction in the computation of income taxes, and income taxes are out-of-pocket expenses. Hence, depreciation is important because of its effect on the income taxes. Income taxes are reduced as a result of deducting depreciation.

Assume that National Machine Company can obtain a new machine costing $220,000 that has a useful life of ten years. To simplify the illustration, it is assumed that the machine will have no residual salvage value. This machine is expected to yield cash savings of $75,000 before income taxes each year. The *net* saving, however, is the saving after income taxes which in this case has been estimated at 40 percent of net income before taxes. The annual estimated saving after income taxes has been computed below at $45,000.

Estimated annual saving before income taxes	$75,000
Less: Income taxes at 40% of the saving	30,000
Net annual saving	$45,000

In the above computation, one very important factor has been overlooked. Depreciation on the new machine has not been considered.

In the illustration given, assume that depreciation of $22,000 will be deducted each year and that the income tax rate is 40 percent. The depreciation deduction will reduce income taxes by $8,800 (40 percent of $22,000). The net annual saving is actually $53,800 ($45,000 + $8,800) and not $45,000 as computed above.

The correct net return after income taxes is computed on the next page.

Estimated annual saving in out-of-pocket costs before income taxes		$75,000
Less: Income tax on out-of-pocket cost savings at 40% of $75,000	$30,000	
Less: Tax benefit from depreciation deduction (40% of $22,000)	8,800	
Net increase in income taxes		21,200
Estimated annual saving in out-of-pocket costs after income taxes		$53,800

In a replacement type of situation, depreciation on the new property may be more or less than the depreciation on the old property that will be traded or sold. The difference in depreciation will cause the income taxes to be higher or lower. For example, assume that a new machine is expected to yield annual cash savings of $30,000 before income taxes. Depreciation on the new machine is estimated each year at $25,000 while the depreciation on the old machine to be replaced would amount to only $15,000 if the old machine were retained. Income taxes are at the rate of 40 percent. The increase of $10,000 in the depreciation will reduce income taxes by $4,000 (40 percent of $10,000 difference). The difference in depreciation can only be considered for the years in which depreciation can be deducted on the old machine. In later years, when depreciation can only be deducted on the new machine, the income tax effect will be computed by deducting the depreciation that is still available on the new machine.

ACCELERATED DEPRECIATION

In the illustration given, depreciation was deducted by the straight-line method. In practice, an accelerated depreciation method probably will be used for tax purposes. Relatively large depreciation deductions are taken in the early years of the life of the asset when an accelerated depreciation method is used, and smaller depreciation deductions are taken in the later years. As a result, income tax payments are lower in the early years.[2] This

---

[2] Federal tax provisions may be designed to encourage or discourage capital investment. The Revenue Act of 1962 provided for an investment credit. Subject to limitations prescribed by law, the taxpayer was permitted to deduct a percentage of the cost of a property from income taxes. The investment credit was a direct reduction against the tax and not a deduction to be used in computing taxes. Furthermore, the investment credit did not reduce the depreciable basis of the property. The investment credit reduced income taxes for the year in which the property was acquired. As a result of this tax credit, the after-tax rate of return on investments was increased. The investment credit was later suspended and, in the future, may be reinstated or suspended again according to the current fiscal policy. If the investment credit is in force, it must be considered. In the example given below with a 7 percent investment credit, the investment credit would be $15,400 (7 percent of $220,000). Income taxes in the first year would be decreased by $1,400.

Income tax on $75,000 savings in out-of-pocket costs (40% of $75,000)		$30,000
Less: Investment credit	$15,400	
Depreciation effect (40% of $40,000)	16,000	31,400
Income tax effect—decrease in first year		$ 1,400

means that the net returns from the investment will be larger in the early years, and the larger net returns received in the early years can be reinvested to earn even larger returns later on.

Assume once again that National Machine Company can obtain a new machine costing $220,000 that has a useful life of ten years with no estimated residual salvage value. Annual out-of-pocket cost savings are estimated at $75,000 before income taxes. Depreciation will be deducted by the sum-of-the-years-digits method (SYD method). The depreciation deduction for the first year by the SYD method is $40,000 (10/55 × $220,000 cost subject to depreciation). With a 40 percent tax rate, depreciation of $40,000 reduces income taxes by $16,000.

Income tax on $75,000 savings in out-of-pocket costs (40% of $75,000)	$30,000
Less: Depreciation effect:	
40% of depreciation of $40,000	16,000
Income tax effect—increase in first year	$14,000

The net return after income taxes for the first year is $61,000 and not $53,800 as it would have been without the benefit of SYD depreciation.

Savings in out-of-pocket costs before income taxes	$75,000
Deduct: Increase in income taxes after the effect of SYD depreciation	14,000
Savings in out-of-pocket costs after income taxes	$61,000

The savings after taxes will not be as large in later years. But the company has relatively large returns in early years that can be reinvested. Furthermore, the risk that the investment will not be recovered is reduced.

The effect of SYD depreciation on investment returns is compared with the effect when straight-line depreciation is deducted.

SYD Depreciation

Year	(1) Savings before Income Taxes	(2) Less Depreciation	(3) Taxable Savings (1) — (2)	(4) 40% Income Taxes 40% × (3)	(5) Savings after Income Taxes (1) — (4)
1 ...	$75,000	$40,000	$35,000	$14,000	$61,000
2 ...	75,000	36,000	39,000	15,600	59,400
3 ...	75,000	32,000	43,000	17,200	57,800
4 ...	75,000	28,000	47,000	18,800	56,200
5 ...	75,000	24,000	51,000	20,400	54,600
6 ...	75,000	20,000	55,000	22,000	53,000
7 ...	75,000	16,000	59,000	23,600	51,400
8 ...	75,000	12,000	63,000	25,200	49,800
9 ...	75,000	8,000	67,000	26,800	48,200
10 ...	75,000	4,000	71,000	28,400	46,600

The discounted rate of return on the investment is a little more than 20 percent when straight-line depreciation is deducted in the computation of income taxes.

Present value of annual returns of $53,800 for 10 years
($53,800 × 4.192 present value of $1 received annually
for 10 years at 20%) $225,530

But the discounted rate of return is a little more than 22 percent when depreciation is deducted by the SYD method. Income taxes are lower in the early years when an accelerated depreciation method is used. As a result, the net returns after income taxes are higher in the early years than they are when straight-line depreciation is deducted. The discounted rate of return is also higher when larger returns are received in the early years.

Year	Savings after Income Taxes	Present Value Factor, 22%	Present Value of Savings (Returns), 22%
1	$61,000	0.820	$ 50,020
2	59,400	0.672	39,917
3	57,800	0.551	31,848
4	56,200	0.451	25,346
5	54,600	0.370	20,202
6	53,000	0.303	16,059
7	51,400	0.249	12,799
8	49,800	0.204	10,159
9	48,200	0.167	8,049
10	46,600	0.137	6,384
Present value of returns at 22%			$220,783

INCREMENTAL RETURNS

The investment producing the highest *discounted rate* of return will not be the most desirable in every circumstance. The investments to be compared may not be the same in amount. The amount of the return from a larger investment in many cases will be larger than the return from a smaller investment, but the smaller investment may have a better rate of discounted return.

This type of situation can be illustrated by assuming that Globe Transit Company has an opportunity to invest in one of two projects. Each project has an estimated life of five years with annual returns as shown below:

	Project I	Project II
Net investment	$75,000	$100,000
Annual return for each of 5 years	30,000	38,000

Investments are expected to yield a discounted rate of return of at least 15 percent.

The discounted rate of return is computed on each project alternative as follows:

	Project I	Project II	Incremental
Net investment	$75,000	$100,000	$25,000
Annual return	30,000	38,000	8,000
Ratio of net investment to annual return	2.5	2.632	3.125
Present value factor from 5-year line of Table II that most nearly corresponds with ratio of net investment to annual return	2.532	2.635	3.127
Rate of return from Table II	28%	26%	18%

It would appear that Project I should be selected because the discounted rate of return is higher. But the discounted rate of return method will not always give the correct solution. The key to the problem is the incremental investment and the incremental returns. If the rate of return on the incremental investment is greater than the cutoff rate of return, the additional investment should be made. In this situation, an additional $8,000 a year is returned on an additional investment of $25,000. The rate of return on the incremental investment is 18 percent, and the cutoff rate is 15 percent.

A solution by the excess present value method follows:

	Project I	Project II
Present value of returns at 15%		
$30,000 × 3.352	$100,560	
$38,000 × 3.352		$127,376
Investment	75,000	100,000
Excess present value of returns	$ 25,560	$ 27,376

Project II should be selected. It yields greater excess returns on a present value basis.

The concept of incremental investment still applies even though the initial investments are the same. The returns are reinvested and may be viewed as potential investments in the future. If one alternative produces larger returns than another in the early years, while the other alternative produces better returns in later years, the problem of incremental investment arises. Should the company forego the more immediate returns for even larger returns in the future? The answer will depend upon the rate at which future returns can be invested and the amount of the future returns as compared with the sacrifice of immediate returns. A solution to the problem is to discount at the lowest acceptable rate of return.

A GRAPHIC SOLUTION

Sometimes the investment problem can be understood better when the returns are depicted on a graph. The returns from each alternative are discounted at various discount rates. The investment is subtracted from the discounted returns, and the excess or negative discounted returns are plotted on a graph.

Conceptually, the graph shown below is not too unlike the P/V graph used in break-even analysis. Positive discounted returns are given on a vertical scale above a zero line, and negative discounted returns are shown below this line.

Data from the previous illustration are depicted on the graph that follows:

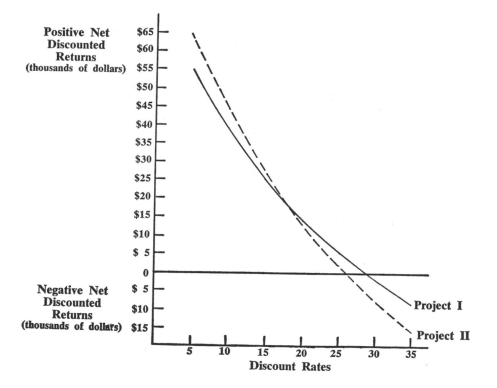

Computations at the 10 percent rate are given below to illustrate the procedure employed:

	Project I	Project II
Present value of returns	$113,730	$144,058
Less: Present value of investment	75,000	100,000
Net positive discounted returns	$ 38,730	$ 44,058

Note that Project II is a better investment candidate when the lowest acceptable rate of return is less than about 18 percent. If the company can reinvest returns at more than 18 percent, Project I is better. The discounted rate of return for each alternative is at the point where the present value line crosses the zero axis on the chart. The cost of the investment is balanced by the discounted returns at the rate indicated at the point of crossover.

THE EVALUATION PROCESS

The task of rating the investment alternatives is usually not as difficult as the task of collecting reliable data that can be used in making an evaluation. Even with experience, it is not easy to make estimates of future returns and the rates that should be used in discounting.

Generally certain policies and procedures are followed in the acquisition of investments of various types. For example, requests for new equipment or for special projects are reviewed by the engineering department or may even be initiated by that department as a result of studies made. The technological aspects are evaluated, and competing pieces of equipment are compared as to performance. Revenues, costs, and savings are identified with each alternative through the combined efforts of the engineers and the accountants.

Ordinarily, special forms are used to record data with respect to the cost of the investment and the anticipated returns. When the evaluation reports have been completed, they are turned over to a screening committee for critical review. Some of the investment expenditures will be approved by this committee and recommended to the project or equipment planning committee of the board of directors who will give final approval or disapproval.

Sometimes the discounted return approach is rejected as an analytical tool because of the difficulty in making estimates. But the problem of estimation cannot be avoided under any method that may be used to evaluate investment alternatives. Giving recognition to time adjustments for monetary amounts does not add uncertainty. Even in a simple payback calculation, the investor must make the same estimates.

THE POST AUDIT

After a piece of equipment has been acquired or after a project has been started, it is watched closely. Its performance, both from a technical and an economic viewpoint, is audited or reviewed at the end of its "shakedown period." During this period, it may be found that certain corrections will have to be made if the project is going to realize its potential. At the end of the period, an audit or review will show whether or not the investment lived up to expectations and may point out ways in which the operation can be improved.

The audit referred to is not an audit in the true sense of the word. It is in reality a general review and like the original evaluation may contain errors of estimation. The review may also be limited by the accounting information that is available. On a special project the operating results may be shown separately in the accounting records. But on an individual piece of equipment, which is only one among many items, there may be no separate accounting. In fact, it would be difficult indeed to identify the operating results with any one piece of equipment. Whether or not additional effort should be exerted to get separate accountability will depend upon the relative importance of the investment and the cost incurred to get the additional information.

The post audit can be quite useful. First of all, it is a means by which errors of operation can be detected and corrected. The audit may also serve as a control in that employees may tend to be more careful if they realize that the equipment is under surveillance. Furthermore, project evaluations may be more thoroughly made if these evaluations are to be given a performance test at some later date. And, of course, the audit may reveal information that can be applied in future investment planning.

Questions

1. How does a capital investment differ from other investments?

2. Why are capital investment decisions so important?

3. What three factors are related in the evaluation of capital investment alternatives?

4. What is the net investment from a decision-making point of view?

5. How are the proceeds from the sale of old equipment used in computing the net investment in a replacement situation?

6. What is an avoidable cost? Explain how an avoidable cost is used in the determination of net investment.

7. How do income taxes affect the net investment?

8. Since cash is a current asset, under what circumstances is it thought of as being a capital investment in decision making?

9. Are the returns from an investment the accounting profits? Explain.

10. The return from an investment is not always in the form of a net inflow of net working capital. Explain.

11. Why is depreciation an important factor in the computation of the annual net returns?

12. Is there any advantage in obtaining relatively large returns from an investment in the early years? Explain.

13. Explain how investment alternatives can be compared by the excess present value method.

14. The investment alternative yielding the highest discounted rate of return is the most acceptable. Will this always be true? Explain.

Exercises

1. Parsons Blending Company plans to replace a mixing machine that was acquired several years ago at a cost of $14,000. The machine has been depreciated to its residual salvage value of $2,000. A new machine can be purchased for $16,000. The dealer will grant a trade-in allowance of $3,000 on the old machine. If a new machine is not purchased, Parsons Blending Company will spend $2,000 to repair the old machine. Gains and losses on trade-in transactions are not subject to income taxes. The cost to repair the old machine can be deducted in computing income taxes. Income taxes are estimated at 40 percent of the net income subject to tax.

Required: Compute the net investment in the new machine for decision-making purposes.

2. A suburban branch of Lopez Brothers is to be located in Blue Ridge Estates. It is estimated that this store will add $600,000 each year to sales revenue. The additional goods sold each year will cost $350,000, and costs to operate this store for a year not including depreciation and allocated costs will amount to $85,000. Depreciation of $50,000 will be deducted each year. Income taxes are estimated at 40 percent of net income before income taxes.

Required: Compute the annual net return expected from the operation of the suburban branch.

3. Van Horn Marine Company plans an investment of $75,000 in new machinery that should produce net returns after income taxes of $25,000 each year for five years. The representative of another equipment manufacturer presents an alternative plan. By investing $160,000 in his company's equipment, Van Horn Marine Company can obtain net returns after income taxes of $50,000 each year for five years. In the future, an investment of this type can be expected to yield a discounted rate of return of 12 percent.

Required: (1) Which investment alternative is more attractive if a discounted rate of return of 12 percent is expected? Show computations.
(2) What is the discounted rate of return on each investment alternative?
(3) What is the discounted rate of return on the incremental investment?

4. Williams Machine Company is faced with two alternatives. It can invest $150,000 in new equipment that is expected to yield net annual returns after income taxes of $36,000 for ten years, or it can invest $250,000 in equipment that is expected to yield net annual returns after income taxes of $67,000 for ten years. No investment of this type will be made unless it appears that it can earn a discounted rate of return of at least 18 percent.

Required: (1) Discount the annual returns from each alternative at the lowest rate of return that is acceptable, and compute the excess present value of the returns.

(2) What is the discounted rate of return on each investment alternative?

5. New equipment costing $60,000 is to be purchased by McMurray Windings Company to replace equipment that is now in service. If the new equipment is acquired, the equipment that is now being used will be sold for $22,500. A loss of $12,500 will be recognized on the sale.

The new equipment should produce annual cost savings as follows:

Materials and supplies cost reduced by	$ 8,000
Labor cost reduced by	11,000

These savings will be offset to an extent by higher maintenance costs each year of $4,000.

The new equipment has an estimated useful life of five years with no residual salvage value at the end of the five years. Depreciation on the new equipment will be recorded at $12,000 each year. If the old equipment is to be used, depreciation of $7,000 will be recorded each year. Income taxes are estimated at 40 percent of the net income before taxes.

Investments of this type are expected to yield a discounted rate of return of at least 15 percent.

Required: Compute the present value of the annual returns at 15 percent and determine the excess of the present value of the returns over the net amount of the investment. Does the new equipment meet the minimum rate of return requirement?

6. The president of Gustine Automation, Inc., plans to abandon a project that will probably yield annual cash flow returns of $45,000, after income taxes, for each of the next eight years. If the project is abandoned, he estimates that the company will receive $200,000 and a loss of $80,000 can be deducted for income taxes. No salvage recovery is anticipated if the project is continued for eight years.

A new project may be substituted for the present project if it appears that it will produce better results. The new project will cost $350,000 and is expected to yield $65,000 in annual cash flow returns, after income taxes, for each of the next 15 years. At the end of 15 years, the company will probably recover $50,000, net of taxes, from the sale of salvage materials.

A 15 percent discounted cash flow return is the lowest rate of return that is acceptable. Income taxes have been estimated at 40 percent of net income before taxes.

Required: Should the company abandon the old project and substitute the new project? (Show computations to support your answer.)

7. A company that specializes in services for tourists plans to invest in recreational facilities at Sea Breeze Point. At the present time they are considering providing short cruises along the coastline in a sightseeing boat.

A dealer in marine yachts offers them a double-decker boat that will carry 100 passengers a trip. This boat costs $160,000 and is conservatively estimated to have a useful life for 5 summer seasons. At the end of 5 seasons it can be traded in on a replacement or can be sold for $40,000.

Costs of operation, consisting of salaries, sales promotion, maintenance, fuel, licenses, rentals, taxes, and insurance are fixed costs for the season and will not be influenced to any great extent by the hours of operation or the number of passengers carried. These costs have been estimated at $78,000 for a season. Passengers will pay $3.50 a ride.

It has been agreed that the venture must yield discounted returns of at least 18 percent if it is to be competitive with similar investment situations.

Depreciation will be computed using the SYD method, and income taxes are estimated at 40 percent of net income before income taxes.

Required: (1) Can the rate-of-return objective be met if tickets are sold to only 32,000 passengers a season? Show computations.

(2) Can the rate-of-return objective be met if tickets are sold to 40,000 passengers a season? Show computations.

8. Bob's River Moldings, Inc., plans to invest $90,000 in automatic equipment that should produce net returns before income taxes each year of $30,000. The equipment has an estimated useful life of five years with an estimated residual salvage value of $15,000 at the end of five years. Depreciation will be deducted by the SYD method. The investment will not be made if the discounted rate of return will be less than 15 percent. Income taxes are estimated at 40 percent of the net income before taxes.

Required: (1) Evaluate the investment by the excess present value method using a 15 percent minimum rate of return.

(2) Make the evaluation that was made in (1) above assuming straight-line depreciation.

9. Lincoln Institute plans a research project that will require additional staff, supplies, books, and so forth. The estimated cost of the project is $132,000. It is estimated that the results of the research project will yield annual returns to the Institute of $42,000 each year for five years.

Required: (1) How long will it take to recover the costs invested in the project? In other words, what is the payback period?

(2) What is the discounted rate of return on the project?

Problems

18–1. Modern automatic equipment costing $340,000 can be acquired by Sully Tool Company to replace equipment that is now being used. The freight charges on the new equipment have been estimated at $9,000, and it is estimated that the equipment can be installed for $17,000. Special attachments to be used with this unit will be needed and will cost $35,000. The equipment that is now in service can be traded in on the new unit. The dealer will allow $60,000 on the trade-in. The old equipment can also be sold for $45,000 with a loss on the sale of $50,000. Income taxes are estimated at 40 percent of net income before taxes. A loss on the trade-in transaction will not be deductible in computing income taxes.

Required: Compute the net investment for decision-making purposes.

18–2. Three investment alternatives are being evaluated by Jason and Fries, Inc. If one alternative is accepted the others will be rejected. Data with respect to each alternative follow:

	Net Amount Invested	Net Annual Return after Income Taxes	Estimated Life of Project
Alternative 1	$175,000	$40,000	10 years
Alternative 2	210,000	80,000	5 years
Alternative 3	280,000	90,000	10 years

Required: Which of the three alternatives if any should be selected if investments in the future are expected to yield a discounted rate of return of 20 percent? Show computations.

18–3. The president of Arnold Milling Company, Inc., has been considering an investment of $250,000 in machinery that should have a useful life of ten years with a terminal salvage value of $30,000. The company can expect a discounted rate of return on investments of this type of 18 percent.

The president believes that this investment will barely meet the rate of return requirement. According to estimates made, the net income before income taxes from this investment will probably amount to $58,000 a year. In making this computation, depreciation of $22,000 has been deducted. Income taxes are 40 percent of net income before taxes.

The president has been informed that depreciation may be deducted by the SYD method. He doesn't understand how a "bookkeeping method," as he calls it, can help to improve the rate of return on the investment.

Required: (1) Compute the discounted rate of return on the investment using straight-line depreciation.

(2) Compute the discounted rate of return on the investment using SYD depreciation.

(3) Explain to the president how a "bookkeeping method" can help to improve the rate of return on the investment.

18–4. The product development department of Olean Industries, Inc., has formulated a plan for the introduction of a new type of recording instrument. To manufacture this instrument in sufficient quantity, it is estimated that an investment of $4,000,000 must be made in production facilities and that additional working capital of $400,000 must be retained to support the operation. The project is expected to have a useful life of ten years. At the end of the ten years the additional working capital can be released, and the productive facilities will have an estimated residual salvage value of $430,000.

After the first five years, a total outlay of approximately $600,000 will be needed over the remaining five years to rehabilitate the production facilities used for this new product.

The company expects projects of this type to yield an annual return of 20 percent after income taxes. Income taxes are to be estimated at 40 percent of net income before taxes.

Sales for each year has been estimated at $3,000,000 and additional costs (excluding depreciation) have been estimated at $1,800,000 a year.

A schedule of depreciation to be deducted in the computation of income taxes is given on the next page.

Required: Will this project meet the rate-of-return requirement? Show computations. Round computations to the nearest thousand dollars.

Years	Initial Investment	Additional Investment
1	$ 800,000	—
2	640,000	—
3	512,000	—
4	410,000	—
5	328,000	—
6	262,000	$240,000
7	210,000	144,000
8	168,000	84,000
9	134,000	66,000
10	106,000	66,000
Totals	$3,570,000	$600,000

18–5. New product line opportunities are being investigated by the product engineering division of Satterline Manufacturing Company. A recreational product has interesting possibilities, but it is likely to be a style type of product that may yield returns for only 5 years.

New equipment can be obtained for the production of this product line at a cost of $145,000 installed. During the 5 years that the equipment is used, additional working capital of $22,000 will be required, consisting primarily of cash and inventories of materials and finished products. At the end of the 5 years, the working capital can be released, and the equipment can be sold for $10,000 net of the estimated cost of removal. This new product line should result in an increased cash flow before income taxes of $112,000 each year.

Instead of selling the equipment at the end of 5 years, the company, by spending an additional $75,000 can convert this equipment and use it to manufacture another product line that is expected to add $20,000 to annual cash flows before income taxes for an additional 5 years. If the equipment is held for a total of 10 years, the working capital will be held for 10 years, and the expected residual salvage value of the equipment will be $2,000 at the end of the 10 years.

There is still a third possibility; another product line appears interesting. The company, however, must select either one product line or the other. It is believed that the market for this line of product will last for 10 years. However, it will develop slowly with anticipated cash flow returns before income taxes of $90,000 each year for the first 5 years and $150,000 each year for the last 5 years. The cost of the equipment as quoted by the manufacturer is $234,000. Shipping and installation costs are estimated at $2,500, and the cost of auxiliary parts is estimated at $3,500. Additional working capital of $28,000 will be required to support this project, and this working capital can be released at the end of the 10 years. At the end of 10 years, the equipment should have a residual salvage value of $20,000.

Depreciation is to be deducted by the sum-of-the-years-digits method. Income taxes are estimated at 40 percent of net income before income taxes.

A minimum rate-of-return objective has been established at 20 percent.

Required: Determine which of the three alternatives would be best for the company. Use the excess present value method and show computations.

18–6. The management of Stellar Metals Company is considering introducing a new product line. A survey has been made in an attempt to estimate the potential demand for this product. A special type of equipment will be required for the manufacturing process, and one or more units of this equipment will be acquired if the project is accepted.

Data with respect to the production and sale of the product are given below:

Number of Equipment Units	Product Unit Capacity	Estimated Selling Price per Product Unit	** Variable Product Unit Costs Materials	Labor	Overhead
1	80,000	$5.00	$2.00	$1.00	$.50
2	150,000	5.00	1.80	1.00	.50
3	200,000	5.00	1.60	1.00	.50
4	240,000	5.00	1.50	1.50	.80
* 5	270,000	5.00 4.00	1.40	1.50	.80

* Any units sold in excess of 240,000 will have to be sold at a unit price of $4.00, thus 240,000 at $5.00 and 30,000 at $4.00.
** Pertains to the entire production at the level indicated.

The new product line will increase fixed costs (excluding depreciation) for the year by $50,000. According to estimates made, this increase can be expected regardless of the number of product units manufactured.

Working capital required to support the project has been estimated as follows:

Number of Equipment Units	Working Capital
1	$ 40,000
2	75,000
3	100,000
4	120,000
5	132,000

The company with its present plant capacity can install any number of machines from one to five to handle production.

Cost estimates furnished by an equipment dealer are given below:

Number of Equipment Units	Total Installed Cost of Equipment	Total Estimated Residual Salvage Values
1	$ 240,000	$15,000
2	450,000	30,000
3	645,000	45,000
4	840,000	60,000
5	1,035,000	75,000

A better price is offered by the dealer if more than one unit of equipment is purchased. Each machine is estimated to have a useful life of five years.

If the equipment is purchased, depreciation will be computed by using the sum-of-the-years-digits method.

The lowest rate of discounted return that the company will accept is 15 percent. The income tax rate is 50 percent.

At the end of five years, the working capital required to support the project will be released.

Required: Calculate the excess present value (or deficiency) associated with each alternative number of machines that might be acquired and determine how many machines (if any) should be purchased. Assume that the company can sell all units that can be produced under the conditions stated. Show calculations.

18–7. Equipment used in current operations is evaluated on a periodic basis by Ewing Blenders, Inc. The method of analysis, referred to as "value analysis," compares the present resale value of the equipment with the present value of the stream of cash flow returns expected from its continued use in operations. On the basis of this analysis, the equipment may be continued in service, sold, or replaced by more efficient units.

The company has set a minimum rate-of-return objective of 20 percent. The income tax rate on capital gains is 25 percent and 40 percent on ordinary income.

Data with respect to two units of equipment are set forth below:

	Unit #1	Unit #2
Original cost	$135,000	$225,000
Accumulated depreciation	80,000	155,000
Net book value of equipment	$ 55,000	$ 70,000
Resale value at the present time	$ 83,000	$ 50,000
Estimated remaining life	5 years	5 years
Estimated salvage value at the termination of useful life	$ 10,000	$ 20,000
Estimated annual cash flow returns before income taxes	24,000	25,000
Estimated annual depreciation over remaining useful life	9,000	10,000

The company is considering a new unit of equipment (Unit #3). This unit will cost $370,000, installed, and is estimated to have a useful life of 10 years with an estimated residual salvage value of $60,000 at the end of 10 years. The annual cash flow return before income taxes from this unit of equipment has been estimated at $92,000.

Depreciation is to be deducted as follows:

Year	Depreciation
1	$74,000
2	59,000
3	47,000
4	38,000
5	30,000
6	24,000
7	20,000
8	16,000
9	1,000
10	1,000

Required: (1) Should Units #1 and #2 be sold or continued in service? (2) Should Unit #3 be acquired? (Show all computations.)

18–8. Tanello Patterns, Inc., plans to invest $17,500,000 in a new production process. The total investment is as follows:

Depreciable assets	$12,000,000
Assets not subject to depreciation (to be recovered at termination of project)	5,500,000
Total	$17,500,000

If the company accepts this investment situation, equipment in service having a net book value of $3,300,000 will be sold for $1,500,000. This equipment, if continued in service, would yield a depreciation deduction of $900,000 for each of the next three years.

The pattern of depreciation to be deducted on the new equipment over the estimated 10-year life of the project follows:

Years	Depreciation Deduction
1	$2,400,000
2	1,920,000
3	1,536,000
4	1,229,000
5	983,000
6	786,000
7	629,000
8	173,000
9	172,000
10	172,000

At the end of the 10 years, the equipment is expected to have a residual salvage value of $2,000,000.

The additional cash flow returns before income taxes that are expected from this investment situation are set forth below:

Years	Additional Cash Flows Before Income Taxes
1	$8,000,000
2	6,000,000
3	5,000,000
4	4,000,000
5	4,000,000
6	3,000,000
7	2,000,000
8	1,000,000
9	1,000,000
10	1,000,000

The expected returns from the equipment currently in use including the recovery of the residual salvage value have been taken into consideration in estimating the additional cash inflow returns before income taxes.

The lowest acceptable rate of return is 20 percent. Income taxes are estimated at 50 percent of net income before taxes.

Required: Does this investment meet the rate-of-return requirement? **Show** computations and round answers to the nearest thousand.

18–9. Plans are being made by the management of Fortune Paper Products, Inc., to introduce a new type of paperboard product that sells for $12.20 a unit. According to market surveys, the company should be able to sell 50,000 units of this product each year.

Two alternatives for equipment acquisition are available if this project is adopted.

One equipment manufacturer offers a type of equipment that can be used to produce this product line. Each unit of equipment, however, can only produce 10,000 units a year. Hence, if this equipment is acquired, it will be necessary to buy 5 units to meet the anticipated demand. Each unit of equipment costs $85,000 installed and is expected to have a useful life of 5 years with no residual salvage value at the end of the 5 years. The costs of operating each unit of equipment have been estimated as follows:

Production capacity	10,000 units of product per year
Rate of production per hour	5 units of product.

Costs per unit of product:

Direct materials	$	6.00
Supplies		.20

Costs per hour of operation:

Direct labor	.80
Maintenance	.50
Repairs	.10
Power	1.00
Lubrication	.60

Fixed cost for the year:

Repairs and maintenance	$2,500

Another equipment manufacturer offers a larger unit of equipment that has the capacity to produce 50,000 units of product a year. This equipment costs $380,000 installed. It also has an estimated useful life of 5 years with an estimated residual salvage value of $40,000 at the end of the fifth year. The costs of operating the larger unit of equipment have been estimated as shown below:

Production capacity	50,000 units of product per year
Rate of production per hour	25 units of product.

Costs per unit of product:

Direct materials	$	6.00
Supplies		.20

Costs per hour of operation:

Direct labor	4.00
Maintenance	2.00
Repairs	.60
Power	5.00
Lubrication	1.00

Fixed costs for the year:

Repairs and maintenance	$6,000

Management estimates that if this project is undertaken, it must be supported by additional working capital of $120,000 that can be released at the end of the project.

Capital investments are expected to earn a discounted rate-of-return of 20 percent. In evaluating investments, depreciation is computed using the straight-line method.

Income taxes are estimated at 50 percent of net income before income taxes.

Required: Does the project meet the minimum rate-of-return requirement? The company will either buy one large unit of equipment or five small units of equipment if it undertakes the project. Which of the two alternatives appears to be better? (Show computations and round to the nearest dollar.)

18–10. The president of Fayetteville Liners, Inc., has been considering two investment opportunities. One of these opportunities will yield high returns in early years but will produce no returns after five years, while the other opportunity will be developed slowly and will yield higher returns in later years.

The investment in each opportunity will be $200,000. If one alternative is selected, the other alternative must be rejected. The company can earn a discounted rate of return of 15 percent on its investments.

The returns from each alternative after income taxes have been estimated as follows:

	Alternative			Alternative
Years	1	2	Years	2
1	$100,000	$10,000	6	$ 80,000
2	80,000	10,000	7	100,000
3	50,000	20,000	8	100,000
4	20,000	30,000	9	100,000
5	20,000	50,000	10	100,000

Required: Which investment alternative is more desirable when a discounted rate of return of 15 percent can be expected? Show computations.

18–11. Meridian Instrument Company manufactures 40,000 valve assemblies each year. These assemblies are used in the production of a pressure gauge. The cost to manufacture each assembly has been estimated as follows:

Direct materials	$1.80
Direct labor	.30
Variable overhead	.15
Unit variable cost	$2.25

These assemblies can be purchased from a supplier at a unit cost of $2.60.

If Meridian Instrument Company purchases the valve assemblies, equipment used to produce it can be sold for $25,000 with no gain or loss on the sale. This equipment can be used for five years but the salvage recovery at the end of five years will be negligible. Depreciation of $5,000 will be deducted each year if the equipment is kept in service.

The company receives a 15 percent discounted rate of return from investment opportunities, and income taxes are at the rate of 40 percent on net income before taxes.

Required: Should the company sell the machine and buy the assemblies, or should the company continue to manufacture the assemblies? Show computations.

Chapter 19

THE CONTROL OF DECENTRALIZED OPERATIONS

One of the most striking characteristics of business operation and organization during the past 15 years has been the tendency toward decentralized operations. This movement has been going on at the same time that the number of business combinations and mergers has been increasing. It seems that many companies are simultaneously seeking the advantages of bigness through combinations and of smallness through decentralizing the management of the combined operations.

In general, a *decentralized company* is one in which operating divisions are created. Each division is staffed with a management that has some authority for making decisions and thus becomes responsible for a segment of the company's profit. Even though the actual delegation of decisions may differ from company to company, the spirit of decentralization is quite clear and that is to divide a company into relatively self-contained divisions and allow these divisions to operate in an autonomous fashion. The amount of decision-making authority granted to division management will, of course, vary among companies. Decisions as to capital investment are usually centrally controlled; but decisions as to selling price and quantity and method of production are frequently delegated to the division management.

Two of the alleged advantages of a decentralized organization are:

(1) To provide a systematic means of delegating a portion of the decision-making responsibility to operating people below top management.

(2) To motivate managers in charge of certain company activities by bringing them more closely in touch with the company's profit objectives.

Of course, top management wants to know whether these advantages are being realized. This desire creates a problem of how to control and evaluate division management. This problem of division control and evaluation is usually more complex than the problem of controlling a single activity within the company. For example, in a centralized company a problem of control may exist with respect to certain production activities. A cost center may be established and reports may be generated to assure top management that the product is being produced at the lowest possible level of cost. The problem is usually one of *cost control*. In decentralized divisions, the division management may have authority over selling prices of the finished product, make or buy decisions, some investment decisions, and so forth. The problem here is mainly one of *profit control,* which is much broader and often more complex than a problem of cost control. The fact that the division manager usually has more freedom than a production foreman in making decisions usually means that a simple cost index is not an adequate control device. Control over cost will not indicate how efficient the division manager is as a price-maker for the finished products.

THE CRITERIA NEEDED FOR A CONTROL SYSTEM

In general, in order to control anything it is necessary to have:

(1) An index of overall actual performance.
(2) A standard by which to measure the actual performance index.

A comparison of actual performance with standard performance produces variance information that can form the basis for corrective action.

The selection of an evaluation index is rarely an easy problem. The main underlying criterion in this selection is quite clear: the index chosen must encompass as many of the operating variables as possible. Of course, the operating variables that are important are those over which the supervisor, foreman, or manager has control. Rarely, if ever, can one single index of performance be established that will encompass all of the factors that are considered important in evaluating an operation.

In evaluating a production operation, cost is usually considered to be a fairly good evaluation index. The cost that should be used is the controllable cost. However, this index, although useful, may not tell the entire story. The cost in a certain activity may be high because the supervisor spends much time on developing his personnel. If this supervision helps to provide a good training ground for future managers, perhaps the supervisor is being more efficient than his cost performance indicates. From a long-run viewpoint, this situation may be quite desirable.

In a decentralized operation, the selection of the index used to evaluate division performance is usually a complex problem. The main complexity is that a division manager usually has quite broad decision-making authority.

When the manager has more authority, there will be more decision factors under his direct control; consequently, a greater burden will be placed on the evaluation index. Cost as an index is usually not broad enough for evaluating division operation.

Profit as an index of division performance may also be inadequate. This index is broader than cost because it includes revenue considerations. In this sense, the price-making authority of the division manager will be reflected in the index. However, the ability of the division manager to build good customer relations, to secure employee loyalty, and to provide a good training ground for future top management prospects may not be adequately reflected in the profit figure, especially in the short run. Furthermore, the ability of the division manager to produce a given level of profits with a minimum capital investment will not be reflected by looking at profits alone. This problem may be partially solved by assigning capital investment to the division and calculating a rate-of-return index by relating profit to investment. This rate-of-return index, which is broader than profit alone, may be especially useful and desirable if the division manager has some authority and control over increases or decreases in the amount of capital invested in his division.

The problem of selecting an appropriate index is further complicated by the fact that one division may furnish goods and services to another division; hence, the divisions are not completely autonomous. In order to use division profit as an index where goods or services are transferred between divisions, it is necessary to develop a solution to the intracompany or transfer pricing problem. For example, if a warehouse division furnishes services to an operating division, a decision must be made as to the price at which the services are to be transferred. This is necessary to determine the warehouse division's revenue and the operating division's cost.

The overall problem is even more complex because division profits, rates of return, and transfer prices are frequently used as an aid in making decisions as well as in evaluating performance. A transfer price that is satisfactory for performance evaluation may be poorly suited to decision making and may actually lead management to wrong decisions.

When the index has been chosen, it is then necessary to settle on a standard against which to measure or compare the actual performance. The standard can be based on last year's results or the results of similar divisions within the company. However, these standards presume that the respective operations are somehow performing at the best possible efficiency. A better solution may be to choose a standard that is arrived at independently. This standard may be a budgeted profit for the division or a budgeted rate of return. If the profit is budgeted, it is possible to consider the capital invested in the division in establishing the budget. Hence, it may be that the investment can be effectively considered without actually budgeting a rate of return.

Having described an overall system of control for division operations, the remainder of this chapter will be used to discuss more completely the following parts of the problem:

(1) The selection of a profit index.
(2) The problems encountered in using division controllable profit as an evaluation index.
(3) The problems encountered in determining division investment.
(4) The intracompany pricing (transfer pricing) problem.
(5) The possible conflicts that may arise in using transfer prices for both performance evaluation and decision making.
(6) The selection of the standard against which to compare the actual performance.

THE PROFIT INDEX

The choice of the profit index is not simple. However, there really is no question of whether a performance index is needed. It is rather a question of how to construct the best one, and several different profit concepts can be used. These concepts can best be illustrated through an example. It is possible for a particular division to have the following profit and loss data assigned to it:

Revenue from division sales	$1,000
Direct division costs:	
Variable cost of goods sold and other operating costs....	700
Fixed division overhead, such as the cost of certain indirect labor and perhaps certain operating supplies	100
Fixed division overhead that is noncontrollable at the division level, such as the division manager's salary	50
Indirect division costs:	
Allocated (fixed) general office overhead, such as the division's share of the cost of the president's office	60

The above data make it possible to select several different profit calculations. The summary calculation at the top of page 546 presents some of the commonly suggested alternatives.

The four profit calculations given above are not the only possible ones, but they are the most reasonable. The names or titles assigned to each are descriptive of each calculation, but the terminology in this area has not been standardized. The important thing is to recognize what is included and excluded in each calculation.

	Division Contribution Margin	Division Controllable Profit	Division Direct Profit	Division Net Profit
Revenue	$1,000	$1,000	$1,000	$1,000
Direct cost:				
Variable cost	$ 700	$ 700	$ 700	$ 700
	$ 300			
Fixed controllable cost		100	100	100
		$ 200		
Fixed noncontrollable cost			50	50
			$ 150	
Indirect cost: Allocated home office overhead				60
				$ 90

Division net profit. It may appear that the best profit calculation to use in measuring division performance is the division net profit. Unfortunately, however, net profit is usually calculated by deducting some pro rata share of the home office overhead. An example of this cost would be the cost of operating the president's office. It is true that each division benefits from the incurrence of such a cost; but rarely, if ever, is this type of cost controllable at the division level. Although benefit received is the main criterion used to allocate cost for income reporting to outside investors, there is a real question as to whether this criterion is the proper one for performance evaluation purposes. If controllability is accepted as the main criterion in assigning cost for evaluation purposes, then net profit is a poor measure of performance.

Probably the main argument for using net profit, which implies an allocation of home office costs, is that it makes the division manager aware of the full cost of operating his division. Even though part of this full cost is not controllable by the division manager, it may be that reporting the full cost will make him work harder to control the cost over which he does have some jurisdiction. However, this argument rests largely on how the division manager is motivated. Perhaps a better approach would be to assign only controllable costs to the division and then to establish a rigorous standard in hopes that the manager will be highly motivated to meet the standard. If this works out, the manager will be concentrating his entire attention on costs that he can control rather than having his energies diluted by analyzing costs that he cannot influence.

The other obvious difficulty in using division net profits is that some method of allocation must be found for assigning the home office costs to divisions. Whatever method is chosen is likely to be arbitrary and open to question by the division managers. In order for the allocation procedure to have the desired motivational results, it will be necessary to find an allocation procedure for home office costs that is acceptable to the division managers. If this is not done, a division manager may spend much of his time attempting to reduce his costs by getting top management to change the allocation procedure.

Division direct profit. This profit calculation is defined as the total division revenue less the direct cost of the division. This concept avoids the main difficulty of net profit in that the home office costs are not allocated to the division. However, as will be noted from the calculation summary given on page 546, there may still be some direct costs that are included in the calculation but that are not controllable at the division level; that is, some costs that can be directly traced to the division may not be controllable. Costs such as the division manager's salary may be controllable only at the top management level. Also, some division overhead, such as insurance, taxes, and depreciation on fixed assets, may be established because of past investment decisions that were made by top management. If costs are to be assigned to the division on the basis of controllability, then these above-mentioned costs should be excluded from the profit calculation. If this is not done, the division profit used for performance evaluation may be increased or decreased by actions of someone who is not in the division. If this happens, it is difficult, if not impossible, to argue that the profit is really a measure of the division manager's performance.

Division controllable profit. This profit calculation is defined as the total division revenue less all costs that are directly traceable to the division and that are controllable by the division management. It would seem that, for performance measurement, this calculation is the desired one since it best reflects the results of the division manager's ability to carry out his assigned responsibility. Changes in the profit figure from year to year should be a reflection of how management responsibility is being carried out at the division level. Provided the standard used for comparison is valid, any variances between actual and standard can be explained in terms of factors over which the division manager has decision-making responsibility. It may be, of course, that some of these factors are difficult for the division manager to influence. For example, the prices of raw materials may be increasing. If the standard (budget) is not revised each year, unfavorable price variances will result. Even though the price cannot be influenced, perhaps alternate raw materials can be used or alternate sources of supply can be found. Problems of this nature may be difficult to solve, but this is part of the division management's responsibility. Failure to solve such a problem successfully is different from being unable to take any action at all because there is no authority. The latter situation almost always arises with respect to costs that can be controlled only at the top management level; that is, the division manager, regardless of whether he can solve the problem, rarely has the authority to attempt a solution.

In calculating controllable profit, some fixed costs are included. It may appear that the cost is noncontrollable if it is fixed. This is not necessarily true. "Fixed" does not mean fixed in *amount*. It means fixed with respect to changes in volume. Perhaps the division manager can reduce the *level* of supervisory salaries by reorganizing certain parts of the division operation. The new level of cost may still be fixed with respect to volume changes, but profits will increase because the new level is less than the old level. The point is that the level of fixed cost may be controllable. If fixed controllable costs are not included, important spending variances may be overlooked.

Division contribution margin. The contribution margin or marginal income of the division is calculated by deducting variable costs from total revenue. The main argument for this concept is that contribution margin is useful in decision making. This point has been demonstrated throughout the book. However, for performance evaluation the defect is obvious, namely, there are some controllable items of fixed cost that are excluded from the calculation. As a performance evaluation index, therefore, contribution margin is incomplete in its coverage.

It is true that contribution margin is useful in decision making. The fact that controllable profit is used in overall performance evaluation should not be taken as an indication that contribution margin has to be given up as a decision-making technique.

The following report shows both the contribution margin and the controllable profit:

Division A
Profit Report

Revenue	$1,000
Variable cost	700
Contribution margin	$ 300
Fixed controllable cost	100
Controllable profit	$ 200

In this report both the contribution margin and the controllable profit are available as a management tool, and there is no need to have to choose one or the other. Furthermore, the controllable profit may be the best guide for some decisions. If a particular decision will change the level of fixed cost, then these costs should be considered as variable costs for that particular decision. For example, if the division manager decides to eliminate a department, it may be possible to reduce supervisory salaries that are included in fixed controllable cost. If this is the case, the entire profit statement will be used as a basis for establishing the necessary data for the decision.

SOME PROBLEMS IN USING DIVISION CONTROLLABLE PROFIT AS AN EVALUATION INDEX

Deciding on the best index to use for evaluation purposes does not solve all the problems of actually measuring the index. There are several accounting problems that must be solved in order for controllable division profit to be a good index for evaluating performance.

There are several ways in which the division manager can increase the short-run profits of his division to the detriment of the company as a whole. For example, it may be possible to delay maintenance costs. Such an action will inflate profits, but the long-run profitability of the division and the company may be affected adversely. Expenditures that engender employee loyalty may be delayed or simply may not be made at all. In the short-run, division profits may increase, but at the expense of long-run division and company profits. If the division manager is motivated to cut down supervision costs, he may not develop long-run top management personnel. In short, a solution must be found to the problem of the ability of the division manager to create division profits that will cause a long-run decline in company profits.

Other accounting problems may arise if profit comparisons are made between similar operating divisions. In this case, all profit calculations should rest on the same inventory and depreciation procedures. A problem also arises with respect to cost items that sometimes are inventoried (and written off as used) and other times are expensed directly. For example, the purchase of indirect operating supplies may create a problem in interpreting profit differences between divisions as well as profit differences between accounting periods for the same division. If potential inventory items such as indirect production supplies are expensed when purchased, it may be that an increase in a division's profit this period came at the expense of a large purchase of supplies the previous period. Likewise, differences in profit between divisions during a given period may be caused by a difference in the timing of purchases and the failure to reflect inventories. If these differences are significant, the profit figure will be distorted and may be difficult to analyze.

Problems of revenue recognition may require attention before the division profit can be used effectively in evaluating performance. When the sale is only a matter of delivery, as can be the case for some precious metals and agricultural products, for example, the ability of the division manager to influence the amount of profit and the profit pattern by choosing the time of sale may destroy comparisons between years and between divisions. It may make sense, for example, to evaluate division performance in gold mining by recognizing revenue when the gold is produced rather than when it is sold.

If controllable profit is to be used as an evaluation index it is, of course, necessary to be able to define and measure controllable cost. This problem was mentioned earlier and it is not a trivial one. Whether a cost is controllable depends on the level of management under consideration. The cost of owning a building may only be controllable at the division manager level; the operating department manager may have very little influence over such cost.

Controllability also has a time dimension. If the time horizon is very long, some costs may be controllable which would not be controllable in a short time period. For example, the cost of owning a machine may be controllable by a department manager if the time horizon is at least as long as the life of the machine. On the other hand, if the time horizon for the profit calculation is one year, perhaps only the cost of operating the machine (as opposed to the cost of owning the machine) is controllable. Supposedly, all costs are controllable at some level in the organization if the time horizon is sufficiently long. However, this does not resolve the problem since profit reporting periods may be as short as one month or one quarter of a year. In distinguishing controllable from non-controllable costs, it is necessary to consider the time horizon as well as the level of management for whom the profit report is prepared. This applies not only to cost and revenue items but to investment items as well.

DETERMINING DIVISION INVESTMENT

If divisions are to be evaluated on the basis of rate of return on investment, it is necessary to determine the investment base to be used. There are many problems connected with this determination.

The first problem that arises is to decide which assets should be assigned to the division. Many assets can usually be traced directly to the division. For example, a division may handle its own receivables and inventory and may even have jurisdiction over its own cash balance. Also, much of the physical property used may be traceable to a particular division. Sometimes, traceable assets such as receivables, inventories, and cash are centrally administered and controlled. However, by proper account coding it is usually possible to trace receivables and inventories to the division operation even though these assets are administered centrally. Cash, on the other hand, if it is centrally administered, is usually very difficult to trace to division operations.

In most cases, there is bound to be some investment that is common to several divisions. In such a case, no amount of coding, sorting, or classifying will provide a basis for directly tracing this investment to a division. If this type of investment is to be assigned to the division, a basis of allocation must be found. An example of common investment would be the investment in building, furniture and fixtures, and so forth used by the central corporate administration. Any basis of allocation used to assign this type of investment is bound to be an arbitrary one. If such an assignment is made, the division investment is no longer the traceable investment but is the traceable investment plus some allocated share of common investment.

One author has suggested that the relevant investment base for division evaluation is the amount of investment uniquely devoted to the support of the particular division operation.[1] If this criterion is applied to common investment, the amount of the common investment allocated to a division would be that part of the total common investment which could be avoided if the division were not present. This is a difficult concept to apply, but perhaps its application can be approached by seeking relationships between the level of common investment and the level of certain division activities. For example, perhaps a relationship can be established between the level of common investment in a personnel department and the number of employees in each division.

If the above procedure cannot be applied, it is difficult to see any justification for the allocation of common investment. At best, the procedure used is likely to be quite arbitrary. If divisions are compared with one another, this comparison will probably be affected by the basis of allocation chosen. In fact, the basis of allocation could well determine the ranking of each division. In an earlier section of the chapter it was stated that the best profit calculation for performance evaluation was the one based only on factors under the control of the division management. If this same criterion is used in determining investment, the common investment should not be allocated. Traceable investment should be a better measure of controllable investment than traceable investment plus some allocated share of common investment.

---

[1] Gordon Shillinglaw, *Cost Accounting, Analysis and Control*, Revised Edition (Homewood, Illinois: Richard D. Irwin, Inc., 1967), p. 790.

Once the method of assigning investment to divisions has been determined, it is necessary to decide whether plant assets will be stated at gross, meaning original cost, or at net, meaning original cost less accumulated depreciation. (It is assumed for purposes of this discussion that the original cost of an asset is the relevant base and not the replacement cost or some other measure. This problem will be discussed later.)

The use of gross plant assets for calculating a division rate of return on investment is justified in three ways by Research Report No. 35 of the National Association of Accountants. They are: [2]

(1) Some companies who participated in the study used gross fixed assets because duPont and Monsanto Chemical Company use it.

(2) Using undepreciated cost is sometimes defended on the grounds that it tends to compensate for the effect that inflation has had on historical costs. The report indicates that those companies who gave this justification admit that this base is a rather haphazard method for approximating replacement cost.

(3) The gross base is used to prevent the rate of return from rising as the net book value of depreciable assets is reduced by depreciation.

Of these three reasons, only the third seems to have any real validity. A fourth reason often given for the use of the gross base is that different depreciation methods used by different divisions are washed out and interdivisional comparisons are more effective.

With regard to the third reason, namely the rising rate of return, the reader is referred to Chapter 5. In this chapter, the problem of an increasing rate of return was discussed in some detail as the problem pertains to the business as a whole. The N.A.A. research report mentioned above indicates that the main problem with respect to division profit has to do with the recovery of capital. The capital recovered through operations is ordinarily reinvested elsewhere in the business and so there is no real tendency for rate of return on net investment for the company to increase. On the other hand, if capital recovered in a division operation is reinvested in some other division, then the net asset base, which is decreasing, will cause the rate of return on net assets for a division to rise. These observations, of course, rest on the assumption that the earning power of the asset is fairly constant from year to year or, more precisely, that the earning power declines less rapidly than does the net book value.

_____

[2] *N. A. A. Bulletin, Research Report No. 35,* "Return on Capital as a Guide to Managerial Decisions," 1959 (New York: National Association of Accountants), p. 13.

The observation that for the business as a whole (because of the reinvestment of capital) there is no tendency for the rate of return on net assets to rise with the passage of time is a statement that borders on being in error. The straight line method of depreciation always has a tendency toward giving an increasing rate of return over time. In the early years of an asset's life, the rate is understated, and in later years the rate is overstated. If the firm has plant assets, some of which are new and some of which are old, the understatement will tend to offset the overstatement and the overall rate will not tend to rise. This occurs not simply because the capital is reinvested but because the assets are well-seasoned in age. Therefore, even if the funds recovered by operation in a particular division are reinvested in that division, there will be a tendency for the rate of return on net assets to rise with the passage of time if straight-line depreciation is used and if the assets of the division are predominantly of the same age group. If the division has predominantly new assets, the rate of return calculated on net assets will be lower than the rate of return in a similar but older division.

This problem was discussed in Chapter 5 and the annuity method of depreciation was proposed. There is no particular reason why this same method cannot be used to depreciate divisional assets, and this procedure would then allow the use of net assets as an investment base. There would be no tendency for the rate of return to rise simply because of the depreciation method used.

The above discussion presupposes that either net or gross original cost is used in the determination of the division investment. One might argue that replacement cost or perhaps original cost adjusted for changes in the price level should be used. It may seem that, if rate of return is to be used as a measure of division efficiency, the investment should be stated on some current value basis rather than on some historical basis, or perhaps even worse, on the basis of several different historical bases as is usually the case if historical cost is used. The obvious difficulty is the measurement problem. How would replacement costs be approximated? What happens when the specific plant or equipment asset is not replaced? If a common-dollar base is desirable, which price level index should be used? It is easier to raise questions than to give answers in this problem area.

THE INTRACOMPANY OR TRANSFER PRICING PROBLEM

In calculating division profit, problems arise when the divisions are not completely independent. If one division furnishes goods or services to another division, a transfer price must be established in order to determine the profit of the divisions involved. This is because the transfer price represents the buying division's cost and the selling division's revenue. Both revenue and cost are necessary to calculate profit. There is a possible conflict in establishing transfer prices because the data may be used in making decisions as well as in calculating a profit index for performance evaluation. In this section of the chapter, it will be assumed that the transfer price is used only for performance evaluation. Some of the possible areas of conflict will be investigated and discussed in the next section.

There are many possible transfer prices that may be used. Some of the commonly recognized possibilities are as follows:

(1) Market price.
(2) A negotiated or bargained market price.
(3) A transfer price based on a cost calculation that can be either full cost or marginal (variable) cost.

Market price. There may be real difficulty in determining a market price. First of all, the use of a market price assumes that a market exists at the transfer point. Even if this is the case, the appropriate market price may be difficult to establish. Frequently, the list price is only vaguely related to the effective market price. Often the market price will be a fluctuating one. The selling division may incur less cost in selling to the buying division than would be incurred if the product were sold to outsiders. This occurs when the buying division is a captive market. In such an instance, if the market price is not adjusted downward, the selling division will get the entire benefit of the savings in selling costs.

A more difficult problem exists where there is no real market at the transfer point. If the selling division furnishes repair, research, or storage services to the buying division, how can a satisfactory market price for such service be established? This is certainly not an easy problem to solve.

In spite of the problems of arriving at market price, there is general agreement that, if a market price can somehow be determined, it is probably the best price for use in performance evaluation. The underlying justification for this statement is as follows. The use of a decentralized organization arrangement is largely motivated by a desire to create smaller, autonomous operating divisions that will conduct their business as separate entities. The use of a market transfer price, where possible, will create the actual market conditions under which these divisions would operate if they were actually separate companies, rather than divisions of one organization. Furthermore, to the extent that market prices can be established on the basis of outside forces, they form an excellent performance indicator because they cannot be manipulated by the individuals who have an interest in the resulting profit calculation.

For purposes of illustrating the above comments, assume that the company has two divisions, a producing division and a marketing division. The operation might be a corporation farm. The producing division is to produce a bushel of wheat, which can be sold as soon as it is produced or transferred to the marketing division where the decision will be made as to the future date to sell the wheat. This situation is diagrammed below:

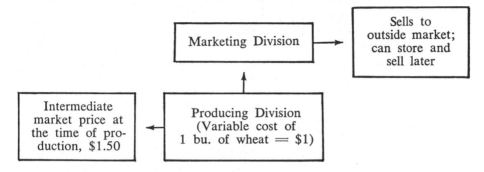

If management desires to evaluate each division manager, the $1.50 market price should be used as a transfer price. This price compared with the $1 variable production cost gives a 50 cents profit. This profit is dependent on the efficiency of the production operation. It also depends on the ability to produce the proper grain crop (wheat, corn, etc.) at the right time. These decisions are within the jurisdiction of the producing division manager. The marketing division should buy from the producing division only if it is felt that the grain can be stored and sold at some later date at a profit. These decisions are the responsibility of the marketing division. If the marketing division buys the bushel of wheat and sells it six months later at $2, having incurred interest and storage costs of 30 cents, the profit resulting from this operation is 20 cents. A summary calculation is as follows:

	Producing Division	Marketing Division	
Sales	$ 1.50		$ 2.00
Cost	1.00	($1.50 + $.30)	1.80
Profit	$ .50		$ .20

The total profit for the company is 70 cents; but by using a market transfer price, the total profit is divided into a producing and a marketing profit. These separate profits will be a good basis on which to evaluate each division's operation.

Negotiated or bargained market price. One of the early writers on transfer pricing, Joel Dean, strongly recommends the use of negotiated or bargained prices as a refinement in the market pricing scheme.[3] Dean urges that there are real advantages in allowing the two division managers, who must have complete freedom to buy and sell outside, to arrive at the transfer price through arm's-length bargaining. Dean stresses that the selfish interest of the division managers in the division profit and their bonuses will serve the company objectives as long as the following three principles are observed:

(1) All transfer prices should be determined by negotiation between the buyer and the seller.

(2) Negotiators should have all the data on alternative sources, markets, and market prices.

(3) Both the buyer and the seller must be free to buy and sell outside the company.

This scheme suggested by Dean has much appeal. A negotiated market price may solve some of the problems encountered in trying to base the market transfer price on a list price, which may have no meaning, or on a market price, which is really not applicable because the selling costs of selling to the division are much less than selling outside the firm. Furthermore, much of the friction and bad feeling that may arise by a centrally controlled market transfer price may be eliminated without incurring any misallocation of resources. It may be that this method will demand much of the division managers' time to negotiate the transfer prices. If this is undesirable, a possible remedy would be to negotiate these prices for a certain time period instead of for each transfer that takes place. Also, it has often been observed that many of the problems that arise in transfer pricing are created because the buying division is a captive customer and is unable to bargain effectively with the selling division. Real competition can probably be injected into the situation by encouraging the division managers to buy and sell outside and, of course, praising them when their results are favorable.

However, a word of caution is also in order. Bargained or negotiated price may solve some of the problems encountered in transfer pricing, but such a method will probably not eliminate all of them. If the buying division can obtain a lower price by purchasing outside, it is true that the buying division's profit will be increased. However, the selling division's decrease in profit because of a loss in volume may more than offset this profit increase. In such an instance, the total company may suffer. In the long run, the selling division manager would probably lower his price so as not to create large losses because of unused capacity. If this happens, the ability to negotiate market price is certainly superior to a centrally administered market price from which the division managers cannot depart.

---

[3] Joel Dean, "Decentralization and Intracompany Pricing," *Harvard Business Review*, XXXIII, 4 (1955), pp. 65-74.

Transfer prices based on cost. For performance evaluation, it is difficult to justify transfer prices based on cost—either full cost or marginal cost—except as a last resort. A price based on marginal or variable cost is useful in decision making, as will be discussed later, but for performance evaluation such a figure usually produces a loss for the selling division. Where no intermediate market exists, perhaps a price based on cost is the only possibility. In such a case, *for performance evaluation,* full cost or full cost plus some profit allowance is probably superior to variable or marginal cost. If this is not done, there will probably be no profit on which to evaluate the selling division. Such a scheme is not without its problems. Probably the most serious problem will be the long arguments that will undoubtedly be generated on just what is the cost. Also, as will be shown later, a full cost is almost useless as an aid in decision making.

If cost is to be used as a transfer price base, it should probably be a standard cost rather than an actual cost. If this is done, the inefficiencies in the producing (selling) operation will not be passed on to the buying division. Such inefficiencies should not be passed on because the buying division probably has no control over such factors.

TRANSFER PRICES FOR DECISION MAKING—A SYSTEM OF INFORMATION AND COMMUNICATION

As was pointed out earlier, one of the basic reasons for decentralization is that decentralization makes it possible to spread the decision-making responsibility and authority throughout the firm. If one man or a small group can efficiently make *all* decisions for the entire firm, then much if not all of the impetus for decentralization will disappear. Hence, one of the basic assumptions in decentralization is that the firm-wide decision process is too big and complex for one man to handle and that this important process can be carried out better by decentralizing some of the decisions that must be made, and having these parts of the process carried out by managers of subunits.

If this type of delegation of decision-making responsibility is to work, a communication system must be set up within the firm. The need for a system of communication on which decisions can be based will usually vary directly with the degree of decentralization involved. If all decisions are made centrally, the only need for communication is so that the submanagers can implement the decisions. On the other hand, if the submanagers *make* and *implement* decisions, the need for a system of communication within the firm is greater.

In a decentralized operation, if the divisions are *interdependent,* a system of transfer prices can provide a communication system or a set of signals which the submanagers can use as a basis for their decisions. In such a setting, the system of internal prices serves the same purpose in facilitating internal transactions as the external price system does in facilitating transactions between the firm and external parties.

To develop this point, consider the role of the external price system as a system for providing information and communication for facilitating transactions *between* firms. If a make or buy decision is to be made by Firm A, the first step in the decision would probably be to compare the outside prices of labor and raw materials (and other factors of production) with the *outside price* of the part. The decision will depend primarily on how these "costs" compare with each other. Note that the external price system furnishes the information which guides the actions of the decision maker. Note also how much more difficult it would be to make a decision if the information on costs were not available in the form of external prices. It is in this sense that a system of prices is a powerfully efficient information system.

In a decentralized operation, where divisions are interdependent, the manager of a division needs information which will enable him to decide when to deal with a sister division and when to deal with an outside firm. For example, assume that Division B can buy a component part from Division S or from an outside firm. This problem is just another version of the make or buy example given earlier. The decision will depend primarily on a comparison of the costs of acquiring the component from Division S (which is given by the internal transfer price) or from the outside firm (which is given by the external price). If the internal transfer price is higher than the external price, the manager of Division B has a *signal* to buy outside the firm and vice versa. It is, therefore, important that the transfer prices give the right signals, for otherwise the decision process will not be carried out efficiently.

Before discussing the problem involved in using internal transfer prices in decision making, it is useful to observe that even the external price system sometimes breaks down as an information system for decentralized operations. As an example, suppose that Firm F has several divisions, say Divisions A, B, C, and D. Suppose that Division A needs to buy a fabricated steel part to be used in its final product. Two outside companies (X and Y) bid on the job and Company X quotes a price of $100 and Y a price of $110. However, if Y gets the order for the fabricated part, it will buy the raw steel from Division C. This order will amount to $40, of which $12 will be profit to Division C. In this case, the external price system breaks down as an information system.

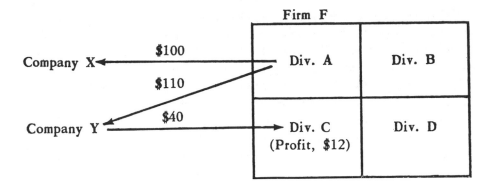

As shown in the above diagram, the net cost to Firm F is $100 if A buys the part from X and $98 (i.e., $110 — $12) if A buys the part from Y. Yet, the external price which A uses does not reflect the advantages to the firm of buying from Company Y; that is, the external price system does not give A all the information. In such a case, A will probably choose the wrong course of action.

Since the external price system is sometimes inefficient as an information system, it should be obvious that an artifically created internal price system rarely can be completely trouble free. However, in a decentralized operation where divisions deal with each other as well as with outsiders, there is no choice as to whether transfer prices should or should not be used. The various division managers need an information system and internal prices are, for the most part, inevitable.

The following discussion of the problems and difficulties in using transfer prices is offered in hopes that a clear understanding of these problems will lead to better internal price systems and practices.

It is difficult to anticipate and describe all potential problems, but it is possible to describe some of the general problems that management should be aware of. Two distinct cases will be distinguished: They are (1) a situation where a market exists at the transfer point and (2) a situation where a market does not exist at the transfer point.

The intermediate market case. In the case of division operation, two general types of decisions may be called for. They are (1) how to produce and (2) how much to produce. The second type of decision includes the decision as to both price and quantity. Assume that Division A is the selling division and Division B is the buying division. One decision made by B is to decide whether or not to buy from A. B will be encouraged to buy from A as long as the price quoted by A compares favorably with the outside market price.

If the market is a perfectly competitive one, it may make little difference in the overall profit picture even if B does buy outside. This is because A should be able to sell all of its output on the outside market; hence, B's decision to buy outside will not cause A to have any idle capacity. Furthermore, if the market is prefectly competitive, the selling costs of selling outside are likely to be about the same as the cost of selling to B.

When the market is not a perfectly competitive one, the situation changes somewhat. If market price is used as the transfer price, it would be undesirable for the price to be so rigid and inflexible that B might possibly go outside to find a somewhat lower price and not buy from A without A's being allowed to lower its price. Such an action might cause A to have idle capacity, and the overall company profits would be lower than if A dropped the price to encourage B to buy inside. Actually, B should buy inside so long as A's marginal cost is below the outside market price. In such a situation, then, a possible conflict arises. Some authorities have advocated that the transfer price should be a dual one; that is, the transfer price to A should be the market price and the transfer price to B should be A's marginal cost. This feeling arises because many of the decisions to be made by B should be based on marginal or variable cost. The example given is one such decision. Such a practice will undoubtedly destroy some of the advantages of decentralization. By using a dual standard, some of the competitive atmosphere will be destroyed. A system of negotiated market price would seem to work much better. A would probably not allow idle capacity to persist in the long run. Rather, the market price to B would probably be negotiated at a low enough price so that B would not continue buying outside.

For most decisions of how to produce, even where there is capital investment involved, the proper calculation is the marginal cost. This is so because, from the viewpoint of the entire company, the how-to-produce decision should be made so as to achieve the minimum cost possible. Costs that change with volume are the relevant costs, and these costs are the marginal (or variable) costs. Any time a market transfer price is used, there is a potential conflict that may arise in connection with how-to-produce problems. In some cases a negotiated market price may accommodate the situation (as in the example); but, in any case, the safest transfer price for the decision is the marginal or variable cost. Such a transfer price, however, is generally a poor one for performance evaluation.

In pricing and output decisions for the end product, again it is the marginal or variable costs that are relevant. This is particularly true when the intermediate market is not a perfectly competitive one. If the intermediate market is perfectly competitive, the market price will suffice. For example, assume that Division A produces unprocessed meat and Division B can buy from Division A and sell the meat processed. In order to justify processing, the variable cost of processing in Division B plus the opportunity market price as determined by the intermediate (unprocessed) market must be less than the selling price of processed meat. Hence, market price will accommodate a sell-or-process-more decision in a competitive market.[4]

In the case of an imperfect intermediate market, the following decisions must be made with respect to output:

(1) What price should be charged for the final product?
(2) What price should be charged for the intermediate product?
(3) How much of the intermediate product should be produced for sale on the outside market and how much for sale to Division B?

All of these decisions must be made on the basis of a marginal cost and a marginal revenue schedule for the several products involved. Neither market price nor a transfer price based on full cost will suffice in making these decisions. Hence, a conflict is bound to arise between choosing a transfer price for performance evaluation and one for decision making.

The following example will illustrate the imperfect market situation. Assume that Division A sells to Division B. The output of Division A is Product X_1, which can be sold at the intermediate market stage or can be transferred to Division B and processed and sold as Product X_2. The marginal revenue and the variable cost situation is as follows:

| | Division A | | | Division B | |
Number of Units	X_1 Marginal Revenue	X_1 Variable Cost	X_2 Marginal Revenue	X_2 Variable Cost	X_2 Marginal Revenue Less X_2 Variable Cost
11	$ .25	$1.50	$ .50	$1.00	$—.50
10	.25	1.50	.50	1.00	—.50
9	.50	1.50	1.00	1.00	-0-
8	.75	1.50	1.50	1.00	.50
7	1.00	1.50	2.00	1.00	1.00
6	1.25	1.50	2.50	1.00	1.50
5	1.50	1.50	3.00	1.00	2.00
4	1.75	1.50	3.50	1.00	2.50
3	2.00	1.50	4.00	1.00	3.00
2	2.25	1.50	4.50	1.00	3.50
1	2.50	1.50	5.00	1.00	4.00

---

[4] In terms of economic theory, the market price and the marginal cost in a perfectly competitive market should be equal; that is, if the division manager maximizes profit, he should produce and sell until marginal cost and marginal revenue are equal. In a perfectly competitive market, the demand curve is horizontal because the division can sell any output at the market price. Hence, marginal revenue and market price are equal. If production is expanded until marginal cost and marginal revenue are equated, marginal cost will equal the market price.

This example is simplified by using a constant variable cost as a measure of marginal cost. In comparing the marginal costs and revenues, it can be seen that six units of X_2 can be sold in the final market before the net marginal revenue equals the variable cost of X_1 of $1.50; therefore six units of X_1 should be sold to Division B for processing into X_2 and sale in the final market. But five units of X_1 can also be sold in the intermediate market before the marginal revenue equals the variable cost of $1.50. Hence, 11 units of X_1 should be produced.

The reader will note that this output decision has been made by using the marginal revenue of Product X_1 and the *net* marginal revenue of Product X_2. A unit of X_1 has a marginal production cost of $1.50, and it should be sold in that market where the profits are the highest. In the case of the intermediate market, no further processing is necessary. The production cost of $1.50 represents the total additional cost to be incurred in selling Product X_1 in the intermediate market. However, if X_1 is processed and sold as X_2, the additional processing cost is $1 per unit and this amount should be deducted from the marginal revenue of X_2 to arrive at the net amount of additional revenue that will eventually accrue to the company.

In the above example, the total production schedule calls for 11 units of X_1 to be produced by Division A. It was assumed that the capacity of Division A was such that at least 11 units of X_1 could be produced. This may or may not be the case. Suppose, for example, that the capacity of Division A was limited to less than 11 units. In this case, a priority schedule must be developed to decide which units of X_1 should be sold to the intermediate market and which units should be sold to Division B for further processing and sale in the final market.

This priority schedule can be determined by comparing the marginal revenue schedules of the two divisions. For example, the first three units of X_1 should be transferred to Division B since the net marginal revenue of this division is greater than the marginal revenue of Division A. On the 4th and 5th units, the marginal revenue of X_1 in either the final or the intermediate market is $2.50; so there is a point of indifference. The 6th unit should be allocated to the intermediate market, the 7th and 8th units have equal value in either market, the 9th unit should stay in Division A, and the 10th and 11th units have equal value in either market. The 12th unit should not be produced, since the marginal revenue in either market is lower than the marginal cost of $1.50. The schedule on the next page, where the unit numbers are in parentheses, summarizes the priority for each unit. If for some reason the productive capacity of Division A is restricted to less than 11 units, this priority schedule can be used.

Units of Product X_1	Marginal Revenue if X_1 Is Sold in the Intermediate Market	Net Marginal Revenue if X_1 Is Sold to Division B for Sale in the Final Market
1	$2.50 (4 or 5)	$4.00 (1)
2	2.25 (6)	3.50 (2)
3	2.00 (7 or 8)	3.00 (3)
4	1.75 (9)	2.50 (4 or 5)
5	1.50 (10 or 11)	2.00 (7 or 8)
6	1.25	1.50 (10 or 11)
7	1.00	1.00
8	.75	.50
9	.50	-0-
10	.25	—.50
11	.25	—.50

As can be seen from the example, the allocation problem in an imperfect market situation requires marginal cost transfer prices. A market transfer price may cause Division B to restrict production. This restriction could cause Division A to stop short of the most profitable level of production. Yet a marginal cost transfer price is a poor one for performance evaluation. In the imperfect market situation, therefore, a conflict will undoubtedly arise where the data must also be used for pricing and output decisions.

The no intermediate market case. If, in fact, no intermediate market exists for the product of Division A, then Division A is really not a profit center. Such a division may still be set up as a decentralized independent operating unit, but it is more like a cost center within a centralized firm. To treat such a division as a profit center requires the determination of a transfer price that may be quite arbitrary. Furthermore, there is no real possibility for negotiation between Divisions A and B since Division A has no outside market alternative.

For decision problems, the proper transfer price for Unit X_1 would be its marginal or variable cost. Since no market price exists, the main alternative is likely to be the full cost. The full cost may be an acceptable transfer price for performance evaluation, but such a figure will undoubtedly lead to poor decisions, because the buying division will be more likely to buy outside and in doing so may create excess capacity in the selling division. It is probably better to recognize the cost center as a cost center and to evaluate Division A on the basis of a controllable cost budget or standard. The variable or marginal cost should be used as the transfer price to Division B. This figure can be used as a basis for evaluating Division B on a profit basis and it also will be useful to Division B in making output and production decisions.

THE EVALUATION CRITERION OR STANDARD

The main indexes of division performance discussed earlier in this chapter were (1) division profit and (2) division return on investment. Where no intermediate market exists, it is difficult to calculate profit, and cost may be the best performance index. However, standards for cost control have been discussed in earlier chapters and this problem will not be reviewed here.

If profit alone is used as an evaluation of division performance, the standard for measurement will probably be a profit budget for the division. This budget can be constructed by referring to other similar division operations within or outside the company. If this is done, the factors that are unique in the operation of a particular division should be taken into consideration. If the market is temporarily depressed and if this factor is not controllable by the division manager, this factor should receive proper consideration in establishing the budget. A detailed division profit budget should show, after a comparison with the actual performance, the parts of the division operation that are the weakest and on which a concentrated managerial effort is justified. Only the factors that are controllable by the division manager should be included in the profit budget.

This approach has been criticized on the grounds that the division manager also has responsibility for the invested capital and that a profit budget may relieve him of this responsibility in the evaluation process. This criticism has probably been the main reason for trying to use rate of return on investment as a performance index. This scheme, however, is not without its problems. First of all, it is probably a mistake to compare a division's rate of return with the overall average rate *desired* by the top management. It may be that the division can never measure up to the desired overall average rate of return. Just because management desires a 20 percent rate of return is absolutely no guarantee that a particular division can ever hope to earn this rate. Also, a division that earns 15 percent should not necessarily be liquidated. Even if other parts of the company can earn 20 percent on additional investment, the 15 percent division should not be liquidated unless the division investment is based on liquidation value and unless the 15 percent division can be liquidated without affecting the other operating divisions of the company. To the extent that the 15 percent return is based on historical investment, it is probably a poor guide for capital budgeting decisions, and depending on the standard used, it may be a poor index of performance. If a rate of return is used for judging performance, a standard of comparison should be established for the division being evaluated and should not be based on the desires of management.

Another problem encountered in using a rate of return for judging performance can arise when the division manager does not have control over investment decisions. If the capital budget is administered centrally, it is more effective to control division investment by making the division manager's new projects compete for funds by using as a standard the best projects that exist elsewhere within the company. In this respect, the division rate of return budgeted for performance evaluation may be an extremely poor guide for additional investment because the money may find a better use elsewhere in the company.

Even though the division manager may not have complete control over all of his division investment, he is likely to have a good deal of control over the working capital requirements of the division. The performance index should allow for this aspect of division operation. However, instead of calculating a rate of return on working capital investment, it is probably easier and more effective to include a charge for this investment in establishing the profit budget. This charge may be based on the rate that could be earned on working capital investment elsewhere in the company. If such a procedure were followed, the division manager would be reluctant to demand excess working capital. Furthermore, top management can also tell whether a particular division's use of working capital is as profitable as other divisions.

The problem of controlling and evaluating division operations in a decentralized company is exceedingly complex. Yet, top management really has no choice as to whether or not control is needed; it is rather a question of finding the most effective control device. Every manager must have some means of answering the question, "Where are the problems and the weak spots in the overall operation?" In a decentralized operation, the contact with the various parts of the operation is likely to be quite impersonal. Usually some reporting system must be used. Accounting concepts are useful because they can facilitate management by exception. If a good standard can be established and if a good index of actual performance can be calculated, the two can be compared and the exceptional case demanding management's attention can be found. However, since the control problem is a difficult but an important one, it behooves the manager to be very familiar with the strong features of a particular system as well as the troublesome problems that will undoubtedly be encountered in using accounting information.

Questions

1. What are the advantages of decentralization?

2. Why isn't cost a good control index in evaluating a division manager who has decision power on prices and combination of products?

3. Briefly state the difference between division controllable and division direct profit.

4. What are some of the disadvantages of using division profit as an evaluation index?

5. Should investment which is common to several divisions be allocated to those divisions for purpose of calculating a rate of return?

6. Under what conditions are transfer prices necessary?

7. If a market transfer price can be determined why is it that such a price is usually considered the best one to use?

8. If cost is used as a transfer price for a "service" department, why is standard cost usually preferred to "actual" cost?

9. If the intermediate market is perfectly competitive, will a market-based transfer ever lead to excess capacity in a producing division?

10. What is the disadvantage of using negotiated transfer prices where no intermediate market exists in which the producing division can sell its products?

Exercises

1. In evaluating the performance of the Lang Company, the President, Mr. Lang, says that the return on investment has been running about 5 percent. He reasons that he can earn more than 5 percent by investing in alternative investments and the company should therefore be sold.

Last year (which was typical), the net profits were $50,000 and the total assets as per the balance sheet amounted to $1,000,000.

Required: Explain to Mr. Lang one of the important reasons why his analysis may not be correct because of the investment base he is using in his calculation.

2. Given the following data, compute division contribution margin, controllable profit, direct profit, and net profit.

Revenue from sales	$7,280
Division variable costs	4,100
Fixed overhead directly traceable to the division:	
Controllable	600
Noncontrollable	380
Allocated home office overhead	1,310

3. Division B buys components from Division S and uses these components in manufacturing a product which is sold to outside customers.

A customer offers $100 for an order of two units. Division B's variable cost of producing the order, including the components from S, is $70 per unit. Division S uses a full cost transfer price of $60 per unit which includes $25 of allocated fixed overhead.

Required: What is Division B likely to do in this situation? If both S and B have excess capacity would this action be good from the viewpoint of the whole company? What kind of a transfer price could be used to avoid this problem?

4. Company X has two divisions, M and S. Division M manufactures a product and Division S sells it. The intermediate market is perfectly competitive, but the product can be stored and sold later or processed and sold in the final processed market. Once the product is manufactured, some of it is sold by Division M and some is transferred to Division S which decides whether to hold or process the product. The following transactions pertain to 1972:

1. Manufacturing costs incurred by Division M in producing 1,000,000 units $4,700,000
2. Of the 1,000,000 units produced:
    400,000 sold by M in intermediate market 3,300,000
    200,000 (No additional processing work has been done on these units in Division S.) held by S for sale later 1,900,000
    400,000 processed by S and sold 4,000,000
3. Sales value of 600,000 units at the time they were transferred to S 4,950,000
4. Total additional processing costs of S 1,400,000
5. No beginning inventories

Required: (1) Prepare an income statement for the whole firm.
(2) Prepare separate income statements for each division using a market value transfer price.

5. Describe why an internal transfer price information system would not be needed in a decentralized operation if the divisions were independent.

6. The Quirin Company is going to build an office building for itself in a large city. The company has a construction division which builds all buildings and equipment for the entire company. The construction division has requested bids on the elevators for the building from two companies. The O Company gives a bid of $3,000,000 and the U Company bids $3,250,000. However, the U Company would buy raw materials for the elevators from a fabricating division of the Quirin Company. This order would result in the fabricating division earning $300,000 after covering all costs. Since the Quirin Company is decentralized, the construction division is not aware of this possibility.

Required: Which bid would you expect the construction division to take? Which bid would the Quirin Company prefer to have the construction division accept? If these sorts of transactions are important, should the Quirin Company be decentralized? Explain.

7. The Boyd Company has a producing division which is currently producing 50,000 units and has a capacity of 100,000 units. The variable cost of the product is $6 per unit and the total fixed cost is $200,000 or $4 per unit based on current production.

A selling division of the Boyd Company offers to buy 50,000 units from the producing division at $5.80. The producing division manager refuses the order because it is below variable cost. The selling division manager urges that the order should be accepted, even though his price offer is below variable cost, because by taking the order the producing division manager can lower the fixed cost per unit from $4 per unit to $2 per unit since output will double. This decrease will more than offset the 20 cents difference between the variable cost and the price.

Required: (1) If you were the producing division manager would you accept the selling division manager's argument? Why or why not?

(2) From the viewpoint of the overall company, should the order be accepted if the selling division manager intended to sell the units in the outside market for $6.25 after incurring additional processing costs of 30 cents per unit?

8. The tailor shop in a men's and women's clothing store is set up as an autonomous unit. The transfer price for tailor services is based on the variable cost which is estimated at $4.00 per hour. The store manager feels that the men's department is currently using too much tailor time and that this department could cut down on hours used by taking more care in fitting the suits, coats, etc. The manager decided to double the hourly tailor rate (to $8) even though this new rate is no reflection of the real variable cost. His idea is to simply provide an incentive to the men's department to conserve on tailor time.

Required: What possible disadvantages do you see in the store manager's action? Do you agree or disagree with this means of stressing the need to conserve tailor time?

9. The Alpha Company has a central heat, light, and power department which furnishes utilities to other operating divisions. The transfer price is based on "actual" full cost. The actual cost is determined at the end of each month and is simply the actual variable cost incurred plus the actual monthly fixed cost divided by actual production.

One of the operating division managers argues that a standard cost transfer price should be used so that cost variations due to volume fluctuations and spending inefficiencies are localized in the utility department.

Required: Do you agree? If so, why would such a system be superior to the one now in use? If you do not agree, why not?

10. The Christie Company allocates central office overhead to its operating divisions. One of the central services is a computer facility. The cost of this facility is fixed and amounts to about $500,000 per year. This amount is allocated to the divisions based on the percentage of time each uses.

Required: In what sense is this allocation a transfer price? Could this practice lead to wrong actions if the operating divisions have no actual authority to buy computer time outside the company? Do you agree with the general practice?

Problems

19–1. The Wester Company has a producing division (Division P) which produces a metal that is used by a processing and selling division (Division S) in the production of a sub-assembly unit sold to aircraft companies. The metal is produced in a rolling type process and is then cut into strips and, after the edges are trimmed, is sent to Division S. The variable cost of a ton of metal that has been through the rolling process is $50 for labor and raw materials. The cutting and trimming variable cost is $5 per ton. The fixed overhead on a ton of metal that has been through the rolling process is $500,000 per year or $10 per unit (ton) based on a maximum capacity of 50,000 tons. The fixed overhead associated with the cutting and trimming operation is $100,000 per year and is assigned to units based on the maximum capacity—$2 per ton. The transfer price to Division S is a full-cost price of $67 which is the sum of the variable costs and fixed costs per unit.

An outside vendor approached the manager of Division S and offered to rent him a machine which could cut and trim the metal. The cost of the machine would be $300,000 per year. Of the $67 transfer price, $7 is attributed to the cutting and trimming process. Thus, there would be $350,000 annual savings to Division S if the price is reduced by $7 per unit (i.e., 50,000 tons times $7). This savings is extremely attractive to the manager of Division S.

Required: (1) If the fixed cost of the cut and trim overhead in Division P cannot be reduced, how should the vice president of operations advise the manager of Division S? Assume the equipment used by Division P has no salvage value.
(2) Would the manager of Division S be justified in arguing that the price of metal from Division P should be lowered to reflect the cheaper prices available through renting?

19–2. The Kyle Company has a central power generating plant which furnished electric power to all of the manufacturing divisions. The cost of operating this facility is virtually a fixed cost since it is a highly automated operation. The cost data for the year is shown below:

	Budget	*Actual*
Depreciation	$1,000,000	$1,000,000
Labor and supervision	100,000	110,000
Maintenance	500,000	600,000
Total	$1,600,000	$1,710,000
Units of production	8,000,000	7,000,000
Cost per unit	$.20	$.244

The majority of the costs are fixed. The variances from budget are primarily spending variances resulting from the use of overtime.

Required: (1) Assuming that the transfer price is to be used in the performance evaluation of the division managers, should it be based on the budget or actual? Why?
(2) Suppose the budget rate per unit is used as a transfer price. Is it possible that such a per-unit rate might adversely affect the decisions of a division manager? Give an example. If your answer is "no," then explain.

19–3. A large farming company has two divisions, one produces grain, the other sells the grain. As soon as the grain is produced, it is transferred to the selling division where it is stored in anticipation of future sale at a higher price.
During the year, three grain crops of 1,000,000 bushels each were produced. All three have now been sold although some were held in inventory for various periods of time. The market price at production time was $1.50 per bushel for the first crop, $1.80 for the second, and $1.60 for the third. There were no beginning inventories.
The annual income statement for the entire company appears as follows:

Revenue		
Sales (3,000,000 bu.)		$4,800,000
Cost		
Manufacturing labor and materials	$2,000,000	
Selling division labor	100,000	
Manufacturing overhead	1,500,000	
Selling division overhead	20,000	3,620,000
Income (ignore taxes)		$1,180,000

Required: The company president is very pleased with the total profits but he wants to determine whether the price speculation activities of the selling division are earning a profit. He requests that you prepare divisional income statements for the manufacturing division and the selling division. Decide what type of transfer price, market or cost, to use. Explain which transfer price is better. Are the division income statements useful? Explain.

19–4. The Aimco Company has several divisions. Division S produces (among other products) a metal container which is sold to customers who use it for shipping liquid chemicals. The main raw material used in manufacturing these containers is a metal which can be purchased from Division M, one of the other divisions of the company, or from several outside sources. Division S has received a customer order for 100 containers at $125 each. The manager of Division S requests bids for the raw material required to produce the containers from Division M and from two outside companies. Division M, bidding a transfer price on full cost, bids a price of $90 per ton on the raw material order. Division M's variable cost is only $45 and there is excess capacity. However, Division M regularly bases price bids on full cost whether the order is from a sister division or from an outside customer.

The two outside companies bid $78 and $76. However, Company A, which bid $78, would buy the manufacturing supplies necessary to produce the raw material from Division P, another division of Aimco. The supplies would amount to $10 per ton of raw material required and the profit to Division P is about 40 percent of selling price.

Required: (1) What would you expect Division S to do?
(2) Will S accept the right outside bid?
(3) Should Division M's transfer pricing policy be changed? If so, how?
(4) Does the outside price system work efficiently in this case?

19–5. The Long Company has several departments which operate quite autonomously as far as decision making is concerned. The company allocates "central office" overhead to all these operating departments based on the total labor dollars incurred by each division. The central office overhead budget and the allocation rate are shown below:

Central Office Activity	Amount
Executive offices	$100,000
Legal	20,000
Advertising	25,000
Personnel	40,000
Accounting	15,000
Total	$200,000
Total estimated payroll in all operating departments	$400,000

Allocation rate ...... $200,000/$400,000 = $.50 per labor dollar

The central office overhead of $200,000 is considered to be a fixed cost. Also, once the rate is established, it is not changed for one year.

The manager of the engineering research department has several employees on his staff. This department does research on certain engineering problems on the company's products and issues reports to clients who request this service. The department is faced with a need to hire two more secretarial people because of an increased work load. If the manager works through the company's personnel department, these positions can be filled at a cost of $400 per month for each secretary. However, the usual 50 cents per dollar of payroll will also be charged against the research department's budget for central office overhead. The manager discovers that he can hire the services of an outside secretarial service, "Eastern Girl," which will furnish two secretaries for as long as they are required and the cost is not added to the payroll. The cost will be $450 per girl per month.

Required: (1) Is the central office overhead cost a transfer price? Explain.

(2) What is the manager of the research department likely to do? Show your calculations.

(3) If the Long Company wants to continue to allocate central office overhead advise the president how this might be done so as not to affect the hiring decisions of the various departmental managers.

19–6. The Martin Company has a producing division (No. 1) that supplies several parts to another producing division (No. 2) which produces the main product. These component parts are listed below with relevant cost information:

Component Number	Variable Cost per Unit	Quantity Produced
1	$ 4	20,000
2	6	20,000
3	10	30,000
4	1	10,000

The fixed costs (which are out-of-pocket costs) of Division 1 amount to $100,000. These costs consist of the salary of the division management, indirect labor, payroll, and the like. In addition, the fixed cost which is not out of pocket (consisting mainly of depreciation on machinery) amounts to $60,000 per period.

In calculating unit cost, the total fixed cost of $160,000 is allocated to units to arrive at a *full* cost. This calculation is shown below:

Component Number	Variable Cost per Unit	Fixed Cost per Unit	Full Cost per Unit
1	$ 4	$2	$ 6
2	6	2	8
3	10	2	12
4	1	2	3

In establishing transfer prices, the full cost is used. In Division 2, which uses the four components, the manager has authority to buy inside the company or to buy from an outside supplier. The outside prices vary somewhat throughout the year. At the present time, the outside prices are as follows:

Component Number	Outside Price
1	$ 6.00
2	8.50
3	12.50
4	2.90

The manager of Division 2 notices that the outside purchase price on Component 4 is 10 cents lower than the transfer price and places an order with an outside supplier. Division 1 stops producing Component 4, reallocates the fixed cost to the remaining units, and adjusts the full cost transfer prices.

Required: (1) Reallocate the fixed costs and determine the adjusted transfer prices based on full cost. If there is no communication between the two divisions, what action will the manager of Division 2 be likely to take?

(2) Comment on the deficiencies of the full cost transfer price system. What changes would you recommend?

(3) Devise a method of assigning the fixed cost of Division 1 to Division 2 that will not cause Division 2 to buy outside when the components should be produced by Division 1. Consider the possibility of charging Division 2 a flat rate regardless of the volume purchased plus a charge per unit for the number of units purchased.

19-7. Division A produces Product X, which can be sold to Division B or in an outside market. Division B processes Product X into Product Y and sells this product in the outside processed market. The variable cost of making X in Division A is $11 per unit, and the additional variable processing cost in Division B is $2 per unit. The marginal revenue function for each market is given below:

Number of Units	Product X	Product Y
12	$ 9.25	$ 9.50
11	9.25	9.50
10	9.25	9.50
9	9.25	10.00
8	9.25	10.50
7	12.00	11.00
6	12.00	11.50
5	12.00	12.00
4	12.00	12.50
3	13.00	13.00
2	13.00	13.50
1	13.00	14.00

Required: (1) How many units of X should be produced? How should these units be distributed between the intermediate market and Division B?

(2) Give a priority schedule for distributing units of X between the intermediate market and Division B.

(3) What problems would be involved in using a market transfer price for Product X? Under what conditions would a market transfer price be better than a transfer price based on variable cost?

19-8. The Conway Company has a central computer facility which is used by several operating departments for data processing and problem-solving purposes. The cost structure of this center is given below:

Cost	Budget—1972
Rentals	$ 800,000
Payroll—operators	40,000
Payroll—programmers	70,000
Payroll—supervision and secretarial	30,000
Miscellaneous supplies	20,000
Utilities	100,000
	$1,060,000

It is estimated that 10,000 time units will be available for 1972 during which the computer will be available for use.

All of the costs shown in the budget are considered to be fixed, except for utilities and miscellaneous supplies which are variable.

During the past five years, the computer facility has not been operated at full capacity. The percentage of capacity has increased from 50 percent in the first year of operation to about 70 percent of capacity estimated for next year (1972).

A transfer price policy has been established which calls for the use of a full cost per unit of time. Thus, an operating department that needs one half of a time unit would be charged at the rate of $106 \left(\dfrac{\$1,060,000}{10,000} \right)$ per unit or $53. All operating units do most of their own programming. The central staff has four programmers who are used to solve special problems as they arise in the center.

The associate director of the center has approached the director to revise the transfer price policy to include only the variable costs. His argument is that the operating departments would thereby be encouraged to make greater use of the facility. The director's response is that he sees no reason why this should be so. "After all," he points out, "the operating departments need only so much time anyway and, besides, the various managers cannot buy computer time outside the company; so how could the transfer price affect their behavior?"

The associate director's response is that he knows of several instances where the operating departments have secured additional outside-the-company programming services so that the program finally submitted would require less running time. "In fact," he says, "I know of one case where the operating manager spent $100 on additional programming to save an estimated two time units of running time." The director's response is, "He should have—after all, it cost us $106 per time unit to run the program!"

Required: (1) Do you agree with the associate director or the director? Explain.

(2) Was the behavior of the operating manager (as described by the associate director) optimal so far as the whole company is concerned?

(3) Assuming that the additional programming effort could not have been done inside the company, what is the maximum price that the operating manager should have paid?

(4) Can you think of other possible examples that might support the associate director's argument?

19–9. The H and S Packing Company has two divisions. Division 1 is responsible for slaughtering and cutting the unprocessed meat. Division 2 processes meat such as hams, bacon, etc. Division 2 can buy meat from Division 1 or from outside suppliers. Division 1 can sell at the market price all the unprocessed meat that it can produce. The 1972 income statement for the company appears on the next page.

The ending inventory of $100,000 is at the cost of production incurred in Division 1. This inventory is as yet unprocessed. The market value unprocessed is $120,000. The sales for the year can be broken down as follows:

Division 1	$ 400,000
Division 2	1,400,000
	$1,800,000

The market value of the unprocessed meat actually transferred from Division 1 to Division 2 (exclusive of the ending inventory) was $1,000,000.

The H and S Packing Company

Income Statement

For the Year Ended December 31, 1972

Total sales			$1,800,000
Cost of goods sold:			
Beginning inventory		—0—	
Manufacturing costs:			
Raw materials, Division 1	$500,000		
Labor, Division 1	300,000		
Overhead, Division 1	200,000		
Processing supplies, Division 2	150,000		
Labor, Division 2	200,000		
Overhead, Division 2	100,000	$1,450,000	
Cost of goods available for sale		$1,450,000	
Ending inventory at cost:			
Division 1	$ —0—		
Division 2	100,000	100,000	1,350,000
Gross margin			$ 450,000
Operating expenses:			
Sales and administrative, Division 1	$110,000		
Sales and administrative, Division 2	120,000		
Central office overhead	140,000		370,000
Net income before taxes			$ 80,000

Required: (1) Prepare division income statements that might be used to evaluate the performance of the two division managers.

(2) Explain the transfer pricing policy you have used in preparing the statements.

(3) Can you see any conflict in the policy you have used if this same transfer price is to be used for decision making?

19–10. The Mackey Manufacturing Company has five divisions producing the same general line of paper products. The mills (divisions) are located in different parts of the country. The age and type of assets used differ from mill to mill. Also, the cost of labor differs with the location.

The method used to evaluate the performance of each mill is to calculate a unit cost based on the actual production. The unit cost for each mill is then compared with other mills. The cost report for 1972 is given below:

Cost Report

For the Year Ended 1972

Mill	Cost per Ton	Difference from Best Performance	Rank
1	$156	$11	4
2	150	5	3
3	146	1	2
4	145	—0—	1
5	171	26	5

The company president is disturbed at the great difference in cost performance between mills. This great a difference has not existed before. The output of all the mills is sold through a single selling division (the transfer price is based on full cost). The product may be shipped directly from a given mill to a customer, but the shipping order comes from the selling division. The amount of production for each mill is scheduled by the sales division.

The following detail data are available for each mill for 1972:

	MILL				
	1	2	3	4	5
Tons produced	50,000	100,000	100,000	100,000	20,000

Costs:

Variable labor and raw materials costs per ton	$ 140	$ 146	$ 138	$ 142	$ 141
Fixed out-of-pocket costs .	200,000	200,000	200,000	200,000	200,000
Fixed plant and equipment depreciation costs	600,000	200,000	600,000	100,000	400,000
Cost per ton	156	150	146	145	171

The market value of a ton of product is $150 of which $10 per ton represents the selling costs of the selling division.

Required: (1) Ignoring any freight cost, is the existing production of 370,000 tons scheduled among the five plants in the best way possible? If not, indicate how you would reschedule the production. Assume that the capacity of each mill is 100,000 tons per year but that it is necessary to produce at least 10,000 tons at each mill for marketing reasons.

(2) Recalculate the unit costs and revise the cost report as it is presently being used by the company.

(3) Devise a reporting system that will give a better indication of mill performance.

(4) Is the full cost transfer price most useful for deciding where to schedule production? If not, suggest an alternative.

19–11. A Company has a division which manufactures and sells bedroom furniture. The income statement of this division is given below:

Furniture Division
Income Statement
For the Year Ended December 31, 1972

Sales		$10,000,000
Division costs:		
Variable cost	$7,000,000	
Fixed cost	2,000,000	9,000,000
		$1,000,000
Allocated central office overhead		800,000
Net income		$ 200,000

Investment allocated to division—$3,000,000
Return on investment—6.7%

The management is disturbed at the low return on investment. The corporate treasurer indicates that the company can earn at least 20 percent on additional investment in any number of other projects. Furthermore, the treasurer points out, "The investment is really understated because the plant and facility carried at cost of $3,000,000 could be disposed of easily for twice that."

An investigation reveals that the division fixed cost of $2,000,000 could not be eliminated even if the division were sold. The allocated central office overhead is a prorata share of operating the corporate offices, and sale of the division would not effect this cost either.

Required: (1) Assuming that an expenditure of $1,000,000 annually would maintain the facility in good operating condition for at least ten years, should the division be sold?

(2) If not, is there a better way to report the return on investment so as to alert the management to consider selling if volume began to decline?

19–12. The Ray Company has a division that manufacturers shafts, some of which are used by other divisions and some of which are sold on the outside market. This division is organized in two sections, which are described below:

Section 1, *Machining and Grinding.* This highly mechanized section has much heavy equipment that is used to give shape to the shafts and to perform grinding operations on shafts that have special requirements.

Section 2, *Cleaning and Packing.* This section consists primarily of laborers who clean and pack all shafts.

The costing system used by the company charges raw materials, direct labor, and overhead to each unit of product. The labor and the materials are considered to be variable costs, but the overhead is 75 percent fixed and 25 percent variable. The overhead is allocated on the basis of the labor cost required to produce each product. Furthermore, the rate is a division rate and not a section overhead rate. This rate is developed from the following information:

	Direct Labor Payroll	Overhead
Section 1	$250,000	$800,000
Section 2	200,000	100,000
Totals	$450,000	$900,000

Overhead rate: $\dfrac{\$900,000}{\$450,000}$ = $2 per dollar of labor cost

Average wage rate for Section 1 is $2 per hour; for Section 2, $1 per hour.

A full cost transfer price is used for selling services to other producing divisions. If an order is placed by another producing division that calls for $20 of raw materials and two hours of labor time in each section, the price that is quoted would be arrived at as follows:

	Hours	Total
Labor:		
Section 1	2	$ 4
Section 2	2	2
		$ 6
Overhead:		
$2 × $6		12
Raw materials		20
Transfer price		$38

The assistant to the controller has been considering a change in the costing system whereby an overhead rate would be developed for each section. He believes that such a system would give a more equitable price for the work done for other divisions. He is confident that he would have a better basis for determining the profit from sales to outsiders. Since the shaft sold on the outside market is standardized, the price is determined by the customs of the industry and the primary decision that must be made is whether to accept or reject orders at a given price. At times, the division is near enough to capacity that outside work must be stopped if inside work is to be done.

At the moment, two orders are being considered. These orders are from another division that can buy either inside or outside the company. The details on the two orders are given below:

	Order 1	Order 2
Raw materials	$30	$25
Labor: Section 1	3 hours	5 hours
Section 2	3	1

Required: (1) Calculate transfer price for orders under the present system.
(2) Calculate the transfer price under the proposed system.
(3) Explain the difference in the prices.
(4) Calculate a section overhead rate based on *variable* overhead only.
(5) Recalculate the transfer prices for the two orders.
(6) Which of the three systems do you prefer? Why?

Chapter 20

BUDGETS-SALES AND PRODUCTION

A plan showing how resources will be acquired and used over a specified time interval is called a *budget*. The act of preparing a budget is called *budgeting,* and the use of a budget as a means for controlling activity is called *budgeting control.*

Management sets objectives and makes plans for their realization. Obviously, the plans will have to be designed to fit the objectives. The objectives as viewed by different levels of management will differ, but they are not conflicting and can be reconciled in the preparation of a budget for the firm. Top management is not interested in profits alone but considers profits in relation to the investment. In other words, top management tries to maintain and improve rate of return on investment. Rate of return can be increased by increasing profits, and it can also be increased by reducing the amount invested. For example, inventories should be at an adequate level, but an excessive investment in inventories tends to hold down the rate of return. If inventories can be reduced and profits maintained, the rate of return will increase. Management at the plant operating level probably will not be concerned with the rate of return. Foremen and shop superintendents are not responsible for selling the products at a profit or for the investment in assets. Instead, they will concentrate on minimizing the costs of production. However, if costs of production are minimized, the effect on profits and rate of return will be favorable. Hence, the limited objectives at lower levels of management are in harmony with the objectives of top management.

The plans of management are incorporated into a budget for the company, and the actual results of operation are measured and compared with the budget. Significant variations are reviewed and an investigation is made to determine the causes for variation, if it appears that the benefits to be derived would be greater than the costs of investigation. Corrective steps are taken. Perhaps tighter control may be exercised over operations; or if conditions have changed, this should be recognized in a revision of the original plan. The feedback of information is then applied in the preparation of further plans for the future.

Budgeting and budgetary control can be viewed broadly as essential features of a total management system. The system is set forth in the diagram that follows:

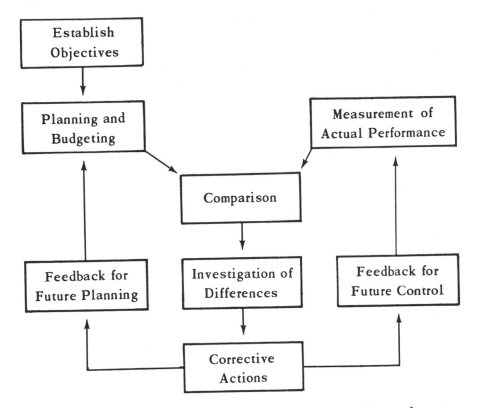

If investigation reveals that the plan is satisfactory but that performance can be improved, steps are taken to bring future performance into line with the plan. If investigation reveals that the plan is unsatisfactory, the plan is corrected. These corrective actions are shown on the diagram as the feedback loops.

THE ADVANTAGES OF BUDGETS

Budgets are tools that are made and used by management. Benefits can be derived from the budgeting process, although budgeting is not an end in itself. By preparing a budget, management is forced to look ahead and to consider how the various functions of a business fit together. Some of the more significant advantages to be derived from budgets and budget preparation are listed below:

(1) Budgeting is a means of coordinating activities through the cooperation of those who seek to achieve a common goal.

(2) Budgeting helps to make the various members of management aware of the problems faced by others and the factors that interlock in running a business organization.

(3) A budget is more than speculation; it is a workable pattern to be followed.

(4) A budget places an obligation upon the enterprise to maintain adequate financial records that can be tied in with the budget.

(5) With a budget, all people in the organization become conscious of the need to conserve business resources.

(6) Efficient or inefficient use of resources is revealed by budgets intended for that purpose.

(7) A budget gives management a means for self-evaluation and can be used to measure progress.

THE SCOPE OF BUDGETING

Budgeting and budgeting control are at the heart of the managerial planning and control concepts that have been discussed in the preceding chapters. For example, budget estimates are made of flows of future net working capital and cash receipts and disbursements. In product costing and control, manufacturing overhead is assigned to the products by means of a budget, standards may be incorporated in budgets, and the concept of variable costing is applied in the budgeting process. Also, operational budget plans include segments of long-range planning that apply to a particular year.

Budgets, which are prepared in different ways to serve specialized purposes, may be generally classified by type as follows:

(1) A budget for a division or other segment of a business, a project, or a product line.

(2) A budget for the individual who controls the revenues and costs.

Project or product budgets. A budget for a particular segment of a business, a project, or a product line serves as a general guideline to probable results of that particular activity. For example, expected total costs of construction of a power plant can be established and actual costs compared to the budget. Similarly, revenues and costs can be budgeted for various product lines. Fixed costs may be allocated, as a separate item, to determine

580

whether the activity or product line can carry its share of total fixed costs. Budgets prepared in this way are useful because they provide an overall picture of various functions and projects. However, an overall picture may not be suitable as a means of personalized control. Various persons may be responsible for individual costs of a function or project with no one person being responsible for the total operation.

The human factor. A budget that identifies revenues and costs with an individual responsible for their incurrence, a *control* or *responsibility* budget, is more suitable for control purposes. In this type of budget, as discussed in Chapter 9, revenues and costs are not allocated but are identified directly with the responsible individual. A departmental supervisor, for example, has a budget for his department which includes only the revenue and the costs that are subject to his control. Actual data from operations are then accumulated and a comparison with the budget shows whether or not the supervisor achieved what was expected. A budget of this type localizes differences between the budget and the actual operations, making it possible to measure individual performance.

The concept of a control budget is distasteful at best, bringing to mind restrictions and critical evaluations of expenditures. If management places too much emphasis upon the inhibitive aspects of budgeting, there will be a tendency to play it safe and to assume few if any risks. As a result, the company may become too budget conscious and fail to make the most of its potential. Yet if budgeting and control are neglected, there is financial chaos. There should be a point of balance between the two extremes.

In responsibility accounting the manager budgets the costs that he controls and thus has a valuable tool for evaluating his own performance. Top management is becoming aware of the importance of human behavior in an organization and budget policy is being formulated so that individuals will be motivated to cooperate in achieving company objectives. When the needs of the individual are brought into balance with the goals of the organization, the budget will no longer be viewed as a necessary evil. Instead, it can be a valuable guide and a means of self-evaluation to the individual manager.

Master budget plan. The type of budgets discussed in the preceding paragraphs are not separate in the sense that they are unrelated. Costs that are budgeted by project or product line can also be budgeted according to the individual responsible for incurring the cost. The costs may be collected and reported in various ways, but they are brought together in one coordinated master budget for the firm. The master budget plan will be discussed in greater detail in the next chapter.

The computer has made it possible to rearrange costs and other data in many different ways with relatively little clerical effort. If basic information is entered on a punched card, magnetic tape, or other input media, it can be processed to serve different purposes. For example, actual and budgeted costs can be classified by the individuals who authorize their incurrence; they can be classified by product line, by territory, or by any other relevant basis and can be brought together in a total budget report for the firm. The realignment of costs for different cost reports would be a formidable task if it were carried out manually, but the task is relatively easy for a computer. Furthermore, the costs can be reconciled with little risk of error.

THE BUDGET PERIOD

The length of the budget period may be a week, a month, a quarter of a year, a year, or even more than a year. There is no set interval of time. It all depends upon how the budget is to be used. In any case it should be complete, tracing an activity or a project through from the time it is started until it is ended. The operating budget, for example, should cover at least one cycle of operations. Plans for the purchase of merchandise are only a part of the budget. The budget should be extended to show that the merchandise will be sold, that cash will be collected on the sales, and that any debt arising from the purchase will be repaid. Perhaps the operating cycle can be completed in a week, in which case a budget could be drawn up on that basis. If the business has an unusually long operating cycle, the budget may extend beyond a year.

A budget for the acquisition of capital investments may be made for five or more years into the future. The plans for later years will probably be somewhat indefinite, based as they are upon long-term prospects. With the passage of time, the plans will be revised as necessary, with the maturing installment being inserted in the budget of operations for the next year.

Ordinarily, budgets of regular operating activity are drawn up for a period of a year, with the year being divided into quarters or months. The budget year, of course, corresponds with the fiscal year so that comparisons of actual results with the budget can be made. If the budget is restricted to a month or a quarter, it places a limit upon advance planning and tends to encourage a short-term outlook. On the other hand, a budget extended far into the future is apt to be less accurate. As events are projected further into the future, there is a greater chance for miscalculation. For instance, it may be fairly easy to predict sales for the next month from a backlog of customers' orders, but it is difficult to come up with a reasonable estimate of sales for a month that is almost a year away. Events that cannot be foreseen at the present time are apt to arise and upset even the short-term estimates, let alone those covering a longer period of time. A compromise is often reached by preparing a budget for the year by quarters, but as the immediate quarter approaches it will be divided into months.

Generally, some provision is made for revising the budget and bringing it up-to-date. After a few months have elapsed, it may be quite evident that the budget for the year will no longer apply. Usually at the end of the first quarter or at some other designated time the budget will be reviewed and corrections will be made as necessary.

Sometimes a *rolling* or *progressive budget* is used. When a month goes by, the budget is extended one more month into the future. At the end of February, for example, a budget for the following February is added; and at the end of March a budget for the following March is added, and so forth. Budgeting is then a continual process. There will always be a budget for a year in advance, and as time passes, the budgets for future months will be adjusted as circumstances warrant.

Often it is desirable to compare one month with another; but the comparison may be distorted merely because of the variations in the lengths of months. Perhaps more business may be transacted in January than in February because there are more days in January. On a comparable time basis, the business volume may be constant. Some companies eliminate these arbitrary differences by dividing their fiscal year into 13 periods of four weeks each, thereby making it possible to compare one period of the year with another.

THE TIMING CONCEPT

In business planning, however, time is not looked upon only as a means for measuring intervals such as months or years. Allowance must also be made for the sequential flow of events and the time required for events to unfold and influence different parts of the total operation. Activities and transactions are not translated into results right away in many instances, but instead they develop and reach fruition at some later date.

Timing the logical progression of events is also important in nonbusiness situations. Heavy mountain snowfalls, for example, may result in spring floods for downstream areas, but the conditions leading to the floods precede them by several weeks. Steps may be taken to prepare for the floods, or, if possible, to prevent them.

Similarly, in business, plans are formulated so that all activities will be synchronized. If a new plant is to be built, weeks or months may elapse before products can be manufactured and sold. When a new product line is to be added, it may take several months or years to develop its profit-making potential. Even in the normal course of operations, there will be a natural sequence of events. If large purchases are made in certain months, some arrangement will have to be made to pay the suppliers. Cash may be borrowed from the bank, or presently held cash reserves may be reduced. As cash is realized from subsequent sales, it may be applied to reduce loan balances, it may be retained, or it may be used in various ways.

PREPARATION OF THE BUDGETS

In budgeting, all functions and activities of the business are carefully interlocked. The plans for the manufacturing division must be tied in with the plans for the sales division. If large shipments are to be made to customers during particular months, the manufacturing division should have the products ready at that time. At a still earlier date, the materials to be used in production will have to be ordered, allowing enough time for their receipt from suppliers and their conversion into finished products. This concept of timing and coordinating activities applies in all areas of budgeting.

A budget is prepared by combining the efforts of many individuals. Those who are in charge of a particular function or activity will make up the budget estimates. The estimates for separate departments or divisions that perform a similar function are adjusted as necessary and are summarized in one budget for that function. For instance, sales estimates may be made by regional sales managers, with the approved estimates being combined into one sales estimate for the company. At the same time, the functions such as sales, production, product engineering, purchasing, and so forth, will be coordinated so that all of the budgets will fit together properly.

Ordinarily a person will prepare his own budget or, at the very least, will be consulted before any budget is assigned to him. This is particularly true if the budget is to be used in controlling his activities. The self-imposed budget has certain very distinct advantages, as follows:

(1) A person who is in immediate contact with an activity should be able to make reliable estimates.
(2) He will tend to feel that he has been recognized and that he is a member of the team.
(3) Most likely he will make every effort to fulfill a budget that he has imposed upon himself.
(4) The self-imposed budget has its own peculiar control. The individual is forced to blame himself if he cannot operate within its limits.

The self-imposed budget, however, is not necessarily accepted as it stands. If too much freedom is allowed, there is a possibility that the budgets will be too easy and that they will offer no challenge. Undeserved credit may be taken for favorable budget comparisons. Before the budgets are accepted, they are reviewed by higher levels of management. If changes are to be made, they can be discussed and compromises can be reached that will be acceptable to all concerned.

The person in immediate contact with any activity is in a good position to make budget estimates, but he is also apt to have a narrow viewpoint. When a man devotes his energy to one thing, he is very likely to exaggerate its importance, forgetting that it is only a part of a bigger activity. For instance, a regional salesman may wonder why a product line that he has sold successfully has been discontinued. His company, however, may have discovered that the sales in total were not sufficient to justify further production.

Top management and the lower levels of management work together to produce the budget. As a general rule, those who are in higher positions are not familiar with the details of any activity and will depend upon their subordinates for underlying information. On the other hand, the top executives of the firm know more about the business as a whole, are better informed with respect to the general business outlook, and take a broader point of view. Each member of the management group, acting in his own capacity and cooperating with others, makes a contribution to the budget.

SALES FORECASTING AND THE SALES BUDGET

Sales are often the limiting factor in budgeting. In many cases the company can deliver whatever goods or services it can sell. Consequently, the sales budget will be prepared first, with other budgets that are dependent upon sales being prepared later. But even before a sales budget in units of product or dollars can be developed, there must be a sales forecast for the next year. The forecast will depend upon a variety of factors, among which are the price policy, the general economic outlook, regional differences, conditions in the industry, and the position of the company in the economy.

Methods used in forecasting sales vary widely. Each industry and company has distinctive characteristics, which in themselves tend to create differences in outlook. In general, the sales forecast is based upon an analysis of past sales and an estimate of future economic prospects.

Sales from past years can be broken down by product lines, regions, and salesmen to provide a basis for estimating possible future sales. The regional sales managers and salesmen will prepare sales estimates for the coming year in the light of their knowledge of the past and their expectations for the months that lie ahead. Higher echelons of management who are better informed with respect to the total economic picture will review these estimates and fit them into a composite forecast for the company, making adjustments wherever necessary.

A sales forecast is sometimes made on a more scientific basis by fitting the business activity of the company to published indexes and reports on the economy at large. A given company may find that its activity tends to follow the Federal Reserve Board's Index, statistics on bank deposits, national income, population trends, and so forth. From relationships that have been developed, it will be possible to predict future sales trends.

Many factors operate to complicate the forecasting problem. A company may appear to fit into a particular industry grouping, yet upon closer examination it may be found that the company handles many different lines of products and in reality has the attributes of several industries. In addition, products may be sold through various channels in different territories or even in different countries. Some products, such as food staples and clothing, will be produced for sale to the consumer, while other products will be indirectly related to consumer demand. For example, basic products such as glass, steel, and aluminum are not sold to the consumer directly but are used in the manufacture of other products, which are then sold to the final consumer. The demand for basic products that are used in making other products is said to be a *derived demand*. Sales forecasts for these products will depend upon forecasts and data prepared for other industries. The demand for paint and lumber, for example, will be influenced to a large extent by the number of new housing starts planned. If products are sold to automobile manufacturers, then the demand will be derived from forecasts of new car sales.

Sometimes a computer is used in working out forecasts. The computer, of course, adds nothing to the forecast itself but is a means by which diverse information can be brought together in various combinations and tested for validity. A watch manufacturer, for example, knows that watches are often purchased as graduation gifts and that sales bear a relationship to the number of students who will graduate in any particular year. But the manufacturer may not know just what correlation there is between watch sales and the number of students graduating. Various factors that have a bearing on watch sales can be brought together in weighted formulas and can be tested on the computer. Experimentation and testing will reveal whether or not the weights used in any of the formulas are valid. If a reasonable degree of correlation is found to exist in any formula tested, the formula may be used in estimating the sales potential.

A forecast of sales on an industry-wide basis must be broken down so that it will apply to a particular company. Each company will look at its position relative to the total market and will calculate its share of the market. In some areas and in certain product lines one company may dominate, while in other areas and in other product lines the sales may be divided in different proportions. Market studies will show customer preference by locality and may reveal why one brand sells better than another. Market surveys are not made so that they can be used in budgeting, but data taken from surveys can often be applied in budget preparation.

PROFIT ESTIMATION

The sales forecast provides a foundation for profit planning and eventually a sales budget. Sales budgets, like sales forecasts, are usually broken down by product line, regions, customers and salesmen. Ordinarily, planning future sales is difficult because of changing conditions in the economy and in the company itself.

Models may be built that incorporate various assumptions with respect to economic conditions, volume of sales, prices, and costs. By means of a computer, the models may be tested in simulation studies to determine what can be expected if certain probabilities are attached to the assumption. Information can be derived for realistic budgeting, and at the same time the effect of a particular change in any factor can be determined. In other words, the sensitivity of profits to changes in factors such as sales volume and prices can be tested, thus providing management with not only budget data but also data that can help to identify areas of the operation that will require close attention.

A simple illustration is given to show how probabilities can be applied in determining the expected value of sales, costs, and profits. Assume, for example, that a company plans to sell one product line next year at a price of $20 a unit. Probability estimates have been made for sales volume and variable unit costs.

Sales Volume (Number of Units)	Probabilities
150,000	.40
120,000	.30
100,000	.30
	1.00

Variable Unit Costs	Probabilities
$16	.60
12	.40
	1.00

Fixed costs, both the managed and committed costs (as defined in Chapter 9), are estimated at $300,000 for the next year, and income taxes are estimated at 50 percent of net income before income taxes.

The expected value of the contribution margin for the next year is computed below. The sales volume probabilities and the variable unit cost probabilities are independent of each other. The probable value of the contribution margin under each condition is the joint probability of the sales volume and the variable cost. For example, there is a 40 percent probability that 150,000 units will be sold and a 60 percent probability that the unit variable cost will be $16. The joint probability is 24 percent (.40 × .60). The total expected value of the contribution margin is the sum of the expected values of the contribution margins for all conditions given. Stated another way, it is the weighted contribution margin that takes into account the joint probabilities of all stated conditions and is the value that best represents the combination of possibilities.

Contribution Margin
(In Thousands)

Events	Sales Revenue	Variable Costs	Contri- bution Margin	Probabilities Sales	Probabilities Variable Costs	Joint	Ex- pected Value
Sales of 150 units Unit variable costs:							
$16	$3,000	$2,400	$ 600	.40	.60	.24	$144
12	3,000	1,800	1,200	.40	.40	.16	192
Sales of 120 units Unit variable costs:							
$16	$2,400	$1,920	$480	.30	.60	.18	86.4
12	2,400	1,440	960	.30	.40	.12	115.2
Sales of 100 units Unit variable costs:							
$16	$2,000	$1,600	$400	.30	.60	.18	72
12	2,000	1,200	800	.30	.40	.12	96
Total expected value, contribution margin							$705.6

Similarly, the total expected value of sales and variable costs can be determined, as shown on the next page.

Sales Volume	Probabilities	Expected Value
150,000	.40	60,000
120,000	.30	36,000
100,000	.30	30,000
Total expected value		126,000

Sales revenue (126,000 units × $20) $2,520,000

Unit Variable Cost	Probabilities	Expected Value
$16	.60	$ 9.60
12	.40	4.80
Total expected value		$14.40

Total variable cost (126,000
  units × $14.40) $1,814,400

The expected value of the profit plan is given below:

Sales	$2,520,000
Variable costs	1,814,400
Contribution margin	$ 705,600
Fixed costs	300,000
Net income before income taxes	$ 405,600
Income taxes, 50%	202,800
Net income after income taxes	$ 202,800

The probabilistic approach to budgeting, can provide a general guideline to the possible outcome of a combination of different factors under conditions of uncertainty. Past experience coupled with a careful analysis of the future can serve as a basis for establishing probability estimates. Admittedly, probability estimates will not be precise, but they should be more accurate than rough approximations or intuitive judgments.

In each particular circumstance, the profit will vary according to the combination of conditions. The expected value, however, results from assigning weights to the various conditions in combination and is a weighted value.

THE SALES BUDGET ILLUSTRATED

The general approach to budgeting is illustrated in this chapter and in the chapter that follows by assembling a master budget plan for Reed and Company. To keep the illustration within reasonable limits, budgets for departments and smaller units of the business are omitted and the annual budget is broken down by calendar quarters and not by individual months.

Reed and Company sells two product lines, which are manufactured in one plant. During the year 1973 it plans to sell the following quantities of each product:

Reed and Company
Sales Budget—Units of Product
For the Year Ended December 31, 1973

	Total	First Quarter	Second Quarter	Third Quarter	Fourth Quarter
Product 1	450,000	60,000	150,000	200,000	40,000
Product 2	300,000	90,000	70,000	50,000	90,000

Each of these two products is sold on a seasonal basis. Product 1 tends to sell better in summer months, while Product 2 sells better during the winter.

By handling product lines that sell heavily in different seasons, Reed and Company hopes to be able to even out production over the year. The extent to which Reed and Company can realize its goal of balanced production will depend upon the time required to manufacture a unit of one product as compared with another, the sales volume of each product line, the manpower and facilities required in manufacturing, and other factors related to the peculiarities of the products themselves.

Prices established for the various product lines are applied to the sales budget in units of product to produce a sales revenue budget. If price changes are expected during the year, then the budget should be altered accordingly. Reed and Company plans to sell its products at uniform prices throughout the year: Product 1 at $40 a unit and Product 2 at $50 a unit. The prices are attached to the physical units and the following budget of sales revenue is prepared:

Reed and Company
Gross Sales Revenue Budget
(In Thousands of Dollars)
For the Year Ended December 31, 1973

	Total	First Quarter	Second Quarter	Third Quarter	Fourth Quarter
Product 1	$18,000	$2,400	$6,000	$ 8,000	$1,600
Product 2	15,000	4,500	3,500	2,500	4,500
Total sales revenue	$33,000	$6,900	$9,500	$10,500	$6,100

The gross sales as budgeted will not be realized even if the actual sales are made according to plan. Some of the customers will return products or will expect allowances for one reason or another. Still other customers will fail to pay what they owe, and their accounts will have to be written off as uncollectible. Management will be reluctant to admit that accounts cannot be collected or that allowances of any consequence will be granted. Nevertheless, if the budget is to be realistic, provision must be made for deductions from gross sales revenue.

A study of past experience shows that Reed and Company has lost about 3 percent of its billed revenue each year because of returns, allowances, and uncollectible accounts. The returns and allowances have averaged about 2 percent of gross sales, while uncollectible accounts have averaged about 1 percent. From all indications, future revenues will be reduced in approximately the same proportions, and the budget that appears below has been prepared on that basis.

Reed and Company

Sales Revenue Budget

Net of Returns, Allowances, and Uncollectibles

(In Thousands of Dollars)

For the Year Ended December 31, 1973

	Total	First Quarter	Second Quarter	Third Quarter	Fourth Quarter
Gross sales	$33,000	$6,900	$9,500	$10,500	$6,100
Returns and allowances .	$ 660	$ 138	$ 190	$ 210	$ 122
Uncollectible accounts ..	330	69	95	105	61
Total deductions	$ 990	$ 207	$ 285	$ 315	$ 183
Net sales	$32,010	$6,693	$9,215	$10,185	$5,917

SALES AND PRODUCTION

The sales budget is the foundation for the production budget. From an estimate of sales, it is possible to draw up plans for the manufacture of the products that will be needed. In making its plans, the manufacturing division will schedule production so that deliveries can be made to customers promptly. Therefore, the plans for production will have to be synchronized with the sales budget.

Also, the sales division will be limited in its planning by the capabilities and the capacity of the manufacturing division. It may be possible to sell a particular product, but perhaps it cannot be manufactured at a reasonable cost. The company will then have to abandon prospects for the sale of the product or find a way to cut the costs. When products are required to meet exacting standards and specifications, the sales division and the manufacturing division will have to join forces in working with the customers. The sales potential exists, but the company will not get the order if the manufacturing division cannot meet the stringent standards imposed. Sales estimates must also be tied in with manufacturing capacity. It is possible, of course, to sell more than the factory can normally produce by depleting inventories, by subletting the work, or by producing at overcapacity. At some point a limit will be reached, and the company will be forced to add to its productive capacity if it expects to increase its sales volume.

Sales and production must be coordinated closely. Neither function can be planned in isolation. The sales division depends upon the plant for its products, and the manufacturing division will be guided by sales estimates.

INVENTORIES AND PRODUCTION

Assuming that a workable sales budget has been agreed upon, plans can be drawn up to produce the quantities of products specified. If the products are relatively perishable or if they cannot be stored, they will have to be manufactured at about the time they are to be sold. On the other hand, if it is possible to store the products, the production schedule can be more flexible.

Given a choice, a company may choose to operate at a fairly uniform level throughout the year; or, conversely, it may prefer to manufacture products as they are needed. With variations in sales volume throughout the year, inventories will increase or decrease if production is held at a constant level. When production is tied in closely with sales, the inventories will not vary to any extent, but production will go up or down with sales. Each approach to the production problem has its cost advantages and disadvantages, and the decision will generally be made on a least cost basis.

When production is stabilized at a certain level, the manufacturing costs tend to be more uniformly distributed throughout the year. In all likelihood, the manufacturing costs will also be lower. Plant facilities will not be overworked in some months, only to remain idle at some later time. By employing workers steadily throughout the year, the company can retain good employees and avoid the cost and the nuisance of hiring and laying off temporary personnel. Probably the company will attract a better type of employee who will be more satisfied with a steady job and as a result will be more productive.

However, other problems arise when production is stabilized. Inventories of finished product will be built up when sales volume is low and will be liquidated during the busy sales season. The variations in inventory will create a storage problem and will add to carrying costs. Funds may be invested in inventories when they could be used elsewhere to better advantage. The interest cost of this nonproductive investment must be taken into account. Furthermore, there is a risk that the inventories will deteriorate in storage, will become obsolete, or will not sell in the quantities anticipated. This general type of problem is also encountered in planning raw materials inventories.

Some compromise should be made. If sales volume is irregular, it will not be possible to schedule production evenly throughout the year and to maintain a constant level of inventory at the same time. A middle position can be reached at which costs and inconveniences will be at a minimum. The plant should be operated at a fairly even rate throughout the year without allowing the inventories to pile up beyond reason. Peaks and valleys in the operating cycle can be leveled out to some extent by selecting product lines that will sell heavily in different seasons.

If at all possible, a flexible position is usually taken. Moderate inventory reserves may be held so that unexpected increases in demand can be filled. In planning how plant facilities and other productive factors are to be used, some leeway should be allowed so that production can be increased or decreased within limits while using the existing manpower and facilities. In order to have flexibility, the flow of work must be carefully planned by cost centers. A bottleneck in one department can hold up production for the entire plant, thereby creating rigidity.

THE PRODUCTION BUDGET ILLUSTRATED

The production budget stems from the sales budget, but, as explained in the preceding paragraphs, there is some degree of latitude. Inventories may be built up or liquidated depending upon the policy adopted by management and the outlook for future sales. The sales budget, on a unit basis related to the desired inventory level, can be converted into a budget of units to be manufactured.

In the budget for Reed and Company, given at the top of the next page, sales and production for the year are equal, although there are variations within the year. If sales volume were expected to increase in the first quarter of the following year, some increase in inventory would be likely in the fourth quarter of the budget year. Production varies with sales volume for the most part with some differences in inventory. However, with seasonal products that complement each other, the plant may still be used rather evenly throughout the year.

Reed and Company
Production Budget—Units of Product
(In Thousands of Units)
For the Year Ended December 31, 1973

	Total	First Quarter	Second Quarter	Third Quarter	Fourth Quarter
Product 1:					
Units to be sold	450	60	150	200	40
Less: Inventory planned at beginning of quarter	15	15	40	50	10
Total	435	45	110	150	30
Add: Inventory planned at end of quarter	15	40	50	10	15
Units to be produced	450	85	160	160	45
Product 2:					
Units to be sold	300	90	70	50	90
Less: Inventory planned at beginning of quarter	20	20	15	15	20
Total	280	70	55	35	70
Add: Inventory planned at end of quarter	20	15	15	20	20
Units to be produced	300	85	70	55	90

Questions

1. What is a budget?

2. What is budgetary control?

3. Give some of the advantages to be derived from budgets and budget preparation.

4. Explain two general ways budgets may be classified.

5. In some circumstances, fixed costs may be allocated in budgeting and in other circumstances they should not be allocated. Explain this difference.

6. If budgets are prepared to serve special purposes, how can the differences be reconciled?

7. Can a comparison of actual results with a budget lead to better future budgets? Explain.

8. What is a budget period? Is a budget prepared for a month, for a year, or for some other interval of time? Explain.

9. What is a rolling or progressive budget?

10. How does the concept of timing enter into budgeting?

11. What are the advantages that can be derived from a self-imposed budget? The disadvantages?

12. How does a sales forecast differ from a sales budget?

13. Point out some of the factors that must be considered in sales forecasting.

14. Why does the budgeting operation generally begin with sales forecasting?

15. Explain briefly how probabilities can be used in the budgeting process.

16. Why must sales and production be coordinated?

17. When products sell on a seasonal basis, how can production be evened out over the year?

18. What limitations will influence the extent to which production can be stabilized?

Exercises

1. Hayes and Goldman, Inc., sell two lines of product. An estimate of the number of units of each product line that should be sold in the fiscal quarter ended September 30, 1973 follows:

	Products	
	A	B
July	3,400	900
August	3,100	1,100
September	2,700	1,400
Totals	9,200	3,400

Product A sells for $5 a unit and Product B for $8 a unit. Past experience indicates that sales returns, allowances, and losses on uncollectible accounts amount to approximately 5 percent of gross sales revenue.

Required: Prepare a budget showing gross sales revenue, estimated deductions from sales, and net sales for each month and for the quarter.

2. Two types of humidifiers are sold by Emmaus Electric Company, model H-25 and model A-14. During the first six months of the year sales were as follows: 8,000 units of H-25 and 8,000 units of A-14. Consumer demand is expected to shift over to H-25 in the last six months of the year. In the last six months of the year, sales are estimated as follows: 11,000 units of H-25 and 5,000 units of A-14. Model H-25 sells for $190 a unit with variable costs of producing and selling a unit estimated at $160. Model A-14 sells for $135 a unit with variable costs of producing and selling a unit estimated at $95.

Required: Does it appear that the total contribution margin in the last six months of the year will be as large as it was in the first six months? Show calculations.

3. The economic forecasting department of Tupelo Products, Inc., has made a thorough study of the factors that are expected to influence the general economy and the fortunes of the company during the coming year.
Probabilities have been estimated for sales volume, selling prices, and variable costs. Data for one particular product line appears on the next page.

Sales Volume		Selling Price		Unit Variable Cost	
Units	Probability	Price	Probability	Unit Cost	Probability
250,000	.20	$30	.40	$15	.70
200,000	.80	25	.60	20	.30

Required: Compute the expected value of the contribution margin.

4. Ward Cambridge, as president of Cambridge Metals, Inc., states that he believes that the company has as much chance to sell 60,000 units of product next year as it has to sell 50,000 units. The product line will be sold for $50 a unit.

According to estimates made by the production department, there is a 60 percent probability that the unit variable cost will be $30 and a 40 percent probability that the unit variable cost will be $35.

Mr. Cambridge states that executive bonuses will be $50,000 higher if the sales volume is 60,000 units. If only 50,000 units are sold, the fixed costs are estimated as follows:

Fixed Cost	Probability
$200,000	.80
150,000	.20

The executive bonuses will be included in fixed costs if 60,000 units are sold.

Required: Compute the expected value of the net income before taxes.

5. Marchak Blending Company has estimated sales of a certain product line for each quarter of the coming year as follows:

First Quarter	240,000
Second Quarter	252,000
Third Quarter	270,000
Fourth Quarter	276,000
First Quarter (next year)	288,000

At the beginning of the year there were 40,000 units of product in inventory. At the end of each quarter, the company plans to have an inventory equal to one-sixth of the sales for the next fiscal quarter.

Required: How many units must be manufactured in each quarter of the current year?

6. Lilac Hills, Inc., processes various food products, one of which is usually sold heavily in the summer months. A packaged assortment of this product sells for $12 a unit, and the variable costs of manufacturing and selling this unit amount to $8. At the beginning of the year, 600 packages were in stock. The company plans to have enough units in stock at the end of each month to meet one-third of the sales demand for the next month. Fixed costs identified with this particular manufacturing operation have been budgeted at $26,000 for the first six months of the year. Sales demand for the first seven months of the year has been estimated as shown on the next page.

Required: (1) Compute the number of units that must be processed each month for the first six months of the year to meet the sales demand and to maintain the desired inventory level.

	Number of Units			Number of Units
January	1,800		April	1,740
February	1,500		May	2,880
March	1,200		June	3,600
			July	4,500

(2) Compute the contribution margin from estimated sales for each month.

(3) In what month, if any, will the contribution margin become equal to or exceed the fixed costs of the manufacturing operation?

7. A fire at Fenway Supply Company on May 5, 1972 not only damaged tangible properties but also caused a loss of potential sales by disrupting normal production. Fortunately, the company has insurance protection for profits lost as a result of fire. An inventory of 3,000 completed units of product were stored in a separate location and were not damaged by the fire. In the month of May only 7,000 units were manufactured. In June, production was up to 60 percent of maximum capacity, and in July production was up to 70 percent of maximum capacity. In subsequent months the company produced 40,000 units a month or operated at maximum capacity. At the time of the fire, the company had orders for the sale and delivery of 28,000 units in May. New orders for 32,000 units were received in May for June delivery, orders for 34,000 units were received in June for July delivery, and in July orders for 36,000 units were received for August delivery. Customers will not accept delivery after the scheduled month for delivery. Each unit of product sells for $12.

Required: You have been asked to furnish information to the insurance company showing the loss of sales in units and in dollars by not being able to fill customer orders. This is to be part of the loss claim filed with the insurance company.

8. In late September, the sales manager of Franklin Chemicals, Inc., realized that the original sales forecast for the last three months of the year must be revised. The original forecast showed that 515,000 pounds of an industrial chemical would be sold in October, 525,000 pounds would be sold in November, 560,000 pounds would be sold in December, and 580,000 pounds would be sold in January. It now appears that sales will be as followings:

	Pounds			Pounds
October	500,000		December	530,000
November	510,000		January	550,000

Normally 500 pounds of this chemical can be produced in one of the departments in an hour. An inventory equal to 20 percent of the estimated sales for the next month is to be on hand at the end of each month, and the company plans to have 100,000 pounds in the inventory at September 30.

Required: (1) Prepare a revised production budget for each of the last three months of the year.

(2) How many hours of production can be released each month for other work in this department by the expected reduction in sales? (Assume that the inventory is to be 100,000 pounds at September 30 in either case.)

Chapter 21

THE COORDINATED BUDGET

The master budget plan for the year is made up of many separate budgets that are interrelated. In budgeting, various limitations have to be considered. Ordinarily, the sales forecast as translated into a sales budget for the company is looked upon as the limit that will be used in establishing production budgets, selling and administrative budgets, cash budgets, and so forth. But this may not always be the case; shortcomings in production may force the company to turn away sales. Lack of productive capacity, shortages in materials, inability to meet specifications on the orders, or other reasons, may create a situation where the sales budget will be determined by production rather than the other way around.

BUDGET RELATIONSHIPS

As mentioned in the previous chapter, the sales budget that fits the limitations stated above serves as the keystone for the total budget. All other budgets are then related to the sales budget either directly or indirectly. The individual budgets and their relationship to one another are set forth on the next page.

Since the activities and the budgets for all phases of the business operation are influenced by sales, plant production is geared to the expected demands of the customers as set forth in a budget of sales, and the costs of selling the product and administering the business are also planned in relation to sales activity. Selling expenses such as advertising, travel, and entertainment are not only dependent upon sales activity but also help to create it. There is a certain degree of interdependence. Capital expenditures, on the other hand, are only indirectly related to the sales of any one year. Ordinarily, long-range plans for asset acquisitions are not curtailed because of estimates of reduced sales in any given year. The plans, however, may be postponed or revised if there is little prospect for sales recovery over the long run.

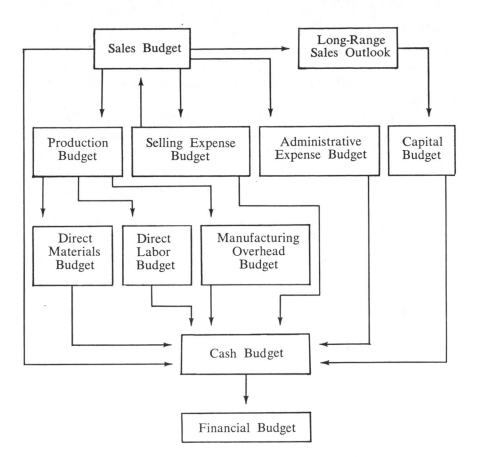

The detailed budgets underlying the budgets of production, selling expenses, administrative expenses, and capital expenditures are prepared from the summary budgets to which they are related. Finally, the various budgets are drawn together in the cash budget. For example, a budget of materials to be used can be prepared only after a decision has been reached as to what types and quantities of products are to be made. The budget of products to be made is, of course, derived in turn from the sales budget. The materials consumption budget is then translated into a purchases budget by estimating materials inventory levels and relating them to budgeted consumption. The purchases budget is then converted to dollars. Plans are made to pay for the materials purchased, and these plans are a part of the cash budget for the year. Thus, the budgeting process that begins with sales fans out in all directions and is tied in eventually with the cash budget.

The cash receipts and disbursements from all sources are estimated according to period of time and they form what is called the cash budget.

Probably there will be times when cash disbursements exceed receipts, or times when receipts exceed disbursements. In a given month, for example, an insurance policy may come up for renewal or an extraordinarily large tax payment may fall due. During this month, cash may flow out faster than it comes in.

Variations in the flow of cash over the year can be evened out by making use of short-term credit. A line of credit will be drawn upon during the months in which cash outflows are heavy. Loans will then be repaid with interest at a later date when the cash inflow exceeds the outgo. Planning short-term credit is a part of the financial budgeting operation.

The financial budget is based upon estimates of the cash flow, which in turn depend upon anticipated revenues and expected costs. Long-term debt is planned in the same manner, with projections being extended further into the future. In the final analysis, this budget like all the others is based upon sales in the immediate or distant future.

After a sales estimate has been drawn up and coordinated with plans for production, individual cost budgets can be prepared. Costs are usually accounted for along functional lines, that is, according to whether they pertain to manufacturing, selling, or administration. This same manner of classification is usually followed in budgeting, with the costs being broken down by activity and department. In this chapter the discussion will be centered around the cost budgets and the ways in which they are prepared and interlocked to form the master budget plan for the company.

THE MANUFACTURING COST BUDGET

The production budget is the key to the manufacturing cost budget. After decisions have been reached as to what quantities of products will be manufactured, the manufacturing costs can be estimated. Manufacturing costs are budgeted in the same way that they are accounted for, by cost element. The manufacturing cost budget is nothing more than the summary of the direct materials budget, the direct labor budget, and the manufacturing overhead budget.

The direct materials budget. The quantities of materials that will be required for manufacturing the products next year are estimated, with the estimate being translated into a budget of purchases for the year. Purchases, like production, are planned in relation to the inventories. If materials can be stored, the purchasing department has a certain amount of freedom and is not forced to follow the ups and downs of the production cycle. Perhaps materials can be purchased in advance at a particularly favorable price, or savings may be obtained by purchasing in large quantity lots. The purchasing department, however, cannot be permitted to operate without restraint. Savings that are obtained by purchasing under favorable conditions can be more than offset by the costs of carrying excessive quantities in inventory. Ordinarily a company will try to seek a compromise position, one in which neither the costs of purchasing nor the costs of storing an inventory are excessive.

The materials inventories are balanced so that there will not be too much of one item and not enough of another. If inventory control is inadequate, quantities of one type of material may be built up beyond any reasonable need while some other material may be in short supply. The investment in aggregate inventory may be large, yet production may have to be curtailed merely because some essential part is not available.

Inventories should be planned so that they will vary only within maximum and minimum limits. These limits are set for each item of material by estimating how much will be needed during a procurement period. There is no point in carrying a supply that is greatly in excess of current need. On the other hand, inventory balances can be trimmed to a point where there is a real risk that shipments will not be received in time for use in the factory.

Careful estimates must be made of how many units of different types of materials will be needed to make the various products. If standards have been established, they can be used and adjusted as necessary in reaching a reasonable estimate of how much material will probably be used. The materials requirements are then translated into a budget of materials to be purchased by subtracting the inventory planned for the beginning of the period and by adding the ending inventory estimate.

The purchases budget. In the illustration given for Reed and Company, two materials are used to manufacture the two products. Two units of Material A are used for each unit of Product 1, and two units of Material B are used for each unit of Product 2. A purchases budget for these two materials expressed in physical units is given on the next page.

Unit costs are estimated and used in converting the purchases budget to a dollar basis. The budget expressed in dollar amounts will aid the treasurer in his planning of future cash disbursements and will also be a step in the collection of the manufacturing costs that will eventually appear on the estimated income statement and balance sheet. The purchasing department is in the best position to furnish data with respect to estimated costs. It maintains contact with suppliers and knows what prices are offered by competing firms. Even so, the task of estimating future prices is difficult. To a certain extent, past records of materials consumption can be used in

Reed and Company

Purchases Budget

(In Thousands of Units)

For the Year Ended December 31, 1973

	Total	First Quarter	Second Quarter	Third Quarter	Fourth Quarter
Material A:					
Production requirement	900	170	320	320	90
Less: Inventory planned at beginning of period	50	50	110	110	40
Total	850	120	210	210	50
Add: Inventory planned at end of period	50	110	110	40	50
Units to be purchased	900	230	320	250	100
Material B:					
Production requirement	600	170	140	110	180
Less: Inventory planned at beginning of period	60	60	50	30	60
Total	540	110	90	80	120
Add: Inventory planned at end of period	60	50	30	60	60
Units to be purchased	600	160	120	140	180

planning a materials requirement budget; but historical prices will not necessarily hold in the future. Published price schedules and announcements of effective dates for price changes will help in immediate planning, but beyond this point estimates will have to be based upon a forecast of conditions in the market that may force suppliers to raise or lower their prices.

In addition to the cost of the material itself, there are other costs that should be included as a part of the material cost. In Chapter 12 it was stated that freight on incoming materials and the cost of purchasing, receiving, handling, and storing materials are a part of materials cost. Usually it is difficult to relate these costs to any specific item of material purchased; as a matter of expediency, they are often budgeted as a part of manufacturing overhead.

The purchases budget in dollars for Reed and Company is given at the top of the next page. It is assumed that costs such as freight, handling, and other costs related to materials have been estimated and applied to the billed cost of materials by using a predetermined rate that has been developed.

The direct labor budget. Direct labor, like direct materials, is first estimated on a physical quantity basis. Production quotas are translated into manpower requirements. There is no inventory planning problem as such,

Reed and Company
Purchases Budget
(In Thousands of Dollars)
For the Year Ended December 31, 1973

	Total	First Quarter	Second Quarter	Third Quarter	Fourth Quarter
Estimated cost of materials to be used	$4,200	$1,020	$1,200	$1,080	$900
Less: Inventory planned at beginning of period	340	340	420	340	320
Total	$3,860	$ 680	$ 780	$ 740	$580
Add: Inventory planned at end of period	340	420	340	320	340
Estimated cost of materials to be purchased	$4,200	$1,100	$1,120	$1,060	$920

but there are many other problems that in some respects bear a resemblance to it. Workers meeting the qualifications set by the production division will be hired by the personnel department if it appears that more help will be needed. The new employees may have to be trained, in which case they must be hired in advance of the time when they will be put to work on the production line. Hiring plans will be coordinated closely with the plans for production. A careless, haphazard employment policy can be costly. With improper timing, there is a risk that trained workers will not be available when needed or, conversely, that they will be ready before they can be used. If too many employees are hired or if anticipated increases in production are not permanent, there will come a time when some of the workers will have to be laid off. This represents the loss of an investment in training costs and may help to boost unemployment tax rates, not to mention the damage to reputation that a company suffers in the labor market by hiring and laying off workers repeatedly.

The labor time required to manufacture the products can be estimated from standards that have been set or from records of past performance. In either event, adjustments will most likely have to be made. New production methods may bring about savings in labor time, thus making past records of performance obsolete. Some allowance will also have to be made for idle time, setup time, and other expected variations from the standards in setting up a budget of total labor hours.

Labor hours will be broken down by pay classifications, with estimated rates being applied in the calculation of a labor cost budget. Rates are often specified by jobs in labor contracts, with provisions being made for adjustments in pay under given circumstances. Estimates will be more difficult to make if a contract change is anticipated during the year or if cost-of-living increases and other indefinite factors play a part in the determination of wage rates. Various fringe benefits, such as pensions, group insurance, and vacations, add to labor cost and may create uncertainties in budgeting. Labor costs are sometimes projected from average standard rates used in product costing, with the rates being adjusted as necessary.

A direct labor budget in hours has been assembled for Reed and Company and has been converted to direct labor dollars on the assumption that labor will be paid at a uniform rate of $5 an hour. The direct labor budget is reproduced below:

Reed and Company

Direct Labor Budget

(In Thousands)

For the Year Ended December 31, 1973

	Total	First Quarter	Second Quarter	Third Quarter	Fourth Quarter
Budget of hours:					
Product 1	91	17	32	32	10
Product 2	305	85	70	55	95
Total estimated hours ..	396	102	102	87	105
Total estimated labor cost	$1,980	$510	$510	$435	$525

The manufacturing overhead budget. Ordinarily manufacturing overhead costs are given considerable attention. Individual cost classifications are examined closely to see how the costs react to changes in volume or in relationship to other factors. Past records may show that a cost will generally follow a certain pattern of increase or decrease in response to a change in some other cost or activity. One company may find that certain overhead costs are influenced by indirect labor hours, while another company will base estimates of overhead on direct labor hours or even on materials cost or machine hours.

For many companies, the best opportunity for cost savings lies in the manufacturing overhead area. Direct materials costs and direct labor costs are often determined by factors that are beyond the control of management. For example, materials of a specified quality may be required and may be obtainable only at set prices, or labor contracts may prescribe what rates will have to be paid for various types of work. Whenever possible, of course, management will search for ways to save materials, to substitute cheaper materials, or to reduce labor cost by improving methods of production. In addition, there probably will be opportunities to trim overhead costs. An apparently insignificant saving on a unit basis can be surprisingly large when the total effect is appraised. A small waste in the use of some lubricant, for example, is unimportant if only one machine is considered; but when this waste is multiplied by all machines in the plant, the loss may be substantial. By paying attention to details, management can control overhead costs and thereby increase profits.

The forecast budget of manufacturing overhead, unlike the budget used to cost products or to control costs in the plant departments, is an estimate of the costs that can be expected during the next year. Products, however, are usually costed with overhead budgeted at the normal capacity level even if it is reasonably certain that the plant will not operate at that level in the coming year. Relatively tight budgets that can be used for controlling plant costs should be adhered to in practice if the company is to achieve its aims. Yet, if it appears that variances will develop in spite of all efforts, the variances should be included in a forecast budget so that all costs can be anticipated before they arise. A falsely optimistic budget can create difficulties in other areas of planning. For instance, the cash disbursements budget and the financial budget for the year will be incorrect to the extent that cash requirements have been understated.

The forecast budget of manufacturing overhead for Reed and Company for the next year appears below in summary form:

Reed and Company
Manufacturing Overhead Budget
(In Thousands of Dollars)
For the Year Ended December 31, 1973

	Total	First Quarter	Second Quarter	Third Quarter	Fourth Quarter
Variable:					
Supplies	$1,842	$ 478	$ 450	$ 385	$ 529
Power	116	28	27	26	35
Heat and light	346	88	86	79	93
Repairs and maintenance	725	190	224	154	157
Total variable overhead	$3,029	$ 784	$ 787	$ 644	$ 814
Fixed:					
Supervision	$1,300	$ 325	$ 325	$ 325	$ 325
Indirect labor	1,872	468	468	468	468
Insurance	60	15	15	15	15
Taxes	56	14	14	14	14
Heat and light	32	8	8	8	8
Repairs and maintenance	44	11	11	11	11
Rent	96	24	24	24	24
Depreciation	720	180	180	180	180
Total fixed overhead	$4,180	$1,045	$1,045	$1,045	$1,045
Total manufacturing overhead	$7,209	$1,829	$1,832	$1,689	$1,859

The overhead costs anticipated for the year have been distributed to the calendar quarters on an accrual basis. At this point, no relationship between the costs and the cash disbursements has been established. For example, insurance cost of $60,000 has been spread over the year at the rate of $15,000 a quarter. Probably payments for insurance protection will not follow this pattern. The entire cost may be paid at one time, or payments in varying amounts may be made throughout the year or even in later years. The budget only reveals that the insurance cost for the year will probably amount to $60,000. There is no indication as to whether the cost has been paid or whether it is a reasonable cost.

THE SELLING EXPENSE BUDGET

The costs of promoting, selling, and distributing the products, or in other words the selling costs, are budgeted in much the same way as the manufacturing costs. Although the selling costs are not included as a part of product cost, they are frequently broken down by lines of product, sales regions, customers, salesmen, or some other significant unit basis. Analysis may reveal that it costs too much to sell a certain product or that the company would do better by concentrating on a particular customer group. Perhaps the cost of operating a retail unit is not justified by the return, in which case it may be better to close the unit or to seek more profitable sales outlets. Cost analysis can be applied in planning sales activity, revealing what it will probably cost to sell different quantities and combinations of products. Furthermore, if costs are budgeted and accumulated on a unit of responsibility basis, it is possible to spot differences by sales region, salesman, customer group, and so forth. Thus selling costs, like manufacturing costs, can be identified by area of responsibility and can be used as a means for control.

It is not as easy to budget selling expenses for the year as it might appear. Some of the expenses, of course, can be estimated with little or no difficulty. For example, the relatively fixed costs of operating a sales office, such as rent, sales salaries, heat and light, and depreciation of equipment, present little or no problem. Similarly, sales commissions based upon a stipulated percentage of net sales can be calculated directly from a budget of net sales. Many of the selling expenses, however, bear no direct relationship to sales and in some cases will be somewhat arbitrarily determined by managerial policy.

Promotional expenses and shipping expenses, for example, are dependent upon sales, but they are also influenced by other factors. Promotional expenses such as advertising, travel, and entertainment not only are governed by sales but also help to determine sales. Shipping expenses vary according to the destination of the products and agreements reached with customers.

Often budgets for sales promotion are made on an appropriation basis. A certain amount is allowed during the year, with the amount to be spent depending upon the sales objectives set by management and estimates of what will be required to realize these objectives. Sometimes promotional expenses are budgeted at a certain percentage of sales, although this policy is not generally recommended. With a decline in sales, there would be a reduction in sales promotion. This could lead to further decreases in sales, aggravating a condition that is already unsatisfactory. Perhaps even greater expenditures for promotion can be justified when sales are falling off.

Selling expenses for Reed and Company have been estimated and summarized in the budget given below:

Reed and Company
Selling Expense Budget
(In Thousands of Dollars)
For the Year Ended December 31, 1973

	Total	First Quarter	Second Quarter	Third Quarter	Fourth Quarter
Variable:					
Sales commissions	$ 992	$ 208	$ 283	$ 291	$ 210
Advertising	573	176	154	121	122
Sales supplies	144	32	42	44	26
Telephone	8	2	3	2	1
Shipping expense	187	33	52	77	25
Delivery expense	96	22	28	25	21
Total variable costs	$2,000	$ 473	$ 562	$ 560	$ 405
Fixed:					
Sales salaries	$ 940	$ 235	$ 235	$ 235	$ 235
Advertising	856	214	214	214	214
Travel and entertainment .	340	85	85	85	85
Sales office rent	40	10	10	10	10
Utilities	4	1	1	1	1
Depreciation	20	5	5	5	5
Total fixed costs	$2,200	$ 550	$ 550	$ 550	$ 550
Total selling expense	$4,200	$1,023	$1,112	$1,110	$ 955

THE GENERAL AND ADMINISTRATIVE EXPENSE BUDGET

The costs of administration and the costs of maintaining a corporate form of business are frequently looked upon as fixed costs. While these costs are less directly related to sales, they are nevertheless dependent upon sales volume in the long run. With minor variations in business activity, the costs of operating the administrative offices will remain fairly constant. However, during prolonged periods of inactivity, these costs will be reduced. Office personnel will be laid off, officers' salaries will be cut, and various economy measures will be instituted during a business slump. In relatively prosperous times, costs will tend to creep up and excesses may be overlooked. The result is that changes in administrative cost tend to lag behind changes in business conditions.

Administrative costs, like manufacturing and selling costs, are broken down for use in control. Budgets of costs chargeable to individual administrative supervisors provide controls against which actual costs can be compared. By following the general principles of cost accounting, it is also possible to set standards of work performance for various activities and to establish cost standards. For example, the cost to process specific accounting data or the cost to assemble data for reports can be calculated by using techniques similar to those employed in job order manufacturing operations. The costs are either directly or indirectly identified with the activity, and the actual costs are then compared with a predetermined budget. If variations are unfavorable and material in amount, steps will be taken to correct whatever is responsible for the differences.

A budget of estimated general and administrative expenses for Reed and Company is given below. This budget along with the budget of manufacturing costs and the budget of selling expenses will be used in planning cash disbursements and in the preparation of an estimated income statement.

Reed and Company
General and Administrative Expense Budget
(In Thousands of Dollars)
For the Year Ended December 31, 1973

	Total	First Quarter	Second Quarter	Third Quarter	Fourth Quarter
Variable:					
Supplies used	$ 597	$150	$151	$156	$140
Heat and light	19	4	5	4	6
Telephone	4	1	1	1	1
Total variable expenses .	$ 620	$155	$157	$161	$147
Fixed:					
Officers salaries	$ 760	$190	$190	$190	$190
Office salaries	820	205	205	205	205
Professional services ...	184	46	46	46	46
Corporate taxes	168	42	42	42	42
Donations	40	10	10	10	10
Rent	20	5	5	5	5
Heat and light	36	9	9	9	9
Telephone	4	1	1	1	1
Depreciation	248	62	62	62	62
Total fixed expenses	$2,280	$570	$570	$570	$570
Total general and administrative expenses	$2,900	$725	$727	$731	$717

THE CAPITAL BUDGET

A plan for the acquisition of various properties such as buildings, machinery, equipment, and other long-term investments is sometimes referred to as a *capital expenditure budget* or as a *capital budget*. For purposes of this discussion, assume that plans for the acquisition of capital assets have been approved by top management, and that these plans are ready to be interlocked with the budget plans for the year. Each year a provision must be made in the current annual budget for the portion of the plan to be carried out that year. Expenditures for minor additions and replacements will probably not be planned far in advance nor will they require the approval of top management. Ordinarily, supervisors at the lower levels will be granted appropriations that can be used in acquiring properties whose costs lie within prescribed limits.

Although properties that will be used in operations for long periods of time are not acquired on the basis of current sales estimates, the prospects for immediate sales will have some influence. If the outlook for sales is not promising, projects that have been planned for the current year may be postponed or cut back, or the original schedule may be followed so that the company will be ready to capture opportunities when conditions are favorable. Replacements and minor additions are more likely to be influenced by the current sales picture.

During the coming year, Reed and Company expects to go ahead with plans for modernization and in the first quarter probably will spend $3,000,000 for new machinery. Part of the cost is to be financed by the issue of $1,500,000 in equipment notes. Other additions to plant assets have been planned by calendar quarters as follows: $160,000, $180,000, $100,000, and $80,000.

The capital budget is set forth below:

Reed and Company
Capital Budget
For the Year Ended December 31, 1973

	Total	First Quarter	Second Quarter	Third Quarter	Fourth Quarter
New machinery	$3,000,000	$3,000,000	—0—	—0—	—0—
Other acquisitions	520,000	160,000	$180,000	$100,000	$80,000
Capital budget	$3,520,000	$3,160,000	$180,000	$100,000	$80,000
Less: Cost of new machinery to be financed by notes	1,500,000	1,500,000	—0—	—0—	—0—
Current cash expenditures	$2,020,000	$1,660,000	$180,000	$100,000	$80,000

THE CASH RECEIPTS BUDGET

Normally sales activity is expected to produce the bulk of the cash receipts. If sales are made on a credit basis, accounts receivable will eventually be translated into cash as the customers pay their accounts. The time required to collect outstanding accounts will have to be estimated, and provision must be made for discounts, returns, allowances granted, and uncollectible accounts. From a study of past records and recent experience in the rate of collections, it should be possible to predict approximate receipts on account. The collection pattern for Reed and Company is given below:

65% of the net sales for the quarter are collected during the quarter with a 2% discount allowed for prompt payment.

10% of the net sales for the quarter are collected during the quarter with no discount allowed.

10% of the net sales for the quarter are collected during the next quarter with a 2% discount allowed.

10% of the net sales for the quarter are collected during the next quarter with no discount allowed.

5% of the net sales for the quarter are collected during the second quarter following with no discount allowed.

Returns and allowances do not necessarily fall in the quarter in which the goods are sold, but Reed and Company find that about 2 percent of gross sales for any quarter are returned or reduced by allowances granted. Net sales for the third quarter of the present year, 1972, amounted to $9,870,000; it is anticipated that net sales will amount to $5,240,000 in the fourth quarter, the quarter in which the budget for the next year is being prepared.

A partial budget of cash receipts is drawn up by applying the collection percentages to the appropriate net sales for each quarter. At the same time, accounts receivable balances are estimated as they will probably appear at the end of each quarter net of returns, allowances, and uncollectibles. The accounts receivable collection schedule for Reed and Company is given at the top of the next page.

In addition to sales, there are many other potential sources of cash. All of these sources must be examined for possible additions to cash in setting up a total cash receipts budget for the year. Dividends and interest may be collected on investments, or cash may be received from an incidental operation such as the rent of a lot or a building or from the sale of scrap material. Ordinarily cash will be realized from the sale of investments in stocks and bonds and from the sale of machinery or other assets not dealt with in the normal course of trade. Stock may be issued or debt may be incurred with cash flowing in as a result.

During the coming year, Reed and Company expects to receive $100,000 in the first quarter from the sale of equipment that cost $300,000 with

Reed and Company
Schedule of Estimated Collections on Accounts Receivable
and Computation of Net Receivable Balances
(In Thousands of Dollars) *
For the Year Ended December 31, 1973

	Total	First Quarter	Second Quarter	Third Quarter	Fourth Quarter
Net accounts receivable, beginning of period ...	$ 2,600	$2,600	$ 2,731	$ 3,434	$3,803
Net sales	32,010	6,693	9,215	10,185	5,917
Total	$34,610	$9,293	$11,946	$13,619	$9,720
Collections:					
Sales of current quarter:					
65% of net sales, less discounts	$20,391	$4,264	$ 5,870	$ 6,488	$3,769
10% of net sales, no discounts	3,202	669	922	1,019	592
Sales of preceding quarter:					
10% of net sales, less discounts	3,071	514	656	903	998
10% of net sales, no discounts	3,133	524	669	921	1,019
Sales of second preceding quarter:					
5% of net sales, no discounts	1,552	494	262	335	461
Total collections	$31,349	$6,465	$ 8,379	$ 9,666	$6,839
Discounts	477	97	133	150	97
Total reduction of receivables	$31,826	$6,562	$ 8,512	$ 9,816	$6,936
Net accounts receivable, end of period	$ 2,784	$2,731	$ 3,434	$ 3,803	$2,784

* Adjusted to even thousands.

accumulated depreciation of $250,000. In that same quarter, marketable securities are to be redeemed at $400,000. Bank loans are to be made as needed, but cash receipts from this source will be planned after both receipts and disbursements have been budgeted. The cash receipts budget for Reed and Company appears at the top of the next page.

THE CASH PAYMENTS BUDGET

The various cost budgets, plans for capital acquisitions, commitments for the discharge of debt, and plans for dividend payments are brought together in a cash disbursements budget. If at all possible, payments will

Reed and Company
Summary of Cash Receipts
(In Thousands of Dollars)
For the Year Ended December 31, 1973

	Total	First Quarter	Second Quarter	Third Quarter	Fourth Quarter
Collections on accounts receivable	$31,349	$6,465	$8,379	$9,666	$6,839
Proceeds from sale of machinery	100	100	—0—	—0—	—0—
Redemption of marketable securities	400	400	—0—	—0—	—0—
Interest received	26	2	12	—0—	12
Total cash receipts	$31,875	$6,967	$8,391	$9,666	$6,851

be scheduled at convenient times, that is, when cash balances are expected to be sufficiently high. Frequently the demand for cash is not spread evenly throughout the year. Several large payments may become due in one particular month, in which case the company will either plan to hold back cash for these payments or will borrow if cash receipts in that month are not expected to be sufficient.

It is unlikely that disbursements will be made in every instance when costs are incurred or when materials and services are used. Advertising, insurance, and rent, for example, are often paid in advance with the cost being absorbed against future operations. Payments for materials, labor, supplies, and other costs of operation frequently follow acquisition and use. A budget of cash disbursements is made by scheduling payments that must be made for materials, labor, other operating costs, dividends, debt service, and so forth.

Freedom in planning is restricted somewhat by customary practice and by commitments that have already been made. Ordinarily, employees will have to be paid at periodic intervals, and rents will usually be paid on a monthly or on an annual basis. Some payments, however, can be made ahead of time or can be delayed somewhat as desired. If discounts are allowed, however, payments should be made within the discount period.

The cash payment schedule for Reed and Company given at the top of the next page shows that disbursements will be unusually large during the first quarter. Insurance and factory rent for the year will fall due in that quarter. In addition, a large down payment must be made on new equipment purchased.

Schedule of Cash Payments

(In Thousands of Dollars)

For the Year Ended December 31, 1973

	Total	First Quarter	Second Quarter	Third Quarter	Fourth Quarter
Material purchases	$ 4,180	$1,130	$1,120	$ 980	$ 950
Direct labor	1,980	510	510	435	525
Manufacturing overhead	6,478	1,645	1,648	1,505	1,680
Selling expenses	4,253	1,118	1,100	1,090	945
General and administrative expenses	2,645	665	662	658	660
Plant asset acquisitions	2,020	1,660	180	100	80
Income tax payments	5,325	1,200	1,375	1,375	1,375
Interest on equipment notes..	120	30	30	30	30
Dividends	2,800	700	700	700	700
Total payments scheduled ...	$29,801	$8,658	$7,325	$6,873	$6,945

FINANCIAL PLANNING

Budgeted cash receipts and disbursements are brought together to form a total cash budget. From this summary of estimated cash flows, it will be possible to anticipate future cash balances. In some months, receipts may not be large enough to cover disbursements, in which case the cash balance will be reduced. If the outflow of cash is too great, plans will have to be made to borrow funds. In other months when receipts are greater than disbursements, loans can be repaid and cash balances can be built up.

Financial plans are drawn up so that a minimum balance of cash will be available at all times. The amount to be held will depend upon estimated future cash flows and the financial policy adopted. In general, the cash balance should be large enough to enable the company to meet its payrolls and to pay its operating costs for the next month with some allowance being made for contingencies and miscalculations in planning. By holding adequate cash balances, management is able to cope with small adversities and is not forced to borrow under unfavorable conditions. When trouble strikes, there is a reserve that can be drawn upon. While the reserve is being used, management can make alternate plans and can secure additional cash from other sources to meet future needs.

Opinion will differ as to what amount of cash should be held. Some companies will maintain fairly substantial cash balances and in addition will have a secondary reserve consisting of government securities that can easily be converted into cash. Many other companies, however, will prefer to operate with smaller cash reserves, depending upon bank credit when cash is needed. Often a line of credit is established at a bank. Cash up to a certain limit can be borrowed when needed, with arrangement being made for repayment.

The management of Reed and Company believes that the cash balance at the beginning of the year is too low to support the expected level of operations. Plans are made to build the cash balance up to a level of approximately $3,600,000. A bank loan of $2,000,000 is to be obtained in the first quarter when disbursements are expected to exceed receipts by $1,691,000. This loan is to be repaid with interest in the third quarter.

The summary cash budget for Reed and Company given below has been designed so that the financial plans will stand out separately. The bank loan, its repayment, and the interest on the loan are shown beneath the planned increases or decreases in the cash balance. The resulting cash balances as they should appear at the end of each quarter are then shown on the last line of the budget.

Reed and Company
Summary Cash Budget
(In Thousands of Dollars)
For the Year Ended December 31, 1973

	Total	First Quarter	Second Quarter	Third Quarter	Fourth Quarter
Cash balance, beginning	$ 1,540	$1,540	$1,849	$2,915	$3,678
Budgeted receipts	$31,875	$6,967	$8,391	$9,666	$6,851
Budgeted disbursements	29,801	8,658	7,325	6,873	6,945
Excess of receipts	$ 2,074		$1,066	$2,793	
Excess of disbursements		$1,691			$ 94
Bank loans		2,000			
Repayment of bank loans ...				2,000	
Interest on bank loans	30			30	
Cash balance, ending	$ 3,584	$1,849	$2,915	$3,678	$3,584

A plan showing how cash will flow in or out of the business is dependent upon the other budgets and is in itself important enough to justify much of the effort expended in budget preparation. Preliminary estimates may reveal that disbursements are lumped together and that, with more careful planning, payments can be spread out more evenly throughout the year. As a result, less bank credit will be needed and interest costs will be lower. Banks and other credit-granting institutions will be more inclined to grant loans under favorable terms if the loan request is supported by a methodical cash plan. The business that is operated on a casual day-to-day basis is more likely to borrow funds at inopportune times and in excessive amounts. Furthermore, with no plans, there is no certainty that the loans can be repaid on schedule.

THE ESTIMATED INCOME STATEMENT

An estimated income statement can be prepared from the budget data for the year. The estimated income statement is a summary of the results expected and shows whether or not plans for profits as reflected in the budgets can be realized. It brings together the various revenue and expense budgets, making it easier to evaluate the overall operation. Management can compare its actual income statement with the estimated statement both during the year and at the end of the year. If budgeted profits are to be realized, adjustments may have to be made as operations progress. Perhaps the budget itself will require revision. At the end of the year, a comparison of actual results with the budget may point out areas of operation that deserve more attention in the future, or comparison may reveal ways in which better budgets can be prepared.

The estimated income statement is broken down by quarters and by months and, in addition, may be broken down according to product lines sold, sales regions, and customer groupings. From an analysis of the statements, management can determine which products, regions, or customer groups are likely to be the most profitable. Plans for the year may be revised if it appears that better alternatives are available, and actual operations will be conducted so that profits will be maximized.

The estimated income statement for Reed and Company given on page 616 has been prepared in the conventional manner. The costs of manufacturing are matched against net sales, with inventories being carried forward at standard costs. The standard variable cost of Product 1 is $15 per unit, and the standard variable cost of Product 2 is $8 per unit. The selling expenses and the administrative expenses have been taken directly from the expense budgets.

The variable manufacturing cost (in thousands of dollars) as taken from the manufacturing cost budgets are given below:

	Total	First Quarter	Second Quarter	Third Quarter	Fourth Quarter
Materials used	$4,200	$1,020	$1,200	$1,080	$ 900
Direct labor	1,980	510	510	435	525
Manufacturing overhead	3,029	784	787	644	814
Total variable manufacturing costs	$9,209	$2,314	$2,497	$2,159	$2,239
Add: Beginning inventory	385	385	720	870	310
	$9,594	$2,699	$3,217	$3,029	$2,549
Less: Ending inventory	385	720	870	310	385
Variable manufacturing cost on the income statement	$9,209	$1,979	$2,347	$2,719	$2,164

The variable manufacturing costs on the income statement each quarter are equal to the total variable manufacturing costs adjusted by inventory differences during the year as shown above. The inventory quantities are given in the production budgets shown in Chapter 20.

Reed and Company
Estimated Income Statement
(To the Nearest Thousand Dollars)
For the Year Ended December 31, 1973

	Total	First Quarter	Second Quarter	Third Quarter	Fourth Quarter
Net sales (discounts deducted) ..	$31,533	$6,596	$9,082	$10,035	$5,820
Variable costs:					
Manufacturing	9,209	1,979	2,347	2,719	2,164
Selling	2,000	473	562	560	405
General and administrative ...	620	155	157	161	147
Total variable costs	$11,829	$2,607	$3,066	$ 3,440	$2,716
Contribution margin	$19,704	$3,989	$6,016	$ 6,595	$3,104
Fixed costs:					
Manufacturing	$ 4,180	$1,045	$1,045	$ 1,045	$1,045
Selling	2,200	550	550	550	550
General and administrative ...	2,280	570	570	570	570
Total fixed costs	$ 8,660	$2,165	$2,165	$ 2,165	$2,165
Net operating income	$11,044	$1,824	$3,851	$ 4,430	$ 939
Add: Gain on sale of equipment .	50	50	—0—	—0—	—0—
Interest earned	26	8	6	6	6
Total	$11,120	$1,882	$3,857	$ 4,436	$ 945
Less: Interest expense	150	30	45	45	30
Net income before income taxes .	$10,970	$1,852	$3,812	$ 4,391	$ 915
Income taxes	5,485	926	1,906	2,195	458
Net income after income taxes ..	$ 5,485	$ 926	$1,906	$ 2,196	$ 457

Details with respect to interest income, interest expense, and the loss on the sale of equipment have been gathered from the cash budget and from information furnished with respect to the sale of equipment. Income taxes are estimated at approximately 50 percent of the net income before taxes.

THE ESTIMATED BALANCE SHEET

The estimated balance sheet tells where the company should stand financially at some later date. Like the estimated income statement, it is a summary budget statement that depends upon the various individual budgets which have been prepared. It can be compared with actual statements from the past to show how the assets and the equities will be affected by operations

616

during the budget year. Balance sheets from past years may reveal unfavorable trends. Does the budget for the next year help to reverse these trends? Perhaps debt has been increasing beyond a safe limit. This should have been recognized in the preparation of the budget for the year, and any remedial action taken should be reflected in the estimated balance sheet for the end of the budget year.

The estimated balance sheet also serves as a point of reference during the year. Interim statements prepared at various dates can be compared with corresponding budget statements. It may be possible to detect some unfavorable variation that should be corrected during the year, or the budget itself may require revision.

A comparison of the budget statements with the actual statements can be put to use in the preparation of future budgets. Knowledge gained by experience can be applied in making better estimates and in controlling operations more effectively so that they will tend to conform to the budget.

The differences revealed in a comparison between budget and actual statements reveal the fact that the company cannot earn the profits it hopes to or have the financial position it wants without paying close attention to the budget during the year. These statements clearly show that the desired profits and financial position can be achieved only by making careful plans that are carried out by the concerted effort of all individuals concerned.

The estimated balance sheet for Reed and Company is given at the top of the next page.

WORKING PAPERS

Financial statements for the next year can be prepared directly from the budgets, but it may be much easier to gather all of the data on working papers before attempting to make up the statements. Working papers that summarize the transactions for the budget year for Reed and Company are given on page 619. By following the same general methods of summarization, quarterly financial data can be drawn together for use in interim statements.

The transactions for the year are taken from the budgets indicated below and are shown on the working papers opposite the numbers given in parenthesis:

(1) Sales—from budget of net sales. Deduct sales discounts shown on budget of collections on receivables.

(2) Variable costs—from cost budgets.

(3) Fixed costs—from cost budgets. Prepaid insurance has been decreased by $15,000 during the year. Depreciation for the year has

Reed and Company
Estimated Balance Sheet
(To the Nearest Thousand Dollars)

Assets	Jan. 1, 1973	Mar. 31, 1973	June 30, 1973	Sept. 30, 1973	Dec. 31, 1973
Current assets:					
Cash	$ 1,540	$ 1,849	$ 2,915	$ 3,678	$ 3,584
Marketable securities	800	400	400	400	400
Accounts receivable, net ...	2,600	2,731	3,434	3,803	2,784
Inventories:					
Materials	340	420	340	320	340
Finished goods	385	720	870	310	385
Prepayments	60	54	50	45	45
Total current assets	$ 5,725	$ 6,174	$ 8,009	$ 8,556	$ 7,538
Plant and equipment, net of depreciation	5,200	8,063	7,996	7,849	7,682
Total assets	$10,925	$14,237	$16,005	$16,405	$15,220
Equities					
Current liabilities:					
Accounts payable	$ 2,800	$ 2,645	$ 2,676	$ 2,775	$ 2,750
Notes payable—bank	—0—	2,000	2,000	—0—	—0—
Accrued interest payable ...	—0—	15	15	—0—	—0—
Estimated income tax liability	1,200	926	1,457	2,277	1,360
Total current liabilities	$ 4,000				
Equipment notes payable	—0—	1,500	1,500	1,500	1,500
Owners' equity:					
Capital stock—$1 par	5,000	5,000	5,000	5,000	5,000
Retained earnings	1,925	2,151	3,357	4,853	4,610
Total equities	$10,925	$14,237	$16,005	$16,405	$15,220

been taken from the fixed cost budgets and has been deducted against plant equipment. Other costs flow through accounts payable.

(4) Cash receipts—from budget of collections on accounts receivable, summary cash receipts budget, and summary cash budget.

(5) Cash disbursements—from budget of cash payments, summary cash budget, and capital budget for plant additions. Exclude payments for plant assets, income taxes, interest on equipment loans, and dividends in computing charge of $19,536,000 to accounts payable. Income taxes as taken from the income statement are credited to estimated income taxes payable.

(6) Transfer of net income to retained earnings—computed from revenue and expense data.

Reed and Company
Budget Working Papers
(In Thousands of Dollars)
For the Year Ended December 31, 1973

	Balance Sheet Jan. 1, 1973		Budgeted Transactions		Estimated Results Dec. 31, 1973	
	Dr.	Cr.	Dr.	Cr.	Dr.	Cr.
Cash	$ 1,540		(4)$ 33,875	(5)$ 31,831	$ 3,584	
Market securities .	800			(4) 400	400	
Accounts receivable	2,600		(1) 31,533	(4) 31,349	2,784	
Inventories:						
Materials	340				340	
Finished goods	385				385	
Prepayments ...	60			(3) 15	45	
Plant equipment, net	5,200		(5) 3,520	(3) 988 (4) 50	7,682	
Accounts payable		$2,800	(5) 19,536	(2) 11,829 (3) 7,657		$ 2,750
Notes payable, bank			(5) 2,000	(4) 2,000		
Accrued interest payable						
Estimated income taxes payable .		1,200	(5) 5,325	(5) 5,485		1,360
Equipment notes payable				(5) 1,500		1,500
Capital stock ...		5,000				5,000
Retained earnings		1,925	(5) 2,800	(6) 5,485		4,610
Sales				(1) 31,533		
Variable costs ..			(2) 11,829			
Fixed costs			(3) 8,660			
Interest earned .				(4) 26		
Interest expense .			(5) 150			
Gain on sale of equipment ...				(4) 50		
Income taxes ...			(5) 5,485			
Net income			(6) 5,485			
	$10,925	$10,925	$130,198	$130,198	$15,220	$15,220

THE USE OF BUDGETS

It may appear from the illustrations given that budgets can be drawn up quite accurately and brought together into financial statements. Unfortunately, this is not so. The mechanical process of bringing the data together on working papers can be carried out exactly, but all of the data used has been taken from estimates that may or may not prove to be correct.

Thus, the budget summaries and the statements are only as good as the estimates upon which they rest.

By preparing a budget, management learns more about the business and with experience can make suprisingly accurate estimates. Management will learn how costs vary with the volume of sales and production and will be able to see how certain peculiarities in some aspect of the operation influence costs. With continued practice, it will be possible to avoid errors that were once made and to arrive at better budget estimates.

Budgets are used as a guide in conducting operations; and when actual operations are compared with the budget, discrepancies reveal the need for further attention in the areas where the discrepancies are located. Usually reports are prepared showing actual data in one column and budget data in an adjoining column. Differences are then computed and shown in still another column. Often the variations are also expressed in percentages. If variations are material, they are traced to determine underlying causes. Sometimes outside factors beyond the control of the company are responsible for budget variations, in which case the budget may have to be revised. On the other hand, it may be found that the budget is in error and that it will have to be corrected, or it may be that operations were not carried out properly.

Questions

1. The manufacturing cost budget is derived from the production budget which in turn is derived from the sales budget. Explain the budget relationships.

2. Is it possible to have an excessive inventory investment while running the risk of inventory shortages? Explain.

3. Manufacturing costs can be budgeted by cost element. What are the cost elements?

4. How is a direct materials budget translated into a purchases budget?

5. Why might a haphazard employment policy be costly?

6. What are labor fringe benefits?

7. How can a labor hour budget be translated into a labor cost budget?

8. Why are relatively small cost savings on a unit basis important?

9. Is the manufacturing overhead budget equivalent to a budget of cash disbursements for manufacturing overhead? Explain.

10. Selling costs may be broken down by product lines, sales regions, customers, salesmen, and so forth. Why are these costs broken down in various ways?

11. Why is it a poor policy to budget promotional expenses at a certain percentage of sales?

12. Are general and administrative costs dependent upon sales activity? Explain.

13. What is a capital budget?

14. How are long-range plans for the acquisition of plant assets included in current budgets?

15. Point out factors that must be considered in budgeting the cash receipts from sales activity.

16. What budgets are combined in planning a cash disbursements budget?

17. Why might cash disbursements fluctuate during the year even with relatively uniform sales and production?

18. Are there advantages in holding large cash reserves? disadvantages?

19. How is a cash budget used in planning short-term bank loans?

20. How can management benefit from the experience gained in the preparation of a budget?

Exercises

1. Scott Products, Inc., normally produces and sells 8,550,000 pounds of a plastic product each month. The materials used in the processing operation cost 16 cents a pound. In the past, the company has exercised strict control over temperature, pressure, and other aspects of the operation and has obtained a 90 percent yield from materials input. Some of the materials input is unavoidably lost by transfer in pipelines where it forms a skin in the pipes and in the storage containers. The company plans to reduce some of the operating loss by installing automatic regulators that are more sensitive to changes in temperature, pressure, etc. It is estimated that the automatic regulators can reduce the loss to 5 percent of materials input.

Required: If the new automatic regulators are installed, how many pounds of input will be required for 8,550,000 pounds of product? Calculate the savings in dollars that can be expected each month with an output of 8,550,000 pounds of product.

2. Market studies show that 15,000,000 units of a certain consumer product should be sold in 1973. Pinella, Inc., produces a part used in this product. Five units of this part are required for each unit of product manufactured. Pinella, Inc., estimates that it will supply parts for 40 percent of the products manufactured. There is also a replacement parts market. Over the past three years, the company has sold the following number of replacement parts:

$$1970— \ 8,500,000$$
$$1971— \ 9,350,000$$
$$1972—10,285,000$$

This trend is expected to continue. The parts are sold for 30 cents apiece in both markets.

Required: Estimate the total number of parts to be sold in 1973 and the amount of expected revenue.

3. The manufacturing cost budget for one of the departments of Klinger and Boyd Company shows that three parts costing 40 cents apiece are required for the manufacture of each unit of product. In July, 1972, the company made 60,000 units of product to meet the budget requirement, but the parts used in production cost 43 cents apiece. The materials purchased and used during the month cost $79,550.

Required: (1) Compute the budgeted materials cost for 60,000 units of product.

(2) Compute the budget variance for July, 1972. How much of the variance was attributable to a difference in the unit cost of the material used? a difference in the quantity used?

4. A labor cost budget for the second quarter of 1973 has been prepared by one of the departments of Wonder Products, Inc. Each employee is paid a regular rate of $5.20 per hour and receives an overtime rate equal to 1½ times the regular rate. The company has estimated that vacation pay is equal to 20 cents for each regular hour of work and that other fringe benefit costs are approximately equal to 15 percent of the regular hourly wages. (Overtime hours are excluded in the computation of vacation pay and other fringe benefit costs.) Labor hours have been estimated as follows:

	Regular	*Overtime*	*Total*
April	4,000	200	4,200
May	4,000	300	4,300
June	4,500	—0—	4,500

Required: Compute the total labor cost per month including all fringe benefit cost. Then, classify the total labor cost for regular hours, overtime, vacation pay, and other fringe benefits.

5. The treasurer of Jay Loft, Inc., plans for the company to have a cash balance of $91,000 on September 1. Sales during September are estimated at $800,000. August sales amounted to $650,000, and July sales amounted to $500,000. Cash payments for September have been budgeted at $680,000. Cash collections have been estimated as follows:

50% of the sales for the month to be collected during the month.
30% of the sales for the preceding month to be collected during the month.
15% of the sales for the second preceding month to be collected during the month.

The treasurer plans to accelerate collections by allowing a 2 percent discount for prompt payment. With the discount policy, he expects to collect 60 percent of the current sales and will permit the discount reduction on these collections. Sales of the preceding month will be collected to the extent of 25 percent with no discount allowed, and 10 percent of the sales of the second preceding month will be collected with no discount allowed. This pattern of collections can be expected in subsequent months. During the transitional month of September, collections may run somewhat higher. However, the treasurer prefers to estimate collections on the basis of the new pattern so that the estimates will be somewhat conservative.

Required: (1) Estimate cash collections for September and the cash balance at September 30 under the present policy.

(2) Estimate cash collections for September and the cash balance at September 30 according to the new policy of allowing discounts.

6. In the first calendar quarter of 1973, Zipin Specialties Company plans to sell 400,000 units of product at a unit price of $5.50. There are no inventories on hand at January 1, 1973. In the first quarter, the company will operate at normal capacity producing 500,000 units. These units will be assigned manufacturing overhead costs of $500,000 and direct labor costs of $250,000. Actual manufacturing overhead and direct labor costs are estimated at $500,000 and $250,000 respectively. Included in manufacturing overhead is depreciation of $40,000. Payments of $687,000 are to be made during the quarter for manufacturing overhead and direct labor.

Materials costing $600,000 will be purchased and used to make the 500,000 units of product. Payments for the supplies of materials during the quarter are estimated at $580,000.

The company plans to collect 60 percent of the total amount billed to the customers during the quarter and will probably collect $420,000 on sales made in previous quarters.

Required: (1) Prepare an estimated income statement for the manufacturing operation for the first quarter of 1973.

(2) Prepare an estimated statement of cash receipts and disbursements for the quarter from the information furnished.

Problems

21–1. A sales budget for the first five months of 1973 is given for a particular product line manufactured by John Huebner, Inc.

	Sales Budget in Units
January	10,800
February	15,600
March	12,200
April	10,400
May	9,800

The inventory of finished products at the end of each month is to be equal to 25 percent of the sales estimate for the next month. On January 1, there were 2,700 units of product on hand. No work is in process at the end of any month.

Each unit of product requires two types of materials in the following quantities:

Material A	4 units
Material B	5

Materials equal to one half of the next month's production are to be on hand at the end of each month. This requirement was met on January 1, 1973.

Required: Prepare a budget showing the quantities of each type of material to be purchased each month for the first quarter of 1973.

21–2. Hixson Machine Company plans to sell 150,000 units of a certain product line in the next six months at a unit price of $14. There are 12,000 units of the product in the inventory at January 1, 1973, and the inventory is to be increased to 16,000 units by June 30, 1973.

Two types of materials are used to make the product. Four units of Material A each costing 50 cents are required for each unit of product, and three units of Material B each costing 20 cents are required for each unit of product. At January 1, 1973, there are 80,000 units of Material A in the inventory and 60,000 units of Material B. Plans for the next six months indicate that 90,000 units of Material A are to be in the inventory at June 30 and that 75,000 units of Material B are to be in the inventory at June 30.

Each unit of product can be produced in 15 minutes of direct labor time. Direct labor is paid at the rate of $5 an hour. The variable manufacturing overhead varies at the rate of $3 per direct labor hour, and the fixed manufacturing overhead for the year is estimated at $420,000 and is to be distributed to the months on a uniform basis.

Required: (1) Prepare a production budget for the first six months of 1973.

(2) Prepare a materials purchase budget for the same six months in units and in dollars.

(3) Prepare an estimated statement of manufacturing profit on a variable costing basis for the first six months of 1973.

21–3. Production estimates for the last six months of 1973 have been prepared by Willow Products Company along with the estimates for January 1974. Two product lines are to be manufactured in the following quantities:

	Product A	Product B
July	3,700	10,400
August	3,400	10,800
September	3,000	9,500
October	3,800	8,600
November	4,700	5,800
December	5,500	5,500
January	6,000	5,000

The purchasing department buys materials in the month before they are required in production. At July 1, for example, the inventory is expected to be sufficient for July production. Materials requirements per unit of product and prices are given below:

Materials Code	Product Line	Requirements per Unit of Product	Unit Materials Price
208	A	8 lbs.	$.50 per lb.
215	B	5 lbs.	$.70 per lb.

New equipment to be installed on November 1 is expected to reduce the waste of Material 208. Only five pounds of the material should be required after November 1 for each unit of Product A.

Required: (1) Prepare a purchases budget in units of material and in dollars for each month from July to December inclusive.

(2) Compute the total savings in the cost of materials purchased that can be expected from the new equipment in 1973.

21–4. Three lines of product are manufactured by Hastings and Wilcox, Inc. It has been estimated that the following quantities will be produced in October, November, and December:

	Standard	Special	Custom
October	1,500	2,600	500
November	2,200	3,700	800
December	3,100	4,500	1,200

The direct labor time required for the production of each unit of product has been estimated as follows:

Standard .... 12 minutes
Special 15
Custom 30

Direct labor is paid at a uniform rate of $5.20 an hour.

Required: Prepare a budget of direct labor hours for each of the three months and convert it into a budget of direct labor cost.

21–5. Danvers Medical Supplies, Inc., produces two types of vaccines that are sold to hospitals and physicians.

Budget plans are being prepared for the next fiscal year. A survey of the market indicates that there will be a total demand in United States for 25,000,000 units of the vaccine type designated as D4587 by Danvers. It is estimated that Danvers should be able to obtain 30 percent of this market. Recently a foreign market has developed, and it is estimated that an additional 4,000,000 units will be sold in that market with Danvers supplying 20 percent of the units sold.

The other type of vaccine, identified by Danvers as D0650, will be sold only in the United States. There should be a total market for 10,000,000 units. The sales manager believes that Danvers will have 30 percent of this market. Sales representatives in the field, however, believe that a more realistic estimate would be 2,300,000 units.

The cost of materials, per thousand units, used in the production of these two vaccines have been estimated as follows:

	D4587	D0650
Active and inert materials	$370	$460
Container	40	50

Direct labor time and cost have also been estimated.

D4587 (per batch of 1,000 units)

2 persons, 2 hours each, labor rate per hour—$3.60
3 persons, 5 hours each, labor rate per hour—$4.80

D0650 (per batch of 1,000 units)

2 persons, 2 hours each, labor rate per hour—$3.60
3 persons, 8 hours each, labor rate per hour—$5.20

Most of the manufacturing overhead cost is fixed, but part of the maintenance cost and part of the cost of electric power vary with time. Variable manufacturing overhead has been estimated as follows:

	D4587	D0650
Maintenance materials for each batch of 1,000 units	5 hours @ $ .80	8 hours @ $ .80
Maintenance labor for each batch of 1,000 units ...	1 hour @ $2.80	1 hour @ $2.80
Electric power	5 hours @ $ .06	8 hours @ $ .06

Shipping and delivery costs amount to $8.00 per thousand units in the domestic market and $12.00 per thousand units in the foreign market.

Product D4587 is sold in the United States for $.79 per unit and in foreign markets for $.55 per unit. Product D0650 is sold for $.95 per unit.

Required: Prepare a budget showing the contribution margin per unit of product and in total for each product line in each market. Use the more conservative market estimate.

21–6. Data given below pertain to the manufacturing overhead costs budgeted by Singer Styles, Inc., for 1973.

(1) The company plans to purchase indirect materials and factory supplies during the year at a cost of $238,000. The inventory of these materials and supplies is to be increased by $16,500 by the end of the year.

(2) The accounts payable consist of obligations arising out of the purchase of direct and indirect materials used in manufacturing operations. Approximately 70 percent of both the beginning and the ending balances of accounts payable represent amounts due for direct material purchases. The accounts payable were $85,000 at January 1, 1973, and are expected to be $100,000 at December 31, 1973.

(3) Payments for indirect labor are planned at $83,000. The liability for indirect labor is expected to increase by $7,000 during the year.

(4) The payroll taxes on the indirect labor for the year are estimated at $6,300. The liability for payroll taxes will probably be $500 lower at the end of the year than at the beginning.

(5) Property taxes were $8,600 for the fiscal year of the city ending June 30, 1973. It is anticipated that taxes for the fiscal year ending June 30, 1974, will be $9,200. The company pays its property taxes for the next fiscal year of the city during June of each year.

(6) Prepaid factory insurance of $3,200 at January 1, 1973, provides insurance coverage up to and including March 31, 1974. Another policy costing $6,480 is to be taken on February 1, 1973. Payment of the total premium will be made in February, 1973, and the insurance coverage extends from February 1, 1973 to January 31, 1976.

(7) Electric service costing $580 is to be used each month and will be paid for at the rate of $580 a month.

(8) The company owed $480 at the beginning of the year for fuel oil purchased. Nothing is to be owed at the end of the year, and the inventory of oil is to be increased by $600 by the end of the year. During the year, purchases of oil are estimated at $8,780.

(9) The inventory of repairs and maintenance materials will be reduced by $1,500 during the year. Payments for repairs and maintenance are estimated at $38,600. Included in the payment estimate is a provision for reduction of the liability for repairs and maintenance in the amount of $800.

(10) Prepaid rent on the factory building at January 1, 1973, amounts to $4,800. The factory is rented for a monthly charge of $1,600. Rent of $3,200 will be owed at the end of the year.

(11) Depreciation of $31,000 is to be taken on factory equipment.

Required: (1) Prepare a manufacturing overhead cost budget for Singer Styles, Inc., for the year ended December 31, 1973.

(2) Prepare a budget of cash payments for manufacturing overhead for the year ended December 31, 1973.

21–7. Selling expense and general and administrative expense data for Rosslyn Sales Company have been estimated as follows for 1973:

(1) Net sales for the year estimated at $2,640,000 are subject to sales commissions of 15 percent. Payments to be made during the year for sales commissions are planned at $375,000.

(2) Payments of salaries to sales personnel are estimated at $93,000. The liability for sales salaries at the beginning of the year amounts to $6,800 and will amount to $7,500 at the end of the year.

(3) Advertising was prepaid at the beginning of the year in the amount of $7,000. Advertising to be charged to operations during the year will probably amount to $216,000. Prepaid advertising at the end of the year is estimated at $5,500.

(4) Travel and entertainment costs pertaining to the selling division are budgeted at $46,000 for the year. The liability for travel and entertainment costs is to be increased by $3,800 during the year.

(5) Other selling expenses with the exception of depreciation are estimated at $23,000 for the year with payments budgeted at $24,300.

(6) Office salaries of $3,100 were accrued at the beginning of the year, payments of $57,800 are to be made on office salaries, and office salaries of $3,800 will probably be accrued at the end of the year.

(7) Office supplies on hand at January 1, 1973, are recorded at $7,400 and will probably amount to $6,200 on December 31, 1973. Payments for office supplies are estimated at $43,700.

(8) Other administrative expenses, with the exception of depreciation, are estimated at $16,200. Payments for the other administrative expenses are estimated at $15,600.

(9) The building is used for both selling and administrative activities. Depreciation of $15,000 is to be charged to 1973. The sales offices occupy 60 percent of the building, and the balance of the space is occupied by administrative offices.

(10) Depreciation on sales furniture and fixtures is to be recorded at $9,500, and depreciation on the office furniture and fixtures used in general office administration is to be recorded at $7,300.

Required: (1) Prepare a budget of selling expenses and a budget of administrative expenses for 1973.

(2) Prepare a budget of payments to be made for selling expenses and a budget of payments to be made for administrative expenses during 1973.

21–8. The treasurer of O'Keefe Fabricated Products, Inc., in planning a budget of cash receipts and disbursements for the first six months of the next year, is trying to anticipate the need for additional borrowed funds or the temporary investment of excess cash.

Actual and estimated sales data are given on the next page for the two product lines that are produced and sold.

All variable costs are out-of-pocket costs. Eighty percent of this cost is to be paid during the month of sale, and the remaining twenty percent is to be paid in the following month. (Round payments to the nearest $1,000.)

Collections on sales are estimated as follows:

20% collected in month of sale, less 2% cash discount.
50% collected in the first month after the sale, less 2% cash discount.
15% collected in the second month after the sale with no cash discount.
10% collected in the third month after the sale with no cash discount.

Each month the company must pay $1,400,000 for fixed operating costs.

	Product 1			* Product 2		
	No. of Units Sold	Unit Selling Price	Unit Variable Cost	No. of Units Sold	Unit Selling Price	Unit Variable Cost
Actual data:						
Nov.	740,000	$12	$8	146,000	$24	$12
Dec.	740,000	12	8	151,000	24	12
Estimated data:						
Jan.	750,000	12	8	148,000	24	12
Feb.	820,000	12	8	142,000	24	12
Mar.	860,000	12	8	131,000	22	12
Apr.	880,000	12	8	126,000	22	12
May	910,000	12	8	104,000	22	12
June	920,000	12	8	105,000	22	12

* Product 2 is a seasonal type of product with large sales volume in the winter months. In March, the selling price is to be reduced to $22.

In addition to the regularly scheduled sources and requirements for cash, there are other receipts and other payments that must be made in certain months.

Estimated receipts from sale of equipment in January ... $1,350,000
Estimated disbursements:

Jan.—Income taxes	$1,400,000
Construction contract	1,000,000
Feb.—Construction contract	1,000,000
Mar.—Income taxes	1,400,000
Dividends	1,200,000
Construction contract	1,500,000
Apr.—New equipment	1,200,000
May—Principal due on 6% debenture notes maturing ...	3,000,000
Interest on total notes outstanding	1,500,000
June—Dividends	1,200,000
Insurance	800,000

A cash balance of $12,500,000 is to be maintained. Cash in excess of this amount is to be invested in short-term securities, and cash deficiencies are to be taken care of by short-term loans.

At January 1, the company had a cash balance of $12,500,000 and no short-term securities. For the purposes of the problem, ignore interest collected on short-term investments and interest paid on short-term loans. Also disregard the effect of the timing of cash receipts and payments within a month. If there is a deficiency of cash and if there are short-term securities available, redeem the short-term securities before obtaining short-term loans.

Required: Prepare a cash budget for the first six months of the year.

21-9. A combination of poor business judgment and misfortunes has placed Delhart Distributors, Inc., in a precarious financial position. Obsolete merchandise has been retained as inventory, and debt has increased to a point where the company is having difficulty with creditors.

A new management has been brought in to reverse the unfavorable trend. A balance sheet at the end of the year is given on the next page.

Delhart Distributors, Inc.
Balance Sheet
December 31, 1972

Assets

Current assets:

Cash	$ 874,000	
Accounts receivable	1,292,000	
Inventory	1,361,000	$3,527,000

Plant assets:

Land		$ 86,000	
Buildings	$3,850,000		
Less: Accumulated depreciation	1,120,000	2,730,000	
Fixtures and equipment	$3,680,000		
Less: Accumulated depreciation	1,540,000	2,140,000	4,956,000
Total assets			$8,483,000

Equities

Current liabilities:

Accounts payable	$ 932,000	
Notes payable	450,000	
Interest payable	342,000	
Income tax liability	83,000	
Other current liabilities	115,000	$1,922,000
Notes payable, 7%, due April 30, 1976		3,500,000

Owners' equity:

Capital stock	$2,400,000	
Retained earnings	661,000	3,061,000
Total equities		$8,483,000

A budget has been prepared for 1973, and an estimated income statement, excluding extraordinary gains and losses, has been prepared as follows:

Delhart Distributors, Inc.
Estimated Income Statement
For the Year, 1973

Net sales	$6,240,000
Cost of goods sold	3,510,000
Contribution margin	$2,730,000
Fixed operating costs	984,000
Net operating income	$1,746,000
Interest expense	280,000
Net income before income taxes	$1,466,000
Income taxes	724,000
Net income after income taxes	$ 742,000

Some former product lines have been discontinued, and different lines have been substituted in their place. If possible, the management hopes to be able to realize the following objectives during the next year.

1. Equipment costing $1,700,000 with accumulated depreciation of $640,000 is to be sold for $780,000.

2. Inventory costing $700,000 is to be sold for $340,000.

3. Accounts receivable of $284,000 are judged to be uncollectible and are to be written off during the year.

4. The losses on the equipment, inventory, and accounts receivable have not been included on the estimated income statement. The income tax saving from these losses is estimated at 50 percent of the losses. During the year, the company plans to pay a total of $155,000 for income taxes.

5. Purchases of merchandise for resale have been budgeted at $3,420,000.

6. Accounts payable consist solely of obligations arising from merchandise acquisitions. Management hopes to be able to pay $3,870,000 on accounts payable.

7. Notes payable (current liability) are to be reduced by $160,000.

8. Other current liabilities are to be reduced by $30,000.

9. Interest payable is to be reduced by $147,000.

10. The agreement under which the notes maturing in 1976 were issued permits advance redemption of the notes without penalty. During the year, management plans to reduce the liability for these notes by $2,000,000.

11. Collections on accounts receivable are estimated at $6,580,000.

12. Depreciation on the buildings has been included in the estimated fixed operating costs at $95,000, and depreciation on fixtures and equipment has been included at $230,000. All fixed operating costs with the exception of depreciation are credited to other current liabilities.

Required: (1) Prepare an estimated statement of cash receipts and disbursements for 1973.

(2) Prepare a budgeted balance sheet at December 31, 1973.

21–10. A summary balance sheet is given for Automated Tools, Inc., on June 30, 1972.

Automated Tools, Inc.
Balance Sheet
June 30, 1972

Assets

Cash	$ 215,000
Accounts receivable	110,000
Inventories	178,500
Plant and equipment, net of accumulated depreciation of $285,000	915,000
Total assets	$1,418,500

Equities

Accounts payable	$ 115,500
Income taxes payable	56,000
Other accrued liabilities	8,000
Capital stock	1,050,000
Retained earnings	189,000
Total equities	$1,418,500

The company had made remarkable progress during the relatively short time that it has been in existence. Recently, a new specialized tool (Product line 3) has been introduced; and the demand for this tool is expected to increase rapidly.

Three main lines of product are manufactured and sold and a sales budget for July, August, September, and October, 1972 is given below:

Product Lines

	1	2	3
Unit selling price	25	16	42
Unit variable costs	15	10	24

Sales Estimate (Units)

Product lines	1	2	3
July	7,500	3,000	1,500
August	8,200	3,000	2,500
September	9,300	3,000	3,000
October	9,700	3,000	3,500

The products are manufactured in the month prior to the month of sale. The materials are purchased during the month that the products are manufactured and are paid for in the next month. All other variable costs are paid for in the month that the products are manufactured. The costs of materials per unit of product are as follows:

Product 1—$10
Product 2— 6
Product 3— 15

The fixed costs of operation assignable to the third fiscal quarter of 1972 are estimated at $195,000. Included in these costs is depreciation of $63,000. Payments of the fixed costs have been estimated as follows:

July   —$62,000
August   — 34,000
September— 31,000

Balances owed on the fixed costs are shown on the balance sheet as other accrued liabilities while the liability to suppliers of materials is shown as accounts payable.

It is estimated that 5 percent of the sales revenue will not be collected as a result of customer adjustments and uncollectible accounts. One half of the balance of sales revenue will be collected during the month of sale, and the other half will be collected in the following month.

Income taxes are estimated at 50 percent of net income before income taxes. The income tax liability on the June 30 balance sheet is to be paid in September.

Management plans further expansion in the near future and hopes to build up cash reserves that may be used for this purpose. With the increase in sales in the third fiscal quarter, management hopes that the cash balance can be increased to $400,000 by September 30.

Required: (1) Will the cash balance be increased to $400,000 by September 30? Prepare a budget of cash receipts and disbursements for the third fiscal quarter of 1972 by months.

(2) Prepare an estimated income statement for each month and for the quarter in total.

(3) Prepare an estimated balance sheet at September 30, 1972.

Appendix A

THE ACCUMULATION OF FINANCIAL DATA

The American Institute of Certified Public Accountants has defined accounting as follows:

Accounting is the art of recording, classifying and summarizing in a significant manner, and in terms of money, transactions and events which are, in part at least, of a financial character and interpreting the results thereof.[1]

In this appendix and the one that follows, the recording, classifying, and summarizing aspects of accounting—that is, the accounting process—will be described and illustrated.

Duality. The properties of an entity and the rights in those properties are accounted for as they enter or leave the business, as they circulate within the business, or as they stand at any point in time. The properties are called *assets,* and the rights in the properties are called *equities.* The rights or equities of outsiders are called *liabilities,* and the rights of the owners are called the *owners' equity.*

Some typical assets of a business enterprise are listed and described below:

Cash—cash on hand or on deposit in banks.
Accounts receivable—amounts owed by customers of the business.
Inventory—materials to be used in manufacturing products, and finished or
  partly finished products and merchandise to be sold to customers.
Land—real estate owned and used by the business.
Building—building owned and used in conducting business activities.
Equipment—equipment owned and used in conducting business activities.

Some typical equities are also listed and described below:

Accounts payable—amounts owed to trade creditors of the business.
Notes payable—promissory notes owed to the bank or to other outsiders.
Mortgage payable—debt owed and secured by a mortgage on business
  property.
John Adams, capital—designation of the interest in a business of an owner
  named John Adams.

Both the assets and the equities are accounted for simultaneously. A business transaction does not affect just one item alone. There are at least

---

[1] *Accounting Terminology Bulletin No. 1,* "Review and Résumé" (New York: American Institute of Certified Public Accountants, 1953), p. 9.

two items to be considered in each transaction. It would not be possible, for example, for a business to have a transaction that resulted only in the increase of the asset cash. There must be some explanation as to why cash increased. Cash may have been received in exchange for some other asset that left the business, or the cash may have entered the business as a result of a loan made by some outsider or as a result of investment by the owner.

The dual aspect of each transaction forms the basis underlying what is called *double-entry accounting*. In double-entry accounting, it is recognized that no asset can exist without someone having a claim or a right to it. Therefore, both the specific assets and the equities are accounted for at the time that transactions are recorded.

The assets of a business can be increased by:

(1) Donations.
(2) Investments by the owners.
(3) The work performed by the business.
(4) Loans or credit furnished by outsiders.

Assets obtained through loans or credit result in an addition to liabilities. In all the other situations listed above, the owners' equity is increased. Both the increase in the assets and the increase in the rights to the assets are recorded.

The total assets of a business can be decreased by:

(1) Losses such as fire or theft.
(2) Withdrawal of assets by owners, such as dividend payments.
(3) The use of assets, such as inventory, to conduct operations.
(4) Donations to others.
(5) The settlement of the claims (liabilities) of outsiders.

The use of assets to settle the claims of outsiders results in a reduction in liabilities. In all the other situations listed, the owners' equity is decreased. The decrease in the asset and the decrease in the equity are both recorded.

One asset may be exchanged for another, or one type of equity may be converted to another form. For example, an account receivable from a customer in the amount of $2,000 may be collected. Totals assets remain unchanged in amount. There has only been a change in the composition of the assets: cash has increased by $2,000, and the account receivable from the customer has been reduced by $2,000. The holder of a note against the company may be given rights of ownership in exchange for his rights as a creditor; that is, the liability for the note payable is eliminated and in its place there is an addition to the owners' equity. The total equity in the firm is the same in amount as it was before, but the form of the equity has changed.

The evidence for a transaction. A business transaction is ordinarily supported by some paper form or document. This form or document serves as evidence or proof of the transaction and gives information about what has happened. It may be received from an outsider, or it may originate within the business unit. A bill or an invoice received from a supplier of materials supports an entry to record an increase in the materials inventory asset and the accounts payable liability. Sometimes materials are transferred within the company. A paper form is usually prepared to support the transfer and to give the essential facts of the transaction. The materials inventory of one division is increased, while the materials inventory of the other division is decreased. Forms originating within the enterprise are also sent to outsiders. Bills or invoices are mailed to customers when sales are made, and checks are sent to creditors in payment of amounts owed.

Accounting for transactions. The accounting process is illustrated by assuming that Frank Sanders begins business on August 1, 1972, by investing $80,000 in cash. After this transaction, the business has cash as an asset in the amount of $80,000, and the owners' equity, that is, the claim of Mr. Sanders on the assets is $80,000. This transaction can be shown on a balance sheet. A *balance sheet* is essentially a formal classified listing of assets and equities at one particular time. As time passes and as other transactions take place, the balance sheet becomes outmoded; but at the balance sheet date it is a statement of the financial position of the enterprise. A balance sheet for Mr. Sanders on August 1 is given below:

Frank Sanders
Balance Sheet
August 1, 1972

Assets	Equities
Cash $80,000	Frank Sanders, capital $80,000

On August 2, Mr. Sanders borrows $20,000 from his bank and signs a note promising future payment. The asset cash is increased, and the liability notes payable is increased. A balance sheet on August 2 is given below:

Frank Sanders
Balance Sheet
August 2, 1972

Assets		Equities	
Cash	$100,000	Liability:	
		Notes payable	$ 20,000
		Owners' equity:	
		Frank Sanders, capital ..	80,000
Total assets	$100,000	Total equities	$100,000

On August 3, Mr. Sanders pays $540 for the rent of a store for three months. He trades $540 of the asset cash for the asset prepaid rent. This is shown on the balance sheet on August 3 below:

Frank Sanders
Balance Sheet
August 3, 1972

Assets		Equities	
Cash	$ 99,460	Liabilities:	
Prepaid rent	540	Notes payable	$ 20,000
		Owners' equity:	
		Frank Sanders, capital ..	80,000
Total assets	$100,000	Total equities	$100,000

Equipment costing $45,000 is purchased for the store on August 7 and cash in that amount is paid for the equipment. Once again there is a trade of assets. Cash is traded for equipment, as shown by the balance sheet on August 7:

Frank Sanders
Balance Sheet
August 7, 1972

Assets		Equities	
Cash	$ 54,460	Liabilities:	
Prepaid rent	540	Notes payable	$ 20,000
Equipment	45,000	Owners' equity:	
		Frank Sanders, capital ..	80,000
Total assets	$100,000	Total equities	$100,000

On August 10, Mr. Sanders purchases merchandise costing $18,000 on credit terms. The asset merchandise inventory increases and the liability accounts payable increases by $18,000 as shown on the balance sheet on August 10:

Frank Sanders
Balance Sheet
August 10, 1972

Assets		Equities	
Cash	$ 54,460	Liabilities:	
Merchandise inventory ...	18,000	Accounts payable	$ 18,000
Prepaid rent	540	Notes payable	20,000
Equipment	45,000	Total liabilities	$ 38,000
		Owners' equity:	
		Frank Sanders, capital ..	80,000
Total assets	$118,000	Total equities	$118,000

On August 16, payments of $12,000 are made to the creditors from whom merchandise was purchased. The asset cash is reduced by $12,000 and the liability accounts payable is reduced by $12,000, as shown on the balance sheet on August 16:

Frank Sanders
Balance Sheet
August 16, 1972

Assets		Equities	
Cash	$ 42,460	Liabilities:	
Merchandise inventory ...	18,000	Accounts payable	$ 6,000
Prepaid rent	540	Notes payable	20,000
Equipment	45,000	Total liabilities	$ 26,000
		Owners' equity:	
		Frank Sanders, capital ..	80,000
Total assets	$106,000	Total equities	$106,000

Merchandise is sold to customers on August 21 on credit terms. The customers promise to pay $25,000 at some date in the future. The asset, accounts receivable, representing the customers' promises to make payment, is increased by $25,000. The owners' equity is also increased by $25,000. A service is performed by the business, and the owner earns the right to the asset received. Ordinarily, a direct increase in the owners' equity is not recorded under these circumstances. A classification telling how the asset was earned, in this case sales, is usually increased. Sales are called a *revenue* item. Revenue tells how assets are increased as a result of the services performed by the business. Revenue can be defined as the consideration received by the business for rendering goods and services to its customers.

At the same time that the sale is made, merchandise costing $15,000 is delivered to the customers. The asset account merchandise inventory, is reduced by $15,000. An asset is used in performing a service; therefore, the owners' equity decreases. This decrease, however, is usually not recorded directly as a decrease in the owners' equity. Instead, it is recorded in an account classified as an *expense*. Expense tells how assets are decreased as a result of the service performed by the business. Expense can be defined as a measure of the assets given up in the process of rendering goods and services or in the process of producing revenue.

A statement of revenues and expenses is called an *income statement*. Expenses are deducted from revenues. If revenues exceed expenses, the difference is called net income. If expenses exceed revenues, the difference is called net loss. The income statement shows the net change in net assets or owners' equity that results from operating at a profit or at a loss.

On August 21 a balance sheet is prepared along with an income statement for the first 21 days of August. The balance sheet is as follows:

Frank Sanders
Balance Sheet
August 21, 1972

Assets		Equities	
Cash	$ 42,460	Liabilities:	
Accounts receivable	25,000	Accounts payable	$ 6,000
Merchandise inventory ...	3,000	Notes payable	20,000
Prepaid rent	540	Total liabilities	$ 26,000
Equipment	45,000		
		Owners' equity:	
		Frank Sanders, capital ..	80,000
		Add: Net income	10,000
Total assets	$116,000	Total equities	$116,000

Mr. Sanders sold the customers merchandise costing $15,000 in exchange for their promises to pay him $25,000. Accounts receivable are recorded at $25,000, and the merchandise inventory is reduced by $15,000. The equality of assets and equities is maintained on the balance sheet by adding the net income of $10,000 to Mr. Sanders' capital.

A separate income statement is given below:

Frank Sanders
Income Statement
From August 1, 1972, to August 21, 1972

Sales	$25,000
Cost of merchandise sold	15,000
Net income	$10,000

The net income shown at this stage is in reality the gross profit or gross margin. *Gross margin* is the difference between sales revenue and the cost of merchandise sold. *Net income* is the final result after all other expenses have been deducted from gross margin. The other expenses of Mr. Sanders' business will be computed presently.

Mr. Sanders recognizes that certain adjustments must be made at the end of the month. He has had the use of bank credit for most of the month but has paid no interest. The interest cost is $150 even though it has not been paid. He has received the benefit from the use of the borrowed funds and must now match the interest cost against revenue in the calculation of his net income for the month. The amount owed to the bank for interest must also be recorded as an increase in the liabilities. Mr. Sanders also used the equipment in his business during the month, and he estimates that $750 of the cost should be deducted from the asset and should be recognized as expense for the month. This expense, which is the cost of the equipment assigned to the month, is called *depreciation*. Rent of $180 has expired by the end of the month. Part of the prepaid rent now becomes expense. The asset prepaid rent is reduced, and rent expense for the month is recorded on the income statement.

Two of the adjustments that are necessary have to do with writing off assets that have been used up in producing revenue. Assets were defined earlier as the properties owned by the business. Some assets may also be viewed as prepaid expenses or costs of benefits to future accounting periods. For example, the equipment will give Mr. Sanders services that cost him $45,000. As these services are used in producing revenue, part of the cost is written off as an expense of producing revenue; that is, part of the benefit is recognized as being received. Another example is the prepaid rent. When rent is paid in advance, it is recorded as an asset. The rent is an asset because it represents a cost of future benefit to Mr. Sanders. The benefit is received as revenue is produced, and at the end of the month the rent that is no longer prepaid is written off as an expense.

Financial statements for Frank Sanders on August 31, 1972 are given below and at the top of the next page.

Frank Sanders
Balance Sheet
August 31, 1972

Assets		Equities	
Cash	$ 42,460	Liabilities:	
Accounts receivable	25,000	Accounts payable	$ 6,000
Merchandise inventory	3,000	Notes payable	20,000
Prepaid rent	360	Interest payable	150
Equipment	44,250	Total liabilities	$ 26,150
		Owners' equity:	
		Frank Sanders, capital ..	88,920
Total assets	$115,070	Total equities	$115,070

The net income shown on the income statement has been added to Mr. Sanders' capital, and the balance sheet is in balance. The income statement is used to measure revenues and expenses for a given interval of time, designated as an accounting period or as a fiscal period. The period of time may be a month, quarter, year, or other significant time interval. Assets and equities on the balance sheet will be carried forward and will serve as

Frank Sanders

Income Statement

For the Month of August, 1972

Sales		$25,000
Cost of merchandise sold		15,000
Gross margin		$10,000
Expenses:		
Rent	$180	
Depreciation	750	
Interest	150	1,080
Net income		$ 8,920

a cumulative record, but the revenue and expense measurement process will start from zero again at the beginning of a new fiscal period. Revenue and expense classifications are like meters that measure the flow of liquids or gases for an interval of time. When the time interval has lapsed, the dials on the meters are set back to zero so that new measurements can be made for the next period of time.

Accounts. The method of accumulating data just illustrated will work, but it is very cumbersome. It is not designed so that information can be collected easily. Furthermore, Mr. Sanders does not need new financial statements after each transaction. He will be satisfied with financial statements prepared at the end of the fiscal period he chooses.

Data can be collected by classification in *accounts*. In essence, accounts are pages or cards divided into two halves by a vertical line and may appear somewhat as shown at the right.

There is an account for each asset, liability, owner's equity, revenue, and expense that is to be accounted for. The left side of the account is called the *debit* side of the account, and the right side of the account is called the *credit* side. Debit and credit are the terms used for left and right in accounting. A book of accounts or a file of account cards is referred to as a *ledger*.

Increases in accounts are recorded on one side of the account, and decreases are recorded on the other side. The balance of the account is the difference between the sum of the items on both sides of the account. There is a debit balance if the amounts on the left side are greater, and there is a credit balance if the amounts on the right side are greater.

The accounting equation. Special rules for recording increases and decreases are employed for each basic type of account: assets, liabilities, owners' equity, revenues, and expenses. These rules are summarized below in what is called *the accounting equation.* This equation is basic to double-entry bookkeeping.

Assets			Liabilities			Owners' Equity			Temporary Owners' Equity					
									Revenues			Expenses		
+		−		−		+		−		+		−		+		−
debit	credit		debit	credit		debit	credit		debit	credit		debit	credit

The increases and the decreases are arranged so that every transaction can be recorded and classified properly by account classification while maintaining an equality of debits and credits. If the recording process is carried out properly in the mechanical sense, the sum of the accounts with debit balances will equal the sum of the accounts with credit balances.

Note that the equation itself can be stated as follows:

$$\text{Assets} = \text{Liabilities} + \text{Owners' Equity} + (\text{Revenues} - \text{Expenses})$$

This merely says that assets are equal to the claims that individuals or other entities have in those assets. Revenues and expenses measure how assets enter or leave the business in performing services for customers, and the net result is eventually added to the owners' equity.

The rules to be followed for debiting and crediting accounts are arbitrarily defined but are logically consistent. For example, a debit means an *increase* in any asset, but a debit will also *decrease* any liability or owners' equity account. The rules of debit and credit have been set up so that the accounting equation will hold true and so that debits will always be equaled by credits. Therefore, assets will always equal equities, and the sum of the amounts shown as debits will always agree with the sum of the amounts shown as credits. Note that a revenue account is credited to increase it. This is logical inasmuch as an increase in revenue is an increase in the owners' equity, and therefore an increase in revenue is handled in the same way as a direct increase in owners' equity. Similarly, increases in expense reduce owners' equity and, like direct reductions in owners' equity, are recorded by debits.

The use of accounts. Instead of preparing a new balance sheet and a new income statement for Mr. Sanders after each transaction, it is more convenient to analyze the transactions and to enter them in ledger accounts according to the rules of increase and decrease shown by the accounting equation. The transactions given for Mr. Sanders in the previous illustration are listed and numbered as shown on the next page.

(1) Mr. Sanders invested $80,000 in cash to begin business operations.
(2) Cash of $20,000 was borrowed from the bank on a note payable.
(3) A $540 payment was made for rent of a store for three months.
(4) Equipment was purchased at a cost of $45,000 in cash.
(5) Merchandise costing $18,000 was purchased on credit terms.
(6) Cash of $12,000 was paid to the creditors from whom merchandise was purchased.
(7) Merchandise was sold to customers on account for $25,000.
(8) The cost of the merchandise delivered to customers was $15,000.
(9) Interest cost of $150 was chargeable to the business in August, and the liability to the bank for interest owed had to be recognized.
(10) Equipment was used to conduct operations in August. The estimated depreciation of the equipment used was $1,500.
(11) Rent of $180 expired during August and became expense.

The ledger accounts for Mr. Sanders with the transactions entered according to the rules of the accounting equation are given on the next page. The entries are numbered so that they can be identified with the transactions.

The reader should trace each transaction through the ledger accounts to satisfy himself that the rule of increase and decrease for each type of account has been followed and that the debit entry is equal to the credit entry in each case. Balances can then be taken from the ledger accounts and used to reconstruct a balance sheet and an income statement that will agree with the statements given on pages 638 and 639. The balance of the cash account, for example, is equal to the sum of the debit entries of $100,000, less the sum of credit entries of $57,540, or is a debit balance of $42,460.

The journal. The direct recording of transactions in the ledger accounts is inconvenient and errors are difficult to find. It takes time to leaf through the ledger pages or cards, and if there are many transactions, there is no time to enter each transaction as it takes place in the ledger cards. Furthermore, there should be some chronological record of the transactions with the entire transaction being shown in one place. Errors can then be located with less difficulty by tracing transactions from the chronological record to the ledger accounts.

A preliminary analysis of transactions is made in books of original entry called *journals*. In its simplest form the journal consists of a book with a column for dates at the left, a wide column for account titles and explanations, and two columns for entering monetary amounts. The first of the two money columns is called the debit column, and the second is called the credit column. A simple journal of this type is usually called a *general journal*. The preliminary record entered in the journal is called a *journal entry*.

Each transaction is analyzed to identify the accounts that are to be debited and credited. The transaction is then recorded as follows on pages 642 and 643.

Assets				Liabilities				Owner's Equity	
Dr.	Cr.	=		Dr.	Cr.	+		Dr.	Cr.
+	−			−	+			−	+

Cash			Accounts Payable			Frank Sanders, Capital	
(1) 80,000	(3) 540		(6) 12,000	(5) 18,000			(1) 80,000
(2) 20,000	(4) 45,000						
	(6) 12,000						

Accounts Receivable			Notes Payable	
(7) 25,000				(2) 20,000

Plus
Revenue

Dr.	Cr.
−	+

Merchandise Inventory			Interest Payable	
(5) 18,000	(8) 15,000			(9) 150

Sales	
	(7) 25,000

Prepaid Rent	
(3) 540	(11) 180

Minus
Expenses

Dr.	Cr.
+	−

Equipment	
(4) 45,000	(10) 1,500

Cost of Goods Sold	
(8) 15,000	

Rent Expense	
(11) 180	

Depreciation Expense	
(10) 1,500	

Interest Expense	
(9) 150	

(1) The date is entered in the date column.

(2) The name of the account to be debited is entered in the account titles and explanation column, and the dollar amount is entered in the debit money column.

(3) The name of the account to be credited is entered in the account titles and explanation column on the next line in an indented position, and the dollar amount is entered in the credit money column.

(4) A brief explanation of the transaction is written beneath the account titles.

The general journal entry on August 1 for Mr. Sanders' first transaction would appear as shown below:

General Journal   Page 1

Date		Accounts and Explanations	F.	Debit	Credit
1972 August	1	Cash Frank Sanders, Capital Investment of $80,000 by Frank Sanders		80,000	80,000

The information shown in the journal is copied into the ledger accounts. This copying process is called *posting*. The narrow column headed "F" in the journal is a cross-reference column or, as the "F" indicates, folio column. The page numbers or folios of the ledger accounts to which the entries are posted are entered here so that a transaction can be easily traced to the ledger accounts if that should become necessary at a later date. Space is also provided in the ledger accounts for page numbers of the journal where the transactions were first entered. Thus a transaction can easily be traced from the journal to the ledger or from the ledger back to the journal.

Posting is a process of organizing data according to account classifications from the chronological record contained in the journal. After the data have been classified in the accounts and summarized, they can be used in the preparation of financial statements and reports.

While the two-column journal does provide a chronological record of transactions with both parts of the transaction in one place, it is not very helpful as a labor-saving device. In fact, there is more accounting work because the transaction must be entered first in the journal and then it must be posted to the ledger accounts. Mr. Sanders would have to make journal entries for each of his transactions, then he would have to post the information from the journal to the ledger accounts before his ledger would contain the debits and the credits shown on page 642.

Columnar journals. Often business transactions of a certain type are repeated time and again. There will likely be many purchases of materials, sales to customers, cash receipts, and cash disbursements. To record each transaction separately in a two-column journal as an increase or as a decrease to a given account would be unduly burdensome. Transactions of a similar type should be classified together, summarized for a period such as a month, and posted as one aggregate transaction for the month.

There are several types of journals, each type being designed to serve a special purpose. For example, all sales transactions could be entered in a sales journal. Similarly, purchases, cash receipts, and cash disbursements would be entered respectively in a purchases journal, a cash receipts journal, and a cash disbursements journal. Other specialized journals can be used if transactions occur frequently enough to warrant their use. A manufacturing company, for example, may use a special journal to record materials withdrawn and transferred to production. Miscellaneous transactions that do not occur often enough to merit the use of a special journal are entered in the two-column general journal referred to earlier.

The special journals have columns so that similar transactions can be conveniently added together and posted as one transaction. Completed journals for Ray Fulton for the month of April are given on pages 645 to 648. The journal columns have already been totaled, and postings have been made to the ledger accounts for the month.

The design of the sales journal indicates that sales are made on both cash and credit terms, inasmuch as the sales journal has a column for cash debits, a column for accounts receivable debits, and a column for sales credits. At the end of the month the sum of the two debit columns should be equal to the sum of the credit column. It is just as though one big sale for the month had been entered in a general journal, except that the detail for all transactions appears in the special journal.

Cash	980	
Accounts Receivable	3,920	
Sales		4,900
Sales for the month of April.		

Obviously, no general journal entry such as the one given above is made. It is not necessary to repeat what is already journalized through the columnar journal. The columnar journal is a means for summarizing similar transactions and serves as a posting medium itself.

It should not be implied from the example given that all sales journals will be designed with three columns. Perhaps only the credit sales will be recorded in a one-column sales journal, and the column total will be posted at the end of the month as a debit to Accounts Receivable and as a credit to Sales. The cash sales would then be entered in the cash receipts journal with a special column being provided for offsetting credits to sales. If all cash receipts are recorded in the cash receipts journal, daily receipts can be compared with the amounts recorded and with bank deposits quite easily without reference to other journals. On the other hand, the sales will not all appear in one journal. There are various accumulation techniques that may be employed, and the choice of any particular method is dependent upon circumstances and individual preferences.

The cash receipts journal is designed so that cash debits can be entered in a special column with credits being recorded in columns for accounts receivable, interest income, and rent income. Presumably cash is not only collected frequently on accounts with customers but is also collected frequently as a result of interest and rent earned. The two general ledger columns provide flexibility so that cash receipts from other sources can be entered in this journal along with the other accounts that are affected.

A one-column purchases journal is used. The column total is posted at the end of the month as a debit to merchandise inventory and as a credit to accounts payable.

The cash disbursements journal has a column for cash credits and columns for offsetting debits to accounts payable, advertising expense, supplies used, and office expense. The design of the journal indicates that Ray Fulton pays cash when he acquires advertising service, supplies, and items chargeable to office expense. These services and materials must be used up at about the time they are acquired, since the cost is entered directly in expense accounts

Sales Journal Page 4

Date		Customers	Cash Dr.	V	Accounts Receivable Dr.	Sales Cr.
1972						
Apr.	3	Hall Bearings, Inc.		V	830	830
	4	Ott Parts Co.		V	960	960
	7	Cash	400			400
	10	Layser Machine, Inc.		V	620	620
	17	Cash	580			580
	24	Cole and Engle		V	480	480
	27	Ott Parts Co.		V	760	760
	27	Layser Machine, Inc.		V	270	270
			980		3,920	4,900
			(1)		(3)	(11)

Cash Receipts Journal

Date	Explanations	Cash Dr.		Accounts Receivable Cr.	Interest Income Cr.	Rent Income Cr.	General Ledger			
							Accounts	F.	Dr.	Cr.
1972 Apr. 8	Ott Parts Co.	960	✓	960						
13	Loan from bank	1,940					Interest Expense	20	60	
							Notes Payable	9		2,000
15	Int. on U.S. Treas. Bonds	30			30					
17	Hall Bearings, Inc.	1,430	✓	1,430						
18	Rent collections	200				200				
20	Int. on savings	150			150					
21	Sale of supplies	80					Supplies Expense	17		80
24	Layser Machine, Inc.	620	✓	620						
28	Rent collections	300				300				
		5,710		3,010	180	500			60	2,080
		(1)		(3)	(13)	(14)			(X)	(X)

Cash Disbursements Journal

Date	Explanations	Cash Cr.	Accounts Payable Dr.	Advertising Expense Dr.	Supplies Expense Dr.	Office Expense Dr.	General Ledger Accounts	F.	Dr.	Cr.
1972 Apr.										
3	Globe-Times	120		120						
6	Stemm, Inc.	250			250					
7	Bass & Co.	680 ✓	680							
13	Office Supply, Inc.	60				60				
14	Morning Call	110		110						
17	Krieger Bros.	770 ✓	770							
20	Office Supply, Inc.	30				30				
21	Harding Co.	170			170					
21	Wilson Bank	80					Interest Expense	20	80	
24	Auto Rental, Inc.	130					Rent Exp.	19	130	
		2,400	1,450	230	420	90			210	
		(1)	(8)	(16)	(17)	(18)			(X)	

rather than being entered first as assets and later being transferred to expenses. Two general ledger columns are also furnished in the cash disbursements journal so that cash disbursements other than those affecting the accounts with special columns can be entered.

A two-column general journal is used for transactions that do not fit into any of the other journals. In the first entry, a customer has returned merchandise that was unsatisfactory. The entry is made in the general journal. The sales return account, an offset to the revenue account, is debited because revenue has been reduced. The asset accounts receivable has been decreased and is credited. In the second entry, the cost of goods sold for the month has been computed and is recorded in the general journal.

Purchases Journal Page 6

Date			Creditor	V	Mdse. Inv. Dr. Accts. Pay. Cr.
1972 Apr.	3	Bass & Co.		V	680
	3	Mennig Machine		V	820
	14	Krieger Bros.		V	770
	17	Ronda Parts, Inc.		V	510
					2,780
					(4) (8)

General Journal Page 7

Date		Account Titles and Explanations	F.	Debit	Credit
1972 Apr.	27	Sales Returns	12	130	
		Accounts Receivable—Cole and Engle	3/ V		130
		Return of merchandise by customer.			
	28	Cost of Goods Sold	15	2,640	
		Merchandise Inventory	4		2,640
		Cost of goods sold in April.			

At the end of the month the journal columns are totaled. The totals of the debit columns in each journal are added together and are compared with the sum of the totals of the credit columns in that journal to provide a check on the equality of the debits and the credits before any amounts are posted to the ledger accounts. For example, the cash receipts journal shows total debits of $5,770, the sum of the cash debit column total of $5,710 and the general ledger debit column total of $60. The totals of the four credit columns also add to $5,770.

The totals of the columns headed with account titles are posted as indicated to the general ledger accounts named, and the appropriate ledger page numbers are shown in parentheses beneath the column totals. The general ledger column totals in the special journals have no significance aside from their use in checking the equality of total journal debits and credits. The total is meaningless because it is a mixture of amounts affecting various accounts. The column totals are not posted. An "X" is placed in parentheses beneath a general ledger column total. Each account named must be posted separately from the general ledger columns with the ledger posting reference being given in the narrow column labeled "F." Separate postings are also made from the general journal. Once again the column totals do not pertain to any one account. The check mark (∨) shown beside the accounts receivable entries will be explained later.

As can be seen from the above discussion, special journals are labor-saving devices. The form and the design of a special journal, as well as the number of special journals used, will vary from company to company. The procedures discussed above should be viewed as a general indicator of how large amounts of quantitative data can be easily processed. The actual procedure used must be tailored to the specific needs of the company.

Ledgers. In addition to having special journals, a company may have special ledgers. The *general ledger* is a summary record for each account classification. Underlying details with respect to any given account may be kept in a *subsidiary ledger*. A summary account in the general ledger that is supported by a subsidiary ledger is referred to as a *control account*. By using subsidiary ledgers, detail can be eliminated from the general ledger. Quite often subsidiary ledgers are used in connection with accounts receivable from customers, the inventory of materials to be used in production, equipment, and accounts payable to creditors. This would be expected inasmuch as these summary accounts are comprised of many individual items. There are many customers to be accounted for under the general classification of accounts receivable, the inventory consists of many different types of materials, equipment is the aggregate of many individual pieces of equipment, and there are several creditors. The details with respect to an account are posted individually to the subsidiary ledger accounts, and the journal column is posted in total to the general ledger control account. Obviously, the sum of the balances in the subsidiary ledger should be in agreement with the balance of the general ledger control account. The data appearing in the subsidiary ledger in detail appears in summary in the control account. As in the case of special journals, the subsidiary ledger is a data processing convenience, and the number of different subsidiary records that are used as well as their design will depend upon the needs of the particular company.

The general ledger, the subsidiary accounts receivable ledger, and the subsidiary accounts payable ledger of Ray Fulton with the posting completed for the month of April are given on pages 650 to 652. In the folio columns in the ledger, references are made by letter abbreviation to the journal from which the posting was made and to the page number of that journal.

A check mark is made opposite each individual account receivable and account payable shown in the accounts receivable columns and the accounts payable columns of the journals to indicate that the item has been posted to the subsidiary ledger account. As the general journal provides no special column for accounts receivable, the credit to accounts receivable will have to be posted individually to the accounts receivable control account and to the account of the customer in the subsidiary ledger.

General Ledger

	Cash		1
1972		1972	
Apr. 1	Bal. 2,100	Apr. 30 CD12 2,400	
30	CR7 5,710		
30	S4 980		

	Marketable Securities	2
1972		
Apr. 1	Bal. 7,000	

	Accounts Receivable		3
1972		1972	
Apr. 1	Bal. 1,600	Apr. 27 J7 130	
30	S4 3,920	30 CR7 3,010	

	Merchandise Inventory		4
1972		1972	
Apr. 1	Bal. 2,300	Apr. 28 J7 2,640	
30	P6 2,780		

	Land	5
1972		
Apr. 1	Bal. 12,000	

	Building	6
1972		
Apr. 1	Bal. 84,000	

	Equipment	7
1972		
Apr. 1	Bal. 16,000	

	Accounts Payable		8
1972		1972	
Apr. 30	CD12 1,450	Apr. 1 Bal. 1,000	
		30 P6 2,780	

	Notes Payable		9
		1972	
		Apr. 1 Bal. 3,000	
		13 CR7 2,000	

	Ray Fulton, Capital		10
		1972	
		Apr. 1 Bal. 121,060	

Sales			11
		1972	
		Apr. 30	S4 4,900

Advertising Expense		16
1972		
Apr. 30 CD12	230	

Sales Returns		12
1972		
Apr. 27	J7	130

Supplies Expense			17
1972		1972	
Apr. 30 CD12	420	Apr. 30	CR7 80

Interest Income			13
		1972	
		Apr. 30	CR7 180

Office Expense		18
1972		
Apr. 30 CD12	90	

Rent Income			14
		1972	
		Apr. 30	CR7 500

Rent Expense		19
1972		
Apr. 24 CD12	130	

Cost of Goods Sold		15
1972		
Apr. 28	J7 2,640	

Interest Expense		20
1972		
Apr. 13	CR7	60
21	CD12	80

Accounts Receivable Ledger

Cole and Engle			
1972		1972	
Apr. 1	Bal. 1,000	Apr. 27	J7 130.
24	S4 480		

Layser Machine, Inc.			
1972		1972	
Apr. 10	S4 620	Apr. 24	CR7 620
27	S4 270		

Hall Bearings, Inc.			
1972		1972	
Apr. 1	Bal. 600	Apr. 17	CR7 1,430
3	S4 830		

Ott Parts Co.			
1972		1972	
Apr. 4	S4 960	Apr. 7	CR7 960
27	S4 760		

Accounts Payable Ledger

Bass & Co.							Mennig Machine			
1972				1972				1972		
Apr.	7	CD12	680	Apr.	3	P6	680	Apr.	3	P6	820

Krieger Bros.							Ronda Parts, Inc.			
1972				1972				1972		
Apr.	17	CD12	770	Apr.	14	P6	770	Apr.	1	Bal.	1,000
									17	P6	510

The trial balance. After the posting has been completed, the ledger account balances can be computed. A list of the balances of the general ledger accounts is called a *trial balance*. If the accounting process has been carried out properly in a mechanical sense, the sum of the debit balances should be equal to the sum of the credit balances. A trial balance is proof that the ledger is in balance and that steps can be taken toward the preparation of the financial statements. An equality of debits and credits on the trial balance should not be interpreted to mean that the account balances are correct. It is quite possible that an incorrect amount may be included both as a debit and as a credit or that some transaction may have been entered in the wrong account or left out entirely. The equality of debits and credits is verified, indicating that the debit and credit principle has been followed correctly, but there is no assurance that all transactions have been recorded properly.

A trial balance for Ray Fulton at April 2 is given at the top of the next page.

Schedules. Balances from the subsidiary ledgers should be listed and totaled, and the sum of the balances should agree with the control account balance. Agreement indicates that all transactions entered in the individual subsidiary accounts have also been accounted for in total. Error is still possible. A transaction may be entered in the wrong subsidiary account, and this would not be revealed by a comparison of the total of the subsidiary balances with the control balance. It is also possible that a batch of transactions may not have been entered in either the subsidiary ledger or the control account. A trial balance or a schedule of subsidiary ledger balances shows that the mechanics of accounting for debits and credits have been followed properly, and it provides a starting point for the verification of account balances and the subsequent preparation of financial statements.

Ray Fulton has subsidiary ledgers for accounts receivable and accounts payable. The sum of the individual account balances in the accounts receivable ledger is $2,380, and this is equal to the accounts receivable balance in the general ledger control account. This is shown on the following page.

Ray Fulton
Trial Balance
April 30, 1972

	Dr.	Cr.
Cash	$ 6,390	
Marketable Securities	7,000	
Accounts Receivable	2,380	
Merchandise Inventory	2,440	
Land	12,000	
Building	84,000	
Equipment	16,000	
Accounts Payable		$ 2,330
Notes Payable		5,000
Ray Fulton, Capital		121,000
Sales		4,900
Sales Returns	130	
Interest Income		180
Rent Income		500
Cost of Goods Sold	2,640	
Advertising Expense	230	
Supplies Expense	340	
Office Expense	90	
Rent Expense	130	
Interest Expense	140	
	$133,910	$133,910

Ray Fulton
Schedule of Accounts Receivable
April 30, 1972

Cole and Engle	$1,350
Layser Machine, Inc.	270
Ott Parts Co.	760
Total accounts receivable	$2,380

The sum of the individual account balances in the accounts payable ledger is $2,330, which is equal to the accounts payable balance in the general ledger control account.

Ray Fulton
Schedule of Accounts Payable
April 30, 1972

Mennig Machine	$ 820
Ronda Parts, Inc.	1,510
Total accounts payable	$2,330

Mechanical accumulators. If business volume is fairly substantial, bookkeeping or accounting machines may be used to eliminate the drudgery and the cost of maintaining manual records. Some machines are essentially a series of adding machine accumulators that make it possible to add several different classifications at the same time. The machine may then take the place of columnar journals. A machine, for example, may have 12 adding machine accumulators. It would then be possible to add amounts pertaining to 12 different classifications at the same time. A machine with 12 accumulators at any given time could perform the same function as a 12-column journal.

At the end of each day, the various totals are drawn from the machine and are posted directly to ledger cards that are inserted in the machine at that time. The machine then serves not only as a journal but also as a posting medium. The risk of error in posting is reduced since the machine prints the totals directly on the ledger cards.

Some machines print a proof sheet of the day's transactions. This proof sheet is a journal of the day's business and may be filed in a binder for future reference.

The work of classifying and summarizing financial data can be performed even more rapidly by using equipment that reads patterns of holes in cards or tapes. The holes are punched in a pattern according to a code established for letters and numbers. Each letter or number is translated into a hole or holes positioned properly on the cards or tapes. The reading process is performed by a machine that makes electrical contacts through the holes. Data drawn from the hole-punched forms are classified according to the account code numbers indicated and are accumulated. The classified and accumulated data can then be punched into summary cards, which serve as ledger accounts. A whole series of operations can be carried out by the equipment without human interference. A program of instructions can be given to a machine on a punched tape, and the machine will operate according to the coded instructions.

Direct transactional recording. It is possible to eliminate the need for journals or preliminary accumulations altogether. Electronic data processing equipment can take original transactional data and transfer them to summary records that correspond to ledger accounts. Transactional data are recorded on punched cards, punched tapes, or magnetized tapes before being entered in the data processing equipment. With no preliminary classification or accumulation, the data is stored in memory sections of magnetized discs or cylinders. The locations on the discs or cylinders are the ledger accounts.

The electronic data processor operates very rapidly with a language of its own. It does not accumulate numbers according to the conventional decimal system, but instead it operates according to the binary numbering system. In the binary system there is only a 0 and a 1. A spot on the disc or cylinder is either magnetized (1), or is not (0). Therefore, by an arrangement of tubes or transistors, any number or letter can be recorded according to whether or not the tube or transistor carries a charge. When the data are needed, they can be translated into the familiar decimal form and withdrawn from the machine.

The financial transactions of a business are sorted out according to type, recorded, classified, and summarized. This process may be carried out manually through the use of journals and ledgers, or it may be carried out by equipment that can accumulate data that have been entered in coded form in hole-punched or magnetized media. The data drawn from ledger accounts or from the summary of hole-punched cards or from the storage areas of electronic equipment are used in the preparation of the financial statements and reports.

The financial statements and reports, however, are not prepared directly from the information shown in ledger accounts after all transactions for a fiscal period have been accumulated. Recognition is first given to adjustments that must be made to record information not entered in the normal course of accounting operation or to revise and bring up-to-date information already recorded. The adjustment process is discussed in Appendix B.

Forms of business ownership. There are various legal forms of business ownership. The three most important forms are:

(1) The proprietorship.
(2) The partnership.
(3) The corporation.

A business that is owned by one person only is a proprietorship. In the illustration previously presented, Frank Sanders owned his own business and operated as a sole proprietor. His equity as the owner of the business was shown on the balance sheet in one amount and was identified by his name. The owner's interest in the assets of a sole proprietorship is labeled, for example, as "Frank Sanders, Capital" or as "Frank Sanders, Proprietorship."

A business is sometimes owned jointly by two or more individuals or entities who share ownership. This form of ownership is a partnership. Each partner's interest is identified by his name and is designated as his capital.

A business may also be incorporated, that is, the business is given an existence apart from its owners through a charter issued by a state. The corporation is like a person at law, being able to transact business in its own right and having the legal rights and responsibilities of individuals in the commercial field.

The owners' equity in a corporation is not identified according to the persons who have ownership rights, that is, the stockholders. Instead, the owners' equity is shown under two broad general classifications:

(1) The investment of the owners, which under ordinary circumstances will remain as a permanent investment.

(2) The accumulated retained earnings of the business. In general, the accumulated retained earnings will be the total of all profits reduced by losses and by cash dividend payments.

In the formation of a corporation, the organizers agree that a certain stated amount shall be invested for each share issued. This original investment constitutes a permanent investment, assuming, of course, that there is no reorganization or other drastic change in the corporate structure. The amount of this stipulated investment is designated as *capital stock* if only one class of stock is issued. If more than one class of stock is issued, the stated amount for each class is shown separately and is appropriately designated as *preferred stock* or as *common stock* as the case may be.

Often a corporation will receive more than the legal minimum investment per share. For example, it may be agreed that for each share issued there will be $1 invested and credited to capital stock. The shares are issued, however, for $5 each. The amount of the investment in excess of the stated value, in this case $4 per share, is credited to paid-in capital in excess of the stated value. Ordinarily, the amount credited to paid-in capital in excess of the stated value cannot be withdrawn and is looked upon as a part of the permanent investment.

The accumulated net earnings of the corporation as reduced by net losses, distributions to the owners, or transfers to paid-in capital are called *retained earnings*. Barring restrictions that may be imposed by law or by contractual agreement, the retained earnings establish the amounts that may be withdrawn by the owners as cash dividends. Sometimes retained earnings become a permanent part of the capital structure. Shares of stock may be issued against retained earnings, with a transfer of an agreed amount to capital stock and paid-in capital in excess of the stated value. Transfers of this sort are made in connection with stock dividends. Instead of receiving cash or other property as a dividend, the stockholders may be given additional shares of stock.

Formation of the corporation. A business may be started as a corporation, or an existing proprietorship or partnership may be converted into a corporation. The conversion of a proprietorship into a corporate form of ownership is illustrated by assuming that Joe Leeman had been operating a small plumbing supply business as a proprietorship. On February 1, 1972, the business is incorporated.

The corporation is authorized to issue 15,000 shares of capital stock, each having a stated legal value of $5; that is, for each share issued, at least $5 in value must be received. The capital stock account will be credited for $5 for each share issued, and any additional amount received upon the issuance of shares will be credited to the paid-in capital in excess of stated value account.

Mr. Leeman contributes the following assets to the new corporation, and the corporation assumes his business liabilities:

Assets:

Cash	$ 7,300	
Accounts receivable	8,250	
Merchandise inventory	9,650	
Equipment	11,500	
Total assets		$36,700

Liabilities:

Accounts payable	$ 4,300	
Notes payable	8,000	
Total liabilities		12,300
Net assets		$24,400

The assets and the liabilities are accepted at the valuations shown. Each share of capital stock has a stated legal value of $5, but it has been agreed that the shares will be issued at an assigned value of $20 per share. In short, capital stock will be credited for $5 for each share issued, and paid-in capital in excess of stated value will be credited for $15. According to this arrangement, Mr. Leeman receives one share for each $20 he invests, or for an investment of $24,400 he receives 1,220 shares.

Cash in the amount of $16,000 is invested by other individuals, who receive 800 shares as evidence of their ownership. Their shares also have been assigned a value of $20 each. As long as the legal stated value is received, it does not matter what particular value is assigned to each share.

The opening entry on the books of the corporation, to be known as The Leeman Supply Company, Inc., would appear in the general journal as shown on page 658.

Business transactions for the new corporation will be recorded in journals and posted to ledger accounts or will be recorded by data processing equipment in the same way as they are recorded for a proprietorship or a partnership.

```
Cash  .......................................  23,300
Accounts Receivable  .........................   8,250
Merchandise Inventory  .......................   9,650
Equipment  ..................................  11,500
    Accounts Payable  .........................            4,300
    Notes Payable  ............................            8,000
    Capital Stock  ............................           10,100
    Paid-in Capital in Excess of Stated Value  ......     30,300
        Investment by Mr. Leeman and others in The
        Leeman Supply Company, Inc.
```

Appendix B

THE ADJUSTING AND CLOSING PROCEDURE

Types of adjustments. Business transactions are accumulated over an interval of time designated as an accounting period or a fiscal period. The period may be a month, a quarter of a year, a year, or any other designated time interval. Ordinarily, financial measurements are made over a period of a year, with the year being divided into months or quarters. During the course of a fiscal period, a company records purchases, sales, cash receipts, cash disbursements, returns of materials to suppliers, returns of merchandise from customers, payrolls, transfers of materials and labor into production, and other events that arise in the normal course of its operation.

But other important information may not be recorded at all, or the information may be recorded but with the passage of time may require adjustment. Before the financial statements are prepared, adjustments should be made so that the statements will be as accurate as possible. The adjustment process is important in the measurement of net income for the period and in the determination of the asset and equity balances at the end of the period. The adjustment process should be looked upon as a part of the income determination process. The mechanical part of the adjustment process should be understood; but in addition the reader should ask himself how the accounting flows, balances, and statements are made more useful by each particular adjustment.

Many of the adjustments to be made can be classified under the following three general headings:

(1) The accrual adjustment.
(2) The prepayment adjustment.
(3) The valuation adjustment.

Accrual adjustments. Often wages, rent, interest, and the various costs of business operations are recorded only at the time they are paid. However, the costs grow or accrue with the passage of time. For example, wages are earned by the employees each working day even though they may be paid only at designated times. If a fiscal period ends between pay periods, an adjustment should be made to record the additional wages expense since the last date of payment and record. The corresponding obligation to make payment to the employees, that is, the liability, should also be recorded. Assume that wages earned and paid during the year amounted to $18,000. The wages expense account would show the following balance:

Wages Expense

18,000

The $18,000 would also appear as a credit to cash if the payroll were paid in cash. But the employees earned another $1,200 since the last entry was made to wages expense, that is, since the last payroll was paid. An adjusting journal entry is made at the end of the year as follows:

Wages Expense 1,200
    Wages Payable   1,200
       To record wages earned but unpaid at the end of the year.

The ledger accounts as adjusted would then appear as shown below:

Wages Expense		Wages Payable	
18,000			1,200
1,200			

The wages payable of $1,200 would appear as a liability on the balance sheet, and the wages expense of $19,200 would be shown on the income statement. If this entry were not made, the net income for the period would be overstated by $1,200 and the liabilities would be understated by $1,200.

Looking at the accrual problem in another way, assets and revenues also grow or accrue. Revenues from rents or interest on investments, for example, are often recorded only when collected. But rent and interest are being earned with the passage of each day. If revenue has been earned from the last collection date to the end of the fiscal period, it should be recorded by adjustment. An asset account would be debited for the amount receivable, and a revenue account would be credited for the additional amount earned. To illustrate, assume that rent for ten months of the year at $250 per month has been collected and recorded as rent income. Rent for the last two months of the year is still owed by the tenants. Before adjustment, the balance of the rent income account would appear as shown on the next page.

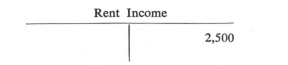

Rent Income

	2,500

The following adjusting entry is made at the end of the year to record the amount receivable from the tenants and the additional rent earned but not collected:

```
Rent Receivable ..................................  500
    Rent Income ...................................         500
    Adjustment to record rent earned since last collection
    date.
```

Rent Receivable			Rent Income	
500				2,500
				500

The rent receivable of $500 would appear as an asset on the balance sheet, and rent income would be shown at $3,000 on the income statement. If this adjusting entry were not made, the assets at the end of the year would be understated by $500 and the net income for the period would also be understated by $500.

The need for *accrual adjustments* arises when all of the data pertaining to the fiscal period have not been recorded. Expenses that increase with the passage of time must be recorded, whether paid for or not, and the liability for unpaid expenses must also be recognized. Similarly, revenues that increase with the passage of time must be recorded, whether collected or not, and the asset representing the amount due must be recognized.

In the following accounting period, when the $500 rent receivable is collected in cash, the entry would be as follows:

```
Cash ..........................................  500
    Rent Receivable ...............................         500
    Collection of rent.
```

The collection is viewed as a conversion of assets; that is, the asset cash is increased and the asset rent receivable is decreased. The income was recognized in the prior accounting period even though the cash was not actually received until the subsequent period. Income and revenue are viewed as being the result of an earning process. The cash collection may or may not take place at the same time that the income or the revenue is actually recognized (recorded).

Prepayment adjustments. Business events should be properly analyzed and recorded as they occur. For example, an asset may be recorded at the time it is acquired for cash; or a liability may be recorded when an advance collection is received from a customer. By the end of the fiscal year, however, the situation may have changed. An adjustment may be required to show the part of the asset that was used in profit-making activity. The expense will be recorded, and the asset previously entered will be reduced. Likewise, deliveries of products may have been made against advance collections received from customers. The liability initially entered in the records will be reduced, and the portion earned will be recorded as revenue. Adjustments made to separate expenses from assets and revenues from liabilities are referred to as *prepayment adjustments*.

Assume that a company pays $450 at the beginning of a fiscal year for insurance protection for three years. The insurance protection would be recorded as an asset in the prepaid insurance account, as follows:

Prepaid Insurance
_____

450 |

At the end of the fiscal year, however, one third of this protection has been used and should be recognized as expense. An adjusting entry is then made as follows:

Insurance Expense 150
    Prepaid Insurance 150
        Adjustment to record use of insurance during the year.

The accounts would then show the information brought up-to-date, as follows:

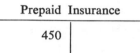

Prepaid Insurance   Insurance Expense

450 | 150   150 |

Prepaid insurance remaining as an asset to be shown on the balance sheet is $300, and the insurance expense to be shown on the income statement for the year is $150. If the adjusting entry were not made, the assets at the end of the year would be overstated by $150 and the net income for the period would be overstated by the same amount.

Viewing this problem from the standpoint of the insurance company, the advance collection of premiums from the policyholders would add to liabilities. This liability will be discharged by rendering a service to the policyholder. When the collection is made, an entry is made to credit the unearned insurance premiums account.

Unearned Insurance Premiums
_____
                    | 450
                    |

The insurance company is obligated to give insurance protection to its policyholder for three years upon collection of the $450 premium at the beginning of the policy period.

Assume that the policy year coincides with the insurance company's fiscal year. At the end of the year, the insurance company has provided protection for one year and has earned one third of the total premium. The adjusting entry appears below:

Unearned Insurance Premiums 150
    Insurance Premiums Earned 150
        Adjustment to recognize insurance premium earned for
        the year.

Unearned Insurance Premiums   Insurance Premiums Earned
_____   _____
150 | 450 | 150
   | |

The liability has been reduced to $300, the amount of the insurance service still to be given to the policyholder. The earned revenue of $150 will appear on the income statement for the year.

It should be noted that the adjustments make it possible to report financial data more accurately. In the example just given, the adjustment results in the assignment of revenue of $150 to the period benefited and restates the liability to the policyholders at $300, the amount of service owed to them at the end of the period.

The depreciation adjustment. To conduct business operations, a company normally requires the use of buildings, fixtures, machinery, and equipment. Assets of this type have a relatively long useful life and are classified on the balance sheet under the general heading of *plant assets* or *fixed assets*. The expense resulting from the use of these assets is designated as *depreciation expense*.

Plant assets are somewhat like prepaid expenses. The cost of a plant asset, like the cost of an insurance policy, for example, is allocated over its useful life. Ordinarily the plant asset has a longer life than the prepaid expense, but the adjustment procedure is somewhat similar. Unlike the prepayment, however, the plant asset may not be paid for at the time it is acquired. Debt may have been incurred to finance the cost of the asset. But the way in which it was financed will have no effect upon the allocation of its cost to operations. The cost is allocated or assigned to time periods according to the flow of benefits received from the use of the asset over its useful life.

An asset such as a building or a piece of equipment will have a limited useful life; it will not yield benefits indefinitely. It will eventually wear out, it will become outmoded with the passage of time and changes in technology, and it may become inadequate as the company grows and requires the use of larger assets or assets with greater productive capacity. Over the total period of time the asset is in use, its cost is allocated to the various fiscal periods as depreciation expense.

Generally, the cost of a plant asset is substantial, and the asset may be in service for a number of years. Often detailed underlying records are maintained to show the original cost of the asset, the name of the company from whom the asset was purchased, the history of maintenance and repair service, the depreciation that has been recorded each year, and other pertinent details with respect to the asset and its operation. Ordinarily the plant asset account itself is not credited directly when depreciation adjustments are made. Instead, a special asset reduction account called "Accumulated Depreciation" or "Allowance for Depreciation" is credited. The original cost is then preserved in the plant asset account, and the reductions because of depreciation are shown in a separate offsetting account. The remaining cost to be charged against future operations, or the *net book value* of the asset as it is called, is equal to the balance shown in the plant asset account minus the balance shown in the accumulated depreciation account. The accumulated depreciation account has a credit balance and is frequently referred to as a *contra-asset account*.

Assume, for example, that a truck having an estimated useful life of five years was acquired at the beginning of the year at a cost of $8,000. Assume also that the truck will have an estimated residual salvage value of $2,000 at the end of five years. The difference between the initial cost and the estimated residual salvage value is to be allocated equally over the five years the truck is to be in service. When an equal amount of cost is assigned to each year, the company is said to be recording depreciation according to the *straight-line method*. The truck when purchased would appear in the accounts as follows:

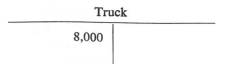

Truck
| 8,000 | |

At the end of the first year, a depreciation adjustment is made to record $1,200 (one fifth of $6,000) as depreciation expense. The plant asset is indirectly reduced by a credit to accumulated depreciation.

```
Depreciation Expense .........................   1,200
    Accumulated Depreciation ...................         1,200
        Adjustment to record truck depreciation for the
        year.
```

After this adjusting entry is posted, the ledger accounts appear as follows:

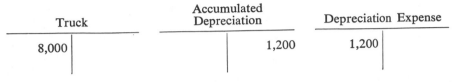

Truck	Accumulated Depreciation	Depreciation Expense
8,000	1,200	1,200

The truck will be shown on the balance sheet at $8,000 with accumulated depreciation of $1,200 deducted, or at a net book value of $6,800. Depreciation expense of $1,200 will appear on the income statement.

At the end of the second year, another adjusting entry would be made to record depreciation for that year:

```
Depreciation Expense .........................   1,200
    Accumulated Depreciation ...................         1,200
        Adjustment to record truck depreciation for the
        year.
```

When this entry is posted at the end of the second year, the ledger accounts would then appear as follows:

Truck	Accumulated Depreciation	Depreciation Expense
8,000	1,200	1,200
	1,200	
	2,400	

The net book value of the truck at the end of the second year is $5,600 ($8,000 — $2,400). Depreciation expense is shown on the income statement for the second year at $1,200, the same amount as was shown on the income statement for the first year.

There is no necessary connection between the net book value of a plant asset and its market value. At the end of the second year the company might be able to sell the truck for more or less than $5,600. Depreciation policy is not intended as a device for the valuation of plant assets. It is merely a means of allocating the cost to the fiscal periods during which the assets are in service. The allocation of cost is made to facilitate the determination of net income for the period.

Depreciation procedure in accounting is an *estimating* process and is filled with uncertainty. An estimate of the useful life and the salvage value is required, and a judgment on how to assign the cost must be made. Consequently, accounting data are not as precise as they may appear. Estimates and human judgments enter into the processing operation, depreciation policy being a good example. The user of accounting information must be aware of these underlying judgments and estimates when using accounting data. The student of accounting should be constantly on the alert for other areas in the accounting process where estimates and judgments are filled with uncertainty.

The inventory adjustment. Some companies maintain *perpetual* inventory records, recording purchases as additions to inventory and withdrawals or sales as deductions from inventory and as increases in cost of goods sold. The inventory records should then show the proper balances on hand at all times. At the end of the fiscal year, a physical count may reveal errors in the book record that should be corrected. However, if the accounting system is operating properly and if there is proper control over the physical inventories, the corrections should not be substantial in amount.

Many companies do not keep a perpetual record of inventories. The purchases are recorded, but there is no record of the cost of items withdrawn or sold. As a general rule, it is impractical to record the cost of items sold if merchandise is sold to customers over the counter in relatively small lots. At the end of the fiscal year, the physical quantity remaining as inventory can be determined by count. Costs are then identified with the inventory according to the particular costing method that is employed. The cost of goods sold during the year is then computed indirectly as the sum of the beginning inventory and purchases minus the inventory at the end of the year. This method of arriving at inventory costs and the cost of goods sold is called the *periodic* inventory method.

A variety of practices may be employed in making the periodic inventory adjustment. The essential point is that the cost of goods sold should be determined as accurately as possible and that the inventory at the end of the year should be valued properly.

The inventory adjustment may be made by setting up a new account entitled "Cost of Goods Sold." The balance of inventory at the beginning of the year and the purchases for the year are closed out by credits, with the debit being entered in the cost of goods sold account. At this point, the cost of goods sold account has a balance representing the cost of goods available for sale. It is converted to cost of goods sold by removing the cost attached to the inventory remaining at the end of the year. This is accomplished by a debit to the merchandise inventory account in an amount equal to the cost of the inventory at the end of the year and by a credit to the cost of goods sold account.

To illustrate, assume that a company had an inventory at the beginning of the year costing $15,000. During the year, purchases of $100,000 are recorded. At the end of the year, a count of the inventory reveals that the merchandise on hand at that time cost $18,000. The adjustment could be recorded as follows:

(1) Cost of Goods Sold	115,000	
Merchandise Inventory		15,000
Purchases		100,000
Transfer of beginning inventory balance and purchases to cost of goods sold.		
(2) Merchandise Inventory	18,000	
Cost of Goods Sold		18,000
To record balance of inventory at end of the year.		

Merchandise Inventory		Purchases		Cost of Goods Sold	
15,000	(1) 15,000	100,000	(1) 100,000	(1) 115,000	(2) 18,000
(2) 18,000					

The balance of the cost of goods sold account is $97,000, representing the cost of the goods available for sale less the inventory carried over for sale into the future. The inventory balance of $18,000 is in agreement with the amount determined by the count at the end of the year.

The valuation adjustment. There is another type of adjustment that may be looked upon as being a valuation adjustment. Certain assets, such as marketable securities, accounts receivable from customers, and inventories are to be realized in cash in the normal course of events. But the assets may not be realized at the amounts shown in the ledger accounts.

Accounts receivable, for example, show the amounts due from the customers, but all of the customers will not pay their accounts. There will be uncollectible accounts. At the end of the year, there is no way of knowing which customers will default. Yet, sales should be charged with the *estimated* uncollectible accounts arising out of sales operations for the year. An adjusting entry is made to record the estimated uncollectible accounts chargeable to the year, and the credit is made not to accounts receivable but to an account that may be entitled "Allowance for Doubtful Accounts."

Assume that sales for the year amount to $240,000 and that the accounts receivable at the end of the year amount to $47,000. It may be estimated that 1 percent of the sales for the year, or $2,400, will not be collected because of uncollectible accounts receivable. At the time the estimate is made, no specific accounts receivable have been identified as uncollectible. The credit is therefore made to an allowance account. The adjusting entry appears as:

```
Uncollectible Accounts Expense ................. 2,400
    Allowance for Doubtful Accounts ..............       2,400
        Estimate of bad debts chargeable to the operations
        of the year.
```

The ledger accounts after adjustment are given below:

Accounts Receivable	Allowance for Doubtful Accounts	Uncollectible Accounts Expense
47,000	2,400	2,400

The accounts receivable are shown on the balance sheet at the gross amount of $47,000 with the allowance of $2,400 being deducted to arrive at a net balance of $44,600.

In the next year, as accounts are identified as being uncollectible, they will be written off against the allowance for doubtful accounts. Assume that an account with Robert Davis in the amount of $600 is judged to be uncollectible in the following year. The entry to write off the amount is as follows:

```
Allowance for Doubtful Accounts ................... 600
    Accounts Receivable—Robert Davis ..............       600
        Write-off of uncollectible account.
```

Both the control account and the subsidiary ledger account of Robert Davis would be reduced by $600.

The estimating procedure illustrated above is subject to errors in judgment but nevertheless tends to produce more useful data than would be the case if the estimate were not made. There is no logical reason why losses on customers' accounts should be matched against revenues of the fiscal period in which the losses are detected. The losses should be matched against the revenue recorded when the initial transaction took place. Unfortunately, no exact determination of the losses can be made at that point. It should be possible, however, to make reasonable estimates based on past experience. Hence, this device is a method for recognizing the doubtful account expense in the period in which the sale was made and not in a subsequent period when the account receivable is actually judged to be uncollectible.

Marketable securities and inventories are also subject to valuation adjustments. It is customary to value marketable securities and inventories at the lower of cost or market. If market values are lower than cost, an adjustment may be made to charge a loss to the year in which the market decline occurred. The offsetting credit may be made directly to the asset account or to an adjunct allowance account similar in concept to the allowance account used with accounts receivable.

Other adjustments. Entries are sometimes made to correct errors that have been detected. It may be discovered, for example, that advertising expense of $600 has been recorded in the current year as expense when it should have been charged as expense the year before. Therefore, the owners' equity at the beginning of the current year is overstated as a result of transferring too much income to the owners at the end of the previous year. Expenses of the current year are overstated, with the result that net income for the current year is understated. The correction would be made as follows:

```
Owners' Equity ...................................   600
    Advertising Expense .............................        600
        Correction of error in recording advertising expense
    of the previous year in the current year.
```

Taking the two years together, there would be no error. The overstatement of net income in one year would be offset by the understatement of net income in the next year. But the income statements for each individual year would be incorrect, and the owners' equity on the balance sheet at the end of the first year would be incorrect.

The adjustment procedure illustrated. Assume that the trial balance shown at the top of page 670 was taken from the general ledger of Barry Stone before adjusting entries were made on December 31, 1972.

No adjusting entries have been made since the end of the preceding year. When the accountant examined the records and the underlying data, he found that adjustments were required as follows:

(1) Interest of $300 was earned on the marketable securities but was neither collected nor recorded.

(2) The market value of the marketable securities was $21,000 at the end of the year with the loss in market value taking place during the year. Investments are to be reduced directly for market declines. No offsetting allowance account is used.

(3) It was estimated that doubtful accounts chargeable against the sales of 1972 should be provided for in the amount of $1,500. No individual account can be identified as being uncollectible, and an allowance will be offset against the total accounts receivable.

(4) Inventory on hand at December 31, 1972, was counted and costed at $16,940. This amount is approximately equal to the current replacement cost of the inventory.

	Dr.	Cr.
Cash	$ 31,620	
Marketable Securities	25,000	
Accounts Receivable	20,980	
Merchandise Inventory, January 1, 1972	18,630	
Prepaid Rent	600	
Land	7,300	
Building and Equipment	152,000	
Accumulated Depreciation		$ 30,400
Accounts Payable		9,320
Notes Payable		10,000
Advance Payments Made by Customers		2,500
Barry Stone, Capital		103,230
Sales		326,400
Sales Discounts	4,650	
Sales Returns and Allowances	5,820	
Purchases	173,800	
Wages and Salaries Expense	26,300	
Advertising Expense	14,100	
Insurance Expense	1,200	
Heat and Light Expense	950	
Interest Income		1,700
Interest Expense	600	
	$483,550	$483,550

(5) Barry Stone rented storage space from Goldsmith Parts Co. for $150 a month, beginning on November 1, 1972. Rent for four months was paid in advance at that time.

(6) The land is used as a building site and presumably can be used for that purpose indefinitely. Therefore, the cost of land will not be matched against revenues as depreciation. Instead, the cost of $7,300 will be carried forward as an asset on future balance sheets until the land is finally disposed of.

(7) The building and equipment cost of $152,000 is being written off at the average rate of 5 percent a year. Residual salvage value is to be ignored.

(8) Interest owed on the notes payable at the end of the year was $100.

(9) Customers paid $2,500 in November for deliveries to be made to them over the next three months. By December 31, Barry Stone had delivered merchandise to these customers at a billed amount of $1,600.

(10) An investigation of the accounts showed that wages and salaries and all other items were properly stated in the ledger accounts and that no further adjustments were necessary.

The adjustment data were analyzed and entered in the general journal at December 31 as shown below:

(1) Accrued Interest Receivable	300	
Interest Income		300
Accrued interest earned on marketable securities.		

(2) Loss Due to Market Decline of Securities . . .	4,000	
Marketable Securities		4,000
To reduce marketable securities to lower		
of cost or market.		
(3) Uncollectible Accounts Expense	1,500	
Allowance for Doubtful Accounts		1,500
Estimate of uncollectible accounts arising		
out of 1972 sales.		
(4) Cost of Goods Sold	192,430	
Merchandise Inventory (January 1)		18,630
Purchases		173,800
Transfer of inventory at the beginning of		
the year and purchases to cost of goods		
sold. Cost of goods sold now shows the		
cost of goods available for sale.		
Merchandise Inventory (December 31) . .	16,940	
Cost of Goods Sold		16,940
To record inventory on hand at the end		
of the year and to remove the cost from		
cost of goods sold.		
(5) Rent Expense	300	
Prepaid Rent		300
Adjustment of prepaid rent. Two months		
out of the four months have expired.		
(6) (No depreciation recorded on land).		
(7) Depreciation Expense	7,600	
Accumulated Depreciation		7,600
Depreciation estimated for the year 1972.		
(8) Interest Expense	100	
Interest Payable		100
Interest accrued on notes payable.		
(9) Advance Payments Made by Customers	1,600	
Sales		1,600
Revenue recognized because of deliveries		
made against advances received from		
customers.		

The adjusting entries were then posted to the ledger accounts. A new trial balance, called the adjusted trial balance, was prepared from the ledger and is shown at the top of page 672.

The income statement for 1972 and the balance sheet at December 31, 1972, prepared from the adjusted trial balance, are given on page 673.

Note that the owner's equity on the balance sheet is $87,390 higher than the amount shown on the adjusted trial balance. This difference is the amount of the net income for the year. On the balance sheet at the end of the year, the amount of the owner's equity is the owner's interest at that time after all net income for the year or net losses for the year have been added or subtracted from any previous balance shown.

The financial statements should be made available as soon as possible after the close of the year. If the accountant takes time to enter all of the

Barry Stone
Adjusted Trial Balance
December 31, 1972

	Dr.	Cr.
Cash	$ 31,620	
Marketable Securities	21,000	
Accrued Interest Receivable	300	
Accounts Receivable	20,980	
Allowance for Doubtful Accounts		$ 1,500
Merchandise Inventory, December 31, 1972	16,940	
Prepaid Rent	300	
Land	7,300	
Building and Equipment	152,000	
Accumulated Depreciation		38,000
Accounts Payable		9,320
Notes Payable		10,000
Accrued Interest Payable		100
Advance Payments Made by Customers		900
Barry Stone, Capital		103,230
Sales		328,000
Sales Discounts	4,650	
Sales Returns and Allowances	5,820	
Cost of Goods Sold	175,490	
Wages and Salaries Expense	26,300	
Advertising Expense	14,100	
Rent Expense	300	
Insurance Expense	1,200	
Heat and Light Expense	950	
Uncollectible Accounts Expense	1,500	
Depreciation Expense	7,600	
Interest Income		2,000
Loss Due to Market Decline of Securities	4,000	
Interest Expense	700	
	$493,050	$493,050

adjustments in the journal and to post the adjustments to the ledger, the publication of the statements will be unnecessarily delayed. In practice, a short cut is frequently taken. A pair of debit and credit adjustment columns is added at the right of the original trial balance taken from the ledger. As the adjustment data are analyzed, the debit and the credit amounts are entered in the new pair of columns opposite the items affected. The debits and the credits on the trial balance are combined with the debits and the credits shown in the new pair of adjustment columns to yield an adjusted trial balance. Sometimes other pairs of columns are added at the right not only so that an adjusted trial balance can be set forth but also so that amounts on the adjusted trial balance can be distributed to a pair of columns headed "Income Statement" and to a pair of columns headed "Balance Sheet" according to the statements in which they appear. Financial statements are then prepared directly from these papers, which are referred to as *working*

Barry Stone
Income Statement
For the Year Ended December 31, 1972

Sales		$328,000
Less:		
Sales discounts	$ 4,650	
Sales returns and allowances	5,820	10,470
Net sales		$317,530
Cost of goods sold		175,490
Gross margin		$142,040
Operating expenses:		
Wages and salaries	$ 26,300	
Advertising	14,100	
Rent	300	
Insurance	1,200	
Heat and light	950	
Uncollectible accounts	1,500	
Depreciation	7,600	51,950
Net operating income		$ 90,090
Add: Interest income		2,000
		$ 92,090
Less:		
Loss due to market decline of securities	$ 4,000	
Interest expense	700	4,700
Net income		$ 87,390

Barry Stone
Balance Sheet
December 31, 1972

Assets

Cash		$ 31,620
Marketable securities		21,000
Accrued interest receivable		300
Accounts receivable	$ 20,980	
Less: Allowance for doubtful accounts	1,500	19,480
Merchandise inventory		16,940
Prepaid rent		300
Land		7,300
Building and equipment	$152,000	
Less: Accumulated depreciation	38,000	114,000
Total assets		$210,940

Equities

Liabilities:		
Accounts payable		$ 9,320
Notes payable		10,000
Accrued interest payable		100
Advance payments made by customers		900
Total liabilities		$ 20,320
Owner's equity:		
Barry Stone, capital		$190,620
Total equities		$210,940

papers. After the statements are released, the accountant will then journalize the adjustments and post them to the ledger accounts.

The closing procedure. At the end of the year the revenue and expense accounts have served their purpose. Measurements of the extent of the net increase or decrease in net assets resulting from profit-making activity during the year have been taken. Now the revenue and expense accounts can be closed, that is, the balances can be removed so that new measurements can be made in the following year.

The closing entry for Barry Stone at December 31, 1972 would be made as follows:

Sales	328,000	
Interest Income	2,000	
Sales Discounts		4,650
Sales Returns and Allowances		5,820
Cost of Goods Sold		175,490
Wages and Salaries Expense		26,300
Advertising Expense		14,100
Rent Expense		300
Insurance Expense		1,200
Heat and Light Expense		950
Uncollectible Accounts Expense		1,500
Depreciation Expense		7,600
Loss Due to Market Decline of Securities		4,000
Interest Expense		700
Barry Stone, Capital		87,390

Entry to close revenue and expense accounts for the year and to close net income to Barry Stone's capital account.

The closing procedure can actually be performed very easily by removing the ledger cards for all revenue and expense accounts and by adding the net income to the owner's equity or by deducting any net loss from the owner's equity. The revenue and expense ledger cards for the old year are filed for future reference, and new ledger cards are labeled and inserted for the new year.

Generally, the closing procedure is formalized by journal entries and postings to the ledger accounts. The balances in the revenue and expense accounts are in effect erased by making an entry equal to the balance on the opposite side of the account. Revenue accounts, for example, normally have credit balances. To remove the balances, a debit equal to the credit balance is made to each account. Expenses normally have debit balances. To remove the debit balances, credits are made to each account in the amount of the previous balance. The net difference, that is, the net income or the net loss for the year, is credited or debited to the owner's equity.

The revenue and expense accounts may also be closed out separately to a summary account entitled "Revenue and Expense Summary." The balance of the summary account is then closed to the owner's equity account.

If the business had been incorporated, the net income would have been subject to income taxes, which would have to be computed and recorded as a debit to income tax expense and as a credit to income tax payable. The income tax expense would be closed at the end of the fiscal year like all of the other expenses. The liability for income tax payable would be debited when cash was disbursed in payment of the tax.

Assume also that the corporation declared dividends; that is, the board of directors authorized the distribution of a portion of the net earnings to the stockholders. If dividends of $1,000 were declared in each of the four quarters of the year, each declaration of dividends would have been recorded as follows:

Dividends	1,000	
Dividends Payable		1,000
Quarterly dividend declared.		

When the dividends are paid, the liability to the stockholders shown as dividends payable is debited and cash is credited. The dividends account is closed to retained earnings at the end of the fiscal year.

Retained Earnings	4,000	
Dividends		4,000
Dividends closed to retained earnings.		

The post-closing trial balance. After the revenue and expense accounts are closed, only the asset, liability, and owner's equity accounts have balances to be carried forward to the next year. The balances after closing are listed on a *post-closing trial balance*. The purpose of this final trial balance is to prove that the general ledger is in balance before transactions are entered for the new year.

The post-closing trial balance for Barry Stone at December 31, 1972, is given at the top of page 676.

The ledger is now ready to receive entries for the next fiscal year, and the cycle of processing accounting data is repeated again.

Barry Stone
Post-Closing Trial Balance
December 31, 1972

	Dr.	Cr.
Cash	$ 31,620	
Marketable Securities	21,000	
Accrued Interest Receivable	300	
Accounts Receivable	20,980	
Allowance for Doubtful Accounts		$ 1,500
Merchandise Inventory (December 31, 1972)	16,940	
Prepaid Rent	300	
Land	7,300	
Building and Equipment	152,000	
Accumulated Depreciation		38,000
Accounts Payable		9,320
Notes Payable		10,000
Accrued Interest Payable		100
Advance Payments Made by Customers ..		900
Barry Stone, Capital		190,620
	$250,440	$250,440

Appendix C

PROBLEMS—
THE ACCOUNTING CYCLE

C–1. Ellen Thomas began business on September 1, 1972, at a store on College Street. She sells records, books, and supplies to students. Ellen deposited $2,200 in a separate bank account for store operations. Rent of $200 was paid by check for use of the store in September. A check for $1,600 was written for store fixtures and furniture. Various items of merchandise were purchased on credit terms at a cost of $1,900. During the month cash sales of $2,300 were recorded on the cash register and deposited in the bank account for the store. A check in the amount of $130 was issued for supplies that were used during the month, and a check for $180 was for wages paid to a student who worked in the store during the evenings. A check for $1,100 was mailed to the supplier from whom the merchandise was purchased. At the end of the month, merchandise costing $700 was on hand. Depreciation on the furniture and fixtures for the month has been estimated at $15.

Required: (1) Record the transactions for the month of September directly in the ledger accounts. Use the ledger account titles given below:

Cash	Sales
Merchandise Inventory	Cost of Goods Sold
Furniture and Fixtures	Wages
Accumulated Depreciation	Rent
Accounts Payable	Supplies Expense
Ellen Thomas, Capital	Depreciation

(2) Prepare a trial balance at September 30.
(3) Prepare an income statement for the month of September.
(4) Prepare a balance sheet at September 30.

C–2. Ben Pasquine purchased the assets of Brodhead Photo Shop on July 1 of the current year for $23,200 payable in cash. The assets were valued as follows:

Inventory of merchandise	$11,600
Store equipment	7,400
Delivery equipment	4,200
Total	$23,200

On July 1, Pasquine rented a store, paying rent of $250 for the month of July, and began business under the name of Pasquine Art Supplies.

Transactions for the month of July are summarized on the next page.

(1) Invested cash of $2,600 by depositing this amount in a bank account for the store.

(2) Purchased merchandise on credit terms at a cost of $6,100.

(3) Acquired additional store equipment costing $2,000. The store equipment was financed by a non-interest bearing note for $1,500 due on November 1, and the balance was paid in cash when the equipment was acquired.

(4) Sales to customers:

Credit	$8,200
Cash	4,600

(5) Cost of merchandise sold, $5,300.

(6) Collected $6,800 on customers' accounts.

(7) Paid salaries for the month of $800 and made payments of $4,900 for merchandise purchased on credit terms earlier in the month.

(8) Other payments made for services and materials acquired and used during the month were as follows:

Utilities	$ 70
Advertising	480
Supplies expense	210
Delivery expense	140

(9) Depreciation for the month has been estimated as follows:

Depreciation of store equipment	$50
Depreciation of delivery equipment	60

Required: (1) Record the transactions for Pasquine Art Supplies directly in the ledger accounts, using the following account titles:

Assets:

Cash
Accounts Receivable
Inventory
Store Equipment
Accumulated Depreciation—Store Equipment
Delivery Equipment
Accumulated Depreciation—Delivery Equipment

Liabilities:

Accounts Payable
Notes Payable

Owners' equity:

Ben Pasquine, Capital

Revenue:

Sales

Expenses:

Cost of Goods Sold	Rent
Salaries	Utilities
Advertising	Supplies
Delivery Expense	Depreciation

(2) Prepare a trial balance of the ledger account balances at July 31.

C–3. A trial balance of Santos Parts Company after the books were closed at December 31, 1972, appears below:

Santos Parts Company
Trial Balance
December 31, 1972

	Dr.	Cr.
Cash	$ 6,340	
Accounts Receivable	11,280	
Allowance for Doubtful Accounts		$ 470
Inventory	10,620	
Prepaid Rent	800	
Store Fixtures and Equipment	8,200	
Accumulated Depreciation		820
Accounts Payable		3,650
Withheld Income Taxes		560
Payroll Taxes Payable		230
Jose Santos, Capital		31,510
	$37,240	$37,240

Transactions for the month of January of the following year are summarized below by weeks:

January 2–6:

 (1) Cash sales, $2,350.

 (2) Sales on account, $3,280.

 (3) Payments to creditors, $2,150.

January 9–13:

 (4) Cash sales, $3,750.

 (5) Sales on account, $4,130.

 (6) Collections on account, $9,200.

 (7) Purchases of merchandise on account, $6,500.

 (8) Payment of $80 for heat and light.

 (9) Paid $930 to employees for salaries. Gross earnings of employees amounted to $1,200. Deductions were made for income taxes withheld of $200 and payroll taxes withheld of $70.

January 16–20:

 (10) Cash sales, $2,830.

 (11) Sales on account, $3,450.

 (12) Collections on account, $7,820.

 (13) Payments to creditors, $5,900.

 (14) Payments to Radio Station WLRN for advertising, $150.

 (15) Payments to *The Eagle* for advertising, $120.

 (16) Paid telephone bill of $45.

 (17) Paid electric bill of $85.

January 23–27:

(18) Cash sales, $3,180.

(19) Sales on account, $2,760.

(20) Collections on account, $2,330.

(21) Purchases of merchandise on account, $10,350.

(22) Paid $320 for office supplies.

(23) Paid $930 to employees for salaries. Gross earnings of employees amounted to $1,200. Deductions were made for income taxes withheld of $200 and payroll taxes withheld of $70.

January 30–31:

(24) Cash sales, $860.

(25) Sales on account, $1,180.

(26) Collections on account, $2,000.

(27) Paid withheld income tax and payroll tax liability outstanding at December 31.

(28) Withdrawal of cash by Jose Santos, $7,000.

Additional information:

(29) The prepaid rent at December 31 applies equally to January and February.

(30) The accounts receivable have been reviewed at January 31, and it is estimated that uncollectible accounts arising out of January sales will probably amount to $300.

(31) Depreciation on store fixtures and equipment should be recorded at $80.

(32) The employer's share of payroll taxes amounts to $120.

(33) The inventory of merchandise has been counted at January 31 and costed at $4,230.

Required: (1) Open the following general ledger accounts and record in them the balances shown on the December 31 trial balance:

Cash	Sales
Accounts Receivable	Cost of Goods Sold
Allowance for Doubtful Accounts	Purchases
Inventory	Salaries Expense
Prepaid Rent	Payroll Tax Expense
Store Fixtures and Equipment	Rent Expense
Accumulated Depreciation	Advertising Expense
Accounts Payable	Heat and Light Expense
Withheld Income Taxes	Telephone Expense
Payroll Taxes Payable	Office Supplies Expense
Jose Santos, Capital	Uncollectible Accounts Expense
	Depreciation Expense

(2) Record the transactions for January directly in the ledger accounts.

(3) Prepare a trial balance of the ledger accounts at January 31, 1973, showing the balances as they would appear after adjustments are recorded but before the accounts are closed at the end of the month.

Managerial Accounting / Appendix C

C–4. A trial balance of the general ledger at March 31, 1972, for **Brennan** Stores, Inc., is given below:

Brennan Stores, Inc.
Trial Balance
March 31, 1972

	Dr.	Cr.
Cash	$10,320	
Accounts Receivable	7,670	
Inventory	6,130	
Store Equipment and Vehicles	11,600	
Accumulated Depreciation		$ 1,750
Accounts Payable		1,640
Withholding Tax Payable		300
Payroll Taxes Payable		90
Walter Brennan, Capital		12,720
Sales		76,000
Sales Discounts	800	
Purchases	31,200	
Salaries	16,400	
Payroll Taxes	950	
Advertising	3,170	
Delivery Expense	1,260	
Rent	3,000	
	$92,500	$92,500

The accounts receivable subsidiary ledger shows the following balances at March 31:

Jay Andrews	$2,430
William Clark	1,750
Howard McCabe	1,690
Milton Weinstein	1,800
	$7,670

The following transactions were completed by Brennan Stores, Inc., during April of the current year:

April 3 Collect amount owed by Jay Andrews. No discount was allowed.
4 Sale on account to Milton Weinstein in the amount of $1,200.
4 Acquired a panel truck for business deliveries at a cost of $6,800.
5 Collected amount owed by Howard McCabe. No discount was allowed.
6 Purchased merchandise on credit at a net cost of $5,300.
7 Sale on account to Jay Andrews in the amount of $2,500.
7 Paid rent for April in the amount of $500.
7 Collected amount owed by Milton Weinstein. A discount of 2 percent was allowed for prompt payment.
10 Paid withholding tax payable and payroll taxes payable balance at March 31.
11 Sale on account to William Clark in the amount of $6,000.
11 Collected balance owed by William Clark at March 31. No discount was allowed.
12 Paid for gasoline and oil used in operation of automotive equipment, $80.

13 Collected amount owed by Jay Andrews resulting from the sale of April 7. A discount of 2 percent was allowed.
14 Paid for merchandise purchased on April 6.
14 Sale on account to Howard McCabe in the amount of $4,000.
17 Purchased merchandise on credit at a cost of $7,200.
20 Paid $150 for advertising.
21 Sale on account to Milton Weinstein in the amount of $3,000.
24 Collected amount owed by Howard McCabe resulting from the sale of April 14. A discount of 2 percent was allowed.
25 Sale on account to Jay Andrews in the amount of $1,500.
28 Paid salaries of $1,600. Gross salaries were $2,000. Deductions were made for income taxes withheld of $300 and payroll taxes withheld of $100.
28 The employer's share of payroll taxes amounts to $130.

Required: (1) Enter the transactions for April in a general journal.
(2) Open general ledger accounts and subsidiary ledger accounts for accounts receivable. Enter balances at March 31 in the ledger accounts.
(3) Post the journal entries. Post the debits and credits to Accounts Receivable in the general ledger and to the individual subsidiary ledger accounts.
(4) Take a trial balance of the general ledger accounts at April 30 and prepare a schedule of the accounts receivable ledger balances at April 30.

C–5. Transactions for Weaver Machine Company for the first month of its operation, June of the current year, are summarized below:

(1) Capital stock was issued for cash of $63,000 invested in the corporation.
(2) Equipment costing $37,000 was purchased. A payment of $5,000 was made in cash, and the balance was financed on a note payable.
(3) Materials costing $9,400 were purchased on credit terms.
(4) Materials used during the month in manufacturing operations cost $7,700. (Transfer the cost of materials from Materials to Work in Process.)
(5) The cost of labor used in production amounted to $5,200. (Charge the cost directly to Work in Process.) No payment has been made to the employees, and the income taxes to be withheld and payroll deductions will be determined later.
(6) Other manufacturing costs pertaining to operations for the month were paid as indicated below:

Factory rent	$ 600
Repairs and maintenance	140
Heat and light	120
Indirect labor	3,500

(7) Selling and administrative costs were paid in the amount of $3,800. Included in this amount is rent of $600 prepaid on the sales office for July.
(8) At the end of the month, additional repairs and maintenance cost for the month amounting to $170 was unpaid. Depreciation on the equipment was estimated at $400. The repairs and maintenance cost and the depreciation pertain to manufacturing operations. Interest of $180 accrued on the note.
(9) Transfer the manufacturing costs indicated in (6) and (8) to Work in Process.
(10) Work completed during the month and transferred to Finished Goods cost $12,300.

(11) Finished goods costing $8,200 were sold to customers on credit terms for $15,800.

(12) Collections from customers amounted to $9,300.

Required: (1) Record the transactions given above in a general journal under date of June 30.

(2) Post the journal entries to the ledger accounts using the following account captions:

Cash	Sales
Accounts Receivable	Cost of Goods Sold
Materials	Indirect Labor
Work in Process	Factory Rent
Finished Goods	Repairs and Maintenance
Prepaid Rent	Heat and Light
Factory Equipment	Depreciation
Accumulated Depreciation	Selling and Administrative
Accounts Payable	Expense
Notes Payable	Interest Expense
Interest Payable	
Wages Payable	
Accrued Expenses Payable	
Capital Stock	

(3) Take a trial balance from the ledger at June 30 before the revenue and expense accounts are closed.

C-6. A trial balance taken from the general ledger of Wahl and Epstein, Inc., at July 31, is given below:

	Dr.	Cr.
Cash	$12,320	
Accounts Receivable	6,030	
Inventory	8,650	
Equipment	10,500	
Accumulated Depreciation		$ 1,300
Accounts Payable		1,930
Capital Stock		10,000
Retained Earnings		24,270
	$37,500	$37,500

The company uses a one-column sales journal, a one-column purchases journal, a two-column general journal, a cash receipts journal, and a cash disbursements journal with provision made for a columnar distribution as shown below:

Cash Receipts Journal:

Cash, Dr.
Accounts Receivable, Cr.
Sales, Cr.
Commissions Earned, Cr.
General Ledger, Dr. and Cr.

Cash Disbursements Journal:

Cash, Cr.
Accounts Payable, Dr.
Wages Expense, Dr.
Income Taxes Withheld, Cr.
Payroll Taxes Withheld, Cr.
General Ledger, Dr. and Cr.

Transactions for the month of August were as follows:

August   2   Sales on account, $2,840.

        3   Collection of amounts owed on account, $2,150.

        4   Purchased merchandise on account, $5,200.

5   Cash sales, $1,200.
7   Paid $800 on accounts payable.
9   Borrowed $5,000 from Union Bank on a note payable due on November 8.
10   Returned merchandise to suppliers and received $700 credit.
10   Paid $6,000 for new equipment.
12   Collection of $2,620 on accounts receivable.
13   Sales on account, $3,480.
14   Commissions earned and collected, $1,100.
16   Wages earned, $1,500. Deductions of $300 were made for income taxes withheld and for payroll taxes withheld in the amount of $80. The net amount was paid to the employees.
17   Cash sales, $1,550.
18   Purchases on account, $4,100.
19   Collection of $4,080 on accounts receivable.
20   Paid $3,820 on accounts payable.
23   Sales on account, $2,350.
24   Cash sales, $1,280.
25   Commissions earned and collected, $1,350.
26   Paid $2,900 on accounts payable.
30   Paid selling and administrative expenses of $750.
30   Sold additional shares of stock for $5,000.
31   Wages earned, $1,500. Deductions of $300 were made for income taxes withheld and for payroll taxes withheld in the amount of $80. The net amount was paid to the employees.

Wahl and Epstein, Inc., records merchandise acquisitions in a purchases account.

Required: (1) Enter the transactions in the appropriate journals.

(2) Enter the balances from the trial balance at July 31 in ledger accounts. Add the journal columns and post to ledger accounts. (Choose ledger account captions that you believe to be appropriate.)

(3) Prepare a trial balance of the ledger at August 31.

C–7. Jensen and Anderson, Inc., uses a bookkeeping machine to process accounting data. Cash remittance forms supporting cash receipts and invoices approved and paid are delivered during the day to the bookkeeper in batches for processing. The machine has several adding machine accumulators that serve like columns in special journals.

When cash remittance forms are processed, entries are made in the first five accumulators, that are used to accumulate the following data:

Cash, Dr.
Sales Discounts, Dr.
Accounts Receivable, Cr.
Sales, Cr.
General Ledger, Cr.

In processing a collection from a customer, for example, the bookkeeper will enter the cash received in the first adding machine accumulator, the sales discount allowed in the second accumulator, and the credit granted to the customer in the third accumulator.

The machine prints a proof sheet of all transactions, with credit entries in the general ledger accumulator being coded by account number so that separate postings can be made to ledger accounts for which no special accumulator has been provided. At the end of the day, totals are drawn from the machine and are posted by the machine to the appropriate ledger cards, which are inserted at that time. Entries appearing in the general ledger column of the proof sheet are posted manually.

The next six accumulators are used in processing cash disbursements:

Cash, Cr.
Purchases Discounts, Cr.
Accounts Payable, Dr.
Selling Expense, Dr.
Office Expense, Dr.
General Ledger, Dr.

Sales to customers on account are processed in the billing department with the total of the credit sales for the day being given to the bookkeeper for entry in the general ledger accounts.

Invoices for purchases of merchandise that have been received and approved are processed in the accounts payable department with the total purchases for the day being reported for entry in the general ledger accounts.

On January 10, cash remittance forms delivered to the bookkeeper from the 11 o'clock mail contained the following information:

(1) Collected $1,470 from New Castle Fixtures, Inc. The gross amount of the bill was $1,500. A discount of $30 was granted to the customer for prompt payment of the account.
(2) Collected interest of $75 on a note receivable taken from James Olsen.
(3) Cash sales were reported by North Side Branch in the amount of $950.
(4) Collected $784 from Mancini Brothers. The gross amount owed was $800. A discount of $16 was allowed for prompt payment.
(5) Received $120 rent from garages rented to Bryant Taxi Company.
(6) Cash sales in the amount of $830 were reported by South Side Branch.
(7) Cash sales in the amount of $1,720 were reported by the main office.
(8) Collected $2,100 from Brooks Machine Company. This balance has been outstanding for several months, and no discount is allowed.
(9) A refund check for $52 was received from Hamilton, Inc., for overpayment of advertising. The original payment was charged to Advertising Expense.
(10) Invoices paid on January 10 are listed below:

(a) Paid $1,862 to Morgan Appliances for merchandise purchased. A discount of $38 was deducted. The gross amount of the bill was $1,900.
(b) Paid $980 to Paulsen Supply Company for merchandise purchased. A discount of $20 was deducted. The gross amount of the bill was $1,000.
(c) Check written for the net amount of $1,430 owed to sales employees. (Debit Wages Payable.) The complete payroll has already been recorded by a general journal entry.
(d) Paid $55 to Westport Art Supplies for advertising materials to be used in January.
(e) Paid $31 to Harvey Stationery Company for letterheads and envelopes purchased for use in the general office in January.
(f) Paid $63 for advertising to appear in *The Morning Call* on January 14.
(g) Paid $40 to Naylor Office Equipment for maintenance and repairs to typewriters used in the general office.
(h) Paid $500 on the principal of a note payable owed to Ace Finance Company.

A report from the billing department reported total sales on credit for the day in the amount of $4,250.

The accounts payable department reported purchases of merchandise in the amount of $3,430.

Required: (1) Prepare machine proof sheets for cash receipts and cash disbursements for January 10. Total the columns.

(2) What amount would be posted for the day as a debit to Accounts Receivable? As a credit?

(3) What amount would be posted for the day as a credit to Accounts Payable? As a debit?

C–8. A trial balance from the ledger of John Crosby and Son, Inc., follows:

John Crosby and Son, Inc.
Trial Balance
December 31, 1972

	Dr.	Cr.
Cash	$ 15,320	
Marketable Securities	30,000	
Accounts Receivable	21,300	
Allowance for Doubtful Accounts		$ 320
Inventory, January 1, 1972	23,270	
Prepaid Rent	2,500	
Furniture and Fixtures	18,700	
Accumulated Depreciation		1,760
Accounts Payable		12,840
Wages Payable		3,000
Withheld Income Taxes		730
Payroll Tax Liability		180
Notes Payable		10,000
Capital Stock, $10 par value		20,000
Retained Earnings		28,390
Dividends	900	
Sales		186,200
Sales Returns and Allowances	1,200	
Sales Discounts	2,000	
Purchases	93,400	
Purchases Returns and Allowances		650
Purchases Discounts		830
Wages	31,700	
Payroll Taxes	2,300	
Advertising	15,100	
Licenses and Taxes	1,100	
Rent	5,000	
Heat and Light	1,320	
Office Supplies Expense	640	
Interest Earned		1,400
Interest Expense	550	
	$266,300	$266,300

Adjusting entries have not been made, and the books are closed annually at December 31. Adjustment data appear below:

(1) The marketable securities, which have been held for the entire year, bear interest at 6 percent on a par value of $30,000. Interest earned as reported

on the trial balance includes only the interest earned and collected on these investments.

(2) It has been estimated that 1 percent of the sales net of sales returns and allowances and sales discounts will be uncollectible.

(3) The cost of the inventory on hand at December 31, 1972, has been determined at $25,300.

(4) The prepaid rent includes rent at $500 a month from November 1, 1972, to March 31, 1973.

(5) Depreciation of 5 percent is taken annually on furniture and fixtures.

(6) The employer's share of payroll taxes for the year should be shown at $2,800.

(7) Unpaid heating bills amounting to $120 have not been recorded.

(8) Interest has not been recorded on the notes payable outstanding at December 31. Three months interest at an annual rate of 8 percent has accrued on these notes.

(9) Estimate income taxes at 40 percent of the net income before taxes.

Required: Prepare working papers for 1972.

C–9. A trial balance taken from the ledger of Bedford Machine Company, Inc., is given below. No adjustments have been made to the accounts for the fiscal year ended June 30, 1972.

Bedford Machine Company, Inc.
Trial Balance
June 30, 1972

	Dr.	Cr.
Cash	$ 38,730	
Accounts Receivable	21,220	
Notes Receivable	5,000	
Allowance for Doubtful Accounts		$ 680
Inventory, June 30, 1972	24,600	
Prepaid Insurance	1,500	
Land	6,400	
Building	93,700	
Accumulated Depreciation-Building		8,780
Equipment	36,400	
Accumulated Depreciation-Equipment		11,300
Accounts Payable		7,300
Withheld Income Taxes		1,600
Payroll Tax Liability		900
Unearned Revenue		15,000
Capital Stock, $1 par value		30,000
Premium on Stock		25,000
Retained Earnings		85,690
Dividends	3,000	
Sales		286,000
Cost of Goods Sold	142,300	
Wages	46,800	
Payroll Taxes	3,900	
Supplies Expense	12,000	
Advertising	16,500	
Repairs and Maintenance	8,600	
Heat and Light	7,400	
Insurance and Property Taxes	4,200	
	$472,250	$472,250

Adjustment data appear below:

(1) Past experience in the collection of accounts and notes receivable shows that 1 percent of the sales will not be collected. All sales are made on credit terms, and the notes receivable arise out of credit sales to customers.
(2) Interest of 6 percent should be accrued for the year on the notes receivable.
(3) An error was found in the inventory records. Merchandise costing $1,780 should have been charged to cost of goods sold; but, instead, $1,870 was charged out.
(4) The prepaid insurance is for the calendar years 1972, 1973, and 1974.
(5) Depreciation is to be recorded on the building at 4 percent a year.
(6) Equipment is estimated to have a residual salvage value of $6,400 after the expiration of its useful life. Depreciation is to be recorded on a straight-line basis at a 10 percent rate.
(7) Advances received from customers in the amount of $15,000 were credited to Unearned Revenue. At June 30, deliveries were made against these advances to the extent of $6,000.
(8) A dividend of 10 cents a share was declared by the board of directors on June 15, payable to stockholders of record on July 3.
(9) Income taxes are to be estimated at 50 percent of net income before taxes.

Required: Prepare working papers for the fiscal year ended June 30, 1972.

C–10. A trial balance taken from the ledger of Omega Company is given below:

Omega Company
Trial Balance
December 31, 1972

	Dr.	Cr.
Cash	$ 32,630	
Accounts Receivable	41,280	
Inventory	48,670	
Supplies	3,120	
Furniture and Fixtures	56,000	
Accumulated Depreciation		$ 8,000
Accounts Payable		11,700
Withheld Income Taxes		2,300
Payroll Tax Liability		1,570
Accrued Rent Payable		800
Capital Stock, $10 par value		15,000
Retained Earnings		142,330
	$181,700	$181,700

A schedule of the balances from the accounts receivable ledger follows:

Adams and Black, Inc.	$ 5,450
Cameron Parts Co.	6,720
Dugan Forge, Inc.	4,250
Layton Patterns, Inc.	10,400
Solt Machine Co.	14,460
	$41,280

Transactions for the month of January, 1973, are given on the next page. Operating expenses are classified either as selling expenses or as office expenses.

January 2 Sold merchandise costing $9,150 to Adams and Black, Inc., on credit terms for $11,720.
   3 Collected amount owed by Cameron Parts Co.
   4 Paid office rent owed at December 31.
   4 Paid $4,900 on account owed to Belle Machine Company. A discount of $100 was deducted from the invoice in computing the amount of the payment.
   5 Purchased supplies for cash at a cost of $1,300.
   5 Collected amount owed by Solt Machine Co.
   9 Sold merchandise costing $8,300 to Cameron Parts Co., on credit terms for $12,600.
   9 Paid freight of $370 to Fast Transit Service on merchandise purchased.
   9 Purchased merchandise costing $12,500 from Tedesco, Inc.
   10 Billed Solt Machine Co. $18,200 for merchandise that cost $11,300.
   11 Collected amount owed by Layton Patterns, Inc.
   12 Collected amount owed by Adams and Black, Inc., at December 31.
   12 Sold merchandise on credit terms to Layton Patterns, Inc. Sales price, $15,400. Cost, $9,600.
   16 Purchased merchandise costing $10,500 from Belle Machine Company.
   17 Paid WLRN for advertising in the amount of $380.
   18 Paid Tedesco, Inc., for purchase of January 9. Deducted a 2 percent discount in making payment.
   19 Collected amount owed by Cameron Parts Co. resulting from sale of January 9. A discount of $252 was allowed.
   19 Paid sales commissions of $890.
   23 Collected amount owed by Layton Patterns, Inc., resulting from sale of January 12. A discount of $308 was allowed.
   24 Paid $430 for various office expenses.
   25 Paid freight of $230 to Express, Inc., for merchandise received from Belle Machine Co.
   26 Received $1,250 from Dugan Forge, Inc., and a non-interest bearing note for the balance owed.
   26 Billed Layton Patterns, Inc., $16,000 for merchandise that cost $10,300.
   30 Payroll for January:

Sales salaries	$6,000
Office salaries	4,000
Withheld income taxes	3,000
Payroll taxes payable	600
Net payroll	6,400

   31 Check drawn for net amount shown on payroll.
   31 Check drawn to Internal Revenue Service to pay withheld income taxes and payroll tax liability at December 31.

Adjustment data for January follows:

(1) Supplies expense in the general office operation was $1,750, and supplies expense in the sales office operation was $1,420.
(2) General office rent of $400 was not paid for the month of January.
(3) Depreciation of $600 is to be recorded on furniture and fixtures. (Charge $400 to the office and the balance to sales.)

(4) The employer's share of payroll taxes is to be recorded at 7 percent of the payroll.

(5) Income taxes are estimated at a rate of 40 percent of net income before income taxes.

Special journals are used with columns as indicated below:

Sales Journal:

> Col. 1—Accounts Receivable, Dr. and Sales, Cr.
> Col. 2—Cost of Goods Sold, Dr. and Inventory, Cr.

Purchases Journal:

> Col. 1—Inventory, Dr. and Accounts Payable, Cr.

Cash Receipts Journal:

> Col. 1—Cash, Dr.
> Col. 2—Sales Discounts, Dr.
> Col. 3—Accounts Receivable, Cr.
> Col. 4—General Ledger, Dr.
> Col. 5—General Ledger, Cr.

Cash Disbursements Journal:

> Col. 1—Cash, Cr.
> Col. 2—Purchases Discounts, Cr.
> Col. 3—Accounts Payable, Dr.
> Col. 4—Freight In, Dr.
> Col. 5—Selling Expense, Dr.
> Col. 6—Office Expense, Dr.
> Col. 7—General Ledger, Dr.
> Col. 8—General Ledger, Cr.

General Journal:

> Col. 1—Debit
> Col. 2—Credit

Required: (1) Enter the balances at December 31, 1972, in ledger accounts.

(2) Enter the transactions for January in the journals.

(3) Post the journalized transactions to the general ledger accounts and to the accounts receivable subsidiary ledger.

(4) Journalize and post the adjustments.

(5) Prepare an income statement for January and a balance sheet at January 31.

(6) Journalize and post the closing entries.

(7) Prepare a post-closing trial balance and a schedule of accounts receivable.

Appendix D

THE PRESENT VALUE CONCEPT

An amount of money to be received in the future is not equivalent to the same amount of money held at the present time. When confronted with a choice, anyone would rather have $100 today, for example, than the prospect of receiving $100 two years later. The $100 that is available today can be invested to return more than $100 two years later. For example, if $100 is invested at 10 percent compound interest per year, it will be worth $121 at the end of two years.

$100 initial investment $\times$ 1.10 = $110 value of the investment at the end of Year 1

$110 value of the investment $\times$ 1.10 = $121 value of the investment at end of Year 1 at the end of Year 2

The investment plus compound interest is called the *compound amount*. The compound amount of $100 in two years with interest compounded at the rate of 10 percent annually is $121. The formula for the compound amount of $1 follows:

$$\text{Compound amount} = (1 + i)^n$$
$$i = \text{interest rate}$$
$$n = \text{number of years}$$

In the example given, the compound amount could have been computed as follows:

Compound amount of $1 = $(1.10)^2$
Compound amount of $1 = $(1.10) \times (1.10)$
Compound amount of $1 = $1.21
Compound amount of $100 = $100 \times $1.21 or $121

If a person can earn 10 percent compound interest, he will look upon the receipt of $121 in two years as being equivalent to $100 today. He will be indifferent as to whether he has $100 today or $121 in two years.

Obviously, many business decisions involve the investment of dollars with the expectation that more dollars will be received at some future time. The returns are compared with the investment in making the investment decision. The returns and the investment, however, are not on the same time basis. Before a comparison can be made, the present and future dollars must be stated on an equivalent time basis.[1] Present dollars may be placed on a future dollar basis, that is, the compound amount of a present investment may be computed. If a businessman has $100 available for investment and believes that he can earn a 10 percent return with interest compounded annually, he will expect to receive $121 at the end of two years from a present investment of $100. Hence, an investment opportunity that is expected to yield $115 in two years from a present investment of $100 is unacceptable if $121 can normally be expected from a $100 investment. In short, the potential investor does not believe that $115 in two years is equivalent to $100 today if he can expect to receive $121 from other investment opportunities that are available.

The present value of a future amount. It is also possible to move in the other direction and to compute the present value of an amount of money that is to be received in the future. Expressed in another way, how much money must be invested today in order to receive a certain amount of money in the future? Or a debtor may look at the situation from a different point of view. How much money must be paid now to settle a debt that will become due in the future? In business, a choice must often be made between having a given amount of money now or the prospect of receiving a monetary return in the future. Does the expected future return justify the investment? This can be determined by computing the present value of the future return and comparing it with the amount invested.

The present value of a future amount of money can be computed by multiplying the future amount by the present value of $1. The formula for the present value of $1 follows:

$$\text{Present value of } \$1 = \frac{1}{(1 + i)^n}$$

i = interest rate
n = number of years

Assume, for example, that $121 is to be received two years later with interest compounded annually at 10 percent. How much money must be invested today to get $121 at the end of two years?

---

[1] The adjustments to place monetary amounts on an equivalent time basis should not be confused with price-level adjustments. The adjustments are made for different purposes. Adjustments for differences in time are required even if the price level remains the same.

Solve for the present value of $1 in two years with interest compounded annually at 10 percent.

$$\text{Present value of \$1, 2 years, 10\% interest} = \frac{1}{(1.10)^2}$$

$$\text{Present value of \$1, 2 years, 10\% interest} = \$.826444$$

$$\text{Present value of \$121, 2 years, 10\% interest} = \frac{\$121 \times \$.826444}{\text{or \$100}}$$

The computation may also be made as follows:

	Year 1		Year 2	
Present				
value, \$100		\$110		\$121

$121 = 110\%$ of the amount invested by the end of Year 1
$121 \div 1.10 = \$110$ amount at the end of Year 1
$110 = 110\%$ of the amount invested at the beginning of
    Year 1 (present value)
$110 \div 1.10 = \$100$ amount invested at the beginning of
    Year 1, or the present value

This is summarized below:

$$\frac{\$121/1.10}{1.10} \quad \text{is equivalent to} \quad \frac{\$121}{(1.10)^2}$$

or

$$\frac{1}{(1.10)^2} \times \$121 = \$100 \text{ present value}$$

In the computation of a present value, the interest is removed from a future amount to arrive at the initial amount invested. The process of reducing future values to present values is called *discounting*. The present value is sometimes called the *discounted value*. The interest to be subtracted is called the *discount*, and the rate of interest is called the *discount rate*.

It is seldom necessary to compute either the compound amount or the present value of a $1. The compound amounts of $1 at various interest rates for various years and the present values of $1 at various interest rates for various years are listed in published tables. A table for the present values of $1 is given on page 700 as Table I. The table gives the decimal equivalent for $\frac{1}{(1+i)^n}$. For example, the value of $\frac{1}{(1.10)^2}$ is .826. Thus, the present value of $121 received two years hence at 10 percent is $100 ($121 $\times$ .826 [slight difference due to rounding decimal equivalent]). By using the tables, it is possible to determine the present value of any amount of money to be received in the future by multiplying the future value by the figure given in the table.

The present value of a series of future amounts. Often it is necessary to compute the present value of a series of amounts that will be received at periodic intervals in the future. For example, management may be considering the acquisition of new equipment or the addition of a new product line. Do the expected future returns from the investment in the equipment or the new product line justify the investment? The future returns can be discounted at the rate of return expected from similar investments, and the result can be compared with the amount to be invested. In other words, the future returns are converted to present value equivalents so that they can be compared with the investment.

It would be possible, of course, to compute the compound (future) amount of the investment by adding compound interest to the investment and to compare this amount with the compound (future) amount of the returns. The comparison would then be based on future values. The normal practice, however, is to make comparisons in the present. Hence, future dollar amounts are usually discounted to a present value.

The present value of a series of returns to be received at periodic intervals in the future is nothing more than the sum of the present values of the individual returns. Assume that $1,000 is to be received at the end of *each* year for five years with interest compounded annually at 10 percent. What is the present value of these five annual receipts of $1,000? The present value of five annual returns of $1,000 received at the end of each year with interest compounded at 10 percent can be computed as shown at the top of page 695.

The same result can also be computed as shown below:

$$\$1,000 \left(\frac{1}{1.10} + \frac{1}{(1.10)^2} + \frac{1}{(1.10)^3} + \frac{1}{(1.10)^4} + \frac{1}{(1.10)^5} \right) = \$3,790$$

The decimal equivalents of the fractions in the equation can be found in the table of present values of $1 (Table I):

$$(.909 + .826 + .751 + .683 + .621)$$

The sum of the present values is 3.79, and the present value of $1,000 received each year for five years at 10 percent interest compounded annually is $3,790.

$$1,000 \ (3.79) = \$3,790$$

End of Year	Returns	Computation		
1	$1,000	$1,000 \times \dfrac{1}{1.10} =$	$ 909	present value of $1,000 received at end of Year 1
2	1,000	$1,000 \times \dfrac{1}{(1.10)^2} =$	826	present value of $1,000 received at end of Year 2
3	1,000	$1,000 \times \dfrac{1}{(1.10)^3} =$	751	present value of $1,000 received at end of Year 3
4	1,000	$1,000 \times \dfrac{1}{(1.10)^4} =$	683	present value of $1,000 received at end of Year 4
5	1,000	$1,000 \times \dfrac{1}{(1.10)^5} =$	621	present value of $1,000 received at end of Year 5

Present value of $1,000 received at the end of each year for 5 years $3,790

Note that the factor, 3.79, can be read from Table II on page 701. The difference between this amount and the amount appearing in the table is due to rounding. The values in Table II are the sums of the values given in Table I.

The present value concept applied. The concept of present value is applied whenever future dollar amounts are to be compared with present dollar amounts. A dollar to be received at some future date is not equivalent to the dollar received today because of the time difference. The dollars to be received in the future are discounted at an appropriate discount rate so that they can be compared with the dollars in the present.

For example, a company may be planning to invest $50,000 in a project that will probably yield $10,000 after income taxes each year for ten years. If the company has other investment opportunities that will yield a 12 percent return after taxes, should it make the $50,000 investment in this project? The solution to this problem can be obtained by discounting the annual returns of $10,000 at the 12 percent rate and comparing the result with the $50,000 to be invested. In other words, the anticipated annual returns of $10,000 are reduced to a present value, and the present value of the returns is compared with the amount to be invested. If the present value of the returns is greater than the amount of the investment, the investment will earn more than the 12 percent minimum rate-of-return requirement and is desirable. On the other hand, if the present value of the returns is less than $50,000, the investment in the project should be rejected. It will not earn as much as other investment opportunities. The method briefly described above is applied in making investment decisions and is referred to as *the excess present value method*. This method is discussed more completely in Chapter 18.

The $10,000 annual returns received for ten years are discounted at 12 percent as shown below:

$10,000 annual return $\times$ $5.65 present value of $1 received each year for 10 years with interest compounded annually at 12% (See Table II on page 701.)

= $56,500 present value of annual returns of $10,000 for 10 years at 12% interest compounded annually

The project should be accepted. Returns on a present value basis are greater than the amount invested, indicating that the project is earning more than the minimum rate of return established at 12 percent.[2]

Another approach may be taken in making investment decisions. The discounted rate of return on the investment project may be determined and compared with the minimum rate of return. The discounted rate of return approach is also discussed in Chapter 18. The rate-of-return calculation is illustrated by using the data from the previous illustration. What is the discounted rate of return when $10,000 is received each year for ten years on an investment of $50,000? Stated in another way what discount rate will equate the $50,000 investment with the $10,000 annual returns?

$$\$50,000 = \$10,000 \times \text{discount rate}$$

To calculate the discounted rate of return, divide the investment by the annual return, that is, find the ratio of the investment to the annual return:

$$\frac{\$50,000 \text{ investment}}{\$10,000 \text{ annual return}} = 5$$

This ratio is compared with the values appearing in the table of the present values of $1 received annually for the number of years involved, in

---

[2] The returns from business investments are not necessarily received at the end of each year. Usually, they are received throughout the year while operations are being conducted. A more accurate calculation can be made by using a continuous discount rate. However, this is not necessary. In making business decisions, management must compare alternatives and select the best alternative from among those that are available. For this purpose, annual discounting is acceptable, it being assumed that the pattern of the returns within the year will be the same for all of the alternatives.

this case ten years. Select the value in the table that most closely corresponds with the ratio. The value in the table for ten years that most closely corresponds with the ratio is 5.019 in the 15 percent column.

The discounted rate of return on the investment is a little more than 15 percent. Multiply the annual return of $10,000 by the value in the table for 15 percent for ten years.

$10,000 annual return $\times$ $5.019 present value of $1 received annually for 10 years with interest compounded annually at 15%

= $50,190 present value of annual returns of $10,000 with interest compounded annually at 15%

The present value of the annual returns amounting to $50,190 is somewhat greater than the investment of $50,000 when the annual returns are discounted at 15 percent. This indicates that the discounted rate of return is somewhat more than 15 percent.

Sometimes the discounted rate of return cannot be computed so easily. The returns for each year may not be equal. For example, an investment of $90,000 is expected to produce returns for five years as follows:

Years	Returns
1	$ 40,000
2	40,000
3	30,000
4	20,000
5	20,000
Total	$150,000

The average return is $30,000 and may be used in computing a ratio of the investment to the annual return.

Total returns of $150,000 ÷ 5 years = $30,000 average annual return

$$\frac{\$90,000 \text{ investment}}{\$30,000 \text{ average annual return}} = 3 \text{ ratio of investment to average annual return}$$

This ration is compared with the value in Table II, page 701, and is closest to 2.991 on the 5-year line for 20 percent.

In this illustration, the returns for the earlier years are larger than the returns for the later years. Therefore, the discounted rate of return will be higher than 20 percent. More immediate returns have a greater present value than returns that will be realized in later years. This would be expected considering that these relatively large returns will be available for investment at an earlier date. A trial rate of 24 percent may be used. The present values for each year are then computed at 24 percent from the table showing the present values of $1.

Years	Returns		Present Values of $1 at 24%		Present Value of Returns
1	$40,000	×	$.806	=	$32,240
2	40,000	×	.650	=	26,000
3	30,000	×	.524	=	15,720
4	20,000	×	.423	=	8,460
5	20,000	×	.341	=	6,820
	Present value of the annual returns				$89,240

The discounted rate of return is slightly less than 24 percent. Ordinarily, the approximate discounted rate of return can be calculated with no more than three trials. If the discounted returns are less than the present value of the investment, use a lower rate for the next trial. If the discounted returns are greater than the present value of the investment, use a higher rate.

When the returns for the later years are large in relation to the returns for the earlier years, the same general procedure can be followed. However, the first trial should be made with a rate that is somewhat lower than the rate computed by using the average annual return. Later returns have less power than earlier returns because they cannot be reinvested as soon. The discounted rate of return, therefore, will be somewhat lower.

An investment illustration. The Wilcox Mining Company plans to invest $1,650,000 in further mine development. This investment should produce $500,000 after income taxes each year for five years, after which the mine will be worthless. Should this investment be made if alternative investment situations can be expected to yield a discounted rate of return after income taxes of 18 percent? What is the discounted rate of return on the mine development alternative?

The first question can be answered by discounting the annual returns at the lowest rate of return that will be accepted, that is, at 18 percent.

$500,000 annual return × $3.127 present value of $1 received annually for 5 years, interest compounded at 18%

= $1,563,500 present value of annual returns, 5 years, 18% compound interest

The mine development plan should be rejected. It will not yield the desired rate of return. The discounted returns are only $1,563,500, and the investment is $1,650,000.

The second question can be answered by solving for the discount rate that will equate the annual returns with the investment. Find the ratio of the investment to the annual return.

$$\frac{\$1,650,000 \text{ investment}}{\$500,000 \text{ annual return}} = 3.3 \text{ ratio of investment to annual return}$$

The table of present values of \$1 received annually shows that 3.352 is closest to the ratio of 3.3. This value is on the 5-year line for 15 percent.

\$500,000 annual return $\times$ \$3.352 present value of \$1 received annually for 5 years, interest compounded at 15%

= \$1,676,000 present value of annual returns, 15% compound interest

The discounted rate of return is more than 15 percent, but it is less than 16 percent.

\$500,000 annual return $\times$ \$3.274 present value of \$1 received annually for 5 years, interest compounded at 16%

= \$1,637,000 present value of annual returns, 16% compound interest

TABLE I

Present Value of $1

Years Hence	4%	5%	6%	8%	10%	12%	14%	15%	16%	18%	20%	22%	24%	25%	26%	28%	30%	35%	40%
1	0.962	0.952	0.943	0.926	0.909	0.893	0.877	0.870	0.862	0.847	0.833	0.820	0.806	0.800	0.794	0.781	0.769	0.741	0.714
2	0.925	0.907	0.890	0.857	0.826	0.797	0.769	0.756	0.743	0.718	0.694	0.672	0.650	0.640	0.630	0.610	0.592	0.549	0.510
3	0.889	0.864	0.840	0.794	0.751	0.712	0.675	0.658	0.641	0.609	0.579	0.551	0.524	0.512	0.500	0.477	0.455	0.406	0.364
4	0.855	0.823	0.792	0.735	0.683	0.636	0.592	0.572	0.552	0.516	0.482	0.451	0.423	0.410	0.397	0.373	0.350	0.301	0.260
5	0.822	0.784	0.747	0.681	0.621	0.567	0.519	0.497	0.476	0.437	0.402	0.370	0.341	0.328	0.315	0.291	0.269	0.223	0.186
6	0.790	0.746	0.705	0.630	0.564	0.507	0.456	0.432	0.410	0.370	0.335	0.303	0.275	0.262	0.250	0.227	0.207	0.165	0.133
7	0.760	0.711	0.665	0.583	0.513	0.452	0.400	0.376	0.354	0.314	0.279	0.249	0.222	0.210	0.198	0.178	0.159	0.122	0.095
8	0.731	0.677	0.627	0.540	0.467	0.404	0.351	0.327	0.305	0.266	0.233	0.204	0.179	0.168	0.157	0.139	0.123	0.091	0.068
9	0.703	0.645	0.592	0.500	0.424	0.361	0.308	0.284	0.263	0.225	0.194	0.167	0.144	0.134	0.125	0.108	0.094	0.067	0.048
10	0.676	0.614	0.558	0.463	0.386	0.322	0.270	0.247	0.227	0.191	0.162	0.137	0.116	0.107	0.099	0.085	0.073	0.050	0.035
11	0.650	0.585	0.527	0.429	0.350	0.287	0.237	0.215	0.195	0.162	0.135	0.112	0.094	0.086	0.079	0.066	0.056	0.037	0.025
12	0.625	0.557	0.497	0.397	0.319	0.257	0.208	0.187	0.168	0.137	0.112	0.092	0.076	0.069	0.062	0.052	0.043	0.027	0.018
13	0.601	0.530	0.469	0.368	0.290	0.229	0.182	0.163	0.145	0.116	0.093	0.075	0.061	0.055	0.050	0.040	0.033	0.020	0.013
14	0.577	0.505	0.442	0.340	0.263	0.205	0.160	0.141	0.125	0.099	0.078	0.062	0.049	0.044	0.039	0.032	0.025	0.015	0.009
15	0.555	0.481	0.417	0.315	0.239	0.183	0.140	0.123	0.108	0.084	0.065	0.051	0.040	0.035	0.031	0.025	0.020	0.011	0.006
16	0.534	0.458	0.394	0.292	0.218	0.163	0.123	0.107	0.093	0.071	0.054	0.042	0.032	0.028	0.025	0.019	0.015	0.008	0.005
17	0.513	0.436	0.371	0.270	0.198	0.146	0.108	0.093	0.080	0.060	0.045	0.034	0.026	0.023	0.020	0.015	0.012	0.006	0.003
18	0.494	0.416	0.350	0.250	0.180	0.130	0.095	0.081	0.069	0.051	0.038	0.028	0.021	0.018	0.016	0.012	0.009	0.005	0.002
19	0.475	0.396	0.331	0.232	0.164	0.116	0.083	0.070	0.060	0.043	0.031	0.023	0.017	0.014	0.012	0.009	0.007	0.003	0.002
20	0.456	0.377	0.312	0.215	0.149	0.104	0.073	0.061	0.051	0.037	0.026	0.019	0.014	0.012	0.010	0.007	0.005	0.002	0.001
21	0.439	0.359	0.294	0.199	0.135	0.093	0.064	0.053	0.044	0.031	0.022	0.015	0.011	0.009	0.008	0.006	0.004	0.002	0.001
22	0.422	0.342	0.278	0.184	0.123	0.083	0.056	0.046	0.038	0.026	0.018	0.013	0.009	0.007	0.006	0.004	0.003	0.001	0.001
23	0.406	0.326	0.262	0.170	0.112	0.074	0.049	0.040	0.033	0.022	0.015	0.010	0.007	0.006	0.004	0.003	0.002	0.001	—
24	0.390	0.310	0.247	0.158	0.102	0.066	0.043	0.035	0.028	0.019	0.013	0.008	0.006	0.005	0.003	0.003	0.002	0.001	—
25	0.375	0.295	0.233	0.146	0.092	0.059	0.038	0.030	0.024	0.016	0.010	0.007	0.005	0.004	0.003	0.002	0.001	0.001	—
26	0.361	0.281	0.220	0.135	0.084	0.053	0.033	0.026	0.021	0.014	0.009	0.006	0.004	0.003	0.002	0.002	0.001	—	—
27	0.347	0.268	0.207	0.125	0.076	0.047	0.029	0.023	0.018	0.011	0.007	0.005	0.003	0.002	0.002	0.001	0.001	—	—
28	0.333	0.255	0.196	0.116	0.069	0.042	0.026	0.020	0.016	0.010	0.006	0.004	0.002	0.002	0.002	0.001	0.001	—	—
29	0.321	0.243	0.185	0.107	0.063	0.037	0.022	0.017	0.014	0.008	0.005	0.003	0.002	0.002	0.001	0.001	—	—	—
30	0.308	0.231	0.174	0.099	0.057	0.033	0.020	0.015	0.012	0.007	0.004	0.003	0.002	0.001	0.001	0.001	—	—	—
35	0.253	0.181	0.130	0.068	0.036	0.019	0.010	0.008	0.006	0.003	0.002	0.001	0.001	—	—	—	—	—	—
40	0.208	0.142	0.097	0.046	0.022	0.011	0.005	0.004	0.003	0.001	0.001	—	—	—	—	—	—	—	—
45	0.171	0.111	0.073	0.031	0.014	0.006	0.003	0.002	0.001	0.001	—	—	—	—	—	—	—	—	—
50	0.141	0.087	0.054	0.021	0.009	0.003	0.001	0.001	0.001	—	—	—	—	—	—	—	—	—	—

TABLE II

Present Value of $1 Received Annually for N Years

Years (N)	4%	5%	6%	8%	10%	12%	14%	15%	16%	18%	20%	22%	24%	25%	26%	28%	30%	35%	40%
1	0.962	0.952	0.943	0.926	0.909	0.893	0.877	0.870	0.862	0.847	0.833	0.820	0.806	0.800	0.794	0.781	0.769	0.741	0.714
2	1.886	1.859	1.833	1.783	1.736	1.690	1.647	1.626	1.605	1.566	1.528	1.492	1.457	1.440	1.424	1.392	1.361	1.289	1.224
3	2.775	2.723	2.673	2.577	2.487	2.402	2.322	2.283	2.246	2.174	2.106	2.042	1.981	1.952	1.923	1.868	1.816	1.696	1.589
4	3.630	3.546	3.465	3.312	3.170	3.037	2.914	2.855	2.798	2.690	2.589	2.494	2.404	2.362	2.320	2.241	2.166	1.997	1.849
5	4.452	4.330	4.212	3.993	3.791	3.605	3.433	3.352	3.274	3.127	2.991	2.864	2.745	2.689	2.635	2.532	2.436	2.220	2.035
6	5.242	5.076	4.917	4.623	4.355	4.111	3.889	3.784	3.685	3.498	3.326	3.167	3.020	2.951	2.885	2.759	2.643	2.385	2.168
7	6.002	5.786	5.582	5.206	4.868	4.564	4.288	4.160	4.039	3.812	3.605	3.416	3.242	3.161	3.083	2.937	2.802	2.508	2.263
8	6.733	6.463	6.210	5.747	5.335	4.968	4.639	4.487	4.344	4.078	3.837	3.619	3.421	3.329	3.241	3.076	2.925	2.598	2.331
9	7.435	7.108	6.802	6.247	5.759	5.328	4.946	4.772	4.507	4.303	4.031	3.786	3.566	3.463	3.366	3.184	3.019	2.665	2.379
10	8.111	7.722	7.360	6.710	6.145	5.650	5.216	5.019	4.833	4.494	4.192	3.923	3.682	3.571	3.465	3.269	3.092	2.715	2.414
11	8.760	8.306	7.887	7.139	6.495	5.988	5.453	5.234	5.029	4.656	4.327	4.035	3.776	3.656	3.544	3.335	3.147	2.752	2.438
12	9.385	8.863	8.384	7.536	6.814	6.194	5.660	5.421	5.197	4.793	4.439	4.127	3.851	3.725	3.606	3.387	3.190	2.779	2.456
13	9.986	9.394	8.853	7.904	7.103	6.424	5.842	5.583	5.342	4.910	4.533	4.203	3.912	3.780	3.656	3.427	3.223	2.799	2.468
14	10.563	9.899	9.295	8.244	7.367	6.628	6.002	5.724	5.468	5.008	4.611	4.265	3.962	3.824	3.695	3.459	3.249	2.814	2.477
15	11.118	10.380	9.712	8.559	7.606	6.811	6.142	5.847	5.575	5.092	4.675	4.315	4.001	3.859	3.726	3.483	3.268	2.825	2.484
16	11.652	10.838	10.106	8.851	7.824	6.974	6.265	5.954	5.669	5.162	4.730	4.357	4.033	3.887	3.751	3.503	3.283	2.834	2.489
17	12.166	11.274	10.477	9.122	8.022	7.120	6.373	6.047	5.749	5.222	4.775	4.391	4.059	3.910	3.771	3.518	3.295	2.840	2.492
18	12.659	11.690	10.828	9.372	8.201	7.250	6.467	6.128	5.818	5.273	4.812	4.419	4.080	3.928	3.786	3.529	3.304	2.844	2.494
19	13.134	12.085	11.158	9.604	8.365	7.366	6.550	6.198	5.877	5.316	4.844	4.442	4.097	3.942	3.799	3.539	3.311	2.848	2.496
20	13.590	12.462	11.470	9.818	8.514	7.469	6.623	6.259	5.929	5.353	4.870	4.460	4.110	3.954	3.808	3.546	3.316	2.850	2.497
21	14.029	12.821	11.764	10.017	8.649	7.562	6.687	6.312	5.973	5.384	4.891	4.476	4.121	3.963	3.816	3.551	3.320	2.852	2.498
22	14.451	13.163	12.042	10.201	8.772	7.645	6.743	6.359	6.011	5.410	4.909	4.488	4.130	3.970	3.822	3.556	3.323	2.853	2.498
23	14.857	13.489	12.303	10.371	8.883	7.718	6.792	6.399	6.044	5.432	4.925	4.499	4.137	3.976	3.827	3.559	3.325	2.854	2.499
24	15.247	13.799	12.550	10.529	8.985	7.784	6.835	6.434	6.073	5.451	4.937	4.507	4.143	3.981	3.831	3.562	3.327	2.855	2.499
25	15.622	14.094	12.783	10.675	9.077	7.843	6.873	6.464	6.097	5.467	4.948	4.514	4.147	3.985	3.834	3.564	3.329	2.856	2.499
26	15.983	14.375	13.003	10.810	9.161	7.896	6.906	6.491	6.118	5.480	4.956	4.520	4.151	3.988	3.837	3.566	3.330	2.852	2.500
27	16.330	14.643	13.211	10.935	9.237	7.943	6.935	6.514	6.136	5.492	4.964	4.524	4.154	3.990	3.839	3.567	3.331	2.853	2.500
28	16.663	14.898	13.406	11.051	9.307	7.984	6.961	6.534	6.152	5.502	4.970	4.528	4.157	3.992	3.840	3.568	3.331	2.854	2.500
29	16.984	15.141	13.591	11.158	9.370	8.022	6.983	6.551	6.166	5.510	4.975	4.531	4.159	3.994	3.841	3.569	3.332	2.855	2.500
30	17.292	15.373	13.765	11.258	9.427	8.055	7.003	6.566	6.177	5.517	4.979	4.534	4.160	3.995	3.842	3.569	3.332	2.856	2.500
35	18.665	16.374	14.498	11.655	9.644	8.176	7.070	6.617	6.215	5.539	4.992	4.541	4.164	3.998	3.845	3.571	3.333	2.856	2.500
40	19.793	17.159	15.046	11.925	9.779	8.244	7.105	6.642	6.234	5.548	4.997	4.544	4.166	3.999	3.846	3.571	3.333	2.857	2.500
45	20.720	17.774	15.456	12.108	9.863	8.283	7.123	6.654	6.242	5.552	4.999	4.545	4.166	3.999	3.846	3.571	3.333	2.857	2.500
50	21.482	18.256	15.762	12.234	9.915	8.304	7.133	6.661	6.246	5.554	4.999	4.545	4.167	4.000	3.846	3.571	3.333	2.857	2.500

Index

Capital stock, 27, 656
Capitalization, leases, 55
Cash budget, 599
Cash flow, and net working capital, 232; illustrated, 236; value of, 242
Cash payments budget, 611
Cash receipts and disbursements statement, 196
Changes in financial position, 12
Changes in retained earnings, 12
Closing procedure, 674
Coefficient of determination, 297
Columnar journals, 643
Combination decisions, 462
Combined cost curve, illustrated, 302
Committed cost, 263
Common-size statements, 164; illustrated 165, 166
Comparability, 160
Compound amount, 691
Conservatism, 20
Consistency, 17
Consolidated financial statements, 79; illustrated, 81, 82
Consumer price index, *see* Price index
Contribution margin, 403
Contra-asset account, 664
Control, 8; and planning. decisions, 3; budget, 580, 581; criteria needed, 543; limits, 293; responsibility accounting, 267, 270, 581; standard costs, 378
Controller, 6
Controllable costs, 266
Controllable variance, 377
Convertible debt, 75
Coproducts, 328
Corporate formation, 656
Correlation, 296; graphic presentation, 297
Cost, 14; and control, 265; and planning, 271; committed, 263; controllable, 266; decision-making, 275; decremental, 272; differential, 272; direct, 265; elements, 261, 323; estimation, 288; fixed, 263, 438; flow, 322; incremental, 272; indirect, 265; marginal, 272; noncontrollable, 266; of capital, 516; of goods sold, 28; opportunity, 275; or market, 44; period, 259; procedure, 262; product, 259; programmed, 263; reports, 267, 326; segregation, 289; semivariable, 263; standard, 352, 378; sunk, 273, 330; transitions, 260; variable, 263
Cost accounting, 259; nonmanufacturing, 260
Cost increases, passing to customers, 443
Cost savings, sharing with customers, 442
Credit, 639; short-term planning, 178

Current assets, 21; capital investment, 521; turnover, 171
Current liabilities, 25
Current ratio, 172
Curtailment decision, 472

D

Debit, 639
Decentralized company, 542
Decisions, by function, 5; by time element, 5
Decision making, abstraction, 456; costs, 275; model, 455; relevant cost data, 460; variable costing, 411
Decremental costs, 272
Deferred income taxes, 71
Deferred revenues, 26
Deficit, 27
Deflation, 96
Demand function, 487
Depreciation, 50, 638; accelerated, 53, 100, 525; adjustment, 663; annuity method, 135; double rate, 52; income taxes, 52, 524; production unit, 51; straight line, 51, 664; sum-of-the-years-digits, 51
Derived demand, 586
Differential, calculus, 301; costs, 272
Dilution of earnings, 75
Direct costing, *see* Variable costing
Direct costs, 265
Direct materials, budget, 600; cost, 261; costing, 312
Direct labor, budget, 602; cost, 261; costing, 312
Direct transactional recording, 654
Discount rate, 693
Discounted rate-of-return method, 517
Discounted value, 693
Discounting, 693
Distress pricing, 500
Division, budget, 580; investment, 550
Double-entry accounting, 633
Double rate, *see* Depreciation
Duality, 632

E

Earnings per share, 75, 143
Earning power, 168
Economics of pricing, 487
Efficiency variance, 377; labor, 364
Electronic data processing, 654
Elimination of product line, 472
Equity, 12, 632; relationships, 175
Equivalent units, 322
Evaluation, criterion or standard, 564; of capital investments, 530
Excess present value method, 517, 520, 696

Expected value, contribution margin, 588
Expense, 13, 636; related liabilities, 71
Extraordinary gains and losses, 30, 74

F

Feedback, in budget control, 579
Financial planning, 613
Financial position, statement of changes, 196; illustrated, 212
Financial statements, 11
First-in, first-out, 17, 48
Fiscal year, 16
Fixed assets, 24
Fixed charges against income, 176
Fixed costs, 263, 438; problem in pricing, 495; troublesome, 263
Flexible budget, 375
Flow statements, 196; illustrated, 199
Forecasting sales, 585
Franchises, 24
Fringe benefits, 355
Full cost, 400, 494; acceptance of, 499; adjusting, 498

G

General and administrative expense, 30; budget, 607
General ledger, 649
Going concern, 14
Goodwill, 25, 79
Graphic solution, capital investments, 529
Gross fixed assets, 552
Gross margin, 28, 637; statement illustrated, 47

H

High-low point method of cost estimation, 289
Historical cost, 95, 97, 316
Holding gains, 100; or losses, 45
Human factors, in budgeting, 581

I

Incentives, 356
Income statement, 12, 196; classifications, 28; estimated, 615; illustrated, 29; relationships, 169
Income taxes, 30; depreciation, 52, 524
Incremental, costs, 272; returns, 527
Index, conversions, 103; division controllable profit, 549; for control, 543; profit, 545
Indirect costs, 265
Inflation, 96
Information, need for, 6
Intangible assets, 24

Integrated company, 470
Interest, times earned, 176; undivided, 21
Interlocking data, 160; factors, 13
Intermediate market, 559; case, 559
Intracompany pricing, 553
Inventory, adjusted lifo, 98; adjustment, 666; and production, 592; costing, 48; level, 346; turnovers, 174; valuation, 45
Investments, see Capital investments and Marketable securities
Investments, 23
Investment credit, 525

J

Job order cost system, 311; illustrated, 316
Joint costs, 328
Joint products, 328; costing, 326
Journal, 641; columnar or special, 649

L

Labor cost control, 355
Labor efficiency variance, 364
Labor price variance, 363
Last-in, first-out, 17, 49
Lease, or purchase, 54; capitalization, 55
Least squares method, 291
Ledger, 639; general, 649; subsidiary, 649
Leverage, 139
Liabilities, 12, 632
Line of regression, 290, 293; graphic presentation, 296
Linear programming, 466
Long-term liabilities, 26
Lowest acceptable rate of return, 516

M

Machine accounting, 654
Make or buy, 470
Management, 1; by exception, 359
Managerial accounting, 1
Manufacturing cost budget, 600, 606
Manufacturing overhead, 261; budget, 313, 375, 604; costing, 312; rate, 313
Marginal analysis model, 492; limitations, 492
Marginal cost, 272, 490
Marginal revenue, 489
Market price, 554
Market value, limits for inventories, 46; of stock, 143, 145
Marketable securities, 44
Markup pricing, 494